Liberalism

THE LIFE OF AN IDEA

Liberalism

THE LIFE OF AN IDEA

SECOND EDITION

Edmund Fawcett

Princeton University Press
Princeton & Oxford

Published by Princeton University Press,
41 William Street, Princeton, New Jersey 08540

In the United Kingdom: Princeton University Press,
6 Oxford Street, Woodstock, Oxfordshire OX20 1TR

press.princeton.edu

COVER IMAGES: *Row 1*: Wilhelm von Humboldt; Sir Isaiah Berlin (Library of Congress, Prints & Photographs Division, reproduction number LC-USZ62-112715);
Walter Lippmann (Walter Lippmann Papers, Manuscripts and Archives, Yale
University Library). *Row 2*: John Maynard Keynes, 1883–1946 (print collection,
Miriam and Ira D. Wallach Division of Art, Prints and Photographs, The New
York Public Library, Astor, Lenox and Tilden Foundations); Alexis Charles Henry
de Tocqueville (lithograph, 1848, by Théodore Chassériau. Rosenwald Collection,
1952.8.215. Courtesy of the National Gallery of Art, Washington); Franklin Delano
Roosevelt, photograph by Harris & Ewing (Library of Congress, Prints & Photographs Division, reproduction number LC-DIG-hec-47325). *Row 3*: Friedrich von
Hayek (Courtesy of the Ludwig von Mises Institute); John Stuart Mill.

Original edition published 2014
Fifth printing, and first paperback printing, 2015
Second edition published 2018

Library of Congress Control Number 2017954566
ISBN 978-0-691-18038-0

British Library Cataloging-in-Publication Data is available

This book has been composed in Kepler Std

Printed on acid-free paper. ∞

Printed in the United States of America

10 9 8 7 6 5 4 3 2 1

TO MARLOWE,

AND IN MEMORY OF ELIAS

CONTENTS

Preface to the Second Edition xi

Acknowledgments xv

INTRODUCTION   The Practice of Liberalism 1

PART ONE   THE CONFIDENCE OF YOUTH (1830–1880)

1   Historical Setting in the 1830s: Thrown into a World of
Ceaseless Change 33

2   Guiding Thoughts from Founding Thinkers: Conflict,
Resistance, Progress, and Respect 39
   i. Humboldt and Constant: Releasing People's Capacities and
Respecting Their Privacy 39
   ii. Guizot: Taming Conflict without Arbitrary Power 49
   iii. Tocqueville and Schulze-Delitzsch: The Modern Powers
of Mass Democracy and Mass Markets 61
   iv. Chadwick and Cobden: Governments and Markets as
Engines of Social Progress 69
   v. Smiles and Channing: Personal Progress as Self-Reliance or
Moral Uplift 77
   vi. Spencer: Liberalism Mistaken for Biology 82
   vii. J. S. Mill: Holding Liberalism's Ideas Together 88

3   Liberalism in Practice: Four Exemplary Politicians 101
   i. Lincoln: The Many Uses of "Liberty" in the Land of Liberty 101
   ii. Laboulaye and Richter: Tests for Liberals in Semiliberal
Regimes 108
   iii. Gladstone: Liberalism's Capaciousness and the Politics
of Balance 115

4   The Nineteenth-Century Legacy: Liberalism without
    Caricature   120
    i. Respect, "the Individual," and the Lessons of Toleration   120
    ii. The Achievements That Gave Liberals Confidence   135

PART TWO   LIBERALISM IN MATURITY AND
THE STRUGGLE WITH DEMOCRACY (1880–1945)

5   Historical Setting in the 1880s: The World Liberals
    Were Making   139

6   The Compromises That Gave Us Liberal Democracy   147
    i. Political Democracy: Liberal Resistance to Suffrage Extension 147
    ii. Economic Democracy: The "New Liberalism" and Novel Tasks
    for the State   160
    iii. Ethical Democracy: Letting Go Ethically and the Persistence
    of Intolerance   167

7   The Economic Powers of the Modern State and
    Modern Market   173
    i. Walras, Marshall, and the Business Press: Resisting the State
    on Behalf of Markets   173
    ii. Hobhouse, Naumann, Croly, and Bourgeois: Resisting
    Markets on Behalf of Society   186

8   Damaged Ideals and Broken Dreams   198
    i. Chamberlain and Bassermann: Liberal Imperialism   198
    ii. Lloyd George, Clemenceau, and Wilson: Liberal Hawks
    of 1914–1918   214
    iii. Alain, Baldwin, and Brandeis: Liberal Dissent and the
    Warfare State   226
    iv. Stresemann: Liberal Democracy in Peril   235
    v. Keynes, Fisher, and Hayek (i): Liberal Economists in the Slump 243
    vi. Hoover and Roosevelt: Forgotten Liberal and Foremost Liberal 264

9   Thinking about Liberalism in the 1930s–1940s   272
    i. Lippmann and Hayek (ii): Liberals as Antitotalitarians   272
    ii. Popper: Liberalism as Openness and Experiment   276

PART THREE   SECOND CHANCE AND SUCCESS (1945–1989)

10 Historical Setting after 1945: Liberal Democracy's New Start   283

11 New Foundations: Rights, a Democratic Rule of Law,
    and Welfare   287
    i. Drafters of the 1948 Declaration of Human Rights: Liberal
       Democracy Goes Global   287
    ii. German Postwar Liberals: The 1949 Basic Law as Liberal
        Democracy's Exemplary Charter   299
    iii. Beveridge: Liberalism and Welfare   308

12 Liberal Thinking after 1945   313
    i. Oakeshott and Berlin: Letting Politics Alone
       and "Negative" Liberty   314
    ii. Hayek (iii): Political Antipolitics   324
    iii. Orwell, Camus, and Sartre: Liberals in the Cold War   328
    iv. Rawls: Justifying Liberalism   335
    v. Nozick, Dworkin, and MacIntyre: Responses to Rawls,
       Rights, and Community   345

13 The Breadth of Liberal Politics in the 1950s–1980s   352
    i. Mendès-France, Brandt, and Johnson: Left Liberalism in the
       1950s–1960s   352
    ii. Buchanan and Friedman: Liberal Economists against the State 365
    iii. Thatcher, Reagan, Mitterrand, and Kohl: Right Liberalism in
         the 1970s–1980s   375

PART FOUR   LIBERAL DREAMS AND NIGHTMARES
IN THE TWENTY-FIRST CENTURY

14 Two Decades That Shook Liberal Democracy   389
    i. The Rise of the Hard Right   389
    ii. Economic Discontents   399
    iii. Geopolitical Loneliness   410
    iv. Nationhood, Citizenship, and Identity   421
    v. Intellectual Doubts and Disaffection   439

15 The Primacy of Politics   454

Works Consulted   467

Name Index   495

Subject Index   507

PREFACE TO THE SECOND EDITION

To shore up a weakened building, you need to understand its foundations. You need to grasp what it rests on, why it arose, and what it is for. So it is with democratic liberalism, or to use the more familiar name, liberal democracy. Nobody who witnessed recent political shocks and watched antiliberal successes in Europe and the United States can doubt that liberal democracy is under challenge from inside and out. As discrepancies of wealth and power widened in recent decades, disaffected citizens questioned liberalism's aims and ideals. A great structure of historic wealth and shelter that lately appeared to be the envy of the world showed weaknesses and flaws. As the pride of its occupants gave way to self-doubt, people on all sides asked, were those flaws reparable or fatal? Across the world, liberalism's geopolitical prestige was dimmed by rising powers that offered attractive-looking nonliberal paths to material progress and stability. The liberal democratic world itself appeared to be splitting as the United States and Britain took illiberal paths politically and unilateralist paths internationally, leaving a shaken France and Germany as European standard-bearers for the liberal order.

The original edition of *Liberalism: The Life of an Idea* in a final chapter mentioned, without dwelling on, the present weaknesses of liberal democracy. The book's aim was to show what liberalism is, the better to see what we should be worrying about. This updated new edition contains an expanded final part, written after the upsets of 2016–17, on liberalism's present ills and doubts about its prospects. A new Introduction makes clearer the book's underlying assumption that liberalism, although complex and diverse, is easy to recognize and distinguish from its rivals, especially in times as now when liberalism looks as if it is in jeopardy and needs defending.

Liberalism is an enduring practice of politics guided by distinctive aims and ideals. It began in the early nineteenth century, not before as often claimed, in a previously unimagined predicament. Amid the ceaseless change of capitalist modernity, the first liberals sought durable new ways to secure ethical and political stability. That liberal search, then as now, was guided by four broad ideas: acceptance that moral and material conflict in society cannot be expunged, only contained and perhaps in fruitful ways tamed; hostility to unchecked power, be it political, economic or social; faith that social ills can be cured and that human life can be made better; and law-backed respect by state and society for people's lives and projects, whatever they believe and whoever they are.

More follows in the Introduction about each of those ideas—in shorthand, *conflict, power, progress* and *respect*. They distinguish liberalism point-for-point from its chief rivals in the nineteenth century, conservatism and socialism; from fascism and communism in the twentieth century and from their diverse twenty-first-century competitors: authoritarians, populists of right and left, theocrats and one-party state-capitalists. Much of the unending conflict among liberals that runs through this book is about how to think about their ideals and realize their aims. Because liberalism's guiding ideas set such high hopes, they also cause swings of mood from triumphalism to despair— and back.

Despite its wide variety of parties, camps, interests, philosophies and dominant characters, liberalism has for two centuries shown a high degree of unity and continuity. In secure times, liberalism's variety has struck people as too bewildering to count as variation in a single political practice. Surely, it is said, the term "liberalism" names different practices. Surely, there are many liberalisms. Surely, there is no one settled concept *liberalism* or *liberal*. Although arresting when first heard, such claims are much exaggerated and hard to press without raising the suspicion that the claimant recognizes liberalism well enough but is foxed by the wealth of diverse ways to think and talk about liberalism. Fear of loss, however, sharpens the mind. In insecure times, as now, definitional puzzles are less worrisome than the blunt matter of liberalism's survival.

In aiming for a rounded picture, the story here does not start with liberty, as books on liberalism often do. It does not labor back upstream to track liberal ideas to a remote preliberal past. It does not sequester liberal thought within economics or moral philosophy. It distinguishes liberalism from democracy and describes the arduous, ever negotiable compromise that produced liberal democracy. It does not treat liberalism provincially as a British and American monopoly but gives due weight to liberal traditions in France and Germany, treating all four countries together as a representative but nonexclusive core. Polemical energy is wasted on showing that liberalism's aims and ideals are narrowly Western, secular-Enlightened, bourgeois-individualist, procapitalist or—to use a fashionable term of abuse—rootlessly cosmopolitan. None of these slurs or labels stick. No sect or party owns liberalism's aims and ideals. They serve every nation, gender and class. If that brands liberals as universalists, so be it. They may wear their scarlet "U" with pride.

This is a book for the concerned common reader. There are no regular footnotes and no endnotes. The speed and generosity of the web has lightened the task of checking facts or following up quotations. Save for recent books not translated, titles of works are given in English with the date of original publication. A list of works consulted and drawn upon can be found at the end.

Liberals have been searching for acceptable points of stability amid bewildering change for 200 years. No point of stability has lasted. New ones, as now, were in time always needed. Conflict was never resolved, only mitigated. The search goes on, and liberals can blame themselves if they stop looking. They are not searching blindly. For behind them they have arguments, traditions, and experience. They have a history. That history is vital for understanding what liberalism is, why it matters and what, amid the shocks of the present, we risk losing. To recall that history is why I wrote this book.

Edmund Fawcett
January 2018

ACKNOWLEDGMENTS

For this chronicle of liberalism, I have plundered widely from the works of many writers and scholars. I am in their debt and thank them all. In person, I thank wholeheartedly Oliver Black, Donald Franklin, Charles Hope, Howard Naish, Chaim Tannenbaum, Tony Thomas, and David Wiggins, who read all or part of drafts, caught errors, and made valuable suggestions; Catherine Clarke, my agent, who encouraged me to "tell a story"; Al Bertrand at Princeton University Press, who saw the point and who urged me to update the story with liberalism's present travails in this new edition; my editor, Sarah Caro, and her ever helpful Princeton University Press colleagues; Marlowe Fawcett, who shared his film skills; and Natalia Jiménez, my wife, who gave unflagging support and never shied, on reading drafts, from "I don't get it" and "Where is this going?"

Liberalism

THE LIFE OF AN IDEA

Introduction

The Practice of Liberalism

If you think that liberalism is in jeopardy and worth defending, then it matters to see liberalism for what it is. To see something for what it is, you need to recognize its kind. If you ask what kind of thing liberalism is, you are likely to be told that it is a political ideology, an ethical creed, an economic picture of society, a philosophy of politics, a rationale of capitalism, a provincial Western outlook, a passing historical phase or a timeless body of universal ideals. None of that is strictly wrong, but all of it is partial. Each of those answers makes one aspect of liberalism the whole of liberalism. None puts liberalism in its proper category. Seen in the round, liberalism is to be taken as a practice of politics.

Liberalism has no foundation myth or year of birth. Its intellectual and moral sources go back as far as energy or curiosity will take you, but it arose as a political practice in the years after 1815 across the Euro-Atlantic world and nowhere significantly before. Liberalism responded to a novel condition of society, grown suddenly larger with expanding populations, energized by capitalism and shaken by political revolution in which, for better or worse, material and ethical change now appeared ceaseless. In that unfamiliar setting, the first liberals sought fresh terms for the conduct of political life that would serve their aims and honor their ideals.

People before them had not imagined such an ever-shifting world. Thinkers of the eighteenth-century Enlightenment had encouraged the idea that people might understand and change society. Hume and Kant had welcomed liberty from ethical tutelage. Adam Smith had spied the first fruits of modern capitalism. None had experienced the true force of either. None had understood, let alone felt, a new state of affairs in which society was changing people, often at unprecedented speed and in ways nobody understood. That restless novelty, welcome in some ways, bewildering in others, argues for an early nineteenth-century opening to the liberal epic. To look for political liberalism before then is like searching for the seventeenth-century carburetor or the eighteenth-century microchip.

Neither dynasties, presidencies nor revolutions mark liberalism's life. Four rough periods, given sharp dates for clarity, stand out. The first (1830–1880) was a time of youthful self-definition, rise to power and large achievements. In its second period (1880–1945), liberalism matured and struck a historic compromise with democracy. From that compromise, hard-fought and unstable as it was, liberalism emerged in a more inclusive form as democratic liberalism, better known as liberal democracy. After near-fatal failures—imperial overreach, globalized rivalries and world wars, political collapse, economic slump—liberal democracy in 1945 won itself a second chance with the military defeat and moral ruin of fascism, its twentieth-century rival on the right. That third period of reparative success and intellectual vindication (1945–89) ended in seeming triumph with the surrender of Soviet Communism, liberal democracy's twentieth-century rival on the left. In a fourth period (1989 to the present), self-doubt returned amid bewildering shocks and anxious concern that liberal democracy's many recognized complaints might no longer be treatable on their own but were threatening to run together and become fatal.

Liberalism's Sources

The four broad ideas that have guided liberals in their history had roots of various kinds. The first idea, acknowledgment of conflict's inescapability, drew on fresh memories of religious warfare and on the realization that economic change and intellectual fragmentation were together throwing stable societies into upheaval.

The second liberal idea, distrust of power—be it the power of the state, of wealth or of the social community—drew on old human wisdom that power grew implacable if not checked, as well as on the modern realization that undivided authorities could not command complex societies.

Faith in human progress, the third liberal idea, rose out of a human urge to improve, tidy, and repair, but more immediately and more articulately out of religious awakening and Enlightenment zeal in the seventeenth and eighteenth centuries, each a version of this-worldly hopefulness, often found together in one and the same liberal. No more than Kant did early liberal statesmen such as Guizot or Gladstone take faith and reason to exclude each other.

Lastly, civic respect—that is the law-backed respect by state and society for people and their projects, whatever they thought and whoever they were—had roots in religious acknowledgement of people's intrinsic worth and insistence on their moral responsibility for themselves. It had roots also in law, particularly laws of property and inheritance. The political demands of liberal respect, however, were wider in range and more specific in content. Liberals enjoined power not to intrude on people's privacy, not to obstruct their aims and not to exclude anyone from those first two promises whether by debarment or neglect. In fortifying and extending civic respect, liberals built on the modern emergence of toleration for unorthodoxy as well as on the yet newer thought, promoted in political economy, that law and tradition ought not to stand in the way of people's fruitful innovations and productive enterprises.

Insisting that state and society must respect everyone, whoever they were, was a democratic seed in an otherwise undemocratic creed. Liberalism promised the boons of divided power, human progress and, in its several domains, civic respect. Only democratic liberals insisted on those boons for everyone. Liberalism laid out the feast. Democracy drew up the guest list. Much of the liberal story has involved an unending struggle between liberalism for some and liberalism for all. That contest is described in its three domains—political, economic and cultural—in Part Two (1880–1945). Not till the twentieth century's second half could democratic liberals claim to have won. The twenty-first century fear was that success might have been a passing phase.

Once liberalism had found footing and spread, liberal thinkers spun from a shared frame of mind a more articulate outlook. They mixed disputed legal, philosophical and economic terms of art—rights, individuals, free markets—with the loose banner language of the political street, notably "Liberty!" They drew on intellectual precedents going back past sixteenth- and seventeenth-century defenders of toleration and anti-monarchical republicanism through the conciliarism and ethical ratio-nalism of the scholastic church doctors to arguments about power, duty and justice of the ancient Greeks, all of which gave rise to unsettled ar-guments about when liberalism began.

No one version of the liberal outlook ever became canonical. Liberal-ism had no accredited doctrinalists, no Congregation for the Propaga-tion of the Faith, no Marx-Engels Standard Edition. No one philosophy spoke for its ideas. Millian Utilitarianism and Hegelian idealism served alike in the nineteenth century as justificatory narratives. In the English-speaking world after 1945, a rights-based liberalism came to dominate political philosophy. Given such variety of common terms and suggested vindications, liberalism's outlook was bound to be loose fitting, open to interpretation and unsettled argument. Liberal philosophers strive to justify liberalism. The rivals of liberalism strive to defeat liberalism. Lib-erals vie among themselves to own liberalism. In the thicket of liberal ideas, it is good to be clear which argument you are having.

Hopes and Fears in a Strange Predicament

Liberalism began in a predicament. The first liberals were looking for a new political order after the upheavals of early industrial capitalism and two late eighteenth-century revolutions—American and French—had thrown society into fruitful but unending turmoil. The principal liberal challenge was that order from now on would be dynamic, not static. When thrown out of balance, society might come to rest again but never, save by remotest luck, in its former place. Continuity of life imagined as a comforting return home was gone for good. Thrown into an unfamiliar world of nomadic modernity, liberals were thrilled and horrified. Nei-ther their political temperament nor their political ideas can be under-stood without seeing the hold on them of that thrill and horror together. In searching for an acceptable political order in a destabilized world of ceaseless change, liberals had accordingly a hopeful dream, a nightmare and a daytime picture of human society that combined both good and bad dreams in an unsteady, creative tension. Liberalism from the beginning was as much a search for order as a pursuit of liberty.

The hopeful dream imagined a myth of order in a masterless world: a peaceful, prosperous place without father figures or brotherhood, chieftains or comrades, final authorities or natural-born friends. It was an appealing myth shaped by distrust of powers, monopolies and authorities, by faith that the worst human ills of warfare, poverty, and ignorance were corrigible in this world, and by unbreachable respect for the enterprises, interests and opinions of people, whoever they were. Those convictions attracted and were first voiced by educated, propertied men keen to get ahead and to prevent existing elites from standing in their way, but the appeal of liberal ideas was not confined to such people, and in democratic times the appeal broadened without limits of social category. Liberalism's ideas served as guides in a world of ever-shifting novelty where interests clashed and argument never ended. Liberals were not sleepwalkers. They worked hard to convince themselves that their guiding ideas, ambitious and exacting as they were, might interlock and reinforce each other.

Liberals hoped for *ethical* order without appeal to divine authority, established tradition or parochial custom. They hoped for *social* order without legally fixed hierarchies or privileged classes. They hoped for an *economic* order free of crown or state interference, monopoly privileges and local obstacles to national markets. They hoped for an *international* order where trade prevailed over war and treaty prevailed over force. They hoped lastly for a *political* order without absolute authorities or undivided powers that all citizens might understand and accept under lawful arrangements honoring and fostering those other hopes.

The liberal nightmare pictured a world in disorder. The nightmare drew on the direct experience of revolution and warfare in 1789–1815 as well as on collective memory of the fratricidal conflicts of the sixteenth and seventeenth centuries. It mingled fears of a return to historic intolerance and religious strife with revulsion at the terror and counterterror, popular unrest, vengeful repression, *levée en masse* and unlimited warfare that had recently swept over the European and Atlantic world. European liberals shuddered at riotous mobs in burgeoning cities. American liberals feared reprisal for the cruelties and wickedness of slavery. Ever deeper poverty in the countryside was bleakly forecast as growing populations threatened to outstrip agricultural capacities. Liberals everywhere worried that whereas the benefits of progress were commonly diffuse and would be seen over time, the costs of progress tended to be local, sharply felt and abrupt.

Liberalism resolved hope and nightmare into a desirable picture of society as an unfraternal place without natural harmony from which clashing interests and discordant beliefs could never be removed but where, with luck and wise laws, unceasing conflict might nevertheless be turned to welcome ends in innovation, argument and exchange. That picture of conflict channeled into peaceful competition made a mystifying, fluid and constantly surprising society intelligible to liberals, and thence in some sense justifiable or acceptable.

Appealing reasons existed to suppose the elements of the liberal dream might work together and hopes might be achieved. Ethical order would become self-fulfilling with the spread of education and material independence, as people learned to take responsibility, to choose well and wisely for themselves and to respect each other's choices. Social order would be self-sustaining as the cumulative benefits of technical and economic change outweighed their costly disruptions. Economic order would be self-correcting, for when one market failed, another market could provide, and when a whole economy faltered, prosperity would return so long as the economy was left to rebalance itself without lasting or ineffective interference. International order similarly would prove self-imposing as the mutual gains from trade and openness outgrew the spoils of war. Political order, finally, would be self-fulfilling as subjects became rulers, the master-state became a servant-state and the only rules citizens had to obey were those they had in some sense accepted for themselves. As hopes go, those were big hopes.

Liberalism's ambition struck its rivals from the start as extravagant if not Utopian. Hope for masterless order among contented people asked a lot of steady material gains, which came, but not steadily. It asked a lot of rising forbearance among reasonable citizens within nations, which was visible in good times but vanished with frightening speed in bad. It asked a lot of declining belligerence between nations, which did indeed lessen for the kinds of reasons liberals gave only to return to their consternation in ever more destructive forms. In new guise, those same challenges are as stark now as in the nineteenth century. Hope for order from horizonless innovation, open borders and limitless social freedom asks a lot of people who do not all share the gains, who long for stability and who do not always want to be reasonable or forbearing with neighbors they do not particularly like.

Dream and nightmare, success and wreckage mark the liberal story and, with them, wide swings of mood: politically, from over-confidence to self-doubt; intellectually, from unbounded universalism to worldly-wise damage limitation. At the top of the cycle, liberals could always be found spying calamity ahead. At the bottom of the cycle, liberals could always be found reminding shaken colleagues of the upturn to come. Like up-and-down capitalism itself, liberalism's mood swings are comforting only to a point. Cycles in history, like trends in nature, can come to an end.

Liberalism's Four Guiding Ideas

Liberalism's first guiding idea—conflict—was less an aim or ideal than a description of society, though hardly a neutral description. Conflict of interests and beliefs was, to the liberal mind, inescapable. If tamed and turned to competition in a stable political order, conflict could nevertheless bear fruit as argument, experiment and exchange. By treating society not as an extended tribe or a household writ large but as a field of peaceable competition, liberals put constraints on what prescriptive ideals to follow. Their ideals, that is, had to suit a competitive society. When liberals took conflict for inevitable and competition, its peaceable form, for desirable, they excluded or demoted social virtues that their political rivals favored. To liberals, competition in the town square, laboratory or market place encouraged bargaining, creativity, and initiative, whereas social harmony stifled or silenced them. Conservatives, who saw harmony in tradition, and socialists, who saw harmony in fraternity, were each quick to insist that liberal ideals grossly distorted the true picture of society. The liberal picture was, to their minds, a portrait painted to flatter liberalism's self-image, a picture not of how society was but of how grasping liberals wished it to become.

In thinking about conflict, American and British liberals have tended, in hopeful imitation of economists, to treat it individualistically as involving two single bargainers or contestants that could without distortion be magnified to social scale. French and German liberals have tended to treat conflict more socially as taking place among shared mentalities and self-standing groups. With that contrast in mind, it will be suggested at the end of Part One that liberalism can be but does not need to be defended in contentious "individualist" terms.

Hopeful early liberals such as Constant, Tocqueville and Mill welcomed diversity and distrusted social unity. They saw in modern fragmentation the sunny potential of material and intellectual creativity. Liberalism, however, soon had to reckon with people who would rather fight than trade. It had to find something to say to people with little or nothing to trade, nothing, that is, of the marketable kind that liberal capitalism characteristically valued. Faced by those difficulties, later liberals, particularly after 1945, often tried to fool themselves that society was not after all in inescapable conflict. With a measure of bad faith, they were tempted to fall back on the fond belief that modern people's interests and convictions were converging on the common goals of social peace and material plenty. On that wishful picture, conflict in liberal modernity was not so much tamed as expunged.

To shaken liberals in the twenty-first century, it is not the least clear that modern society reliably turns conflict to net advantage or that liberal capitalism has achieved a wished-for steady-state of concord in discord. Theirs is not the sunny view taken by mid–nineteenth century liberals of vigorous argument and fertile competition. Nor is it the self-confident post-1945 liberalism of moderate government-aided economic convergence in a nevertheless open and diverse society, but a bleaker view of unremitting conflict and division reinforced by doubts about the liberal foundations. Rattled liberals nowadays are likelier to see the intellectual and material fractures of society more with the eyes of Jean Bodin or Thomas Hobbes, though without the recourse to absolute powers, a plausible solution in the sixteenth and seventeenth centuries but in liberal modernity neither acceptable nor achievable.

As for liberalism's second guiding idea, human power was implacable. It could never be relied on to behave well. Whether political, economic or social, superior power of some people over others tended inevitably to arbitrariness and domination unless resisted and checked. Power might stop people from doing what they chose or make them do what they would rather not. The kind of power that mattered first in politics was public power, of state over citizen, wealth over poverty, majorities over minorities. Public power took a variety of forms. Power might come as hard, lawful coercion by the state. It might come more softly as overbearing economic pressure in the market or socially as constricting orthodoxy. Each form carried a characteristic "or else," exacting compliance by threatening respectively punitive restraint, the infliction of penury or social ostracism.

Power might on occasion be resisted by open violence or, in the thrilling *grand soir* of radical imagination, by popular uprising. But power for liberals could be peacefully and durably resisted only by law and institutions, themselves forever contested by competing interests eager to capture lawful authority. Liberal resistance to power needed accordingly to be watchful in several domains. It was best understood by what it excluded and what was proposed instead: not autocratic rule, but division of constitutional authority; not economic monopoly, but economic competition; not intellectual orthodoxy, but free enquiry and open argument.

Liberal resistance called, demandingly, on citizens one by one not to submit to undue power. The ideal liberal citizen was self-possessed and ready to answer back to authority. Yet liberalism was not a call to martyrdom. Effective resistance had to be collective. Liberalism called accordingly for a shared commitment to laws and institutions that prevented any one interest, faith or class from seizing control of state, economy or society and turning it to their own domineering purposes. Liberal resistance, that is, required lasting arrangements that recognized "the radical illegitimacy of all absolute power" in Guizot's words. Creating institutions, however, was but a first step in collective resistance. The liberal task of standing up to power was never over. Resistance was rarely secure, for power was remorseless and cunning.

The first defense against arbitrary power, law and government, was itself a power, hence an abiding problem for liberals. The problem dogged them in the nineteenth century as they strove to make government not smaller or weaker, as appropriative later caricature insisted, but more capable and less corrupt. It dogged liberals in the mid–twentieth century, by when they had come to accept wide socioeconomic responsibilities for government but at growing cost and with open-ended demands for government to do ever more. It dogged small-government liberals in the late twentieth century who forgot the powers of wealth and orthodoxy and became fixated on government as the only power to resist. The task of finding a balance between containing and empowering the state dogged the liberal democracies in the twenty-first century, by when it had become clear that denying, belittling and neglecting government's responsibilities did not magically make them go away.

In thinking about the proper level of state power, liberals throughout staked a lot on progress, their third guiding idea, which they trusted would make society and its citizens less unruly. The first liberals stressed progress in various ways, as their story will show. Humboldt, Guizot and Mill emphasized the progress made possible by education. The economists Cobden, Marshall, and Walras stressed the progress of economic advance and spreading prosperity. Smiles and Channing saw progress in personal advance, respectively as self-improvement or moral uplift. High officials such as the Benthamite Chadwick looked to government to answer social ills and improve the common welfare. That social-minded tradition of liberal progress was taken up and widened by the "new liberals" early last century, Hobhouse, Naumann, Bourgeois and Croly. The scope and timing varied, but after 1945 the social tradition of liberalism—whether written as in France and Germany, half-written as in the United States or unwritten as in Britain—was constitutionally embedded in Western politics. Welfare capitalism, which included universal education and cradle-to-grave social security, became the liberal model of human progress across the Atlantic world. For the next 70 years it often seemed as if the deep, enduring question in Western politics was the cost and sustainability of liberal progress.

The fourth liberal idea was that there were limits to how superior power could treat and above all not mistreat people, or exclude people. Liberals called on state and society to respect people themselves, whoever they were, whatever they believed. Liberals were not repeating the banal truth that might was not right. They were neither inventing the idea that moral restraints existed on power nor rediscovering the ancient maxim that sensible rulers must avoid cruelty, theft and disregard for the people's will. Liberals were applying a common moral and prudential inheritance in new circumstances where a new kind of citizen was making new demands. As Constant, Tocqueville, and Mill all grasped, modern citizens demanded ample room for public maneuver together with a secure private space, and had the self-possession to stand up for what they wanted.

As people faced a variety of impositions from state and society, the demands of civic respect came in several domains and took various forms. Again, they could best be put negatively. In setting limits to what superior power of some over others should not do, liberal respect insisted on nonintrusion, nonobstruction and—the democratic "whoever"—nonexclusion. Intrusive power might intrude on people's private world, interfere with their property or gag their opinions. Obstructive power might block creative aims, entrepreneurial ventures and technical innovations. Exclusive power might deny protections and permissions to the poor, to women, to the unlettered or the unorthodox. Power might deny them to anyone that is typed undemocratically for inferior citizenship by markers of social difference.

Civic respect promised people reliable protection from oppressive or unwanted power. It was a public, not personal, requirement addressed to state and society, hence the "civic." It called impersonally for restraint from the powers of those "cold monsters": state, wealth and society. It set high standards on what those behemoths owed each of us. It did not call on power to like, admire or take a personal interest in people, a misplaced hope like asking gravity to be nice to us. Taken democratically, civic respect was demanded for everybody, whoever they were. So understood, it was to be extended without the discriminations of favor or exclusion, neutrally, impartially and in blindness to people's given or adopted social clothes, a requirement of complexity and ambition, giving rise to unending dispute in thought and practice.

Particularly after 1945, liberals began to think of the permissions and protections offered by civic respect less in Utilitarian terms of their general benefits than in terms of personal rights. The shift involved a conceptual reduction and a pragmatic inflation. Philosophically, in looking for legitimizing answers to why power must desist from intruding on or obstructing us, liberal thinkers re-elaborated new contractarian versions of old natural-rights doctrines. Described in chapter 12, that modern search for the bedrock on which to rest inviolable rights started in the United States where methodological individualism dominated the social sciences, law courts played a leading part in politics, and every kind of social conflict could be framed as a legal dispute between two parties, often one of them an agency of the state. The so-called rights explosion, however, was neither confined to the university world of political philosophy, nor was it purely American. Politically, post-1945 liberals everywhere tended to fall into a habit of treating any aspect of what state and society owed us by way of respect as a matter of personal rights that could be legally codified and in principle defended in court, an inflationary sequence described in chapter 11 on human rights after 1945.

The liberalism of rights was in time flanked by a neo-Hegelian liberalism of recognition. It too involved a reduction and an inflation. As his twentieth-century interpreters read him, Hegel described a contest between the unrecognized and powerless against the recognized and powerful until all recognized all in equal acceptance of a law-governed state. History, in that picture, became a struggle for recognition. The metaphor electrified neo-Hegelian liberals, who likened the impersonal respect owed by power towards people to the personal recognition that people owed each other. It was but a step to treating every public intrusion, obstruction or exclusion as a denial of recognition, and to a blurring of the line, precious to political liberals, between the public and the private spheres, between the political and the personal.

Intellectually, whereas the liberalism of rights had succored mid–twentieth century movements for non-discrimination and civil rights, the liberalism of recognition succored a problem stepchild of those great campaigns, the politics of identity. As described in Part Four in the chapter "Nationhood, Citizenship and Identity," unifying campaigns to end exclusion and win civic respect for all risked becoming divisive campaigns to celebrate difference. When pursued in separatist spirit, identity politics, for all its virtues, divided the left, gave weapons to the right and weakened the democratic idea of equal citizenship.

It's about more than liberty.

The triple structure of civic respect made it irresistible for liberals to simplify. Faced by the historic intrusions of rulers, bailiffs, tax collectors, book censors and priests, reliable protection from undue power was what people had immemorially spoken of as liberty. In their several contests against unchecked power—political, economic and social—the first liberals seized on the idea of liberty, borrowing heavily against the moral capital of the parallel movement to free slaves. Eager to release vigorous new enterprise from old strictures against unequal bargains and unfair wages, liberal economists and lawyers worked hard to embed into nineteenth-century commercial law the idea of free contract. In facing down its twentieth-century rivals, fascism and communism, liberal democracy fought a successful contest of geopolitics and principle under the all-purpose banner of freedom.

Liberals, it is said, believe in liberty. Indeed, they do, but so do most nonliberals. Standing up for liberty does not distinguish liberals or what they believe in. Just about every modern rival to liberalism has claimed to stand somehow on the side of liberty. *Le Conservateur*, a French journal founded in 1818 to promote tradition and reaction, announced its aims as a defense of "king, religion and liberty." In *The Communist Manifesto* (1848), Karl Marx and Friedrich Engels looked forward to a classless society in which "the free development of each is the condition for the free development of all." In 1861, the American Confederacy's vice president, Alexander Stephens, defended the newly formed government of the slave-holding South as securing "all our ancient rights, franchises and liberties." The encyclical *Libertas humana*, which Pope Leo XIII addressed to Roman Catholics in 1888, held that shaping human law so that everyone might better conform to "the eternal law of God" comprised the "true liberty of human society." The charter program of the Nazi Party in 1920 announced its goal as "Germany's rebirth in the German spirit of German liberty. Benito Mussolini described Italian fascists as "libertarians" who believed in liberty, even for their enemies.

Maybe so, but those nonliberals were surely thinking of different things from what liberals think of when they invoke liberty. That objection, telling perhaps on its own, would have more weight if liberals themselves agreed on what liberty amounted to and why it mattered in politics. But they don't. Although often spoken of interchangeably, freedom and liberty are not quite the same. Freedom implies absence of obstruction or constraint, which may be natural (a tree across the path) or social (a police officer's "Stop!", a no trespassing sign or a ticket barrier). When liberals talk of liberty politically, they have in mind freedom of the second, social kind, particularly freedom from the prohibitions and intrusions of coercive authority. Yet even here, liberals do not all agree.

Some liberal thinkers would ask more of liberty in politics than simply the absence of outside constraint. Liberty would be of small worth in their eyes without capacities and resources to exercise liberty or without the assurance that liberty might not at the whim of power be snatched away. Other thinkers would push liberty yet further, taking it as the civic ideal of a self-possessed, autonomous citizen who chooses their own path in life but accepts nevertheless public responsibilities in the society to which they belong. Whichever of those several conceptions of liberty—negative, positive, or republican, to use labels from political philosophy, or some combination of the three—the democratic question would remain whether liberalism's promises of permission and protection were to be taken as extended to some people or to all people. Democratic liberals would take liberalism's promises as made for everyone. If driven to allow liberals one and only idea, democratic liberals would say that equality, not liberty, was its dominant idea. Other liberals, refusing to be driven, would deny that liberalism had one idea, be it equality or liberty, that somehow dominated the others and on which liberalism could be made to rest.

Liberty has held the stage in the monodramas of liberal history. In its Hegelian or Whig variants, the tale is essentially the same. History as Hegel imagined it was a kind of super-agent for the ever fuller realization of human liberty—for whatever counted in practice, that is, towards the extension of people's powers and capacities, both mental and material, in successive stages of society. As the common focus of people's drive for freedom, history on Hegel's account moved stage by stage towards its end or goal in an enlightened and law-governed constitutional monarchy. Only such a state, to his mind, could provide the ordered liberty that citizens needed to best achieve their proper ends. A twentieth-century Italian liberal, Guido de Ruggiero, told a Hegelian story of liberty's advance in his classic *History of European Liberalism* (1924), though with a different goal in view. For Ruggiero, the spread of liberty was tending to a condition of society in which each citizen had bankable opportunities to develop their capacities and realize their aims, a democratic commonwealth, that is, where everyone's hopes and chances in life were equally respected.

In the Whig epic of emancipation, liberty's agents were flesh-and-blood particulars—early Christians, medieval townspeople, reforming Protestants, seventeenth-century parliamentarians, anti-Stuart 1688-ers, anti-tax American colonists, French 1789-ers—knocking away one barrier or another to their advancement, motivated willy-nilly by private conscience, urge for gain or an expansive sense of self. Liberty on such accounts was a common human possession, ever at risk of hostile capture and in need of protection or release. The Protestant Macaulay's *History of England* (1848–61) celebrated the anti-Stuart revolution of 1688 in England as a restoration of ancient liberties lost to absolutism and intolerance. The Catholic Acton's posthumous *History of Freedom* (1907) tracked from antiquity to modern times a long campaign by personal faith to fend off suffocating authority. In the medieval contest for supremacy between church and crown that neither were in position to win, Acton spied a modern recovery of liberty and the creation of a lasting space for civic freedom.

Liberty-driven history survives in the recent fashion for books that recount modernity's unstoppable success as a happy *ménage à trois* of free enquiry, unobstructed new technology, and liberal politics. In biological mode, such tales make liberty an all-purpose reproductive advantage in the evolution of social forms. They credit just about every aspect of human betterment and social progress since Galileo spotted Jupiter's moons through a handmade telescope to liberty's selfless sharing of her bounty. The tale has dazzling appeal. But are the boons of universal schooling, democratic suffrage, and penicillin all forms or consequences of liberty?

There are simpler versions of the liberty narrative. They follow a memorable rule of three: political liberty's first victory was constitutional freedom (early nineteenth century), its second victory was economic freedom (later nineteenth century) and its final victory was democratic freedom (mid–twentieth century). That tidy sequence helps itself to the disputable claim that liberty is the one underlying value that representative institutions, free markets and democratic participation all embody. History is wilier than attempts to catch it in one trap allow. It concerns itself solely with liberty no more than liberals do. Obviously, you cannot leave liberty out of the liberal story. Like the king in chess, liberty comes into its own, but nearer the end of the game. For all its crowning appeal, liberty is the wrong place to begin.

The "L" Word

An irksome verbal difficulty must be faced. It would be neat if all and only liberal politicians, thinkers, parties and voters called themselves "liberal." The word itself would then mark who was a liberal and who not. Most liberals, however, have called themselves something else. Apart from Britain's long-lived Liberal Party (1859–1988), most small-*l* liberal parties in the four countries under focus here never took the capital-*L* name "Liberal" at all. In addition, "liberal" is not an all-or-nothing term. You can be more or less liberal. You can be liberal*ish*. The word, besides, had non-political uses before there were ever liberals in politics. It could mean generous, open-handed or lenient, even to a fault. When used of trade as by Adam Smith, for instance, it meant unrestricted trade. The word, lastly, had a bewitching etymology, linking "liberal" with freedom as if by definition, whereas the word entered politics more by accident.

The first to adopt the term "liberal" openly in politics were the Spanish *liberales*, members of the Cortes or parliament demanding a return to constitutional rule. In 1814 Spain's vacillating Bourbon king suspended the two-year-old constitution under the combined pressures of Catholic resistance, European reaction and colonial revolt against Spanish rule in Latin America. The *liberales* hoped that reviving the constitution would restore customary liberties and persuade the colonies to remain Spanish in a new commonwealth. They contrasted themselves with the *serviles*, slavish supporters, as they saw them, of the crown. European reaction defeated Spain's constitutionalists, but as a label for an emerging outlook, the term "liberal" itself survived. Quickly it spread from Spain to France and thence across Europe.

To begin with, "liberal" characterized constitutional opposition to autocracy. On Napoleon's return from exile in March 1815, Benjamin Constant wrote in his journal that however "liberal" the ex-emperor's intentions, the results would more likely be "despotic." After Napoleon's final defeat, the term "liberal" was a pejorative to conservatives restored to power. In 1819 Austria's chancellor, Prince Metternich, told his political secretary, Friedrich von Gentz, that "ultraliberalism" was to be extirpated without pity. Britain's Tory foreign secretary, Viscount Castlereagh, called Whig advocates of electoral and other reforms in the 1820s "our English *libéraux*," as if the Frenchness of the word was itself enough to damn the parliamentary opposition as disloyal and unsound.

By 1830, there were not only liberal views, but people who embraced such views: liberals. In France *un libéral* meant loosely anyone, monarchist or republican, who favored constitutional government and opposed a return to the *ancien régime*. In *The Charterhouse of Parma* (1839), the French novelist Stendhal wrote mockingly of his fictional Italian tyrant, Ernest IV, alone at night and afraid, who had only to hear the parquet squeak to "leap for his pistols, fearing a liberal under the bed."

Germany's liberals took many names. The first liberals called themselves Progressives. They split into right-wing National Liberals and left-wing *Freisinnigen* or Independents, who split in turn into an Independent Union and an Independent People's Party before in 1910 becoming Progressives again. In the Weimar Republic after 1918, the National Liberals renamed themselves with wounded pride the German People's Party and the left liberals became the German Democratic Party. After 1949, in the western half of a divided Germany embarked on recovery from national shame, the liberals renamed themselves Free Democrats.

The mainstream of French politics in the Third Republic (1870–1940), Fourth Republic (1944–1958) and Fifth Republic (from 1958) was liberal in character, though never in name. Many have fallen for the bluff assertion of Emile Faguet, a French literary critic who wrote in 1903 that there were no liberals in France and never would be. Elie Halévy, a French historian of English thought, who understood politics better than Faguet, grasped that you could be liberal without calling yourself liberal. Halévy described himself in 1900 as being "anti-clerical, democratic, republican, not socialist, against intolerance—a 'liberal', in other words." With the rediscovery of French liberalism in the 1970s and 1980s, such verbal puzzles came to seem less taxing. A French historian of ideas, Cécile Laborde, judged in 2003 that "the dominant language of politics in France is republicanism, not liberalism," but added the decisive rider that republicanism had "historically occupied the ideological space of liberalism." Different words, that is, might voice the same ideas. The bad odor of liberalism has, all the same, never left. Neo-liberalism in particular is widely taken in France for foolish and unfrench. The word "libéral" itself has come to mean a heartless, mindless free-marketeer even on the lips of the former banker and centrist liberal Emmanuel Macron, who campaigned successfully for the presidency in May 2017 on the slogan "Ni libéralisme, ni nationalisme."

With the two exceptions of the short-lived Liberal Republicans, led to defeat in the presidential election of 1872 by the redoubtable newspaper editor Horace Greeley, and the mid–twentieth century Liberal Party of New York, a moderate wing of the local Democrats, the main parties in American politics avoided the name. After the 1850s, two loose coalitions, the Republicans and Democrats, each with liberal and less liberal wings, monopolized the nomenclature of party competition.

By 1945, "liberal" in the United States had taken on a local and an international use. When used of politics in the United States, "liberal" indicated a supporter of the New Deal and civil rights, normally a Democrat. Internationally, "liberal" contrasted an American-led West with a Communist East. The term in the use was interchangeable with "free," "open" and "democratic." The label "liberal democracy," barely recorded before the 1930s, became common, its share of occurrence in publications jumping, according to Google Books Ngram, five times between then and 1980 and another seven times in the next two decades.

The conservative right in the United States was by then using "liberal" as a term of abuse for almost anyone it disagreed with, and the ending of the Cold War soon, as it seemed, robbed "liberal" of use as a term of geopolitical contrast. Partly in result, "liberal" became scarcely usable in serious political studies without asterisks, qualifications and neck-covering disclaimers about separate referents or conflicting senses.

Never lost to view, despite the verbal and conceptual puzzles, was a recognized practice of politics that four notably varied Western societies serving here as an exemplary core—France, Britain, Germany and the United States—all uncontroversially converged upon after 1945. That familiar, stable-seeming practice became in the first decades of the new century, a focus of anxious concern, not because it was hard to define, but out of fear that it might not survive. The practice merited a label, and "democratic liberalism," or more conventionally "liberal democracy," has struck most people as apt. Difficulties with the word "liberal" or with the concept *liberal* are as big or small as you want to make them. Particularly in times as now, when some people are thrilled by liberalism's travails and others are afraid for its life, everybody can be taken to know what they are talking about. The challenge is not to identify liberalism but to describe and understand it well.

Liberalism's Distinctiveness

Liberalism's four guiding ideas were distinctive. Taken one by one, they distinguished liberals from nonliberals and antiliberals. Taken together they stood out in relief against the competing outlooks of liberalism's chief nineteenth-century rivals, conservatives and socialists.

Both arose in reaction to liberalism, which they pictured as source and celebrant of blind, restless change. In the name of stability, conservatives appealed to the fixity of the past. They took society for a harmonious, orderly whole before critical modernity promoted self-seeking disaffection and liberal capitalism sowed discord between classes. They believed in the unchallengeable authority of established rulers and custom. Power, to the conservative mind, was to be obeyed, not questioned or made to justify itself. Conservatives took human capabilities for largely fixed and society's scope for wholesale improvement as small or nonexistent. They looked on liberal respect for people's chosen enterprises and opinions, especially when those took unwelcome or disruptive form, as harmful to orthodoxy and good order. Civic respect, to the conservative mind, undersanctioned human willfulness, overcelebrated private choice and scanted the demands of duty, deference and obedience.

Socialists also disagreed with liberals, point for point. In the name of brotherhood, socialists appealed to the fixity of the future. Conflict divided society at present, they accepted. But conflict was neither enduring nor ineradicable. For conflict, they believed, would end once its sources in material inequity were overcome. Socialism here stands for the many nineteenth-century families of the left that grew out of Jacobinism and popular radicalism to include Utopian collectivists, Fourierists, Marxists and early labor unionists. Socialists, like liberals, believed in resistance to power, but not all power. Wealth's power was their primary target, and to contain that power socialists flanked and blended with democratic movements for suffrage extension and political reform.

Socialists trusted by contrast the power of society, thought of as coextensive with the working people. Anarcho-socialists took society for self-organizing, hence in no need of protection from its own power. State-minded socialists took state power to express popular power, intuited by elected or self-appointed tribunes. Liberals, by contrast, distrusted all power, including the power of the people, however thought of or spoken for.

Like liberals, socialists had faith in human progress, but taken in contrary ways. For socialists, progress meant radical transformation of society, whereas liberals took progress for gradual improvement within society as it largely was. Some socialists would reach their goal gradually by the ballot, others in a revolutionary leap. All hoped for a postcapitalist society of effective material equality assured by commonly owned or collectively managed property. For socialists, lastly, liberal respect for people one by one overplayed privacy and self-interest at the expense of comradeship, class loyalty and solidarity. Nor were socialists persuaded that liberal respect operated evenly across its several domains. Liberals, in socialist eyes, respected private enterprises and private property above all else and, despite cries of denial, stood accordingly athwart genuine progress.

The early twentieth century was generous to liberal self-understanding with two defining Others: fascism and communism. Both rejected liberal values and adopted but perverted the democratic promise of universal inclusion. Fascism appealed to a false unity of nationhood, particularly nationhood based on the fiction of race. Communism appealed to a false unity of class, particularly the unity of the working class as somehow representative of humankind. To fascism there was no higher power than nation or race, to communism none than the working people. The mystical authority of each, as interpreted by an elite party, was absolute. Personal progress was thought of in terms of socially imposed templates rather than as a growth of capacities along privately chosen paths. Social progress was equated to progress of nation, race or class, from the benefits of which those in the wrong nation, race or class were excluded. Neither fascism nor communism offered benchmarks for civic respect, or indeed any clear lines that society might not overstep in its pursuit of the common good. As the more thoughtful liberals recognized, communism was an extremism of hope, fascism an extremism of hate. They were nevertheless alike enough on those four counts to provide liberalism with a captivating image of itself in negative.

The comprehensive disgrace of fascism (1945) and a closing of the book on Soviet communism (1989) left liberalism, as it seemed, without a global rival against which to compete historically or define itself conceptually. That sense of an ending was short-lived. In the expanded field of the twenty-first century, it was soon clear that liberalism had attractive, competing "isms" that overplayed power, underplayed civic respect and acknowledged fault on neither score: one-party authoritarianism, state capitalism, democratic nationalism, theocratic Islamism and illiberal populist movements of left and right.

Unity and Shape of the Liberal Outlook

Liberalism's four guiding ideas may be taken for liberal answers to hard questions facing any political outlook. Is the conflict of interests and faiths in society inescapable? Is power implacable and, if so, is it controllable? Are human society and human capacities static or dynamic? Are there moral or prudential limits on how those with more power may treat those with less? Answers give political outlooks a characteristic shape.

Liberals accepted the fact of conflict but distrusted power and sought to limit power. To provide for order, they counted accordingly less on power to impose control on society than on human progress to foster self-control among citizens. Liberalism's rivals, conservatism and socialism, made themselves simpler choices, given their contrasting pictures of society's true character. For conservatives, society was an organic harmony, social conflict was a malady, and people were not at root improvable. In a harmonious society, progress was not needed to create order, and, if temporarily lost, order could be restored only by power, not by progress. Progress to the conservative mind, that is, was unnecessary or ineffective. For socialists, society was a fraternal harmony, distorted at present by resolvable conflict provided material inequity was removed. Radical progress for socialists, unlike gradual progress for liberals, meant a leap out of conflict into fraternity. Once arrived in fraternity, people and power would merge, removing any need to protect the one from the other. There was a pattern here. To the hard questions about conflict among people and about tension between people and power, conservatives and socialists alike each answered in ways that lightened the burdens of containment and resolution placed on political action. Liberals, with their answers, made the burden on politics heavier.

There is no tidy answer to what made liberal answers liberal. If a satisfying, noncircular definition of "liberalism" is still wanted none is available. Looking for liberalism in semantic space or conceptual space is looking in the wrong places. Historically, liberal answers to the hard questions of politics were answers liberals gave. In addition, liberal answers and the outlook that came with them marked out clear differences with rivals on a familiar ideological map. Neither point will satisfy someone demanding the essence of liberalism or a decisive specification of the cultural kind *liberal*. The liberal outlook can, nevertheless, be seen for distinctive in a third, more helpful way.

Just as liberals would not simplify the hard questions, so they would not subordinate some guiding ideas to others, despite their inner tensions. Liberals held to all of them together, neglecting none. Whether taken as pragmatic open-mindedness or pluralism of a more theoretical kind, that second-order acceptance of tension and conflict among their own guiding ideas was itself characteristically liberal. Liberals, when being liberal, did not drop one requirement from their outlook in order to make that outlook neater to formulate or easier to follow. The liberal outlook is not a cohesive structure like the chemistry of a natural element. Some parts of the liberal outlook cohere, some conflict. Nor can the outlook be given intellectual coherence or persuasive appeal by reducing all its requirements to one overriding idea, such as liberty or equality. Liberals give their outlook coherence when pursuing its discordant aims together, and they are not acting like liberals unless they do.

Among liberalism's guiding ideas, resistance and civic respect reinforced each other. Respect and progress pulled against each other in tension. As to that first pairing, resistance and respect each bore on the proper relationship between power and people, but a relationship viewed from different sides. Resistance enjoined citizens to restrain power by law and institutions, and if that failed, by dissent. Respect enjoined power to desist from undue use of power against citizens. There was one play but two roles, rulers and ruled, each with distinct kinds of duties to the other that did not neatly reflect each other, unlike counterpart duties between spouses or friends or the inverse exchanges of buyers and sellers. Civic respect was about what power may not do to people. Resistance was about how people together could arrange matters so that power acted with respect. Out of resistance came arrangements and institutions for constraining power: divided authority, representative elections with the negative sanction of removing unwanted governments at the ballot, laws to restrain wealth and provide for need, independents courts to defend the exercise of those arrangements. Out of respect came guaranteed permissions and protections from power that people could count on by right or law.

As for the tension, respect conflicted with progress. Liberal respect stressed a negative aspect of human power, the harms it could do to people when not checked. Human power had positive aspects, however. Not only was human power, when expressed as skill, excellence, or virtuosity, valuable in itself. Human power, like natural power, could do work and yield results. It could bring benefits, including benefits needed for social and human progress. To improve society, power was needed, imposing here, obstructing there. To improve people, particularly by education, you had to shape or interfere with their chosen ends or those of their families, the "you" here being the familiar agencies of state and society. To improve the world, in short, you had to interfere with the world. Liberals were sincere in prizing diversity and individuality. They were sincere in wanting to let people alone and protect them from power. In the liberal breast, however, was also to be found the domineering teacher and liberal imperialist. With characteristic pith, Lord Acton nailed the difficulty in a letter to a friend in 1887: "My liberalism admits to everyone the right to his own opinion and imposes on me the duty of teaching him what is best."

Liberal Deviations and Alliances

The complexity of the liberal outlook allowed for deviations and alliances. Among deviations, anarchism in the nineteenth century and its late twentieth-century cousin, libertarianism, both promoted respect for people on their own into a super-principle, to the neglect of liberalism's other guiding ideas. Despite their local appeal, neither idea was practical in large, complex societies. Libertarian thought, particularly of a strong free-market kind, has nevertheless stamped present-day sensibilities, encouraged underestimation of the need for countervailing powers, and fed distrust of politics and government.

An opposite pull, towards progressive authoritarianism, fostered the liberal goal of social progress at a cost to civic respect, especially the inclusive, democratic element in respect. Social progress pursued in illiberal ways has often tempted liberals as a temporary second-best, as nineteenth-century examples will show. In good economic times, twentieth-century liberal economists tended to relax with the thought that economic progress, whatever the cost, would in time meet other liberal goals.

As open-minded negotiators at the political center, liberals were ever available for party alliances to their right and left. By the late nineteenth century, right-wing liberals had allied with market-minded conservatives in a defense of wealth and property against economic democracy. That rightward tendency in liberalism was noted early. After the German liberals' rout in their failed revolution of 1848 against absolute rule and princely privilege, Helmut von Moltke, the future Prussian field marshal and creator of Germany's general staff, wrote about liberal prospects in a letter to his sister-in-law. For all their stormy talk of change, Moltke told her, liberals would quickly see where their true interests lay. Before long, he predicted, "the most radical deputy will be carrying on like a monocled toff." Moltke was only half right. By the late nineteenth century, as will be seen, many left-wing liberals had embarked on the historic compromises that led after 1945 to democratic liberalism. In that compromise, government parties of the right soon joined. However, by the twenty-first century, a hard right, illiberal in its disregard for countervailing powers and undemocratic in its economic exclusions, had reemerged and reasserted its distinctiveness.

Who Is Liberal and Who Isn't

There was always a question of who was and who wasn't a liberal. Every liberal had to hold to all four liberal ideas without sacrificing one to the others, but that left scope for variation, degrees of liberalism and marginal cases. Tocqueville yes, Marx no, although some have thought he was a liberal. Being or not being liberal came in degrees. Guizot and Mill were both unmistakably liberals, but Mill, who admired Guizot as a thinker and historian but not as a politician, was more liberal. Herbert Hoover was a liberal of a kind but less liberal than Franklin Roosevelt. Much had to do with who you took for allies. Business-minded liberals by the end of the nineteenth century were, as just noted, often hard to tell from business-minded conservatives. Social-minded liberals were similarly often hard to tell after 1945 from liberal-minded socialists.

If exemplars are demanded, Gladstone and Lincoln were exemplary liberals in the nineteenth century, Beveridge and Lyndon Johnson in the twentieth. Mill, Weber and Rawls were exemplary liberals among thinkers. There were also intriguing outliers and marginal cases. Among nineteenth-century politicians, Richter in Germany and Laboulaye in France were minority liberal voices in illiberal regimes. Among thinkers, neither Sartre nor Oakeshott were straightforwardly liberal. Each scorned the label. Mentioning either of them in a work on liberalism provoked dismay or charges of incomprehension from reviewers of this book's first edition. It would be odd, however, not to hear something liberal in Sartre's philosophical veneration of sovereign personhood or in Oakeshott's mocking suspicion of systems and planning.

Liberal Passions

Speeches, talk and fiction have mattered for liberalism as well as treatises. To follow liberalism's story, you need a scalpel for its ideas, but also an ear for the moral sentiments, passions and attachments that gave those ideas force. In *Anna Karenina* (1873–78), Tolstoy described "the true liberalism" of Anna's amiable, shambolic brother, Stiva Oblonsky, as being "in his blood." Oblonsky's was not the doctrinal liberalism he read about at the club in his liberal newspaper, but a deep-rooted set of moral sentiments. That temperamental liberalism, Tolstoy told us, rested on "a leniency founded on a consciousness of his own defects" and on a profound sense of human equality which "made him treat all men alike whatever their rank or official position." The American poet T. S. Eliot took a less flattering view of the liberal temperament. "He is a liberal,"

Eliot said of his friend and fellow poet Stephen Spender, "and therefore tends to intolerance and to judging others; and he tends to take an unctuously superior tone on the basis of very imperfect understanding." There are many feelings in the liberal breast.

Characteristic social sentiments and moral emotions lent strength to liberalism's guiding ideas: hatred of domination (resistance); pride or shame in your society (progress); outrage at maltreatment and exemplary wrongs (respect); zest for competitive challenges (conflict). None were liberal property. When such feelings were brought into politics, liberalism gave them a characteristic voice. Those liberal feelings had also darker counterparts. The powers that came with strength, excellence, wealth or moral splendor provoked liberal envy and resentment. Liberal zeal for progress could mask self-punishing scrupulosity towards blameless collective ills. Insistence on civic respect for people was ever open to the distortions of selective indignation. Blithe acceptance of conflict could tip to its opposite, undue fear of disorder and anxious longing for calm. Liberalism's sharper critics to left and right—Joseph de Maistre, Karl Marx, Friedrich Nietzsche, Charles Maurras, and Carl Schmitt, for example—all made hay with that shadow side of liberal sentiment. Liberalism's great orators, Guizot, Lincoln, and Gladstone; liberalism's great talkers, Clemenceau and Lloyd George; and liberalism's great writers, Orwell, Camus, and even semiliberal Sartre, all understood liberal sentiments, the bright and dark ones alike. To understand liberalism, you need to keep in mind its characteristic temperament and its shifting moods.

Liberalism as a Practice

As a practice of politics, liberalism can be taken naturalistically for a norm-governed adaptation to modern historical circumstance. Like any broad human practice, liberalism has a history, practitioners and a distinctive outlook to guide them. Practices are familiar. They may be thought of as cultural kinds, whose members are open to observation and inspection much like natural kinds. Law, marriage, religion and art are examples. Politics is another. As politics is a practice, liberalism strictly is a subpractice or the practice of a practice. So are its rivals, conservatism and socialism, each of them being ways to practice a practice. Once that is understood, it is simpler to avoid the stutter and speak of liberalism as a practice without ado. By "practitioners" is meant simply liberals, the men and women who have engaged in, voted for and thought about liberal politics. The term "practice" could be replaced by "tradition." Which one is preferable depends on the ear. If a term of art is wanted, "ideology" could replace "outlook." Talking of a liberal ideology rather than a liberal outlook is harmless so long as it is remembered that liberals *have* guiding ideas but that liberalism itself, taken as a practice or tradition stretched out in historical time, cannot *be* a set of guiding ideas, something abstract and in need of mental labor to pull to earth.

Nor, to avoid a related mistake, is liberalism a philosophy of politics. To take it for one involves a confusion of levels between politics and history on the one hand and philosophy on the other. Political liberalism has had high-order justifications for its guiding ideas in abundance: Kantian, Hegelian, Utilitarian, neo-idealist, neo-Lockian, Popperian, Rawlsian, neo-Hegelian and pragmatist. Without first identifying the liberal outlook, you cannot analyze or justify that outlook philosophically, indispensable as both tasks are to liberalism's higher self-understanding. To identify the liberal outlook without tying it to particular philosophies, you need to see how that outlook has guided liberal practice historically. The same is true of other attempts to anchor the liberal outlook in some nonpolitical discipline. Liberalism as such may, but has no need to, appeal to speculative anthropology, sociological methodology or, as the chapter on Spencer will suggest, evolutionary biology.

The Liberal Story

Part One (1830–1880) of this book recounts liberalism's arrival in political argument and ascent to government power. After a sketch of the historical setting, its first seven chapters describe the lives and thoughts of the founders of liberalism, often in contrasting pairs to dramatize a contest of ideas. Humboldt, a professor, stressed human advance through education, Constant, a social outsider, the growth of individuality in private pursuits. Against the looming power of mass society,

Tocqueville promoted voluntary association; against that of the mass market, Schulze-Delitzsch promoted economic localism and coopera-tives. Chadwick worked for social progress by government action, Cob-den by expansion of free markets. Smiles took personal progress for self-improvement, Channing for moral uplift, each distinct from socialist class advance or from conservative doubt that people deeply change at all. Mill made a philosophic attempt to square liberal respect for people with social progress understood as expansion of the general good. Lin-coln and Gladstone, great users and expanders of government, exempli-fied liberal ideas in office.

Part Two (1880–1945) describes liberalism in command together with its successes and failures as it compromised with democracy. Lib-eralism in this period went a long way to meeting its aims and honoring its ideals. It also survived, barely, calamities of its own making. Consti-tutionally, state power was segmented and controlled even as the reach of government grew. Chapters on Walras, Marshall and the business press illustrate how states were resisted on behalf of markets. The power of the market was tempered by the beginnings of a welfare state, as the parallel careers of the "social" liberals, Hobhouse, Naumann, Croly, and Bourgeois, will show.

Liberalism (1880–1945) made peace with democracy. From that his-toric compromise emerged the practice of liberalism known as liberal democracy. The grand bargain between liberalism and democracy in-volved political choice, economic power and ethical authority. In each area liberals abandoned whatever monopoly hopes they may once have entertained as a rising elite of educated, propertied men intent on sup-planting previous régimes. Liberals accepted popular sovereignty across those three domains. In return, popular forces accepted liberal rules of procedure, protections of property and respect for personal choice. The compromise was neither smooth nor automatic, but grudging and hard fought. Least of all was it historically inevitable or conceptually neces-sary. Liberal democracy is contingent and reversible.

In the decades after 1880s under pressure of class conflict, govern-ments enacted sweeping social reforms and gave the state new tasks, welcomed by most liberals as an application of liberal principle to new circumstance, though resisted by an unconvinced minority as an aban-donment of liberal principle. Education and cultural progress did not, first of all, eradicate prejudice and intolerance or create reasonable, dispassionate citizens as reliably as liberals had hoped. Aggressive nationalism, jingo imperialism, anti-Catholicism, white racism, anti-Semitism and other exclusionary hatreds proved winning vote-getters, to which liberal elites often responded opportunistically when not offering active encouragement. The varied early twentieth-century careers of Bouglé, Alain, Baldwin and Brandeis illustrate the challenges of embedding civic respect for all and protecting unorthodoxy and diversity against society's pressures, challenges not met until the human rights and civil rights movements after 1945.

Trade and economic interdependence, secondly, did not ensure peace and amity. They brought a rivalry of liberal imperialisms, illustrated by the parallel careers of Joseph Chamberlain and Ernst Bassermann. In 1914 came an unexpected and bewildering world war that many took to mark liberalism's end. That war introduced two new political types that came to prominence in the twentieth century, the liberal hawk defending liberal values by military strength, and the liberal internationalist, promoting multilateral negotiation and peaceful cooperation among competing nations. Nor, lastly, during the decade-long slump of the 1930s could liberals convincingly persist in the laissez-faire doctrine that when markets capsized, they righted themselves. Their after-runners have made of them warring prophets, but as the chapter on them makes clear, Keynes, Fisher, and Hayek were all aiming to save capitalism.

Part Three (1945–1989) describes liberalism's restabilization and success. Liberal democracy survived economic collapse, world war and moral ruin to enjoy a second chance after 1945. The liberal world took that chance, and succeeded beyond expectation. The story opens with human rights, liberal democracy restored in full to Germany and the expansion of the liberal welfare state. Representative liberal thinkers of the 1950s–80s occupy the next five chapters, followed by the turn of liberal economists against the state. Three politicians each from the liberal left and the liberal right close the years 1945–89.

Were 1989 the end, the narrative arc would be simple: liberalism is up, it's down, it's up. The liberals of 1830–80 drew the blueprint. The liberals of 1880–1945 built the house and then almost burned it down. Liberals took their second chance in 1945 and by 1989 liberalism was the pride of the neighborhood. That was then.

Part Four, "Liberal Dreams and Nightmares in the Twenty-First Century," recounts liberal democracy's upheavals and disappointments in the century's first two decades. It recalls the dream of masterless, self-fulfilling order with which liberalism began and asks how pursuable the dream continues to be in its several domains. It describes the rise of a hard right, both illiberal and antidemocratic, economic travails, liberal democracy's growing geopolitical loneliness and apparent division into unfriendly European and Anglo-American camps, as well as widespread intellectual disaffection, all of which shook liberal confidence in the democratic achievability of their hopes. The conclusion is bleak, not despairing. The book ends with a plea to resist the lure of mechanism, those beguiling stories that tell us that irreversible social, economic, historical or even evolutionary trends ensure that democratic liberalism is bound to fail or must succeed. It urges liberals to accept instead the primacy of politics, the availability of options and the thought that whether liberal democracy survives or fails depends to no small degree in how well it is understood and defended.

Democratic Liberalism in the Round

Liberalism arose as a practical response to the predicament of capitalist modernity. It offered an ethically acceptable order of human progress among civic equals without recourse to undue power. It appealed especially to modern-minded, self-possessed people who would not be bossed about or pushed around by superior power, be it of state, wealth or society. Liberalism offered to improve people's lives and to treat them and their enterprises with equal respect. Liberals took moral and material conflict in society as inevitable but hoped that conflict could be made fruitful in argument, experiment and exchange. Their four guiding ideas—conflict, resistance to power, progress and civic respect—underlay and gave point to liberalism's familiar and contested banner terms, "liberty," "the individual," "rights," and "equality." Liberalism's promises were not narrowly Western or bourgeois. Their appeal was universal. It remains a matter of conflict how far liberal promises may be met democratically, that is, for everyone whoever they are.

PART ONE

The Confidence of Youth (1830–1880)

1

Historical Setting in the 1830s

Thrown into a World of Ceaseless Change

On April 12, 1835, Wilhelm von Humboldt—diplomat, linguist, advocate of universal education, and liberal pioneer—was buried beside his wife, Caroline, in a small plot overlooked by a statue of Hope in the park of their estate on the northwestern edge of Berlin. Through the oak trees lies Tegelsee, one of many lakes that give the city its sparkling light. A short walk away stands the family's elegant villa, rebuilt to a neoclassical design by Prussia's leading architect of the day, Karl-Friedrich Schinkel. The calm and seclusion give little clue that Humboldt lived in a world turned upside down. He was born into a Prussian noble family in 1767 before liberalism was dreamed of. By the time he died, revolutions in the Americas, the Dutch Republic, and France had shaken the Atlantic world and liberalism was on its way to becoming what it is today, a common practice of politics for market societies in perpetual motion.

At the time of Humboldt's birth in the court and barracks town of Potsdam to the southwest of the city, an enlightened warrior king, Frederick the Great, ruled Prussia, the American colonies were British, and the Bourbon monarchy ruled, or attempted to rule, France. Most Europeans lived and worked on the land near where they were born, dying as a rule before they were forty. Most could not read or write. In Britain four in ten men and seven in ten women could not sign their names at marriage. Urbanization, like industry, lay in the future. In the German Ruhr Valley, Düsseldorf was a tiny town and Essen little more than a village. London, Bristol, and a few small cities aside, England was a place of countryside and market towns. In a flash of scientific imagination,

James Watt had grasped how an efficient piston might work, but a reliable steam engine had yet to be perfected and harnessed in industry. To satisfy a flourishing new social type, the middle-class shopper, Europe relied on trade and on slaves sold by Africans for work in New World colonies. Enlightenment thought thrived on hopes for human betterment but also on sugar, coffee, and tobacco.

Law and custom commonly limited where you could work or live, what associations you could form with like-minded friends or fellow workers, and what moneymaking enterprises you could start. Serfdom of a kind, tying laborers to their villages, survived in rural Prussia. Close to a quarter of Britain's two million American subjects were slaves or indentured servants working payless for a fixed term in return for their Atlantic passage and keep. Non-Anglicans could not teach in British schools or universities, nor marry legally without a vicar's dispensation. Catholics could not vote or sit in parliament. Jews in Britain, France, and Prussia lived on sufferance, without political or civil rights. Protections of speech and press were precarious. Prior censorship, where it existed, was spotty and haphazard, but the threat of reprisal was enough to make people think twice before speaking their minds. Punishments were frequently cruel and spectacular, especially if you were poor, defied power, or flouted orthodox opinion.

Such was the old world of Humboldt's birth in 1767. It was not as stunted or backward as critics made out. The world of Humboldt's birth was above all not fixed or frozen, but a world in movement. After centuries of creeping up and falling back, Europe's populations were exploding with growth. Pressure was on to find new ways to feed and provide for more people. The term would not be heard for another eighty years or so, but the first shoots of industrial capitalism—investing in productive machinery for private profit—were already visible. Pressure was also on to find new ways to do what wise and effective rulers had always done: listen to the people.

For voices were being raised against ills and encumbrances of the old world: against absolute and arbitrary monarchs, against backwardness, neglect, and illiteracy, against slavery and intolerance, against not being able to say and print what you wanted or make money as you pleased, against not having a voice. Established ethical authorities and accepted models of conduct, once as pervasive and weightless-seeming as air, felt suddenly burdensome and had to explain themselves. To practices and conditions previously taken for natural or irremovable there were, many now insisted, alternatives. There was, though, no one party of change, no one focus of opposition, no one vehicle of progress. There were in particular no liberals. In Humboldt's youth the word "liberal" meant generous, open-handed, or perhaps lenient to a fault. The phrase "a liberal" was a grammatical mistake and the term "liberalism" would have met blank stares. By the time of Humboldt's death, in a world transformed, a new approach to politics was emerging to welcome and, it was hoped, to channel breathtaking change.

Humboldt was too young and distant to witness the first great upheaval of his life, the American Revolution, when Britain's fractious New World colonies won a war of independence in 1783, imposed a disputed constitution on themselves and founded a divided, experimental new republic, the United States. For the lasting aftershocks of another upheaval, the French Revolution, Humboldt was present in person as a high official, diplomat, and liberal dissident in an enlightened but autocratic Prussian government.

In the summer of 1789 young Humboldt was on a European tour with his old tutor when news reached them of revolution in France. They rushed to Paris, and three weeks after its fall visited the Bastille, which workmen were beginning to demolish. The "grave of despotism," as the tutor solemnly put it, impressed them both, but the idea of revolution did not sweep young Humboldt away. He asked himself what revolution would do for the sick and poor of the city, whose condition appalled him. Nobody knew what lay ahead. In Paris, as on the rest of the trip, Humboldt mostly saw sights and visited brothels, carefully noting what he spent there in his day book.

Humboldt welcomed what he took for revolution's higher aims: an end to arbitrary rule and a historic release of human capacities; but he thought the means, rewriting society's ground rules, were sure to fail. Foreign invasion, civil war, counterinvasion, and state-led terror—against foes of revolution rich or poor and soon against any who murmured a word against terror—seemed to confirm Humboldt's worst fears. They left him also with a historic challenge. Revolution and war had shattered Europe's old political order. Humboldt's generation and those that followed faced a long search for a new one.

The French declared a republic, executed their Bourbon king for treason, won and lost again control of most of Europe under a corporal-turned-emperor, Napoleon Bonaparte, lived through fifteen years of reaction after his defeat in 1815, and then shook Europe a second time by throwing out a restored Bourbon monarchy in 1830. The British and Germans caught the mood. In November, the liberal Whigs replaced the conservative Tories in power after almost half a century in opposition, and an era of economic, social, and political reform began at Westminster. In the German lands—the nation was unified only in 1871—absolute princes, whether despotic or enlightened, faced demands for civil liberties, constitutional rule, and representative government. Everywhere the brutalities and excesses of the old order began to pass. In the United States a wave of campaigning improvement, both political and moral, swept the fractious new republic. It took in many causes—temperance, women's rights, and slavery, the most divisive of all—but animating each of those causes was a fervent, often religious, conviction that American life on earth should be less wild, more orderly, and more reformed.

In Europe half a century of conservative attempts to sit on change, to maintain or restore the old order, was ending. Restrictions on speech, press, travel, residency, association, trade, commerce, and the public practice of religion came under challenge and were in many places lifted. In the new American republic, restrictions of like kind rejected in the federal constitution but surviving in state law or custom were by now also disappearing. It was a motley of causes pressed by clashing voices with rival interests and conflicting priorities. The word meant different things in different mouths. But a flag of convenience that swept up many of those separate causes was the banner term "liberty." A vast and loose party of movement began to form. Its followers started to call themselves liberals.

In 1835, the year Humboldt died, Germany's first steam train, the *Adler*, puffed up a section of line from Nuremberg to Fürth. That same year French navvies began laying railway track from Paris to the Atlantic port of Le Havre. Samuel Morse devised a code to shorten messages on the newly invented electric telegraph, and Samuel Colt took out a patent for his revolver. The German chemist Justus Liebig synthesized a precursor for the artificial material known as plastic, which before long would transform what people wore, sat on, and ate off. Plate-glass mirrors began to appear in ordinary homes and William Fox Talbot exposed the first photographic negatives, two devices that changed how people saw themselves and gave spurs to demanding new routines of self-improvement as well as to the fashion industry. Money was becoming an all-purpose solvent and a common standard of value. In France the Laffitte bank financed liberal ministries. The British state borrowed from the Rothschild Brothers to pay £20 million in compensation for "property" lost on the abolition of empire slavery the previous year. Bank of England notes became an unrefusable means of settlement in trade and were soon Britain's only legal tender. Factory production, with its rough standards but massive quantities, was replacing craft work. In 1835 there were fewer Prussian hatters per head of population than there had been in 1767, the year of Humboldt's birth, but many more new hats.

As the summer of 1835 ended, a Rhineland merchant's son entered the University of Bonn, where he threw himself into the drinking and gaming clubs. His father soon harried him to pursue serious studies at the new university that Humboldt had founded in Berlin. The boy was Karl Marx, and before long he would alter ideas about historical change. In September a British naval ship, *HMS Beagle*, carrying a naturalist on a four-year geological survey docked at the Galapagos Islands. He was Charles Darwin, and he would soon alter ideas about natural change. Marxism challenged inclusive liberal gradualism with a rival picture of historical progress as a sequence of dominant classes superseding one another. Darwinism, though not Darwin himself, tempted liberals to think of politics as a kind of biology.

In Boston in 1835, Ralph Waldo Emerson began a career as a lecturer preaching the higher values of self-cultivation in a grubbily commercial world. In Paris, Honoré de Balzac, a writer who professed to hate liberals but found their drive and sense of social freedom irresistible, published the first installment of *Père Goriot*, his novel of ambition, betrayal, hidden powers, and "egoism" in a suddenly fluid society. On a tour of America young Richard Cobden, the future British champion of free trade, decided that go-getting Americans had found the secret of a strong economy. On an equally enthusiastic German visit three years later Cobden would see nothing strange in rhapsodizing in a letter to his brother about Prussian government. A flourishing society, Cobden thought, needed both. Also in 1835, a young nobleman in France's prefectural service, Aléxis de Tocqueville, published the first part of *Democracy in America*, his puzzled reflections on a new country where he had seen firsthand a society turning its back on tradition, status, and privilege. Lucid about much else, on slavery Tocqueville's prose became opaque, though America's irrepressible conflict was stirring. In October a mob chased William Garrison, the abolitionist publisher of *The Liberator*, through the Boston streets.

2

Guiding Thoughts from Founding Thinkers

Conflict, Resistance, Progress, and Respect

i. Humboldt and Constant: Releasing People's Capacities and Respecting Their Privacy

It is tempting to wonder how Humboldt would have responded to this new world had he lived on like his younger brother, the explorer and naturalist Alexander, into the 1850s. Though some have taken Humboldt for an open-minded but conservative friend of the old world, he voiced a conviction that runs like an arrow through nineteenth-century liberal thought. His leading idea—dashed off in a youthful essay, *The Limits of the Effectiveness of the State* (1792), but published in full only after his death—had a head and a tail, a positive and a negative part: developing human capacities to the full in their diversity and individuality was an urgent task, but a task for which laws, government, and regulation were generally inept.

For anyone who did not get past his essay's title, it was easy to miss what Humboldt was saying. He was not thinking so much of government intervention in markets as of how state and society, which were not distinct in his mind, could stifle the true end of human life: finding and making full use of your talents in your own way. Humboldt certainly took a narrow view of the state's capacities. It had a job, he wrote, to defend people ("negative welfare") but not to support them ("positive welfare"). The state's holding property was a poor idea, as it was virtually bound to end up owning too much, and there was no future in levying sales taxes, which cost almost as much as they brought in. To pay for tasks the state could and should carry out, defense and justice, it might on the other hand tax income. It should not try to improve morals and should leave private conscience alone, for Humboldt believed everyone should be able to follow whatever religion they chose, or none. Humboldt was open-minded about constitutions. Different ones suited different places. The key everywhere was to have a constitution with "the least possible positive or special influence on the character of the citizens." His friend and contemporary Benjamin Constant (1767–1830) echoed and amplified the protective, negative aspect of Humboldt's leading idea. In *Principles of Politics* (1815) Constant wrote, "There is a part of human existence that remains of necessity individual and independent, and which lies by right utterly beyond the range of society."

Clustered here in celebration of people's independence are thoughts that lie at the liberal core. The first is that everybody—but especially those with power—must respect the deep-held aims and beliefs of others and not intrude on them by imposing purposes and ideals people have not chosen for themselves. The second thought is that people have within them an open-ended capacity for betterment and reform: to grow, to improve, to progress, with help or direction from others if need be. Constant, a more laid-back and permissive spirit, stressed more the first, nonintrusive thought. Humboldt, a born teacher, stressed the second, more educative thought. Though both men saw unique worth in people, Constant thought of that worth as something private that modern people now had ever more means to defend from intrusion; Humboldt saw it as a germ of potential to be cultivated and encouraged to grow. In theory both convictions—respect for personal privacy and zeal for human progress—sped together in parallel. In practice, they often got in each other's way, as liberals soon had to confront. Hardly a topic in nineteenth-century liberal thinking about politics did not turn in some way on the intrusive business of improving people's capacity to choose the aims of life well for themselves—on education that is, thought of in the broadest terms.

Both men were outsiders among insiders, Humboldt by temperament, Constant by temperament but also birth. Constant the man together with his defense of liberal privacy will appear in turn. We need to see first how, on turning from diplomacy to education, Humboldt put his ideals about nurturing human potential into practice.

After Prussia's capitulation to Napoleon's armies in 1806, Humboldt lost his post as envoy to the Holy See and soon left Rome, where for six years he had happily drunk in and written about the classical past. On return to chilly Berlin, he took charge of the section in the Interior Ministry that set up Europe's first full system of centrally administered state schools and founded a university teaching the nontechnical subjects of humanities and law. A strange step, you might think, for a pioneer liberal who insisted that the state was a "body of laws, not a school." Humboldt saw no conflict, for what mattered to him was the kind of school a state provided. Education that imposed purposes and limited choices should be discouraged, he believed, particularly if they were a state's purposes or those of its elites. With that in mind Humboldt tried, without success, to close Prussia's military academies and schools reserved for nobles. He opposed also vocational schools that taught chiefly crafts and trades. The trouble with them all in Humboldt's mind was that such schools aimed at a final product: soldier, state official, artisan. They narrowed life's choices. They put or kept people in boxes. He favored by contrast an open, nonimposing "liberal" education, rich in Greek and Latin, of the whole man, whatever he might turn out to be—women were not as yet part of the liberal story.

The ideal was not easy to realize. Humboldt was in his education post less than two years. Prussia's state schools were quickly stratified in content and selection on class lines. The elites read Homer and Virgil. The poor did craft work. Liberals like Cobden visiting in the 1830s from backward Britain were nevertheless struck with admiration all the same that Prussia, unlike Britain, had state schools at all.

Shining as it was, the ideal of humane well-roundedness left liberalism with an open question. Was it that pursuing many aims and interests without overspecialization was good for each of us? Or that a society with "diversity of stations" was healthier and more creative? Many-sidedness in people and social diversity were distinct. Generalists might lead richer lives but contribute little to society. The division of labor enriched society but narrowed people's lives. Questions of whom "individuality" benefited—people one by one or society as a whole?— passed down to an admirer, John Stuart Mill, who cited Humboldt with enthusiasm in his essay *On Liberty* (1859). Later in the democratic times of the 1880s to 1940s, "new liberals" raised a different question about people's capacity for personal growth along lines they chose for themselves. What did it serve, they asked, to celebrate that capacity unless everyone had the means—the health, time, space, and money—to exploit it?

Humboldt returned to diplomacy as second to the Prussian chancellor Karl-August Hardenberg in the peace talks of 1813–15 in Paris and Vienna that ended the Napoleonic Wars, but as helpmate and companion to his near-deaf superior more than as active participant with a say of his own. Humboldt had hoped for a loose confederation of self-governing German lands each with a representative constitution suiting its character and place. His arguments against princely absolutism immediately went nowhere. The powers at the Congress were after peace and stability among Europe's nations, not liberal change within them. When in 1819 the Prussian authorities followed those of Austria in suppressing the press and arresting radicals, Humboldt objected, the king sacked him, and he left public service for good.

In likenesses of him, young or old, Humboldt stares out at us through large eyes with a look of unreadable detachment. Letters to his many women friends brim with warm abstractions or passionate anxieties but few particulars. It was somehow typical that, hard as he argued for the emancipation of Prussia's Jews, he had almost no Jewish friends. In the closed circle of Prussian public life, Humboldt was arrogant and shy, too lofty for intrigue and too impatient for maneuver. Perhaps nobody was less suited to understand the rough-and-tumble of commerce that was transforming his country and its elites. Rather than ask, he waited to be given. When no offers came, he made sudden unmeetable demands and was surprised when his superiors or his friend, the king, turned him down. After the final rebuff, Humboldt retired to his estate at Tegel, where he added to his large collection of classical sculpture, widened an already astonishing range of tongues including Basque and Javanese, and elaborated his remarkably modern picture of human language as tightly rule-governed but open and endlessly fertile. Unbounded creativity within dependable order was not far from Humboldt's beguiling but strikingly detail-free picture of an ideal liberal society. His claim to rank among pioneer liberals lies in his insistence on the need for finding and releasing the unique potential in each of us.

Humboldt's belief in the human capacity for growth was sunlit, phil-hellene, and in the air among German writers of the day, including Goethe and Schiller, who knew Humboldt and admired his learning. His confidence spoke of a class and a time. Benjamin Constant's insistence on personal independence came from his own fluid personality, from his Protestant faith, and from observation of modern life. He was a lifelong gambler, weathervane in party politics, and restless seducer of other men's wives. His foibles and absurdities gave opponents ample ammunition for mockery: ridiculous duels, interminable court cases, groveling to the Laffittes and to the king to pay his gaming debts. "The Weather-vane," a satirical song of 1815, taunted Constant for spinning round in his attitudes to Napoleon, first foe, then ally, then foe again on the French emperor's final defeat at Waterloo. Late in 1830 Louis Philippe, France's "citizen king" in the July Monarchy (1830–48), named the dying Constant to the Conseil d'Etat in return for support in France's liberal revolution earlier that year. Constant, the story goes, took the opportunity to touch the new king for a draft to pay his gambling debts, adding that he would still have to be among the first to criticize if the sovereign erred. "Just so, just so," Louis Philippe murmured indulgently as he waved for Constant's money.

Constant was born in Swiss Lausanne to a family of French Huguenot origin. His mother died soon after his birth. His father, a colonel in the Dutch service, spent much of Benjamin's youth trying to clear himself of responsibility in the death of a soldier under his command during an off-duty fracas. By background, Constant was oddly like the silent opponent he often found himself arguing with in his writing, another motherless boy with a weak but affectionate father from nearby Geneva who turned himself into a Frenchman, Jean-Jacques Rousseau. Both were clever young men, both Protestant outsiders who adopted a Catholic country. Neither was conventionally religious, but both took faith, in a large sense, as vital for humankind and necessary for society. Both brimmed with erudition without being scholars, although unlike the self-taught, polymathic Rousseau, Constant had a lengthy formal education. At Oxford he learned English, at Erlangen drinking and gaming, and at Edinburgh a lesson of the Scottish Enlightenment to pay close attention to the human content of moral ideas and the historical context of political arrangements.

Constant made two marriages of convenience but, possibly on the lookout for a mother, had several affairs with older women. An early protectress, Mme de Charrière, well understood his quicksilver temperament. "As soon as he expressed a feeling," she said, "it meant that it was about to vanish." Constant's longest affair was with the writer and essayist Germaine de Staël, the daughter of the Swiss banker, Jacques Necker, who had tried to save the French crown from bankruptcy. In her opposition to Napoleon Bonaparte she was firmer than Constant, but less liberal in outlook and shallower in her understanding of the times.

Unlike Mme de Staël, Constant had no money of his own. Nor had he roots in the *ancien régime* or complexities about its passing of a kind the Norman squire Tocqueville never fully lost. Service as a minor flunky at the stifling court of Brunswick in his early twenties had convinced Constant that princely authority was unequal to the problems of his times. He was neither surprised nor disappointed when in September 1792 an army of regulars and volunteers raised to defend republican France rebuffed the Duke of Brunswick's undermotivated, counterrevolutionary forces at Valmy.

At moments of turmoil Constant rallied to the side of conservative order, only to regret it soon after. In 1799, now established in Paris, he supported Bonaparte and joined the Tribunate, the representative bauble in an otherwise autocratic regime, but was out again two years later when Napoleon took advantage of the Tribunate's term limit and in its first rotation got rid of his most tiresome carpers, Constant included. Constant spent much of the next years writing a compendious universal history of religion, dutifully published by his wife after his death. In 1814–15 at the restoration of the Bourbon monarchy, Constant backed the revival of the peerage, only then to revert to his earlier conviction that there was no place for noble privilege in a liberal state. He drafted a liberal constitution for Napoleon during the ex-emperor's one-hundred-day return in the spring of 1815, though with few illusions that Napoleon would stick to it should he defeat France's conservative enemies and recover power. During the White Terror against Bonapartists, republicans and Protestants that followed Napoleon's defeat, Constant spoke out against the villainous excesses. Though his health had gone, he continued in the 1820s to defend goals that gave body to his liberal principles, goals that were securely reached in France only in the Third

Republic after 1870: careers open to talents, responsible government, jury trials, a free press, separation of church and state, religious toleration, and a choice of lay or religious schools.

Constant believed that a new kind of society was emerging and that it was altering politics for good. It was bringing benefits of progress on its own, and so reducing the need for active reform. It was putting older forms of popular government out of reach, so facing people with novel tasks in restraining undue power. Above all, this new kind of society was peopled by a new kind of person of uninhibited character and demanding expectations. This new sort of person was changing what was expected from state and society by way of civic respect.

The new sort of person that Constant took to be changing politics was remarkably like Constant: flexible in character, not to be pinned down with labels, concerned with his own private world. In the antihero of his novel *Adolphe* (1816), Constant created an extreme specimen, without roots, fixed aims or lasting attachments, but possessing a sharp and distinctive sense of self. As a fictional character, Adolphe took life not only from Constant's awareness of his own personality, but from shrewd observation of the world around him. Interests were now diverse, Constant wrote, and people were becoming harder to pigeonhole or stereotype. People in different countries, for example, shared interests that might bring them closer to foreigners than to their compatriots. The world to that extent was growing cosmopolitan. People generally hated interference of every kind, especially if they sensed it singled them out unfairly. People, it is true, had always hated interference. The difference now was that people were readier to complain about interference, to stand up against interferers and demand that interference stop. More people had money. They knew and read more. Power now had to persuade them more than bully or threaten them. People could and did talk back to power.

Constant was looking to the wings where a demanding new personage was waiting, the private citizen. He was urging state and society to respect this personage and refrain from intruding on its life aims and profoundest beliefs. Constant made his argument less from grounds of higher principle than from prudence. High-end, speculative defenses of *all* people and their rights came to dominate liberal thinking much later after 1945. By then liberals had come to accept, often reluctantly and after much shoving, that everyone enjoyed the common rights and privileges that came with human personhood. Constant was saying something less ambitious and more limited: because of how society was changing, old forms of interference with people's interests and beliefs were ceasing to be practical or effective.

About progress, Constant sounded blithe. In the new society that was emerging, progress could be counted on for several reasons. Unless interfered with, the benefits of progress were likely to flow easily and naturally. Society did not greatly need reform, for it was reforming itself. The big obstacles to progress, to Constant's mind, were attempts to stop it or channel it in chosen directions. To take particulars, experience suggested that human knowledge and intellectual vitality increased unless interference got in their way. Dogmatic ways of thought were vanishing as people turned away from authorities in spiritual and moral matters. Warfare and its cousins, despotism and empire building, were out of keeping with the commercial spirit of the times. Destructive and oppressive forms of life would diminish as people turned to making, buying, and selling.

The thought that more trade might encourage war or that large movement of peoples and contact with foreigners, far from creating amity, could provoke hostile passions gave Constant little pause. The next century and a half would make liberal faith in the reliability of progress look overtrusting. In his enthusiasm, Constant tended to talk of progress as automatic and self-driven. By writing as if modern society were now likely to generate prosperity and peace on its own, as if disagreement and competition could now be counted on to yield fruitful results, Constant voiced what became a liberal fault: underplaying how much people had to do to bring the boons of progress about, and how easily they might slip away unless worked for.

In thinking about how to restrain power, Constant also started from how society was changing. Societies were growing more complex. People were less directly in touch with each other. Lines of supply between buyers and producers were lengthening. Government's reach was widening, but from ever further away. Trying to hold back such changes was pointless, Constant thought. The thing was to find apt ways to resist power in the new context. What could surely no longer restrain power was direct democracy. Far-flung, mass society was putting that ancient ideal beyond reach. Constant was here arguing with that inner opponent of his, Rousseau.

Rousseau's picture of small republics where citizens took personal part in the conduct of their common life in a way appealed to liberals. In theory, a direct say in affairs with fellow citizens was an attractive defense against outside domination and tyrannical rule. Under the label "republican," that ideal of active citizenship among equals without a single domineering power had defenders in Machiavelli in the sixteenth century, English radicals in the seventeenth century, and Jeffersonians in late eighteenth-century America.

Constant's conviction that modern society had put the ideal out of reach was clearest in his essay *Liberty Ancient and Modern* (1819). By ancient liberty Constant meant the direct say in government that everyone in a Greek city-state was believed to have had. Theirs, Constant suggested, was the liberty to take part and not to be imposed on without taking part. Modern liberty in contrast was protection from unwanted interference by state or society. Each kind of liberty had advantages and disadvantages: a direct say but little personal leeway under ancient liberty, or little direct say but a lot of leeway under modern liberty. Representative democracy rested on an implicit bargain: citizens gave up direct powers over their lives; the state compensated them by letting them alone. Was it a good trade? Here again, politics on Constant's story tracked society. Modern people, he was saying, wanted privacy more than they wanted a direct say in public life. Those were now facts of social life that liberal politics should take account of. Constant saw risks, without having clear remedies, in too much disengagement from public life, an idea that struck deep with a fellow liberal who developed it more fully—Tocqueville.

Constant was not blithe about power. Another of his fertile suggestions tossed out for later liberals to exploit recalled the old wisdom that despotism had no dates and came in many guises. Tyrannous power, Constant held, took various forms and could occur in any age. Society could be counted on to improve, Constant believed, but the risk of overweening power would remain. Progress, in other words, could not be counted on to exclude undue power. Constant left it to a historian and fellow politician, François Guizot, to build on his thoughts about power and to draw a lesson for liberals: the job of resisting it never ends.

Constant's works were out of fashion by the end of the nineteenth century. John Stuart Mill, a keen observer of French politics, admired Constant as a defender of the press and a true liberal among "intriguers." In a newspaper obituary in 1830, Mill called Constant's death a "misfortune for the world." Constant's objections to autocracy passed down to later French liberals in the economically liberal but politically despotic Second Empire, such as Jules Simon and Edouard Laboulaye, who republished Constant's lectures on politics. Constant was less read in the Third Republic, not only because of his eighteenth-century tone and inattention to economics but because his ideas about undue power, a free press, and personal privacy were by then widely absorbed into the French liberal outlook. When Constant's writings were re-edited and republished in the 1980s, he joined François Guizot, Aléxis de Tocqueville, and Mill in the modern canon of liberal founders.

Neither Constant nor Humboldt were democrats in an electoral sense or friends of the worker. Humboldt's liberalism was that of an elite expecting to govern without serious interference from below. Constant opposed privilege and favored a society open to talent. He thought people, ethically speaking, should go their own way. He believed neither in strict equality at the ballot box nor in industrial democracy. The world of Humboldt and Constant was changing in ways neither fully grasped. Politically, people without Humboldt's background or Constant's connections wanted a say in government. Economically, class struggle had begun between bosses and workers. Liberals who came after Humboldt and Constant faced fresh lessons. They learned that civic respect for people might have to apply to everyone "whoever they were" in a new and unrestricted way—that is, democratically.

In the same month that Humboldt died, April 1835, a mass trial got under way in Paris of *canuts*, silk workers from Lyon, and their supporters. The workers had occupied their factories the previous year in protest against low wages and bad conditions. France's liberal minister of the interior, Adolphe Thiers, had sent troops to dislodge them at the mill owners' behest. Workers who survived the slaughter went for trial, and most were deported or given heavy prison terms. In their search for order, conflict between capital and labor was to preoccupy liberals for the rest of the century and beyond. The long-lived Thiers would be remembered on the French left both for Lyon in 1834 and as the man who ordered the bloody suppression of the Paris Commune of 1871, leaving a picture, and not only in French minds, of the typical liberal as given to kindness when convenient and butchery when necessary.

ii. Guizot: Taming Conflict without Arbitrary Power

If Thiers was the most hated liberal of nineteenth-century France, François Guizot (1787–1874) was probably the most despised. A professor of history turned politician, he was the brains of the July Monarchy, the liberal interlude between Bourbon reaction and the autocratic rule of Louis Napoleon (1848–70). When in February 1848 the July Monarchy ended in débâcle, Guizot became a scapegoat for its failures. His career was over and his reputation vanished. A dim figure though he may be to British and American readers, Guizot takes first rank in the liberal story. In his day, Guizot was among the acclaimed liberals of Europe. Young Tocqueville attended his Sorbonne lectures in the early 1820s, taking copious notes. John Stuart Mill wrote in 1840 that Guizot "now stands before the world as immeasurably the greatest public man living." Mill changed his mind not long after about Guizot the politician, disappointed as were many fellow liberals by Guizot's "low tricks" and illiberal conduct in office. For Guizot the historian and thinker, Mill never lost esteem, and it is not hard to see why.

Guizot spelled out for liberal minds the enduring threat of unchecked power and the urgency of preventing any one class, faith, or interest from dominating society. His grasp of both ideas was historical and dynamic. Power was subtle, was fluid, and returned in ever fresh forms. Politics was about forever finding new points of balance among conflicting interests. Guizot wrote against the background of the French Revolution that had torn his country and much of Europe apart. He grasped that societies were not harmonious, but riven by conflict. He grasped it with a vividness of earlier thinkers such as Bodin and Hobbes, shaken by religious discord and civil war in the late sixteenth and early seventeenth centuries. Guizot grasped it with a strength that the young Marx admired and that more complacent liberals were later in danger of losing. Guizot's answer to conflict and disorder, though, was not power, as it had been for Bodin and Hobbes and as it was soon to become within the Marxist canon. Power for Guizot was the problem, especially when supreme or unchecked. Restraining power was for Guizot the first task of politics.

Guizot's overarching conviction was, as he put it, "the radical illegitimacy of all absolute power." Government was stablest and left people most alone, Guizot thought, when power was not held in single hands and when rulers, wise or foolish, had to listen to those they ruled whether they wanted to or not. Absolute power by contrast was concentrated and had only to listen to itself. The term "absolute" was a legalism and historical term of art, but what Guizot had in mind was familiar enough to everyone as despotism or tyranny. Such unchecked power could be, and often was, arbitrary, unresponsive, and oppressive. The trouble was not what power chose to do but what power was capable of doing. Absolute power could, as its defenders argued, be enlightened, beneficial, and benign. To liberals that was not enough. Absolute power could also change its mind when it wanted. It could turn harmful and malign. Intentions changed. Capacities lasted. Power was not to be trusted.

To support his thoughts about the differences between good government and tyranny, Guizot plunged as a historian deep into Europe's past. In tracing his lessons to obscure or possibly mythical early forms of representative government in the Lombard councils and the Saxon Witenagemot, Guizot had a double purpose. To his French hearers he was recommending reconciliation in a nation divided into supporters and opponents of the French Revolution. Like most early French liberals, Guizot saw good in the revolution as well as bad. He appealed accordingly to both sides. To the forces of reaction, with their veneration for the past, Guizot sought to show that divided power and representative government had their place in French tradition. To the forces of progress, he hoped to recover history for use by liberals in the cause of constitutional government and reform.

Guizot's other lesson about power applied broadly and was not limited to France. The historian's time in the archives had confirmed Constant's thought that despotism could occur in any age and took no single constitutional form. It could arise, as the ancients had known, from the rule of the one, the few, or the many. Classifying governments as monarchies, oligarchies, or democracies was proper but superficial. Each kind might be tyrannous if power was unlimited. What mattered to liberals was not who or what ruled but how. Here for liberals determined to resist power was a demanding lesson. One power hid another. The job of resistance was never over. It was always work in process.

Guizot and fellow French liberals also had the lessons of their recent past. The removal of an absolute monarchy had not ended unbridled power. There followed the unchecked power of the Jacobin street in the "bad" revolution after 1792 when control of the republic passed to Robespierre and the revolutionary sections of Paris speaking through the Convention in the name of the people; there followed the unchecked power of a military strongman, Napoleon Bonaparte, who restored order in 1799, first as consul, then consul for life, and soon as emperor; there followed on his fall in 1815 the restoration of the crown and the unchecked power of Bourbon kings supported by vengeful conservative Ultras. From the time he was a small boy, Guizot had seen it all.

He viewed politics in the grand sweep, not the personal or small scale. Even allies said of him that he lived in thought and lacked imagination about other people. The right distrusted him as much as the left despised him. His pale face looking away from us in Paul Delaroche's portrait (1837) is noble, grave, and off-putting. Honoré Daumier's sketch of him (1833) crouched and dark on the parliamentary benches with thick, knobby features, as much aging boxer as *éminence grise*, may be nearer the truth. He lacked a light touch, answering hoots from opponents with "Your jeers will never reach the heights of my disdain." Whether or not he actually said it, nobody forgot the peremptory advice to workers and radicals demanding the vote on the same terms as men of property that was hung on Guizot's name: "Get rich by work and thrift!" A republican crowd that burst into the royal palace at the Tuileries during the revolution of 1848 was reported to have heard an old parrot, coached no doubt by a conservative prince, crying "Down with Guizot!"

As prime minister Guizot saw none of that coming. Earlier that February at her evening salon, his confidante, Dorothée Lieven, a Russian aristocrat and reputed tsarist spy, was talking anxiously to Paris's chief of police about unrest in the streets. They called over Guizot to ask his opinion. "Oh, don't worry," he told them, "You needn't lose sleep over *that*." Within days a bewildered king had sacked Guizot, who fled disguised as a German footman on a coach for England, a recent enemy of

France whose supposedly well-balanced institutions he, like many continental liberals, admired without fully understanding.

It was Guizot's second midnight flight. The first had come when Guizot was still a small boy. In April 1794 the guillotine took away his father, a Calvinist lawyer in Provence who had sided with the Girondins, the protoliberals of the French Revolution vainly trying to resist the power of Jacobin Paris. The widow of Guizot senior fled for safety to Geneva with six-year-old François and his younger brother. There François got an excellent, polyglot education and after his return to France in 1805 quickly won eminence as a historian of new range and daring. Guizot fell in with an influential Paris coterie of politicians, professors, and intellectuals opposed alike to the despotism of Bourbons, Jacobins, and Napoleons. They were France's first liberals, though commonly called *doctrinaires*, a mocking name put into circulation by a satirical pro-Bonapartist magazine in Brussels, the *Yellow Dwarf*. When in 1815 France faced defeat at the hands of Britain and the reactionary empires of Austria, Prussia, and Russia, French liberals had to decide between two kinds of despotism. With exceptions, they picked the lesser evil as they saw it and threw in against Napoleon with the restored Bourbon king: fat, amiable Louis XVIII.

In theory the king held a balance between liberals at the center and Ultras on the right. In practice his thoroughly reactionary regime tried to stifle change. Tory governments in Britain, in power since 1783 but shaken by the American and French revolutions, attempted to do the same. So did the German princes, absolute rulers in their nearly forty kingdoms and principalities, restored to rule by Europe's victorious powers in 1815. France was the first to crack. Guizot was at the center of the story. He and his fellow liberals had a suppler view of revolution than that of French Bourbons, British Tories, or German princes. Guizot had a suppler view than that of the conservative Anglo-Irish Whig, Edmund Burke, whose *Reflections on the French Revolution* in 1790 stressed the perils of abandoning established custom and disregarding the wisdom of tradition without adequately netting those perils against the benefits of change or the sagacity of its advocates.

Guizot and his fellow *doctrinaires* were neither republicans nor democrats. They believed in representative government by consent on a narrow, property-based franchise and in a constitutional division of powers under a monarch who reigned but did not rule. They believed in divided control, speaking back to power and party competition. They took politics, in other words, for a contest. They did not believe that people en masse were capable of taking part in that contest.

Such views were reflected in the *doctrinaire* understanding of the French Revolution as "good" until Robespierre and the Terror turned it "bad." Against the Ultras of 1815–30, the liberals argued historically. French society had moved on and the *ancien régime* was not reimposable. The revolution of 1789 had brought palpable gains liberals wished to hold on to. A uniform, well-administered rule of law now favored private property and commerce, two prerequisites of social order and economic progress. The spread of land ownership with the revolutionary sale of church and noble estates had not created a property-owning democracy of twenty million as the liberal historian Jules Michelet enthusiastically claimed in his *History of the French Revolution* (1847–54). It had entrenched a social pillar of nineteenth-century rural France, the rich "peasantry." The "good" revolution had also embraced Enlightenment ideals of religious toleration, civil liberties, and free speech, which the old regime had taken cautious steps toward and which the extremes of revolution and counterrevolution had then ignored or thrown away. Such was the common understanding of the 1789 revolution that passed from French liberals to liberals generally.

When during the late 1820s Bourbon Ultras appeared to threaten those gains of the "good" revolution, France's liberal opposition recovered its nerve. In 1830 its moment came. Rather than listen, an obdurate king rashly dissolved the legislative chamber. The liberal press, led by Thiers at *Le National*, stormed in protest. The common people of Paris took to the streets and persuaded troops to fraternize, an episode fixed in our imaginations and vocabularies by Eugène Delacroix's painting *Liberty Leading the People*. Once the streets were safe, Guizot and his allies swept the king and the Ultras out and put on the throne the Orleanist claimant, Louis Philippe, son of the man who had voted in 1793 for the execution of his cousin, Louis XVI.

France's "glorious three days" in July 1830 shook Britain and Germany. In November, Britain's opposition Whigs—the loose coalition of enlightened landowners and city radicals that eventually fed into the modern Liberal Party—took office in Westminster alone for the first time in almost half a century. Across the German lands calls were heard to replace the unchecked power of kings and princes with constitutional rule and representative government. A liberal phase in Europe had opened, with France and Guizot in the lead.

There was not the least aura of majesty to the July Monarchy. Daumier depicted Louis Philippe, barely a year on the throne, as an inert, cavern-mouthed Gargantua swallowing bribes by the sackful. Guizot, Thiers, and other liberals took charge of the ministries. To Karl Marx, graduated from Berlin and author with his friend Friedrich Engels of *The Communist Manifesto*, the *doctrinaire* professors and liberal newspaper editors were a front for the true power: money. Writing after the regime's fall in 1848, Marx described the July Monarchy as "a joint-stock company for the exploitation of France's national wealth."

The July Monarchy brought France food shortages, corruption, and repression. It also brought greater press freedom, state schools for boys, and growing, but uneven, prosperity. The 1848 revolution that did for Guizot mattered more politically than socially or economically, burning out almost before it began. By the summer of that year, the radicals were dashed. Economic progress and social order returned, though it was not a liberal order. A second Napoleon established himself as an elected despot. As did Chancellor Bismarck later in Germany in the 1860s to 1880s, the new Napoleon squeezed liberals politically by meeting liberal goals in an illiberal way.

Restless in English exile, Guizot turned down an offer of a professorship at Oxford and returned to France in 1849. Where other liberals succeeded, Guizot tried but failed to re-enter parliament. Not only did he carry the blame for the fiasco of the July Monarchy's collapse, he had in office betrayed his highest liberal ideals. He had muzzled the press and barred Michelet from public lecturing—as in the 1820s the Ultras had stopped Guizot. Perhaps most damagingly of all, Guizot had given foes to left and right cause to think him un-French. A devout and lifelong Protestant who prayed every morning, he was neither anticlerical nor atheistical in the manner of an eighteenth-century *philosophe*, and saw no clash between Christian faith and liberal ideals. Not only did the cosmopolitan Guizot speak the main European languages with ease. Foes attacked him when foreign minister for being soft on Britain and mockingly referred to him as "Lord Guizot," deaf to his liberal conviction that conciliation with a former enemy in the cause of trade was better than armed rivalry. Guizot never lived down the charge from the republican and pro-Napoleonic left that—when visiting Louis XVIII in 1815 at Ghent, avowedly to plead for a constitution—he had betrayed military secrets to France's enemies. He began a long retirement, wrote his memoirs, and sank, politically, into oblivion. Resisting the authoritarian rule of a seductive second Napoleon fell to a new generation of French liberals.

Guizot in truth loved France with passion, and he expressed that love in a way that had lessons for later liberals, foreign as well as French. Guizot did not deny national attachments or try to wash them out with universal principle. Rather he hoped to encourage a sense of the French nation that did not rest only on foreign glory, exclusion of others, or military prowess. As minister of education in 1833 he supervised the central reforms that set up state schools for boys in every French commune, training schools for teachers in every department, and the beginnings of a national curriculum. On the rough benches of their schools, French boys began to learn that they were French, not least by learning to speak French. Second, Guizot created in 1830 an inspectorate for identifying and preserving historical sites and national monuments. The phrase did not take wing for another century and a half, but Guizot was one of the first and most dedicated champions of France's *lieux de mémoire*—sites of memory or places where people could begin to think of themselves as sharing a common past and hence to some degree a common present.

Guizot's place in liberal thought rests on his ideas about resistance to absolute or undivided power. He gave them clear expression in the sixth and eighth of his *Lectures on Representative Government* given in Paris in 1820–22. Guizot started those lectures when the reactionary government of Count Villèle snuffed out hopes of constitutional change. His lectures were stopped and he was fired from the Conseil d'Etat. When allowed again to lecture in 1828, Guizot resumed, "You may recall that six years ago we were saying . . ." and the cheers rang.

The tasks of containing power, Guizot argued, flowed from what was known about power from experience. Unlimited power tended to perpetuate itself. Few or none who claimed to rule by right had shared their powers. Whatever was insisted otherwise, sovereignty belonged by right to none. Nobody was capable of its unlimited exercise, neither kings nor citizens. "Sovereignty belongs as a right to no one person whatever," he wrote, "since the perfect and continued apprehension, the fixed and inviolable application of justice and of reason, do not belong to our imperfect nature." Neither singly nor together did what we happen to want at any given moment underpin just decisions or proper choices. Guizot was here attacking the weakness of left and right alike for believing in final says. He was rejecting the idea, dear for example to Rousseau, that we were in command of ourselves and could not be countermanded. No, Guizot believed, reason and right were in charge, not our wishes. Ideally, people's wishes would be coherent and proper. But people were not ideal, and politics had to work with people as they were. At the same time, Guizot was attacking Legitimists who clung to the doctrine of the absolute right of kings. The very idea of sovereignty as the exercise of supreme power had to be abandoned in Guizot's view. The only sovereigns in politics were law, justice, and reason. The consequences were momentous. All exercise of power had to be shared. Governments had to be removable in elections. The press had to be unrestricted and political meetings freely permitted.

For Guizot that last requirement mattered most. Power needed to be talked back to, to be asked "Why?" and to be made to give answers. Without scrutiny and criticism, the division of powers and the sanction of intermittent elections might prove inadequate checks on power. For law could underpin tyranny and voters might elect despots. Guizot's idea was that nobody should count on power to follow rules by itself. Power needed another voice. Being talked back to was for Guizot as necessary to the responsible power as it was to the exercise of reason itself. The contrast with absolute power was clear. Those with absolute power might find it wise or expedient to listen to those it ruled or explain to them its conduct, but they were not under any necessity. If it so chose, absolute power might be opaque, when power ought to be transparent; mystical, when power ought to be accessible; irrational, when power was obliged to give reasons. The practical upshot lay less in institutions or laws than in forceful, unending argument. Guizot thought of mentalities first, institutions second. Though Guizot the politician disregarded his belief in public argument when in office, Guizot the thinker tirelessly repeated that the sharpest weapons of resistance to power were a critical press and public meetings allowing for unlimited debate.

In Guizot's strictures against absolute power we clearly see the first difference between liberals and their nineteenth- and early twentieth-century rivals, conservatives and socialists. To schematize, conservatives revered traditional or established power. Authority was to be obeyed and orders followed without question. To the conservative mind, the very idea of limited power or divided sovereignty involved a confusion. For sovereignty was no more or less than supreme power of command without having to answer "why."

Socialists were different. Like conservatives, they revered absolute power and recognized sovereignty as supreme power. Unlike conservatives, they located absolute power not in dynasty or tradition but in the people. The people's voice was supreme and final. Here and in what follows, "socialist" is a cover-all term for the antiliberal left including latter-day Jacobins and populist republicans as well as collectivist followers of Fourier or Marx. Whatever particular line they took, socialists had no good answer as to who was to intuit or channel popular power. So liberals at any rate insisted. Their complaint generalized in democratic times to include populists of the right as well as the left. To the liberal mind, nobody claiming to intuit the popular will or to speak for "the people" was to be trusted.

As a liberal, Guizot disagreed about power with both conservatives and socialists. Whereas conservatives rejected, Guizot accepted the power of the people, albeit understood in a subtly negative way. Whereas socialists made the power of the people absolute and conclusive, Guizot thought of popular power as essentially dispersed and provisional. The people, on Guizot's view, should not have the final say. For nobody should. Guizot knew perfectly well that decisions had to be taken. Rather, he was saying that public argument about decisions should never stop.

Guizot's theory of popular sovereignty resembled that of James Madison, the American constitutionalist, in being at root negative. Popular sovereignty for Guizot was in effect the nonsovereignty of any one section, class, faith, or interest. None should dominate or have the last word. Nobody should claim to speak for all, just as no one reason should end a public argument. The power of the people, like public reason itself, was for Guizot just over the horizon. Both were to aim for but beyond reach, and nobody should claim to have either in their grasp.

From the nonsovereignty of any one class, belief, or interest it was an easy step to thinking of politics as a search for balance, as finding compromises among competing interests or at any rate preventing any one of them from prevailing. Looking back in old age, Guizot saw France riven by conflict between, as he put it, "hats and caps, cassocks and jackets"—bosses and workers, priests and mayors—which he nevertheless still hoped could be bridged or balanced off in a politics of what he called the *juste milieu*, the happy medium.

Guizot's soggy phrase was treated with derision to left and right. Yet his thoughts about a future classlessness paralleled those of Marx. History revealed there to be many factions, many conflicts, and many paths to stable compromise. France, on Guizot's story, had had a weak crown that allied itself with towns against a strong nobility. England's crown by contrast had vied and lost against an alliance of towns and nobles. The one pattern led to liberal modernity through absolutism, the other to the same point of arrival through constitutionalism. The existence of two paths encouraged the mistake of thinking that they led to different destinations. Constitutions depended on balance and compromise, not the other way around. To Guizot the point of balance required would depend on the forces involved, which change with time. In his day, class was a relevant force. No conflict was more pressing than that among the poor, the rich, and those in between. Guizot hoped that one day a middle class, neither envious nor neglectful, might hold the balance. In time it might become the main, perhaps the only class, at which point society would, more strictly, be classless.

To call it happy would be too much, but in looking for a social "medium," Guizot saw ahead to the future shape of France. He did not put people in partisan boxes. He thought society might improve as people grew more tolerant and accommodating. He took cosmopolitan pride in a Europe of which France was a shining, not dominant, part. He believed that diversity and tension brought strength, not weakness. Europe's achievement, he believed, lay in having combined distinct traditions into a single civilization: Roman law, Christian inwardness and Germanic equality.

Splendid as his liberal ideals were, Guizot's understanding of their scope was thoroughly undemocratic. After 1848, Guizot was remembered as a reactionary less because he was a liberal than because he was not a democrat. Liberalism lived on in the French Republics and became, in democratic form, the mainstream of progressive politics known as "republicanism." The "extinction" of French liberalism in the later nineteenth century was a verbal, not an actual, extinction. By then "liberalism" in France had taken on a narrow sense as a name for an alien, inhumane doctrine associated with Englishness, hard-driving Manchester-school mill owners and the Lockean fantasy of membership in society as involving a kind of choice.

Liberal attitudes to conflict made a second point of contrast with their conservative and socialist rivals, following that over power. For liberals, conflict was ever present. It was unceasing and ineradicable. Whatever form it took, over interests, beliefs or ways of life, the thought was that conflict must be tamed, transformed into competition, and made fruitful in trade, experiment, and argument. Too much could be made of whether liberals welcomed conflict as healthy and productive or feared it as dangerous and destructive. They did both. Conflict, for liberals, was a fact of life. Politics was about how conflict might serve useful ends and not break society apart.

Conservatives took a different view of conflict. To them society was not by nature divided. Society was at root harmonious and unified. The myth of class conflict in particular was put about by resentful agitators and disaffected intellectuals. Diversity of opinion was not the welcome result of an unending conversation among open-minded equals but the regrettable consequence of wisdom's failure to prevail over ignorance among imperfect humans. There were not many equally worthwhile paths in life to choose from but one path, that of virtue and tradition. Conservative eyes were no worse than liberal eyes. Conservatives could see divisions in society. But to conservatives those divisions were not of society's essence. To the extent that divisions existed within society, they represented for conservatives a fall from grace, a lapse into modernity, a loss of past unity.

The socialist left's attitude toward conflict was different again. The left agreed with liberals that conflict in society was wide and deep, not that it was endless or inevitable. It disagreed with liberals also about how many sides were involved. For liberals, conflict involved many, many sides and many, many matters. Conflict's subject matter, in a sense, was unbounded. To socialists, conflict involved only two sides, rich and poor, and one topic, material inequity. Conflict would cease, they held, once its sources in material inequity were removed. Socialists disagreed with conservatives that society was harmonious until foolishly interfered with. They faulted liberals for refusing to see where the roots of one, overarching conflict lay. Those roots lay for the socialist mind in differences of material interest among unequal classes, differences from which other conflicts, notably of faith and opinion, invariably stemmed. Remove inequity and harmony came in all life's departments. That, in crude summary, was the socialist dream of one-stroke emancipation. Although divided and denatured at present, society for the socialist left was by nature harmonious. There it agreed with conservatives, though not about structure or timing. For conservatives, harmony lay in a hierarchical past, for the socialist left in a brotherly future.

Society for liberals was always in conflict. To liberals there never had been and never would be a time of harmony. The best hope was for a frame of order and stability that was flexible enough for adjustment as the forces in conflict changed. Such a frame would be "artificial" and "man-made." It would be neither God-given nor natural but reliant on common interests in peace, stability, and prosperity. Within it, private conflicts could be bargained away leaving no one with festering regrets that might threaten common interests.

In anxious moods, liberals looked on unending conflict with stoical dread. In calmer moments, they welcomed conflict as zestful and energizing, the opposite of sterile harmony and dull uniformity. In tense times, liberals pictured conflict as terror, riot, and religious war. In tranquil times, they rethought conflict as competition, diversity, and individuality, welcoming them all. When giving in to hope, liberals pictured conflict as tamed and productive, the arena replaced by market and forum. Later, as the terminology of liberalism crystallized, "market" liberals persuaded themselves that conflict, softened into competition, was an unalloyed good, only to have to relearn, again and again, that interfering rules of order and credible government to defend them were required after all. Similarly, "social" liberals persuaded themselves that open-ended conflict was an avoidable harm, only to have to relearn time after time that conflict, in the guise of competition, could also be fruitful, and its absence stultifying. Whatever the liberal mood, the task of containing and utilizing conflict was never over, just as the task was never over of resisting power. For liberals, unlike for conservatives or socialists, there was no escape from politics.

iii. Tocqueville and Schulze-Delitzsch: The Modern Powers of Mass Democracy and Mass Markets

Guizot experienced the arbitrary power of absolute monarchy, the Jacobin street, and the military strongman. A generation later, Aléxis de Tocqueville in France and Hermann Schulze-Delitzsch in Germany preoccupied themselves with new forms of power. Tocqueville looked for a counterweight to the pressure of mass democracy. Schulze-Delitzsch for a middle way between the new power of the industrial market and the growing weight of the central state. Both hoped for an answer in local and voluntary collectivities of public life becoming known as civil society.

Though attached to his class, Tocqueville was a liberal of the left in the July Monarchy and briefly foreign minister in the Republic of 1848–51. He was known across Europe for his writing on politics, praised by Mill and credited with introducing the term "individualism" to public argument in France as something more than an antiliberal term of abuse. Schulze-Delitzsch was a leading member of the liberal Progress Party and founder of German cooperativism, a vigorous movement of local financing and self-help that spread and survived well into the twentieth century, especially in German cities.

Aléxis de Tocqueville (1805–59) saw the spread of democracy in broad terms of ethical and cultural change, and not simply a matter of voting. Authority in matters of belief and taste was disappearing, just as hierarchy was vanishing socially. Everyone was becoming his own arbiter. So it seemed to Tocqueville. He did not think that democracy in his large sense could be stopped. Society was evolving, and with it outlooks and attitudes. There were costs as well as benefits, and the large question was how to handle democracy's costs: an overpowered modern state and an underpowered modern citizenry. Both were connected in Tocqueville's mind and both were to be resisted. At its most lurid, his fear was that society was turning into an atomized mass of willful, self-interested egos that an intrusive state could suborn, especially a state with benevolent motives. Tocqueville's alarming picture, retouched for novel conditions, bewitched many twentieth-century liberals.

Of frail health, Tocqueville lived on his nerves, working in bursts followed by frequent collapses. The surface calm of the books, with their balanced contrasts and untroubled assurance, was a deception. As his British biographer Hugh Brogan has described him, Tocqueville was less a cool-headed analyst than an impulsive Romantic, able to write well only when his feelings were engaged. He feared and loathed the Paris crowd, adored his run-down family manor in the Cotentin Peninsula, and loved France almost to the point of jingoism. He found religious belief absurd on the whole, but—another echo of Constant—he took some unquestioned faith or other as necessary to serve as society's ethical glue. Since it was familiar and available, Roman Catholicism, Tocqueville believed, met that purpose well.

Cool as he might sound, Tocqueville was a man of attachments. Though lucid about their failings, Tocqueville was proud to belong to the secular twin peaks of old France, the landed *noblesse d'épée* and the professional *noblesse de robe*. His father came from a line of Norman squires claiming a warrior ancestor who sailed to England in 1066 with William the Bastard to claim the Saxon crown. His maternal great-grandfather was Guillaume de Malesherbes, a lion of the Paris bar who defended Louis XVI for abandoning his country during the French Revolution. The Terror swept away Malesherbes and several of his family. Tocqueville's father, jailed with them, escaped only because the guillotine caught up with Robespierre first.

The son respected many of his family's attitudes but flouted others. His legitimist father had flourished in the Bourbon restoration, but at its fall in 1830, young Aléxis, then a government lawyer, faced a choice. Officials had to take an oath to the new Orleanist king. The cynical old Etienne Pasquier, who had run Napoleon's police in Paris, laughed off the oath as a harmless "ticket to the spectacle." On point of honor, many legitimists, who had sworn fealty to the Bourbons, refused. Tocqueville agonized, and took the oath. Yet more daringly for a man of his milieu, in 1835 he married an Englishwoman who was not noble, Catholic, or rich.

Tocqueville's arias to excellence and warnings about democratic mediocrity have misled people into thinking him a snob, the sort of person who looks disdainfully down at the crowd but insecurely up at their supposed betters. Tocqueville, on the contrary, was a nob—an aristocrat, that is—with a strong sense of *noblesse oblige*. Public office, though no longer a privilege, was still to his mind a duty. A poor speaker and hopeless party man, Tocqueville was elected deputy at second go in 1839 and he sat with the center-left. In 1848 he was briefly foreign minister and drafter of a republican constitution that lasted barely a year.

His *Recollections* (1850) record his part in France's unhappy second republic (1848–52). During the bloody June days, Tocqueville, a member of the National Assembly with parliamentary privileges, went to see the street fighting for himself. There was no doubt whose side he was on. The forces of order, Tocqueville wrote, "delivered the nation from the oppression of Paris workers and restored its self-possession." Other liberals thought differently. Tocqueville neglected to report that on his excursion he apparently ran into a platoon of soldiers who had just arrested the exiled left-wing liberal, Alexander Herzen, a Russian nobleman's son. Herzen was also out observing events, though with more sympathy for the people's cause. The radical Russian baron asked the liberal French count to intercede. Detainees were vanishing, Herzen explained, and many were being shot. Tocqueville listened politely to his plea for help but, as Herzen told it, declined to intervene, priggishly explaining that a member of the legislative branch could not interfere with the business of the executive branch. The soldiers took Herzen away. He won release several nervous hours later after persuading an intelligent and sympathetic police captain that he was not a foreign agitator.

A liberal of Tocqueville's outlook had more to fear than the Paris street. His fears that a modern despot might manipulate the popular ballot came true under Bonaparte's nephew, Louis Napoleon, president from December 1848. Three years later Napoleon closed parliament, made himself emperor as his uncle had done, and rigged a plebiscite to make it seem legitimate. Although the Second Empire promised France stability and prosperity, the price in despotism to Tocqueville was too high.

In retirement from politics he began a history of the French Revolution but finished only the part on the *ancien régime* before tuberculosis killed him at fifty-three. Tocqueville had hoped to show that, under the old monarchy, the French state was centralized but weak and that the Revolution had kept it centralized but made it strong. Tocqueville saw advantages and disadvantages. A centralized state with an effective administration under a rule of law favoring property and commerce created a stable basis for economic progress. Such a state also limited direct or local control. Most seriously, a centralized state increased the risks of bad government. For a liberal, progressive state might fall into illiberal hands.

In Tocqueville's *Democracy in America* he created an indelible picture of something fast emerging but as yet not wholly familiar, middle-class society. He did so especially in the second volume (1840), when thinking as much of France as of America. As sketched by Tocqueville, middle-class society had neither a noble elite with high standards nor a pauper class with unmet needs. Such a society was probably how Europe would be before long. Americans were competitors with each other on equal footing in a contest anyone could win or lose. Rewards were to achievement, not rank. As it was a middle-class contest, the stakes were narrowly material and insatiable. They were material in that the contestants were interested in wealth, not excellence. They were insatiable because the contestants were none of them poor: they had already met their material needs, and were using wealth as a token in an unending contest of social one-upmanship. To use present-day terms, they were grading each other on the curve using money as a common standard. Here was restless change bred into the wishes of the human heart. In the competitive spirit of commercial America, Tocqueville thought he had spied a new form of enduring, many-sided conflict, though one among rough equals that, in a suitably loose set of basic laws, could be contained and made peaceable and productive as a self-regulating, masterless order. Disguised as social description and misleadingly named, Tocqueville's book was an exercise in guarded praise for liberal modernity and its guiding ideas: endless but peaceful competition, limitation on powers, and civic respect among roughly equal citizens.

Liberal, middle-class society had drawbacks in Tocqueville's eyes. As everyone's voice counted, majority opinion could stifle minorities. It could crush the lone wise voice or despised but worthy outsider. In addition, governments elected on the majority principle swung between being over-strong and being weak, unstable, and inconsistent. Voting, on the other hand, was educational, Tocqueville allowed. It also encouraged participation, although national voting was not the most important way for citizens to turn from private concerns to take part in the common life of society. Following another of Constant's hints, Tocqueville stressed the value of voluntary associations, local government and town meetings of the kind he had seen or heard about in New England. A vigorous civil society, Tocqueville thought, could act as a source of resistance to the counterpart novel tyrannies he feared of stultifying majorities and over-strong modern states. Together those tyrannies could give much of what liberals also hope for—social order and prosperity—but at the illiberal cost of silencing minorities and stifling initiative.

Hermann Schulze-Delitzsch (1808–83) shared the kind of hopes Tocqueville had for a middle way between state and market, but in more down-to-earth manner. He was a commercial judge from a small Saxon town near Leipzig. Politically, his long career as a German liberal was a search for balance among forces that were not yet ready for durable compromise. His dream was of an ark from the rising waters of modernity. Neither big nor small, with few rich or poor, it would be an ideal home for the "golden middle ranks" freed of envy and pity, living on equal terms. His liberal Utopia was to have a large say in its own affairs, a strong commitment to cooperative self-help and a flourishing voluntary life of clubs, unions, and associations.

That powerful and attractive picture of a neighborly society, neither frozen in the past nor hurtling uncontrollably into the future, appealed to nineteenth-century liberals almost everywhere. In his *Principles of Political Economy* (1848), sometimes misremembered as a narrowly free-market handbook, Mill's picture of a desirable society that he spelled out in book six is similar. Wendell Phillips (1811–84), the American abolitionist and Republican radical, thought that certain New England towns had come close to such an ideal in his boyhood. As dreamer and practical man of affairs, Schulze-Delitzsch strove to realize the vision in contemporary Germany. Though virtually forgotten by the twentieth century, Schulze-Delitzsch was a large figure in his day, not least for the socialist left, who saw him as a dangerous rival whose ideas had to be confronted and exposed.

Schulze-Delitzsch grasped that his ideal society would have to feed and pay for itself. There was no escape from production, work, and trade. Professional experience, the disappointments of 1848 and careful reading of the political economists convinced him of the need to find a civic path between reaction and revolution. The kingdom of Saxony had doubled its population since 1750. Once a place of farms, it was now at mid-century among the fastest industrializing regions of Europe, importing more food than it exported. Perhaps half the labor force worked in textiles or in something related. Lutheran by confession, Saxons divided more by class than religion. Recent laws of free-market inspiration had relaxed old restrictions on the movement of labor and the building of factories. In the trade disputes that came into his court, Schulze-Delitzsch saw the plight of artisans and small businesses under pressure from new manufacturers and big firms.

Schulze-Delitzsch drew the lessons of the failed German revolution of 1848 in terms of "realms." Politically, the revolution was a defeat for German liberals from which there was no early recovery. They had wanted constitutional and representative government in a peacefully united Germany but had secured none of those things. Economically, the task was promoting industry and trade. That was a job for business, not politics. Economic growth did not depend on political reform. Liberals still had work to do. Socially, liberals might moderate the impact of factory work and city crowding. By relieving hardship, liberals might deflect working-class demands for more say in government.

Schulze-Delitzsch read the socialists from the small-scale Utopian Charles Fourier to the large-scale Utopian Karl Marx. He read the vividly written popular free-market books of the French economic liberal, Frédéric Bastiat. Neither a socialist nor a market economy could work on its own, Schulze-Delitzsch concluded. Capitalism was there to stay. It was beneficial but disruptive. It could flourish only if collective ways could be found to contain its boisterous energies. Collective solutions, if thought of as central solutions, were bound to do more harm than good. Marx's doing away with the state, though anarchist in aim, suffered as did all central solutions, from trying to do too much. Solutions could be collective, Schulze-Delitzsch believed, without being central.

The answer lay in mutualism. Schulze-Delitzsch set up his first trade cooperative in 1849. Voluntary welfare schemes and mutual banks that he inspired spread rapidly. By the early twentieth century perhaps five to six million Germans benefited directly or indirectly from cooperatives of some kind.

Mutualism struck many liberals as a more attractive, less costly route to social peace than the socialist alternatives of trade unionism and universal franchise. The socialist left treated mutualism as more of an obstacle to working-class advancement. Across Europe, both sides in 1863 followed Schulze-Delitzsch's public dispute with Germany's leading socialist, Ferdinand Lassalle. Mutualism presumed a society of artisans and the self-employed too far from the present-day facts. It offered the German industrial worker no durable home. Nor did it promise them a vote. Schulze-Delitzsch was no electoral democrat. In 1862 he told a working-class audience who had come to hear about liberalism that rather than press for a vote, they should join a worker's self-help association and better their lot. Once they could stand on their own feet, liberals parties would welcome them, and if they brought money to the party, so much the better. Guizot could not have said it with less tact. What appealed to mutualists drove away socialists. An early protégé of Schulze-Delitzsch was a Leipzig button-maker, August Bebel. In time mutualism struck him as more dodge than ideal. In 1863 he was among the founders of the party that became the German Social Democrats. Liberals had a challenger for the torch of progress.

Soon Bismarckian state welfare was overtaking Schulze-Delitzsch's fatherly vision as means of deflecting working-class political demands. A high relief on a monument of 1899 to Schulze-Delitzsch by Hans Arnoldt in Berlin's Mitte district shows the burly liberal reformer as a benign and solid guardian, leaning over a grateful artisan on a bench, as if to raise him up. Schulze-Delitzsch was by then a dated figure. Business and finance were outgrowing the capacities of his cooperative ark. A more democratic culture was impatient with paternalism.

Schulze-Delitzsch's vision of a balanced but localized liberal society won attention outside Germany. Mill urged a British fellow liberal, the economist and later minister Henry Fawcett, to take note of German cooperativism, though Mill was cautious about its prospects as a general answer to the taming of industrial conflict. The French economist

Léon Walras praised cooperativism but doubted whether it could meet the scale of activity needed in a modern society. Looking back in his *History of Economic Doctrines* (1909), the French champion of cooperativism, Charles Gide, praised Schulze-Delitzsch's "magnificent progress," but judged that his movement had helped chiefly "the small shopkeeper, the well-to-do artisan and the peasant proprietor."

Schulze-Delitzsch's broader ideal of capitalism tempered by attention to society's needs lived on in the liberal vernacular of the social market that underpinned Europe's post-1945 success, though stripped of localism. The other element of Schulze-Delitzsch's vision of middle-way progress, voluntarism, also lived on. Joining in became a strong element in late nineteenth-century German politics both for local action and to influence power at the center. Ministries, general staffs, and parliament were not the only actors in German public life. Germans were great joiners. There were leagues, unions, federations, associations, lobbies, interest groups, and brotherhoods of every kind: avocational, confessional, professional, conservative, liberal, left-wing, pro-navy, and antimilitary. On German unification, laws on associations formed a muddle of permission and control. Bismarck's system encouraged nationwide interest groups but discouraged national parties. After 1899, laws were harmonized and relaxed, permitting both to operate more freely. For Germany's growing but diverse middle class—and more and more for the working classes—associational life was part hobby, part duty, part mania. Some of it was for clubbableness, some to win favors from government, some to run government. Local association and national parties cross-influenced as much as competed with each other.

Schulze-Delitzsch's experiments with cooperativism and Tocqueville's thoughts about the twin threats of state and mass society suggested the strengths and limits of liberal "middle ways." Fears that voluntary associations and civil society were under threat became a liberal preoccupation, stronger at times, assuaged at others, but never wholly mastered. A more balanced way for liberals to take Tocqueville's hopes for civil society and Schulze-Delitzsch's promotion of cooperativism amid mass society was to see that neither voluntarism nor localism was an end in itself. States did some jobs well. Voluntary bodies did some jobs well. Private companies did some jobs well. None could be counted on to do a good job of anything forever. None had a permanent license for the sole performance of any given task. Job descriptions changed with circumstances. The trick was to know which of the three was likely to do well at a task for long enough to avoid the need for ceaseless interference by the other two, but not so long as to lock in failure. Similarly, central policies and solutions were good for certain purposes at certain times, local policies and solutions for others at other times.

In the continual churn of liberal capitalism, it was to grow ever clearer that the institutions of society—state, market, or civic—and the instances of government and commerce—central or local—were in a sense secondary. They were tools, subject to technical improvement, decay, and repair. What did not change and what mattered for liberals was to gauge which arrangements in any period better served the liberal ideals of containing monopoly powers, promoting human betterment, and showing people due respect.

iv. Chadwick and Cobden: Governments and Markets as Engines of Social Progress

The early liberals shared their immediate eighteenth-century forebears' hopes in progress. There was something called society, liberals believed. It was intelligible, and once understood, it was open to improvement. Some liberals found reforming strength in Christian zeal, others in Enlightenment reason, many in both. Some were perhaps simply adapting to circumstance by putting a purposeful face on the brute fact of ceaseless change. Whatever drove them, liberals kept faith with progress. They saw it in economic and social terms, but also in terms of human capacities and human character. Liberals wanted to improve society. They wanted even more to improve people. Progressive reform accordingly had distinguishable streams: reform of society and reform of the self. They were hard to separate in the nineteenth-century liberal mind. But they were not the same task. Both merit scrutiny.

It is worth stepping back first, though, to notice with progressive reform a third point of contrast between nineteenth-century liberals and their conservatives and socialist rivals, having seen already those to do with power and with conflict. Conservatives did not believe in progress. They thought the room for genuine human betterment small or illusory.

Social reform was at best a tactical indulgence, at worst a heedless interference with rooted social patterns whose scope for change was small. Hopes for improving people's character were equally dim. Human beings were pretty well what they were, and the average was low. Excellence to conservatives was an absolute, not a relative notion. Social improvement, if it came at all, was less advance than making up lost ground, a matter less of reform than repair. Conservatives were not morally blind or heartless. In their sensitivity to local wrongs and particular outrages many conservatives claimed with some justice to be more modest, and so more successful, doctors of human ills than were liberal apostles of overambitious reform.

Socialists took a brighter view of human prospects. They believed with liberals in social betterment, but thought of it differently. Progress for socialists called for a leap into a brotherhood of equals, nothing short of which would count as a genuine improvement. Socialists believed in creating a new society, liberals in gradual improvement to an existing society. Socialists were progressives of transformation. Liberals were progressives of reform. Shared belief in progress made liberals and socialists potentials allies, although shared suspicion of popular power in democracy made liberals equally potential allies of conservatives.

Liberals had ample room for disagreeing about social reform among themselves. To simplify, a pair of spiritual guides dominated the thoughts of nineteenth-century liberal reformers and they did not always give the same advice. One was the public interest, the other was the free market. A powerful theory of the first was the Utilitarianism of Jeremy Bentham, and of the second, the political economy of Adam Smith. Bentham had asked of any law or customary social arrangement, did it foster the greatest good of the greatest number? Smith had taught that markets were most productive when left to themselves. The reforming message to government of Utilitarianism was interference and control in the service of bettering society. The reforming message to government of political economy was noninterference and removal of controls in the service of spreading prosperity, greater freedom for producers and wider choice for shoppers. The messages, it was hoped, converged. Broader prosperity, the aim of political economy, contributed to the common good. A better society, the goal of Utilitarians, included greater freedom and more choices. So it looked, but the messages commonly conflicted in practice. Reconciling the messages of the common interest and the free market has occupied liberal minds virtually ever since.

A good early British example of the contrast exists in the lives and careers of Edwin Chadwick (1800–90), a Benthamite drafter of the 1834 Poor Laws and representative of top-down Victorian reform through government, and Richard Cobden (1804–65), who led the campaign for free trade in Britain.

Chadwick grew up in the Benthamite milieu of Philosophical Radicalism. His father was a radical journalist, his grandfather a Wesleyan preacher. Educated privately, he caught Bentham's notice with an article in the *Westminster Review* calling for better policing, and became his secretary. Reform Whigs, in power at Westminster since 1830, were creating a new administrative culture of reports, commissions, and statistics. They needed young men like Chadwick. In our time he would have been a technocrat or policy wonk. He was scrupulous, hardworking, impatient, dogmatic, and without a shred of humor or tact. His fear of disorder was unusually strong. City police were necessary, he believed, to stop urban crime from seeping into the countryside. Schoolchildren, he thought, should do military drill to prepare them in case of fire. He wanted queuing at coach stops to show more discipline. Chadwick believed propertied women should have the vote, but he rejected Bentham's more radical views, which included universal suffrage for all and term limits for members of parliament in a postmonarchical republic.

Chadwick nevertheless pictured society and government much as Bentham did. Society was an aggregation of people responding alike only to pleasure and pain. By juggling incentives and penalties, law and government could gradually purge society of the bad habits and false beliefs that obstructed the smooth achievement of the greatest pleasure for the greatest number, the Benthamite understanding of the common good. After such reforming groundwork, government could indeed be "quiet." Until then, government must needs interfere with undreamed of ferocity. Chadwick's personal reputation as a measurer and meddler became so great that people credited him as author of almost any reform. The compulsory civil registration of births, marriages, and deaths, previously a parish responsibility, was not Chadwick's doing. In a country that was only just beginning to think of itself as a society in any sense, let alone one of totals and averages, people took registration as another of his centralizing reforms and called it "being Chadwicked." Known as "England's Prussian minister," he was said to be the most unpopular man in the country. It was said that the government pensioned him off early in 1854 because colleagues would no longer work with him.

A lump of a man with long hair and a huge, domed brow, Chadwick was more than a Victorian character. His campaigns for urban sanitation did much to reduce disease, save money, and prevent deaths in the workforce. Although real wages began to rise after the 1840s, they were not enough to raise living standards on their own without public action of Chadwick's kind. Chadwick's insistence led, for example, to an early statutory limitation of children's hours of work. His fear of disorder had a neurotic side, but the scourges he fought were genuine. Cholera and typhus were not projective figments of a terrorized bourgeois mind.

Chadwick exemplified two running threads in liberal reform. They recur in different guise throughout the liberal story. One was a conflict between centralizers and localizers. The other had to do with the moralization of poverty. As to the first, Chadwick was a centralizer. With the economist William Nassau Sr., he drafted the government report in 1834 that led to the replacement of parish relief with centrally administered workhouses. The new workhouses were cruel, poorly supervised, and corruptly run. In deference to untested theory, they replaced a patchwork of neighborly aid with a rigid system under control of remote officials out of touch with local conditions. So Chadwick's critics complained. The truth was more complicated. Neither old nor new systems were much good. The earlier one was also punitive and open to abuse. Frequently altered, its cost was hard to control, particularly when food prices soared as they did during the long years of war with France (1792–1815). Whether or not poverty was in fact growing in Chadwick's day, as twentieth-century historians of the industrial revolution long argued over, politicians and officials at the time viewed with alarm the thought that living standards might be declining. To a reforming liberal mind like Chadwick's, poverty was too large a problem to leave pell-mell to localities.

Chadwick's centralizing attitudes illustrate a general point about how market-minded liberals looked at the state in the nineteenth century. The point applies also in France, Germany, and the United States. These were attitudes not to one thing but to many. "The state" is a tidy term in political thought and political sloganeering. In practice, market-minded liberals confronted not one coherent, coercive power, but shifting networks of overlapping authority, local and central, customary and statutory, voluntary and mandatory.

In Chadwick's time, the *central* British state was indeed small and comparatively well run. Its controlling hand used a high degree of delegation to voluntary bodies such as schools, hospitals, orphanages, and friendly societies for mutual insurance. Private at first, these blended with local authorities, which in turn were "coordinated" by growing use of statute and central administration. Pressure to centralize came less from those two bugbears of twentieth-century free-marketeers, bureaucrats keen to increase their sway and misguided collectivist thinking, than from legal and economic forces. First, as cities grew and pressed into country jurisdictions, a need for adjudication arose between competing authorities. Second, businesses and banks wanted large, national markets. They wanted public goods such as roads, canals, and railways. Above all they wanted the uniformity and predictability that came with common standards and enforceable nationwide rules. Local practices, discrepant measures, haphazard legal judgments, and regional barriers blocked commercial opportunity and economic progress. Commerce, in short, wanted a single market. But to create a single market took a centralizing state.

Viewed from a business office in Manchester or Bristol, creating a single market might well look like the removal of barriers. It was natural to present such a creation in negative terms as the clearing away of obstacles, a freeing from encumbrances. Viewed from localities, creating a single market commonly felt more like an alien imposition, as loss of liberty. Wherever you stood, all was in movement. Vanishing fast were the humanly intelligible communities whose passing Thomas Carlyle lamented in *Past and Present* (1843). Vanishing were points around which self-managed localities might organize and protect themselves of a kind Schulze-Delitzsch still hoped for in Saxony. The use of the term "regulation," which came in during Chadwick's day, was a telling metaphor borrowed from engineering. It implied a picture of nation and market as smoothly running and well-coordinated as a machine.

As to the moralization of poverty, when in his Poor Laws report Chadwick distinguished the deserving poor from the undeserving poor, he reflected an ambivalence that liberals have never resolved. Chadwick argued that the standard of living in the workhouse should be "less eligible," that is lower and less appealing, than that of a gainful worker's. Otherwise the workhouse would appeal as a better alternative to honest labor. Chadwick's report was plain: "In abolishing punishment," it said, "we equally abolish reward." Liberal attitudes to poverty seem to run in cycles of charity and penalty, entitlement and conditionality, indulgence and stigma. The distinction between deserving and undeserving poor survived after 1880 among the social-minded "new liberals" such as Leonard Hobhouse, but vanished with William Beveridge's welfare reforms in the 1940s, when state aid came to be seen as a benefit to do with status or right, not need and reproof. In the 1970s, liberal attitudes changed again as free-market liberals identified "welfare dependency" as perhaps not a sin but a weakness or malady that in turn needed the state's intervention, correction, and cure. The growth of poverty in rich societies during the early decades of the present century provoked a counterconcern among liberals, suggesting another turn of the cycle. Liberals showed less readiness to stigmatize poverty by blaming it on the poor but little clarity about how politics and government should respond.

Cobden's father was a Sussex farmer who left to run a shop in Hampshire after the farm went under. He died when Richard was young. On leaving school at fifteen the boy worked in his uncle's warehouse in London and then set up a calico-printing business of his own in Manchester. Its fortunes rose and fell. Cobden, keener on journalism and politics, handed it over to his brother. A visit to the United States in 1835 was his turning point. On his American trip four years before Tocqueville had worried about the deleterious pressures of mass society. Cobden returned in wonder. He saw natural security, social openness, plentiful land, and an economy creating unbounded wealth. His enthusiastic picture of the young republic was for him an obverse of Britain, warlike, privileged, feudal, fettered. Cobden threw himself into a life of campaigning against old Britain.

His causes formed a square, each side of which faced one of liberalism's enemies. Against war and military spending, first, twin enemies of prosperity. "As little intercourse as possible between the governments, as much connection as possible between the nations of the world," Cobden wrote in 1836. For local self-government, second, to end the hold of country squires on city affairs, with a rousing call to "Incorporate Your Borough" in 1837. For free trade, third. Ending protection against foreign grain imports occupied him and his colleague, John Bright, from 1838 to 1846, when Robert Peel split the Tories by agreeing to repeal the corn laws. Cobden became a popular hero. Handkerchiefs printed with his face went on sale. In 1860 he was nationally feted as negotiator of the Anglo-French trade agreement. Finally, land reform. A flourishing economy could not exist, Cobden believed, without wide land ownership. He backed land-distribution schemes for breaking Britain's "land power" and achieving his vision of a property-owning democracy.

Behind each of Cobden's foes lay a single interest: landed aristocrats. They soldiered rather than traded. They earned from urban rents without working. They kept out cheap food. They monopolized land. Cobden, it should not be forgotten, was fighting a liberal class war and landed aristocrats were the enemy. Liberals were perfectly sincere in setting out universal propositions and principles. They were also out to win power, which meant seizing it from those who held power. They wanted them and theirs to rule, and liberal ideas were both objects of principled commitment and weapons in the contest.

Cobden's class war had mixed success. Britain's "feudal" establishment, as militant liberals liked to think of it, fought a long, successful retreat in battle order. Free trade on the other hand became a matter of official faith and, as bringer of cheap food, widespread popular devotion. It survived the turn toward protection during the 1870s in France, Germany, and—most strongly of all—the United States. Free trade's untouchability in Britain weakened as support grew for empire preference in the late nineteenth century burst of liberal imperialism. It gave way altogether in the crisis of the 1930s. As of much interest as his causes themselves, however, was Cobden's legacy to public argument.

Cobden's genius was dialectical. He took sides and had a position, but he did not argue as a partisan. He argued as if for everyone, including aristocrats. To shoppers and housewives he argued that tariffs were a brake on consumption that kept food prices high. To businessmen he argued that opening British ports to European grain would raise continental demand for British manufactures. To owners of land growing grain he argued that competition from foreign suppliers would make

British farmers more efficient, thus increasing investment in land and pushing up the value of the landlords' estates. Cobden was saying, in short, that everyone wins.

To those not convinced, Cobden had weapons in reserve. To non-economists, he argued that holding out against free trade was resisting a natural necessity. "To make laws for the regulation of trade," he said in 1836, "is as wise as it would be to legislate about water finding a level or matter exercising its centripetal force." To economists Cobden appealed to a new theory of value. It was not labor content that fixed a good's market value but supply and demand. By substituting the utility theory of value for Ricardo's labor theory, Cobden was able to answer one of the protectionists' strongest arguments: cheaper food would enable owners to pay lower wages, which would be bad for workers and encourage social unrest. No, Cobden explained, what you paid a worker did not depend as Ricardo had thought on the cost of maintaining him. Supply and demand for labor fixed the level of his wage. The price of food did not come into it. Third, to Christians—most of his hearers—Cobden added that free trade was virtuous. In his maiden speech to parliament in 1841, he argued movingly that relieving hardship in factory towns by lowering tariffs was an obligation for any good Christian.

A proposal that was at once a benefit to all, a natural necessity and a Christian duty was hard to resist. The free-trade gospel in Britain won wide and enduring appeal. Cobden's nobody-loses argument readily generalized to other free-market proposals. It became a valued part of liberalism's dialectical arsenal. Brisk, assured, and backed by expertise, Cobden sharpened an all-purpose, rechargeable weapon. It suggested an ideal condition of society in which everybody was a winner, or at any rate, as the small print told you, there were fewer losers than in any competing arrangement. In neutral-sounding technical terms, that ideal returned within liberal thought in many guises. Whether in the language of Cobden's day or in that of welfare economics and game theory, "everyone wins" became a cudgel for the silencing of nonwinners. It shut down argument and forestalled a question that recurred to nag the liberal conscience: "What do we say to the losers?" "Everyone wins" fitted awkwardly also with liberal insistence on the virtues and benefits of competition. If everyone was a winner, there was little value in victory and scant cost to defeat, hence in truth scarcely a competition at all.

With his evangelical temperament, Cobden was the John the Baptist of free enterprise. He reflected an upturn of mood in political economy. Smith had been cautiously hopeful about the chances of widening prosperity. Malthus and, more guardedly, Ricardo had taken the dismal view that it could not be counted on and that poverty was likely to endure. By Cobden's time, confidence had returned. Economic growth, higher wages, fewer mouths for each family to feed, and more investment seemed to be following each other in a virtuous cycle.

Cobden fashioned a weapon for publicists and dogmatists but was not himself dogmatic. No anti-government zealot, he argued for state schools, saying, "Government interference is as necessary for education as its non-interference is essential to trade." He praised Prussian absolutism as the "best government in Europe" for raising up its subjects "mentally and morally." In a minority among British Liberals, Cobden backed the Union in the American Civil War. When the commercial consequences of that war caused misery in Lancashire, Cobden appealed loudly to Christian conscience for public help. He argued tirelessly against Britain's many wars and supported congresses for peace, though he favored the use of force in what came to be called humanitarian intervention. Cobden's eminently liberal life was a warning to distrust labels and to beware of economists who, unlike Cobden, claimed to be arguing from a neutral point of view.

v. Smiles and Channing: Personal Progress as Self-Reliance or Moral Uplift

Hard as it became for later liberals to reimagine, when their nineteenth-century predecessors thought about human progress they thought of improving human character. Mid–twentieth century liberals felt unhappy with something as fixed and stereotypical as character. They recoiled from interfering with people in order to perfect something people were no longer held to possess. Latter-day liberals were just as doubtful as their forebears about the cultural and moral fiber of their fellow citizens, but they faced those anxieties in suppressed and roundabout ways. Liberals of the nineteenth-century felt little need to conceal the liberal urge to teach, correct, and improve. Reforming human character was a burning preoccupation, for many reasons.

Some bore on the benefits that better character might bring to society. Self-possessed citizens, for example, would be stronger at standing up to power. Educated ones could be better trusted with the vote. Self-reliant people lifted burdens of support from others. Better people, above all, caused less trouble and let anxious liberals sleep sounder. In his *Autobiography* (1873), Mill predicated his boundless hopes for a progressive transformation of society on a "change of character" both "in the uncultivated herd who now compose the labouring masses, and in the immense majority of their employers."

Other reasons bore on the benefits that better character could bring more directly to people themselves. These could be material or moral. The message of material self-improvement was that through hard work and good habits you could get ahead and stand financially on your own. The message of moral self-improvement focused on the elevation of taste and conscience. It taught that beauty and virtue, in a broad, this-worldly sense, were the true ends of life and preached a gospel of social engagement. Samuel Smiles is an exemplary British advocate for the material kind of self-improvement. William Ellery Channing, an American Unitarian preacher, illustrates the moral kind of self-improvement.

"True liberty rests on character," wrote Samuel Smiles (1812–1904), one of the most widely read nineteenth-century authors in English. One of eleven surviving children from a modest Scottish family of strict Presbyterians, Smiles pulled himself up and made himself rich by selling books that advised others to do likewise. "The greatest workers have sprung from the ranks," Smiles wrote in *Self-Help* (1859), the best known of his many books. By the time of his death, it had sold a quarter of a million copies. Hostile to privilege and exclusion, Smiles made the *Leeds Times*, which he edited, a platform for radical causes. He supported the Chartists' call for universal male suffrage, paid members of parliament, and regular parliamentary sessions, though drew back from what he took for violent Chartist methods. No socialist, he preached not solidarity and counting on your fellows, but relying on yourself. It was Smiles who put the French neologism "individualism" into English currency as a term of praise, and not, as it had largely been until then, a pejorative. It was, Smiles wrote, "strong individualism which makes and keeps Englishmen really free."

Smiles preached a gospel of hard work. *Self-Help* praised doers and achievers, particularly engineers, scientists, and entrepreneurs. The flaw in Smiles's gospel of hard work was not hard to spot. Almost everyone worked hard in life. Few were highly paid. Many went without the satisfaction of recognized or worthwhile work. Tiny numbers knew success in Smiles's sense. Winning was a matter of luck, and his prizes were lottery prizes. Smiles, who disapproved of gambling, saw the difficulty. With admirable candor, he took the hard line. Great rewards could not be counted on, and it was deceitful to promise them, he thought. They were an unmerited bonus for the lucky few, indeed a highly improbable bonus. The only deserved and reliable reward was hard work itself. Smiles was franker than many later liberals attempting to soft-sell harsh economic measures in the democratic marketplace or to defend unacceptably big executive pay as somehow worthy or merited.

In defending the virtues of drudgery for its own sake, Smiles went to implausible lengths to erase the difference between painting the Sistine ceiling, say, and scrubbing its floor. Shakespeare, Smiles claimed, preferred running a theater and keeping account books to writing good plays. As if purpose and talent were of small consequence beside work and application, Smiles cited with approval Beethoven's judgment that pleasure-loving Rossini could have written great music if only they had flogged him harder as a boy. Among poets, Smiles ranked Southey above Coleridge because Southey, he calculated, put in more hours. Smiles's contorted attempts to treat work of whatever kind as a value in itself, regardless of what work produced, echoed Bentham's refusal to acknowledge hierarchy in cultural values. It looked forward also to the modern economic approach to work as a neutral measure of undifferentiated effort, a uniform minus for which money pay was an all-purpose, compensating plus.

Self-Help is all the same a remarkable book. Smiles's admirations and excitements, especially for difficult technical achievements, soften its philistine edge. A feel for daring roof spans, bridges, and rail lines betrays his claim that results matter less than the labor. Smiles read hugely, and wrote simply and well. As an editor he understood pace. On business and engineering, he wrote with the experience of someone who had run a railway company and an insurance firm. A Victorian believer in progress, Smiles was proud of what intelligence and hard work could bring to those who used them, a further silent admission that results also counted. He was not blind to the faults of his day, but he strongly believed that for most people life in England was far better than it had been. In *Thrift* (1875) Smiles contrasted the condition of England in his time and a century earlier, around the time of Humboldt's birth, with which this liberal story opened. Smiles pictured that late eighteenth-century world as fetid and lacking: no steam engine, manufactures, or coal, perilous roads, loutish aristocrats, corrupt middlemen, and feckless lower orders diverted by cock fighting and public hangings. "The 'good old days' have departed," Smiles wrote, "we hope never to return."

Character mattered also in the nineteenth-century United States, where it mattered especially to liberals. In party political terms, the first American liberals were the Whigs, who pictured themselves as a movement of resistance to the "tyranny" of Andrew Jackson, president in 1829–37. Socially the Whigs emerged from the liberal-minded elites of the early republic. As with Europe's first liberals, these were men—and to begin with almost no women—to whom leadership came naturally. They expected to lead congregations, head colleges, run businesses, and make laws. By the 1820s, however, American property qualifications for voting were rapidly disappearing. Wider franchises were throwing up leaders like General Jackson. To his liberal foes, he was a bully with too much popularity and too much power who appealed to the wrong sort. Jackson painted his Whig complainers as an interfering elite defending old privileges. They shot back that he was a first-generation elitist defending new privileges. Both claimed to speak on the people's behalf. But by that they meant different things. Whigs wanted to improve people for their own good. Their Jacksonian opponents wanted to reassure people that their aims and beliefs were fine as they stood.

Culturally, the quarrel of Jacksonians and Whigs was a contest between frontier and parlor, saloon and salon. In a sense it was about the domestication of a rootless settler society. Whigs came to favor women's part not only in church, but in politics. Emerson's friend Margaret Fuller, the Boston leader of the women's movement, and Elizabeth Cady Stanton, organizer of the Seneca Falls congress for women's rights in 1848, came out of the same milieu of liberal Protestant social action. To Whig reformers the rest of America was not the Wild West but the Wild Everywhere, scarred by dueling, drinking, whoring, and rioting. In the 1830s only one American in fifteen lived in a town of more than eight thousand. Compared to Paris or London, the biggest cities—New York, Boston, and Philadelphia—were provincial towns without metropolitan culture. Like early nineteenth-century Germany, the United States had no single urban focus. Unlike Germany it had no princely courts with their cultural traditions, and only a handful of university towns. In such a society, reforming American character meant first of all encouraging manners, morals, and civility. In American popular memory the reform of character was often pictured as a battle by hearth and market against wildness and isolation in which the losers—the western cowboy and the southern rebel—became mythical heroes.

The foremost Unitarian preacher of his time, William Ellery Channing (1780–1842) was an outstanding representative of American liberal Protestantism. He rejected the gloom of strict Calvinism, preached earlier in New England, that taught of a distant but vengeful and arbitrary God who left man alone to deal with his own depravity. Channing had a buoyant Enlightenment confidence in the progress of people and society, democratic hopes for general education, and faith in the relevance of the Christian gospels. There was on Channing's telling no Fall, only earlier man, no divine plan only human history, no covenant of man with God nor social contract among men, only society into which everyone is born and where they remain.

Channing himself was born into upper-crust Boston. A grandfather had signed the Declaration of Independence. Emerson found him cold in person but electric in the pulpit. As a Christian humanist, Channing was preacher, lecturer, and public educator in one. He would have found himself at home in Germany. Like Humboldt, he advocated Latin and Greek as the ground of a rounded education. He viewed the figure of Christ, much as did Enlightened German Protestants, as a moral exemplar with a universal message and showed no interest in the stage machinery of supernatural theology. In the lecture he was proudest of, "Self-Culture" (1838), Channing pictured human existence as a kind of further education in all departments of life during which people might attend to the unceasing growth of their faculties. It sounded arduous, but part of Channing's appeal was to make self-cultivation sound almost like gardening.

Growing the self did not for Channing mean neglecting society. Civic action was for Channing a vital part of self-fulfillment. A reformer rather than a firebrand, his "liberal faith" was an engagement in social causes in a spirit of toleration and acceptance, without punishing moral zeal. An early antiwar group, the Massachusetts Peace Society, was founded in Channing's house in 1815. Moral development called for political engagement. He urged his listeners to join the reforming drives of the time. Channing lived his own message as a campaigner for prison reform, temperance, women's rights, workers' education, and help for the poor. Like other Whigs, he was against the extension of southern influence to the West and spoke out against the annexation of Texas. Though slow to adopt outright abolitionism, from 1835 Channing became a public voice of opposition to slavery itself, to the discomfort of conservative parishioners who disapproved of the moral offense, but saw, as southerners were quick to argue, how closely southern slavery and northern commerce were tied. Channing organized the meeting at Boston's Faneuil Hall in December 1837, when the radical Wendell Phillips established his preeminence as an antislavery orator. A generation younger than Channing, Phillips went on after the Civil War to campaign for equal rights for women and for economic democracy. As with Channing, his political engagement grew smoothly from moral convictions themselves rooted in a modern religious faith. Our next liberal represents a post-Christian nineteenth-century liberal looking for a new faith and finding it in science.

vi. Spencer: Liberalism Mistaken for Biology

The long-lived Herbert Spencer (1820–1903) merits attention in the liberal story for misleading but seductive metaphors he sewed into liberal thought. He took politics for natural history and treated the market as the arbiter of social justice. He began as a youthful reactionary, putting laissez-faire maxims into a pamphlet of 1843, *The Proper Sphere of Government*. His best remembered work, *Social Statics* (1851), contained many radical ideas. There followed voluminous writings blending morals, politics, and biology into a single smooth mass. In age, Spencer returned to reaction. His weaker ideas lasted best, a disconfirming instance of the principle of "survival of the fittest," a phrase Spencer coined but which is often wrongly fathered on Darwin. Spencer was at liberalism's edges, but he was still liberal. He turned himself into a character as if to show the worth of the human possession he prized most, individuality. He stressed the protean nature of the danger that to his mind most threatened such individuality, namely coercive power.

"While old kinds of coercive government are dissolving," Spencer wrote in his *Autobiography* (1904) published a year after he died, "new kinds of coercive government are evolving." His age was experiencing "a social exuviation, and the old coercive shell having been cast off, a new coercive shell is in course of development." Exuviation was the shedding of a skin or an outer layer of shell, which then grew again. As the power of some humans over others is forever shed and renewed, Spencer was suggesting, resistance to it must be ever vigilant and never ending.

Spencer was an autodidact, valetudinarian, and amateur inventor who sought patents for a telescoping fishing rod, an articulated hospital bed, and a "cephalometer" for phrenological measurement. By turns indolent and hugely productive, Spencer dabbled in civil engineering and worked for train companies in the rail boom of the early 1840s. Exposure to the "trickeries of trade" left him with a distrust of businessmen as caustic as Smith's. Contented moments gazing at the stratified beds of railway cuttings awakened, Spencer tell us, an interest in natural change and evolution. In 1848 a well-to-do uncle, who knew the editor, helped him to a first job as a subeditor on the free-market *Economist* newspaper. The editor, James Wilson, told him that the post required daily office attendance, but "no heavy duties." In London Spencer fell easily into a circle of progressive, scientific-minded intellectuals. When his uncle bequeathed him a small legacy, he left the rigors of weekly journalism to devote himself to writing.

In his *Autobiography* Spencer writes with pride that he had inherited from Derbyshire Methodist forebears an aversion to submission and a repugnance for every kind of authority. Likenesses concentrated on Spencer's puckishness: runaway pork-chop whiskers, lively eyes, and deep smile lines bracketing a broad mouth that looks ready to deliver a quip. He refused to wear formal dress and when on trains tied his manuscripts to himself with yards of thick string. The novelist George Eliot fell in love with him, but he not with her, though they remained good friends. She once asked why, given that he thought so much, his brow had no wrinkles. Because, Spencer told her, nothing ever puzzled him. As to why he had stayed a bachelor, Spencer told a friend that when young he was not financially secure enough to support a wife and once he was secure it was too late. In 1856, Spencer seems to have had a complete nervous collapse, afterward nursing his frail health with vegetables, tobacco, opiates, and salt-water compresses.

In *Social Statics* (1851), Spencer imagined society in Benthamite fashion as an agglomerate of independent, self-interested human units. Each such unit, he wrote, sought pleasure and shunned pain. Humans hence shared a motive for cooperation. Spencer called its governing rule the principle of equal freedom: "Every man has freedom to do all that he wills, provided he infringes not the equal freedom of any other man." Spencer next drew out specific liberties: not to be intruded on in the home or interfered with in trade or in what you say or print. Rights of noninterference extended also to women and children, who should be protected from "coercive education"—laws obliging parents to send children to school. Spencer defended a right to "voluntary outlawry," that is dropping "all connection with the state, including its protection." He argued that everyone, women as well as men, should have a vote, and that the state should hold title to land as a monopolist, letting it to tenants who could put it to the most productive use.

Classical writers had tended to treat bad government as a failure of virtue or an imbalance of social forces. Medieval thinkers had taken it for divine punishment on human wickedness. The political rationalists of the Enlightenment and the English Utilitarians had encouraged people to think of misgovernment as the result of corrigible ignorance and avoidable error. Spencer spoke of bad government, as he came to speak of bad anything, as a kind of maladaptation: "All evil results from the non-adaptation of constitution to conditions."

Using the language of biology, Spencer joined Utilitarian happiness, human progress, and government inaction into a single story that sounded to the unwary like science. He gave the story an irresistibly suggestive name, "evolution," which he put into circulation in "The Development Hypothesis" (1852). Spencer was far from the first thinker to equate "right" with "natural." In a flash of imagination, he did see a new way to tell a very old story. He gave an ancient but gnomic ethical injunction a modern spin by turning "Follow nature!" into "Follow evolution!"

The label "Social Darwinist" was untrue of Spencer and unfair to Darwin. Spencer's improvisations on biology drew on the work of Jean-

Baptiste Lamarck, who unlike Darwin believed in the inheritance of acquired characteristics. Darwin doubted that clear moral or political consequences could be drawn from evolutionary theories of natural change. Spencer, in addition, had a pseudo-factual nineteenth-century way of making the eighteenth-century distinction between civilized and uncivilized peoples. Under Spencer's editorial supervision, assistants put out volumes of "descriptive sociology" that partitioned humankind with spurious exactitude into higher and lower races. Many liberals of the day shared such superstitions. Spencer's speciation of humankind should be kept in mind when reading his homilies to "the individual."

In *Principles of Ethics* (1879–93) Spencer wrote that all natural forms, including societies and their moral ideals, evolved continuously without breaks. Forms moved from simple to complex. Hunter societies became farming societies. Warfare made way for commerce. Whereas militant societies were simple, industrial societies were complex. As complexity followed simplicity in the order of history and since later was better, it followed for Spencer that industry was better than warfare. So for human character. People have improved from homogenous beings in interchangeable predatory groups to more individuated, sharply defined characters in diverse societies. Among adults, Spencer tells us, "the individuals best adapted to the conditions of their existence shall prosper most" and the "individuals least adapted . . . shall prosper least." That was a "law which, if uninterfered with, entails the survival of the fittest."

The Cambridge moral thinker and Utilitarian liberal Henry Sidgwick concentrated devastating fire on Spencer's evolutionary story of ethics in a paper in the opening issue of the philosophical journal *Mind* in 1876. He followed it in the same journal four years later with a heavy shelling of Spencer's *Data of Ethics*. To neutral readers, Sidgwick left Spencer's edifice roofless and tottering. First, looking for guidance in ethics from "evolution" was vain. For all that evolution told us, Sidgwick wrote, was that human norms had evolved naturally. None, that is, came with divine or supernatural authority. We still needed to know which of many surviving norms was the one to follow. All in some sense were ancient. We needed to know which was right.

The distant future, second, gave little or no guidance either. To be told "Follow the norm best adapted to nature's final goal" was empty.

Not knowing the goal, we had nothing to aim at. Older moralists had sketched an ideal person against which to judge conduct and called the ideal "natural." Spencer's natural ideal was not an imaginary person but a supposed destination for the social part of nature inhabited by man, a destination, Sidgwick insisted, about which we knew nothing.

Another difficulty for Sidgwick lay with progressive ethics, of which Spencer's evolutionary ethics was a subvariety. Proponents disagreed on which features of the present were improvements on the past. The French social philosopher Auguste Comte, for example, approved of and expected more social control. Spencer, who disapproved of it, expected less. As Sidgwick nicely put it, those who made ethical progress their test in ethics commonly disagreed about the "next term in the series." Spencer's rejoinder did not impress Sidgwick. Spencer claimed that complexity, which came later, was better for people than simplicity, which came earlier. Complexity, that is, made people happier. But, Sidgwick objected, one outstanding mark of "complexity," the division of labor, contributed also to unhappiness by replacing skill and control with dull, subservient, and repetitive work.

Sidgwick's final salvo was that in talking of "evil" as "maladaptation" and making "adaptiveness" or "fitness" the all-purpose test of right and wrong, Spencer was promising us either no judgments or wrong judgments. No judgments if "unfitness" turned simply on the banality that how things are need not be how they ought to be. And wrong judgments whenever what was "fit" or "adapted" to present circumstances was visibly wicked.

Spencer's theory only sounded Darwinian. In Darwin's theory of natural selection evolutionary change had no purpose. Nor strictly speaking had it direction. Later in Darwinism did not mean higher or better. It meant simply later. Natural change was pointless. In any period, the species that existed, including humans, were, strictly speaking, leftovers. They were species that, thanks to tiny chance reproductive advantages operating over very long stretches of time, did not die out. It was Spencer with his gift for a seductive phrase who spoke, well before Darwin used such language, of "survival" and "competition," as if virtue and intention were in play, not cell mechanics. Had Spencer called later species such as humans not "survivors" but "remnants," his running together of survival and success would have sounded less appealing. As fiercely as had Sidgwick in ethics, Thomas Huxley criticized Spencer's misunderstandings of evolution and his attempt to derive politics from biology in his lecture "Administrative Nihilism" (1871). Biologism in social thought re-emerged, nevertheless, and was on its way to achieving priestly authority in certain quarters by the late twentieth century.

Spencer's mélange of ethics and biology was seductive. His tale of justice as desert offers a telling example. Justice, for Spencer, was giving merit its due. His rule of social justice was that the "superior shall have the good of his superiority; and the inferior the evil of his inferiority." "Superiority," he wrote, "profits by the rewards of superiority." Justice rewarded merit. Merit came from what a person contributed to society. Forces of supply and demand fixed the market worth of a person's social contribution. Their contribution was fixed by their capacities, and nature fixed those. Spencer had set up a smooth linkage among justice, natural selection, and competitive markets, so crafting an all-purpose riposte to complaints of injustice in the social status quo.

"Such high pay is not merited," you might say. Or "Low pay like that is not deserved." No, the Spencerian could reply. Nature rewarded the dim and weak with unfitness. Their capacities were lower and they produced less. Nature rewarded the clever and strong with fitness. Their capacities were higher, and they produced more. Markets rewarded the unproductive with low pay, the productive with high pay. As everyone got their deserts, justice was met. Unmerited winners and undeserving losers—there were ever plenty of both kinds—dropped out of account.

In old age and ill health, Spencer's earlier hopefulness—"Evil perpetually tends to disappear"—narrowed to a morose, defensive conservatism. His doubts about businessmen softened. He joined the homeopathist Lord Elcho in the Liberty and Property Defence League (1882). An early example of a moneyed lobby in democratic politics, the league brought together landowners, railway directors, and rate-payers' associations to press for their interests against, as they saw them, municipal socialists, tyrannical county councils, and liberal reformers. Spencer pulled back from the unorthodoxies of *Social Statics*. No, he now accepted, people were not free to make themselves "voluntary outlaws," as no one in practice could deny themselves the state's protection. No, public ownership of land was neither right in principle nor practicable. No, women should probably not have the vote at once because—Spencer here fell back on bewhiskered liberal stereotypes—women's evolution-arily "lower" animal nature prevailed over their "higher" rational side and because, being timid and subornable, women would tend to vote for despotic figures of authority.

Strive as he did to turn himself into a reactionary bore, the Derbyshire wag in Spencer never wholly died. In 1882 Spencer was feted on a trip to the United States, where his host and patron gave him a "trying" dinner, as he described it, at Delmonico's in New York. He was sleeping badly and disliked iced water. Called on to speak, Spencer said that Americans worked too hard. Life was not for learning or work: both were for life. A new ideal was needed, as different from industrialism as industrialism was from earlier militarism. It was, Spencer told his startled listeners, "time to preach the gospel of relaxation." That was not what Spencer's admiring wealth creators were expecting to hear. Spencer grew less hos-tile to religion and even began to tolerate babies, a late admission of one of the more basic aspects of human survival.

In "Reflections," the concluding section of his *Autobiography*, he added a telling qualification to his proud assertion of familial noncon-formity. Resisting human powers and authorities, he wrote, presumed that there was a "sovereign norm superior to any regulations made by man." Perhaps even his anti-supernaturalism was weakening. As Sidg-wick had stressed, Spencer's difficulty was that biology constrained the range of our ideals but did not tell us which ideal within that broad range of biologically possible ideals we should pursue. Spencer's politics was open also to the objection that liberalism involved more than resist-ing power and disobeying bad rulers. It involved creating order, and not waiting for nature to create order by itself. Perhaps Spencer's scientific-sounding system was an ersatz faith, created to fill a gap in a godless world and to find broad purpose where there was none.

vii. J. S. Mill: Holding Liberalism's Ideas Together

No one did more than John Stuart Mill (1806–73) to hold together con-flicting elements in liberal thought. Nobody since has offered as many-sided or candid a statement of the conflicting pressures within the lib-eral creed. Mill connected to many liberal tribes but was not captured by any of them. Perhaps because his understanding of other people's ideas was so large and so generous, it was often mistaken for agreement. Men as different in outlook as the progressive Comte and the conservative Scottish historian Thomas Carlyle wrongly took Mill for a disciple. One-sided appropriation did not stop. Free-marketeers and big-government liberals, conservative and left-wing liberals, paternalist reformers and hands-off libertarians have all claimed ownership of Mill. Some deny he was a liberal at all. Others think Mill, typically for a liberal, dodged hard choices and never decided what camp he belonged to. There is no good reply to people for whom camps and labels matter more than answers. Here instead is a rapid sketch of Mill's life and thought.

When in the late 1860s Mill turned to completing his *Autobiography*, he was already a famous figure in Britain and abroad. With the help of his stepdaughter, he was answering a mountainous weekly correspondence sent by well-wishers, favor seekers, and nitpickers from across the globe. His candor was legendary and winning. At an 1865 election rally before his brief turn in the House of Commons as a liberal independent, he was asked if he had written that the lower orders were for the most part habitual liars though ashamed of their lying. Looking firmly at his questioner Mill answered that indeed he had, and his mainly working-class audience broke into stormy applause. His death in Avignon, where he had lived in retirement, was flagged in Britain on newspaper placards.

He grew up on a ferocious regime of learning from the time he could speak, watched over by a trinity of Utilitarians: Jeremy Bentham, Francis Place, a radical tailor, and James Mill, his father. Mill senior was the son of a shoemaker from near Dundee in northeastern Scotland. He had made good, reached London, and married a wife with money from her parents, who ran a lunatic asylum in Hoxton on the far edge of London. James Mill called his firstborn John Stuart after the Scottish patron in whose carriage he had ridden southward. Mill junior was to recall that in his father's care he was "never a boy" but grew up in "the absence of love and presence of fear" without protection from his mother. She is present as a dim, submissive drudge in early drafts but missing altogether from the published *Autobiography*.

A spell in southern France at 14 and meeting at a London debating club Romantic and conservative friends almost as clever as he was melted some of that early frost. His father nevertheless put young Mill to the cause, getting Bentham's sprawling scripts into order for the press and writing for the radical-reform *Westminster Review*, the third point in a politico-literary triangle with the Whig *Edinburgh Review* and the Tory *Quarterly Review*. Whether from overwork or depression there followed a passing crack-up in the "melancholy winter" of 1826–27, the first of two watersheds in Mill's life.

Mill recorded his "dull state of nerves" less in medical terms than as a crisis of faith and an intellectual turning point. Bentham and his father had raised him with an overarching ideal. The only gauge of right or wrong, they taught him, was how far what people do or the laws they follow add or take away from overall human happiness. Here was the core of Utilitarianism: the greatest happiness as an overriding test for morals and society. The idea's appeal was electrifying. Its challenge to competing ideas of right and wrong was stark. What else but human well-being should guide our lives, our moral rules, our sense of justice? What other test of moral rules or political arrangements could serve but their "utility"—their contribution to the happiness or well-being of hu- mankind? Not unexplained duties or unquestioned custom. Not well- being as judged by moralistic guardians or subject to exacting standards of virtue or excellence, but well-being as experienced in "pleasure," the pursuit and satisfaction of our chosen aims, high and low. Young Mill had accepted that test with little difficulty. It gave content and a metric to the liberal ideal of progress. It gave liberal aversion to hierarchy and distrust of tradition an iron-hard wrecking ball with which to work. In editing Bentham's writings, Mill had seen for himself how the Greatest Happiness Principle knocked away the justifications from under ob- structive laws and pointless customs that frustrated and did not make people happy. So it had all seemed. Now a terrible question struck him.

Suppose his Utilitarian ideal were met. Suppose the greatest happi- ness were achieved. Would that make him happy? Mill's answer was no. To his scrupulous intellect, the consequences seemed shattering. If great happiness for many would not make him happy, how could such an achievement be counted on to make anyone happy? And if—as Ben- tham and his father had supposed—all that could bind any *one* person to the Utilitarian ideal of general happiness was the confidence that achieving the ideal would make *that* person happy, had Mill's realization not stripped the creed of its only appeal? Gone was the tie that was supposed to bind people to Bentham's ideal. Gone was the tie supposed to bind them indeed to any aim beyond their own happiness—their own immediate interests and well-being. A gap that his teachers had obscured or encouraged Mill to think did not exist had opened between the personal and the political, between the private and the public interest. Mill found himself pulled between liberal progress and liberal respect with no way to slacken the tension. Might it not be wrong to make someone pursue the good of society? Why, on the other hand, should the progressive betterment of society bow to private whim?

Mill's mental world—the world of a liberal reformer—had come apart. He set about trying to rebuild that world, and with it a liberalism that gave due weight to social reform and to respect for persons. He began to look for a liberalism of social betterment that did not impose on people's own aims and beliefs. He began to look for a liberalism of progress for all with protection for each from the weight and power of mass society. It was only a glimmer to begin with. But an idea that guided him was this. Perhaps a large element in human happiness was itself to be let alone and allowed to flourish in ways of your own choosing. Putting his mental world together again took him the rest of his life.

The first step was to mark the ground. In a pair of lucid but passionate essays that still read as if from yesterday—"Bentham" (1838) and "Coleridge" (1840)—Mill imagined a great contest between his teachers and their critics. On one side was the "party of civilization." This was Bentham and the Utilitarians together with everything they revered: facts, rationality, system, moral calculation, cool reckoning of benefits and harms, reform, intervention, and progress. On the other was the "party of independence." That was the poet-thinker Coleridge and the Romantic conservatives, with all they revered: imagination, intuition, moral feeling, outrage at particular wrongs, custom, tradition, stability. Neither side was wholly right nor wholly wrong, Mill thought. Their mistake was to ignore each other. Bentham could learn from Coleridge that right and wrong were not all that counted. Imagination and sympathy—beauty and "fellow feeling"—mattered too. The Romantic mistake was to set imagination and sympathy above right and wrong. Sentiment counted for much in morality, but it was a first word, not the last. Bentham's error, as with moralists generally, was to sink imagination and fellow-feeling altogether. The aim for Mill was not to weaken morality but to fix its limits.

Mill married Harriet Taylor, his companion of two decades, after the death of her husband in 1851. Hard as later writers found it to accept, their long affair, though scandalous to friends and taxing to her complaisant husband, was probably not sexual. Harriet confided as much in letters. Carlyle, with his keen eye and sharp tongue, nicknamed her "Platonica." Mill, ever open-handed with acknowledgments, credited the radical-minded Harriet with pushing him leftward toward democracy, feminism, and trade unionism. The compliment was generous to a companion he loved. The tendencies were present in Mill to begin with.

In 1858 came the second watershed of Mill's life. In July he left the administrative post he had held for thirty-five years. Given his intellectual output, it is astonishing to recall that he also had a day job at the East India Company, where his father had worked. An early example of public-private enterprise, the company supervised courts and tax raising in colonial India. As the Mughal Empire decayed in the eighteenth century, it had filled a gap in the administration of the Indian states. The company had filled also the pockets of shareholders, among them Edmund Burke, a would-be reformer of its notorious corruptions. To Mill senior (1773–1836), the company was, by contrast, an agent of progress that stood up both against rich landowners who obstructed commerce and prosperity, and against antique cruelties such as infant sacrifice, widow burning, and debt slavery.

Even in Mill senior's time, the East India Company's position was weakening. It lost its trade monopoly in 1813, and the Indian Mutiny of 1857 finished it off. The following year, parliament closed the company, and indirect rule of British India gave way to direct rule from Westminster at the India Office. In a sense the change marked the end of British imperialism by economic happenstance and the beginning of British imperialism by liberal policy. Mill, who had risen to chief examiner, was pensioned off. In a brief for his superiors defending the company and lamenting its end, Mill attempted a vindication of colonial rule itself: it was a temporary imposition, to teach Indians to govern themselves. Here was a Millian thought to loosen the liberal tension between social reform and respect for persons: masters might be needed for a time to teach self-mastery. As will shortly be seen, Mill thought something like that about democracy at home.

Later in 1858 came a different blow. While in southern France during October, Harriet caught fever and died within days. At fifty-two Mill was a widower without a job. Although he was now free to think and write, with Harriet's death, he told a friend, his "spring of life" was broken. Her twenty-seven-year-old daughter, Helen Taylor, stepped quickly and smoothly into Harriet's place as Mill's letter drafter, household manager, diary secretary, and editorial adviser. With astonishing perseverance and Helen to help, Mill finished his building. Its three parts are outlined below, though out of order of their publication.

In *Utilitarianism* (1861), Mill defended and revised his father's Benthamite creed. The most obvious objection to Utilitarianism was the crudity of its idea of happiness as pleasure minus pain, where pleasure was thought of as a measurable staple like sugar without significant variation in kind and tasting the same to everyone. Mill opened up that idea of happiness. First, human character was varied. Second, pleasure lay less in feeling things than in doing things, that is in pursuits and activities. Last, certain kinds of pleasure were "higher" than others. It was better to be "a human dissatisfied than a pig satisfied; better to be Socrates dissatisfied than a fool satisfied."

For Mill's campaign to rebuild his liberal world, the lessons of *Utilitarianism* were these. Happiness was varied and complex. Each of us had to pursue it for ourselves in our own way. In that search, education and experience were vital, for without them nobody could begin even looking. Finally, the search mattered as much as the arrival, a Romantic thought indeed. Here Mill sounded as if he was leaning toward a surrender of kinds to the second common objection to Utilitarianism: it offered happiness and made happiness a gauge of life, whereas happiness, as ancient wisdom and experience taught us, was unobtainable. Mill's play with happiness, satisfaction, and need was indeed open to confusion, but he had not abandoned faith in Utilitarian progress and reform. Given intelligence and will, neediness could be met. "Most of the great positive evils of the world are in themselves removable," he wrote in a ringing passage. He looked forward with confidence to a time when serious diseases were reduced and poverty "extinguished." With needs met, happiness, too, was attainable, Mill believed, so long as people were critical in their desires and material plenty, once achieved, was recognized as plenty, not as a way station on the path to ever more.

The third and final objection to Benthamite Utilitarianism was Mill's own. It was the terrible question at the time of his breakdown. If Bentham's mechanical picture of humans as pleasure-seeking units was correct, what bound us to the ideal of general happiness? What bound us, more troublingly, to any authoritative standards of right and wrong, justice or morality? Without an answer, Utilitarianism looked, as critics claimed, a doctrine of pure, if well-intentioned, expediency. In a long, intricate chapter, "On the Connection between Justice and Utility," Mill struggled to explain how by a gradual extension of sympathy and "fellow-feeling" self-interest might be expected to grow into solidarity with society.

The argument was knotted and inconclusive. Was Mill telling us to be more careful in matters of justice when applying the test of greatest happiness? Was Mill, that is, leaving justice in privileged subordination to the calculation of best outcomes? Or was he telling us *fiat justitia, ruat caelum*—let justice be done though the heavens fall. Was he saying in other words that when justice is at stake, we were to abandon the Utilitarian test altogether and give a person justice—give whatever was his or her due—regardless of general utility, the common good, or indeed any broad consequences? The two approaches lead in quite different directions. One looks back to recognized duties and accepted obligations, the other forward to expected results. Mill's rejoinder that those two discordant approaches commonly came together in practice was neither reassuring in itself nor convincing as a guide for reconciling the two approaches when they clashed, especially in novel, unfamiliar conditions—the kind that ceaselessly changing modern society was forever producing.

With *On Liberty* (1859) Mill pursued the conflict that had preoccupied Tocqueville. The conflict lay between individuality, which Humboldt and Constant had prized, and the stultifying power of mass society, which Mill feared for its pressures of "apelike imitation" and "intrusive piety." On his title page Mill quoted Humboldt's insistence on the "absolute and essential importance of human development in its richest diversity." Humboldt had left hanging who such open-ended diversity was good for.

Had he meant that being well-rounded generalists was good for each of us? Or that to have a rich variety of diverse human types was good for society?

Mill seemed to be saying that both were desirable. Whether for society as a whole or for its members one by one, individuality and originality were to be cherished, not stifled by the powers of conformity. "Experiments in living" were to be encouraged, not forbidden. The only ground that society, state, or law had for coercive interference with people's chosen practices or beliefs was when they threatened harm to others. Another question was why individuality and originality were good at all. Were they good in themselves? As a Utilitarian, Mill seemed committed to saying that only happiness was good in itself. Perhaps then individuality and originality were good because denying them by means of bigoted convention and oppressive laws made people unhappy. The details and ambiguities of the arguments Mill made for the preciousness of individuality ought not to obscure the strength and scope of the claim itself. In *On Liberty*, Mill was doing more than echo Constant's idea of an untouchable private realm. He was passing down to later liberals an ethical conviction that fortified their distrust of power and their insistence on civic respect for people, whoever they were.

It was not just that people differed in their tastes and aims. They should be encouraged to embrace and nurture such differences. People, Mill suggested, were not like sheep, who had a common sheepy way to live. People's "sources of pleasure" and even "susceptibilities of pain" differed. Their "higher" aims varied, and a liberal society in Mill's view should recognize that diversity. How Mill's promotion of individuality and human difference fitted with the "science of human nature" that he had looked forward to in his *System of Logic* (1843) was not clear. He still held that similarities existed among people that were open to empirical study. In *On Liberty* he was objecting rather to the idea that such similarities added up to a common nature of the kind that might then be used as the standard of natural or unnatural—that is right or wrong— ways to flourish in maturity. To think so in Mill's eyes was to treat raising and schooling people like tending sheep or pruning trees.

Mill went further and rejected any ethical standard that a person had not somehow embraced for themselves. A person's choice of how to live was not to be gainsaid, Mill argued, because it failed to meet some external standard of excellence, because it was unworthy in itself or because it was frowned on by society. Overall happiness remained for Mill the one ethical standard, but it was a goal that everyone had to shape and find for themselves. If Mill was right and those two thoughts could be made to cohere, the consequences for society were large. Mill was calling on society to withdraw claims to ethical authority except where one person's conduct threatened to damage another. Mill's "harm" test offered to show where society's authority was to stop: "The individual is not accountable to society for his actions insofar as these concern the interests of no person but himself."

Mill's crowded thoughts about individuality had little immediate impact, though in time their influence on liberal society and liberal thinking was momentous. In Mill's day, the ethical climate was unsympathetic. Group conflicts of class and nation were coming to the fore. Among liberal progressives, team players were more admired than originals. Flouters of convention tended to be cultural modernists, who were apolitically conservative or antiliberal like Friedrich Nietzsche. In Britain, the loudest reaction to Mill was negative. A ferocious response came from a fellow Utilitarian of illiberal temper, the Queen's Bench judge James Fitzjames Stephen. In his attack on Mill, *Liberty, Equality, Fraternity* (1873), Stephen seized on the seeming circle in Mill's "harm" test and worried at it like a hound. "How can the State or the public be competent to determine any question whatever," Stephen roared, "if it is not competent to decide that gross vice is a bad thing?" Not long afterward the imprisoned homosexual poet Oscar Wilde ironized in *De profundis* (1897) on the hypocrisies of a supposedly liberal society that prized economic self-reliance but defended bigoted convention. His own ruin, Wilde wrote, "came from not too great individualism of life but from too little." Wilde was implying that liberal society took Stephen's view of private conduct, not Mill's.

In *On Representative Government* (1861) Mill made his peace with electoral democracy. A new power—the people—was to have its say, even if the middle classes were dull and greedy, the lower orders ill-informed and unreliable. All should have a vote, including women—excluding them was as reasonable, he wrote, as excluding red-headed men. But, he added, educated citizens with property, who knew more of affairs and had a greater stake in society, should have more voting weight than the uneducated masses. Proportional representation was necessary to bring minority voices into Parliament. Legislation was now too complex to leave to members of Parliament and commissions should draft it instead. Civil servants should be professionally competent and independent.

Mill was here touching on a point about nineteenth-century government that later market liberals found easy to miss. Central government in Mill's day was a small, often corrupt affair with scant peacetime responsibilities and few means for meeting them. To most liberals, it needed modernization and improvement. In those last recommendations of Mill's about the writing and the administering of laws lay formidable new tools for a rapid increase in the state's powers and capabilities, as would soon be called on, chiefly by liberals, for fighting wars, administering a growing empire, and taming class struggle with social welfare. Mill was farsighted also in spying in the distance the economic weaknesses that twentieth-century liberals would hold against democracy: free-riding, interest-group capture, and the absence of hard budget constraints.

In 1865 Mill made an experiment in living of his own: he entered Parliament. He refused to stand as an official Liberal but agreed to campaign as an independent liberal on condition that he would spend nothing on his campaign, take no bribes, and speak his own mind, not a party's. To the confusion of radicals, Mill spoke in the House for conservative causes: for a strong defense and for lowering the national debt. Though he argued passionately to save from hanging two Irish Fenians he thought wrongly condemned, he supported the death penalty. The balance of Mill's interventions, though, was on the radical side. He spoke in favor of self-government for Ireland, confiscation of absentee Irish estates, asylum for political refugees and women's rights. He wanted Governor Eyre of Jamaica, who had punished an uprising there with the hanging of over four hundred people, to face prosecution for murder. Like Cobden, Mill took the North's side in the American Civil War, unable to see how any liberal could be in doubt about slavery. He had a poor political nose. Robert Lowe, a Liberal and fellow economist of conservative temper, called a speech of Mill's against a farm compensation bill, turning on a subtle point about costs and prices, "too clever for this House." The Tory leader, Benjamin Disraeli, mocking Mill's teacherly tone, called him "a finishing governess." His mind, all the same, was of its time. In his first two administrations (1868–74 and 1880–85), Gladstone passed a package of liberal reforms with a strong Millian stamp on each: disestablishment of the Church of England in Ireland, Irish land reform, married women's property acts, a national education act, and the abolition of religious tests in universities.

After Mill's failed bid for re-election in 1868, he retired to the south of France, a country for which he had deep affection and whose liberal traditions he admired. At this house in Avignon, he finished his essay *On the Subjection of Women* (1869) and worked on his thoughts about socialism. His sympathy for women's emancipation was strong, but characteristically careful. During the debate on the 1867 electoral reform, Mill had moved, unsuccessfully, that the word "man" be replaced by "person"—in effect to grant educated women with property the vote. He pursued the topic in his 1869 essay. There were, he argued, no natural differences of capacity between men and woman that bore on public and social life. The progress of society suggested an advance to greater equality between men and women, bringing with it greater happiness in all. Companionable marriages were preferable to those in which the husband domineered—he was thinking, flatteringly perhaps, of his own. Excluding women from public and professional life halved the pool of talent in society and corrupted men by giving them an artificially superior status that encouraged bullying.

Mill came to favor trade union rights and treated the power of capital over the working man as a despotism that needed tempering by the power of the state. As he watched social conflict intensify, Mill added radical details to successive editions of *Political Economy*. He abandoned the "fixed wage fund" theory, which wrongly claimed that a limited stock of money was available for wages and that, if union workers pushed up their own wages, others were bound to get less. He opposed obligatory overtime and favored land and inheritance taxes, as well as Chadwick's failed proposal for a proto-welfare state to help the sick, old, and needy. By the end of his life, some liberals took Mill for a socialist.

Mill was becoming a left-wing liberal of the kind that plays a large role in the next part, when liberalism in Europe and the United States takes a more active and interventionist turn. Mill shared many of the socialists' narrower aims about tempering the strength of capital, but without their dreamy talk of brotherhood or submissiveness to collective power, as his biographer Michael St. John Packe nicely phrased it. At the same time he never abandoned his beliefs in the necessity for private property or in the benefits of free markets as the best engine of prosperity and provider for social progress that he had spelled out in *Political Economy*.

In its fifth book he had given lasting arguments as to why laissez-faire or nonintervention should be the general practice for state and government. He saw no reason to retract them in later editions, and they have served the cause of economic liberalism ever since. Each focused on bad consequences. They were, in turn, the *atrophy argument*: interfering with people and restricting them stunted their faculties; the *risk-of-abuse argument*: any extension of powers added to the likelihood of abuses by power; the *overload argument*: adding responsibilities further burdened an overloaded state; the *better-grasp argument*: people knew their own business better than state or government; the *initiative argument*: overzealous government sapped commercial enterprise and initiative. As to his reasons not to interfere, Mill immediately added exceptions where he thought state or government should intervene: supplying public goods in default of private provision; protection of children, minors, and "lower animals"; regulations on work hours, poor-law support, protection for shoppers against unfair marketing, and colonial rule, an exception to laissez-faire, but justifiable for benefits in educating and raising up subject peoples. In both lists, Mill was giving reasons or considerations that weighed one way or the other, not stating hard-and-fast rules, a distinction free-market zealots have tended to overlook.

That progress depended on prosperity, Mill recognized, but he did not confuse the two. In book 4 of *Political Economy* he pictured a "stationary state" when an economy, having reached a broad level of wealth, ceased to grow. In a balanced state of society without very rich or very poor, even though material prosperity itself ceased to grow, human flourishing could continue to advance, he suggested, more fully and more openly than before. That ideal appealed to Wendell Phillips and Schulze-Delitzsch, indeed to many liberals who were beginning to think not only of how to produce greater wealth but how it might be better shared and better used. That same ideal pulled together much of what mattered to

Mill in the practice of liberalism: social progress, social balance, and respect for people's own aims while raising their sights.

Mill's idea of a "stationary state" in which material satisfaction permitted higher pursuits was present in the thought of Adam Smith, whose whole outlook presumed an ethical stability that underpinned commercial progress and gave it purpose. The thought that commercial progress might slow or stop alarmed later political economists, preoccupied by overpopulation and scarcity. The thought by contrast attracted Marx, who sought an escape for society from the unstoppable forward drive of capitalism. The thought that prosperity might falter or vanish haunted postwar economists after the world slump of the 1930s. Mill's stationary state returned as a theme at the end of the twentieth century, when liberals began asking, "Enough for us?" and "Too much for the planet?"

3

Liberalism in Practice

Four Exemplary Politicians

i. Lincoln: The Many Uses of "Liberty" in the Land of Liberty

Abraham Lincoln (1809–65) is one of the political giants looming over this first part of the story. Another is William Ewart Gladstone (1809–98). Each shaped and led a long-lived party of government, the Republicans in the United States, the Liberal Party in Britain. Without them the story might lose track of the ringing words that have moved liberals. A practice of politics needs not only an outlook with ideas but also an oratory to lend those ideas force. Lincoln and Gladstone appealed to liberal sentiments noted in the Introduction: hatred of domination, pride and shame in one's society, outrage at mistreatment, zest in effort and action, and longing for tranquility. Effective preachers, they played also on the darker, less uplifting side of such feelings: envy and resentment, self-punishing scrupulosity, selective indignation, interfering recklessness coupled with undue fear of risk. Both men pointed ahead to the liberalism of 1880–1945, Lincoln in the creation of a warfare state and the long-lived Gladstone in the challenge to liberalism of mass politics.

With Lincoln, it is no longer possible to talk about liberalism while pretending to ignore liberty. For with Lincoln we are in the land of the Liberty dollar and the Liberty Bell; the land of Liberty Enlightening the World with her torch and law book in New York Harbor and of Armed Freedom with her sword and shield, facing a rebellious South on the dome of the Capitol in Washington, D.C. We are in the land where "liberty" stood for something—a virtue, a natural possession, a cause—that was sacred enough to die for. It is the land of "Give me liberty or give me death" and "As he died to make men holy, Let us die to make men free."

"We have a genius for liberty," the temperance preacher and abolitionist Theodore Parker wrote in "The Political Destination of America" (1848) and few American politicians have risked neglecting or abusing an idea that seemed so perfectly to catch the national spirit. In *Liberty and Freedom* (2005) David Hackett Fisher gave a masterly survey of the place those nonidentical twins played in American oratory and political symbolism. Without seizing and controlling the slogan "Liberty!," Fisher wrote, no serious movement ever imposed itself in the United States for long. Few if any prospered once rivals had tarred them as liberty's foes.

The slogan "Liberty!" has evoked different things in the United States at different times. Abraham Lincoln, who knew the power and malleability of words, saw the point. When dedicating a military cemetery at Gettysburg in 1863 Lincoln spoke of the United States as "a new nation, conceived in liberty." With his usual clarity in a speech at Baltimore the following year he added the telling rider: "We all declare for liberty but in using the same word we do not all mean the same thing."

Jefferson imagined America's westward expansion as extending "an empire of liberty," and on Jeffersonian tongues in the first two decades of the nineteenth century "liberty" evoked a spacious idyll of independent farms and small government. In the long Republican domination from the Civil War until the 1890s, "liberty" meant chiefly emancipation, national progress and freedom for businesses not to have to listen to the demands of their workers or the complaints of their customers. In the heyday of Democrat liberalism from 1932 to 1980, "liberty" and "freedom" pointed to what government was trying to secure for all citizens: a fairer economic shake and a more equal voice in politics. After the Republican realignment of 1980, the words again evoked freedom from government, especially in the selective sense of lower taxes and less red tape.

"Liberty" evoked contrasting things at one and the same time. At the nation's birth, American rebels wanted to free themselves from the British parliament's campaign to pay for Britain's wars by taxing the colonies. The rebels wanted to be free of British creditors who lent money to pay for the war of independence. On victory, the Americans wanted to be free of British attempts to restrain the seizure of Loyalist property and to protect native Indian lands on the northwest frontiers from grasping American settlers. That frontier impulse continued to give "liberty" an American edge. To Jackson's followers in the 1830s, "liberty" meant freedom for a young nation to expand with its slaves across Indian lands and into Mexico. It meant freedom for self-made men to get ahead in the world by whatever it took. For Jackson's opponents, the first American liberals known as Whigs, the term had other associations. To Whigs "liberty" evoked self-mastery, freedom from warfare with the nation's neighbors and, hard as Whigs found it to reach one, an answer to the scourge of slavery.

In 1860, on the verge of civil war, all four presidential candidates spoke of "liberty" and "freedom." To John Bell, the Whig would-be reconciler of the sections, "liberty" meant public order and respect for the constitution. To Stephen Douglas, who still hoped the extension of slavery to the West could be left to popular decision in the new territories, "liberty" meant democratic choice. To John Breckinridge, the southern candidate, "liberty" meant the natural or constitutional right—take your pick—of the states to be let alone. To the radical Wide Awakes, who led pro-Lincoln torchlight parades in northern cities, "liberty" meant emancipation of southern slaves and freedom from southern obstruction of progressive legislation in the Congress. In the election of 1912, four candidates—Taft, the conservative Republican, Debs, the social democrat, Roosevelt, the Progressive Republican rebel, and Wilson, the "New Freedom" Democrat—each had their own distinctive vision for the country under the banner of "Liberty." Examples multiply. Then came Herbert Hoover's "ordered liberty," Franklin Roosevelt's "Four Freedoms," and Martin Luther King's hoped-for nation "free at last, free at last" from the injuries of racialism.

Americans were not arguing past each other in mutual incomprehension. To think that is to cheapen and mystify disputes of substance into crass but persistent misunderstandings. Theirs was not a verbal or conceptual confusion. They could understand the lexical grammar of "free from" and "free to." They could see the difference between being free (as when an unblocked river is free to flow) and being at liberty (as when a person is not stopped or inhibited by authority). To the extent that they meant different things by "liberty" and "freedom" their differences were pragmatic. Americans were not in conflict over the meanings of terms or the content of an idea. They were not, without realizing it, deploying different ideas. Their conflicts bore rather on the political focus of the same idea and the diverse uses that idea might be put to in public argument. Americans did not agree on which freedoms mattered most. They differed on the urgency, directness, and salience of a variety of political freedoms. In particular, two sets of contrasting freedoms stood out in Lincoln's time. One was the sovereign freedom of the Union from foreign powers as against the freedom of the states from the Union. The other was liberty for slaves against the liberty to keep slaves.

Before turning to Lincoln himself, however, a final thought about liberty in American political argument is worth noting. The language of freedom has encouraged an alluring but lazy picture of American politics as framed by a collection of absences. How often have we heard of what the new republic was free of: densely settled land; customary property rights; feudal ties; religious disabilities; an established church; patterns, traditions, and inheritances of a long national history; social hierarchies; habits of deference; a radical workers' movement; class conflict of a kind to shape the national politics.

A classic example of such *tabula rasa* thinking was Louis Hartz's *The Liberal Tradition in America* (1955). America was liberal at birth, Hartz argued, and had remained liberal ever since. Never feudal, it created neither a class-conscious left nor a status-conscious right defending its privileges and reforming society paternalistically. Americans did not look to government or state for help in shifting an old ruling class out of the way. Americans had no court or country grandees, no tradition-proud army, no established church, no munificent patrons. Improving, paternalist Whigs and agrarian Jacksonian radicals were for Hartz all liberals applying Locke's doctrine of self-government whether they realized it or not in a virgin land. Not only did Hartz blur the difference between liberalism and democracy. His was a class explanation of American history, only class was missing.

Whether or not the United States was, as Lincoln claimed, "conceived in liberty," the American land and American society were tendentiously pictured as borderless, empty and unfurnished, blank and "free," waiting to be filled at choice. Nothing comes of nothing, however. Allow—a large and purely temporary concession—that the familiar catalogue of absences above is historically fair and correct. After listing the burdens and clutter of the Old World that the New World was providentially free from, we would still need a story about the growth and endurance of the powerful presence around which American politics has largely turned and which American liberals, Lincoln in the lead, did much to shape: law and government.

He is a towering but puzzling figure, a great liberal and a warrior-unifier, an American Gladstone and American Bismarck combined. To many Americans Lincoln is the national reconciler who ended slavery and preserved the Union. To others he is the great separator who in saving the republic perpetuated its sharpest divisions. Most can agree that, like them or not, Lincoln summed up the aims and ideals of the American liberal in fewer words than anyone else. At Gettysburg, he described the United States as dedicated to the idea that "all men are created equal" and declared its mission as preserving a new form of politics, "government of the people, by the people, for the people." In his Second Inaugural speech, he announced with the fierce gravity of Cromwell that a just and godly cause, even war, must be pursued to the end.

His Gettysburg speech insisted in effect on the weight Americans should give to not excluding anyone from civic respect or social concern. For people merited those no matter who. Under pressure of war, Lincoln silenced his doubts about the feasibility of black and white Americans living together in the same society and drew a large consequence: everyone was due the voice and protections of full citizenship, whoever they were. It was a sweeping claim, heavy with promise and disappointment, but it helped set a new horizon to the shifting scope of liberal principle and opened Europe's way to a compromise with full democracy. If unlettered black field hands could be American citizens, by what argument could scared liberals hold back the claims of women and workers? In Lincoln's second inaugural, he invoked the duty to pursue those goals in God's name with a sword if necessary. Lincoln at Gettysburg pointed toward what to believe in and aim for. On the steps of the Capitol in March 1865 he spoke of how to hold and pursue such aims—"with firmness in the right, as God gives us to see the right." Liberal respect was due to all, but for those who disagreed, liberal progress promised not only the schoolroom but the battlefield.

In its scope, Lincoln's liberalism was democratic. Wherever Lincoln started from, he came in time to think of liberalism's ideals democratically, that is as applying to all. His liberalism was not democratic in a narrower majoritarian sense. He was not a populist. He did not think social or electoral majorities had the last word. In Lincoln's debates of 1858 with Stephen Douglas, his Republican competitor for a Senate seat before the war, Douglas had argued for leaving the question of whether slavery should be allowed in the new western territories to voters there. No, Lincoln had argued, there were higher tests of right and wrong than what majorities decide is right or wrong: the tests of justice and morality.

Plain and humble in outward style, Lincoln was ambitious from the start. Born in the slave state of Kentucky and raised on the frontier in Indiana and Illinois, he bridled at farm life working for a semiliterate father. Two trips on a flatboat down the Mississippi to New Orleans would have shown him the market realities of chattel slavery, though what conclusions the young Lincoln drew are uncertain. At twenty-two he left the family farm for a nearby township, where in 1834 he talked and joked his way to a seat on the Illinois legislature in Springfield. A Whig chieftain spied his talent, urged him to read some law books, and, in 1837, having earned his license, Lincoln went into practice with his patron. He was on the ladder.

The Whigs were a party of those who did well or were hoping to do well in the market economy. The party gathered in upwardly mobile white Protestants, city clerks, and those in skilled occupations as well as farmers near to transportation tying them into city markets. At the heights, the Whigs were bankers and insiders. In the North, their Democrat opponents rallied artisans whose skills were being discarded with the spread of industry, Catholics who resented Whig interference with their saloons and their schools, and up-country farmers who disliked city slickers and bankers.

Lincoln quickly absorbed the progressive values of the Whig elite. In 1842 he married Mary Todd, the daughter of a well-to-do Kentucky banker who owned slaves but disapproved of the institution. Lincoln himself was no firebrand. By the 1850s he was a prosperous star of the Illinois bar, winning tax exemptions for the Illinois Central railway and defending it against accident claims. Though slavery was wrong, he said in 1854, it was politically "a necessity." He opposed its extension West but could see no immediately practical way to end it in the South. Nor was

Lincoln insensitive to the common prejudices of white northerners, which in many places were written into antiblack local laws. Until well into the Civil War Lincoln toyed with compensated emancipation and "colonization," meaning expatriation, as the way to end slavery.

The new Republican Party, which he led from 1860, took over from the Whigs as the voice of commerce and industry. As its leader, Lincoln favored "improvements," that is government spending on transport and public works, but was against a strong and active presidency. In his prewar speeches, Lincoln continually stressed the constitutional rights of states to decide their own affairs. In the White House Lincoln presided nevertheless over a massive expansion in the powers of the federal government. Freed from southern obstruction by the withdrawal of secessionist members, the wartime Congress in 1861–65 created the American elements of a modern state. It as good as gave away public lands to westward settlers and raised an income tax. It provided federal land for companies to build the first intercontinental railways and for states to open free engineering and farm colleges, public seedbeds of invention and prosperity.

Lincoln was not looking to fight a civil war. He had entered Congress in 1846 among Whigs opposed to war with Mexico. In the 1850s he opposed the growing violence among pro- and antislavery forces, and thought John Brown, the marauding northern abolitionist, justly hanged. After election as president in 1860 on the eve of conflict, Lincoln offered the South constitutional guarantees for the preservation of slavery, though not its westward expansion. When war came, Lincoln used the forces of the state with grim purpose. He harried battle-shy generals appalled at the industrial slaughter wrought by modern weaponry. He imposed martial law in fractious Union states and suppressed resistance to the 1863 Union draft by force. As the end neared, he let General Sherman loose to wreak revenge across a stubborn but defeated South.

Had Lincoln in assassination not become a liberal martyr in 1865, what might he have done? It is irresistible to ask, even if there is really no answer. Like the abolitionist Wendell Phillips, might he have pursued liberal respect and concern for all in a deeper, more demanding way by taking up the economic complaints of western farmers and industrial workers, that is, by pursuing economic democracy? Might he have pursued similar treatment in law for everyone, that is legal equality, like the liberal Republicans, Carl Schurz, his German-American backer, and Salmon Chase, his fractious colleague whom he made chief justice? Might Lincoln have changed his original intention to pursue a conciliatory peace and given in to the radical Republicans? They wanted to destroy the plantocratic order of the South and remake the region as a late-starting North. We cannot be sure. By instinct and practice Lincoln was a balancer, a player-off of competing interests. In April 1865 there were many future Lincolns.

What can be said is that in keeping the South in the Union, Lincoln changed the options for American liberalism. The South made American convergence to liberal democracy later, more difficult, and less complete than in France or Britain. It played a part not unlike that of backward East Prussia in Imperial Germany. Over the next century the southern power in Congress resisted votes for women, civil rights for blacks, and the humanization of American punishment. In 1946, in tandem with the American Medical Association, southern conservatives stifled Truman's hopes for a national scheme of compulsory health insurance, which most Americans favored. When Democrats formed a Senate majority, southerners sat immovably as committee chairmen, and when Democrats were a Senate minority, southerners exploited blocking powers under the Senate rules with consummate discipline and skill. Obstruction by southern Democrats, in alliance with antiliberal Republicans in the nation at large, ensured that the United States came later and less completely to state-guaranteed protections against the risks of life that liberal Europeans would uncontroversially soon come to expect as benchmarks of social progress and public expressions of civic respect for all.

ii. Laboulaye and Richter: Tests for Liberals in Semiliberal Regimes

Human progress and civic respect for people often come together, but there is no need for them to do so. There are nonliberal ways to pursue social reform. There are nonliberal ways to show concern for people's needs, which many liberals believe is a material counterpart or even prerequisite of equal respect. A state can nanny people to their benefit while wrongly intruding on them by denying them a say, choices, voice. To put it in latter-day terms, states can do good without doing right. So liberals, who are a demanding lot, believe. Autocratic reform faced nineteenth-century liberals with hard choices.

In France, the authoritarian Second Empire (1852–70) confronted French liberals with the dilemma of working or not with a reforming autocrat. The "empire" was a calamity for French liberals in many ways, surprisingly good for them in others. Louis Napoleon's stolen landslides seemed to confirm everything liberals feared from universal suffrage and what Thiers called "the vile multitude." The agents of the Second Empire closed newspapers. They trampled on other civil liberties that liberals had pressed for since the 1820s. The emperor wooed the unforgiving right, grievously wounded but unready to die. He turned his back on liberal anticlericalism, less because he believed than because he had caught the wind of religious revival in Catholic seminaries and fashionable drawing rooms. Catholicism returned to schools. Liberal attempts to reestablish divorce, abolished in 1816, were abandoned. Though widely popular, Louis Napoleon's foreign ventures (Mexico) and wars (against Austria in Italy, Russia in the Crimea) irked peace-minded liberals who disliked big military budgets.

As its most scornful liberal critics had to admit, the Second Empire did wonders on the other hand for French banking and industry. It supported the free market, promoted the Crédit Mobilier and other investment banks that raised capital for new industries. In 1860 France struck a trade agreement with its old enemy, Britain, followed two years later by one with Prussia. In 1863–67 legislation embedded the joint-stock limited company in French law, permitting a burst of company formation. Not only had it brought prosperity. French liberals could be grateful to the Second Empire for restoring order and silencing the urban "street." During his Paris stay in 1851–52, young Walter Bagehot, later editor of the *Economist*, witnessed the December upheavals there and enthused in published articles about Louis Napoleon's coup d'état as a victory for commerce and calm.

An exemplary French liberal in illiberal times was Edouard Laboulaye (1811–83), a French professor of public law, antislave campaigner, and Americophile, best remembered as the promoter of republican France's tribute to the United States: the Statue of Liberty in New York Harbor.

Unlike Tocqueville, beset by aristocratic hesitations, Laboulaye admired American democracy with little reserve. He translated the liberal reformer Channing's writings into French and marveled at the public schools of Massachusetts. He looked up to Lincoln, supported the Union and, unlike French Bonapartists, abhorred the southern cause. In *The Liberal Party* (1861) Laboulaye set out his ideas for a democratic liberalism. He saw advantages to universal suffrage, for all its "Caesarist" abuse by the Napoleons: mass democracy allowed defeated minorities the hope of becoming tomorrow's majorities and provided a negative sanction in the peaceful removal of unwanted governments. Laboulaye championed personal liberty, social conciliation, and the decentralization of power to break the grip of Paris and Napoleon III's prefects.

Liberal voices such as Laboulaye's were little heard at first, though by the late 1860s they had gained in confidence and strength. In 1867, a liberal Emile Ollivier, became minister of education and two years later prime minister. Despite his pleas, Ollivier was still not able to persuade the emperor to unshackle the press. France was not "ripe" for such liberties, Napoleon told him. Nor could Ollivier restrain France's war hawks who looked with alarm across the Rhine to the growing power of Prussia, where liberals also found themselves in a reforming but semiliberal regime.

An exemplary German liberal who faced such difficulties was Eugen Richter (1838–1906), a Progressive thorn in Chancellor Bismarck's boot. Richter was a German Cobden. He had a beard like a yew hedge and a frown of stubborn ferocity. His vision of the state and its limits was stern. Pedantic but principled, he led the parliamentary opposition to Bismarck first as leader of the Progressives and after that party split, as leader of the Independents. Richter denounced the chancellor's expedient and manipulative approach to power as "socio-autocracy." Bismarck returned the compliment with class disdain, deriding Richter as "the loudest rooster on the progressive dung heap."

To understand Richter, a word is needed about Wilhelmine liberals as well as one about Richter's bugbear, the Iron Chancellor. Liberal splits and recombinations were intricate, but the broad position was simple enough. In 1861, liberals formed the Progressive Party, intent on extension of civic freedoms and above all on parliamentary control of the Prussian budget. Six years later the Progressives split for good into right and left, big business and little business, pro- and anti-Bismarck. The National Liberals (1867) rallied to the chancellor, to German unity through war, to universal suffrage in Reichstag elections, and, before long, to trade protection. The liberal left, which kept the Progressive label, included purist stalwarts of free trade and antimilitarism under Richter as well as welfare-minded social liberals. The left purists and left welfare liberals agreed that the landowning hold on the Prussian Diet must be reduced and that the Reich ministries should be accountable. They disagreed about expanding the state's tasks. Opposition to Bismarck held them together for a time and in 1884 disillusioned Bismarck liberals joined breakaway Progressives in the renamed *Freisinnige* (Independent) party. After Bismarck's dismissal as chancellor in 1890 by young Kaiser Wilhelm II, Germany's left-wing liberals reverted to type, splitting and recombining themselves into ever smaller groupings as the Catholic and Socialist Parties grew.

Otto von Bismarck (1815–98) accumulated power because he had a reputation for power, as he himself grasped. People used him as a landmark in an institutional fog. He was not a spider in a fine-spun web or the pilot of a well-run ship. The central institutions and finances of the unified German Reich were a new and improvised muddle of dynasty and federation, democratic representation and executive fiat. That it worked at all owed much to the professionalism of permanent officials operating under a modern and reasonably open rule of law. A hereditary monarch, at once emperor and king of Prussia, picked a chancellor, who ran two sets of ministries, Reich and Prussian. Two parliaments, the Reichstag, elected for all Germany on universal male suffrage, and the parliament of Prussia, whose elective lower house was chosen on a three-class franchise, completed the tangle.

The liberal-dominated Reichstag proposed reforms and opposed Bismarck. The conservative-dominated Prussian Landtag supported the chancellor and opposed reforms. In such a system, assigning political responsibility was hazardous. Bismarck's foes nevertheless shared in his own myth and credited him for just about everything good or bad that happened in Germany from the 1860s to the 1880s. The myth lived on after he was gone: Bismarck was the gravedigger of German liberalism, a charismatic leader who taught a people nothing, a blinkered conservative who bequeathed to his successors a hugely productive economy distorted by class-fractured politics, the destabilizer of Europe, the forerunner of Hitler.

The myths took new life in 1918 and again after 1945, but they started in Bismarck's life. As his longtime aide and editor Lothar Bucher read drafts of the chancellor's best-selling *Memoirs* (1898), he sighed, "Nobody counts but him." Others in the book did commonly appear as fools, scoundrels, or nonentities. Friedrich Naumann, a left-liberal of the next generation, chided Richter for falling for the Bismarck myth. Richter, Naumann judged, allowed a principled hostility toward power to sour into an obsession, becoming in his words "a typical opponent of whatever Bismarck did, even when the outcome wasn't particularly illiberal."

The son of a medical orderly from Düsseldorf, Richter trained in law, dabbled in journalism, and won a name with a campaign to relax the state regulation of taverns. In parliament from 1867 as one of Germany's first full-time politicians, he spoke up against war and for foreign trade, unfettered markets, tight budgets, and civil liberties. That creed, rooted in hostility to state power and national aggrandizement, set him on collision course not just with Bismarck. Richter's fellow liberals in parliament were most of them ready, when put to it, to scrap free-market principles if other principles promised German power and prosperity more quickly and reliably. Against the distant promise of comparative advantage, international openness, and small government, they followed Bismarck in the here and now of national strength, tariffs, and big navies. Richter inexpediently kept the faith.

Wilhelmine liberals were an awkward coalition and with Bismarck's mischievous encouragement divisive issues soon drove them apart. Richter was on one side of each issue, Bismarck on the other. The first was Bismarck's battlefield route to German unification. German liberals all wanted German unity. Not all wanted it at any cost. Back before the defeat of 1848, a leader of the Baden liberals, Carl von Rotteck, had cried "I prefer freedom without unity to unity without freedom. I do not want unity under the wings of Prussian eagles." Richter thought similarly of Prussia's military prowess. It was a burden to taxpayers, diverted people's efforts from industry and commerce, and strengthened the least progressive elements in Prussian society: military officers and landed nobility. Other German liberals saw Prussian strength differently. To them the benefits of unity—to commerce, to German power abroad—were worth fighting for, and if Prussia could win unity on the battlefield, so much the better. Assured of backing from liberal hawks, Bismarck maneuvered Prussia into victorious wars against Denmark (1864) and Austria (1866). The following year, a large block of liberals, eager for unity and fed up with inconclusive budget fights, left Richter and the Progressives to form the pro-Bismarck National Liberals.

German liberals disagreed also over Bismarck's anti-Socialist laws and the reintroduction of tariffs. In 1878, struggling to contain working-class demands, Bismarck proposed banning and jailing Social Democrats. The next year, he proposed abandoning free trade. After the slump of the 1870s, much of the world, Britain aside, had begun to raise trade barriers. Germany replied in kind. Richter opposed both measures, without success.

Richter had no time for the socialists, whom he saw as pitting class against class. In his satire, *Pictures of the Socialistic Future* (1891), it is hard to make out which revolted Richter more, socialism or democracy. Richter's little book, written in response to the Socialist Bebel's *Women under Socialism* (1879), imagined a society from which the middle classes had fled, papering their trunks with worthless government bonds. The state distributed housing by lot and dispensed food in public kitchens. Criminals went to work camps to repay their debts to society and only socialists might write for *Onwards*, the one daily paper. Public services, theaters, and concerts were communalized. Rationing lead to shortages. Work rates demanded in state factories rose. Riots spread in the countryside. Berlin's ironworkers struck. The police were reinforced. Seizing its chance, France sent troops to reoccupy the German borderlands. The socialist experiment ended in failure and national defeat.

Richter's book suggested a disregard for those who had not scrambled up the ladder as far as he had. Although hostile as a liberal to the Social Democrats, Richter was against suppressing working-class radicalism by bans and imprisonment. To Richter that was wrong on principle and unlikely to work, as he correctly guessed. After Bismarck had gone as chancellor in 1890, the antisocialist laws were left to lapse. By 1912 the Social Democrats were the largest party in the Reichstag with 110 seats, more than a quarter of the total.

Even in the depressed 1870s Richter held out against tariffs, as they discouraged trade and lowered living standards everywhere. Politically, tariffs to Richter's mind fortified a reactionary alliance in Germany of "iron and rye," its older industries and its Prussian Junkers. On anti-Catholicism, repression of Social Democracy, and a return to tariffs, most National Liberals backed Bismarck. A minority, pricked in their consciences and disillusioned by Bismarck's cult of strength, split off and returned in 1880 to Richter and his Progressives.

A fourth "wedge" issue among Germany's liberals was compulsory, state-guaranteed social insurance for working men and women. It was studied, admired, and later imitated, with variations, in Britain and France. To Richter, any social insurance was "communistic," and his anti-Bismarck liberals followed him in voting against the social welfare bills.

In terms of immediate results, Richter's liberalism was a failure. He lost each of his big battles. Yet he stood for what he believed in. His was a liberalism of principle that set him at odds not only with the ever flexible National Liberals of banking and big industry but with intolerant anti-Catholics among the Progressives. On a longer view, Richter laid up liberal credit for the future. In the same spirit as Cobden, he spoke out against militarism, jingoism and colonialism. In the liberal tradition of toleration and respect, he castigated anti-Semitism, a derangement he treated as an affront to humane values and a greater threat to liberal order than the spectre of socialism. He spoke out against exclusion and privilege, twin pillars of an unfair and unequal society, against Bismarck's autocratic and instrumental approach to power, and against the conservative ultras' blind pursuit of national strength together with unthinking worship of its totems. Vainly, Richter warned Germans of the dangers of a naval arms race with the British. That too few listened did not mean that nobody listened. Richter's distrust of underchecked and overconcentrated power reemerged in the constitution of the Weimar Republic and then again in the constitution of the German Federal Republic in 1949.

Laboulaye and Richter offer lessons about nineteenth-century liberalism. It was a broad church, with many sects speaking for many interests. It was not peculiarly British or American, but had strong traditions in France and Germany. The two politicians remind us also that compromise and withdrawal were not the only course for liberals in autocratic or semiliberal regimes. Liberals could also keep alive liberal ideals for more receptive times.

iii. Gladstone: Liberalism's Capaciousness and the Politics of Balance

William Ewart Gladstone (1809–98) was not at the London meeting in June 1859 that created Britain's Liberal Party. The characteristically brisk entry for that day in the lifelong diary he kept does not mention the event. Yet as leader of the party from 1867 and prime minister four times, Gladstone gave British liberalism, perhaps liberalism generally, a focus and sense of character. Gladstone by family and background touched each of the leading British liberal milieus: Whig aristocracy, northern trade, and crusading reform. His father was a wealthy Liverpool man, his mother an evangelical Christian. He went to Eton and Oxford and married into the Welsh Anglican gentry. He began as a Tory determined to defend the Church of England, dominated the Liberal Party in its reforming parliamentary heyday in the 1860s to 1880s, and reinvented himself in old age by adapting to the new campaigning politics as the charismatic "People's William."

As chancellor of the Exchequer four times—twice when he was also prime minister—Gladstone observed the free-market creed of free trade and tight budgets. At the same time, he created in the Treasury a formidable tool of modern government. The Exchequer of the seventeenth century was the crown purse. In the eighteenth century it became a fiscal committee of the ministries. Gladstone recentralized the Exchequer in the Treasury, a place of financial control so trusted that in time it proved equally good at increasing as at restraining public spending. The surface principles of Gladstonian finance were straightforward. Revenues had to be small as both kinds of taxation were harmful. Indirect taxes and tariffs hurt the poor by raising prices. Direct taxes discouraged initiative. As trust, in the form of financial credit, was vital to government by consent, government borrowing could not be large. Spending therefore had also to be small. In practice, the doctrine was something of a rationalization for the incapacities of government in the nineteenth century. In truth, capitalist industry was waiting for government's abilities to catch up. Gladstonian finance was less a measure of fiscal probity for all time than a temporary expedient as the administrative order that a successful economy requires settled into place. Before long, the liberal British state would grow and grow.

Gladstone's failed attempt to win Home Rule for Ireland split the Liberals and distracted them from social reforms. Nevertheless it expressed a conviction, frightening but unavoidable to the liberal mind, that people in the end must govern themselves—a thought pressed by a small but vocal number of anticolonial Liberals. Gladstone spoke for international law, arbitration of disputes, and the self-determination of peoples. He was in theory against expanding Britain's colonial empire, but accepted the annexation of Egypt. After the Reform Bill of 1867 doubled the electorate to roughly a third of the men older than twenty, Gladstone adapted quickly to a widened franchise and became a champion of causes. In the Midlothian campaign of 1879–80 he made forty-eight speeches, stirring up outrage at Ottoman oppression in the Balkans.

Gladstone's campaigning zeal and popular charm reached out to new voters. It won the party fresh life. It also put the Liberal trinity of peace, retrenchment, and reform under strain. Gladstonian reform was a cleansing kind that removed obstacles and abolished corruption. It did not aim to cure social ills directly. It cost tax payers little. Free trade, ending paper duties, lower taxes—as chancellor in the 1880s he still dreamed of abolishing income tax altogether—disestablishment of the Church of England in Ireland, secret voting, opening the universities to nonconformists, and competitive exams for the home civil service: such reforms, with one exception, of Gladstone's first, longest, and most successful ministry (1868–74) came with one exception at little public expense. The exception was the Education Act of 1870.

Late in the day, and long after Germany, with which they were beginning unfavorably to contrast their country, British Liberals began to hear what Cobdenite radicals had long been telling them: the government must follow France and Prussia in paying for schools. The 1870 act provided in effect for local boards to run elementary schools paid for by property taxes. Schooling from the age of seven to twelve was made compulsory, in theory nondenominational—as in France, the nettlesome issue of state support for religious teaching was punted rather than solved—and from 1891, free. By then state schools were costing almost as much as the Royal Navy. Liberals had stepped on to a bridge toward a newer, more expensive liberalism.

Gladstone's enemies judged him better at sounding principled than being principled. Earnest and argumentative, Gladstone was to doubters the kind of politician who could find a plausible reason for most anything and deliver it in the gravest tone. Besides a gift for casuistry, he had a sense of theater and was incapable of not attracting attention. At the age of eighty, he celebrated the centenary of the French Revolution with a speech on the upper deck of the newly opened Eiffel Tower. He was remembered for discipline, energy, and fearsome embodiment of the Victorian ideal of self-mastery. His brains—a first at Oxford in classics and mathematics—and his appetites, especially sexual appetites, were prodigious. His work rate was machinelike: each mouthful chewed a legendary thirty-two times, the *Iliad* read through in Greek three dozen times, twenty-one thousand other books devoured and many of them annotated, roughly two every three days for eighty years.

Gladstone found religion and politics hard to pull apart. A tolerant nation could not impose faith or morals. Yet politics without moral vision was for Gladstone unintelligible, as was morals without religion. His vision combined the egalitarian dicta of the Sermon on the Mount with a Homeric devotion to unflinching and, when needed, ruthless nobility. The notion that his faith might not be the faith of all humankind was foreign to him, and he remained unshaken in that characteristically liberal mix of Enlightenment and Christian universalism. In 1888 he told the writer and suffragist Mrs. Humphry Ward that he had two tasks left: carry Home Rule and prove the intimate connection between the Hebrew and Olympian revelations. Gladstone's ideal of a virtuous liberal commonwealth was a Christian state, not imposed by law but arisen in spirit, and peopled by latter-day Hectors.

As it had been for Guizot, balance was a key to liberal politics in Gladstone's mind. He was a mediator, holding together in one party Whig nobs and Baptist radicals, open-minded pragmatists and free-market zealots, laxists and rigorists, libertines and temperance campaigners. He bridged elite and democratic politics. The vote, to him, was a trust, not a right. To Ruskin's jibe that he was "a leveler," Gladstone shot back that he was "an out and out inequalitarian." He never truly wavered from his conviction, announced in an 1853 budget speech, that a better way to help the poor than redistributive taxation was letting the rich keep their money for saving and investment. Gladstone's patriarchal world was peopled by contrasting kinds of character: active, self-reliant, and rational on the one hand; passive, dependent, and impulsive on the other. He was nevertheless a progressive "inequalitarian." Though inequalities would remain, given education, he thought people could improve. Under pressure, he gave his support to the franchise extensions of 1867 and 1884.

Gladstone contrasted the masses favorably with the "classes." The people were the trunk of a tree. They gave energy and strength. The elites at the top were weaker and liable to exhaustion. So imagined, society was the living frame of common life. Respect for rank and reverence for shared values united people of all stations. Shared values began in the family and church, and spread outward, through municipalities to the nation, and thence to "common humanity." Though he was swimming against a centralizing tide and to a degree against his own practice, Gladstone voiced support for local democracy and local power. Over a dispute in a coal district in 1892, he said that if the community wished for lower miners' hours, the mine owner must give way. Government could not cure human ills. It could help people help themselves. Each of us was a moral prime, but existing only in family, church, town, and nation.

Such oppositions were the stuff of Gladstone's liberal thinking. He spoke a language of rights, but also a language of sympathy. Society was for him a vital whole, growing outward from the domestic cell, and a field of combat riven by selfish pursuit of sectional interest. Progress brings greater wealth, but wealth encourages selfishness. A politician's job was to manage and temper conflict. Perhaps there was no division Gladstone did not think could be overcome. The classical seesaw of his contrasting thoughts well expressed how he pictured politics and society: "Good governance depends on the balance of forces." In avoiding the domination of one power, he was echoing Madison and Guizot.

Gladstone was a devout Christian and consummate politician. The world he lived in was to him far from as it should be. How deeply he saw why is less sure. Industrial capitalism had changed his world. Far from shaking itself to pieces, as Marxian criticism had suggested it would, capitalism was showering benefits on Victorian Britain, and not only on the rich, but on the middle classes and increasingly the working classes as well. At the same time industrial capitalism was creating pockets of misery. It was breaking down old protections, upsetting expectations, and loosening social ties faster than Gladstone could grasp. The same was true in France, Germany, and the United States. Liberals in the last twenty years of Gladstone's long life had to think again about the kinds of tasks their aims and ideals demanded of them.

4

The Nineteenth-Century Legacy

Liberalism without Caricature

i. Respect, "the Individual," and the Lessons of Toleration

It has come to feel natural for liberals to talk of the kind of respect due to men and women from the powers of state, market, or society in terms of cherishing and defending individuals. By a simple slide, it feels then natural to talk of liberalism as characteristically individualist. Slipping further, it is easy to talk of liberalism itself as a kind of political individualism, much as the British constitutionalist A. V. Dicey did when looking back in his *Lectures on Law and Public Opinion in England in the Nineteenth Century* (1898), where he suggested that the two terms had in common usage become virtually interchangeable. Once people tell you that two hard-to-pin-down "isms" are names for the same thing, it is best to stop and ask what is being talked about.

The first part of this book introduced a nineteenth-century liberal who prized the open-endedness of human capacities (Humboldt), one who stressed the absoluteness of people's privacy (Constant), as well as liberals who urged people to show initiative and take responsibility for their lives, either materially by inventiveness and hard work (Smiles) or morally by civic engagement and commitment to great causes (Channing). It has described a liberal who called for open-minded experimentation in worthwhile ways of living and in the promotion of individuality (Mill) and a liberal preoccupied by how unchecked power may grow to dominate unless talked back to by critics with awkward opinions and unorthodox beliefs (Guizot). It has included liberals preoccupied by how obstructive or superannuated rules might interfere with people's innovations and commercial aims (Cobden), how the pressures of majorities might jeopardize the pursuit of excellence (Tocqueville), and how the twin growth of big business and centralizing government might crush small-scale enterprises and local control (Schulze-Delitzsch). All of those liberals were in some way speaking up for the worth of human projects and capacities, and for the need to protect them from cramping or controlling power. It is natural by contrast to ask in which of those many tasks, and in what way, those liberals were all standing up for individuals, let alone whether and in what sense they were all individualists. It is natural to see if there are not clearer, less conceptually fraught ways to talk about the respect for people that liberalism demanded from power.

When putting respect for people at the core of politics, liberals drew amply on the historical experience of religious toleration, on the recognition of diverse opinion amid the spread of literacy, and on a widening acceptance of free speech and free association. That inheritance of enlightened modernity depended on three profound moral convictions with a long, though not uncontested, pedigree in the common tradition. Everyone had moral worth whatever their social rank. Everyone's link with the divine or—to put a parallel thought in secular terms—with what ultimately mattered in life was strictly their own. Everyone, third, had the capacity to take moral responsibility for themselves. Those convictions were neither invented by liberalism nor unique to liberalism. Liberals, however, took them into politics in new ways with momentous consequences.

Individuals took time to enter political writing. Translations particularly in the twentieth century were littered with an anachronistic use of "individuals" that, strictly speaking, were never there. Roman private law concerned the *utilitatem singulorum*. A French translation of 1803 had that as *les intérêts de chacun*. An English translation of 1932 was "the interests of individuals." Hobbes wrote in English of "individual persons"; Locke of "individuals" when the silent "persons" was understood. By the eighteenth century, "individual" stood alone. It was growing banal but losing its innocence. The term no longer served just to separate one person from another. It served to separate each from an implied larger whole—an estate, a corps, the public, society. It served to favor them with a kind of moral or constitutive primacy. "The only true and natural foundations of society," the legal theorist William Blackstone wrote in 1753, "are the wants and the fears of individuals."

The term "individual" was taking on layers of moral and philosophical description borrowed from the silent "person," itself implicitly restricted in range to capable, propertied men. A distributive term stealthily acquired generic uses. A curious character, part particular, part universal, came into view: "the individual." Liberals began to talk of defending the individual much as people today speak of saving the whale or protecting the planet, as if individuals were simultaneously many things and one. A charm of "individual" was that the word smoothly veiled who or what liberals were talking about. Only after 1945, when liberal democratic societies finally acknowledged civil rights for every last grown man or woman, could liberals claim to stand up for "the individual" without provoking laughter.

At birth, the term "individualist" in politics was polemical. It entered public argument early in the nineteenth century as a tool of abuse for deployment by the first conservatives against the first liberals. It suggested egoism, disloyalty or disaffection. It imputed to liberals a fairy-tale picture of society as a join-if-you-wish club, tarring them with the upstart vices of antisocial selfishness and priggish self-celebration. Wilhelm von Ketteler, bishop of Mainz and an intellectual godparent to later Christian Democracy, blamed liberals in *The Labour Question and Christianity* (1864) for a ruinously mistaken picture of society that took people for "atoms of stuff" to be "pulverised" and "blown over the earth."

Socialists took up the term in the long contest over the character of social progress in which they opposed the "individualist" kind. The contest set labor against capital, trade union radicals against business-minded conservatives, defenders against opponents of government intervention. The contest was commonly talked of as between collectivists and individualists. Neither side thought they were arguing about the underlying make-up of society or the metaphysical status of human persons. Such arguments came later. The two sides were arguing about wages and taxes, about how bosses should not mistreat workers, and about who should control the factory floor. When in *The Elements of Politics* (1891) the philosopher Sidgwick defined "individualism," he took it not for a method of thought but a principle for fixing "the nature and limits of governmental interference." Drawing on the nineteenth-century notion of free contract, he defined individualism as the claim that "what one sane adult is legally compelled to render to others should be merely the negative service of non-interference, except so far as he has voluntarily undertaken to render positive services." The "socialistic principle," by contrast, was that "one sane adult, apart from contract or claim to reparation, shall contribute positively by money or services to the support of others." On that understanding, to put it crudely, socialists but not individualists believed in taxes for social purposes. Like Mill, Sidgwick put himself judiciously in the middle, no socialist but, politically speaking, no dogmatic individualist either.

Reading off political positions from economic individualism was no easier. The marginal economists Léon Walras and Alfred Marshall recast economics "individualistically" by picturing economies as grown from simple exchanges between anonymous, isolated, cost-conscious agents. Both godfathered the "individualist" economics of liberal capitalism. But Walras was social-minded, Marshall market-minded. Walras believed, where Marshall did not, in the public ownership of land. Walras was suspicious of big business, whereas Marshall saw benefits in consolidation and scale. Walras favored, whereas Marshall distrusted, trade unions.

The idea was still hazy when Albert Schatz, a French legal theorist, wrote a groundbreaking study, *L'individualisme économique et sociale* (1907). Schatz traced the intellectual roots of what he called democratic liberalism to varieties of individualism in social, political, economic, religious, and moral thought since Thomas Hobbes and Bernard Mandeville. By the 1920s, the new subject of sociology was looking for theoretical letters of credit, and individualism, as championed for example by Max Weber, was soon widely, though not universally, adopted among liberal thinkers as a proper method of social study. Social phenomena, Weber held, were to be explained by the actions of people one by one, and their actions were to be understood in terms of their intentions. As a doctrine of method, individualism became a popular liberal weapon of resistance to outlooks that made impersonal forces the agents of historical change, notably Marxism. As political liberalism and theoretical individualism were run together, an unholy alliance tightened the link. Liberals who held it true hoped to use theoretical individualism against Marxists, socialists, and other collectivists. Conservatives who held individualist doctrine false hoped to discredit liberalism by yoking it to a mistaken picture of people and society. After 1945, when a liberalism of rights replaced Utilitarianism as liberalism's favored philosophy, the individualist linkage was further tightened.

Against that turbid background, Steven Lukes in *Individualism* (1973) offered to clarify which varieties of individualism did or did not matter to liberalism. When drafting the book, Lukes boasted to an Oxford friend, Isaiah Berlin, that he had found eleven distinct varieties. Berlin replied, "So few?" On publication, Lukes had thinned his list to six individualist doctrines. Three bore openly on liberalism. Each was best understood through what it fostered or protected in people. Religious individualism defended the sanctity of personal conscience. Economic individualism promoted free markets and private property. Political individualism insisted on government by "individual" consent, a double idea requiring both representation of people one by one, not in classes, corporations or estates, but also government attention to what people wanted for themselves, not what government wanted them to want.

Ethical individualism straddled a divide between what mattered and did not matter to political liberalism. It was a cluster of like-sounding but distinct claims: the human person, taken separately and on its own, was a bearer of ultimate value, the source of value, or the arbiter of value. Political liberals could happily assent to the first but dissent from common misinterpretations of the other two. Liberals, that is, could follow moral tradition by insisting on the untouchable sanctity of the human person without denying noninstrumental value to shared, collective goods and without falling into the subjectivist error of thinking that each of us choose or create our own values.

Lukes's last two individualisms—epistemological and methodological—were the theoretical kind. Each bore on how to think about society and common life at a high level of abstraction. Neither were required for political liberalism. Each in its field—knowledge and language on the one hand, society and history on the other—gave the isolated person or "abstract individual" a kind of constitutive primacy or explanatory authority. Parallels existed between the claims of political liberalism—don't interfere with people's religious beliefs; count opinions in politics one by one; respect private property—and the claims of theoretical individualism: knowledge of the world depends on distinctive experience of the world; society is made up of separate people taken one by one. The theoretical claims leaned heavily on a picture of isolable people with their own viewpoints and private spaces. In making their political claims, however, liberals could, but did not have to, adopt that picture. In defending their claims to what power should not do to people, liberals did not need to begin with everyone's supposed isolation from each other and singularity of viewpoint, as conservative and socialist opponents claimed they did. Indeed, attempts since to find footing for liberalism's outlook in those theoretical kinds of individualism or in subjectivist varieties of ethical individualism have not carried conviction. Light on civic respect can nevertheless be shed in a lower-level, less ambitious way by seeing in more detail what protections it promised people from power.

The respect demanded was civic in several ways. It was an impersonal relationship between the citizenry and the public powers of state, market, and society. Respect did not call on power to like, admire, or even take a personal interest in anybody, those being selective attitudes people took to each other. Unlike personal respect, civic respect was unconditional. It could, it is true, be limited or withdrawn, from convicted lawbreakers for example, much as respect could be lost or withdrawn between colleagues, friends, or spouses. However, whereas personal respect among people need never arise to begin with, state, market, and society could not pick and choose whom to respect. Unlike personal respect, civic respect was due to people blindly and anonymously. It was to that impersonal feature that liberals pointed when talking of "equal" respect. Respect was required for people, whoever they were. Liberal respect was civic lastly, as due principally to "active" citizens, thought of having counterpart duties to society, and limited, to begin with, to propertied white men.

Of civic respect three promises, nonintrusion was about not compromising people's security. Primarily legal, it enjoined a cluster of restraints on state, market, and society against interfering with people's privacy. The second element in civic respect, nonobstruction, was comparatively new and spoke to a rapidly changing world. Primarily social and economic, nonobstruction appealed to the open-endedness of people's capacities and the productivity of their capital. It enjoined a freeing of paths, a removal of barriers, and a lifting of inhibitions that to the liberal mind got in the way of social progress and personal flourishing. The third, non-exclusion, was at root moral. At the deepest, it demanded acknowledgment of people's intrinsic worth regardless of their social clothes. Nobody, to put the idea in other terms, was to be excluded from the human moral community. From the sphere of religion and fortified by gradual acceptance of toleration, the moral idea of nonexclusion entered nineteenth-century politics, where liberals enthusiastically widened its content while initially limiting its range.

Nonintrusion had to do with securing people and their property from extractive rulers, domineering masters, and grasping neighbors. It was an old protective idea and, in its widening range, primarily legal. It took early form in enforceable local rights and liberties. The idea drew a circle of inviolability around a person, his or her household, his or her things, and, as public argument spread along with literacy and printing, his or her opinions. Constant, Mill, and Tocqueville each invoked the image of a circle or sphere, pressed by unwanted forces from the outside and offering a perimeter of shelter. Mill in *Political Economy* wrote that "under whatever political institutions we live, there is a circle around every individual human being which no government, be it that of the one, the few or the many, ought to be permitted to overstep." Nonintrusion included old protections of person and property against arbitrary search, seizure, and arrest. When people took their private selves into the public sphere, nonintrusion included liberties of speech, censorship-free publication, assembly, and association.

The second promise of liberal respect, nonobstruction, was dynamic and expansive. It drew on an image of people as centers of energy and action, as moving points with purpose and initiative that custom, law, and society threatened to stifle or block. To the comforting image of a private hearth to be sheltered and protected, liberals added an exhilarating image of paths to the unknown that must be cleared and kept open. They added an image of ladders to social heights that anyone might climb. They added an image of money creating more money while it slept, and an image of seeds of potential in everyone that might grow and flourish if properly nurtured. Such pictures promoted initiative, openness, and originality.

Experimenters, engineers, and entrepreneurs were doing things on a scale nobody had done before. They were making discoveries, harnessing inventions, hiring labor, creating wealth, and making things in previously unimagined ways. Old elites were breaking down or being opened to new members. Literacy and education were spreading beyond small minorities. People's opportunities to outgrow the category they were born into, to be unlike their parents and to make something new of themselves, were multiplying and spreading. An overarching liberal thought that promised to bring order and justification to that ferment was that whatever obstructed those happy developments was to be swept away. Social virtues associated with innovation, upward mobility, and human development were to be prized: boldness, initiative, entrepreneurial spirit, and self-command. Mental sloth, lack of ambition, envy, and passivity were correspondingly to be reprobated as social vices. "I were an impostor," Samuel Smiles wrote in 1859, "if I promised any class that they would advance themselves if they were improvident, thoughtless, and idle."

Socially, nonobstruction included equality of opportunity, the borderless ideal of removing barriers to social advance. Economically, nonobstruction found expression in volumes of mid–nineteenth century legislation that broke down old commercial barriers. From the 1850s to the 1860s, new laws embedded freedom from interference in their everyday operations for collectivities such as business firms, and in time for trade unions. Lawyers were less troubled than philosophers or social methodologists as to whether such collectivities were individuals or not. The British social thinker Ernest Barker wryly noted when looking back from 1915, "If we are individualists now, we are corporate individualists," he wrote. "Our individuals are becoming groups."

For the third element of civic respect, non-exclusion, liberals could look to the insistence of common moral tradition on the unimpeachable worth of the human person. People may be excluded from many things for good reason. Everybody but you may reasonably be excluded from your property. Everybody but the winner may be excluded from the prize. Everybody but those in need may be excluded from help for the needy. No good reasons existed to exclude anyone from the recognition due to human worth. Importing that idea into politics had great consequences. Politically, nonexclusion underpinned the equal rights of "active" citizens to vote and hold office, for example, as well as equality before the law: refusal of the idea that faith, rank, or wealth might be good reason to treat one person before a court differently from another. In time, nonexclusion became a weapon against denying anyone equal respect because of their personal status or social clothes.

Civic respect was contested in each of its elements by liberalism's nineteenth-century rivals, socialism and conservatism. For socialists, promising not to intrude on privacy or discourage individuality undervalued to the point of denial the claims that class solidarity had on the loyalty and duties of working people. Conservatives thought that privacy and individuality undermined local attachments and respect or hierarchy. For both opponents, liberal nonintrusion sounded protective but was in fact corrosive.

As for nonobstruction, to socialists, such changes promoted inequalities and jeopardized brotherhood. A common socialist complaint was that industrial capitalism, the day's most salient innovation, was turning society and morality upside down. As liberalism favored innovation and not getting in people's way, liberalism deserved the blame. To conservatives, innovation, initiative, and the removal of barriers to people threatened custom and tradition, a Romantic cry against liberal modernity that has never died away.

Over nonexclusion, socialists and liberals were both allies and rivals, as they were with progress. Both hoped for a society without exclusive divisions of hierarchy, class, estates, or sections. Liberals pictured such an undivided society as classless. Socialists imagined it as made up of a single "universal" class. To use the terms of the French Revolution, undivided society for liberals was one of civic equality, for socialists of working-class fraternity. Liberals saw the end of nonexclusion as diversity, socialists as solidarity. For all their high talk of respecting people by letting them alone to go their own way, liberals in socialist eyes treated people shabbily. For including everyone was empty, they insisted, unless people had means, especially the material means, to make use of civic respect's protections and permissions.

As conservatives, socialists, and liberals all believed in the worth of personhood, theirs was not a moral dispute as such but a dispute about the political implications of a shared moral conviction. Conservatives suspected liberals of smugness and hypocrisy. Liberals had not invented human worth. Conservatives in this connection had ground for their claim that they were more inclusive, better at standing up for ordinary folk and more practiced at treating them properly than were hard-hearted, trade-obsessed liberals with their punishing factories and disruptive reforms. To the conservative mind, there was no problem in recognizing everyone's moral dignity. To import the idea into politics for it there to run free struck them as absurd. Few people, to the conservative mind, were capable of an active part in public life, let alone governing. People, that is, might deserve moral respect whoever they were, but not civic respect.

Despite opposition, the liberal claim that people merited unquestioning respect from power won acceptance in societies where more and more people were demanding such respect and had the means to make themselves heard. In pressing the claim, liberals could call also on a common moral tradition that everyone shared equally in human worth as well as on recent the historical experience of failed religious persecution and breakdown of orthodoxy.

For all its appeal, equal human worth was not straightforward to bring into politics. One aspect had to do with content, the other with scope. They stood somewhat in reciprocal relationship. Human worth had to be the kind of thing everyone shared to do its non-exclusionary work. Whatever everyone shared, given their manifest differences, had to be something as singular and hard to pin down as human worth. The wider the scope, the less tangible the content. The more tangible the content, the more troublesome the scope. That tension never left liberal thought.

The content of equal worth can be put in many ways. For example, people matter for themselves. They are not beasts or tools. Philosophers from Kant onward aimed to buttress such convictions with secular arguments. The conviction itself was old, being present in the Jewish, Christian, and Islamic traditions. The idea of human worth as something cashable in this life was once supposed to have fallen away in medieval Christian thought and been rediscovered with a bang in the Renaissance, popularized in the Reformation, and given democratic voice soon after. Whether that is historically apt or accurate, the intrinsic worth of humans became an organizing marker in political thought during the seventeenth and eighteenth centuries even as belief in the divinity of its origins began to disappear. The idea spread that intrinsic worth was something neither society nor rulers should ignore and became a way to divide political thinkers, to use a hard-working contrast, into idealists, who welcomed morality into politics, and realists, who hoped to keep morality in its place. On the idealist side, Kant made the noninstrumentality of persons a centerpiece of his ethics and politics, tying the one idea closely to another, namely the capacity to give and take reasons. In *Groundwork to the Metaphysic of Morals* (1785) he wrote, "Man, and in general every rational being, exists as an end in himself."

The other aspect of human worth was its distribution. Everyone, the thought ran, had whatever it was that gave a life value. To express the thought negatively, nobody might be denied community in human worth. None of that was easy to put coherently. The idea took many forms. Natural-rights thinkers would say that nobody was naturally a master or naturally a slave. Christians would say that all were equal in the sight of God. Some liberals, echoing Rousseau, might say all shared equally in human dignity. The kind of dignity that commanded unquestioning respect was not, that is, a mark of social rank, personal capacity, or worldly achievement. Others, picking up on Kant's linkage between personal worth and the capacity for sound but independent judgment, might equate dignity with rationality—a claim that Kant's critics, liberal and nonliberal alike, suspected could in the wrong hands easily become a sword of exclusion and inequality. Hegel combined a conceptual and a historical tale in treating the claims of human dignity and the struggle for recognition as different aspects of human advancement.

In less philosophical mode, English Puritans put the thought of equal worth grandly. Archangel Michael tells Adam in *Paradise Lost*, "Man over men he made not lord, such title to Himself reserving." Puritans also put it pithily. Leveler Rumbold on the scaffold at Edinburgh in 1685 after the failed Monmouth Rebellion against James II declared, "I am sure there was no man born marked of God above another; for none comes into the world with a saddle upon his back, neither any booted and spurred to ride them." Although those were not strictly the same thought, their aim was the same. They all pointed to the idea that there is something valuable for itself in each human life that cannot be exploited or transgressed without moral harm.

In taking moral nonexclusion into politics, liberals imported an idea of daunting ambition, the democratic consequences of which they spied at first only foggily. Thought of democratically, the idea of nonexclusion came to apply to civic respect as a whole. For civic respect itself could be taken inclusively, for everyone whoever, or exclusively, for a privileged few. A limited electorate or a legally protected caste could, like an exclusive club, treat its members equally while treating excluded members unequally. Civic respect, when taken democratically, allowed for no such exclusion. On the contrary, respect required that the customary assurances of nonintrusion, the novel permissions of nonobstruction, and the security from discrimination offered by nonexclusion were due without argument to every last person, however lowly, stupid, or seemingly useless to society. As will shortly be seen, honoring that requirement opened a long contest between liberalism and democracy not settled until the mid–twentieth century and ever open to backsliding and renegotiation.

To turn back to look at a second support for civic respect, the history of toleration gave liberals the twin encouragement of reasons and precedents. The liberal picture of the past no doubt exaggerated its unity but was credible enough to serve liberal self-understanding as heralds of the new. Their picture was roughly this. On the path to modernity it had come to be accepted that social order did not require a common faith. Secular and spiritual power had before then blended in shared, uniform control. Social order, as the watchword of the French crown had it, required "one king, one law, one faith." Coercive law backed religious norms and church authority sanctioned coercive law. As law and religion were in effect one, religious unorthodoxy amounted to political dissent. With modernity, that suffocating coherence vanished. The authority of the state and the force of its laws were justified in secular terms of fair-handedness and usefulness to people's various purposes. Such moral authority as churches had, or claimed to have, deserved no backing in law. The aims of life, broad or narrow, were for everyone to find and test for themselves, unimposed on by social authority.

In between premodern unity and modern diversity came a bridge of toleration. The crossing was slow, with much backing up. Toleration amounted first to nonpersecution. Amid confessional strife abetted by dynastic rivalry, sixteenth-century rulers came to see that peace required them to desist from the one-sided support of a dominant faith. With frequent backsliding, Catholic rulers stopped tormenting Lutherans, Lutheran rulers stopped tormenting Calvinists and Calvinist rulers stopped tormenting Anabaptists. Longing for social peace underpinned the religious truce of Augsburg (1555) and the Treaty of Westphalia ending the Thirty Years War (1648).

In preaching and pamphleteering for toleration, its learned defenders leaned heavily on the two organizing themes of ignorance and perversity. Persecutors, they argued first, never knew enough to weed out reprobates justly or successfully. Secular magistrates and church authorities in a fallen world were ignorant of God's deeper designs. The crown's task was to protect the saved and damned alike, and only God knew which was which. So the English proto-Protestant William Wycliffe had argued in the late fourteenth century. That argument from ignorance was condensed by Nicholas of Cusa into a fifteenth-century tag: "One faith, many rites." God, the implication ran, could be honored in many ways, and no prince or priest knew enough to say with authority which way pleased or displeased God more than others. Persecution, secondly, was perverse. Whether practically or morally, it was self-defeating. Practically, coercion did not work. Torturers could make people suffer but not change their minds, and coercion generally stiffened dissent. Morally, persecution injured by its cruelty and arrogance the Christian principles it claimed to fight for.

That double argument against the suppression of unorthodoxy, from ignorance and from perversity, was well known and had won wide acceptance by the late sixteenth century. The great defenders of free thought and liberty of conscience who followed in the seventeenth century—Milton, Spinoza, Bayle, and Locke—drew on the double argument liberally. As reasons against permitting power to attempt to monitor what people thought, those later thinkers amplified but did not greatly add to the invincible ignorance of authorities who did not know what to forbid, or to the moral and practical perversity of trying to monitor people's minds.

Toleration tended to stretch along the line of what it spared people from. Toleration spread from not burning or imprisoning heretics, to lifting fines for the practice of unorthodox faiths, to legal recognition on an equal footing with orthodoxy, and finally to giving the unorthodox the same civic rights as the orthodox enjoyed. That sequence from nonpersecution through decriminalization and legalization to civic equality was not an unbroken grand march. The very existence of stages allowed for compromise and delay. In France, the Edict of Nantes (1598) gave Huguenots only limited religious liberty, and its grant of civic rights was withdrawn in the 1620s, well before the revocation of the edict itself. Assurances of mutual toleration for Lutherans, Calvinists, and Catholics in the Peace of Westphalia (1648) were made between Sweden and the Empire, although not with France. The English Toleration Act (1689) abolished certain religious tests and put Anglicans and non-Conformists on a footing in some areas of public life but excluded Catholics and Unitarians, accepted Quakers only conditionally, and excluded all but Anglicans from many posts. Catholics and non-Conformists in England did not gain equal rights as citizens until 1829, Jews not until 1858. Only at a distance could that sequence from control to nonintrusion appear rapid, smooth, or irresistible.

A mechanism was spied all the same that encouraged the hope that toleration, once adopted, would become irreversible and then quickly self-abolishing. The mechanism was indifference. It was made much of, especially in England. By 1700, after almost two centuries of violent religious conflict, passions of faith were in decline. In 1694 an Adventist preaching the imminent second coming of Christ was not consigned to the stocks or sent to the gallows but urged to seek medical care. In his "Letter on Enthusiasm" in *Characteristics* (1711), Locke's patron, the Earl of Shaftesbury, recommended ridicule as the proper riposte to religious sectarians. During his stay in England that began in 1729, Montesquieu caught what he took for the spirit of the age. Almost nobody attended the regular prayers that opened sittings of Parliament, Montesquieu reported, and in company if religion was mentioned, everyone fell to laughing. A parallel line came from Daniel Defoe (1660–1731), a dissenter persecuted by Anglican judges, who became best known for *Robinson Crusoe* (1719). In squibs and essays Defoe pressed his conviction that squabbles over religion were making way for competition in trade as interest in faith waned, moneymaking became a preoccupation and the shift did everyone good. A couplet in Defoe's "The True Born Englishman" (1701) neatly caught that worldly distrust of religious sectarianism: "Wherever God erects a house of prayer / The Devil always builds a chapel there."

Confidence in the mechanism of growing indifference drew on the very shape of toleration as an idea. As a narrow, heavily trafficked bridge between prohibition and acceptance, toleration was not a place to stop. Toleration spanned a gap between what was legally forbidden and what was morally acceptable. If everything disapproved of were forbidden, or equally, if everything permitted were acceptable, toleration would not be necessary. Strictly, it would not be possible. The gap it spanned would vanish. Toleration was only possible when certain moral offenses were legally permitted. If a moral offense was strong or widely felt, the case for legal prohibition grew. If the moral offense was weak or narrowly felt, the case for frank acceptance grew. In between, toleration was unstable, pressed by rigorism and restriction on one side, by laxism and permissiveness on the other. The state might shrink what was permitted by prohibiting more. Or society might shrink what it found unacceptable by objecting to less. As the balance between those pressures shifted historically in different areas of life, so the space for toleration in those areas grew or shrank.

In the religious sphere, the mechanics of toleration worked in the direction of growing acceptance. As religious indifference spread, faith became private, society was "secularized," and the space of unacceptability shrank. There was less and less to tolerate, as people cared less and less about each other's religion. To the liberal mind, such secular indifference was a welcome triumph of enlightened modernity that might provide a model for principled indifference to other social distinctions, chosen or unchosen, in nonreligious domains.

By the 1880s, much of the content, though not yet the full scope, of liberal civic respect was embedded in law or social practice. In the twentieth century, public power let people go in ever more ways, as people's social clothes came to matter less and less in the eyes of the law and in terms of economic efficiency. Here was something for liberals to take pride in. On the other hand, as the next period of liberalism will amply show, exclusionary passions and sectional hatreds did not die with enlightened modernity and liberal capitalism. Growing indifference to religion among some people coexisted with renewed religious zeal among others. Education spread, as Humboldt and Mill hoped, but the reliably self-governing citizen remained elusive. Society grew more middle class, as Hegel, Constant, and Tocqueville predicted, but material conflicts of rich and poor remained. Society as a whole grew more prosperous, but the natural undersupply of fellow feeling that Hume had described and

Mill had wrestled with did not correct itself in step. There were, liberals learned, no mechanisms of mutual acceptance among people. The protections that liberal respect promised people from the power of state, wealth, or society were never secure. The work of shoring up civic respect for people and keeping it in repair was never over.

ii. The Achievements That Gave Liberals Confidence

The first part of the liberal story has shown that taking nineteenth-century liberalism as a campaign for liberty obscures it with an overgeneral label and that taking it as a campaign for small government guys it by anachronistic caricature. When nineteenth-century liberals spoke for liberty, they were not all standing up for the same things. Government by the 1880s was growing in ways that the first liberals could scarcely imagine, and liberals had done much to bring government's new powers about. When defending "the individual," liberals were conducting many distinct campaigns. Liberalism in the nineteenth century was more than the economic creed of a rising bourgeoisie.

Ethically, Wilhelm von Humboldt and Benjamin Constant took an opening stand on contrasting aspects of civic respect for people: nourishing their capacities and honoring their privacy. Politically, the liberal dream of masterless order took shape in the person of Guizot, historian, thinker, and prime minister. His ideas about the need to contain power and prevent its monopolization paralleled American constitutionalism, given clear expression in the preliberal Madison and the nonliberal Calhoun. Socially, Tocqueville articulated an enduring liberal anxiety about the stifling cultural power of mass democracy. The German liberal Schulze-Delitzsch voiced a counterpart concern about the centralizing power of government and mass markets. William Ellery Channing and Samuel Smiles illustrated two contrasting paths of personal progress: moral improvement and material independence. Economically, the lives of the Utilitarian reformer Edwin Chadwick and the champion of free trade, Richard Cobden, crystallized a lasting "state versus market" argument among liberals about the most reliable means of social progress. Herbert Spencer pictured a liberal political order as the natural but welcome outcome of evolutionary progress. Intellectually, John Stuart Mill gave fullest acknowledgment to the tensions in liberal thought between furthering social progress and promoting human individuality, between pursuit of the common good and respect for people one by one, for their property and their aims. Abraham Lincoln and William Ewart Gladstone personified liberalism's capaciousness and demonstrated the power of liberal words. Each held together large parties combining many liberal streams. Edouard Laboulaye in France under the authoritarian Napoleon III and Eugen Richter in Bismarckian Germany illustrate the challenge liberalism faces when the search for order and pursuit of human betterment are conducted in illiberal ways.

The liberals of 1880–1945 inherited an appealing ideal of an ethically acceptable order of human progress among civic equals without recourse to undue power. Material progress, the spread of education, and the acceptance of middle-class values of moderation and compromise convinced liberals that their dream of masterless order might after all be realizable.

Liberals still had to be made to accept that their dream was to be realized democratically. Liberals in the next period came to accept that what liberalism promised to propertied, educated men was due to everyone, whoever they were. Politically, they came to accept universal suffrage. Economically they came to accept fairer shares. Ethically, they gave up claims to tutorial authority.

A common element that later liberals noted in their nineteenth-century forebears was confidence. The tone was world-weary but clear-eyed in Guizot, wanly victorious in Tocqueville, dogged in Richter and adamantine in Mill. It was biblical in Lincoln and Homeric in Gladstone. In their differing tones, all voiced a confidence that later liberals heard with envy.

Liberals of the next period learned that universal education and cultural progress did not ensure human reasonableness. They learned that modern economies did not always stabilize by themselves. They learned that international trade and financial exchange did not guarantee peace. As they advanced into the twentieth century, liberals discovered that their emerging new order could slide back into war and barbarism on a scale that the very successes of liberal capitalism had done much to make possible.

PART TWO

Liberalism in Maturity and the Struggle with Democracy (1880–1945)

5

Historical Setting in the 1880s

The World Liberals Were Making

On May 20, 1880, a young don at Cambridge University in England asked a nineteen-year-old student of his with whom he was in love to marry him. To his delight, she accepted. He was Neville Keynes, a teacher of economics and philosophy. She was Florence Brown, the daughter of a liberal-minded Congregationalist minister and an early gainer from the waning of prejudice against women in higher education. The couple were soon married, and in June 1883 their first son, John Maynard, was born. Neville went on to write books on logic and economic method. Florence, who campaigned for the reform of juvenile courts and opportunities for women in public life, became Cambridge's first woman city councilor and in time its mayor. Seven decades later in the winter of 1945, the son, now a member of Britain's House of Lords and the world's most famous economist, reluctantly signed terms for an American loan to his struggling country. Britain had wanted $5 billion unconditionally, it got $3.75 billion with strings, and the three months it took to get that felt to Keynes more like begging than bargaining. He left Washington frustrated, exhausted, and ill. Within four months he was dead.

Like Wilhelm von Humboldt, who began this liberal story, Maynard Keynes lived in a world turned upside down. Both men witnessed unparalleled economic advance and unprecedented economic dislocation, warfare on a new scale of destructiveness, the rise and fall of classes, elites and nations, as well as sweeping change in law and politics. Humboldt was born into a preliberal world and died as liberalism was taking root. Keynes lived in a world that was liberal throughout but which, to start with, was in many essentials predemocratic. He witnessed and some of his ideas helped secure the long, grudging compromise that liberalism struck with democracy, economically, politically, and ethically. He died as a stabler version of what had emerged from that historic compromise, liberal democracy, gave liberalism a second chance.

Liberals in Humboldt's time were an opposition of rising men and women, confident in their belief that the wrongs of society belonged to others whereas righting those wrongs belonged to them. The liberals of Keynes's time were no longer an opposition. They ran the governments and dominated the establishments of their day. Liberal ideas were now orthodoxies. Where liberals were not actually in power, politics grew liberal in character. Liberals owned the successes and failures of the 1880s to 1940s. As there were many of both, the democratic liberalism that emerged after 1945 was hardened and chastened.

As with 1835, the year of Humboldt's death, 1883, the year of Keynes's birth, offers a revealing time slice for the period. It was a full one for economists besides Keynes. Joseph Schumpeter was born in February and the following month Karl Marx died. In June, the German Reichstag passed a compulsory health insurance bill drawing on the knowledge of a new breed of social experts such as Gustav Schmoller, founder of Europe's premier economic think tank. In the United States, young Irving Fisher was studying to enter Yale University, where he was to spend his career as a monetary expert and student of business crashes. In Lausanne, the French-born economist Léon Walras refined and defended his mathematical description of market equilibrium, liberalism's dream of a self-stabilizing order rendered in simultaneous equations. In England, Keynes's future teacher, Alfred Marshall, was at work on an early draft of his "study of mankind in the ordinary business of life," *The Principles of Economics* (1890).

Politically, liberals and socialists were beginning to glimpse that in competing for the crown of progress they were allies in its cause. In August 1883, the American labor leader Samuel Gompers told a congressional committee in Washington that trade unions held in check "the more radical elements in society." In Swiss exile from Bismarck's antisocialist laws, Eduard Bernstein was urging Germany's Social Democrats to abandon hopes of a revolutionary leap into brotherhood and to transform capitalism by gradual reform.

By 1883 liberals were under challenge to accept that their high civic ideals might apply nonexclusively to everyone. The Berlin writer Hedwig Dohm opened a campaign to win votes for women. Social distinctions of gender rested, she argued, not on natural differences but on changeable, prejudicial conventions. On a tour of the Eastern United States, an Omaha chieftain, Standing Bear, called for legal protection of Native Americans, then excluded as noncitizens. The rule of law was cruel in its exclusions of American blacks. In October, the U.S. Supreme Court struck down the Civil Rights Act of 1875, which had outlawed the color bar in "public accommodations"—eating or drinking places, coaches, ferries, trains, and theaters.

Intellectually, liberalism's ethical ideal of rational self-reliance was under scrutiny. In 1883 Friedrich Nietzsche published the first two parts of *Thus Spake Zarathustra*, a further step in his equivocal campaign to demolish, as some took it, moralistic faith in liberal progress or, as others read him, to find a humanly wearable ethics in a godless and pointless world. At a psychiatric clinic in Vienna, young Doctor Freud was starting to think out a segmented picture of the human mind that would shake confidence in the comforting thought that the mind's contents were transparent to us and, given the will, controllable. The words *société*, *society*, and *Gesellschaft* were ceasing to mean drawing rooms where you might or might not be welcome and starting to figure in politics as the object of a new discipline, named first in France, *sociologie*. It focused less on private, independent purposes than on irreducibly social phenomena such as imitation, public ritual, and the conduct of crowds. We were less free than supposed, the study of society suggested, and bent to collective pressures we were barely aware of.

Economically, the 1880s were years of recovery between disturbing panics of 1873 and 1893. Alarming as those short cycles were, they occurred within a long late nineteenth-century upswing. From 1869 to 1913, average incomes in France rose in adjusted dollars from $2,000 a year to $3,500, in Germany from $1,900 to $3,600, and in Britain from $3,000 to $4,900. In the United States, between 1870 and 1890 alone, real income per head almost doubled. Even for the poor life improved. From the 1880s onward real incomes rose as prices stabilized or fell, families grew smaller, and medicine and urban sanitation improved. Not everyone gained equally. Debtors, farmers, craftsmen, and small enterprises suffered as groups more than others. Wealth spread unevenly. Germany's pattern of inequality was typical: in 1913 one-tenth of German households took 40 percent of total income, two-fifths took another 36 percent, and half the country made do with 25 percent. Working people responded in self-defense, demanding a fairer share of an expanding economy. From 1890 to 1913 the proportion of the nonfarm workforce in unions rose in Britain from 10 percent to 25 percent, in Germany from under 5 percent to 25 percent, and in the United States from 2 percent to 10 percent.

Rival progressive narratives competed accordingly in the 1880s to 1940s. To use a phrase of the American economic historian Thomas K. McCraw, a socialist narrative told of a House of Have against a House of Want. It told of an exploitative bourgeois machine treading workers and poor into the ground, soon to be replaced by a stabler, more equitable social order. A countervailing liberal narrative told of liberal capitalism gradually assuaging the material conflicts it caused as economies grew and prosperity spread. In history's rear-view mirror it looks clear which story won. Liberals in the 1880s to 1940s were seldom sure which economic story they were in, open conflict or gradual accommodation, especially when their economic world shook in the 1890s and collapsed in the 1930s.

Though nobody knew it at the time, by 1883 the steam-coal-transport revolution was ending and a chemical-engineering-electric revolution was beginning. In January the Southern Pacific Railroad opened from the Gulf of Mexico to the Pacific Ocean. By September the completion of the Northern Pacific had linked the Great Lakes to the American Northwest. Big American firms now had a single national market. In Berlin, Emil Rathenau founded the German engineering company AEG to put the electro-mechanical discoveries of the previous decade to use. In Ohio, John D. Rockefeller combined forty small firms in a giant enterprise, Standard Oil, that refined oil to light and heat homes. In a Mannheim machine shed, Karl Benz was tinkering with the first non-steam automobile. Soon Standard Oil, to Rockefeller's surprise, would be refining oil to fuel cars. The unpredictability of technical change, we shall see at the end of this part, was a centerpiece of Karl Popper's attack on "march of history" theories, especially theories claiming that history was leaving liberalism behind.

Coming fast down Commercial Street arm in arm in 1883 were the company and the consumer. By emancipating the business company, pathbreaking laws of the 1850s to 1870s in Britain, France, Germany, and the United States created an expansive new agent of creativity and change. Companies were made registrable without onerous state approval. Investors' liability, when a firm crashed, was limited to their personal stake. Companies were freed at birth from favoritism, state interference, and bribes. They were freed in life from the inhibiting fear of risk.

As wealth began to spread, not every last cent was spent on necessities. For the first time on any scale, people had material choices. They had economic discretion. Economists began to call people consumers and to attend to their choices. Demand at last entered economic thinking as an equal and active counterpart of supply. Consumers were vital to firms, which courted and cajoled them. Mass consumption, mass advertising, and mass newspapers together helped foster economic democracy and democratic culture.

As wealth continued to spread, not every last cent was even spent. More people saved, and in new ways. Stocks grew popular. In November 1883 a Wall Street reporter, Charles Dow, started a tip sheet, *The Customers' Afternoon Letter*, forerunner of his Dow-Jones stock index. Plutocratic habits spread fast. In 1900, half a million Americans owned stock directly, about one person in 150. By 1950 the share had grown to around one in 12. If you included company pensions funds, a much vaster number of Americans by then had cause to watch the Wall Street ticker and to consider themselves capitalists at one remove.

Rumbling down Commercial Street as well in 1883 came a heavy new vehicle, the modern state. Government spending in the 1880s accounted for roughly 10 to 15 percent of national output in the countries under focus here. By 1945, the peacetime level had settled at 40 to 50 percent. Companies and consumers complained without pause but used the state when convenient, turned to it in need, and felt abandoned when it failed to help. As Adam Smith had grasped, business wanted indulgence from government, not neglect. Although the modern state grew most visibly in war, as states always had, peacetime factors were also in play. Government in the 1880s to 1940s became less corrupt, less a tool of exclusive or extractive elites, more predictable, and more effective. As voters and businesses asked more of government, it grew more capable, and as its capacities grew, more was asked.

All of that, finally, was happening in a settled field of national authority. A more or less integrated modern state presided over a more or less unified nation. Sectional divisions persisted. Socially speaking, Imperial Germany divided into a backward, rural East and a progressive, industrial West. The United States split similarly along a South-North axis, with the additional complication of color. After wars of unification in 1861–70, the two countries had a single national authority that presided over component states committed to settling internal differences without violence. Though its state authority was comparatively centralized, the United Kingdom, to give Britain its proper name, was in a way the least united. Undisputed authority did not extend to poor, mainly Catholic Ireland, which represented a fifth of the United Kingdom's population. By comparison, France, though shorn of rich, industrial Alsace-Lorraine, lost to Germany in 1870, was coherent, and in the Third Republic (1870–1940) found at last a stable liberal order. That "more or less" above needs stressing. National incoherences remained strong enough throughout 1880–1945 to threaten the liberal dream of order. Deeper yet were the incoherences of liberal empire, with its tangle of diverse status and conflicting authorities, and its many challenges to liberal principle.

By 1880 liberals were under pressure to reach a durable bargain with democracy, politically, ethically, and economically. Nothing was fated and divergence was ever possible, but by the end of the nineteenth century, all four nations had begun to converge on the common practice of politics we call liberal democracy. That historic compromise is the topic of this second part from the 1880s to the 1940s.

Politically, it involved liberal acceptance that their aims and ideals applied not just to a worthy, propertied elite but to everyone regardless of how lowly, useless seeming to society, or poor. In particular, it meant accepting electoral democracy. Working-class and popular forces were pressed in return to acknowledge liberal limits on the authority of the people's will, to forsake hopes of a revolution to free people from remorseless capitalist change, and to accept liberal constitutional procedures, the rule of law, and respect for property. As liberal self-confidence waned, liberal democracy came to be looked on less as the governing creed of a progressive elite than as a set of neutral procedures for brokering conflict and managing interest-group bargains.

Ethically, liberals came under pressure to compromise with democratic society. This meant accepting that contempt for rank and refusal of deference could be turned against liberals themselves and not just against previous elites that the first liberals had opposed and largely supplanted. It meant seeing that indifference to tradition and disregard for taboo might demystify ideals and totems that liberals themselves held dear. It meant relinquishing tutorial authority and substituting for the promotion of responsible, self-reliant character as liberalism's ethical aim the celebration of choice. In the long nineteenth-century contest between competing liberal visions of personal enfranchisement, Constant's quicksilver but vigilantly authentic self began to prevail over Humboldt's classical ideal of self-standing, humane civility.

Economically, compromise with democracy was a price liberalism faced to save capitalism. By the 1880s, the outlines of such a bargain were becoming evident. If the few were to share with the many, the many should accept the existence of the few. If it accepted that capitalism was here to stay, labor stood to gain a more equal voice with capital, higher wages, and steadier employment. If capital accepted that a richer, more contented, and more vocal working class was good for business, it could stop fearing for capitalism's survival. Outlining such a bargain was not difficult. Reaching it on stable terms took in practice until after 1945. In liberal thought, the dominant problem became less principle than cost: could liberalism afford democracy? Murmured in Mill, voiced by Schumpeter and Hayek, that troubling query anchored liberalism's economic anxiety about democracy.

In reviewing Tocqueville's second book on America, Mill chided him for wrapping up universal suffrage, cultural leveling, and modern commerce into a single idea and calling it democracy. Mill had a fair "what-do-you-mean?" sort of point, but Tocqueville was also on to something. The spread of spending power and the gradual acceptance of diverse ethical voices were as much a democratic enfranchisement as the extension of the ballot. By the end of the nineteenth century, liberals faced all three democratic demands. They compromised, and liberalism survived, but liberals never quieted their anxieties about the damage that democracy was causing to political good sense, economic vigor, and the ethical health of society.

From the 1880s to the 1940s liberals lost that sense of youthful confidence that their nineteenth-century predecessors had enjoyed. They faced bewildering disappointments that tested their ideas and shook their morale. Education, civic freedoms, and material progress did not end prejudice, intolerance, or sectional hatreds. International trade and finance did not replace warfare. Market economies thrown out of balance did not right themselves. After 1945, liberal democracy got a second chance. It succeeded, not least because of lessons learned from the 1880s to the 1940s.

6

The Compromises That Gave Us Liberal Democracy

i. Political Democracy: Liberal Resistance to Suffrage Extension

If you exclude laborers and women from politics for lack of education, Condorcet wrote in 1790, soon the only people admitted will be those with public-law degrees. The point of his sarcasm was that civic rights ought not to depend on civic "capacity," that is on education or property. Everybody, by implication, should be able to vote and run for office. A pathbreaking advocate of universal suffrage, Condorcet was pinpointing a difficulty that would dog liberals for much of the next 150 years. In *What Is the Third Estate?* (1789), Condorcet's ally, Abbé Sièyes, had called for the removal of noble rank and clerical status as political barriers to bourgeois men. In the constitutional debates of 1793, Sièyes and Condorcet took a large step beyond by demanding that every last person have equal civic status. Although they drew back from votes for women, their proposals were radically democratic for the day. The early liberals were by contrast democratic laggards. Well into the nineteenth century, liberals ingeniously spun out reasons why their lesser fellows lacked the capacity for full citizenship. Only reluctantly did liberalism come to treat citizenship as an entitlement.

As regards voting for those who were to govern them, the United States took the democratic lead on behalf of "free" citizens, that is for men who were neither native Americans nor slaves. Members of Indian tribes were excluded from citizenship. For apportioning seats in the lower house of Congress, the federal Constitution of 1787 counted slaves as three-fifths of a person. Otherwise the new Constitution was silent on who could vote, leaving electoral rules to the states. State constitutions, drafted after independence from a mixture of old rules and new principles, reflected a stratified colonial society. Political rights in many states were limited by religion, color, or property. The Carolinas, for which Locke had drawn up an early colonial charter, denied non-Protestants the right to hold office and denied nonbelievers the right to vote. Massachusetts obliged male citizens to join a church, which meant in practice the Congregationalist church, until the 1830s. After the end of the second British-American war in 1815, as the republic stabilized and spread westward, such restrictions began to loosen and disappear. Pressure for full electoral democracy came, as in Europe, from below but also from the impracticability of maintaining a stratified franchise on an expanding frontier. Jacksonian populism represented both upward and outward pressures. Liberal elites in the cities feared unschooled popular energies but gave in to change. By the 1830s white men in the United States with few exceptions could vote and hold office, whoever and wherever they were, however poor and whatever they believed.

To French nineteenth-century liberals, the "good" revolutionary constitution of 1791 got it right. Tax requirements filtered the franchise by excluding around 40 percent of Frenchmen from voting for electors, some 70 percent from being an elector, and over 80 percent from winning office. The "bad" revolutionary constitution of 1793 had gotten it wrong. It opened civic rights to all men older than twenty-one and to any foreigner who had lived and worked in France for a year. France was by then at war and the democratic 1793 constitution was never applied, which to liberals was just as well. In 1830, under an Orleanist "king of the French" committed to constitutional rule, the liberals did not entrust power to the people. Tax requirements limited voting to roughly one Frenchman in 170. When in the republic of 1848 the vote was at last extended to all men, the autocratic Louis Napoleon kept the practice but debauched its spirit. A plebiscitary landslide in 1851 lent popular legitimacy to his despotic coup, confirming liberal fears of the subornable common voter.

In Prussia, Chancellor Bismarck took note. In 1867 he persuaded the Prussian king and parliament to adopt universal suffrage for voting to the parliament of the North German Federation. Four years later on German unification, a similar rule was carried over for elections to the all-German parliament, the Reichstag. Among the parties of progress, mass democracy served the Catholic Center and the Social Democrats well, but caused liberal parties lasting trouble.

In Britain, the Whig Reform Act of 1832 extended the vote to roughly 7 percent of people older than twenty, a larger share at the time than in France. But when France reverted to universal male suffrage in 1848, Britain became democracy's laggard. In 1866 backbench Liberals brought down the Russell government over a second electoral bill. Leading the revolt was Robert Lowe (1811–92), a businessman's politician and foe of trade unions who had crafted the 1856 Company Act. Few people, especially working-class people, understood the simplest economics, he believed. It was Lowe, as earlier noted, who warned Mill not to overrate the intelligence of their fellow MPs. Extending the vote, Lowe thought, would harm business, jeopardize free contract, and put property rights at risk. His revolt was little more than a delay, though it gave the conservative opposition, which briefly took office, an opening. In 1867, a successful Tory bill widened the electorate to 2.2 million, roughly one man in three. Lowe was unreconciled. He warned parliament that it must now "prevail on our future masters to learn their letters." Repeated as "We must educate our masters," Lowe's remark epitomized nineteenth-century liberal doubts about popular democracy's place in the dream of masterless order.

Liberal doubts had ancient sources refreshed by recent experience. The most obvious was fear of the masses. Classical tradition had taught that the crowd was not to be trusted. Half a century of popular violence appeared to confirm that lesson. Lurid memories included London's "No Popery" Riots in 1780, Shay's rebellion of indebted farmers in Massachusetts in 1787, Captain Swing's farm-machine smashing in Kent, and the seizing of factories by Lyon silk workers in the 1830s, not to forget the murder of two constitutionalist liberal deputies during the Frankfurt uprising of September 1848. Crystallizing every other liberal fear was the Jacobin democracy blamed for terrorizing France in 1792–94. Classical tradition also offered a corollary: popular rule normally ended in chaos, when terrified citizens begged a despot to restore order. The Napoleons, uncle and nephew, seemed to confirm that second lesson.

Liberal opposition to a democratic suffrage was at most a holding operation. As populations grew, wealth spread and literacy rose, pressure of numbers made electoral democracy impolitic to resist. Argumentatively, as champions of government by consent and equal opportunity, liberals were ill placed to deny to others the civic benefits and capacities they claimed for themselves. We have seen how with civic respect in general a liberal "what?" prompted a democratic "who?" The suffrage fight may be thought of as a special case of the "who?" question. Liberals had no good answer to the implicit charge behind the words on a placard that the great twentieth-century American progressive John Dewey had once gleefully seized without reading as he joined a women's suffrage parade down Fifth Avenue in New York: "Men can vote, why can't I?"

The liberal concession to democracy was large. Public administration and diplomatic statecraft required to the liberal mind not just knowledge beyond the average citizen's range. They took gifts of decision and habits of command beyond the capacity of any large collection of people. In time liberals silenced, without abandoning, such doubts about mass democracy. They ceded to universal suffrage itself in a long, strategic retreat and reluctantly accepted that the many would rule, though they never abandoned the search for limits on how the many might govern. A first element in that strategic retreat was to settle on a liberal understanding of popular sovereignty. Government by the people, as liberals saw it, had to be limited in particular by the constraints of *representation, articulation, bureaucratization*, and *insulation*.

Whatever affection they kept for the classical ideal of direct democracy, most liberals followed Madison and Constant in accepting that in modern states of any size direct participation was neither practical nor desirable. Madison, it will be recalled, sketched negative arguments in favor of representative democracy in *Federalist X*. He saw in *representation* a diffusion of the popular will and a protection against domination by any single interest or power. Constant had added a more positive thought in "Liberty Ancient and Modern": "Poor men look after their own business; rich men hire stewards." Delegating politics to others was a fortunate by-product of progress and prosperity, Constant was suggesting. His appreciation of modern administration neglected its complexity, however, and underplayed how little say modern citizens had over their "stewards." Delegation, on his account, sounded more like abandonment. Constant sensed but was not deeply troubled by the difficulty. His thrust was that modern citizens had better, more diverting ways to spend their time than on politics. Prestige and excellence could now be had without governing or holding office. Modern people were acquiring a self-confidence rooted in property and education to send others to do their bidding. If their bidding was not done, the stewards could, in elections, be recalled. In present-day conditions, Constant concluded, the only credible form of democracy was representative.

Some kinds of representation did too little to *articulate* the popular will. They relied on a false equation of the popular will with the will of the majority. Notable as a negative model in liberal eyes was the Jacobin democracy of the "bad" French Revolution. In the republic of 1792, the popularly elected National Convention had in theory expressed the people's will. In practice, a small Committee of Public Safety harried by the radical Paris sections took decisions under Robespierre, which a fractious Convention with luck then confirmed. Jacobin democracy had populist descendants. For liberals, Jacobin or populist democracy was either a free-for-all among false equals or an executive tyranny claiming to act for the majority. Minorities, localities, property, dissent, and public order were left in either case without defense against the unchanneled power of inarticulate or suborned majorities.

The contrasting liberal ideal of popular sovereignty was a "republican" form of representation that articulated and bridled the majority will. Republican representation demanded constitutional intricacy. It demanded supremacy of law overseen by independent courts and bounded by entrenched civic protections. Liberals accepted majority voting as a practical method for taking collective decisions. No actual majority, on the other hand, should be able to dig itself in, let alone make itself supreme. Today's minority should have fair hope of being tomorrow's majority.

That "republican" understanding of popular sovereignty seemed to its critics to turn on a trick. It made the people's voice supreme but passed it through so many filters, actual or theoretical, as to render what came out unrecognizable. Liberals, the charge ran, supported government by consent so long as consent was diluted, tacit, or hypothetical. Their ideal gave the people voice so long as it was not heard.

In answer liberals insisted that the notion of the people's will had to be understood in the right way. The republican idea of popular sovereignty was essentially negative. To say that the people were supreme was to say in effect that nobody was. On such a picture, ultimate power, and with it ultimate responsibility, must lie over the horizon. Were ultimate power locatable, it might be seized and, once seized, it would inevitably be abused. Such thoughts guided Madison and Guizot in their search for ways to resist domination by any single power. Constant spelled out the negative idea with characteristic brio in *Principles of Politics* (1815): "In a society based on the sovereignty of the people, sovereignty belongs to no one person or class. . . . The people as a whole are sovereign in the sense that no individual, no party and no group can claim sovereignty for themselves." The liberal dream of masterless order took political shape in that twin idea of dispersed, unlocatable power and impersonal responsibility.

Which arrangements best embodied "republican" requirements left room for argument. Many early German liberals admired, without fully understanding, Britain's constitution. Carl Welcker, a Baden liberal and coeditor of a multivolume *Encyclopedia of Politics* (1845–49), called it, with no apparent irony, "the most glorious creation of God and nature and simultaneously humanity's most admirable work of art." Other continental liberals took their line more from Kant. He had shrewdly judged Britain's constitution, with its domineering parliament of landowners and rich merchants, as oligarchic and despotic. Seen as a people, Kant is reported to have said, the English were the finest in the world. Seen as a state, England was in Kant's view the "most destructive, self-seeking, despotic and bellicose" of all. Such liberals followed the great Prussian thinker in his admiration for a younger, more hopeful United States. In 1861, not long before Laboulaye called for democratic liberalism in France, Mill gave universal suffrage measured welcome. It could, he thought, combine effective government with civic edification, so long as educated voters had more electoral weight and minority parties were able to win seats.

A year when civil war broke out between North and South in the world's principal democracy was hardly the best time to allay liberal doubts about universal suffrage. Mass democracy was nevertheless coming to look inevitable, especially after the Union won. In 1881, the British liberal historian Lord Acton wrote to Mary Gladstone, the prime minister's daughter, about a proposed further extension in Britain beyond the 1867 franchise. "We are forced in equity," Acton told her, "to share the government with the working class." Acton gave several reasons to smile at the inevitable: a wider suffrage was fair; it fostered economic peace and national prosperity by empowering labor, a source of national wealth; it gave voice to original opinions that might not otherwise be heard; and it lessened the chances of domination by any one section, class, or interest. Acton concluded, in an echo of Constant, that it was not that the working class was unfit to govern: "Every class is unfit to govern."

Laboulaye, Mill, and Acton together handed down a set of reasons that liberals might choose from when reconciling themselves to mass democracy at the polls: nonpermanence of majorities, nondomination by majorities, inclusion of minorities, peaceable change, civic engagement, labor tranquility, voice for unorthodoxy, and, generally, fairness. In more technical garb, those arguments have returned in some combination or other ever since.

Acceptance did not mean embrace. Liberal doubts remained. The British legal historian Henry Sumner Maine, an independent of liberal sympathies, complained in *Popular Government* (1885) that democracy produced legislative deadlock. As "monarchy inverted" it encouraged coups. In *Democracy and Liberty* (1896), the Irish historian W.E.H. Lecky feared that democracy evened the terms of class conflict too much. Trade union representation, he worried, undermined freedom of contract and encouraged interference in industry. Power, Lecky wrote, was falling into the hands of "the most ignorant," driving a terrified middle class to cry out for "despotic order." Mass democracy was unstoppable, Lecky thought, but might be tempered by nondemocratic upper houses. A parallel fear was the fiscal consequence of franchise extension. As late as 1913, the British government statistician Bernard Mallett put the matter neatly. In an electoral democracy, he predicted, spending would be largely controlled by "the poorer" classes while revenue was obtained mainly from a minority of wealthier people. By implication, if everyone was to have a vote, then the tax-paying middle-class minority would demand that the untaxed working-class majority pay their share of taxes.

Liberal students of democracy in France and Germany saw less mass representation than *bureaucratization* under the guidance of elites. French and German sociologists and political scientists looked at how democracy actually worked, in the spirit of Guizot, who had written to a friend in 1851, "You can put down a riot with soldiers and secure an election with peasants," but to govern, he added, "you need the support of the higher classes, who are naturally the governing classes." Guizot was not thinking of an exclusive caste born to govern but of open, middle-class elites with property or brains. By the end of the century, students of politics were putting Guizot's acerbic picture of electoral democracy on a more factual basis. Rather than match mass democracy against an ideal picture, they set to describe its actual mechanics, its sources of power, and its means of control. Instead of an Athenian *agora* or a Swiss town square, such observers saw organization, oligarchy, and bureaucracy. In Joseph Chamberlain's Birmingham caucus and in the boss-run American city machines, Moise Ostrogorski spied with regret a decline of personal responsibility in politics and its replacement with large, uncontrolled forces. In *Political Parties* (1911), the German political scientist Robert Michels proposed an "iron law of oligarchy": for good or ill, bureaucratization and decision-making by elites diluted the democratic will. People en masse, Michels judged, did not make hard choices. "Democracy," he wrote, "characteristically prefers the authoritarian settlement of important questions." Though the French liberal essayist Alain did not share the elite view of democracy, he summed it up with a characteristic epigram: "Hardly a drawing room exists where popular sovereignty is taken seriously."

Liberals who accepted that unexalted picture of "real existing" liberal democracy faced a choice. Michels's teacher, Max Weber (1864–1920), chose guarded hope. Neither the liberal nor the democratic elements were, in his view, sham. They had to be seen for what they were. Rather than recitals of the Sermon on the Mount, the vocation of politics involved "slow, strong drilling through hard boards," Weber wrote in 1919. Power indeed was being centralized. Executives dominated parliaments. Parties were becoming machines. Method and process were everywhere prevailing. On those inevitabilities, Weber insisted. Yet Weber, a lifelong liberal, balanced that picture with less despairing thoughts. Parliamentary criticism was still a vital corrective to power. The negative sanction of throwing out discredited ministries made voting more than an indulgent charade. Politicians' first duty, it was true, was to follow an "ethic of responsibility," by which he meant a methodical attention to consequences. When times demanded it, Weber added, politicians must equally be ready to take a principled stand and say, "I can do no other."

An alternative to Weber's guarded acceptance was angry rejection, the course taken by Georges Sorel (1847–1922), a French engineer from the École Polytechnique and disillusioned exliberal. In *The Illusions of Progress* (1908) and *Reflections on Violence* (1908), Sorel castigated liberal democracy as a suffocating sham. It was sham in masking the true sources of power and vitality. It masked irrationality with procedures, myth with argument, and force with talk. It suffocated by smothering popular energy and violence, which alone were strong enough to break the sham. Sorel's claims sat uneasily together. It was unclear on his account how a liberal sham could be so effective. Sorel faced the difficulty of any I-can-see-better-than-you-can theory that makes the rest of us into dupes. It faced the difficulty of any supposedly progressive theory that treated public reason and political morality as a denial or suppression of people's fundamental irrationality. Sorel's story of liberal democracy as a mask to gull cretins and anesthetize the masses never lost its appeal. It ran with an electric charge into anti-liberalisms of the twentieth century, with calamitous effect. Michels, a disillusioned liberal who like Sorel despised the historic compromise, ended in Italy as a supporter of fascism.

The economic critique of liberal democracy ran in parallel. It was quieter and less impassioned. It proved also to have longer life, surviving as it did the moral catastrophe to which irrationalist rejection of liberal and democratic values amply contributed after 1918. The most formidable exponent of the economic critique of democracy was the economic historian Joseph Schumpeter. A Czech-born Austrian who took American citizenship, Schumpeter laid the foundations in a life of work beginning before the 1914–18 war and culminating in *Capitalism, Socialism and Democracy* (1942). Schumpeter's core idea was that the needs of liberal capitalism and the demands of popular sovereignty did not smoothly mesh.

Schumpeter's "Can capitalism survive? No I do not think so" is well known. Less repeated is his immediate qualification. Democratic capitalism could survive, Schumpeter added, under certain constraints: favoring expertise in the making and administering of laws, promoting restraint from working-class parties by including them in government, and, above all, insulating areas of economic decision from popular oversight. The economic critics of liberal democracy feared in particular the growing weight of taxes and state spending. In modern conditions as the critics saw it, competing interests won favors from the state without heed to upper limits on their demands as a whole. As balancing favors were dispensed to all sides, state spending rose and monetary inflation threatened to run beyond control. Schumpeter's baton passed, we shall see, to Hayek, thence to public-choice theorists such as James Buchanan and the monetary economist Milton Friedman, a trio of thinkers who shaped the neoliberal upheaval of the 1970s.

Try as liberals might to limit the vote, to raise its cost, or to deflate its value, people without the vote continued to demand the vote. City-based liberals objected from the start to a bias that gave rural voters, man for man, more say than city voters, but they resisted extending votes to women, nonwhites, and the laboring poor. Eligible voters became a majority of Britain's adult population only in 1918 when women thirty and older as well as working-class men previously excluded brought the share of voters to 74 percent. Double votes for certain university graduates, an old symbol of liberal distrust for the unlettered masses, were not abolished until 1948. German women got the vote in 1918, British women twenty-one and older in 1928, but French women only in 1944. Black Americans in the South were enfranchised in federal law after the Civil War but denied the vote by ruse and intimidation upheld in state courts until the 1960s. In both Europe and the United States, outright buying of votes declined, making elections less nakedly corrupt, although the weight of lobbying money in politics grew ever heavier. Gerrymandering of districts and compromises involved in any choice of voting system frustrated attempts to perfect electoral representation. Nevertheless on paper at any rate, Britain, France, Germany, and the United States had by midcentury all broadly converged on the ideal of "one person, one vote" and earned the right to call themselves electoral democracies without an asterisk.

One respect in which nineteenth-century liberal fears of universal suffrage proved justified was that liberal parties declined as mass politics spread. In Germany, at the first Reichstag election of 1871, the two main liberal parties won just under 40 percent of the vote in an electorate of more than seven million. By 1912 their vote had fallen to 25 percent, in an electorate almost twice as large. In the Weimar Republic the two liberal parties together, the big business German Democrats and the left-liberal German People's Party, were the strongest winners at the start, taking almost a quarter of the vote in the first Reichstag election in 1920. By November 1932, when even the left liberals had collapsed into a frightened law-and-order party, Germany's two liberal remnants scraped respectively 1 percent and 2 percent of the vote.

The twentieth-century rout was as sudden and severe for Britain's Liberals. From 1831 to 1885 the coalition of free-trade Tories, Whigs, radicals, and reformers that took the name Liberal in 1859 were out of office for barely twelve years and lost the popular vote in only two of fourteen elections, in 1841 and 1874. In the 1860s Liberals could count on 60 percent of the vote and in 1900s still 50 percent. By the 1930s, overtaken on the left by the Labour Party, Britain's divided Liberals were winning less than 10 percent of the vote. After the Labour landslide of 1945, when Liberals won only six seats, the Labour Minister of Health Aneurin Bevan joked that to get to the House of Commons the Liberal Party could now take a taxi.

The reasons for that collapse were many. In progressive spirit, liberals were closer to parties of the left than to those of the right. Economically, business liberals on the other hand were at odds with the union-dominated left. Socially, liberal parties were out of step with mass culture. The radical *notables* of France, the liberal *Honoratioren* of Germany, and Whig grandees of Britain were making way for newer, more professional politicians, wise to organization and advertising. Politics for the new politicians was less ruling than marketing. Even in Germany liberals began to lose their nineteenth-century city bases as small businesses and small shops, a core strength, declined in face of growing industrial and commercial scale. An emerging "white-collar proletariat"—urbanites in shops and offices—had livelier excitements than earnest social causes and liberal discussion evenings. In *Setting the People Free: The Story of Democracy* (2005), the political theorist John Dunn cited H. G. Wells, that mocker of the liberal conscience, who teased a small London gathering of Fabian reformers in 1910: "Measure with your eyes this little hall: look at that little stall of not very powerful tracts: think of the scattered members, one here, one there. Then go out into the Strand.

Note the size of the buildings and business places, note the glare of the advertisements, note the abundance of traffic and the multitudes of people. That is the world whose very foundations you are attempting to change. How does this little dribble of activities look then?"

Some liberals adapted better than others to the bustle of city multitudes and the glare of advertisements. Temperament played its part. Winston Churchill, who first held office as a Liberal and claimed in spirit always to have remained one, wrote a telling essay on Lord Rosebery in *Great Contemporaries* (1937). Rosebery, who briefly led the Liberal Party from the House of Lords during the 1890s, never had to fight an election. Churchill saw here a lesson for modern liberals. "Whatever one may think about democratic government," Churchill wrote, "it is just as well to have practical experience of its rough and slatternly foundations. No part of the education of a politician is more indispensable than the fighting of elections." It was not difficult to harangue a hired crowd from the stage. A democratic politician needed the "bustling experience of a parliamentary candidature, with its disorderly gatherings, its organized oppositions, its hostile little meetings, its jeering throng, its stream of disagreeable and often silly questions." Churchill's lesson sounds obvious now. Liberals had to learn it or pass the torch to those that had. With its fine distinctions, earnestness, and high sensibilities, liberalism was otherwise always going to be a minority taste.

If not for liberal parties, by the end of the nineteenth century mass democracy nevertheless promised a certain compensation for liberalism itself. As opposition parties were drawn into government, those more adept at mass politics absorbed and adapted liberal ideas. As liberalism conceded to democracy, democracy conceded to liberalism. In this give-and-take liberalism stood to gain in one large way more than it lost. For at the heart of the historic compromise was a commitment to compromise itself. With the triumph of liberalism, the idea of politics as a contest for total control was pushed to the margins. That idea lingered on, longingly in a rival socialist picture of order through brotherhood, resentfully in the conservative picture of order through social unity. The modern right was slower to adjust. The interests it spoke for had more to lose than the dispossessed supporters of the left. The right viciously fought rearguard actions. After 1945, it too came round. Eventually the modern right and modern left both accepted the liberal conviction that domineering power was an outdated fantasy, to be resisted and rejected.

Reasons existed to suppose that a liberal spirit of compromise might prevail. Social habits and attitudes were growing among the middle class in a broader sense. On the list of bourgeois excellences, to the personal virtues of hard work, sobriety, and education were now added organizational virtues of the white-collar office: method, negotiation, legalism, written instructions, and disagreement without animosity. Hegel, in *The Philosophy of Right* (1821), had identified a new kind of citizen who neither grew nor made things, but who served the universal interests of society as administrator, facilitator, or middleman. Guizot had looked in similar vein to in-between bourgeois man, who was in a "classless" class of potential reconcilers, as the natural ruler in modernity. Tocqueville saw a classless European future in his imagined America: less aristocratic, less top-down, less hierarchical. What had come to them in a conceptual flash was now historically, it seemed, actually coming to pass. At an intensifying pace, the division of labor was dissolving face-to-face group loyalties and making everyone more dependent on strangers. Society as a whole was growing more cohesive in its interdependencies, but for any single one of its members more open, less fixed, and less stratified. Brains, organization, patience, bargaining—the bourgeois virtues of agents and middlemen par excellence—were accordingly at a premium. In Weber's shrewd judgment, Marx had told essentially the right story of modernity, only he had picked the wrong "universal" class.

The modern exercise of state power was changing in step. Rulers were no longer one or a few atop a pyramid. The field of authority was coming to look less like a military chain of command than a city grid with traffic police at intersections. Although in scale the state's capacity for violence had grown frighteningly, violence against its own citizens—those at any rate who did not challenge the emerging rules of the game—was more threatened than used and more open to negotiation. Constant had guessed rightly that busy, self-assertive people would less and less put up with imperative ways. Threat and command were giving way to inducement and persuasion.

The words would not be heard for a while, but a liberal picture of pressure-group politics in a pluralistic society was taking hold, even in semiliberal Imperial Germany, with its unions, leagues, and associations. Liberal talk and liberal procedure were less gripping than the spellbinding theater of the Marxist left or the sacred oratory of the wounded right. Liberalism's picture of an open but stable order where competing interests and conflicting beliefs were ceaselessly balanced off or bargained away was coming into view by the end of the nineteenth century. Securing and underpinning such an order was another matter. None of what the first liberals had seen at a distance was conceptually necessary or historically inevitable. Little or nothing of liberal progress was automatic or irreversible.

ii. Economic Democracy: The "New Liberalism" and Novel Tasks for the State

A first challenge was finding a common roof for the House of Have and the House of Want to avert what many liberals feared might be turning into economic civil war. That challenge was met by governments in the 1880s and decades immediately after by social legislation, urban reform, and taxation on a new scale, as well as by removal of constitutional barriers to such radical initiatives. Intellectually, liberals divided in their responses. Free-market liberals argued that such interferences were wrong in themselves or would not work. Capitalism, they were saying, could look after itself. The so-called new liberals of Europe and their Progressive cousins in the United States insisted that radical change was not only right in itself and effective in its aims, but necessary for liberal capitalism to survive and thrive. To anchor those arguments in their times, a sketch may help of the outstanding fiscal and legislative changes and their context.

As in liberal thinking, so in liberal-democratic practice, France got there first. In the Third Republic (1870–1940) France found modern normality. Once secure from reaction by the end of the 1870s, France fixed on a liberal-democratic form of public life that persists in essentials to this day. The elements were capitalist enterprise, an effective and professional state, multiparty democracy on a classless suffrage, and a legal order protecting persons and property. The French term for that framework was *démocratie républicaine*. A fair English translation is the later term "liberal democracy." French liberals practiced liberalism without acknowledgment, yet practice it they did. Liberalism in French political talk had acquired an unbreakable association with a discredited economic doctrine, laissez-faire, and a fantastic picture of society as made up from choice by scattered individuals. French liberals talked instead of republicanism and radicalism. Symbols and terms aside, France's dominant parties were liberal in outlook and practice. They reflected the fact that, however haltingly and incompletely, moral and material conflicts were growing less bitter and that French society was growing more middle class. After 1880, the monarchist right was more nuisance than institutional danger. The proto-Communist left offered a sheltering form of minority life but was never close to power. For sixty years, two liberal families—Republicans on the right, Radicals on the left—alternated or combined in government. France's Socialists sang revolutionary songs but pilfered liberal clothes and took office in "bourgeois" ministries. When the socialist leader Jean Jaurès challenged the Radical Georges Clemenceau to say what the ever-flexible radicals stood for, Clemenceau shot back, "You know perfectly well. It's in your pocket. You stole it from me."

Although the Third Republic's 108 governments in seven decades won it an unmerited reputation for ineffectiveness and frivolity, its achievements were genuine and lasting. State secondary schools opened to all and the right of assembly was written into law (1881). Unions became legal and divorce was reallowed (1884). Church and state struck an awkward but workable nonaggression pact that kept, in theory at any rate, the state out of religion and religion out of state schools (1905). A progressive income tax was passed into law (1914). Between 1900 and 1940, compulsory elements of a welfare state—workmen's compensation, child benefit, incapacity payments, old-age pensions—grafted themselves to mutual and charitable practices of social aid. The Popular Front government of Léon Blum (1936–38) added an obligatory two-week paid holiday and a forty-hour week, though its benefits were soon curtailed again under pressure of austerity. Reform came from across the liberal spectrum: from the Republicans Pierre Waldeck-Rousseau and André Tardieu, the radical Joseph Caillaux and the socialist Alexandre Millerand. Technocracy played a large role in the persons of Etienne Clémentel, father of regional planning and farm credit; Louis Loucheur, the elite-trained sponsor of low-cost housing, and Pierre Laroque, begetter of the post-1945 *sécurité sociale*, a rationalization of earlier welfare reforms made piecemeal. One reason it was hard to sell "antistatism" to French liberals was that the French state was comparatively clean, prestigious, and well run.

Liberal Britain was close behind. Confirmed in government by the landslide of 1906, Liberals embarked on a tide of radical legislation that divisions over Ireland and nearly twenty years in the wilderness of opposition had delayed. It was a new Liberal Party, largely shorn of the Whig grandees who had formed the biggest single group in Liberal cabinets as late as the 1880s. The suffrage extension of 1884 had opened the party to newer, city-oriented voices. After 1910 forty, MPs from the growing Labour Party supported Liberal reforms that, as in France, created the modern basis for politics.

That tide of Liberal legislation included school meals, school medical inspections, and reform of juvenile punishment (1906–08); state pensions for those older than seventy (1908); unemployment insurance in shipyards and heavy engineering (1908), stretched to industry as a whole (1911); state sick pay insurance (1911); labor exchanges (1909); town and country planning (1909); shop workers' half-day holiday (1911); pay for MPs (1911); and minimum wages in mines (1912). To pay for it all and cover a mounting deficit, David Lloyd George's "People's Budget" of 1909 raised taxes on the rich, which the anti-reform House of Lords rejected. After a yearlong contest of constitutional authority, the budget passed and the Lords' powers were curbed. All in all, between 1888 and 1913, social expenditure rose sixfold, the top rates of income tax trebled and death duties more than doubled, to 20 percent. Lloyd George's reforms made two Britons in five direct beneficiaries of the state, a proportion that soon grew to include all. For the wealthy, it was a social revolution from which there was no going back. The practice of social intervention by the British state, local as well as central, was grumbled about but not abandoned by subsequent Conservative cabinets, greatly extended by the Labour government of 1945 and not seriously challenged until the 1980s, by when much of the practice was too habitual and popular to shift.

A similar wave of social action and legislation followed in the United States. By 1880, the North had abandoned its attempt to impose "reconstruction" on a resistant white South and the ensuing truce among the sections facilitated an astonishing burst of capital accumulation and industrial progress. As in Germany, the late onset of economic growth was swift and sweeping in its effects, good and bad. Almost everyone grew richer. A few people grew stupendously rich, forming in critics' eyes a smug plutocracy. The last decades of the nineteenth century became known as the Gilded Age, a label taken from a popular 1873 satire of greed and corruption that Mark Twain had written with a friend. Rather than trumpet the good, liberal reformers focused on correcting the bad: foul and chaotically growing cities, unsafe factories, untested medicines, dangerous foods, and corruptions by money in politics, both city and national. The aim, as in Europe, was to save and temper, not replace, capitalism.

The cause of reform split politically into Progressive reform from above and Populist reform from below. The Progressives were liberal and middle class, though they did not limit their attentions to their own kind. They included Alice Paul, campaigner for women's rights, Ida B. Wells, an early force in the National Association for the Advancement of Colored People, H. W. Wiley, a government chemist who campaigned for safe food and medicine, and John Haynes, a champion of direct democracy who got the ballot initiative and the referendum put into California's constitution in 1911. None were socialist. All believed in capitalist enterprise. Many were Christians, driven by moral faith, like Walter Rauschenbusch, who preached a "social gospel." Progressivism crossed party lines. Two presidents, Theodore Roosevelt, a Republican, and Woodrow Wilson, a Democrat, pursued Progressive policies.

The Populists were democratic and working class. Their Omaha Platform of 1892 called for low interest rates, remonetization of silver to push up farm prices by cheapening money, public control of railways, and social use of public land. Their champion was William Jennings Bryan, an antidrink prairie lawyer with a scorching tongue and a talent for political organization. Populism carried the Democratic Party, which three times from 1896 to 1908 chose Bryan for president, who lost on each occasion. Like Reform itself, neither Progressivism nor Populism had one aim, one priority or one voice. As moods and movements, all the same, they had unity enough to make them recognizable currents in American politics.

In the 1910 elections, the anti-reform hold on the House of Representatives was broken, clearing the way for a wave of legislative change that not even an obstructive Senate could block. Two years later Roosevelt's bolt as an independent Progressive split the Republicans and put Wilson into the White House. A former politics professor and president of Princeton, Wilson had taken a liking to politics as governor of New Jersey. His *Congressional Government* (1885) had argued that Congress was too strong, the presidency too weak. As president, Wilson set out to live up to his words that the chief executive should be "free to be as big a man as he can." With the congressional log-jam clear, Wilson signed sweeping reforms that lowered tariffs, introduced a federal income tax, set up the Federal Reserve System, and established antitrust rules that partly exempted labor unions, enabling industrial workers to organize without fear of legal claims. The commerce and labor bureaus were reorganized in departments that became lobbying points for big business and big labor. Regulation of trade and industry grew. Wilson's two terms as president (1913–21) marked a historic shift of power to the executive branch.

For lessons of their own, liberal reformers from abroad rushed to Imperial Germany, incompletely liberal as it was. In quick succession during the 1880s, the Reichstag approved Bismarck's schemes for sickness insurance (1883), industrial accident coverage (1884), and state-run old-age insurance (1889). All were compulsory, a feature Lloyd George copied in Britain and that American liberals resisted until the 1930s and French liberals until after 1945. Costs in Germany were shared two-thirds by firms and one-third by workers, though the state paid one-third for pensions. Motives, as elsewhere, were mixed. Buying off socialists, rationalizing a patchwork of existing schemes, improving the workforce, strengthening the nation, and honoring fairness all played a part. Bismarck saw a chance as well to split the liberals. Richter and his small-business liberals objected, as we saw, on principle. The big-business National Liberals accepted on principle, complained of the costs and reluctantly supported Bismarck's proposals in the Reichstag. The drafting was by Theodor Lohmann, Bismarck's economic adviser. A strong intellectual influence came from the economic professors of the Social Policy Union, the liberal imperialist Gustav Schmoller and the liberal anglophile Lujo Brentano, two reformers both mockingly known as "tenured socialists."

The admiration of foreign liberals for Prussia was mixed. German public administration was widely treated as a model. Cobden, to recall, enthused about its schools and its crack civil servants. In the Franco-Prussian war, many British liberals took the German side. Mill wrote to Henry Fawcett in 1870 that the British could do well to remember whom the Germans were fighting: the despotic Napoleon III, not the French people. The British "new liberal" Leonard Hobhouse remembered his village pub cheering news of the Prussian victory at Sedan. Admiration for Germany cooled, however, in the 1880s as doubts among foreign liberals grew. Germany's central powers were too strong, its imperial aims too wide, Bismarck's temperament too bullying, and the liberal opposition too weak. In economic terms, German liberals were either principled but ignored, like Richter, or barely liberal at all, like the neomercantilist Schmoller. The foreign criticisms were easy to understand and later became unassailable. Did German twentieth-century history not amply confirm its nineteenth-century "liberal deficit"? Matters, in fact, were more complicated.

Wilhelmine Germany was semiliberal, incompletely liberal, or patchily liberal, not illiberal or antiliberal. Thanks to liberal pressure from the 1860s to 1890s, Germany obtained open markets, the rule of law, lay public schooling, civic emancipation of Jews, scrutiny of government by parliament and press, and many civil liberties including freedom of association. After Bismarck's fall in 1890, liberals won a Prussian income tax, though not as yet an all-German income tax. They failed to break the blocking power of an undemocratic Prussian Diet. Both changes had to wait, as did liberal democracy proper, until 1918. By then groundwork was done for which liberals could claim much credit.

Overemphasis on Wilhelmine Germany's "liberalism deficit" rested besides on artificial standards of liberal purity. On certain counts, Germany of the time was more liberal than its neighbors. From 1890 to 1900 it was spending less of its national income on defense than its old enemy, France, and much less than its rapidly industrializing eastern rival, Russia. It started a naval race in 1898 largely because, as Schmoller noted, free-trading Britain monopolized the seas and was unwilling to let its monopoly go. British Liberals raised income tax to pay for battleships as well as pensions. Shortly before the first world war, liberal Britain as good as nationalized the Anglo-Persian oil company in order to supply fuel for its growing battle fleet, now converted to oil from coal. In 1900–10, Germany's manufacturing tariffs were at 13 percent, on average notably lower than the French 20 percent or the prohibitive American 44 percent. As for industrial concentration, another commonly used marker of liberal impurity, only sixteen of Germany's prewar companies had more than £2 million in capital—about £1.5 billion in today's money—as against forty-one in Britain, from which that hero of free-market liberalism, the independent entrepreneur, was vanishing.

Pre-1914 Germany was politically less exceptional than disputed war guilt in 1918 and undisputed moral ruin in 1945 made it appear. The central decision taking of the Reich lacked, it is true, strong and tested parliamentary brakes. The prerogative powers of emperor and chancellor were large. The influence of the army and naval staffs was without due civilian oversight. Nor was the picture of Germany as an expansive power in war-prone hands that developed among liberals in Britain and France after 1871 a fantasy. Defensive harping on "power" and disdain for principle in the name of realism from German politicians and intellectuals alarmed Germany's neighbors and began to convince even the boasters themselves. All that was true. But the German state machinery was so tangled and overlapping that bargaining more than command was needed to effect decisions. Britain's and France's military planners were also hard for civilian politicians to control. Germany's many leagues, associations, and pressure groups played if anything a larger part in public life than their counterparts in Britain and France.

Nor on other scores was Germany such a liberal laggard. The contemporary American students of politics John Burgess judged in *Comparative Constitutional Law* (1890) that German guarantees of personal liberty were stronger than those prevailing in France, where the state was in practice barely checked, and those in England, where whichever government controlled parliament was all powerful. German city government, the envy of the world, was mostly in liberal hands up to 1914 and beyond.

Many Germans felt their country to be more civilized, more advanced, and less belligerent than France or Britain. In those ways they even felt themselves more liberal. When war came in 1914, a German propaganda poster designed by the graphic artist Louis Oppenheim asked, "Are we barbarians?" A table of figures on the poster declared that Germany spent twenty times as much as Britain on social support and three times more on schools, published four times more books, put out six times more industrial patents, and had four times more Nobel Prize winners. Another poster, "Who is the militarist?" noted that Britain had fought three times more wars than Prussia had since 1700 and was currently spending 50 percent more than was Germany on armaments.

The challenge that mass parties posed to German liberals was not unique. Britain's Liberals, we have seen, also shrank to vanishing after the 1920s. Nor were Germany's East Prussian Junkers the only feudal remnant of the liberal world. A conservative blocking power remained in the rural-dominated French Senate, which the liberals of the Third Republic never fully broke. United States senators were not directly elected until 1913 but chosen by unrepresentative state legislatures. Even then the upper chamber continued to delay liberal reform under the skillful obstruction of recalcitrant southern Democrats. Differences of attitude, structure, and process, last, ought not to obscure large similarities of outcome. Wilhelmine Germany's liberal rivals were more imperialist, as quick to use force, and equally overindulgent to their own bigots and nationalists. Complicated Germany belonged inside, not outside, a complicated liberal world.

iii. Ethical Democracy: Letting Go Ethically and the Persistence of Intolerance

Liberals of the period had more to concern them than economic and fiscal conflicts, as the French social thinker Célestin Bouglé recognized. Modern democratic society, he saw, both fostered and threatened liberals' ethical ideals. Welcome acceptance of others was growing as exclusionary hatreds spread. As it freed people from the authority of stereotypes, modernity seemed to lend prejudice new strength. Bouglé (1870–1940) was a collaborator of the sociologist Emil Durkheim and teacher of a younger generation of French liberals, including Raymond Aron. An academic star before he was thirty, an expert on caste in India and later director of the École Normale Supérieure, he was among the founders of the *Revue de Métaphysique et de morale* and an editor under Durkheim of the *Année Sociologique*. As a left-wing liberal, Bouglé was active in radical causes and an early supporter of France's League for Human Rights (1898), founded in response to the anti-Dreyfus campaign. To disillusioned liberals like Sorel, the lapse into partiality and intolerance was exhilarating, an acknowledgment of authentic passion, and an escape from liberal hypocrisy. Bouglé's own sympathies lay entirely on the side of openness and acceptance. Yet he understood the strength of prejudice and exclusion, from which, as he noted, liberals were not immune.

In a brilliant, farsighted essay, "Egalitarian Ideas" (1899), Bouglé pinpointed an outstanding characteristic of the present-day person as a readiness to mix his or her roles at will. Stereotypings of caste, class, and religion, Bouglé indicated, were antithetical to a modern understanding of people. A desirable liberal requirement was, by implication, the willingness to show people civic respect, not only whoever they were, but whoever they chose to be. State and society, on this idealized sketch, were being asked to let go of people in novel and, for many, disturbing ways. As they did, liberals faced a challenge they had not fully prepared for. What if modern people opted in large numbers to be bigots and racists?

Bouglé turned to that question in "The Crisis of Liberalism" (1902). The persistence of intolerance had come as a surprise. For years, he wrote, liberals had used "the conspiracy of circumstances" as a "pillow" on which to fall asleep. Without undue complacency, the first liberals were able to treat intolerance, conceptually and historically, as more or less solved. Tidying up operations remained. But the strategic victory was won. By the early nineteenth century many thoughtful liberals assumed that a modern social order needed neither an overarching creed nor a unifying tribal loyalty. Dogmatic or sectarian relapses looked at worst as temporary, unsustainable deviations from liberal modernity's happy path. Recent trends had woken liberals with a jolt. They were at a loss. Should they open-mindedly tolerate intolerance or use the powers of state to curtail racial and confessional prejudice? Liberals had dreamed of civic harmony amid ethical disharmony. Modern society was not turning out that way.

To start his career, Bouglé did what any serious aspirant in his profession, European or American, had to do. He went to Germany to study social reform. He came away knowing a lot about unemployment insurance, but with a profounder lesson as well. Material inequities were not the only source of conflict. Ethical and cultural differences might in time prove yet harder to bridge. Growing wealth did not seem to drive them away. On the contrary, everywhere Bouglé looked the opposite seemed true. Germans had just lived through a divisive campaign against the Catholic Church, the *Kulturkampf*. Anti-Semitism had burst out in France. Although Bouglé did not focus on them, neither Protestant Britain, with its anti-Irish prejudices, nor the white United States, with its endemic racism, were exempt. Liberals everywhere tended to share an imperial presumption that their countries had lessons in forbearance to teach the rest of the world. Confidence that their own societies had come further on the road from prejudice and exclusion than more backward humankind was so pervasive as to be virtually invisible, not least to liberals.

Liberals were not simply foolish or hypocritical. Their dream of civic peace amid ethical disharmony was genuine and appealing. Morally, the dream gave political shape to sentiments of personal respect expressed in maxims about protecting people's equalities and rights. Historically, the dream had support in an appealing two-stage story, already described, of civic respect growing out of religious toleration. If Bouglé's description of social modernity was apt, liberals were now facing a third stage in that sequence. The present stage was more liberating yet, but also more challenging. People were no longer prisoners of stereotyping categories imposed by accident of birth or by the us-or-them demands of others to join their team. People could choose who to be. Liberal respect for people now appeared to demand a much wider letting go by state and society. That, too, was welcome. There was little in itself wrong with the dream. The mistake was to think that realizing it would be ratchetlike or mechanical, and not a matter of forever finding new points of balance.

In the late nineteenth and early twentieth century plenty of liberals were getting the balance wrong. In Germany, liberals had abetted Bismarck in anti-Catholics laws of 1871–74, which banned political preaching, closed the Jesuit order, put churches under state supervision, instituted civil marriage, and threatened priests who urged Catholics to adopt passive resistance with expatriation. *Kulturkampf*, the name coined for the campaign by a distinguished epidemiologist and liberal politician, Rudolf Virchow, was many things. It was a reaction to a reaction by the Roman Catholic Church against secular modernity and the loss of its ethical influence. It was part, if a misconceived part, of building a national state, a task that invariably encourages a drive to limit or extinguish countervailing powers. Most damaging for liberals, the *Kulturkampf* expressed progressive contempt for "peasant" superstition, which was to be rooted out, as one German liberal put it, like "phylloxera, the Colorado beetle and other enemies of the Reich."

Although a few German liberals, notably the redoubtable Eugen Richter, had opposed the *Kulturkampf* on principle, German liberals in the main supported it, only to regret their mistake. The campaign proved a historic blunder. German liberals failed to persuade Catholic voters that priests were bamboozling and exploiting them. Instead, Catholics tended to treat liberals as the mystifiers and exploiters, sermonizing about freedom while heartlessly grinding the poor. Liberal-minded Catholics, though opposed to their own church's reactionary hierarchy, resented the assault. Soon four Catholics in five were voting for the Catholic Center Party. As if blind to that first mistake, many liberals in the 1880s supported Bismarck's anti-Socialist laws, again with Richter an honorable defender of liberal principle against the misuse of state power. Partly as a result, the progressive stream of German politics had by the 1890s divided. Liberals in the middle formed a historic but shrinking core, squeezed between the world's largest, best organized labor movement and the world's largest, best organized Catholic Party. Liberal hopes that religion would somehow vanish from politics into the privacy of homes and consciences looked fond, if not forlorn.

For French liberals the religious question was simpler. France had one leading church, not two. More neatly than in Germany, progress, the left, and anticlericalism matched up in France against reaction, the right, and Catholicism. On the other hand, the Roman church in France was set, as in Germany, on recovering lost authority. French anticlericalism was a reaction to a reaction, a riposte to clerical fears and hatreds of change. In tones familiar from the moral conservatives of today, Catholic reaction railed against Enlightenment, revolution, and "decadence" on behalf of temperance, discipline, and obedience. Pressure for piety came from above, for example from the militantly antimodern Assumptionists, egged on by Louis Veuillot's ultra-reactionary Catholic paper, *L'Univers*. It came also from below in genuine expressions of popular faith such as devout pilgrimages and the witnessing of miraculous appearances.

French anticlericalism stamped the left unevenly. To the proto-Communist Guesdists, to focus on religion mistook symptom for disease—class exploitation. At the other end of the anticlerical spectrum, militants such as Clemenceau wanted religion expunged from schools and politics. In between were grades of anticlerical tone and compromise agendas. French anticlericalism prevailed by making concessions. Although the Roman church was no longer voice or guide of the French state, much of its cultural authority remained—too much certainly for the most militant anticlericals. In fighting their battles, France's anticlericals often behaved in illiberal ways. As Bouglé noted, some critics feared that liberal intrusions were making the French state into a church-like authority.

Bouglé was in little doubt about which side he was on, but he was not an antireligious ultra. Faith, like patriotism, was not to Bouglé a sign of mental dwarfism. Bouglé distinguished between beliefs and the political mischief made of beliefs. Militant anticlericals were in danger, Bouglé felt, of aping militant clericalism by intruding on people's private sphere. Rather than rail at superstition, Bouglé thought liberals should defend the "principles of 1789," under poisonous attack from the nationalist far right. They should focus their energies, not on the supposed superstitions of the faithful, but on militant clericalists, chauvinists, and anti-Semites. They should rally people to a republican patriotism.

In "Teaching Patriotism" (1904), Bouglé pictured such loyalties as lying somewhere between involuntary attachment and chosen commitment. The healthy patriotism Bouglé hoped for drew on memory, sentiment, and ideals. It was in line of descent from Guizot's allegiance to liberal principle and imaginative reverence for the French past. Bouglé's sense of nation lay between "concrete and actual" attachment to France as land and people, and the idealist commitment to republican ideals. The choice of where to find the line occupied European liberals after 1945, and with better luck than Bouglé's generation they struck on a remarkable and original answer that balanced regional pride, national citizenship, and European unity.

Another of Bouglé's farsighted contributions was the essay "Polytelism" (1914). People's aims, beliefs, and hopes were proliferating and diversifying, it asserted. He called that "polytelism," many-endedness. The plural condition of modern society that Constant had brilliantly gestured at and that Mill had defended with less descriptive detail was in the French sociological manner presented by Bouglé as a social given. To arrive at a workable social order, he suggested, it was too much to expect agreement any longer on the ultimate ends of life. The best to hope for was agreement on fair, common principles of society that left people free and able to pursue their aims. Politics, that is, should be like a building with many uses. Bouglé's thoughts about how people who disagreed profoundly about the ends of life might nevertheless co-exist amid basic laws rooted in mutual recognition and forbearance looked forward as well as back. With notable clarity, his thoughts antici-pated lines of principle pursued and extended particularly by American and German liberals after 1945.

7

The Economic Powers of the Modern State and Modern Market

i. Walras, Marshall, and the Business Press: Resisting the State on Behalf of Markets

By the 1880s, a body of ideas we may call free-market liberalism, or perhaps better business liberalism, formed a triangle. At one point was market economics, consolidated by the late nineteenth-century theorists of marginalism. At another was legal individualism, encapsulated in the doctrine of freedom of contract. At a third was the business press, which popularized market economics and sharpened it into a weapon of public argument.

Two outstanding exponents of marginalism were Léon Walras (1834–1910) and Alfred Marshall (1842–1924). Walras was a Frenchman who taught as a professor at Lausanne. Marshall, an Englishman, held the chair in economics at Cambridge and founded the *Economic Journal*. Walras pioneered the mathematization of economics, Marshall its redomestication as a study of people in the everyday tasks of buying and selling. Both sought to make economics more scientific by making it less historical. They sought to free economics from the variations of period and locality by finding constancies and patterns for everywhere. Walras borrowed from the flows and stabilities of engineering to express market-clearing balance in sets of equations. Marshall put the mathematics in an appendix and explicated sound market reckoning by way of vivid examples. To neither of them was economics a grand march of historical stages or a terminal clash between social classes. Their topic was both more exotic and more familiar. It grew from single shoppers and "representative" firms, as Marshall called them, making material choices one by one. Both men insisted that to think your way into economics, you had to begin with simple exchanges between isolated, cost-conscious agents. If you could do that with two, you could do it with many. If you could do that without assumptions about your cost-conscious pair's other aims and preoccupations, you could isolate what was specifically economic in their behavior.

Most of Walras's and Marshall's key ideas had found voice from other economists before the 1870s in the writings, for example, of Johann Thünen, Antoine Cournot, Hermann Gossen, and John Stuart Mill, though in scattered or as yet pregnant form. Mill's death in 1873 serves as a useful turning point, for marginal ideas were now made explicit and pulled together. Walras and Marshall were not alone. Stanley Jevons in Britain and Carl Menger in Austria did parallel work early in the 1870s. Although priority was disputed, Walras and Marshall did most to shape isolated insights into a coherent body of thought. By the 1880s economics was becoming a research program, a profession, and a body of thought feeding public argument.

The marginalist breakthrough specified the character of economic choice, isolated where that choice occurred and suggested how to tell good economic choices from bad. Economic choice, marginalism taught, worked by substitution. It involved swapping one thing for another, be it goods, money, work, time, pleasure. All economic choice involved trading, even with yourself. Thought of as equal exchange in which you lost to gain and gained to lose, economic choice properly understood was less about the satisfaction of desires than about their rearrangement. Choice, furthermore, took place, in Marshall's words, "on the margin of doubt" as to whether such a trade was worthwhile. That margin of uncertainty straddled an unimprovable point where taking a touch less of some good would leave a person undersatisfied, and a touch more, oversatisfied.

Marginalists then generalized that idea of finding an unimprovable, marginal point of least regrets into an all-purpose rule of prudent economic decision taking: go on doing anything—making, marketing, buying, selling—until the minute extra benefit of continuing equals the minute extra cost of so doing, and then stop. If, marginalists undertook to show, you did that carefully across every transaction, you would leave yourself materially or monetarily speaking most satisfied. You would, in economic language, "maximize utility" at the point where, whatever you were trading or transacting, marginal benefit equaled marginal cost. If shoppers and firms all did that unhindered in free markets governed only by the choices of those involved, then everyone's material hopes and regrets would at that instant exactly balance.

In *Elements of Pure Economics* (1874 and 1877), Walras spelled out that idea of a momentarily satisfying balance between consumers and firms within a market society in succinct mathematical terms. His equations showed with precision what fixed prices for consumer products, rents, wages, capital equipment, and investment capital. Consumers, Walras assumed, aimed to maximize utility or overall satisfaction. Firms aimed to maximize profit. Firms called on factors of production, labor, and capital. Goods markets cleared when consumer demand for goods equaled firms' supply of goods. Factor markets cleared when firms' demands for factors equaled consumers' supply of factors, that is, labor. When goods and factor markets all cleared, an economy was in balance. Walras described market clearance for relative prices of one good in terms of another and then for all goods in terms of money. Competition, finally, would minimize producers' costs and maximize consumers' satisfaction. On large and simplifying assumptions, nobody could be better off. In such an equilibrium, Walras wrote, everyone "can obtain greatest satisfaction of their wants." Walras's flawed proofs were later corrected and refined. Though many dismissed his mathematical approach to economics as too abstract, it became in time the discipline's vernacular. The twentieth-century profession followed Walras in treating economies as engineers treat fluid or mechanical systems, by describing their workings in groups of equations relating rates of change. To a liberal world ceaselessly in movement, Walras offered the thrilling promise of intelligible and measurable order.

Like Mill before and Keynes after him, Walras was an economist's son. Unlike them, he was a wayward student and late developer. He entered France's top engineering school, the École des Mines, but left before his final exams, so sparing himself a conventional career atop French officialdom. He clerked for a railway, wrote magazine articles, dabbled at banking, and drafted a novel. On a summer walk in 1858, Walras later recalled, his father told him that two great intellectual tasks remained in their century. One was to make history scientific. The other, which he pressed on his errant son, was to do the same for economics. The moment, Walras reported, was "decisive." He set to the task and, though professional acceptance was slow, in 1870 secured a chair in economics at Lausanne despite suspicions that he was a socialist. Walras taught there until 1892, publishing little but his *Elements*. As an analytical demonstration of how to seize an idealized economy at one go, that single work alone was enough for several careers. In Schumpeter's eyes, Walras had met his father's Comtean challenge to make economics rigorous, and for that Schumpeter judged Walras the greatest of economic innovators.

In 1906 came a telling final episode. Walras let friends propose him for the Nobel Prize for Peace. His watchwords—free trade and free competition—encouraged peace, they argued, whereas tariffs, government interference, and mercantilism encouraged war. The Nobel committee was not impressed. It saw little provable connection, so dear to hopeful liberals from Constant and Cobden onward, between free markets and peace. Previous winners, after all, had included the founder of the Red Cross and a German peace campaigner. The prize went instead to Theodore Roosevelt for mediation in the Russo-Japanese War.

Another aspect of the marginalist breakthrough was the doctrinal freight it discarded. Marginalism abandoned political economy's one-sided preoccupation with supply, production costs, overpopulation, and subsistence. With them went the Ricardian prejudice, clung to in the Marxist tradition, that only labor gave products genuine economic value. The marginalists treated neither rents from land as an unmerited reward to idleness nor profits from business as a forced extraction of "surplus value" from unempowered workers. The earnings of any factor—labor, land, or capital—equated on the marginalist picture to a balance of demand (what each might add to sales) and supply (what each cost its offerers to provide). In particular, demand and supply fixed the price of labor (wages). Demand and supply fixed the price of capital (interest rates).

That mental shift, implicit in Walras and explicit in Marshall, occurred against a background of mounting plenty. Adam Smith's was not a "dismal science." Smith had thought that real wages might one day rise beyond subsistence levels. Marshall, who attended to pay records and tax returns, could see that real wages were rising. Spending power was growing. Workers were becoming consumers. Within economic thought, demand cried out to be given its equal part in fixing price, and marginalism responded. It was as sensible to ask whether supply or demand set price, Marshall wrote, as to ask which blade of the scissors cut the paper. The thought and image were Mill's, but Marshall gave them new emphasis. On Marshall's telling, any purely supply-side or purely demand-side story in economics was bound to be incomplete.

He was born at Bermondsey near the docks in South London, the son of a butcher's daughter and a cashier at the Bank of England. His intelligence and feel for economy showed early. In Greek class at school he refused to use accents, complaining that they did not repay the time they took. At seventeen he made himself a precocious vow to work in short bursts of fifteen to thirty minutes and never to use his mind "except when it was fresh." At Cambridge his father wanted him to study theology, but Marshall's strength in mathematics prevailed. He became an economist, and on the death in 1884 of Henry Fawcett, took the chair there in political economy, which he held for the next twenty-four years. More dogged than robust, Marshall suffered throughout his career from bouts of ill health. He was sensitive to criticism, avoided controversy, and wrote with a perfectionist slowness that made his great book hard to grasp as a whole. By the eighth edition in 1920 shortly before Marshall's death, he had added twelve appendixes. At Cambridge his pupil Keynes found him an inspiring but chaotic lecturer.

Marshall is remembered with justice as one of modern economics' founders. His *Principles* did not just legitimize demand and supply as the sovereign forces governing all economic transactions. It brimmed with conceptual tools that were either new or that Marshall showed clearly for the first time how to specify and put to use: the price responsiveness of demand (elasticity); cost savings to a single firm from growth or improvements in its industry (external economies); gain from a purchase at less than ceiling price (consumer surplus); a price rise driving you to different products (substitution effect), or leaving you with less to spend on other things (income effect). By distinguishing periods of time over which prices adjust—market, short run, long run, and secular—Marshall pointed out ways to break down a problem that foxed

Walras: price adjustments in practice are never smooth or instanta-neous, but take place over longer or shorter periods of time during which conditions change. Equilibrium was always just out of sight.

A third aspect of marginalism was its aspiration to political neutrality. Left and right have both taken marginalism for weapon more than tool, though that was not how Walras or Marshall saw matters. Were margin-alism as politically loaded as critics claimed, it is hard to explain why the two men's thinking converged in economics but diverged in so much else. Walras was more social-minded, Marshall more market-minded. Walras believed, where Marshall did not, in the public ownership of land. Walras was suspicious of big business, whereas Marshall saw ben-efits in consolidation and scale. Walras felt more sympathy than Mar-shall did toward trade unions. Despite such differences of opinion, both thinkers were nevertheless able to agree on marginalism's core princi-ples: the twin sovereignty of supply and demand, and the fruitfulness of competition. They were able to do all that largely because both grasped how much of life, including political life, marginal economics could not pronounce on.

Walras recognized what his general proof that competition maxi-mized economic satisfaction did not show. For the sake of theoretical gain, his proof made artificial assumptions that were highly contestable when mistaken for ethical resting points. The proof presumed an arbi-trary distribution of income, whose fairness or unfairness was left ex-plicitly to one side. Inequity and inequality mattered to Walras but he did not think economic theory as such addressed them. It told us about how best to equalize the costs of production and the prices of goods, not how fairly to pay workers or distribute wealth. Walras was making a distinction adumbrated in Mill and now spoken of as that between ef-ficiency and equity.

The principles governing the rights and duties of social life, Walras wrote in "The Theory of Property" (1896) were justice, association, and fraternity. Each was needed for social health and none could be reduced to either of the others. Economic reasoning—which bore on exchange and reciprocal obligations—was relevant to the first two, not to the third. Justice, the giving of due, was obligatory and reciprocal. Associa-tion—the making of contracts, forming of clubs, undertaking mutual insurance—was reciprocal but voluntary. Association enriched society, but society itself rested on more than voluntary association. It depended on deeper ties of humanity. Such ties enjoined care and concern for the needy that neither justice nor mutual advantage demanded by themselves.

Though sanguine about capitalism, Marshall witnessed its disruptions and was concerned by poverty. He had socialist and trade union friends, including leaders of the great London Dock Strike of 1889, whom he admired in almost all but their grasp of economics. Marshall's attitudes were less contradictory than might appear. Because alleviating poverty was urgent, he thought it necessary to understand and foster market economics. On his mantelshelf, Marshall kept an oil sketch of a destitute man whom he called a "patron saint," but he was quietly withering about what he took for nonsolutions to bad working conditions and poverty, such as producer cooperatives, government regulation, and nationalization.

The borders between ethics and economics in Marshall's thinking were no clearer than they were for Walras. For each of them, ambiguity floated over whether competition maximized satisfaction for all of us or for each of us. It was unclear for both how their economic agents integrated humane fellow feeling with the mechanical reckoning of cost and advantage. The contrasts were acute in Marshall. With characteristic mixture of warmth and mockery, Keynes, in his memorial essay to Marshall in the *Economic Journal* (1924), thought that inside him was an "imp" with the voice of an "evangelical moraliser." Marshall favored competitive markets not only because they were economically most efficient but in the hope that they would encourage the social virtues of effort, conscientiousness, and prudence. He thought, like Mill, that we were not in the end the final judges of our satisfactions. "A truly high standard of life," Marshall wrote, "cannot be attained till man has learned to use leisure well." In the first pages of his *Principles*, he stated a difficulty that economic thought alone has never solved. Economics was about people in "the business part" of life, Marshall wrote. But, he added, anyone "worth anything" carried a "higher nature" into business, where he would be influenced by "his conceptions of duty and his reverence for high ideals." That was optimistic, to say the least. In their different ways, Walras and Marshall stressed that limits existed to the scope of economic decision-making. They offered universal guidance for making economic choices. They did not make economic thinking universally applicable to all choices.

A second point in the body of ideas forming the free-market triangle was the legal doctrine of freedom of contract. The doctrine won ground among mid–nineteenth century lawyers and courts in the common law tradition of Britain and the United States. Terminology aside, "individualist" freedom of contract came to prevail also in the nineteenth-century continental or Roman tradition of private law. A free contract was free principally from two sorts of previous hindrance. One sort was freedom of content from tradition or custom. The other sort was freedom of the parties from social category.

As to the first freedom, striking bargains and making contracts had been "unfree" in that custom, and law limited where and how you might agree to work, and what, especially land, you might agree to sell. Courts might refuse to uphold agreements judged unequal, unfair, or too remote from common practice. Under freedom of contract, by contrast, parties were at liberty to agree, within law, on whatever they wished. God's will, majority will, tradition, equity, and public interest no longer came into it. Over the content of agreements, parties in a sense were sovereign. So long as the content was lawful, it no longer had to be customary, fair, just, or moral. As to the second aspect, the parties' social clothes ceased to count. Contracts became impersonal. Rich or poor, clever or stupid, it no longer mattered. Courts began to treat parties to a valid contract as responsible grown-ups who came to market with their eyes open. Parties, that is, became equal before the law. That this freedom of contract should become a legal pawn in political battles was inevitable. As between labor and capital, parties were not equal. So social-minded "new" liberals argued in support of social legislation to limit contracts on behalf of weaker parties. In the words of the British social liberal R. H. Tawney, "Liberty for the pike" was "tyranny for the minnow."

The third point in the triangle was the business press. Well before marginalism there had sprung up in the 1830s to 1840s a lively tradition of market popularization on which the late nineteenth-century business press was able to draw. Frédéric Bastiat (1801–50) in France and Harriet Martineau (1802–76) in England wrote highly popular books promoting free-market ideas by way of amusing fables and homely examples. Bastiat's candle makers' petition to remove an unfair competitor by blotting out the sun and Martineau's tales of Brooke village enriched by enclosures were a model of how to convey market ideas in homely terms. Martineau's mixed casts of upstairs, downstairs, and in-betweens offered a core sample of English society presented in simple, everyday dialogue of a kind that still seemed fresh when radio and television adopted the style in popular slice-of-life dramas a century later.

Mill derided the limpid "summary of principles" with which Martineau ended her educational tales, perhaps with a touch of authorial pique. His *Political Economy* sold only three thousand copies in the four years of its first edition. On publication in 1832–34 Martineau's monthly booklets sold a total of ten thousand. Marx and Engels fared yet worse than Mill, whose great work, though slow out of the gate, showed well in the stretch. *The Communist Manifesto* ran quickly through three German editions during the revolutionary year of 1848, before virtually vanishing from sight until the 1870s, when extracts were read in court at a trial of German Social Democrats. Its rediscovery led to new translations, but the *Manifesto* won more than a coterie readership only after 1917 when the Soviet government sponsored huge runs in more than two dozen languages. For anyone in the market for insights into liberal capitalism, palatable free-market fables, an arduous ascent of Mount Mill, and a Marxist morality tale promoted by war-pressed Bolsheviks, each had their attractions and rewards. Readers with investments to make, orders to place, and savings to shift turned for news and practical information to a growing business press.

In Germany, an anti-Bismarck liberal, Leo Sonnemann, founded the *Frankfurter Zeitung*, a business paper, in 1867. A colleague of Schulze-Delitzsch, Sonnemann believed in free markets, workers' rights, and an active state, but was no socialist. His slogan "No dictators, neither Bismarck nor Marx" cost Sonnemann his Reichstag seat in 1884 when Bismarck instructed the right to vote for his socialist opponent, who won. Like many liberals of the day, Sonnemann was active in Frankfurt politics and with the art historian Ludwig Justi founded the city's Städelsches Museum. In the United States, Charles Dow and colleagues turned their small *Customer's Afternoon Letter* into a full newspaper, the *Wall Street Journal*, in 1889 and began delivering market news to investors by telegraph.

Britain led the creation of a weekly business press with the *Economist*, founded in 1843. In France, it was followed in 1862 by *L'Economiste français*. Their best known editors, Walter Bagehot (1826–77) and Paul Leroy-Beaulieu (1843–1916), make a study in parallel. Neither contributed to economics in the manner of Mill, Walras, or Marshall. Bagehot was more shining essayist than systematic thinker. Leroy-Beaulieu was professor of economics at the Collège de France, but his treatise on political economy of 1893 was an antique at publication. Both writers contributed much to liberal politics. They reported the workings of liberal capitalism, put economic issues at the center of politics, and sharpened neutral conceptual tools into dialectical weapons. Bagehot, Leroy-Beaulieu, and their counterparts in Germany and the United States were as vital to the creation of free-market liberalism as were Walras, Marshall, and their university colleagues.

Walter Bagehot (1826–77) was born to a West Country banker with a well-stocked library. Of Dissenting temper, the father sent his gifted son to London University rather than to Oxford or Cambridge to avoid their Anglican doctrinal tests. A star at university, young Bagehot found careers open to him. Though not physically commanding, he was magnetic in his fluency and enthusiasms. Bagehot tried law, which bored him, and moved quickly on to politics and journalism. In December 1851 during a stay in France he witnessed Louis Napoleon's coup, an episode which at twenty-five fixed him for life and gave him, for a liberal, undue respect for established order. A society's first duty was to defend itself against riot and disorder, Bagehot wrote in press articles about the coup. Liberty and representation might have to be sacrificed to prevent revolution, he thought, especially in a country such as France, which was not yet mature enough for either. Young as he was, Bagehot understood something not every market zealot has always grasped: businesses and banks crave stability and predictability. Bagehot felt no urge to radicalize life and turn society upside down for the sake of a libertarian idea. He grasped that business was about making and keeping money, not doctrinal purity or improving morals. He was a matchless example of that large and vital subcategory among market liberals: the business liberal, ethically broad-minded but with a conservative undertow of deference to customary power and established order.

After Paris, Bagehot returned to Stuckey's, the family bank, founded by his mother's uncle and run by his father. There he discovered that banking was "a watchful, but not laborious trade," leaving him time for journalism, for which he had outstanding flair. His outlets included the *Economist*, whose editor, James Wilson, took him up. In 1858, Bagehot married Eliza, Wilson's eldest daughter; he was made a director, and on Wilson's death Bagehot in 1861 became editor. Bagehot had a sense of phrase, a taste for tidy contrasts, and the gift of mental economy. He wrote of a premodern "age of custom" when power was exercised "by tradition" and a modern "age of change" in which power was brokered "by discussion." He wrote fluently about banking and trade from direct experience in terms that people who worked in them could understand. He distrusted abstractions and admired Adam Smith not least, as he put it, for impressing "practical men by his learning, at the same time that he won them by his lucidity and assured them by his confidence." Economics, Bagehot thought, studied actual episodes and arrangements. It should be more historical than hortatory. Walras and Marshall sought to show what economics could not tell us about how to live. Bagehot struggled to heed that same lesson, while finding it irresistible to draw lessons from what economics did say.

No natural democrat, Bagehot feared the mob and the unlettered working class. As a monarchist, he welcomed the British crown's factitious air of tradition as a dignified distraction for the masses from where power really lay: among the "efficient" parts of government, as he called them in *The English Constitution* (1867). His hopes for order lay in the rationality and effectiveness of financial and administrative elites. His emphasis on the theatrical elements in politics and the masking of true power was cool, even cynical. Though expressed in softer terms without a hint of anger or violence, Bagehot's low view of the ordinary person's capacity for sound judgment was little different from the elite "realism" of Marx and Weber or the irrationalism of Sorel. Bagehot thought electoral democracy inevitable all the same while hoping that its deleterious effects might be muted by ensuring that the working class had more schools, better morals, and greater comforts. In the 1870s he came to accept the working-class vote, as well as votes for women, whose work and capacities he believed political thinkers generally had underrated.

"I covet power, influence," he told his fiancée, but he lost three elections and never entered Parliament. Bagehot influenced opinion, rather, through what he knew and wrote. His grasp of banking was unequalled. Gladstone judged him "a supplementary chancellor of the exchequer." In *Lombard Street* (1873) Bagehot urged the Bank of England to acknowledge that it was a central bank and act according to its duties, tightening money in good times, and flooding markets with liquidity in bad.

Bagehot's reconciliation of liberalism and tradition presumed on customary social stabilizers that were vanishing as he wrote. He distrusted presidentialism of an American kind and prized parliamentary government, even as the growing executive power of modern states was making it hard for parliaments to do their supervisory work. The modern state was the preoccupation of Paul Leroy-Beaulieu, Bagehot's French counterpart who lived enough later to face difficulties the English liberal had only glimpsed.

Leroy-Beaulieu's father was a liberal notable in the July Monarchy, a friend of Guizot committed to the interests of an educated, well-to-do bourgeoisie. The elder Leroy-Beaulieu owned land in Normandy, rose to be prefect of the Lot, and after 1848 moved without difficulty into unbroken service of the French state as a conservative supporter of Napoleon III. The son Paul was a German-trained lawyer, journalist, and economist. Like Bagehot, he married into the business. His wife was the daughter of Michel Chevalier, the first professor of economics at the Collège de France and a free-trader who negotiated the Anglo-French commercial treaty of 1860 with Richard Cobden. In 1878, Leroy-Beaulieu took over his father-in-law's chair.

In writing about politics and economics, Leroy-Beaulieu had a new tone and approach: cool, assured, factual. He had no historical grand narrative, save perhaps that liberal capitalism now ran to a horizon beyond which none could see. He made money in the markets and invested in new brands standardizing local specialties such as Roquefort cheese. He tipped stocks and shares, encouraging investors to abandon an old French preference for houses and land. Those who listened made a great deal of money from government and railway bonds, though they were brutally punished by the post-1914 inflation if they had not got out in time. About parliamentary democracy, as opposed to the presidential kind, Leroy-Beaulieu was open-minded to the point of fickleness, though he approved of universal suffrage and, like Bagehot, believed in votes for women. As a carper from the outside, Leroy-Beaulieu viewed the Third Republic's parliament as incurably corrupt, though he softened on finally winning a seat after many tries and some bribery of his own in 1899.

In *The Modern State*, Leroy-Beaulieu accepted that democracy and the modern state were here to stay. The challenge to liberals was to cope with their powers. The rise in state spending was alarming and regrettable, he judged, but in a woeful underguess, thought that at 10 to 12 percent of gross domestic product state spending was reaching a natural limit. Like Bagehot, he had no time for "economic anarchists" who thought that economies organized and stabilized themselves, and he derided "nihilists of government" who dreamed of a minimal state. Pure thought here was little help, he believed. States were good at some things, bad at others.

The power of the modern state was new and disturbing in two ways, he thought. Government was no longer more reasonable and competent than those it governed. It was open to passions and fads. It heeded special interests more than the common good, and its officials had no personal stake in government's success or failure. Either they grew cynical and slack or turned policy to their own ends. The modern state was new, second, in having no competitors. Without competitors to sharpen them, states did too many things badly. Here was public-choice theory in germ: state action tended invariably to be partial, self-serving, or inept.

Where the maxim "Create wealth!" gave no answers, Leroy-Beaulieu was largely at a loss. Raising France's birth rate? Greater social cohesion? National decline? Leroy-Beaulieu exercised himself about them all. An ardent imperialist, he believed that national power lay in colonies: "The nation that colonizes most is the premier nation," he wrote in *Colonization in Modern Nations* (1874), "and if it is not today, it will be tomorrow." Yet, anxious about costs, he asked himself how colonies were to be defended and paid for. Leroy-Beaulieu closed *The Modern State* by tacitly admitting limits to his business liberalism, without being sure where they lay. He fell back on the familiar liberal cure-all of better character. Civilization was not the spreading of knowledge and technology alone, he wrote. True civilization required good habits of initiative, voluntary activity, thrift, and taking responsibility. Here spoke Humboldt and Samuel Smiles, but decades late. For the "new liberals," to whom the story now turns, that old liberal message was no longer credible. Education took too long. Character was too elusive and unreliable. Society's challenges were too urgent. Something new was needed, and the new liberals found it in the state.

ii. Hobhouse, Naumann, Croly, and Bourgeois: Resisting Markets on Behalf of Society

In Britain they talked of "positive freedom," in Germany of "social liberalism," in the United States of "new democracy," and in France of "solidarity." Their banner terms varied, but their cause was the same. Describable collectively as "new liberals," they won the liberal argument between 1880 and 1914 over calling on the power of the state to tame the power of the market. Because free-market purists denounced new liberals as nonliberals, the "new liberals" took pains to stress their continuity with tradition. In freeing liberal thinking from a cramped understanding of liberty and the conceptual snares of individualism, they hoped to show what standing up for people and their freedoms required in the fast-changing conditions of modern life. Economically, the new liberals believed that societies were now rich enough to turn a growing "social surplus" to public uses. Politically, they urged bridge building, large alliances, and middle ways in the spirit of the German new liberal Friedrich Naumann, who liked to say, "In politics, there are no absolute friends or enemies."

Inspiration in Britain came from the Oxford philosopher T. H. Green (1836–82), a teacher of generations of students who absorbed his ethic of social responsibility. Green's pupils included several future liberal politicians—Herbert Asquith (prime minister), Edward Grey (foreign secretary), and Alfred Milner (colonial governor in South Africa)—as well as numerous high government officials and liberal intellectuals. Green's aim was to demythologize Christianity, retain its more pacific and charitable moral messages, and apply them to politics in ways that appealed as much to imperatives latent in the social facts as to exhortatory preaching.

Green's lecture "Liberal Legislation and Freedom of Contract" (1881) gave vivid expression to an idea about the requirements of liberty that served the new social-minded liberals as a sort of pass key in their arguments against small-state liberalism. The idea was this: unless people had the capacity to use liberty for the pursuit of worthwhile ends, it was hard to say what, if anything, liberty on its own was worth.

Historically speaking, liberalism on Green's account had faced negative and positive tasks. The negative tasks—resisting absolute power and privilege, and removing restrictions on production, work, and trade— were now largely achieved. The positive task of empowering people remained unfinished. The question for liberals, Green believed, was no longer, "Do state and society let me alone?" but "Do they help or hurt in my realizing my potential?" The state, he argued, should create "conditions of freedom," that is, conditions for the free exercise of people's capacities. Social constraints on freedom were many: drunkenness, bad housing, shortage of work, and underused land. If the state stood by and did not remove such obstacles, it was a victory for negligence, not for freedom. By freedom, Green wrote, we "do not mean merely freedom from restraint or compulsion." Freedom included rather "a positive power or capacity of doing or enjoying something worth doing." Freedom of contract, the legal element in antistate liberalism, was for Green "valuable only as a means to an end." Liberties, he was saying in sum, had little worth in themselves without capacities to exercise those liberties.

Green was aiming to win recognition for the existence of common duties to promote people's capacities, whoever they were. As laissez-faire liberals had long objected that such duties interfered with liberty, Green had to answer their complaints. His reply was that those common duties did not interfere with liberty properly understood. Liberals could invoke the notion "liberty" in many ways, and none of them dominated though they might well obfuscate. Green's thoughts about obfuscatory liberal uses of the concept of liberty were widely shared. In "Individualism and the Intellectuals" (1898), Emil Durkheim complained of a constrictive, negative understanding of liberty. Naumann in Germany voiced much the same idea in homelier terms: "You can be free only when you know how you'll make it through the month." Different views existed among liberals as to how far state and society had responsibilities to help citizens and not simply step out of their way. It sloganized rather than clarified matters to pose that dispute as an argument about the true character of freedom.

The British Liberal who best popularized the "new liberal" ethos was Leonard Hobhouse (1864–1929). Liberalism ran in the family. His grandfather was a Gladstonian law lord. At Oxford he studied and briefly taught philosophy, but found it too removed from politics for his taste. Next he wrote, edited, and reviewed for the liberal *Manchester Guardian*—322 long pieces in one year, he claimed. He bridled equally at journalism, a profession, he moaned, that "may be carried on by persons of independent means or by people without conviction." He settled down finally in 1907 at the London School of Economics as professor of sociology, a new subject in England, and stayed there until the end of his career. Tall and stocky, Hobhouse wore a walrus moustache shaggy enough to hide the least trace of a smile. He tended to depression, was often ill, and wrote, prolifically, on his nerves. He despised hunting, an emblem of aristocratic excess, and loathed cars, cherishing instead the thrifty freedom of the bicycle.

The attitudes were typical of someone caught between ages. Intellectually, Hobhouse's voluminous writings floated uneasily between bold nineteenth-century synthesis and careful twentieth-century analysis. In *Liberalism* (1911) Hobhouse's experience as a journalist served him well. It gave a short, authoritative statement of new liberal ideas, with their strengths and weaknesses. Hobhouse rose above the contest "individualist versus collectivist." To the extent that the contest marked a disagreement about ethics, liberals, he suggested, were surely both. A healthy society mattered only because it mattered to the people in it, he wrote. To that extent, liberals were individualists. Much that mattered to people, on the other hand, was social. Everyone took or had an interest in society. Liberals to that extent were collectivist. They recognized, in other words, both private and public values. Not all collectivists did. Socialism, Hobhouse thought, went too far in giving public and collective values undue priority.

As for liberty, Hobhouse took it for a historical catchall. Liberalism arose on his telling in resistance to "authoritarian order," be it religious, political, economic, or moral. Liberty's banner had flown over resistance in nine distinct struggles: equality before the law; protection from arbitrary taxation; personal freedom of movement, thought, and religion;

equality of opportunity; the economic freedoms of establishment, employment, and trade; protections of children and family; national independence from control by other powers; world order of stability and peace; and finally for government by consent with a voice for all. Undaunted by such variety, Hobhouse wrote that, in each contest, liberty had removed an obstacle to "personal flourishing." Freedom and unfreedom mattered, Hobhouse was arguing, because they respectively enabled and frustrated the pursuit of worthwhile aims in life.

In scouring the past Hobhouse judged the laissez-faire of Manchester-school liberalism, though influential in the business press, a minor influence on serious liberal thought. John Stuart Mill's subtler Utilitarianism offered Hobhouse a possible ideal in the common good. That, too, he rejected, as pursuing the common good offered each citizen alone too little civic protection, which no liberal could allow. Hobhouse's own ideal "personal flourishing" raised an opposite difficulty. Why should my personal flourishing matter to you? Typically for the time, Hobhouse invoked cloudy organic metaphors of society in which wholes depended on the flourishing of parts. He wrote much on social evolution but, unlike Spencer, did not elide politics with biology. Hobhouse hoped, as had Mill, for the gradual emergence of fellow feeling. In the mutual advantage on which society rested Hobhouse saw potential for the growth of a deeper ethical harmony.

Hobhouse thought that state regulation and social intervention were desirable, though there was to be little or no public ownership. Nor should governments attempt to direct economies. He considered the "official" socialism of the Fabians and the Webbs illiberal, antidemocratic, interfering, paternalist, and technocratic. As to how the "social surplus" of a rich economy should be taxed, Hobhouse carried over the moralized distinction of Ricardo and Mill between hard-earned and lazily earned money. High profits, inheritances, and rising land values all lay within the taxman's grasp, not because they worsened inequalities but because they did not represent work. Hobhouse was no more forgiving about the idleness of the poor. Adopting Chadwick's harsh distinction, Hobhouse thought that the state should help only the "deserving" poor and that the self-pitying sloth of the "undeserving poor" should be discouraged. Politically, Hobhouse welcomed Liberal cooperation with the new Labour Party, which had already begun at Westminster. He pictured Labour as teacher might a pupil with little inkling of how soon Labour would be master. Labour, on the other hand, had little inkling of how thoroughly it would adopt Hobhouse's ideas.

In the United States, the intellectual voice of Progressivism was a small but influential magazine, the *New Republic*. Its editorial core was Herbert Croly, Walter Weyl, and the long-lived Walter Lippmann (1889–1974). The magazine's editor, Herbert Croly (1869–1930), was the son of two free-thinking journalists. His mother wrote a popular column on women's topics. Admirers of Comte, the couple had young Herbert "christened" in the "religion of humanity" and raised him with attentive freedom, teaching him to argue almost before he could talk. It took Croly until his late thirties to find himself, but he did with a bang by writing a book that spoke to his times and made his name, *The Promise of American Life* (1909). He was taken up by a couple of liberal angels, Willard Straight, a self-made investment banker, and his wife Dorothy, the daughter of the reform Democrat William Whitney, one of the nation's richest men. Theodore Roosevelt was a friend, supporter, and purveyor of Croly's ideas. With money from the Straights, Croly in 1913 launched the *New Republic*. The magazine was more political at times, more literary at others. It leaned left and it leaned right. Whatever its exact hue, the *New Republic* was a litmus of enlightened liberal opinion.

The Promise of American Life took aim, as Hobhouse had, at unbridled individualism. By that, however, Croly meant an economic, not an ethical, attitude. Croly took individualism much as Henry Sidgwick had in *The Elements of Politics* (1891) for a standing suspicion of overactive government. Such hostility had been apt in Jefferson's day, Croly wrote. Amid early harmony, the American ideals of democracy, freedom, and prosperity took shape in pioneer spirit, limited government, and trust in the promise of a new life. The present ideals were the same, but in a world of great cities, big corporations, and heavy industry, how to realize them, Croly wrote, was bound to be different. Private go-getting and passive government alone were no longer enough. The nation needed vigorous direction from Washington if it was to promote science, efficiency, personal fulfillment and social justice. Government had to be both democratic and effective: monitored at the polls but executed by unusually able people, saints and technocrats combined. What should happen if voters rejected the improvements to their lives of his social-minded aristocracy, Croly did not say. Nor as an ardent imperialist, like Roosevelt and the Straights, did he linger long on whether the rest of the world wished to be showered by America's liberal bounty.

Croly's weakness was a tone of elegiac carping known as "Crolier than thou." Closer to the ground and to reform politics was Walter Weyl (1873–1919), an early wonk whom Croly hired. Weyl's analytical mind was steeped in German method and German culture. He thought of politics economically, studying railway companies, immigration, and labor. His father, a Rhineland Jew, came to the United States in 1851 at sixteen. Young Weyl took a business degree and visited Germany, whose schools and universities impressed him, as they had Cobden. He noted how far real wages had risen and concluded in "Labour Conditions in France" (1896) that Marxists were wrong to predict progressive impoverishment.

Weyl summed up his own ideas in *The New Democracy* (1912). In wealthy societies there was now a "social surplus," usable to create a fairer, more balanced society. Unlike Hobhouse or Croly, Weyl thought that likely to happen not because of a profound and improbable ethical change but because of society's new shape. Pressure to change came from fifty million middle Americans. Above were twenty million too rich to care and below twenty million too poor to act. As a guess about where middle America would find its center of gravity in the 1930s to 1980s, Weyl was farsighted. Economically, his call for the "socialization of industry" fell predictably on deaf ears in a nation where government's indirect but massive and systematic support for business dared not speak its name. By contrast, Weyl's other causes—regulation, tax reform, "moralization of business," and limits to money's power in politics—were an uncontested part of the Progressive mainstream. Much like a better-known American, Thorstein Veblen, who complained of the economy's dependence on "conspicuous consumption" in *The Theory of the Leisure Class* (1899), Weyl worried about the pointless shopping to which wealthy societies were prone. Such "elephantiasis" was diversionary because excess money was often better spent on public goods like city parks and schools, as well as damaging because spare cash also encouraged unhealthy habits like smoking, binge drinking, and compulsive buying. Liberals, Weyl thought, should find noncoercive ways to discourage people from harming themselves and short-changing society in ways that they did not fully choose. Weyl's *New Democracy* remains remarkably topical.

In Germany itself, a pastor who turned to liberal politics, Friedrich Naumann (1860–1919), was a tireless reconciler, unable to see a disagreement he did not try to bridge. He worked for a progressive grand alliance uniting corporate Germany and the working class that would detach the big-business National Liberals under Ernst Bassermann from their conservative allies and bring them together with the Social Democrats under August Bebel. A minor core of open-minded liberals without ties of their own would arbitrate at the center of a coalition "from Bassermann to Bebel." It proved a fond dream, yet Naumann's hopes for a social-minded liberalism never wholly vanished, resurfacing in Germany after 1945. He preached sympathy for the poor but seemed to believe in a social-Darwinian "struggle for existence." His all-points commitments included democracy and monarchy, liberalism and imperialism. In the 1880s Naumann espoused Christian social aid. In the 1900s he called for a liberalized, democratic Reich. In 1915, he looked forward to a postwar federation in Central Europe under German leadership.

Early photographs of Naumann show a pale, earnest young man with searching eyes and a troubled brow. In an oil study for a portrait of Naumann around 1909, the Berlin painter Max Liebermann caught that same mix of anxiety and determination. He was born in 1860 into a family of pious Lutherans at Störmthal, a hamlet on a sandy lakeside southwest of Leipzig. He escaped to university, studied theology and became a pastor. Troubled, as were many like him, by urban poverty, Naumann did charitable work at Hamburg's Rough House, a North German equivalent to London's Toynbee Hall and Chicago's Settlement House. As a pastor, he won a name for the Lutheran directness of his tongue and pen. It irked him that middle-class liberals in their harshness were less help to the poor than were paternal conservatives and traditional churches. He fell in with and out with Adolf Stöcker, a Jew-baiting court preacher then exploring Christian socialism. Naumann founded a magazine, *Die Hilfe*, promoting similar ideals purged of anti-Semitism. Naumann then met and befriended Max Weber, who persuaded him that in politics national power and economic scale mattered as well as ethics.

Weber taught Naumann to think, like him, realistically in terms of economic interests, both class and national. To Weber, social peace between the classes depended on national prosperity, which depended in turn on German security and international power. Germany was held back in the world, Weber thought, because a "backward" landed class dominated politics. Business and labor were now Germany's natural leaders, though Weber was glum about their chances of working together and facing up to the nation's historic tasks. Naumann was more hopeful. In *Democracy and Empire* (1900) he proposed a grand alliance between business and labor, watched over by a beneficent kaiser, who was to personify not dynasty or caste but civic equality and a democratic sense of nation. This was liberalism of a limited kind. Naumann accepted the facts of conflict in Wilhelmine Germany. His hopes that conflict could be contained within German society as it was were wishful. Something similar affected Naumann's thoughts about German nationhood and position in the world.

His third search, like Bouglé's in France, was for an escape from vindictive kinds of patriotism. Nationhood for the German liberals of 1848 had been a positive idea: principled, inclusive, and progressive. After 1871, the German right had seized the idea of nation, making it atavistic, exclusive, and antimodern. For liberals of Naumann's day, it was becoming difficult to be patriotic without turning into a commercial imperialist if not a war-mongering jingo. Naumann exemplified that problem in small and large ways. An intellectual omnivore, Naumann had a strong interest in art and design. In 1907 he helped found the German Werkbund, an association of businessmen and designers. The aim was to give Germans better design. Antinationalist critics had little trouble turning the Werkbund's aims upside down and deriding it as a chauvinist campaign to make better design German. An equivalent inversion recurred on grander scale in Naumann's *Mitteleuropa* (1915), which looked ahead to a postwar German patriotism. Such a positive nationalism would, Naumann hoped, be liberal and inclusive, not chauvinist or domineering. The book envisaged a free-trading central Europe, federalized by treaty under democratic German leadership. As a guess about what would follow the breakup of the Austro-Hungarian Empire, Naumann's book misread the national aspirations of Germany's eastern neighbors and failed to gauge Slavic resentment at the German presumption of superiority, much as British liberals tended not to hear the resentments of Britain's colonial subjects. The Czech statesman Tomas Masaryk's *New Europe* (1917–18), with its call for self-determination of Slavic nations as a bulwark against "Germanhood," was a surer guide to the conflicting claims and divisive turbulence of postwar Central Europe. By the 1930s, Naumann's vision was understandably but unfairly dismissed as "Hitlerism light." Domination and conquest were not, though, Naumann's purpose. Stripped of its faults and turned West, not East, *Mitteleuropa* could be taken as an early German sketch of the European Union.

If one word catches what French reformers were working for it was "solidarity." A commodious term, stolen and stretched from Roman law, solidarity gathered Jacobin equality, Christian charity, and socialist fraternity into a serviceable modern ideal. Marx had renewed the term's progressive currency in the 1850s by persuading the International Workingmen's Association to use "solidarity" instead of "brotherhood," which sounded to Marx woolly and sentimental. French left-wing liberals took up "solidarity" as the marker for a middle way between working-class militancy and conservative reaction. The movement's little green book was *Solidarité* (1896), written by a radical prime minister, Léon Bourgeois (1851–1925). Its main thought, really its only thought, was simple enough: "Man is born in debt to human society," Bourgeois wrote. Every child came with a rich tool kit of capacities and utilities: language, culture, civilization, safety, security. Great or small, the singular achievements of any one person drew at profit on that common stock of human capital. By rights the achiever owed something in return: he or she should acquit his or her debt. Bourgeois ran with that metaphor of debit and credit in justifying what liberal reformers were doing to promote social welfare, labor peace, and civic protections.

Bourgeois was a man of the middle in more than name. A watchmaker's son, he was born between left-bank and right-bank Paris on the Île Saint-Louis. A clever product of republican meritocracy, Bourgeois at thirty-six was prefect of the Tarn, a southwestern department caught in quarrels between church and state, bosses and workers. He sacked a Catholic mayor who supported recalcitrant priests. When mine owners at Carmaux—later Jaurès's constituency—asked for police to end a miners' strike, Bourgeois refused, and arbitrated instead. As prime minister in 1895 Bourgeois fell afoul of a conservative Senate, much as Lloyd

George in Britain and the Progressives in the United States. The upper house refused Bourgeois's proposal for a progressive income tax, which had to wait in France another twenty years. Other French thinkers attracted to social liberalism included Durkheim, who had a subtler, more worked-though notion of "organic" society than Bourgeois, based on the interdependencies that arise for each of us from the modern division of labor; the economic historian and champion of mutualism, Charles Gide, as well as the legal scholar Léon Duguit, who promoted an idea of the state not as supreme and final power but as public servant.

Fiery as the contest between liberals for and against the state sounded, a great equalizer washed over their disputes. It washed over the subtly different appeals made by the social-minded new liberals. The equalizer was money. By the end of the nineteenth century, the House of Want and the House of Have were coming to agree on the need for a common roof. The harder question was how to pay for it. Social reform meant tax reform, and tax reform meant somebody would have to pay more. Those root tax-and-spending conflicts for liberals, old or new, were similar in Britain, France, Germany, and the United States. In their overall shape, they have changed little to this day.

The conflicts may be put as a trilemma. Liberals could have free trade, low direct taxes, and small government. That was the Gladstonian option. They could have high tariffs, low direct taxes, and big government. That was the Bismarck and American big-business option. Or they could have free trade, high direct taxes, and big government. That was the European "new liberal" and American Progressive option. Nobody could have low tariffs, low direct taxes, and big government for any length of time without running up unsustainable debts.

The Gladstonian option was no longer a serious choice. Liberalism's old fiscal wisdom, anticipated by Adam Smith, repeated by Mill and observed, more or less, by Gladstone was no direct taxes and balanced budgets. By the end of the nineteenth century that wisdom no longer paid the bills, for spending had grown. As in Britain, so in Germany. Business wanted state help in supporting profit and protecting capitalism from labor. The working class wanted state help in supporting living standards and protecting labor from capitalists. Everyone but pacifists wanted guns and battleships. The very idea of small-government liberalism as quintessentially nineteenth-century is, to a large extent, a polemical twentieth-century invention. Virtually all large interests wanted stronger, more effective government in the nineteenth century. It was only at the very end that government became capable of offering what interests wanted. The quarrel was over who paid. The late nineteenth-century budgetary choices narrowed accordingly to tariffs or income tax. The rich hated direct taxes and shared a preference with farmers for tariffs. The city poor hated tariffs, as they meant expensive food, and looked to income tax to soak the rich.

In confronting those choices, liberal Britain had a stronger, more active state than semiliberal, weak-state Germany. Thanks to a centralized treasury and public trust in taxes, Britain was better able than Germany to finesse its fiscal conflicts. British finances in the 1890s were better balanced. Though it spent more absolutely, only 40 percent of the Britain's central budget went on defense, compared to more than 90 percent of the Reich budget in Germany. Around 30 percent of British taxes were direct, whereas the Reich had virtually no direct taxes. Worse, the Reich had to share imperial tariff receipts with the states. When war came, Britain paid for it not just by touching Wall Street for cash but by taxing its own people. Germany paid for war almost entirely by borrowing. It thus created a burden of public debt that hobbled the new republic after 1918. It took time for liberals, new and old, to see the point. The hard and interesting arguments about state and market go nowhere when conducted in overgeneral, either-or terms. Virtually every attempt to turn "state versus market" issues into a matter of principle starts out with a favored answer to "Who pays?" In practice, state versus market issues turn on the structure and burden of taxes, actual or imputed, which once in place liberal democracies find very hard to shift.

That lesson about nettlesome, many-sided fiscal choices can be generalized. The deeper thrust of the new liberalism was that polar thinking—for example, "individualism versus collectivism," "market versus state," and "freedom versus intervention"—were not fruitful ways to think about how to realize liberal-democratic aims. New liberals could offer up polar opposites—negative versus positive liberty, inclusive versus exclusive patriotism, top-down versus bottom-up reform—as well as anyone. At most the poles told you, unhelpfully, to steer between them, but not where. Abandoning polar thinking was the new liberalism's deeper achievement. A counterattack against the new liberalism began, we shall see, at the end of the 1930s. It gained strength in the 1970s and began to prevail in the 1980s. That new attack used a pincer movement that contributed to its success. One thrust was to put polar contrasts— state versus market, individual versus society—back at the center of political argument. The other was to make resisting them sound like intellectual and moral weakness.

8

Damaged Ideals and Broken Dreams

i. Chamberlain and Bassermann: Liberal Imperialism

The liberal world of the 1880s to 1940s was an imperialist world. As the very term "liberal imperialist" has come to sound self-contradictory, it would be nice for present-day liberals to treat the liberal empires of the nineteenth century as a legacy left to reluctant heirs, much as Schumpeter treated it when in 1919 he called imperialism an unwanted "heirloom of the absolute monarchical state." Liberals, after all, resist power and resent domination, whereas imperialism involves domination of one people by another. How much easier for present-day liberals to suppose that empire had offended prudence and weighed on liberal conscience from the start. How much easier to surmise that a liberal West would have abandoned empire sooner had not twentieth-century wars and economic depression got in the way. How much easier, but how wrong. In truth, liberals created or extended the late nineteenth-century colonial empires. They defended them when needed with ruthless force. They abandoned them after 1945 largely out of overstretch and exhaustion, though not without bloody rearguard wars against determined—and equally ruthless—independence movements.

There is, though, a second truth about liberal empire. Colonization was not all rapine, domination, and unequal exchange. It was not only "despotism with theft as the final object," in the words of George Orwell. Liberal empire also brought progress and modernity in the form of schools, medicine, science, trade, and rising prosperity. Liberal empire brought the rule of modern law and property rights. It brought the humanizing aims of Christian missionaries with their gospel of personal respect. Empire, that is, brought things liberals believed in. That those things might have come in nonimperial ways does not mean that because they came in imperial ways they did not come at all. Nor were such benefits invariably imposed on unwilling or uncomprehending recipients. The liberal benefits of modernity were often sought for and welcomed by colonized peoples, a point of significance that introduces a third truth. The very image of active, single-minded imperialists and passive, bewildered subjects is paternalist and out of date. Imperialism involved give-and-take in both directions. Colonized societies were not inert, uniform dough. Their peoples did not live in primitive equality. Their precolonial masters were commonly crueler, more exploitative, and more domineering than the imperialists. Slave traders, it will be remembered, were Africans. Postcolonial elites after 1945 found national independence a boon. Postcolonial non-elites often found national independence a tyranny. To grasp the links between liberalism and imperialism we need subtler, less chalk-and-blackboard terms than "contradiction."

A start is to acknowledge rival longings in the liberal breast. The longings are for distinct homes in which liberals can practice their politics and pursue their dream of order. One home is national, the other global or universal. Liberals on the one hand want a secure and tranquil national home for their rights to be protected in, where money may be made and where capital they have sent abroad can flow back to, a home for people to take pride in and, when necessary, feel ashamed about. They long for a unifying whole without hierarchy to which all can feel they equally belong. They want a place for "us" to sense enough togetherness to be able to settle differences by argument and bargaining rather than by warfare that divides a familial "us" into combatant "thems." Such a home is the liberal nation, a useful, indispensable setting for the realization of liberal ideals but without distinctive value on its own. That idea of the nation inspired the American Federalists in the 1780s and the French republicans of 1789. It inspired the German liberals of 1848 who wanted German unity in peace and—some of them at any rate—in democracy.

Liberals, on the other hand, are also wanderers. They want to be free of home ties, to go anywhere unmolested, to be welcomed to trade, to settle or leave as they choose, and to send passportless money wherever they wish. They want to be at peace with everyone and for everyone to be at peace with them. They want, above all, people to be able to take their gods, attachments, and ideals with them wherever they go and not abandon them in the soil they leave behind. At the same time, they want people to be able to cut their roots and adopt foreign gods and attachments as assimilated immigrants in freely chosen new lands. Liberals, that is, want everyone to be at home anywhere in a homeless world. The liberal wanderer's dream of a universal home is a very old dream. It was a Roman dream and a Christian dream. It was not a Greek dream, for whom home was the *demos*, the city. If you take the Jewish dream of a national home as metaphor for sanctuary from hatred and prejudice, then the liberal wanderer's dream was also a Jewish dream.

Liberal empire was a happenstance creation of missionaries, teachers, buccaneering adventurers, and capitalists, no doubt. But over its unpredictable and improvised making floated those contrasting dreams: of a universal home and a national home. Once those dreams are distinguished, the awkwardness with late nineteenth-century liberal imperialism becomes clearer. For a liberal universalist, *liberal* and *imperial* sit happily together. The stress pulling liberals apart is between *imperial* and *national*, between universal and national homes. The awkwardness is less with *liberal* empire than with *French* Empire, *British* Empire, *German* Empire.

Although the term "imperialism" is frustratingly loose, we recognize land empires when we see them: the Roman or Habsburg Empires, for example. We allow for likenesses, recognizing quasi-empires, whatever we call them. Global reach of a commercial and cultural sort that crosses national frontiers backed by formidable state power and norm-fixing influence—think of the late twentieth-century United States or China now—has imperial aspects without adding up strictly to empire. Around 1900 liberal and Marxist writers gave currency to the idea of economic imperialism. They treated the administrative and territorial aspect of the colonizing empire as secondary or dispensable. The essence of economic imperialism in their minds was the rich world's capacity to exact undue commercial advantage.

It is compressing only slightly to say that though Britain and France had extensive colonial possessions earlier, liberal imperialism in the expansive and administrative sense here began in earnest only in the mid–nineteenth century. Britain's colonial reach included control or sovereignty in Singapore (1824), Hong Kong (1841), and Lower Burma (1852).

Direct administrative responsibility for India was finally thrust on West-minster after the Indian Mutiny of 1857 that ended the East India Com-pany and cost John Stuart Mill his post as a London overseer. West In-dian sugar colonies, a supplier of capital and stimulant of demand for nascent British industry in the previous century, were becoming eco-nomically marginal, threatened by new cane fields in India and Australia as well as by European beet production, falling sugar prices, and deathly conditions on exslave plantations. To the north, Britain had lost its lower American colonies in 1783, an unexpected stroke of fortune en-abling Britain to focus on industry rather than Atlantic trade. In 1868 George Gilbert Scott's Italianate Home and Foreign Office building opened near parliament beside St. James Park, a structure so imposing that it was hard for any who saw it not to suppose that the people in it had an imposing empire to run. In fact, Canada, whose French-English tensions, as well as its size, made it hard to rule from London, had won self-government the previous year. Australia's six colonies managed their own affairs, supervised distantly from London with a return-mail time of months. Britain's Cape Colony, threatened with commercial ir-relevance when the Suez Canal opened to India-bound shipping in 1869, was saved by rapid exploitation of diamond discoveries shortly before and by the gold finds of the 1880s in the Transvaal, the neighboring Boer republic.

For France's part, its colonial governors struggled to impose order in Algeria decades after French troops occupied the country in 1830. Mili-tary rule was in time lifted but reimposed after an Algerian revolt in 1839. On a visit two years later Tocqueville complained of the blood-shed—"They," he said of the Arabs, "not we are the civilised ones"—largely because armed repression was not effective in establishing un-challenged French control, of which he fully approved. While quailing at its methods, Tocqueville strongly supported French colonial expansion, which, as a French nationalist, he thought vital for keeping up with the British. French pacification of Algeria took three decades. Napoleon III's vain support for a conservative Mexican empire under French influence ended humiliatingly in 1867. The more successful elements of his foreign policy focused less on colonial expansion than on European power poli-tics, resisting the Russians in the Crimea and the Austrians in Italy, and striking trade agreements with Britain and Prussia. The French presence in Indochina was so far small. On unification in 1871 Germany had no colonies to speak of. Nor had German a word of its own for them. A language hostile to Latinisms since the Reformation and ever resourceful with Germanic alternatives had no time to invent its own word and used the imported *Colonie*. The United States, recovering from civil war and barely stabilized as one nation, had strictly speaking no colonies at all.

Imperial change was then sudden and rapid. In 1870 Algeria was divided into three *départements* and incorporated into France. French Algerian deputies sat in Parliament in Paris, though Algerian Muslims were denied French citizenship. France quickly spread its colonial hold across Indochina, as well as West and Central Africa. Léon Bourgeois wanted income tax in 1896 partly to pay for the occupation of Madagascar, where French troops had with avoidable but characteristic brutality removed a local slave-owning monarchy. In 1882 Britain took control of Egypt, now strategic for British India. Bullied by German colonial boosters, Bismarck accepted in 1884 that Germany should join the "scramble for Africa." A world power, the boosters shouted, required colonies. Bismarck was dubious but gave in because African colonies struck him as an affordable sideshow to the main game of power politics within Europe. After Bismarck's dismissal in 1890, doubts fell away, politicians demanded Germany's own "place in the sun" and by the end of the century *Weltpolitik* or imperial expansion on a par with Britain, France, Russia, and the United States had become German policy. In 1898, the United States annexed Hawaii, and after victory in the brief Spanish-American War that year, extended its protection to Cuba, Puerto Rico, and, brutally, the Philippines. By the 1900s Western control, through colonies or protectorates, stretched to Africa, Indochina, Central America, and the Pacific. In China, the four powers extended and defended trading rights exacted from the 1860s onward. Liberal empire had earned its name.

The rights and wrongs of the new imperialism wedged themselves among liberals, pushing some to the right as they saw the mass appeal of jingo patriotism and others to the left in a mixture of humanitarian disquiet for subject peoples and anxiety that colonialism was a distraction from social concerns at home. Whether for or against colonialism, all liberals kept an eye on its mounting fiscal costs. Liberal anticolonialists included British followers of Cobden such as the *Economist*'s Bagehot and the German liberal Richter, who likened *Weltpolitik* in a nation to clinical megalomania in a person. Two young radicals, Georges Clemenceau and David Lloyd George, were also among the early critics, although both men embraced empire once in office. Moral protest at imperialism was heartfelt but not widespread. It focused on the human harm of repressive wars and colonial massacres. The impropriety of foreign rule itself was a later concern. A garland of essays by British Liberals from the 1920s included these self-satisfied words about unrest in India from Sir Hamilton Grant, who judged that there was little need to look far ahead, that Mahatma Gandhi's agitations had "become a bore" and that Britain in its duty could continue to hold India "not by the sword but by integrity" expressed in "justice and disinterested efficiency." Few liberals talked of colonial peoples' right to self-determination until colonial peoples obliged them to. In his vision of postwar peace, the progressive Democrat Wilson championed self-determination for the peoples of the Habsburg Empire, but not for the "backward" peoples of the world, nor indeed for black citizens in Wilson's native South.

When the French liberal republican Jules Ferry said in 1884 that the "higher races have a duty to civilize the lower races," he was stating what many liberals took for a banality. They took it for granted that "civilized" peoples should if they could raise up "backward" peoples, and, to their minds, that educative mission justified a temporary tutelage. Mill had so defended British control in India as a self-abolishing exercise in political education. When an early nationalist revolt under army officer Urabi Pasha broke out in Egypt, Gladstone reluctantly lent his weight to a British takeover in 1882 with the thought that British occupation would be a passing lesson in respect for good government and order.

If political education was taken to involve learning by doing, the lesson tended not to include instruction in citizenship. In Britain's "nonwhite" colonies, most people remained crown subjects or "protected peoples," neither of whom had the political rights of British subjects. France offered colonial peoples French citizenship on paper, though only on condition they passed cultural tests of "assimilation," including the speaking of French. The rules were changeable and their application varied widely. The vague but handy French phrase "civilizing mission" gained authority, nevertheless. In *Does Germany Need Colonies?* (1879), the German colonial booster Friedrich Fabri nodded approvingly to

Leroy-Beaulieu's French jingoism and wrote admiringly of Britain's "cultural power." In spreading their national spirit to the world, Fabri urged Germans not to lag behind. Rudyard Kipling, in his poem the "White Man's Burden: The United States and the Philippine Islands," which appeared in *McClure's Magazine* in 1899, urged Americans to join Europe's mission: "Take up the White Man's burden, / And reap his old reward: / The blame of those ye better, / The hate of those ye guard." All of them were respinning in their way what liberal Lord Macaulay had crisply said in 1833 when calling on Britain to improve its rule in India: "By good government we may educate our subjects into a capacity for better government." Macaulay could have been talking of suffrage reform. The liberal-imperial attitude to "backward" peoples was little different from theirs to unlettered, propertyless voters in their own countries, though with a wider field of view. The "capacity" of both needed bettering, and it fell to liberals to conduct the reform.

In liberal tutelage and belief in progress on which it rests, critics came to see liberalism's original sin. The colonial tutor in human progress, they insisted, could not help but turn tyrant. Liberalism and imperialism did not stand in contradiction. Far from it. Liberalism entailed imperialism, and in its cruelest aspects. For pupils will rebel, and teachers must punish them for rebelling. Liberals could reply that there were no necessities here, that some colonialists were worse than others, that the benefits outweighed the costs, and that the native subjects whom liberals punished so harshly in their colonial wars were often doing as bad if not worse to their neighbors. Perhaps so. But how was anyone to weigh all that up, as if totting up a ledger?

The fact is that in raising up backward peoples and showering them with the boons of modernity, the governments of liberal civilization had them killed at the same time in tens of thousands. Between 1871 and 1900 it is estimated that peaceable liberal Britain engaged in twenty-two colonial wars of significant scale. Zulu warriors resisting British troops in South Africa in 1879 fell to modern gunfire in horrifying number. In Sudan in 1898 according to contemporary estimates, several thousand followers of the late Mahdi, Muhammad Ahmad, an anti-British prophet, died in a morning. One witness to the massacre was an adventurous young journalist-politician, Winston Churchill, who called it a "signal triumph" by "the arms of science over barbarians." Pacification slipped easily into annihilation. In German South-West Africa in 1904, General Lothar von Trotha ordered the "rooting out" or "extermination" of rebellious Hereros who refused orders to resettle on barren reservations. An estimated thirty thousand died, perhaps the first genocide of the twentieth century. In German East Africa in 1905–07, resistance to demands for cotton planting led to a war of pacification in which, according to a Reichstag report, seventy-five thousand Africans died. The anti-guerrilla campaign of 1899–1902 by the United States in the Philippines cost the deaths of an estimated twenty thousand independence fighters. Around four thousand American soldiers died, most from disease, while thousands of women and children perished in American concentration camps. Contemporary liberal outrage was fierce but rare. The Social Democrats and the Catholic Party objected to German policy in South-West Africa, but their protests were no match for a conservative press, which scared right-wing voters in the "Hottenot" election of 1907 into preferring safety from "reds" at home to justice and humanity for Africans. France's colonial wars, Britain's war against the Boers in South Africa, and the American war for Spain's excolonies were also popular wars. They became unpopular less for the harm done to "them" than for the cost to "us."

Certain liberal voices were raised against colonial brutalities. Emily Hobhouse, Leonard's radical sister, led protests against the high death rate in British concentration camps in South Africa. The French-English journalist and shipping official Edmund Morel exposed the genocidal management of the Belgian Congo. Theirs was an early recognition of the facts of colonial cruelty and with it an awakening of conscience that did not fully express itself in liberal doctrine until after 1945. That recognition plus awakening was prelude also to a shift in philosophical sensibility after 1945 from comfort with Utilitarianism to unease, and to a friendlier attitude toward rights. As the violences of the twentieth century piled up, doubts grew about the obviousness of the moral claim that great benefits for many outweighed grievous or terminal harm to a few.

Few liberals opposed colonialism on humane grounds alone. Most questioned whether the new colonialism was worth it to the colonizers. They disagreed over how to pay for servicing colonies and protecting them with large oceangoing navies. Should it be by income tax or tariffs? They argued over whether free trade was not outdated. Liberal

206 >> CHAPTER 8

imperialists wanted free trade to be replaced by state promotion of national wealth, much as laissez-faire was being replaced by state promotion of social welfare. The camps were never tidy. But roughly, liberal free-traders fought a losing game against liberal neomercantilism. It took liberal free traders until after 1945 to prevail once more.

Among German liberal economists Gustav Schmoller took a revisionist line on the universal benefits of free trade. Schmoller (1838–1917), who had founded the Union for Social Policy in 1872, was a proponent of historical economics. In *The Mercantile System and Its Historical Significance* (1883), Schmoller argued that England had reached the "summit of its commercial supremacy in 1750–1800" thanks not to free trade but to "tariffs and naval war." It was an irony, Schmoller added, that Britain now preached a narrow laissez-faire, telling the world that "only the egoism of the individual" was justified and that neither state nor nation counted. Schmoller was raising a neomercantilist standard. The "mercantile doctrine" was Adam Smith's term for nationalist policies aimed at strengthening home producers by promoting exports and limiting imports. Smith and Ricardo were taken to have holed and sunk mercantilist doctrine for good. Smith all the same believed strongly in British naval power. He approved of the seventeenth-century Navigation Acts requiring British trade to use British ships, which lasted until the 1840s. Sunken doctrines tend to resurface. After Europe's brief interlude of free trade in the 1850s to 1870s, neomercantilism was gaining ground, and not only in Germany.

France's midcentury experiment with free trade was under scrutiny. In the United States, an economic dynamo was being built behind a high tariff wall. Even in Britain, where free trade was a popular cause, liberal shibboleth and article of economic faith, free trade came under question. An interesting study was Leonard Hobhouse's friend and fellow member of the social-liberal Rainbow Circle, J. A. Hobson. Like other "new liberals," he turned to the state to improve the nation's welfare. He was neomercantilist in questioning free trade. Trade-dependent economies were vulnerable to non–free trade rivals, he thought. They were also structurally weak, as competing for foreign markets tended to depress internal trade and lower wages—an argument made by antiglobalists nowadays. He parted company with neomercantilism in rejecting imperialism. Exporting a nation's problems to the world in colonization and unequal exchange was, he argued, a bad solution.

In *Imperialism* (1902), Hobson described "the economic root of imperialism" as capital's need for foreign outlets. It was, he wrote, "the desire of strong, organised industrial and financial interests" to develop, at public expense and with the protection of "public force," private markets for their "surplus goods and their surplus capital." Imperialism, Hobson was saying, was the outward symptom of an internal crisis. People were spending too little. Business capital had too few profitable outlets in Britain. It was being driven abroad by a weakness of consumption. The idea of imperialism as capital's need for foreign outlets was adroitly purloined by Vladimir Lenin, who reused it in *Imperialism: The Highest Stage of Capitalism* (1917) as further evidence of capitalism's pending collapse. While faulting Hobson for confusing savings and investment, Maynard Keynes later praised him for recognizing a previously unsuspected malady, underconsumption. Once it took hold, an economy could not cure itself but required state help. Hobson's economic case has overshadowed his political concerns. He wrote also of the "political taproots" of imperialism: national lust for power, lack of democracy, and economic inequity at home.

He saw imperialism as a menace to peace, a military drain on national finances, and a tyrannical threat to "the institutions of popular self-government." Though his hopes darkened after 1914–18, Hobson was initially sanguine. A later edition of *Imperialism* (1905) even tempered his doubts about free trade and overseas investment: if pursued on fair, agreed terms and supported by democracy, they could together spread prosperity to lenders and borrowers of capital alike. Hobson's 1905 vision was in its way a global version of Naumann's *Mitteleuropa*. Such prospects were dashed in the liberal ruin of 1914–45, but revived afterward. Such arguments are still relevant. If unquestioning commitment to free trade is made a litmus of economic liberalism, then many of the politicians and thinkers of 1880–1945 who thought of themselves as liberals—as progressive defenders of capitalism, that is, who were neither conservative nor socialist—must be judged to have deluded themselves. A simpler and less dogmatic course excludes fewer from the liberal tent and better fits the historical and biographical facts. Free trade was a favored means to the liberal end of greater wealth for more people—a means to be judged, like any other economic instrument, by how well in any period it actually met that aim.

Two liberals who were both committed imperialists and opponents of free trade were Joseph Chamberlain (1836–1914) in Britain and Ernst Bassermann (1854–1917) in Germany. In many ways, they were counterparts. Both were businessmen-politicians. Chamberlain was leader of the Liberals' radical wing before bolting to the Conservatives as a champion of British rule in Ireland and defender of Empire Free Trade. From 1898 Bassermann was parliamentary leader of the National Liberals. His was the big-business party that had supported Bismarck in 1867 and now made a Reichstag bloc with the German conservatives. Both men thought in down-to-earth terms about economics and national power. Both saw imperialism as a relief from social tensions at home, much as Hobson, though in more favorable light. Hobson saw imperialism as a distraction from tackling social conflict; Chamberlain and Bassermann looked to it as an avenue of release. Chamberlain had begun as mayor of Birmingham, a liberal champion of "municipal socialism." Bassermann led a party that belied its weak national profile by running many of Germany's big cities. Both hoped ineffectually for cooperation between their countries, aware of the risks of mounting tension, but unwilling to abandon the pursuit of national rivalries.

Chamberlain began on the liberal left. In 1885 he put his name to the Radical Programme, the work of a Liberal Party ginger group that shocked Gladstonian traditionalists. The Radical Programme combined old Liberal Party demands (land reform, free schools, religious equality, and local government reform) with new policies focused on cities (rehousing, urban clearance, revaluation of taxable land). A particularly popular idea was for local authorities to acquire land for leasing as farm allotments. Most startling to older Liberals was the program's call for a graduated income tax to pay for social aid to the poor, sick, or unemployed. A very rich Birmingham manufacturer, Chamberlain thought others like him could well afford the tax and he had no qualms about involving government in the progress of his city.

As Liberal mayor Chamberlain took over water companies, cleared slums, and built better roads. Chamberlain's "municipal socialism" was not unique. Talking of "small-government liberalism" in nineteenth-century Britain is an equivocation. In local authorities that burgeoned after the Municipalities Act (1835), British liberalism created more government than most Britons had ever experienced. One aim was to take the running of cities away from Tory squires who owned city land. Another was for city government to do more as urban needs grew. The spending of central government, as a share of Britain's economy, barely grew between 1840 and 1890. Local government spending, however, grew fast, absolutely and relatively. By the end of the century, local government accounted for almost half British public spending. Chamberlain was not dogmatic. If there was a job to do and only government could or would do it, then theories should not stand in the way.

Chamberlain had a businessman's distrust of overbroad ideas and a nose for particulars. At the Great Exhibition in 1851, he saw an American screw-making machine better than anything to be found in Europe and bought it on the spot. Productivity in his plants rose, and he cut his work week. Chamberlain measured and costed everything—parts, times, discounts. On entering parliament in 1876, he took the same approach to policies. Did they deliver? Did they pay out at cost? On a requisite visit to Bismarckian Germany, Chamberlain saw prosperity at work and concluded that prosperity did not depend, as doctrinaire Liberals insisted, on limited government and open markets.

Chamberlain talked a radical line. He spoke of poverty and inadequate schools as a blight holding Britain back. To a degree he meant it, as did Conservatives pricked by paternal concern or attracted to the gospel of "national efficiency." It was becoming a commonplace among right-wing politicians and businessmen, particularly big businessmen, that workers were a national resource not to be neglected, squandered, or presumed on. In Chamberlain's radicalism, there was calculation as well as evangelism. He did not need the tendentious metaphors of the French solidarists or the idealistic sermons of the British new liberals to grasp that laissez-faire did not work, and had never worked. It was a doctrine, put about chiefly by publicists, with little bearing on what made businessmen money and kept their employees in work. Like Germany's Bismarck liberals and America's Progressives, he believed that higher pay and better welfare were good for business. He scared the rich by calling social reform, in Bismarckian tones, a "ransom" that they have to pay in order to hold on to their wealth. Nevertheless, on the toothsome issue of whether to pay for reform by taxing incomes of the rich or by taxing everyone through the restoration of tariffs, Chamberlain changed his mind. He ceased flirting with the idea of taxing incomes and sided with the rich. He abandoned free trade, championing instead open commercial borders within the British Empire and tariff barriers against everyone outside.

No party man, he wanted Gladstone's job and was happy to split the Liberals in half. Home Rule for Ireland, which Gladstone pressed for and Chamberlain opposed, was the immediate cause for their breach. The division ran deeper. They differed in their view of liberalism. Gladstone bridged Whig and Radical, the enlightened patrician with the self-made man. There was no Whig in Chamberlain whatever. Without Latin, Greek, country land, or metropolitan ease, he created his own social polish. He spent extravagantly and dressed ostentatiously with monocle and orchid, a foible of his, grown in one of his big Birmingham greenhouses.

Chamberlain was a new kind of British Liberal in other ways. He understood the needs of mass politics. Grassroots organizing, not stump oratory, was key for him. Like Gladstone, he understood emotion in politics, but in a colder, more openly manipulative way. Gladstone's sense of conviction moved people even if they did not fully take in what he was saying. Chamberlain was happy to appeal to the jingo in voters before appealing to their better natures. Whereas Gladstone was ambivalent and conscience-stricken about the British Empire, Chamberlain was uncomplexedly for.

With characteristic vision, Chamberlain used the empire to solve several equations in one: class conflict, economic weakness, and national decline. Britain would be the core of a strengthened and expanded empire of nations, some colonies, some self-governing, which would trade freely among themselves but keep out everyone else's goods with high tariffs. Revenues were to pay for reforms and battleships. The rich would escape income tax. Ordinary people would get cheap empire food. Without empire, Chamberlain foresaw Britain's slippage toward the status of "a fifth-rate power, existing on the sufferance of its more powerful neighbours." Chamberlain's vision was strategic, but it was overtidy, too business-minded and too expedient. He abandoned the Liberal Party, but his new Tory allies, aware of free trade's enduring popularity, rejected Empire Free Trade. Chamberlain then broke from the Tories again, splitting their support. In 1906 the Tories went down to calamitous defeat. Freed by a landslide, the minority Liberal government became a formidable majority that in a few years reshaped and modernized British politics. Without Chamberlain, but with Lloyd George and Winston Churchill, the Liberals put into law radical ideas that the changeable businessman from Birmingham had first espoused and then abandoned.

Ernst Bassermann (1854–1917) was a compromiser and not a campaigner. His was the liberal party that Bismarck had won over, used, manipulated, and outmaneuvered. Yet Bismarck was gone in 1890 and the National Liberals, like the Catholics, were now a swing power, leaning this moment left, that moment right. Bassermann had a pragmatic vision of liberalism as doing what it takes in a world of conflict and uncertainty. He and his party formed an unsteady bridge between liberalism and Bismarckism, between Germany's industrial west and Junker east, between reform and reaction. His world-weary face reflected his low expectations of what was possible from politics. Liberalism for Bassermann was less progress or reform than the containment of conflict and the brokering of interests. Bassermann had a triple strategy, not unlike Chamberlain's, for containing socialism: state-guaranteed welfare nationally, "municipal government intervention" in the cities, imperialism abroad.

Bassermann came from a cultivated and liberal-minded family that had grown rich in the late eighteenth century from vineyards and orchards in and around Mannheim, a town on the middle Rhine presided over by an enlightened, music-loving court. His father was a Frankfurt delegate of 1848 who killed himself soon after, in despair some claimed at the German liberals' defeat. Gustav Stresemann, the liberal hope of the Weimar Republic, was Bassermann's protégé. Bassermann belonged to a generation in movement from the constitutional liberalism of 1848 to an emergent, much contested liberal democracy.

A full-time politician from 1893, when he entered the Reichstag, Bassermann sat on several company boards and spoke for business interests in Germany's industrial west. As a cosmopolitan Rhinelander he found the hard, back-country world of the typical Prussian Junker culturally alien. Bassermann nevertheless preferred the Junkers as allies to the Catholic Center Party or the Social Democrats. Naumann's hoped-for coalition "from Bassermann to Bebel" would do much for Naumann's small group of brainy, ideas-driven liberals, Bassermann concluded, little for his liberal men of affairs, bankers, and company directors. A German nationalist, Bassermann argued for a big oceangoing fleet, for extending Germany's colonies and for expanding German territories in Eastern and Southeastern Europe. Like national-minded liberals elsewhere, he saw the wider world as a field of release from the dangerous pressures of urbanization and democracy at home. Rapid urbanization was the most visible social change in Imperial Germany, and it fell to liberals, particularly National Liberals, to run city government and spend money on the problems urbanization was causing.

There are grounds for forgetting finer gradations and calling Bassermann without ado a conservative. The National Liberals leaned to the right both on electoral grounds and for reasons of policy. Reichstag elections had two rounds. In city constituencies, socialists could block National Liberals from an outright win. To prevail on the second round, National Liberals needed conservative votes. As his party's leader in the Reichstag, Bassermann had a comically hard time finding safe seats for himself and knew from personal experience about liberal trouble at the polls. As a man of affairs he shared in full his party's distrust of Social Democrats. German big business was ready to pay for social peace, though on its own terms. It was against giving workers a say in how factories ran or letting social Democrats raise taxes. Bassermann was nevertheless thoroughly liberal in his commitment to civil liberties and toleration. In the 1890s conservatives tried again to suppress social democracy by bans and imprisonment. Bassermann's skillful resistance in the Reichstag killed the attempt. Prejudice, especially against Jews, revolted him. Bassermann was conservative with a little "c" for sure, but a conservative *liberal*.

Bassermann's main difficulty was the growing strain of keeping the "national" and the "liberal" bits of his outlook together. He faced the liberal problem of wanting both a national and a universal home. The strain that his father's generation of liberal 1848-ers felt about nationhood had grown worse. For the weight of "national" in Germany had changed. Previously, it was unarguably good to be national. Being national meant being for unity, progress, and legal equality in a shared land. By the end of the century, however, "national" was coming, internally, to mean something altogether different, more defensive, exclusive, and potentially punitive. Conservatives, once hostile to the nation, were now waving the flag against forces asking for more equality, for a bigger say and for less bossing about by others. Externally, "national" was coming to mean an extension of Germany's power, trade, and reputation abroad. Well before, in the late 1870s during the first assault against the Social Democrats, the main newspaper of the conservative right, the *Kreuzzeitung*, had venomously totted up those elements of a less exalted, more aggressive nationalism, throwing in religion and anti-Semitism for good measure. Socialism was the natural outgrowth of liberalism, the newspaper's editorialist wrote. Liberal anticlericalism had undermined religious faith, which bound the nation. As religion declined, materialism grew. Who best exploited material values? Jews in finance and commerce. And, given their divided loyalties—were they a faith or a nation?—Jews were not reliably German. Be a liberal if you wished. But to be a liberal German you must first drop your friends: the internationalist Social Democrats and the un-German Jews. The writer on the *Kreuzzeitung* had drawn a deliberately cruel picture of liberal homelessness within the German nation as conceived by the exclusionary right. The picture was to grow crueler with time.

Bassermann was a Germany-firster, but his chauvinism was not anti-Semitic. His Jewish wife was the daughter of a prominent Mannheim banker. His cousins married into Europe's upper-class Jewry. No, Bassermann's belief in the need to expand German power was not racial but geopolitical. Like many Germans in business and politics, Bassermann feared national encirclement. Breakout became a preoccupation. In a letter to the head of the foreign office in 1911, Bassermann wrote that, as other nations shut their markets to Germany, the nation must "expand if she does not wish to suffocate on her own population surplus, to the point where war remains as the only way out." He added that this was "the feeling of the thinking circles of the nation." When it came, Bassermann, like Georges Clemenceau in France and David Lloyd George in Britain, pressed for war to the finish. It did liberalism in postwar Germany no good that many Germans thought of 1914–18 as a liberal war, not to forget the hated liberal peace that followed. Nor was war damage to liberal hopes and liberal virtue confined to Germany.

ii. Lloyd George, Clemenceau, and Wilson: Liberal Hawks of 1914–1918

Verdun and the Somme were not on liberalism's menu. A liberal order called, surely, for invention and production, shopping and housekeeping, thrifty government, small armies, international fellowship, and peace. Commerce and openness were bringing comity among nations. Passion for your country in exclusive and destructive forms had proved a passing phase that large, prosperous trading nations were outgrowing. Twinned with democracy, liberalism was proving itself a more attractive alternative to class war or authoritarian order. Liberal nations were learning to negotiate their differences in similar spirit. So in August 1914 it was not wholly blind or complacent for Europeans and Americans to believe. By November 1918 it was pressing to ask how much if any of that had been true.

Warfare belonged in the liberal nightmare at its blackest. War was deviant and exceptional, an irrational throwback without place in the day-lit order they were hoping to create. Had not John Bowring—an early British liberal, Cobdenite free trader and Unitarian—got it right back in the 1840s when proclaiming that peace was "the normal, the natural state of human society?" For liberals to believe that in 1914 required, it is true, overlooking seventy years of imperial violence. But colonies were far away, backward and easy to overlook. It meant ignoring also an American civil war in which 620,000 had died. But that conflict did not count in liberal reckoning either, being a war of national unification, as were Germany's wars of 1864–71, which also discolored liberalism's half century of peace. Liberals could still bleach armed violence from their picture of the competitive but peaceful world they were creating by telling themselves that progressive modern nations, once established and stabilized, did not fight among themselves. For such nations had peaceful channels into which to direct their combative spirits. Here was a sensible resting place where liberal values and the persistence of conflict could find reconciliation. So it seemed reasonable to believe in 1914, which made the shock of what followed the greater. In "War Graves," a mocking short verse on the conflict's affront to liberal faith, a British historian, Godfrey Elton, replayed the classical Greek epitaph to the Spartan dead: "Tell the professors, you that pass us by / They taught political economy / And here, obedient to its law, we lie."[1]

It shocked liberals that such a war could be fought at all. The outbreak of war among modern, progressive nations in which both sides proclaimed that they were fighting for prosperity and civilization was surprise enough. A still deeper shock to liberal self-belief was that between the Western combatants in a sense the wrong side won. In their wartime propaganda, liberal Britain, France, and the United States positioned themselves as less autocratic, less militaristic, and more pacific than aggressive Imperial Germany. By the end, having forgotten how far their propaganda rested on misrepresentation of the enemy and self-deception about their own belligerence, they conspired to blame Germany for the war.

More thoughtful liberals saw that there was much explaining to do. The 1914–18 war provided evidence in abundance that liberal states were good at modern warfare, perhaps the best. They mobilized their people. They concentrated executive power and exploited financial leverage. They rallied an obedient press to speak loudly and eloquently with claims of morality and right. Not least, they found outstanding leaders able to pursue warfare with the required ferocity and ruthlessness: David Lloyd George, Georges Clemenceau, and Woodrow Wilson. Each of them began their careers with a genuine abhorrence of war but discovered in themselves, when called on, an implacable liberal warrior. Perhaps knightly and commercial virtues were not so different after all. Perhaps Mars himself was a liberal.

David Lloyd George (1863–1945) entered politics as an anti-elitist and pacifistic Welsh radical. A solicitor from a simple middle-class family, he positioned himself as an outsider standing for the "little man" against established church, landed elite and what he called the "peacockism of royalty." To Labour audiences he presented himself as working class. To Liberals he made out that he and his rival, Herbert Asquith, were from "similar stock and the like environment," although Asquith was a mill owner's son educated at Oxford with a rising career as a London barrister, whereas Lloyd George went straight from school to a provincial solicitor's office. As a young MP at Westminster from 1890, Lloyd George

1 Godfrey Elton, "War Graves," from *Winter of the World*, edited by Dominic Hibberd and John Onions, Constable & Robinson, London, 2008. Reproduced by permission of the publisher.

promoted Welsh causes: against Tory brewers and distillers on behalf of temperance, and against state aid to Anglican and Catholic schools that disfavored Welsh Methodism. Braving prowar hooligans who threatened him with violence, he spoke out against the Boer War.

The Liberal landslide of 1906 brought Lloyd George into the cabinet, first as a peacetime reformer, as we have seen, and then in 1914 as wartime chancellor, head of munitions, war minister, and finally prime minister. At the Treasury he raised taxes to pay for the war. To ensure war supplies, he brought in men of "push and go," commandeered the economy, and subordinated the unions. At the war office he harried "châteaux" generals to rethink their costly, murderous tactics. By 1916, when war fever had gone and volunteering was falling off, the Liberals split over conscription. Asquith fell as prime minister and Lloyd George took his place. Deriding calls for a negotiated peace as "cocoa slop," he pursued a "fight to the finish." When the end came, Lloyd George positioned himself at the peace talks in Paris as a bridge between the obdurate Clemenceau and the idealistic Wilson.

Lloyd George was charming and unbothered by detail. He surrounded himself with experts whose brains he sucked dry and whose advice he frequently ignored. Much of the world was a blur in his mind. At the peace conference when his foreign minister corrected him for confusing Ankara with Mecca, he said, "Lord Curzon is good enough to admonish me on a triviality." Always he kept the larger picture in his mind. Observers as different as Keynes and Churchill were awed by his depth of insight. Lloyd George grasped the power of public opinion and used the press with skill, working not through those who wrote newspapers but those who owned newspapers. In an old-fashioned way he continued at the same time to treat his job as leading, not listening. He was less clubbable, more professional, and more full-time a politician than earlier Liberals. The breach with Asquith, which split the party and began its decline, was partly social. Lloyd George's personal style reflected a broader decline of deference, class leveling and loosening of inhibition. Asquith could pass for a Liberal grandee, the lion of a politico-intellectual dynasty like the Russells or the Lytteltons. Lloyd George's friends were golf-playing businessmen, not writers, top-flight barristers, or scholars. At Westminster, Lloyd George lived openly with his mistress and adviser, Frances Stevenson, while his wife led her own life in Wales.

Together with his wartime cabinet secretary, Maurice Hankey, and his "Garden Suburb" of private advisers, Lloyd George created at Number 10 a new executive machine. It made the British prime minister's office more presidential, though without the irksome check of a balky Congress or an interfering Supreme Court. Critics might fault him for this departure from the liberal ideal of divided powers, but Lloyd George was acting in a long British tradition of unchallenged prerogative and centralized direction that no later prime minister seriously attempted to remedy once at the controls—a leading example of where British facts fell short of the common fiction that British institutions were a liberal epitome.

To many, Lloyd George was a schemer without principles. Margot Asquith complained that he could not see a belt without hitting below it. His friend the newspaper publisher, Max Beaverbrook, quipped that he did not mind where he was going so long as he was driving. A larger way to see Lloyd George is as representative of a new liberal-democratic politics: more blurred, less hortatory, more economic, and less partisan. It was a politics of the broad middle-ground, looking for compromise but aware of pressures from the flanks. "You are not going to make Socialists in a hurry out of the farmers and the traders and the professional men of this country," Lloyd George said in 1906, "but you may scare them into reaction." Unideological perhaps, his politics was not without ideas. After the war, he "brought ideas back to the Liberals," promoting new thinking about economic management, welfare, housing, town, and country planning. As an old lion in his seventies he made a fool of himself over Hitler on a visit to Berlin in 1936, calling him "the George Washington of Germany." But then Lloyd George was far from alone among foreign liberals in admiration for a dictator who, however regrettable his methods, had ended the street fighting, locked up communists, tamed Germany's trade unions, and, as they naïvely believed, silenced his own extremists.

It was not a mistake that Clemenceau would have made had he lived to see Hitler's rise. Suspicion of Germany organized his view of the world, which reached longingly across the English Channel and the Atlantic Ocean but was largely focused on France's rival across the Rhine River. Resistant to authority by background and temperament, Clemenceau used the power of the state, once in office, unremittingly. Though a generation older, Georges Clemenceau (1841–1929) was in many ways Lloyd George's French twin. He came from an old line of backwoods Vendée squires, proud of their independence, conditional in their loyalty to royal power and frankly hostile to the authority of the church. A great uncle had voted for Louis XVI's death and Clemenceau himself kept a bust of Robespierre on his mantelpiece. He knew how much the French Revolution had done for professional men of property like his father and grandfather, and he despised the liberal hypocrisy, as he saw it, of welcoming a "good" revolution with warmth while shuddering in horror at the "bad." He was eager for social reform but laughed at socialist dreams of revolution. A strong believer in capitalism, he was happy to please big business, but hostile to antimodern, less money-conscious forces on the French right: clericalism, monarchism, and xenophobia. For all his romantic attachment to the soil of western France, Clemenceau saw France's future not in farms and countryside but in cities and industry. A tireless reader and copious writer with many intellectual and artist friends, he had too skeptical a mind for liberal sermons about education as a cure-all for social ills and was too shrewd to swallow socialist claims to speak for the working classes.

Short, strong, and compact, he exercised every morning and rode in the Bois de Boulogne. An oil painting shows him in his forties on the hustings with receding hair and telltale moustache, as tough and limber as a lightweight in the ring. He was sharp and grumpy, and he enjoyed disconcerting more clubbable men with an earthy, sarcastic tongue. Of a long-winded socialist in the Assembly, he grumbled, "If I could piss the way he talks!" "All regimes," he would say, "end in crap." He had many mistresses, and he loved food and painting. Together in the Louvre in the 1920s one day he and his friend Monet played "What would you take if you could?" Monet picked Watteau's *Embarkation for Cythera* for its glittering light. Clemenceau chose Gustave Courbet's somber frieze of a country townspeople, rich and poor, come together in a hillside churchyard, *The Funeral at Ornans.*

Clemenceau trained, like his father, for medicine but rather than enter practice went to the United States for three years, where he marveled at American progress and democracy. He learned English, translated John Stuart Mill's critique of Comtean positivism, and married an American wife, Mary Plummer. He was habitually unfaithful and won a divorce once it was legalized again in 1884, though not before he had first shopped her to the authorities for adulteries of her own. Clemenceau's admiration for the "Anglo-Saxon" world, a characteristic of French liberals held against them by their foes, had few bounds. He dressed in English clothes and bought his furniture from Maples, a popular London shop. He was continually frustrated in his hopes that Britain would side with France in its running quarrels with Germany.

On return to France from the United States, Clemenceau entered politics as a radical, a term he defined as "the superlative of liberal." His baptism was the Commune of 1871. As a city councilor in Montmartre, he sought to mediate between the angry Paris crowd and the foolish, vengeful authority of the official government under Adolphe Thiers. When in May Thiers unleashed government troops on a starving city from which many of the rich had fled, Clemenceau barely escaped with his life, passing western checkpoints under the guise of an American. In the 1880s, he pushed for radical social reforms and opposed French colonial expansion, a distraction as he saw it from France's major concern with Germany. A business scandal in 1893 provoked one of several duels he fought during a combative life, lost him his seat in the Assembly, and almost ended his career.

Clemenceau's comeback began with Dreyfus. In 1894 his first reaction to the affair was to ask why a military court had favored a treacherous captain with mere prison when a halfwit corporal in an unconnected case had gone to the guillotine for insulting an officer. When the Dreyfus family began to win support, Clemenceau became their white knight. He put his newspaper, *L'Aurore*, at the disposal of their campaign to prove Dreyfus's innocence. Clemenceau became again a national figure, taking office as minister of the interior and in 1906–09 prime minister. The socialist left and reactionary right detested him alike. He supported the Carmaux miners in their campaign for better pay and safer conditions, and called for an income tax. He won a name at the same time as France's "top cop" by sending national riot police, a proud innovation of his, to put down strikes. He sacked striking mailmen and forbade teachers to take industrial action on the ground that for state employees to strike amounted to treason. Socialists like Jaurès, to Clemenceau's mind, understood little of economics or modern government and in their worship of popular power, which they trusted themselves to intuit and control, were little better than "red Jesuits." Above all, socialists to Clemenceau were weak on Germany, being pacifistic by inclination and further deluded by their faith in working-class internationalism. In the years before 1914, Clemenceau campaigned to raise the term of conscription to three years (lowered to two in 1902), whereas Jaurès and the socialists called for disarmament and a Swiss-like defense force.

In July 1914, Clemenceau, now in the Senate, voted with the right to pass a three-year conscription bill. "When our soldiers march towards the enemy," he explained, "republicans march with the reactionaries." Clemenceau, the mediator of 1871, had been reborn as a liberal hawk. Now in his seventies, he was re-energized by the conflict. In yet another of his many newspapers, *L'homme libre*, he harried the military brass on behalf of common soldiers. His reputation for taking their side told for him when his moment came late in 1917. French will had faltered. Troops were refusing to advance. A French spring offensive had failed at a cost of 150,000 casualties. Liberal doves such as Aristide Briand, Joseph Caillaux, and René Viviani joined socialists in calling for a negotiated peace. Liberal hawks were afraid that a country grievously damaged by war, and moving to the right rather than to the left, would not accept a peace with Germany that did not win back Alsace-Lorraine. Trusting that he was the man to push war to the end, the president named Clemenceau prime minister.

Push he did, though it was German failures in the late summer of 1918 and the final arrival of American troops that brought an end. Clemenceau's loudest supporters were now the nationalist right, his harshest critics liberal doves and socialists. He was ruthless with the "peace party" and shamelessly supported the prosecution for treason of its leader, Caillaux, a former radical ally and father of France's income tax. The liberal fear of Bolshevism that gripped postwar Europe completed Clemenceau's drift to the right. He favored French help for the anti-Bolshevik Whites in Russia's civil war even after the British had abandoned the counterrevolutionary cause as forlorn. This anticlerical radical and mocker of the church lived in Passy, a very bourgeois district of Paris, in an apartment overlooking the playground of a Jesuit school. His grave in the cemetery nearby is a conventional slab of stone, though a legend quickly spread that he had asked to be buried standing up and facing Germany.

Clemenceau's intransigent hostility to Germany was held to blame for the peace treaty presented to the Germans in May 1919. The treaty, its critics complained, was too feeble in its provision for implementation to be so harsh in its terms. The British pictured Wilson as a dreamer and Clemenceau as an obstinate troublemaker, with themselves, as ever, disinterested, practical-minded mediators. In truth, Lloyd George and the British pursued national interests as fiercely as did Clemenceau. Each of the allies pursued their own aims: Clemenceau to contain a cheated, vengeful Germany, Lloyd George to defend a weakened Britain's imperial position, Wilson to impose his ambiguous vision of "a new covenant among nations" in "a world safe for democracy" which his newly powerful, creditor nation would police and arbitrate.

Critics of the Versailles treaty focused on the harsh treatment of Germany and on Wilson's Utopianism. The peace took away German territory and colonies, severely limited German armed force and imposed punitive reparations. Maynard Keynes, now a young economic adviser to the British Treasury who attended the conference, wrote a damning appraisal that made his name. Wilson, in the eyes of his detractors, was an American innocent preaching to cunning, self-serving Europeans: they listened patiently to his sermons and then did what they were intending to do, pursue realpolitik. Wilson, besides, was without support at home. In truth matters were more complicated, as was Wilson himself.

Woodrow Wilson (1854–1924) was tall and bony, wore teacher's glasses, and had awkward false teeth that gave him a grimace in repose and made his smile alarming. Obstinate, sure of himself, and poor at picking his fights, he was, in the words of Hugh Brogan in his *History of the United States* (1985), hard to like but easy to hate. A southerner, with the prejudices of his background, he grew up in Georgia where his Presbyterian father ran a women's seminary. At the elite college of Princeton, he found himself an outsider among sons of the southern rich. Though not gifted for scholarship, he took to books as an escape. He worked his way through further degrees and began to publish academic articles. In 1902 he became the first nonclerical head of Princeton. He democratized the eating clubs but lost a pointless fight about the location of a new graduate school. For a man who gave his name to one of its traditions, diplomacy was foreign to Wilson's temperament. Even after leaving university life in 1910, he was happier at the lectern than the negotiating table. Encouraged by his friend and longtime aide, Edward House, Wilson ran for governor of New Jersey. Regional loyalty made him a Democrat. Under the populist Bryan, the party, however, had changed. It was more open, more national, less concentrated in the South. Democrats included prairie farmers and northern factory workers. The change opened national politics to progressive southerners. Wilson won the New Jersey statehouse and earned a reputation as a reforming governor.

Wilson set down his liberal outlook in *The New Freedom* (1913), drawn from campaign speeches. No one power should dominate, he believed, and government should not be lodged with one class or given over to a single interest. "America," he wrote, "was created to break every kind of monopoly." Liberal emphasis on respect for persons echoed in his worry that society and government had become "large impersonal concerns" and in his conviction that labor conflicts arose from "loss of intimacy." He favored freedom of a "positive" as well as of a "negative" kind, echoing T. H. Green's distinction. A believer in individual enterprise, Wilson nevertheless lamented the lack of "concert" and "common mind" that came with capitalist competition in a mass democracy. Order was as vital as competition to his mind. Like other American liberals, Wilson was troubled by the absence of authoritative elites in a "frontier" nation. Both for the creation of wise policy and to keep government honest, openness and intelligent and well-informed public argument were essential.

The American Founders, Wilson wrote, raised "a beacon of encouragement to all the nations of the world." Their aim was not for themselves but "to serve humanity." Wilson's understanding of his high-sounding principles was rich in ambiguity. He was against votes for women or black Americans in the South and spoke not a word against segregation there. He sent American troops to Mexico and Central America, justifying the intrusions by saying, "I am going to teach the South American republics to elect good men." For all his talk of standing up to power, Wilson used the full reach of the state in wartime against its own citizens, invoking the Espionage, Trading with the Enemy, and Sedition Acts to spy on troublemakers and suppress dissent.

When America did enter the war in April 1917, Wilson presented it to Congress as a noble cause, to "make the world safe for democracy" and, more hyperbolically yet, to "make the world itself free at last." America was not under attack, he insisted, and was not out for conquest. Then, as now, a war of choice by a liberal democracy needed justifying as a moral campaign for the defense of ideals. Such thoughts extended to the coming peace. Almost as America entered the war, his friend House set up a large team known as the Inquiry to think out postwar aims. It included the precocious Harvard-taught Walter Lippmann, who had a hand in drafting what became Wilson's Fourteen Points. Eight concerned territorial adjustments and self-determination of nationalities. Six set out principles for a new world order: open diplomacy, freedom of the seas, free trade, arms reductions, colonial "adjustments," and a League of Nations. Wilson's intentions were hard for Europeans to read. Was it to make a better world or to extend American power? To Wilson it was both. The United States needed to be strong to do good in the world. A better world needed a strong United States. Those aims were hard to disentangle in his mind.

In the American Senate, the League's main opponent was an austere, erudite Republican, Henry Cabot Lodge. Wilson was unlucky in such a foe. Lodge was not for keeping America out of the world. He himself had earlier proposed a League to Enforce Peace. From an old line of Boston shippers, Lodge was no isolationist. He was as committed as was Wilson to liberal internationalism, but of a unilateralist, not a multilateralist, kind. Lodge favored foreign engagements when necessary—on American terms. Lodge was more of a scholar than Wilson, whom he judged intellectually second-rate and whose smugness he detested. Lodge was a hater and Wilson was his biggest hate. Wilson nevertheless could have had his treaty, amended to give the United States leeway when coming or not to a fellow member's aid, had he agreed to compromises Lodge offered. Instead Wilson asked the Senate to take the treaty as it was, daring them to "reject it and break the heart of the world." Wilson's mixture of bombast and miscalculation is baffling even now in a statesman of such caliber over whom grateful Europeans had cheered and wept. On his vain cross-country campaign to win popular support for the treaty in the autumn of 1919, Wilson suffered a crippling stroke and lived out the sixteen months of his term a shadow president, spoken for by his chief of staff and his wife.

The Senate's rejection of American membership in the League of Nations provided historians with one of the early twentieth-century's big what-ifs. Had an active, engaged United States joined the League, might a liberal international order have been restored in the 1920s? America in or out, the liberal world faced many likely futures in 1919. A more tractable question is which futures liberals thought they faced. Their answers depended on how they accounted for the war. Was it intentional? An accident? A weakness of international order? Each answer had its adepts.

With a large measure of bad faith, the victorious allies committed themselves to the first explanation: the war had been intentional. Article 231 of the Peace Treaty, which obliged Germany to pay for the damage of war, implicitly blamed the conflict on German aggression. Germany's patriotic leagues, its Germany-first publicists writing of the inevitability of war, and the ever-changeable kaiser himself did indeed sound frighteningly bellicose at times in the prewar years. So did Britain's imperial jingoes and the revanchists in France. Since 1912, the German staff had planned for war. But war planning is what military staffs do, and though intentions may involve plans, plans themselves are not intentions. Tensions between the three Western nations were easing in 1913. Perhaps, then, they miscalculated, and war was accidental. Until the last hour, it is true, diplomats trusted as diplomats will that war might be avoided. When generals assured the politicians that war could be short, politicians heard that war would be short. The soldiers prepared for the worst, which when it came caused even them surprise. Miscalculation, however, is plausible when explaining the passing blunder of two or three powers. If it was all a mistake, why did the war spread so far and last so long? When the field of view was widened to include the initial combatants, Austria-Hungary, Russia, Serbia, and Turkey, the causes had to lie deeper, in a weaknesses of the international order itself.

Such questions were raw material for a new academic discipline that sprang up after 1918: international relations. Even before the peacemakers had left Paris in 1919 it was clear to thoughtful liberals that the treaty, shorn even of its follies, was at best a crude first sketch. Fresh thinking was needed about securing international order. The Carnegie Endowment for International Peace in Washington, DC, which was founded in 1910 and which had provided Wilson with four advisers in Paris, turned to the promotion of international law and arbitration. In 1918, a wealthy British Liberal and supporter of the League, David Davies, endowed the first chair in international relations at the University of Wales in Aberystwyth. With like purpose, the Royal Institute of International Affairs opened in London (1920), the Institut des Hautes Études Internationales in Paris (1921), and the Council on Foreign Relations in New York (1921).

Liberal thinking about international order was, then as now, divided. Some liberal foreign policy thinkers held a version of Bowring's "natural state of peace." Free-trading liberal states, in their view, did not fight each other. Wars arose because backward autocracies could not solve their internal conflicts. Schumpeter pressed a similar idea in "The Sociology of Imperialism" (1919), where he argued that liberal capitalism was essentially pacific. Other thinkers, less comfortingly, accepted the normality of war. Perhaps humans were by nature foolish and aggressive. Perhaps despite earlier liberal hopes, the scope for changing them by education and material progress was small. Perhaps, even if liberal nations were peaceful, enough autocracies and other politically "backward" states survived to cause war. Perhaps any state, liberal or autocratic, had to fight when the balance of power tipped against it too far. Whatever war's deeper causes, liberal thinkers focused on how to promote peace. So-called idealists, in the Wilson mold, looked to international law, regional and global institutions, and even, in time, world government. Their rivals, the realists, looked to the restoration of a balance of power among sovereign nations held at bay from each other in shifting coalitions out of mutual fear. A third group was the cosmopolitans. As had Constant and Cobden, liberal cosmopolitans placed hopes for peace on growing links among peoples, especially commercial and cultural links, that ran below and around state-state relations.

Liberal idealists, realists, and cosmopolitans were all obliged to face a new fact of lasting relevance to peace and war. The claims of the state had strengthened, not only in wider responsibilities and bigger budgets, but in the urgency with which the state's power was exercised and justified. In 1914–1918 Europeans and Americans had their first full sight of the liberal warfare state. Its profile fell in the 1920s and 1930s but then returned for good in the Second World War. After 1945, liberal citizens lived in a condition of semipermanent alert, governed by armed states ever ready for warfare in defense of liberal democracy. Liberal courts, legislatures, newspapers, and publics now consented with little question to the claims of a national-security state. Even before the First World War, acquiescence to a step change in state power was setting in. The mood was well caught by a moment during the 1911 debate on the Liberal government's proposal for an Officials Secrets Act in Britain. When a member, shocked by the danger to civil rights, objected that the bill "upset Magna Carta," the chamber broke into laughter. In the United States, the progressive senator Hiram Johnson summed up the spirit behind the Espionage Act (1917) and Sedition Act (1918): "You shall not criticise anything or anybody in the government any longer or you shall go to jail." Johnson's mockery did not prevent their passage.

For dedicated liberals it was all very puzzling. A terrible war that peaceable liberalism largely brought on itself contributed to a great expansion of that liberal bugbear, unchallenged state power. Liberal hawks justified war as a crusade for liberal or democratic values, much as Lincoln had first for national and later for emancipationist values. By an odd dialectic it also stimulated liberal dissent, as well as liberal defenders of dissent in court.

iii. Alain, Baldwin, and Brandeis: Liberal Dissent and the Warfare State

In September 1914, a French pacifist, Emile Chartier, volunteered as an ordinary soldier to fight in a war he thought immoral. Other pacifists were refusing to enlist or joined up as noncombatants in the medical corps. Chartier served at the front for three years, first in the artillery and then, after laming himself for life when an ankle caught in the wheel of a gun carriage, as a weather scout at Verdun. To his French newspaper readers and to his clever pupils at the Lycée Henri IV in Paris, Chartier (1868–1951) was better known as "Alain," a renowned teacher and nationally syndicated opinion writer. Nowadays he would be called a public intellectual. In his day Alain was the most famous one in France. His *Propos* or short think-pieces urged readers to challenge authority, distrust "importance," focus on particulars, and shun doctrinal "isms," earning them perhaps inevitably one of their own. "Alinisme," as it was known and spelled, was an everyday liberal distrust of power, a call for obstination and the digging in of heels. "Thinking," Alain liked to say, "is refusing." When war came he saw a hard choice between competing refusals that pulled him in opposite ways: going against his pacific beliefs or letting down his fellows. He picked the first. Others were going to fight, and it was no business of his, Alain thought, to put private conscience above civic duty.

In October 1918, an American civil-liberties campaigner, Roger Nash Baldwin, appeared in federal court in New York to answer charges for refusing to register for the draft. At President Wilson's request the previous year, Congress had passed the Selective Services Act. It introduced the first American military call-up since the Civil War. Playing on terms, Wilson called the draft "in no sense a conscription of the unwilling" but rather a "selection from a nation which has volunteered *en masse*." A social worker, probation officer and Harvard-trained lawyer, Baldwin dismissed such evasions. "Conscription of life," he told the court, was "a flat contradiction of all our cherished ideals of individual freedom, democratic liberty and Christian teaching." Though moved by Baldwin's plea, the judge sent him to jail for a year.

Alain and Baldwin represented distinct aspects of liberal dissent. Both objected to what power was doing, but each responded differently. To Alain, power, especially military power, was implacable. Power was alien. Alain felt allegiance to society, understood as local, collegial, and unthreatening, but wished for little or no part in power. Baldwin distrusted power, especially military power, but thought it could be checked and tamed through legislation and the courts. In that regard, exemplary disobedience could test and improve the laws under which power worked. Alain, the teacher and people's moralist, preached. Baldwin, the lawyer, organized and argued in court. On demobilization, Alain returned to teaching and writing, where his antimilitarism and his politics of "criticism and resistance" stamped generations of pupils headed for France's leading institutes and universities. On release from prison, Baldwin launched the American Civil Liberties Union.

Of blunt, Norman "peasant" stock, Alain looked down on ranks, honors, and fame. Though somewhat of a guru to admirers, he took an almost entirely negative view of authority. He urged readers not to be taken in by "the important personage," his term for the human mask of power that reappears continually in different forms. He urged readers not to be dazzled by specialists, administrators, and technicians, to involve themselves in local affairs, to join local associations, and to stand up to central government. He was for pushing back against the encroachments of state, the arrogance of elites and the stifling impositions of established churches. Business and the state were not so much opposing forces in Alain's eyes as twin expressions of dehumanized social arrangements that could be answered only by personal engagement and direct participation. Alain's negative message to keep technocracy and big government away spoke to radical voters in France, neither factory workers nor big businessmen, but "little" people in between, suspicious of the Catholic Church, socially progressive, and pro–private enterprise.

His positive message of politics as associational life in communities small and coherent enough to share common purposes echoed Rousseau's ideal that Constant rejected and Schulze-Delitzsch in Germany tried to realize. The message appealed more for its tone than its details. You should bring some "monarch" or other before the tribunal of the public every day, he wrote, for by taking a daily stone from the Bastille you saved yourself the trouble of tearing it down. The thought makes a certain sense of Alain's decision to enlist. By 1914, all options were bad in his eyes. He chose the less bad. The thing was for citizens to act in small ways to avoid facing themselves with none but rotten choices. Habits of quiet resistance could avert the unacceptable either-or of mutual slaughter or self-martyrdom.

Alain was vague about what such habits of resistance should be. From Alain's teaching his two most famous pupils drew opposite lessons. Simone Weil (1909–43) took Alain's radical personalism to heart. On finishing at the École Normale Supérieure, she taught in secondary schools, as required of French graduates to acquit society's gift to them of a stellar education. Weil then dedicated herself to confronting social injustice by direct action for workers' rights. She worked on the line at a Renault factory and took part in hunger strikes for the unemployed. She lived, and crippled her frail health, by pursuing a personal code of sacrifice for others and commitment to righting of particular wrongs.

Raymond Aron (1905–83), who became an unbullyable voice of French liberalism after 1945, took a sterner line with Alain's lesson in quiet rebellion. Aron blamed his teacher for encouraging unmerited disdain of authority and for contributing to a damaging separation of France's thinking elites from public life. Alain's high-sounding ethical standards were in Aron's opinion spurious and smug. They incited people not to engagement but to withdrawal. In a liberal democracy, Aron believed, a citizen could not adopt toward legitimate power the same attitudes he or she would take toward a tyrant in a despotic regime. Aron's criticism of his teacher sharpened when in 1934, as the menace of Nazism and fascism grew, Alain organized a French pacifist league.

Roger Baldwin, once free in July 1919, became director of the newly formed American Council on Civil Liberties, which had grown out of a loose alliance of lawyers defending conscientious objectors in the 1914–18 war. The son of a Boston manufacturer claiming old Puritan roots, Baldwin was an enthusiastic reader of Thoreau on civil disobedience and an admirer of the anarchist Emma Goldman's libertarian causes, though not her support for violent methods. Goldman, who was deported for her work, was one of many progressives campaigning for unpopular causes—women's vote, easily available contraception, acceptance of homosexuality—that liberal democrats now easily take for granted as somehow embedded in our societies as if by right. Baldwin grasped that matters were not so simple. What a person might in an abstract sense rightfully claim was one thing. What society and its laws would accept was another. In a liberal democracy, Baldwin concluded, the path to getting right and acceptability into better alignment lay in the courts. The courts were where you could argue out not just what the law was but what it ought to be.

Baldwin and the American Civil Liberties Union (ACLU) had plenty to argue against. In a postwar climate of revived white racism and anti-foreigner prejudice, authorities were rounding up radicals and deporting aliens. Federal courts backed the state's unchallenged authority in national security. State criminal courts if they chose could ignore constitutional guarantees of defendants' rights. Legal protections for trade unions, for sexual privacy, and for free speech were weak or nonexistent. Against that background, Baldwin and the ACLU provided counsel and help for countless liberal causes célèbres. It defended radicals prosecuted during the 1919–20 "Red scares" of the Wilson administration; the publisher of James Joyce's *Ulysses*; the Tennessee teacher John Scopes, prosecuted in 1925 for breaking a state law against teaching Darwinism; and the Italian immigrants Nicola Sacco and Bartolomeo Vanzetti, in their failed seven-year effort to avoid execution for the 1920 murder of two Massachusetts pay clerks. Social resistance to ethical tolerance was one element Baldwin had to face in changing American understanding of the law and what the Constitution should be taken to protect. Political fear of an ill-defined scourge known as "anarchism" was another. Mindful of both anxieties, Baldwin explained that the ACLU's aim was to give legal life to the civic protections declared in the Constitution. In doing so, he said, it had to be remembered that the Bill of Rights protected people you "feared as well as those you admired."

The radical anarchism of which Sacco and Vanzetti were suspected and for which Emma Goldman was deported was not the theoretical anarchism by which certain liberals were tempted. Radical anarchism drew on the thoughts of Sorel about the mobilizing force of random violence and on the hopes of Peter Kropotkin for more brotherly, less coercive sources of order than the oppressive state machinery that existing society had to offer. The anarchism that tempted liberals was by contrast more theoretical, a hypothetical starting point in an intellectual exercise of political justification.

The true line of separation between anarchism and liberalism lay between literalness and metaphor. Anarchists believed in the past or future actuality of society without a modern state. Liberals believed that as a matter of fact state and society were inseparable: you could not in practice have one without the other. A powerful strain in liberal thought continued to exploit nevertheless the old philosophical metaphor of a stateless society for the light it shed to them on coercive authority's limits, on people's moral independence, and on the legitimacy of dissent.

The American libertarian Lysander Spooner (1808–87) was, in the terms above, a literalist. He wrote to a friend in 1882 that the entire U.S. Constitution was an "utter fraud" without a shred of authority, because it had "never been submitted to them, as individuals, for their voluntary acceptance or rejection." Nobody was bound by duties they had not consented to, Spooner believed. "If a man has never consented or agreed to support a government, he breaks no faith in refusing to support it," he wrote in *No Treason* (1867). With that single thin blade of "No contract, no obligation," Spooner razored out whole portions of the familiar sociopolitical map. Great governments were all bands of robbers come together for the purpose of plunder. All taxation without direct consent was "plainly robbery." Spooner's "don't-tread-on-me" confidence and suspicion of experts had deep roots and long echoes in the "anti-intellectualism" that the historian Richard Hofstadter identified on right and left in American politics. Spooner was a reminder that anti-state anarchism was in itself neutral and that libertarianism may come in left- or right-wing varieties. Spooner joined Marx in the First Working Men's International. He loathed slavery, campaigned for abolition, supported trade unions, and called in 1880 for revolution as "the only remedy for the oppressed classes of Ireland, England and other parts of the British Empire." Spooner was interesting both in his own right and for running together and trying to answer at one blow elusive questions of consent—"Why should I obey the law"—with pressing questions of dissent—"When must I disobey the law?"

Anarchy and dissent both challenge power but work differently. The anarchist refuses to accept the existence of authority he or she has not consented to. The dissenter accepts the existence of authority but objects morally to what authority does. One appeals to personal will, the other to public conscience. The anarchist is not primarily concerned with the rightness or wrongness with which power acts but with the legitimacy of its authority. The dissenter is not primarily concerned with power's legitimacy but with the rightness or wrongness of what it does. The anarchist says of state and society, "I am not part of this and they have no hold on me." The dissenter says, "I am part of this and cannot stand aside."

The stance of reflexive dissent, much like anarchism, is a purist position, and liberals when acting in liberal manner avoid purism. Aron's complaint against Alain's antiauthoritarianism echoed Naumann's criticism of Richter's "oppositionism" in Germany. Both Aron and Naumann objected that dissent was being taken to extremes or turned into a habit. Alain, in Aron's view, made a program of dissent, much as Richter, in Naumann's eyes, had looked at what Bismarck was up to and did the opposite. Turning dissent into a policy became, on their view, hard to tell apart from anarchist insistence on prior consent. Making a habit of dissent tended to empty dissent of bite and risked making dissent itself a form of disengagement that could actually strengthen undue power. For rather than standing up to power, habitual dissent became blindly reactive and let power control the agenda. Against Aron and Naumann, on the other hand, it could be pressed that dissent needed exercise if it was not to lose tone, that dissenters ought to stay in practice, and that, without the exercise of dissent, the liberal ideals of personal independence and self-reliance were themselves thin and abstract.

For citizens of present-day liberal democracies, it is fortunate to live in societies where the more salient question of obligation to the state is taken to be "Why should I obey?" rather than "Have I the moral courage to disobey?" When commonly posed in such societies, the question of political obligation is usually made with a presumption that the state in question is reasonably just and that its legitimacy is not seriously in doubt. The theoretical point of asking "Why obey the state?" is to find reasons why you should, not to query whether you should. As posed in the classroom, "Why obey the state?" is put in the spirit of the recruiting officer who, to test loyalty and alertness, asked the peasant, "*Why* should you join the army?" rather than in the pragmatic spirit of the reluctant peasant who replied, "Yes, why *should* I?"

To those of strong nineteenth-century conscience like Thoreau, it was a duty to disobey when law enjoined you to act immorally. It was not that dissent was permissible when consent was absent. Rather dissent was obligatory when the state was wrong. Lawmaking authority might be fully legitimate. It might even have been, in some theoretical sense, consented to. Legitimate authority could still impose wicked laws. "When a sixth of the population of a nation which has undertaken to be the refuge of liberty are slaves, and a whole country is unjustly overrun and conquered by a foreign army, and subjected to military law, I think that it is not too soon for honest men to rebel and revolutionise," Thoreau wrote in *Civil Disobedience* (1849) of the American war against Mexico. When legitimate authority imposed wicked laws, Thoreau believed that higher principle called on citizens to disobey.

As liberals all hope for stable order without recourse to undue power, they are bound to argue about when dissent is called for. One thought to keep in mind is whether you are thinking as a citizen or taking the viewpoint of government. Radical liberals, who favor more dissent, tend to think as citizens, whereas conservative liberals, who prefer less dissent, think like governments. Despite the magical phrase "government by the people," rulers and citizens in liberal democracies occupy different roles with different priorities. Governments rule citizens. Citizens control governments. Regular elections are the most visible form of control. Dissent—be it public protest, conscientious objection, or civil disobedience—is equally vital. Whatever dosage of dissent liberals prefer, almost all now agree that dissent merits the protection of law. That was not always so. Agreement on what now feels part of liberalism's core took long to achieve and was hard fought.

An outstanding American defender of dissent was the liberal Louis Brandeis (1856–1941). As a successful private lawyer he made good money while doing public service work and supporting progressive causes, particularly the legal protection of working men and women. As a Supreme Court justice from 1916 to 1939, Brandeis defended rights of antiwar protest, free expression, and privacy against the intrusive claims of state and society.

He was born in Kentucky to Jewish liberals who had supported the 1848 revolution in Austria and escaped to the United States to avoid the repression and anti-Semitic reaction that followed its defeat. He spent school years in Dresden and on return became top of his Harvard Law School class. He was a ferocious worker, described in looks as "tall, spare, rugged, lightly stooping." As a "people's attorney" he fought unpaid for public interest causes, but earned around $75,000 a year—an income equivalent to perhaps $10 million in today's money. To Brandeis, there was no clash between private earning and public duty. Money for him was a source of independence, not pleasure or ostentation. He was simple in his habits and austere in manner. In person, many found Brandeis remote and exacting.

Brandeis's liberal beliefs were exemplary. He was negative about power, positive about human potential. Anyone entrusted with arbitrary, unchecked power was bound, he thought, to abuse it: "Neither our intelligence nor our characters," he wrote, "can long stand the strain of unrestricted power." Among law's main tasks, he thought, was to defend those with less power against those with more, be they agents of business or government. The positive aim of all public action, he believed, was "the making of men and women who shall be free, self-respecting members of a democracy." The fulfillment of human potential and open-ended personal betterment were overriding goals, above all through "broad and continuous" education. The words could have come from Humboldt or Mill.

Brandeis showed also an opposite thread in liberal thought. Not only ought people to be raised up. Brandeis believed strongly in letting people alone. In an early paper, "The Right to Privacy" (1890), Brandeis and a colleague looked over a number of laws forbidding intrusions of one kind or another on people's lives. What held them together, they argued, was a basic "right to be left alone" by fellow citizens, by law, and by government. That idea also ran through Brandeis's judicial career. In *Olmstead v. US* (1927), Brandeis wrote that government wiretapping was an unwarrantable intrusion on "the right most valued by civilised man": to be let alone. In the setting of American law, the rulings of Brandeis and like-minded judges were a bridging link between Constant's intimations of the need for moral privacy and the "permissiveness" of the 1960s and 1970s and beyond. Only then did liberalism acknowledge in law that moral matters previously policed by society, especially sexual matters, were not society's but men and women's own affair.

In 1916, when Woodrow Wilson nominated Brandeis to the Supreme Court, a former president and future chief justice, William Howard Taft, declared him a muckraker and socialist, throwing in the anti-Semitic slur that he was "unscrupulous" and of "infinite cunning." Brandeis argued for government regulation of workers' insurance by exposing the inefficiencies and anticompetitive practices of private insurers. He also believed that, if labor was not strong enough to bargain for itself, state regulation of hours and wages was required. He believed in freedom of contract but did not take that freedom for absolute or untrumpable. Facts here were Brandeis's starting point. In *Muller v. Oregon* (1908), Brandeis argued before the Supreme Court for a state law limiting women's hours under challenge from employers as an interference with their contractual liberties. Brandeis submitted more than one hundred pages of evidence indicating that long hours injured women's health. His argument was in effect that an otherwise compelling legal principle—freedom of contract—was to be judged among other things by the likely social consequences of applying it in the given case. The Court agreed with him. This kind of argument, which became known as "the Brandeis brief," pushed American law in a new, more social-minded direction and gave it a progressive, protective cast.

Once on the Supreme Court in 1916, his fame lay with the "Brandeis dissent." Within under a year, America was at war. Although Congress cut out the worst intrusions of Wilson's Espionage and Sedition bills, it passed them both, and government's powers to interfere with the press and to limit free speech were unduly widened. Wilson set up a propaganda office, the Committee on Public Information. Several lower-court judges, including the civil-libertarian Learned Hand, threw out the more absurd convictions, but many who spoke out against the war went to jail. By the time cases reached the Supreme Court, Brandeis flanked the great dissenter Oliver Wendell Holmes Jr. (1841–1935) in standing up for the appellants. Especially in war, Brandeis believed, a grown-up, responsible citizenry must argue openly about war's aims, its conduct, and its rights and wrongs. He objected to a Minnesota law banning the advocacy of pacifism. He objected to the continuing effort of his patron, President Wilson, to tame and muzzle the press. Ever suspicious of power, Brandeis saw no reason why in wartime patriotic Americans should rally without question to their president. Whether to change the law or to hold power to existing law, Brandeis took dissent as lawful and vital. Like Alain and Baldwin in their different ways, Brandeis recognized that dissent was in liberalism's lifeblood.

iv. Stresemann: Liberal Democracy in Peril

The enormity of what came after makes it even now very hard to think of Germany in 1918–33 through the eyes of those who lived then. Many Germans were anxious or aggrieved. Few felt fated. Almost everybody who thought about such things worried that Europe might turn on itself again. A minority of revanchists aside, most Germans greeted the international pacts of the mid-1920s with relief and joy. Whatever their hopes or fears, nobody knew that they were living between two wars or on the brink of a moral abyss. Looking back on his Weimar youth decades later, the German historian Golo Mann wrote, "In retrospect one tends to think that one foresaw 'history,' at least in general. In actual fact, I foresaw nothing." As he explained, "We had grown up in a parliamentary republic and took its existence for granted." He allowed that a sharper eye could have spotted dangers he missed but suggests that his placid outlook was the more typical. Take four fictional witnesses, the young Berliners in *People on Sunday*, a silent film shot in and around the city in the summer of 1929.

The two men and two women are on vacation from work. If they are thinking of the future at all, it is about who will end up with who.

Played by nonprofessional actors, the four go for a Sunday outing to Nikolassee, a fine lake with sandy beaches on the western edge of the city. They play, flirt, picnic, argue—one jealously breaks another's favorite gramophone record—watch a gymnastics club, and ride in a boat. The whole seventy-five minutes speaks of innocent, workaday satisfactions. There are no portents, no foreboding. When Robert Siodmak and Edgar Ulmer shot the film, the republic had stabilized. Stock markets had not crashed, banks had not failed, nor had tariff barriers cut off trade. The liberal statesman Gustav Stresemann (1878–1929) was at the height of his reputation as a force for compromise and apparently in good health. Things in Germany might yet have gone right. That is not to say that the message of *People on Sunday* was one of hope. It was not a message picture at all. It had a tone of voice, a quiet sympathy for everyday routines, disappointments, and excitements. The film ends with an inter-title "And on Monday, it's back to work." There is no fade to black, no looming catastrophe. As at the end of a Chekhov short story, life goes on.

Though they let it go again, by accepting the Weimar Republic a majority of Germans accepted liberal democracy. Some did it enthusiastically, some grudgingly, others barely at all. The 1919 constitution, though later pilloried and heavily blamed for what came after, represented liberal democracy's founding compromise: German liberals acknowledged democracy and German socialists accepted liberalism. The constitution swept away the class machinery of Wilhelmine representation and gave universal suffrage to all men and women older than twenty. It divided the state's powers and proclaimed, though without fully entrenching in law, personal and civil liberties. By accepting such liberal principles, socialists were agreeing in effect that claims on behalf of Germany's working class—taxes, welfare, regulating capitalism, public ownership—would have to be argued for, voted on, and pursued according to rules of law. By accepting a full voice in government for previously excluded majorities, liberals accepted modern democracy.

To speak in this connection of a "founding compromise" is more than philosophical metaphor. Late in 1918 as the old Reich dissolved into chaos, liberal-left councils took charge in big German cities. In December, their delegates met in Berlin to decide the shape of the new republic. Was it to be Soviet or parliamentary? The delegates—a mix of proto-

Communists, Social Democrats, and left-wing liberals—voted more than three to one to establish a parliamentary republic and for early national elections to a constitution-drafting assembly. The German masses had never really had a chance before to decide on what form of politics they wanted, not in 1848 nor in 1871. Given the choice in 1918, delegates in Berlin voted by an overwhelming majority for liberal democracy rather than Bolshevism.

What in detail German socialists and German liberals hoped to extract from liberal democracy was not the same. Deep conflicts of interest remained. Neither side trusted the other. Many liberals had supported Bismarck's anti-Socialist laws. Socialists looked for an expansion of social welfare. Liberals spoke for their backers in business, Social Democrats for the labor unions. Extremists on their flanks—Communists to the left and conservative nationalists to right—tempted both sides to abandon compromise and seek domination. A third "pro-Weimar" party, the Catholic Centre, broadened the middle ground but added the complication of Germany's confessional divisions. Though sympathetic to the socialists on questions of social welfare, the Catholics could not forget the early socialists' support for liberalism's anticlerical *Kulturkampf.* Many liberals, whose core strength lay in an educated middle class that was largely Protestant or Jewish, found the Catholic Party, dependent as it was on peasants and small producers, to be socially and intellectually irksome.

Despite those many-sided conflicts, all the pro-Weimar parties agreed on liberal-democratic rules for pursuing the political contest. For most of the 1920s a large majority of Germans wanted it that way. In the six years after 1923, when the republic stabilized, Social Democrats and the Catholic Centre Party dominated elections and governments. The once threatening anti-Weimar forces on the far left and far right became more tiresome than dangerous. Liberal democracy, it seemed, was taking root, and no German politician symbolized its growing strength more than the reassuring, bridge-building figure of Stresemann. When economic calamity struck at the end of the decade, for millions, there was suddenly no more "Monday, it's back to work." The correlation of forces changed rapidly for the worse and Germany's liberal democracy was again thrown into doubt. By then, Stresemann was dead, felled by a stroke at fifty-one, leaving historians with a nagging question of the kind they frown on but find it irresistible to ask anyway: had Stresemann lived, might he have made the difference?

On hearing of Stresemann's death on October 3, 1929, the German diarist and man of the world Harry Kessler, then in Paris, wrote of the popular reaction in the city. It was, he said, as if the greatest French statesman had died. Aristide Briand, the French left-liberal prime minister and Stresemann's ally in Franco-German rapprochement, murmured, "Order a coffin for two." The shock and dismay were greater yet in Germany. An estimated two hundred thousand people turned out to watch the funeral cortège in Berlin. For many Germans Stresemann had come to stand for the survival of liberal, civilized values in a political world that looked in danger of losing them. According to a recent biographer, Jonathan Wright, when seen strolling without a bodyguard in the streets of the capital, Stresemann presented an unthreatening, even vulnerable face of authority, and made people, it was said, feel safer.

Although in death Stresemann was eulogized as a liberal voice of persuasion and conciliation, in life he was a notably less straightforward figure. His ambiguities cast light on conflicts over democracy and nationalism within German liberalism, as on those conflicts within liberalism generally. How fully did Stresemann abandon the Imperial German past and embrace Weimar's liberal democracy? How genuine was his pursuit of peace with Germany's neighbors?

The anti-Stresemann prosecution had a strong case. Cartoonists liked to show him on a tightrope over a chasm or struggling to balance a swaying seesaw. The images became apt, but Stresemann had a distance to travel from the right before reaching even that precarious middle position. In 1914 he backed German entry into war, called for German annexations, demanded all-out submarine war, and in 1917 sided with the High Command against a negotiated peace. Like his mentor Bassermann, Stresemann believed strongly in Germany's colonial empire. As leader of the right-wing National Liberals after Bassermann's death in 1917, Stresemann did little to deflect the party from voting in turn against the armistice, the Versailles peace, and the republican constitution. After the kaiser's abdication in 1918, Stresemann flirted for some years with the fantasy of restoring the monarchy and, though his wife was of Jewish extraction, he was capable of anti-Semitic slurs when he found them politic.

The liberal parties continued to compete, and Stresemann shared blame for their failure to unite, which weakened the solidity of the pro-Weimar forces. Talks for an amalgamation broke down as left- and right-wing liberals indulged their historic weaknesses of poor discipline and an overabundance of chieftains. The left-wing liberals regrouped as the German Democratic Party. It drew the intellectual stars: not only Max Weber but also Hugo Preuss, a principal drafter of the Weimar constitution; Walter Rathenau, the industrialist and foreign minister, soon to be murdered by right-wing thugs; Friedrich Meinecke, editor of Germany's leading historical journal; and Georg Bernhard, who ran the left-liberal *Vossische Zeitung*. At one end of the GDP was its most eloquent mouthpiece, Theodor Wolff, the Francophile, internationalist editor of the *Berliner Tageblatt*. He was suspicious of Stresemann and looked to the socialists as natural allies. On the GDP's other end was the venerable Friedrich Naumann, still dreaming of a grand coalition that would unite socialists, liberals, and the nonextreme conservative right. The liberal business elite gravitated to Stresemann, whose National Liberals now took the name of German People's Party (GPP). It too had a left wing and right wing. The Young Liberals wanted social welfare and sought alliance with the GDP and the socialists. The right wing, led by GPP's caucus leader in the Reichstag, sought allies among conservatives.

Left-liberal doubters could sum up the case against Stresemann's liberalism in the claim that war and Weimar had changed too little in him and that he had not accepted democracy. Like Bassermann, Stresemann had treated social reform and imperial expansion as ways to win the working class to the Reich, much as they had used national pride to win the conservative middle class, soften religious controversy and quiet fears of radical upheaval.

The weakness of the view that Stresemann was no liberal democrat is that it blamed him for his past and stopped in 1923. The truth is that events changed Stresemann's outlook. Nationalist murderers in 1921 killed Matthias Erzberger, the Catholic politician who had signed the armistice. A year later right-wing assassins shot Rathenau to death in his car. After 1923, the year of all crises, even Wolff and Stresemann were partly reconciled. The far left, encouraged by the Comintern, staged uprisings in several cities. Such violence drove left- and right-wing liberals together. The force of events made Stresemann and liberals like him into pragmatic defenders of an embattled democratic republic. Under Stresemann's chancellorship from August to November the republic somehow survived an autumn in which, after German nonpayment of reparations, French troops occupied the Ruhr; the German government called for and subsidized passive resistance, helping cause a hyperinflation; Communists rose in Saxony and Thuringia; and fascists attempted a putsch in Munich. Caught between extremes domestically, the liberal-democratic middle had few alternatives but to try to crush them both. Short of another war, talking with France and its allies was the only visible path that lay open internationally.

Stresemann was born into the lower middle class of Berlin, where his father had a bar and a small business delivering beer. He was the youngest of seven. At school, he was better at writing than mathematics and thought of becoming a journalist. At Berlin University, in a survey of the political scene for a student paper in 1898, Stresemann found no adequate home for a social-minded liberal. He was against the intolerance of conservatives and anti-Semites toward Jews, of Protestants toward Catholics, and of socialists toward nonworkers and non-Germans. Unlike nostalgic liberals, Stresemann had no problem with bigness. In a university thesis on the bottled-beer industry in Berlin, his answer to the threats of big brewers to small delivery men like his father was to join up and build their own brewery. No foe of rapid modern life, Stresemann noted with approval how Berlin *Weißbier*, a drink to savor, was making way for Bavarian beer, a drink to gulp down, much as the slow-burning pipe was giving way to factory-made cigars and cigarettes. Nor did Stresemann lament that department stores were changing shopping. In restless change, there was a balance of minuses and pluses. Regulation, he concluded, was not the answer to the encroachments of big business. Rather, small firms should organize and compete. Stresemann followed through. First he organized Saxon chocolate makers into a league. Then he did the same nationally. It made his name politically. Stresemann's down-to-earth acceptance of an economics of scale marked a difference from the hopeful, Utopianism of Schulze-Delitzsch's localism and cooperativism. On entry into politics, Stresemann represented a new kind of figure, the representative of special interests, the lobbyist. It made his transition to national statesman all the harder.

Stresemann's speeches to the Reichstag and reports to his party offer markers of his political growth. His Reichstag speech of November 1923 defended his record as chancellor in imposing a state of emergency, deposing the Saxon government, and in stabilizing the currency on terms involving pain for debtors and creditors. His watchword was, "Not restoration and not counter-revolution, but evolution and co-operation." Scarcely any country, he said, was as racked by division as was Germany. Only by bridging them could recovery and stability be achieved. There was nothing to put in place of the republic, neither fascism nor Bolshevism. There was, however, a crisis of party, a failure to coalesce in the middle. Stresemann's telling speech against authoritarian nationalism and social revolution did not save him. Next day the nationalist right, the Communists, and the Social Democrats put down no-confidence motions, and when the vote came, Stresemann lost. "What made you overthrow the chancellor will be forgotten in six weeks," President Ebert is reported to have told his socialist colleagues, "but you will feel the consequences of your stupidity for 10 years."

At the end of 1926, in his message to his party, Stresemann spoke with guarded optimism. Now foreign minister, Stresemann was able to look back on his diplomatic achievements, provisional as both were: peaceful revision of Versailles and reconciliation with France. Germany had entered the League of Nations and won back operational sovereignty among nations. Despite hectoring from the right, his party had taken responsibility and made decisions. Not everything was right. There were still too few jobs. Yet the economy had stabilized and the "psychological crisis" of the republic had passed.

In 1929, Stresemann drew a starker balance sheet. A Franco-German alliance looked more distant, given a turn to the right in France. The socialists and his party could not agree on how to pay for a rise in unemployment insurance. Savings flowing from the Young plan for rescheduling German reparations would not fill the growing budget deficit. To the right, nationalist extremism, spurred and promoted by the press magnate Alfred Hugenberg, was again trying to make itself heard. Stresemann's concluding message to his party's Reichstag caucus was unambiguous: "We must work with the left, because parts of the right have gone mad."

By 1929 Stresemann's politics offered a set of clear alternatives to the poison of the nationalist right and the murky goals of now Stalinized Communism: peaceful revision of Versailles backed democratically by parliamentary authority with popular support as against abrogation by German *diktat* after suppression of republic institutions; international equality in Europe as against German domination; trade and cooperation as against national autarky; antiracism and tolerance as against anti-Semitic intolerance; persuasion and inducement as against demonization, threats, and force; balanced compromise; and mutual respect as against maximalism and exclusion.

At the time of Stresemann's death in 1929, the far right was in fact weakening. An anti-European referendum called for by Hugenberg and his extremist allies against accepting the Young plan failed miserably in December. On the other hand, the strains of finding agreement between business liberals and socialists over budgets and welfare were growing. Aggrieved national feeling was strong even among liberals. In *Land* and parliamentary elections, scared liberal voters were bleeding away to the right. With all his gifts for maneuver and persuasion, Stresemann would have found it hard to bridge those divisions, even before economic crisis struck in 1931. Probably Stresemann could not have made the difference. That the question was asked shows itself the peril German liberal democracy was in, for no liberal democracy is in good health if it looks for survival to one strong voice, however liberal.

Though the pro-Weimar forces did not save the republic, their failure was not inevitable. One factor that raised the odds against them was a social change that particularly affected the liberal parties. Whereas liberal parties had spoken most directly to the self-employed, Germany was now a society of factory and office employees. The natural audience for one of Weimar's three main defenders was shrinking. That put an extra weight of defense on the other pro-Weimar forces, the Catholics and the Social Democrats. Each distrusted the other. And both were harried on their flanks—by the nationalists to the right, by the Communists to the left.

Another factor was economic and affected all the pro-Weimar parties, just as it affected liberal-democratic parties elsewhere. The state was now materially involved in people's lives as never before. The state came less as gendarme, recruiter, or spy, more as tax officer, census taker, and welfare clerk. People feared the state less, but relied on it more. The greater risk to state authority was less disaffection or rebellion than exaggerated expectations and disillusion. Not only was the state omnipresent. It could now fail people, and when it did the political consequences threatened to be grave. In the crisis of the 1930s governments failed people in France, Britain, and the United States, where politicians and intellectuals also worried that their societies might not hold together and their way of politics might not survive. In those countries, liberal democracy had had more time and less taxing circumstances in which to embed itself. In fledgling Weimar, economic crisis became a crisis for the republic itself.

v. Keynes, Fisher, and Hayek (i): Liberal Economists in the Slump

By the 1930s liberalism's economic disappointments were acute. Confidence in free markets and limited government was seriously shaken. It took strong nerves in 1936 to agree with Maynard Keynes that capitalism, though given to "severe fluctuations" was not "violently unstable." Keynes proved correct, but for believers in the system the gap between turbulence and self-destruction seemed to have narrowed alarmingly. The crisis of the 1930s was on a new scale. Events were shredding liberal platitudes. Economies were not righting themselves when disturbed. Free markets were not bringing social peace.

Liberal belief in laissez-faire economics, never pure or wholehearted, had already weakened at the end of the previous century. The "new liberals" of the 1900s tempered free-market, small-government economics with insurance and welfare of a limited, if expandable, kind so as to cushion deleterious social effects of the market. In winning the battle for progressive income tax, they had broken a taboo against government redistribution of wealth. Save in Britain, free trade was no longer considered a semireligious mark of liberal principle, but treated as one tool of policy among others, to be judged by results. Thrown together in wartime cooperation, business and government discovered productive affinities of scale and organization neither had suspected, encouraging the idea that both could work together as well in peacetime.

Those were significant changes in liberalism's economic outlook. Yet they did not yet add up to a coherent new vision. In the 1920s much of the old "hands-off" faith returned. Indeed, for a time the course of events caused the old faith little serious challenge. A postwar slump of 1920–21 in Britain and the United States was brief. Germany's finances stabilized after the hyperinflation of 1923 with surprising speed. France in the 1920s broadly prospered. Internationally, a revised gold standard appeared to restore the prewar order.

The crisis of the 1930s broke the spell. Liberalism had confronted nothing like it before. Not only was the breadth and depth of the economic slump unprecedented. Liberalism, in its woes, now faced serious political competitors. Between 1929 and 1932, American output in money terms shrank by 40 percent. Joblessness in 1932 stood at 15 percent in Britain, 17 percent in Germany, and 22 percent in the United States. As liberal parliaments struggled without answers, Bolshevism and fascism loomed as appealing alternatives. Even before the slump, newborn or fledgling democracies in Russia (1917), Italy (1922), Poland (1926), and Lithuania (1926) had collapsed into one-party or strongman rule, or like Greece, had swung between democracy and dictatorship.

A convincing defense of the prevailing order needed accordingly an economic and a political part. The first had to show that capitalism could still be counted on to deliver on its promises: that a return to rising and shared prosperity would continue to underpin liberal democracy. The political defense had to show that the social order and stability that liberals craved was still possible on liberal terms. It had to show that the benefits of prosperity and social peace could be won without concession to domineering power and latter-day tyranny. The political underpinning and defense of liberal democracy takes up much of this book's next part after 1945, with an antitotalitarian prelude in the last chapters of this present part. The economic defense, the topic of the current chapter, preoccupied a new profession in which the voices of Irving Fisher, Maynard Keynes, and Friedrich Hayek stood out.

Each had his own diagnosis and cure for the economic crisis. Keynes treated the slump as a crisis of underspending. The collapse of output and rise in unemployment was in his eyes a failure of "effective demand" or spending power, particularly investment spending. The only immediate answer was state intervention to reprime the pump and make good the spending shortfall. Fisher believed that the depression's cause and cure were chiefly monetary. Bad decisions by central banks had turned a business slowdown into a slump. People who had borrowed cheaply in order to speculate during the pre-1929 boom were failing and defaulting as dropping prices now magnified their debts in real terms. The answer, Fisher thought, was a monetary reflation to raise prices again and reverse a potentially catastrophic downward spiral. Hayek agreed with Fisher that the cause of the depression lay in monetary disturbances but did not believe that government action could help. On the contrary, as artificially cheap money had led to "overinvestment" in the first place, monetary reflation in Hayek's view would make matters only worse. The same was true for him of government spending on public works. Either Keynes's or Fisher's course, on Hayek's view, stored up inflationary trouble ahead. The best answer was to wait for markets to correct themselves, chiefly by allowing money wages to fall.

Governments, it is worth recalling, were piloting by sight. They were improvising in new circumstances without clear ideas or ready answers except to do what they had done before. The notion of "managing" or "rescuing" peacetime economies was new in the 1930s. Politicians, treasury officials, and central bankers found themselves with responsibilities neither they nor voters had expected. They turned to economists for advice, but the advice given was conflicting or simply too new to under stand. In *Booms and Depressions* (1932), Fisher listed fifteen distinct theories of the business cycle. Confronted by such conflicting expertise, it is more understandable why some policy makers trusted to precedent, others like Franklin Roosevelt to improvisation.

In the 1930s, the influence of Keynes, Fisher, and Hayek was indirect. Keynes lectured, published, broadcast, and gave evidence to committees but did not strictly shape policy, except perhaps in Sweden, a forerunner in the economic compromise between liberalism and democracy and a pioneer of the twentieth-century welfare state. Only Fisher, by stressing the danger of falling prices, gave policy makers an overall rationale for choice among a range of discordant options, but principally in the United States and his more specific remedies were broadly ignored. The influence of the three economists became a factor in policy making later, and then on a scale that threw exaggerated light on their impact in the 1930s. Keynes's ideas for economic stabilization by government triumphed in the decades after 1945 and Hayek's anti-interventionism prevailed in the 1980s. Fisher's insight into the depressive risks of financial booms shaped the counterdeflationary money-creating actions of the Federal Reserve after the dotcom minibust of 2000 and the financial meltdown of 2008.

Keynes, Fisher, and Hayek are often treated as competitors. Their champions in later disputes paired each of them off against the others. When taken together, the contests made a confusing circle: do-nothing Hayek against interventionist Keynes; fiscal intervener Keynes against monetary intervener Fisher; monetary intervener Fisher against monetary do-nothing Hayek. There were genuine differences of explanatory focus and serious disagreements over policy. At a deeper level, they were all doing the same thing: looking for ways to limit capitalism's disruptive instabilities without injuring liberal principles, a breadth of shared purpose that is worth bearing in mind.

They grew up in a climate of late nineteenth-century economic ideas that were broadly these. Within nations, prosperity was best ensured when central government was effective but small, markets were open and competitive, and bosses and workers were free of legal interference to agree on wages and terms. Among nations, liberal economists thought that trade and investment should flow freely across borders, and people everywhere looked to the gold standard to provide stable, orderly money. For the understanding of the fundamentals of economic exchange, Walras and Marshall had offered a sharp, mathematical language in which to cast the explanatory idealization of competitive markets "clearing" at equilibrium when supply and demand balanced. The profession's grasp of an entire economy was hazy, however. National economic statistics were rudimentary. The word "macroeconomics" had not been heard of and demand management was unknown. The notion of experts and ministries diagnosing and directing a peacetime economy struck anyone who knew about the actual world of taxation, commerce, or banking—let alone the inept, underpowered, and, in the United States, corrupt condition of government—as apt for Utopian theorizing, not economics.

That mental world in which Keynes, Fisher, and Hayek had grown up was shaken in 1914–18 and changed for good in the 1930s. Like it or not, governments found themselves economically in charge during peace-

time in ways they had not expected and for which they were not adequately prepared. Though hardly in control, governments were now held
to blame. They turned to economists for advice and found that economists had little ready or relevant to offer. Economists in a sense were
having to reinvent their subject. They had in particular to acknowledge
the elephant in their equations, for one thing that had not reverted to
laissez-faire tradition with war's end was the size and weight of government. Particularly in Europe, government spending was now far beyond
the 10 percent of output that the French free-marketeer Leroy-Beaulieu
had at the turn of the century judged a "natural" limit. Average government spending as a share of the economy in France, Britain, and Germany had risen from 15 percent in 1913 to 26 percent in 1920. It was only
12 percent in the United States, but that was almost double the prewar
figure. With some urgency, economists were called on to tell governments what to do with this economic weight and how to meet the cry
from business and people alike, "Do something!"

Keynes and Fisher each represented a distinct line of economic reinvention. Keynes stressed the government's fiscal tasks of taxing and
spending. Fisher stressed the government's monetary tasks of raising
prices in a slump and then keeping prices stable. Hayek, positioning
himself as the keeper of an idealized nineteenth-century faith, insisted
that the older, limited government course was right: no reinvention was
needed, for none was possible. The idea of governments understanding
or diagnosing whole economies was, to Hayek, a presumptuous and
risk-filled delusion.

Those debates of the 1930s remain fresh because they involved different understandings of liberalism's economic compromise with democracy. Those in the free-market, do-nothing school were asking labor to
take the burden of adjustment to a problem of overinvestment, as they
saw it, for which government's monetary tinkering was mainly responsible and capital largely innocent. Keynes called on government, which
meant taxpayers at one remove, to take the burden of adjustment to a
problem of underconsumption caused equally by labor's reluctance to
take lower pay and capital's cyclical loss of nerve. In burden-of-
adjustment terms, Fisher was closer to Keynes's "everyone pays" than to
Hayek's "labor pays." The monetary authorities, Fisher believed, should
reverse the fall in prices and engineer inflation so as to rescue debtors.

Creditors would lose as the real value of their assets was eaten away, but they would lose even more, Fisher reasoned, if debtors did not repay them at all. Keynes, Hayek, and Fisher were all trying to save capitalism. They were not recommending that everyone be asked to pay an equivalent price for the rescue.

After his death, Maynard Keynes was turned into idol, scapegoat, pied piper, confidence man, savior, and sage. In life, he was none of those things. His family exemplified Victorian high-mindedness, hard work, and upward mobility. Its background was a "chapel and trade" nonconformism of this-worldly faith, self-improvement through education, and distrust of establishments, social or intellectual. A grandfather was a market gardener in Salisbury, a grandmother taught school. The Keynes family's move to Cambridge represented the emergence of a new elite, Britain's educated middle class, diverse and as yet tiny, but of growing confidence and sense of authority. Their son Maynard had both to the full.

Underpinning his assurance and self-assertion were brains, charm, focus, and energy, as well as a devastating temper. A scholar at Eton, he was bookish and athletic as a schoolboy, the first sign of what became almost a personal campaign to refute the law of life's excluded middles: practical *or* theoretical, commercial *or* aesthetic, gay *or* straight, left *or* right. After Cambridge, where Keynes shone, he combined often simultaneously the work of Whitehall civil servant, Cambridge don, financial investor, government adviser, and international monetary negotiator all the while editing the *Economic Journal* and pursuing literary-artistic interests amid a wide circle of intellectual and cultivated friends, particularly the members of the pacifistic and anti-imperial Bloomsbury group.

Keynes's economic theories grew out of a broader outlook. He was disenchanted, commonsensical, and skeptical about universal rational principles but not unprincipled in the ordinary sense. His own ethic centered on civilized pleasures, close personal relationships, financial independence, and public service. He stressed the uncertainty of human affairs and, in certain moods, the intractability of economic reasoning itself. In an attempt at encapsulation in 1937 he suggested that the main message of his work was to stress our inevitable ignorance of future interest rates and profitabilities. Despite the hostile misrepresentation of a frivolous radical intent on undermining individuality and destroying

enterprise, Keynes was anxiously concerned to save capitalism and preserve humane standards. He insisted at the same time that those were
distinct tasks. Prosperity, equitably spread, was a precondition for
human betterment but was not to be confused with betterment itself.
Like Mill and indeed most serious thinkers in the liberal tradition,
Keynes thought there was more to the good life than material plenty.
Wistfully he looked forward to a time when economics would matter
less in public affairs than he and his generation were helping to make it
matter.

Politically, Keynes emphasized caution and expediency. He saw himself as a liberal both in the broad sense of combining progressive reform
with respect for persons and in a British party-political sense. In the
1920s he was one of the leading ideas men that Lloyd George brought
back to the Liberal Party. At the time, the party was losing for good its
electoral position but winning the intellectual battle for a middle road.
Using Mill's word, Keynes treated the Conservatives as the "stupid"
party: hereditary, defensive, and bigoted. They offered him "neither food,
nor drink," and he found the thought of twenty years of government
under them appalling. In a lecture of 1925, "Am I a Liberal?", reprinted
in *Essays in Persuasion* (1931), Keynes said that the City and the Conservatives were "incapable of distinguishing novel measures for safeguard-
ing capitalism from what they call bolshevism." Labour by contrast was
the "silly" party. He sympathized wholeheartedly with Labour's passion
for social justice, its sense of public service and its resistance to making
profit society's end-all. He disliked on the other hand its anti-elitist resentments, which he believed obstructed progress by encouraging hostile reaction. Keynes was for leveling up, not down. Although the Labour
Party had a sensible wing that Liberals could work with, it was "flanked
by the party of catastrophists," the "Jacobins, Bolsheviks or Communists," who believed that the capitalist system was violently unstable and
replaceable by something quite other, which they were nevertheless unable to describe. He doubted that the sensible, "intellectual element" in
the Labour Party would ever exercise adequate control and that its path
would continue to be decided by those who "do not know *at all* what
they are talking about."

Between Conservative and Labour there was, he thought, room for a
Liberal Party "disinterested as between the classes." Its international

policies should be "pacifist to the utmost," with a guarded commitment to arbitration and disarmament. It should aim at "controlling and directing economic forces in the interests of social justice and social stability," but also decentralizing government as well as ending "medieval" laws on divorce, contraception, and sexual "abnormalities." In looking for labels, some have taken Keynes for a "new liberal," committed to social justice and economic democracy, others for a government-house, technocratic elitist. He was really an enlightened latter-day Whig, a modern-minded liberal concerned for social balance and keen for law and government to keep out of people's personal lives. In another essay, "The End of Laissez-Faire" (1926), Keynes summed up his attitude to government's proper role in an economy. Its "nonagenda"—what government should not interfere with or try to do better—was what people were already doing themselves. Its "agenda"—what government should do—was what nobody would do unless government did it. Those were not attitudes of a dogmatic or frivolous mind, but practical maxims of an experienced man of the world.

As a young economic official at the Treasury from 1915, Keynes advised the British government on paying for the war. The practical extent of his Bloomsbury pacifism was to side with government Liberals against conscription, which was imposed over their objections in 1916 as casualties mounted and voluntary recruitment fell. Keynes found his limit nevertheless at the Paris peace talks, where the French and British demands made of Germany appalled him. The reparations they were asking were not payable, he believed, and together with other punitive terms were bound to provoke German revenge. Keynes resigned in protest and put his charges into *The Economic Consequences of the Peace* (1920).

The book was a best seller and made Keynes's name. Its central claims about the avoidable errors of the postwar peace became for many people conventional wisdom. It exposed, as it seemed, the folly and weakness of elected politicians, helping in a way Keynes did not fully intend to sap confidence in liberal government. The book combined a grasp of international finances, a wicked gift for observing great men from close to, and a conviction that the peacemakers were preparing the ground for another war. Looking back after Hitler's rise to power in Germany in 1933, Keynes's claims did indeed look prophetic. Historians at longer remove have stressed the ocean of European contingencies in 1919–33, making it hard to plot a direct course between Versailles and Hitler. They have undermined in particular Keynes's principal financial claim that Germany could not have afforded to pay the reparations demanded by treaty, themselves a vastly larger sum than the renegotiated reparations Germany actually paid.

Keynes's fame might have rested there without the slump of the 1930s. Economic crisis drove him to pull together in one radical book his thoughts of two decades on money, jobs, and politics. Like Adam Smith's *Wealth of Nations*, Keynes's *General Theory of Employment, Interest and Money* (1936) was written to fight a tradition, change mentalities, and chart a new course of policy. Like Smith, Keynes did not conceal the moral and political dimensions of his economic thinking. These showed in a pair of ideas that had preoccupied Keynes since the minislump of 1920–21. One was that unemployment was an overriding moral harm, and that hard, immediate decisions were needed to avert its risks. "It is worse in an impoverished world," he wrote in *A Tract on Monetary Reform* (1923), "to provoke unemployment than to disappoint the rentier." A second preoccupation, expressed in the same book, was the sheer unhelpfulness of conventional doctrine in guiding policy makers. "In tempestuous seasons," he wrote, all classical economics could tell us was that "when the storm is long past the ocean is flat again."

As Keynes saw it, the do-nothing, free-market school was, crudely speaking, asking labor to take the burden of adjustment by accepting a drop in their spending power, either through lost jobs or lower wages. Unemployment, on that view, was voluntary: anyone could find work if ready to take a cut in real pay. The market for labor, like markets for anything, would clear at the correct price—at the level of price-adjusted wages, that is, where supply and demand for labor matched. Keynes found that "classical" answer unacceptable. The do-nothing answer, however, came out of a coherent, widely believed story of how economies worked. Keynes accordingly had to find his way into and out of a thick technical wood.

Keynes's argument in *The General Theory* worked by exclusion. The classicals were wrong that the answer lay in lower wages, for money wages were "sticky." Not only would labor resist pay cuts. Even if money wages did fall, the slump would not end, for falling money wages would mean less spending and smaller business profits. Here Keynes introduced the second player in his drama: business investment. Slumps originated in a collapse of entrepreneurial confidence and an attendant drop in spending on capital assets. Businesses invested as a rule when the likely return was more than the cost of borrowing. In a slump, businesses took even very low interest rates as a sign of sagging prices and collapsing profits, not as an invitation to take on cheap debt. In good times, money left over from consumption—savings, in other words—was channeled into capital investments. In bleak conditions of slump, savings were hoarded instead in a "liquidity trap." With wages stuck, business scared to invest, and savings idling in effect as cash, government spending was the one active variable left.

Each of those steps ran against what Keynes presented as traditional wisdom. The entire chain, indeed, worked in reverse to "classical" thinking. Keynes's chain started from an evaporation of "animal spirits" that drove investment and consequent collapse of capital spending that worked through to a drop in output and loss of jobs. His "classical" opponent's chain, as he described it, ran from overinvestment and overemployment to a sudden correction with declining output, and thence to a fall in spending and prices. On that older picture, the value of output offered for sale equaled the value of goods people would buy, whatever the amount of employment. Changes to spending or "demand" were effects, not causes. Less spending came because there was less work, and there was less work when wages rose out of line with business costs. In such conditions, profitability fell and business borrowing for investment dropped away. The machine would correct itself, however, if business costs were left to fall: if markets for labor and money, that is, could work freely and smoothly. As fewer were hired, wages would fall, and as demand for borrowing dropped, interest rates would follow it down. Once business's principal costs had fallen, hiring could begin again. Output would rise. Such self-correction, it was true, took time. The machine, however, could not settle into an "idle" where resources, above all labor, went unused. So-called involuntary unemployment was no more possible than was "underconsumption."

Keynes rejected that entire supply-side picture. Scathingly, he wrote of the doctrine "demand cannot fail to meet supply" that it had "conquered England as completely as the Spanish Inquisition conquered Spain." To the old economic law that "supply creates its own demand," Keynes offered a new one of his own: "Expenditure creates its own income." Close behind Keynes's economic target stood an ethical doctrine on which his whole attack was ultimately directed. Keynes was questioning the cardinal virtues of economic liberalism as then understood, hard money and thrift. Pursued in the wrong circumstances, he believed, such virtues became vices. Risking money, not saving it, drove capitalism, he believed. "If enterprise is asleep, wealth decays, whatever thrift may be doing," he wrote in the *A Treatise on Money* (1930), for "the engine which drives enterprise is not thrift but profit." Keynes's critics complained with some reason that his classical, do-nothing adversary was to an extent his invention, created for dialectical purposes. The economist Arthur Pigou, for example, was more classical in his mechanics than was Keynes, but agreed on the need for government action. A deeper criticism was of Keynes's treatment of wages.

His argument in the *General Theory* depended on the "stickiness" of money wages, on the assumption in other words that even in a slump, money wages do not fall. That assumption could be heard in different ways. Was Keynes saying that money wages do not fall or that they ought not to be allowed to fall? Either way, a line of criticism opened to which Keynes and his Keynesian followers remained ever vulnerable. The first was political: Keynes was too kind to the monopoly power of labor unions. He simply took it for given that unions would resist cuts to money wages in a slump and that resisting unions was neither politically practical nor humanly acceptable. A subvariant of that complaint was that Keynes was paternalist in attributing to people, especially to working men and women, a "money illusion." Was he suggesting that they could not *grasp* that if prices fell, say, 10 percent and wages fell 5 percent, their standard of living would rise? The second charge was economic: Keynes underplayed the risks of inflation. At the time, Keynes had a telling riposte to both complaints. In a falling-price slump, first, business confidence evaporates, whatever is happening to money wages. Joblessness rises, worsening the cycle. In the 1930s, second, mass unemployment, not inflation or union power, was the urgency of the moment. Both Keynesian ripostes became less telling when conditions changed. By the 1970s, the terms of argument had changed. Trade union power was a political issue, and inflation, not unemployment, was judged the bigger economic danger.

Soon after the appearance of the *General Theory*, John Hicks in 1937 compacted Keynes's argument into a clearer model, making the "classical" and Keynesian cases each special, not general. Both, that is, made particular assumptions about interest rates and investment that might not always hold. Classicals stressed conditions in which by pushing up interest rates, government investment crowded out the private kind and did not increase output. Keynes stressed conditions in which government investment raised output without pushing up interest rates. In the low-employment 1930s, Hicks judged Keynes's assumption more relevant for policy.

In stressing the uncertainty of future interest rates and levels of profitability, Keynes's point was partly philosophical, partly historical. Reliable probabilities, which he took for a logical connection between evidence and prediction, were in theory rational and calculable, but in practice elusive. However desirable, measured risk was often unobtainable, leaving us to grope only with uncertainty. The historical point was backward-looking, though not nostalgic. In the nineteenth century, Keynes sensed, investors had shown a sturdier confidence in the future. Like it or not, he was saying, that enviable confidence was gone and capitalist nerves were now notably weaker. He was not saying that they could not recover, which indeed they did after 1945 in one of capitalism's cyclothymic upswings.

Although technical economic arguments over Keynesianism have never stopped, Keynesianism stamped modern liberal politics in broader ways. Its emphasis on consumer spending as the driver of economies may be treated as the economic aspect of liberalism's compromise with democracy. Liberalism had conceded that everyone should have a say in political power. Keynesianism called for the explicit recognition of a corresponding extension of economic power. High wages, to put it crudely, were the Keynesian equivalent of universal suffrage. The Keynesian message was close to what forward-looking businessmen had already glimpsed: high wages were good for business, as high wages meant more spenders and more spenders meant bigger profits. Liberalism had come to terms with voter democracy. Keynes was urging it to accept consumer democracy, which since workers and consumers were really the same, meant worker democracy. This was distinctive. Liberals like Schumpeter made entrepreneurial risk the spirit of capitalism. Keynes added the material zeal of the worker-shopper, without whom the entrepreneur would have no profits to strive for. American businessmen like Henry Ford had seen the point. They offered high wages and steady work in exchange for taking control of the shop floor from unions and giving it squarely to management.

Keynes's life and work, second, exemplified a further shift in the liberal understanding of the tasks of government. It went well beyond the "new liberal" view of government as regulator, reserve, and safety valve. His masterly biographer, Robert Skidelsky, expressed the point well in *John Maynard Keynes: Hopes Betrayed* (1983), taking as a turning point the Paris Peace Conference of 1919. The responsibility of politicians before voters for the condition of the economy was for the first time openly avowed. "The idea," Skidelsky wrote, "that the creation of opulence was the main task of rulers was born in 1919 though it came of age only after the Second World War." Economic "performance" became a minimum standard by which liberals would gauge social progress. Government was made the guardian of that standard and held responsible when performance failed—for some liberals because it interfered too little, for others because it interfered too much. On the authority of the standard itself, both sorts of liberals agreed.

The first signs of official Keynesianism in Britain came in the "White Paper on Employment" (1944), which committed government to maintaining "high and stable" employment. In the United States, the Congress in 1946 committed the administration in law to pursue full employment, defined as adult unemployment of no more than 4 percent. The French Plans of the 1960s and the German Stabilisation Act of 1967 were drafted with similar Keynesian goals. Unspoken was a simultaneous commitment to high wages. Pursuing both aims—full employment and high wages—led in time to unsustainable inflation, as Keynes's earliest critics predicted. Those conflicts of policy and technique should not obscure the larger, unchallenged Keynesian legacy of the 1930s: left or right, monetarist or fiscalist, high-spenders or budget cutters, regulators or deregulators, the governments of liberal democracies were now held responsible for a nation's economic performance. Voters continued to hold national governments to account for economic performance even after globalization, beginning in the 1970s, began to undermine the capacities of governments to determine the course of national economies. By the end of the twentieth century, that mismatch between economic capacity and political responsibility put growing strain on a once happy-looking liberal-democratic compromise.

During the Great Depression in the United States, the first influence on policy was Fisher, not Keynes. Franklin Roosevelt, an instinctive improviser, won the presidency in 1932 on a promise to tighten the budget, not as he is often remembered as a Keynesian deficit spender. The left-wing "planners" in Roosevelt's administration soon lost the argument to pragmatic moderates ready to try whatever would put liberal capitalism back to work. If the moderates had any one guiding idea, it was Fisher's thought that the priority was to stop prices from falling. That strategic aim underlay the New Deal's main lines of action: farm price supports, labor union protection (to underpin higher wages), relaxation of trust-busting (to allow cartelized pricing), and abandonment of the gold standard (a cheaper dollar made goods dearer). All of those, as will be seen, were extensions of experimental rescues attempted by Roosevelt's derided predecessor, Herbert Hoover. The New Deal's public works and social security may be better remembered. As a cure for economic depression, they were a smaller part of the story.

Fisher's broad insight was that overinvestment and speculative asset buying need not be bad in themselves but became calamitously risky when financed by borrowed money. His story of slumps began with Schumpeterian innovation, which fueled a boom. When boom ended, the subsequent recession could turn into a depression when people borrowed to buy financial assets in expectation of continued gains. In a "debt-deflation," Fisher argued, people rushed to cut debt and liquidate, that is, hold their savings in cash. Incomes and collateral shrank, and as prices dropped, the real burden of debt rose, which drove people to reduce even more, pushing prices and production still lower.

Fisher blamed the post-1929 depression on an ill-timed contraction of the money supply. Late in 1928, Benjamin Strong, the head of the New York Fed, whom Fisher knew and admired, died unexpectedly at fifty-five. His guidance was badly missed, for the central bank subsequently blundered by holding interest rates too high as business slumped and prices fell, sending real debts soaring. In 1933, in "The Debt-Deflation Theory of Great Depressions," Fisher described the depressive cycle of "distress-selling, falling asset prices, rising real interest rates, more distress selling, falling velocity, declining net worth, rising bankruptcies, bank runs, curtailment of credit, dumping of assets by banks, growing distrust and hoarding."

Fisher's earlier fame as a monetary economist rested on his formulation of a "quantity theory" of money. According to that theory, the amount of money in an economy affected the overall price level but not relative prices of, say, capital and labor, and hence not the level of output. Money, in a technical sense, was neutral: it affected nominal, not real quantities. Experience showed Fisher how money, above all borrowed money, affected the real economy. It made him an interventionist, though of a monetary kind.

The so-called natural way out of depression, Fisher wrote, was "needless cruel bankruptcy, unemployment and starvation." His alternative to stop or prevent depression was by the "scientific medication" of reflation: raising prices by injections of money up to the average level of prices where existing debts were contracted, and then holding that level stable. Fisher offered various suggestions as how that was to be done, none of which were strictly followed. Little as the Roosevelt administration was doing, Fisher praised it for "the prospect" of an activist policy, providing charts to support his hope, false as it turned out, that in 1933 the worst was past. The American economy recovered, but a second collapse—blamed by Roosevelt's defenders on underinvestment by business, by his critics on government interference—lasted until war preparations in 1940 restarted the engine of employment and growth.

Fisher was a Democrat, a Roosevelt man as early as 1920, and an enthusiast for the early New Deal, while remaining a foe of high taxation. Support for government interference with money markets was not something to expect from his background. The son of a Congregational minister, Fisher went to Yale University, won election to the elite Skull and Bones club, and graduated top of his class. Yale offered him a job, and he taught economics there for the rest of his life. In 1893 Fisher married into a wealthy family and his father-in-law built the new couple a fine house in New Haven. Within five years he was professor.

His attitudes were those of a well-to-do liberal progressive, different in content from those of his conservative classmates and colleagues, but sharing their presumption of responsibility and authority. A believer in top-down reform, Fisher held that "the world consists of two classes—the educated and the ignorant—and it is essential for progress that the former should be allowed to dominate the latter." As "the logical arbiters of the class struggle now beginning," he believed economists had a duty to take part in public argument over policy. In 1930 Fisher was among 1,028 economists who vainly petitioned President Hoover to veto the Smoot-Hawley tariff-raising bill that deepened the world trade crisis.

At the age of thirty-two, Fisher almost died of tuberculosis, a disease that had killed his father. For the rest of his life he remained a health nut. He befriended J. H. Kellogg, the original maker of Corn Flakes, campaigned for fresh air, and militated against hard drink. A book of Fisher's health tips, *How to Live*, became a best seller. His concern with social betterment extended to eugenics and improving "the racial stock." Flirtation with eugenics was a darker though pervasive side of liberal concern for human progress, a version of Lenin's "fewer but better," now commonly downplayed in the liberal epic. Fisher's four great causes, he announced in 1925, were ending war, disease, "degeneracy," and the instability of money. He is remembered for the last, which entailed a life's work of trying to understand money, with its double capacity to create and destroy wealth.

As a teacher and economic theorist, Fisher strove to avoid three dangers: the Social Darwinism of his teacher William Graham Sumner, which threatened to turn economics into a pseudo-science for business interests; an overnarrow focus on a mathematically exact understanding of equilibrium conditions; and the Austrian school's discouraging insistence on economic ignorance and the elusiveness of equilibria. Fisher took economics optimistically in the round as a redoubt to be seized by shrewd thinking, flexible means, and superior force. He believed in the measurement of well-defined values and the precise quantitative statement of key relationships. A pioneer of economic statistics, Fisher later started, with Joseph Schumpeter, a society devoted to their study and in 1933 launched the journal *Econometrica*. Fisher paid equal attention to law, institutions, and history, influenced as he was by the mainly German-trained American economists who in 1885 had founded the American Economic Association.

Fisher had a gift for exposition and a feel for the telling image. On a visit to the Alps he admired a waterfall filling a mountain lake. It struck him that capital, like the lake, was a stock, a quantity that is without a time dimension, whereas income was a flow, a quantity divided by a time. Capital, furthermore, depended on income, the way the lake depended on the waterfall. Without the waterfall, the lake would soon dry up. Without the inflow of income, a stock of capital would quickly dwindle. Capital, as Fisher came to treat it, was an expectation of future income discounted by cost of borrowing—the interest rate. The price of shares in companies reflected, so it seemed to follow, not guesses about the resale value of plant and tools but bets on a company's future income. Here was an insight, amplified in *The Nature of Capital and Income* (1906), that took the study of capital beyond nineteenth-century puzzles as to how capital was economically productive (as opposed to idle, like rent) or ethically acceptable (as opposed to a domineering exaction from the weak by the strong). Returning with his Alpine insight, Fisher built in the basement of his New Haven house a hydraulic model of an economy out of pipes and glass jars of various shapes and sizes through which water flowed at different rates.

In the nineteenth-century United States, money was not only a technical matter for chancellors and bankers but a topic that set class against class and section against section. Soon after the Civil War, the United States disinflated the currency by returning to the gold standard and demonetizing silver. A long farm price deflation starting in the 1870s sparked the Bryan-led campaign to remonetize silver—to reinflate the currency by expanding the monetary base. Falling prices burdened Western farmers with a double load of slumping incomes and rising debt in real terms. Fisher sympathized with Bryan's cause. But the answer, in his view, was not to increase the supply of money by remonetizing silver, but to make the money supply less volatile. Price stability for Fisher was key.

Fisher, like Keynes, was a practitioner of money, as well as its teacher. He invented a card-index system, sold it profitably to the company that became Remington Rand, and amassed a fortune estimated in 1929 at $10 million. In the autumn of 1929, just before the crash, Fisher spoke of stocks as having reached a "permanently high plateau," a call based on unchallenged facts of high corporate profits and reasonable price-earnings ratios, a call that virtually all investors agreed with, but a call nevertheless for which Fisher was mocked as an example of professorial ignorance and market folly. The crash wiped him out. He had bought on margin and owed $11 million. With negative net worth, Fisher was his own instance of debt deflation. He persuaded Yale to buy the family house and rent it back to him for life. Soon Fisher was behind with the rent, sending instead promissory notes, which an indulgent university, proud of its star, agreed in 1939 to forgive.

Fisher's reputation was overshadowed after 1945 by the Keynesians and then in the 1970s by later monetarists such as Milton Friedman who were preoccupied by taming price inflation. Economists began again to take an interest in Fisher during the asset boom of the 1990s. The economist James Tobin wrote of Fisher that, had he pulled his many strands together, he would have been the American Keynes. The chairman of the Federal Reserve, Ben Bernanke, studied Fisher closely. Within three years of the 2008 crisis, the Fed's balance sheet had trebled. In lay terms, Bernanke's Fed flooded the American economy with liquidity in the hope, due to Fisher, that a Great Recession would not turn into a second Great Depression.

Friedrich Hayek (1899–1992) packed the careers of economist, polemicist, and social thinker into a single long life, which is why he appears in three different chapters of this liberal story. As a technical economist in the 1920s and 1930s, he developed a distinctive theory of business cycles and a policy of government inaction during slumps, which cut him off from Keynesians, though not from Keynes. In 1944 he became famous for a popular attack on economic "collectivism," *The Road to Serfdom*. From the 1950s to the 1970s, he produced a comprehensive picture of right-wing liberalism in *The Constitution of Liberty* (1960) and *Law, Legislation and Liberty* (1973–79) rivaling John Rawls's grand construction, *A Theory of Justice* (1971), in its seriousness and ambition. Hayek the economist is the topic here.

Hayek was born in Vienna just inside the century to which, he once said, he more naturally belonged. He never lost a profound, nostalgic connection to an imagined "gone world" that he was forever contrasting with the actual world in which he found himself. He lived through liberalism's great crises—two world wars, economic depression, and cold war. He witnessed the collapse of the liberal international system in 1914, the rise and fall of fascism and communism, the end of European empire, America's rise to dominance, the creation of a European Union, the breakup of the Soviet Union, and the emergence of a capitalist China. Throughout he clung to his liberal dream of a spontaneous, unplanned, self-sustaining order, which he pursued with rare pertinacity. A hostile witness, noting the horror and disorder of the century in which Hayek lived, might rashly conclude that he had seen and understood nothing. Hayek, on the contrary, must be taken seriously because he did see it all and did not abandon his liberal dream.

His parents were well-to-do, liberal-minded conservatives. Their forebears on both sides were from the Catholic Czech lands, but neither went to church or acknowledged its doctrines, and the son absorbed their urbane skepticism. Hayek did not shine at school, though perceptive teachers spotted a wayward originality. In the last year of war, at eighteen, he enlisted and fought on the Italian front as a radio officer. He came back ill from malaria with comic tales of the kind veterans tell civilians with no experience of warfare. When shrapnel took away a piece of his skull, he noticed the hole only days later. The noise of shellfire half deafened him when he forgot to disconnect his headphones. Hayek would later invoke the episode in mock apology for not listening to what others said. At university he studied law and economics, specializing in money and business cycles. From Karl Menger, Schmoller's opponent and founder of Austrian-school economics, Hayek took the idea of spontaneous order: that desirable economic outcomes could arise without anyone seeking them.

As a student Hayek became, in his words, "a mild socialist" by way of exclusion. As best he could see, three strains of unreason threatened a shorn, impoverished Austria, all of which he detested: the nationalists, who had provoked a disastrous conflict and destroyed the Habsburg Empire; the Bolsheviks, who behind their doctrines and slogans were little better than opportunistic gangsters; and an implacable Catholic right that was authoritarian, illiberal, and anti-Semitic. Social democracy was the only reasonable course. Having made his choice, Hayek met Ludwig Mises, head of Austria's Chamber of Industry. Mises was a free-market purist and nineteen years Hayek's senior. He set the young man straight and showed him an alternative.

Mises had settled politically in the borderland between liberalism and libertarianism. Social-minded liberals were in his view not liberals at all.

Mises was among the first of a new kind of intellectual: think tankers paid for by special interests. In his time at New York University, rich backers, notably the Volker Foundation, paid Mises's salary. Before and after his time in London, much the same was true for Hayek, who had absorbed from his mentor several worldly lessons in the combat of ideas: socialists, especially mild ones, were an enemy; tepidity in opinion was a mistake; and liberal individualism, like any polysyllabic creed, would never sell on its truth alone but needed backers. In 1924 Mises's business friends paid for Hayek to start his own think tank, the Austrian Institute of Business Cycle Research. Hayek, the director, had a staff of two secretaries. Thanks to Mises, he was on the way.

Hayck's study of business cycles and his conviction that governments could worsen but not dampen them caught the eye of Lionel Robbins, the head of economics at the London School of Economics, who in 1931 offered Hayek a job. Hayek believed that recessions arose from over-investment encouraged by easy credit foolishly or mischievously ex-tended by central banks. Once in a recession, there was little for govern-ments to do but stop cheapening money, even at the risk of more lost jobs. The cycle had to work itself out.

The contrast of Hayek's economic ideas with Keynes's were obvious. Those with Fisher's were subtler. Both he and Fisher made cheap money a villain, but in different ways. Fisher's mind was multifactorial. Business downturns were not all alike. They happened for various reasons. Why cheap money mattered to Fisher was that it turned downturns into slumps. The downturn's original cause was not the point. Economies ran naturally and well unless disturbed by outside shocks, some unavoid-able, some avoidable. The cause of avoidable shocks was government. The avoidable disturbance that caused slumps was government-cheapened money.

Hayek's detailed story of depressions was different. Cheap money en-couraged businesses to shift from short-term, consumer goods invest-ments to the long-term, capital-intense kind that required heavier bor-rowing. As money was sucked from consumption to investment, people were forced to save. On each count, artificially low interest rates dis-torted the economy's natural rhythms. Businesses moved to big capital projects because borrowing was temporarily cheap, not because they expected strong future profits from their heavy investments. Consumers' demand was frustrated because low interest rates diverted money into investment, interfering with consumers' preferred balance between saving and spending. The crack came when pent-up consumer demand drove businesses in a rush toward short-term production and a painful scramble ensued to abandon overinvestment in long-term capital goods. Hayek's story became standard among faithful Austrian-school economists. Few others adopted it. The implications for policy—stop fiddling with interest rates and then do nothing—struck most people as irrelevant to the crisis of the 1930s. As a theoretical construction, despite Hayek's insights into the rhythms of business investment, the explanatory mechanics seemed to most economists too weak and obscure to support the certitude of his broader narrative: economic nature works unless government interferes.

A similar mismatch of dialectical ambition and argumentative means hovered over Hayek's thoughts about economic ignorance, tantalizingly sketched in "Economics and Knowledge" (1937). It was his manifesto against the path mainstream economics was taking: toward mathematical modeling of conditions under which the main aggregates of an entire economy—income, consumption, investment—balanced. Such equilibrium was an economistical fiction in Hayek's view. All "equilibrium" ever meant was that everyone's plans of spending and saving theoretically cohered. Economies were never in such a state, or at any rate, nobody ever knew enough to be sure that they were, and every pain taken to describe economies in equilibrium, however technically brilliant, was wasted. What some took for deep wisdom sounded to others like poor epistemology masking intellectual exhaustion. Despite Hayek's warnings, the profession took the road to macroeconomics.

"Why," the American conservative William Buckley once asked in mock despair, "does their side have economists who write like Keynes and our side have ones who write like Hayek?" Given that both men agreed so closely on the strengths and virtues of liberal capitalism, it is hard not to think of style as part of why their followers formed such hostile and easily recognized camps. Hayek's writing is plodding and pedantic, unlit by a picture or phrase to catch the attention and save the reader from slumber. Keynes's prose is pointed, quick, and witty, and even in his technical works, lit up by vivid imagery. Though Hayek admired the poised and probing David Hume, he failed to absorb Hume's worldly spirit. Hayek's mental habits reflected more the influences of nineteenth-century German idealism, though with more of Marx's nose for enemies than Hegel's sense of conciliation. Those influences showed themselves in Hayek's fondness for neatly opposed abstractions—nature and artifice, spontaneous order and imposed order, true and false individualism—from which he chose his favored side, to the exclusion of the other. Keynes learned from the Cambridge philosopher G. E. Moore to analyze much and question safe-looking assumptions. Hayek did not find Keynes's homosexuality shocking. Hayek was not a prude and, besides, as a husband who forced a divorce on an unwilling wife, he was in a weak position to preach to others about private conduct. What shocked Hayek in Keynes's ethical outlook was his disregard for convention and rules, and his corresponding trust in his own judgment and that of his friends.

Hayek thought of himself as a Victorian and took Keynes for a sixteenth-century man. Keynes, Hayek once said, disliked the nineteenth century because he found it ugly. To Hayek the nineteenth century was beautiful. Keynes, he suspected, found commerce sordid, though necessary. Keynes in fact had far greater experience of money and markets, a reason perhaps why he exalted them less than Hayek was prone to. There was one way, oddly enough, in which Hayek was more Keynesian than Keynes, at any rate more of a true economic democrat. Keynes was a gifted, wide-ranging Edwardian aesthete. He hoped for economic democracy without an economic culture. Hayek by contrast welcomed the moral and aesthetic dimensions of commerce. Shopping, for Hayek, was an admirable, even beautiful form of life.

vi. Hoover and Roosevelt: Forgotten Liberal and Foremost Liberal

In American historical memory, the Great Depression comes in two guises. One is a drawn-out, many-sided crisis from 1929 to 1941, much longer than that in Europe, whose causes and cures are still in dispute. The slump came from underspending. It came from monetary disturbances. Government intervention saved the day, made things worse, or made no difference. Contrasting defenses in depth by economists and historians exist for each of those views.

In a second guise, the Great Depression has the simplicity of moral drama, a contest between virtue and vice led by heroes and villains. The American presidents of the period, Herbert Hoover, a Republican, and Franklin Roosevelt, a Democrat, pursued lines of policy that are hard at this distance to tell apart. They were nevertheless soon lodged in people's minds as champions of opposing "philosophies" whose colors were pure and clear: Hoover for executive restraint and voluntarism, Roosevelt for expansive government and an interventionist state. Out of that contest, as it came to be imagined, rival camps formed in American politics. They sounded as hostile in tone and as angry with each other as Southerners and Northerners after the Civil War. They exist to this day, called in a local twist of language, "conservative" and "liberal," though those terms disguise hidden likenesses as well as patent differences.

Hoover and Roosevelt were both liberals in the large sense: believers in social progress, as well as in the legal coinage of civic respect—personal rights and private property. Each hoped to restabilize American capitalism on defendable terms for business and labor. Each improvised pragmatically in response to an unprecedented economic conjuncture. Both, as tellingly, contributed to a transformation in economic structure. The change was most obvious in the growth of scale and responsibilities for the federal government. That growth in turn reflected a deeper change that, though less measurable, was quite as real. Hoover and Roosevelt presided over a massive upward shift in expectations of government.

The Hoover-Roosevelt legend obscured their likenesses. Roosevelt's supporters vilified Hoover for doing nothing in frozen panic as slump deepened. They revered Roosevelt as a savior whose New Deal rescued a nation from despair. On Hoover's side, those execrations and celebrations were reversed: Roosevelt destroyed confidence by stirring up frightened voters against business, led the nation from virtues of work and thrift, and by frivolous, ignorant meddling made the slump worse. Hoover's personal unpopularity in 1932 magnified Roosevelt's mandate. Bitter in defeat and abandoned by Republicans, Hoover blamed his obloquy on the "economic hurricane." His standing fell as Roosevelt's rose. So did the prestige of the ideas each was taken to stand for. American success in war here played a significant part by shedding a backward glow on the New Deal. Had Roosevelt left at the end of his second term in early 1941, his standing would have been more disputed. Partisans looked up to him as a defender of working men and women. Detractors saw in him an irresponsible class warrior. To many Americans in between, Roosevelt was a resourceful improviser who had avoided disaster thanks to a large measure of luck. In actuality, dying in 1945 a great war leader much as Lincoln had at the moment of victory, Roosevelt entered the American pantheon.

One of his brains trusters, Rexford Tugwell, told an interviewer long after in 1974 that "practically the whole New Deal was extrapolated from programs that Hoover started." If you allow for Tugwell's exaggeration to make his point, there was much in that. Hoover tried to raise farm prices. Roosevelt tried again. To stop wages from falling, Hoover urged business to make a deal with unions. So as to stop prices from falling, he urged business to club up in "associations." Roosevelt pursued the same aims in effect through law and regulation. Hoover tried to flood dried-out banks with money. Roosevelt tried too. Hoover urged localities, who in 1929 were spending all told twice as much as the federal government, to undertake public works and relief of hardship. As revenues slumped, Hoover perforce ran an un-Republican budget deficit. Roosevelt, who campaigned for a balanced budget, waited until 1935 to extend federal relief on any scale. The truth is neither really knew what to do.

That is not to say that during the Great Depression a composite called Hoosevelt occupied the White House. Both were liberals in the large sense, it is true. Yet their finer conceptions of liberalism were not the same. Nor was their tone. The differences came out less in what each man did than in what he said, how he said it and in particular whom he seemed to be saying it to. Hoover used the White House bully pulpit to tell the country how little the government could do. Roosevelt used it to tell people how much government could do. Hoover, an engineer accustomed to calculating probabilities, understood that the probable benefits of government success had to be netted against the likely costs of government failure. Roosevelt, who better grasped the elements of fear and confidence, sensed what people hoped to hear. Hoover, in addition, seemed to be talking principally to bosses and bankers. Roosevelt spoke as if to all or at any rate all but the very richest Americans.

Those differences arose partly from timing, partly from temperament and partly from ideas. Hoover became president in March 1929. The stock market crashed in October. He did not see clearly what the crash would bring. Nor did anyone else. Polar exploration preoccupied the

New York Times in the last days of December, and in a New Year's forecast the newspaper's business pages judged financial prospects "bright" and industrial conditions "sound." By spring unemployment and bread lines made the depth of crisis clear. With no agreed diagnosis or ready cure, Hoover experimented. He tried many disconnected things without giving business, labor, banks, or farmers a narrative. In June 1930 he signed the calamitous Smoot-Hawley tariff-raising bill. A two-year passage through the Congress had barnacled it with exorbitant rates on more than eight hundred goods, a dismal signal to international trade at a moment of economic peril. Hoover's failure to veto the bill was an undisputed blunder, extraordinary in a man of wide foreign experience whose global mining firm had built up forty offices across the world.

Time, by contrast, worked for Roosevelt. It created urgency and willingness to take risks. By March 1933 when he took office, one in four Americans was out of work and banks were failing. Roosevelt knew no better than Hoover what to do. He knew what to say. He had to convince a shaken country that something could be done. Roosevelt was good at that. Fire was raging behind them. The bridge ahead was insecure. Hoover, who knew about loads and stresses, told the truth, saying in effect, "I cannot guarantee that this bridge is safe." Roosevelt persuaded people to cross, and the bridge held.

They differed in temperament. Hoover was cold and aloof, Roosevelt outgoing and almost artificially sunny. Hoover grew up the child of Iowa Quakers in whose church his strict, God-fearing mother was an ordained minister. Sent away to an uncle in Oregon when his father died, "Bert" Hoover determined to make good. He won a place at the new university of Stanford, earned a degree in engineering, and after laboring in a mine set up his own engineering firm. One of its specialties was fixing mine disasters. Spying Hoover's talents, President Wilson asked Hoover in 1917 to supervise food supply in wartime. He managed the task without resort to rationing. His talents as postwar commissioner for relief in Europe saved countless people from starvation. As Secretary of Commerce in the 1920s he turned the department into a clearinghouse for economic information and a brokerage for what business wanted from government. Few who worked with Hoover liked his bullying manner. Almost all of them admired his effectiveness. An essentially apolitical manager who thought in solutions and worked by commands, Hoover was a doer.

Roosevelt by contrast was a listener. He surrounded himself with advisers of different views, to all of whom he said with an encouraging grin, "Yes, yes, yes." He was born to wealthy, landed parents in Upstate New York. Beside their life of cultivated idleness, characters in the novels of Henry James seem like anxious strivers. After an enjoyable, undistinguished pass through Harvard and Columbia Law School, where he failed to complete a degree, Roosevelt entered state politics as an anti-machine Democrat. A fixer-journalist, Louis Howe, taught him ring skills and knocked away his more irksome patrician tics. Wilson spotted Roosevelt, as he had spotted Hoover, and made him assistant secretary of the navy. In 1921, the charm of Roosevelt's life ended with a crippling polio. His mother urged him to retire. Howe and his wife, Eleanor—a niece of Theodore Roosevelt and Franklin's fifth cousin—encouraged him to stay in politics. He never walked again, but learned enough subterfuges, which his staff cooperated in and which the press courteously respected, for the public not to know. Roosevelt's illness toughened him. It encouraged an inborn talent for dissembling, made him more aware of suffering, and alerted him to the question, "What do we say to the losers?"

Temperament, though, mattered less in the end than the differences between Hoover's and Roosevelt's ideas. Hoover set down his view of politics and government in *American Individualism* (1922) and in speeches he spun off from the book, particularly "Rugged Individualism," given in New York six years later. Those titles, more remembered than the content, were deceptive. Liberals, we have seen, meant so many different things by "individualism" that anyone who used the term was bound to mislead somebody. Hoover spoke up in the New York speech for social justice, wider opportunity, and less economic inequality. Individualism, he told listeners, did not mean laissez-faire or "devil-take-the-hindmost," but "decentralized, local responsibility." There was nothing wrong with government as such. It had wide responsibilities. Those that could be were best handled locally. Public works and transport were examples. Municipalities could even take a successful hand in business such as public utilities, he suggested, because municipalities "are local and close to the people." Defense, medical research—a special concern of Hoover's, who set up the National Institutes of Health—and public lands, naturally needed central government. There Hoover saw a line.

Government should not interfere directly with business, with "the production of commodities." Hoover sounded in all that like a Wilsonian
Progressive, which in a sense he was. Summing up a rather muddled
catalogue of dos and don'ts, Hoover appealed to the core liberal idea of
nondomination by a single interest or power: "The very essence of equal
opportunity and of American individualism," he concluded, "is that
there shall be no domination by any group or combination in this republic." Hoover believed roughly what enlightened American capitalists believed in and what Keynes believed in: high wages and well-run unions
were good for business.

Hoover's larger trouble once president was that people found it hard
to believe such even-handedness, and for a reason. With typical flatness,
he told business visitors to the White House, "When I was Secretary of
Commerce I was devoting myself to your interests, and now that I have
become leader of the nation I must take the view of all the people."
Hoover was sincere in thinking of himself as everybody's president. Too
few took him for such. He never shook his reputation as a lobbyist for
big corporations. A further difficulty was that Hoover contrasted ineffective, distant, interfering big government with local, directly ac-
quainted, personal initiative. He himself had come up from nothing, and
did not see why others should not do the same: "A man who has not
made a million dollars by the time he is 40 is not worth much." Such
contrasts—local action versus centralized action, private initiative versus government interference—were as old as liberalism. Hoover pressed
them too far. Times had changed. The balance of contrast needed ad-
justing, for a new term complicated matters. Allowance was needed for
giant, nationwide companies that dwarfed local effort and individual
initiative.

Hoover was not blind to the difficulty, as he made clear in a speech,
"Business Ethics" (1928). Business, he allowed, was often poorly and
sometimes corruptly run. Better management and fiercer oversight
were needed. Here again, he saw a line. Regulation should be voluntary,
not coerced. The answer to the power of giant corporations, Hoover
thought, was associations of smaller ones, much as his fellow business-
liberal, Stresemann, had created in Germany. Hoover stood not for inaction, but for voluntary action before state action, self-regulation before
state regulation. Liberals had as a theoretical matter always preferred

the first to the second. However, even as Hoover might admit, business-men and bankers were no more honest or averse to free riding than other people were. Evidence that volunteers were rarely if ever in ade-quate supply had, in addition, long been available. By Hoover's day such evidence was overwhelming. Rising democratic expectations had cre-ated demand for action. The action of the American state—inefficient, underinformed, perverse in its consequences—was sucked into the gap left by the failure of "voluntarism." Liberalism was again renegotiating terms in its compromise with democracy.

Roosevelt did not think or talk in such general ideas but knew people who did. For a speech to the Commonwealth Club in San Francisco in 1932, he asked his brain trusters, led by Adolf A. Berle, to write some-thing that was, in effect, a silent answer to Hoover's "Rugged Individual-ism." Berle was coauthor of a groundbreaking study, *The Modern Corpo-ration and Private Property*, published that same year. The book described a historic shift in the character of capitalist enterprise. No longer did "individual" owner-managers run big firms. Ownership was scattered among shareholders. Management fell to hired hands, though hands with ever more power. Hoover, you could say, knew about mining. Berle knew about capitalism. He gave Roosevelt a speech that offered a new take on "liberal individualism."

The modern state, Roosevelt told his listeners, originated in taming Europe's barons. There were no barons to tame in America, but Alexan-der Hamilton had called all the same for a strong state to promote com-merce and banking. His opponent, Thomas Jefferson, argued for a weaker state so that small property and "personal competency"—free-dom of speech, thought, and so forth—might take root and grow. In 1800 Jefferson won the argument. American individualism was born. On the open frontier, it flourished. With the arrival of industry, general abundance was in prospect. Government stood by to help realize the dream. That dream, however, had a shadow: industry's titans, "always ruthless, often wasteful, frequently corrupt." Their growth and power had destroyed the old balance, creating "inequality of opportunity." Big business now called on big government: "The same man," Roosevelt said, "who tells us that he does not want to see the government interfere with business . . . is the first to go to the White House and ask the gov-ernment for a prohibitive tariff on his product." In new conditions, there needed to be a "reappraisal of values." Regulation and government action, were, it is true, a last resort. They were needed all the same "to protect individualism."

Once in the White House, Roosevelt perfected a more direct manner with fewer long words and more takeaway lines. His fireside chats on the radio, which he said took him four or five days to prepare, were small masterpieces of a new genre. Both they and his more formal speeches, given in a high, strong voice, stood out for their memorable phrases: "the forgotten man," "one third of a nation ill-housed, ill-clad, ill-nourished," and "economic royalists" who had "carved out new dynasties." Later speeches stood out for their open vistas of promise: the "four freedoms," of speech, of worship, from want and from fear, "anywhere in the world" (1941); "a second bill of rights" pledging to all Americans a "useful, remunerative job," a decent home, adequate medical care, and security against poverty in old age, sickness, accident, and unemployment (1944).

None of it sounded extravagant. It sounded doable. Extraordinarily, perhaps exceptionally, much of it was done. In looking back at that more hopeful liberal world, it is good to recall that Roosevelt the listener was less creating than responding to expectations. To understand American liberalism in the twentieth century, it is critical to see that rising arc of expectation and its subsequent disappointments. Many Americans who tell you they are against government are the disappointed children or grandchildren of people who taught them, with reason, to expect of it so much.

9

Thinking about Liberalism in the 1930s–1940s

i. Lippmann and Hayek (ii): Liberals as Antitotalitarians

In 1926, the year in which an Italian court imprisoned the Marxist Antonio Gramsci, fascist thugs beat up the journalist Giovanni Amendola, an antifascist liberal. It was his third such beating. His fault had been to attack Italy's dictator in *Il Mondo*, the liberal newspaper Amendola had founded. To describe Mussolini's drive for mastery of society, Amendola put into circulation a new term, "totalitarian." In pursuit of overarching control, the "totalitarian," Amendola suggested, used the state's power to suppress rival parties, close all but submissive newspapers and promote doctrinal loyalty in schools. Amendola died from the final beating, but his coinage lived on. Before long liberals across Europe were using "totalitarianism" as a single term to cover fascism, Hitlerism and Stalinism alike.

Their equivalence as tyrannies became a commonplace idea. The theorist of nationalism Hans Kohn set out the idea at length in *Communist and Fascist Dictatorship* (1935). Comparing the dictatorships, Leon Trotsky wrote of "symmetrical phenomena" in *The Revolution Betrayed* (1937). A difficulty with an otherwise appealing equation was that capitalism was compatible with fascism and Hitlerism, but not with Stalinism. Nor was the dissimilarity theoretical. Business money had bankrolled Mussolini. Germany's big industrial companies bridled at Nazi controls and forced consolidations but quickly accepted that cooperation was the best path to corporate survival and growth. Hitlerist economics was not coherent. But then in the 1930s, whose was? Schmoller's pupil, the economics minister Hjalmar Schacht, favored a civilian economy. Other advisers wanted a war economy. By 1938, the war party had won. Germany no longer had liberal capitalism, but capitalist it was.

If liberal thinkers of the 1930s and 1940s set that awkwardness aside, the shadowing Other of totalitarianism gave them a welcome story in negative to tell of their own creed. The story invoked a *via negativa*, an argument that offered exclusive alternatives and then refuted one of them without offering positive arguments for the other. The argument came in countless varieties, but its common shape was the same. The *via negativa* set the tone for a five-day meeting in Paris of concerned Europeans, including some brave anti-Nazi Germans, late in August 1938. Joining them from the United States was the newspaper columnist and author Walter Lippmann. He was in Paris to promote the French translation of *The Good Society* (1937), his much talked of book on the topic at hand. The meeting was named, in his honor, the Lippmann Colloquium. He had long since left the *New Republic* and found a nationwide readership as a columnist in the daily press. Among journalists, Lippmann was perhaps the leading voice of American liberalism, occupying an intellectual spot on the center-right similar to that of the progressive philosopher John Dewey on the center-left.

Wide as it ranged, within *The Good Society* was a succinct diagnosis of what threatened liberalism from without and what ailed it from within. Liberalism's external foe was collectivism, which had bad and less bad variants. The bad were fascist or communist totalitarians. The less bad were gradualists and well-meaning reformers embarked on a dangerous slope toward the bad collectivism. Liberalism was in trouble within itself, Lippmann added, because it had hit an intellectual dead end. By sticking to a purist doctrine of laissez-faire, it had allowed collectivists to seize the torch of progress. The liberals' challenge was to seize it back.

Most of the Lippmann Colloquium's participants agreed with Lippmann's main idea that doctrinaire liberalism was done for and a new liberalism was needed. As a name for the alternative, the colloquium adopted the German Alexander Rüstow's suggestion, "neoliberalism." As to the character of what it named, agreement ended. Neoliberalism meant different things on different lips. The meeting included technocratic liberal statists such as Ernest Mercier and Louis Marlio, two French business leaders. It included the free-market purists Mises and Hayek. In between were Lippmann and the German pioneers of the postwar social-market model. The final manifesto represented a wearable truce in the unending liberal family quarrel between a little more and a little less state. It had neither visible thread of principle nor practical guidance as to where the line between state and market should come. Liberal intellectuals were going to need more than the Colloquium Manifesto to seize back the torch of progress.

Participants did take away the specter of an antiliberal Other, which Hayek soon brilliantly turned into an anticollectivist tract, *The Road to Serfdom* (1944). Far away in New Zealand, where he had landed a teaching post, Hayek's friend and fellow Austrian Karl Popper began to think how to push liberalism's *via negativa* into original new territory.

Hayek's single best known work, *The Road to Serfdom*, jumbled debating points—socialism begets fascism, economic interventions lead inexorably to totalitarian control—with durable and powerful claims: central planning will not work better than markets; political freedom requires the economic sort. Even sympathizers regretted Hayek's weakness for overstatement and slippery-slope alarms. Yet it was precisely those qualities that gripped readers' imaginations and won the book unexpected attention, especially in the United States, where it became a best seller and was shortened and serialized by *Reader's Digest*.

A noir classic drenched in anxiety, *The Road to Serfdom* was of its time. Hayek's embattled and misunderstood liberal walks the mean streets of a collectivized world, part Philip Marlowe, part Winston Smith, part Bernard Rieux. In many places the prose rises to eloquence. Hayek wrote it in English, taking three years, beginning in 1941. It was the first time he found an English voice that did not sound stilted, professorial, or bitchily Viennese. He said he read the first chapters over and over to himself to perfect the rhythms. You need not find its case convincing to recognize *The Road to Serfdom* as a masterpiece of rhetoric and persuasion in the grand tradition of Ignatius Loyola, Leon Trotsky, and Winston Churchill. Much of the secret is that Hayek speaks openly from the heart. With naked feeling he bares himself as a Utopian, a man lost in mass society, longing for the civilities of his beloved liberal nineteenth century.

As crusading pamphlets must, *The Road to Serfdom* announced a fight for the human soul. Between the bad angel of collectivism and the good angel of individualism, there could be, Hayek warned readers, no choice. "It is necessary now to state the unpalatable truth that it is Germany whose fate we are in some danger of repeating," he wrote. Wartime readers, naïve in the belief that the fight then raging pitted democrats against fascists, would have read that with a jolt. But, no, Hayek explained: subtler than fascism is a villain of many guises, some gentle, some vicious, and which lurked within. Its name was socialism or collectivism, and the key with which it picked people's souls was economic planning. Fascism and communism were the villain's starkest forms, but both were emanations of the same evil spirit now menacing Britain and its allies.

The doctrines of nineteenth-century liberalism, Hayek conceded, rigidified into dogma, opening the way to collectivism, first as socialism, then as Bolshevik Russia and Nazi Germany. Yet redemption lay not in abandoning the old faith but in restoring it to new life. In a few dazzling pages, Hayek had prepared a cunning rhetorical trap that would serve him for the rest of the book: the flaws and inefficiencies of economic overregulation threatened to drive us, directly and unstoppably, to moral ruin and the loss of liberty. In addressing the innocent, if controversial, topic of reformist interventions in the British economy, Hayek could now count on readers to think of Gosplan, Speer's slave workers, Nazi camps, and Stalin's gulag. The book's impact, it must be said, depended on more than lurid association. Hayek gave arguments, or seeds of arguments. They anticipated clearly stated and reasoned themes that he built on in *The Constitution of Liberty* (1960): the inescapability of economic ignorance, the necessity for a rule of law, the intrinsic link between money and liberty, the need for equality under law but not equality of results, and the tensions between order and freedom as well as between liberty and democracy.

At the close, Hayek warned readers that bad ideas might destroy liberal societies. Hayek showed little of Mill's sunny confidence in a vigorous, open contest of opinion. Hayek's doubts about the capacities of democratic societies to defend "liberty" against corrosive beliefs would grow with time. Here he contented himself with identifying the most subversive beliefs. One was a Utopian refusal to accept that scarcity and insecurity would in some measure always be with us. The second was an arrogant faith that we might ever know enough to guide social change. Both mistakes rested, he suggested, on a "rationalist" refusal "to submit to any rule or necessity the rationale of which man does not understand." Here in sketch was an intellectual agenda for post-1945 right-wing liberalism to drawn on.

Critics complained of Hayek's tendentious history, particularly his account of how fascism took hold. The road to Nazism in his native Austria, as Hayek knew, led through authoritarians, anti-Semites, and anti-democrats more than through foolish, overdemanding trade unions. Critics found his appeal to the slippery slope unworthy and his equation of Britain's mild, law-governed collectivism with the chaotic, improvised violence of fascism and communism as bordering the absurd. Keynes characteristically nailed the main difficulty in a friendly, respectful letter. Both men agreed, Keynes suggested, that a line needed drawing between free enterprise and planning. But, Keynes complained to Hayek, "You give us no guidance whatever as to where to draw it."

ii. Popper: Liberalism as Openness and Experiment

Popper's *The Open Society and Its Enemies* (1945) also defended liberal-democratic society along the *via negativa* by attacking its enemies, though in a novel way. Popper's book let air into the increasingly stale more-state-less-state dispute by focusing on critical methods and habits of mind. By making the history of ideas feel politically relevant it vivified the reading of some very old texts. Suitably for a technocratic age, it offered an attractive, high-end analogy between experimental science and open-minded liberal politics. It attacked "deterministic" theories of history, especially *marxisant* ones predicting liberal capitalism's eventual doom, on the ground that history is sensitive to technical change and technical change is inherently unpredictable.

Popper's book, which he dedicated to the war effort, was large and urgent. It spoke less in classic liberal terms of the tensions of order and liberty than of a contest between rival orders, closed and open. The French thinker Henri Bergson had used "closed" and "open" to describe contrasting ethical outlooks in *Two Sources of Morality and Religion*

(1932), but Popper's use of the terms was altogether bolder. His rival orders were both patterns of thought and forms of society. The party of closed order were Plato, Hegel, and Marx, though Popper's drama began fittingly for a liberal with Heraclitus and ceaseless change. In a telling prologue, Popper in effect divided the world into open, liberal-minded spirits who accepted change, uncertainty, and the provisional character of life and knowledge, and closed-up, illiberal spirits who craved sameness, fixity, and security. Good societies came from the first, bad from the second.

Carrying over arguments from a pair of papers of his that Hayek published in *Economica*, "The Poverty of Historicism" (1936) and "Piecemeal Social Engineering" (1944), Popper proceeded along his *via negativa* by attacking liberalism's foes. Their "historicist" story was mistaken in method and hence unproven in its conclusion that liberalism was historically washed up. The foes of liberalism were mistaken also in picturing social progress as a leap to Utopia rather than as acceptance of gradual improvement in step-by-step reform. They were wrong, last, in their "holistic" picture of society as somehow collectively greater, more capable, and more valuable than its component members.

The fault of historicism in Popper's eyes was "the dream of prophecy." Historicists, as he characterized them, denied that there were universal laws in history of the kind met, say, in physics, and since they took moral norms to alter with historical conditions, their denial of historical laws came close to denying universal norms. Historicists did claim to detect trends in history, even directions and purposes. For Popper, that made matters worse. Here was a double fault of moral relativism and predictive arrogance. Unlike laws, trends might last for a time and then cease to last. New technologies ended or diverted trends in ways that reliably surprised us, and future discoveries and inventions were something hard to predict by their nature.

Popper disdained what he called "essentialist" definitions of a kind coming professionally into vogue that offered verbal equivalences for some newly introduced term. He expanded on "piecemeal social engineering" by examples. They ran from banal lessons of everyday life, as when for example we "experiment" by wasting time queuing for a bus ticket and conclude that it would be cheaper to buy one ahead of time all the way to public health insurance and "a policy to combat trade cycles." Popper's list showed how far in practice he was from Hayek. His friend reproved Popper, saying that the very idea of engineering presumed a centralization of knowledge that was never possible. In a wriggling footnote, Popper answered that in their try-and-test approach engineers also allowed for ignorance.

In similarly antidefinitional spirit, Popper did not say what open and closed societies were but gave sets of markers for each. Closed societies were totalitarian, organic, magical, concrete, and organized social relationships according to accident of birth. Open societies were abstract, depersonalized, rational, and governed by exchange and cooperation, and in them social relationships arose by choice, not birth or the decisions of others. Popper did not expand greatly on those terms. Open societies, he allowed, paid a price in lost intimacy, though one worth paying. His image of such separateness was itself a nice example of his theme of the unpredictability of technical change. In an open society, Popper wrote, people went about "in closed cars" and communicated "by typed letters or by telegrams."

Popper made liberalism attractive in a technologically minded time by likening its spirit and practices to those of science, while consigning those of its enemies to semiscience or pseudo-science. He did so in a sophisticated manner by way of high-level analogies of method. The dream of lending politics and history the authority of science captured many thinkers in the nineteenth century. Comte had a tale of the advance of human understanding from "theological" and "metaphysical" stages, where unobservable forces govern the world, to the modern "positive" stage of factually oriented science that both describes nature and guides society. Mill had admired Comte's respect for fact but detested his attempt to lend science the authority of religion. Mill thought that the principles of society might one day be rigorously shown to depend on observable facts of human psychology. Spencer had combined stage-by-stage progress, a speculative theory of a person's mental development and a sweeping analogy between biological evolution and historical change. By Popper's time, such machines looked antique.

Science, Popper told us, aimed at, but never reached, truth. Liberalism progressed from worse to better but never reached an ideal steady state. Science was critical and experimental. Liberalism was open-minded and reformist in a probing, piecemeal way. The analogies did not stop there. Science as a practice advanced by proposing testable theories that were abandoned if falsified by discordant evidence. Liberalism as a practice progressed by testing policies, institutions, and governments and by recasting or removing those that did not work. No theory in science, Popper stressed, was immune to failure. No policy or ministry in politics was above criticism or reform. To Popper's so-called falsificationism in science, there corresponded a *via negativa* in politics, whose guiding maxim was minimize harms rather than maximize the good. A leading example was representative democracy. It enabled people to get rid of unwanted rulers peacefully. That negative benefit was democracy's great appeal and most compelling justification. To complete his grand analogy, which Popper called the unity of scientific method, he likened the incrementalism of science to the gradualism of liberal politics. Popper, who was not a modest man, was deservedly proud of that luminous picture.

With ingenuity, Popper was putting the *via negativa* to new use, less to burnish liberalism by contrast to an enemy than by characterizing the model liberal method. The proper method in politics was not to aim at the achievement of distant, ill-defined ideals but at the removal of local and palpable wrongs. In asking a misleading question, Plato had set political thinking on the wrong line. The pressing issue in politics was less "Who should rule?" than "How can we so organize political institutions that bad or incompetent rulers can be prevented from doing damage?" Do not aim to maximize the good but aim rather to minimize the bad.

If Popper's grand analogy was apt, three common complaints against his picture of science could be directed equally against his picture of politics. Much as verifying and falsifying scientific theories looked like different aspects of the same task, so minimizing the bad and maximizing the good looked like a single task with the signs changed. If scientific knowledge advanced by weeding out failed theories, why was it reasonable to rely, as everyone did, on solid-seeming theories that had not yet failed? Similarly, if a policy in politics was likely to fail in the future, why was it wise to rely on it now? In science, last, there were rarely if ever decisive tests that conclusively discredited a theory. Every theory came with a network of auxiliary theories and assumptions. Failure left experimenters with choices: abandon the theory, reject some auxiliary assumption, or blame a faulty experiment. So it was in politics. Even when it was agreed that a policy seemed not to be working, choices remained: abandon the policy, blame a connected policy, which may in fact be causing the trouble, or reject the original critical findings. There were no mechanisms or guarantees. Judgment and choice were unavoidable. As in science, practice and experience guided the choice of what to correct or reform.

By 1945 there were three grand narratives of liberal capitalism: terminal decline, conditional recovery, and durable success. Lippmann and Hayek spoke for conditional recovery. Popper, a more confident and ebullient spirit, sensed that the problem-solving inventiveness of the scientific and technical mind must somehow spill over fruitfully into liberal politics. Far from a weakness as critics claimed, liberal open-mindedness was to Popper a source of strength and endurance. Within a short time, in one of liberalism's mood swings, both absolute and conditional decline were forgotten. By 1960 or so the liberal narrative that came to sound most persuasive was a tale of historic achievement. In the decades after 1945 liberals began to tell themselves that their dream of order did not look so unachievable after all. Nor was theirs purely a success in negative, a least bad of the bad, a Cold War superiority of the Free World over the Communist Other. The old liberal dream—an ethically acceptable order of human progress among civic equals without recourse to undue power—ceased to look so demanding, so Utopian. The dream began to look achievable, not least as it became less contested and more widely shared.

PART THREE

Second Chance and Success (1945–1989)

10

Historical Setting after 1945

Liberal Democracy's New Start

This was liberals' second chance and they took it. In the West at any rate, winners and losers alike now knew what to avoid. Liberal democracy, outlined in shadow by a Soviet Other and underwritten by the welfare state, became a Western norm. Individuals took center stage outfitted with freshly tailored rights. In age, liberal thought, professionalized in universities, began to look into itself and reflect philosophically on liberalism's higher "whys." Set against the recent past, liberal democracy was for most people a good kind of society to grow up in. To many elsewhere it was an enviable place to live. Its appeal spread.

Much as in the years around 1830 after the divisive Napoleonic upheaval, postwar politicians and businessmen of the West began again to think of their problems in similar ways. They read and translated each other's books and went to each other's universities. They found themselves bound by each other's solutions and began to look for solutions together. They developed common ways of thinking about politics, and stopped taking big decisions—about money, about armies, about laws—in national isolation. They needed to because the costs of rupture and conflict were now too great. They were able to because their societies were growing so alike. In what historically speaking was an astonishingly brief and compressed burst of change, illiterate, rural, farm societies had during liberalism's brief lifetime become first semiliterate, urban, and industrial. Now in a second acceleration, European and American societies were fast converging on fully literate, suburban postindustrialism. In that setting, economic and political cooperation was again possible. The fresh experience of calamitous liberal errors made it necessary.

European and American governments combined in awkward, unequal, but ultimately durable arrangements of tariff reduction, mutual defense, and monetary coordination. Europe turned from 150 years of civil war among its nations to embark on the creation of a postnational union. When Europe's dictatorial outliers—Spain, Portugal, and Greece, and later the ex-Communist countries of Europe—asked to join the game, liberal democracy was a condition of entry. Western liberalism was not a global charity. For Europe's colonies, the 1940s to 1970s were a time of brutal wars of independence to secure what liberals promised themselves—self-rule and defenses against unwanted power—but extended only reluctantly to subject peoples. A shared international practice of politics nevertheless grew up that liberals, reconciled to democracy, hoped to stabilize, extend, and perpetuate.

From the broad liberal center of politics, technically minded men and women created a new international order. They drew on the experience of liberal mistakes. Germany was blamed for the war, with more justice than in 1918, yet reparations were limited and balanced by aid and reconstruction. As American and European prosperity were interknit, monetary cooperation and open trade were vital. As Franco-German rivalry had contributed to two wars, European conciliation was paramount. Through Marshall Aid, the United States dispensed to Europe, including defeated Germany, $13 billion in aid, which as a share of the economy is equivalent to around half a trillion dollars in today's money. From the crash of 1873 to the slump of the 1930s, experience had taught liberals that for open, flourishing trade fixed exchange rates were good and currency wars bad, but that the strains of maintaining fixed rates could overwhelm any one country. Harry Dexter White for the American Treasury and Maynard Keynes for Britain devised a monetary system, favorable to open trade, of fixed but adjustable exchange rates, anchored by the dollar. Robert Schuman for France and Walter Hallstein for Germany laid the groundwork for an economic and political union in Europe that opened a half century of peace and prosperity after 150 years of war. Liberal economists on both sides of the Atlantic drew technical lessons from the 1930s. It was best to fit currency and interest rates to the money supply and the money supply to production and employment, not the other way around. They were recovering the preliberal wisdom of Adam Smith, that a nation's wealth lay in production, work, and skills, not in gold or silver.

The postwar liberal-democratic world was one of growing wealth, but also more widely shared wealth. Per capita income grew and income inequality fell. Lives became longer and healthier. State schools, soon state secondary schools, became universal. Holding and voting for political office was made open to all. Many legal constraints on what people could do or say fell away. Control of press and television eased. Law interfered less with private lives. Prohibitions or limitations on divorce, contraception, and abortion dwindled or vanished. Legal hounding of homosexuals ended. Law interfered more on the other hand to protect workers and not, as before, only shareholders. It stepped in to limit discrimination against women and nonwhites. Suspects got a better shout from police and courts. In Europe—and even briefly in the United States—the death penalty vanished. Judged against liberal ideals, liberal democratic society was in many ways a success. People had more ways than before to resist power. Society and the lives of its members had on many scores improved. Respect and concern for people had deepened and was now widely embedded in custom and law. Conflict among people was more channeled into peaceful competition and contained, and no one power dominated. To the peoples of Western Europe and the United States, the liberal dream in those postwar decades did not look unachievable.

From the 1880s to the 1940s, a democratic liberalism emerged from a historic compromise. In the 1950s to 1970s the terms of that compromise were readjusted and settled. Protections and benefits liberals had claimed for free citizens came to all. Political democracy was finally universal. Everyone but children and teenagers had a vote. Ethical democracy spread as the privacy and permissions that liberals had thought of as for the wise and educated were extended to all. Letting people choose their own path to a good life prevailed over the paternal liberal educator. Constant had prevailed over Humboldt. Economic democracy spread. More people had economic voice. Society grew less like a pyramid and more like a diamond. Between a few rich at the top and a few poor at the bottom grew a thickening middle-class wedge. The kind of economic society Fisher, Keynes, and Hayek had each in his way hoped to rescue had after all come through.

Such welcome developments affected liberal thinking about conflict in society. A thought that had distinguished liberals from their rivals in politics was that conflict was unending and inevitable. The very success of liberal democracy after 1945 now created a temptation for liberals to ignore their own wisdom. As society grew wealthier and more middle class, it was appealing to think that a stage was perhaps approaching at which conflict might ease. The eighteenth-century world of ranks and estates had bequeathed to Hegel, Guizot, and Marx a picture of political conflict as a struggle of classes. That picture was irresistible. It was easy to grasp. It offered a neat way to arrange thoughts about other conflicts in politics. It made sense of the flux of events. Everyone, liberals included, had relied on the picture.

By midcentury, the picture was no longer good. As class conflict was ending, it was easy to think that conflict itself was ending. Liberals in their success had to remind themselves that conflict never ended. Economic disputes did not go away. They became many-sided: governments versus their employees, young families versus pensioners, stockholders versus managements, rich cities versus poor regions, new technologies versus declining industries. As life grew more comfortable, liberal politics grew more complicated. Old political camps broke up and party lines blurred. Political conflict did not go away. Politics became "cross-cutting." Particularly when economic times grew better, people began to quarrel over morals, allegiances—soon to be known as "identities"—and faith. For some liberals the loss of clarity and the absence of a clear narrative were signs that politics was slipping out of people's practical and intellectual control. Had liberalism itself, they asked themselves, not lost its shape and broken up into distinct "liberalisms"? For other liberals, on the contrary, the abandonment of simplifying narratives and recognition of complexity marked not the breaking up of liberalism but a liberal achievement.

11

New Foundations

Rights, a Democratic Rule of Law, and Welfare

i. Drafters of the 1948 Declaration of Human Rights: Liberal Democracy Goes Global

"Intrigue, lobbying, secret arrangements, blocs," Charles Malik wrote in his diary. "Power politics and bargaining nauseate me." Malik, a Lebanese philosopher, was not describing tax fights, arms budgets, or interconfessional war but his work on the postwar Universal Declaration of Human Rights. In late 1946 the UN General Assembly appointed a drafting commission, which duly met in a disused gyroscope factory at Lake Success near New York City on Long Island. As one of the drafters, Malik found the confrontations and technicalities frustrating. For him the force and clarity of human rights shone clear. An Orthodox Christian who took his creed for a celebration of human personhood, Malik knew intolerance and tyrannous abuse first hand. He came from a region laced by confessional divisions in which majorities "handled" or browbeat their minorities. He had studied in Germany under the equivocal Martin Heidegger, but left in 1933 for the United States, though not before Nazi students had beaten him up on mistaking him for Jewish. At Lake Success, Malik learned how arduous it was to codify the human sentiment of outrage into legal terms. He learned how perplexing it was to entrust to the powers of law, government, and popular majorities the task of defending men and women from power's own abuses. The 1948 Declaration of Human Rights continued to cause perplexity, even disdain. As a postwar restatement of liberal-democratic ideals, it nevertheless survived frustration and disregard with remarkable hardiness.

Malik's fellow drafters included another liberal "universalist" of more secular outlook, René Cassin, a French expert in public law and London-based wartime *résistant*. It included a subtle but party-line Soviet lawyer who treated "bourgeois" rights as an ersatz for proletarian solidarity. A non-Communist Chinese scholar, Pen-Chun Chang, found Confucian parallels in Western norms and took pains over translations. The Indian social reformer and independence campaigner Hansa Mehta spoke up for women's rights. Most everyone agreed that human rights were about upholding the worth of personhood and defending people from mal-treatment. Not everyone understood such aims in similar ways. In the chair was Eleanor Roosevelt, the late American president's widow and an experienced campaigner for progressive causes. She entertained the diverse crew with her uncle Teddy Roosevelt's over-the-hill claret and steered them through eighty-one meetings to a near unanimous conclu-sion that had often looked unreachable.

The first task was to draw up a credible list of widely recognized rights. A team under John Humphrey, a Canadian lawyer, scoured the world's codes and constitutions. Humphrey's long list grew upward from liberties and protections that in some form or other were either en-trenched or proclaimed in various enough countries to count as repre-sentative, common, and "universal." The list, however, lacked shape. Practiced in the tidiness of legal codes, Cassin was charged with giving the list a sense of order and rationale. Cassin accordingly drew a picture. He imagined human rights as a classical temple front. Its four columns stood for the prime values of dignity, liberty, equality, and brotherhood. Those values supported rights, solemnly engraved on the pediment. Just what rested on what was, on a closer look, obscure. Cassin's picture served its purpose all the same. Through the subsequent disputes, his order and loose groupings survived.

Article 1 of the final declaration proclaimed those four values to-gether: "All human beings are born free and equal in dignity and rights. They are endowed with reason and conscience and should act towards one another in a spirit of brotherhood." Article 2 required that rights be honored for everyone everywhere, without discrimination or exclusion. Articles 3 to 11 turned on what duties and self-restraints powerful au-thority owed to people as such: the rights of "life, liberty and security of person" as well as equality under a rule of law. Articles 12 to 17 pulled together liberties of people to act as they will within their societies. They demanded respect for privacy, freedom of marriage, and the rights to own property and to move about. Articles 18 to 20 concerned rights of voice and participation in public life and politics: to say and believe what you will, to meet, to speak out, and to hold office. Taken together, those first twenty rights may be seen as reflecting key elements of liberal civic respect, nonintrusion, and nonobstruction taken democratically in a nonexclusive way.

The next seven articles went well beyond old understandings of rights. Article 21 stipulated the kind of legal and political arrangements needed for people to be able to exercise the preceding ones: "The will of the people shall be the basis of the authority of government; this will shall be expressed in periodic and genuine elections which shall be by universal and equal suffrage and shall be held by secret vote or by equiv-alent free voting procedures." In the spirit of the pre-1914 "new liberal-ism," articles 22 to 27 took what we have called civic respect to include common concern for people's needs. Article 22 read, "Everyone, as a member of society, has the right to social security." Other "social rights" followed smoothly. They included social welfare, equal pay, right to work, right to holidays, and right to special care for children and moth-ers. Taken together and at their word, articles 21 to 27 proclaimed a universal right to liberal democracy with a strong "social" cast.

The drafters chose to make no mention of "laws of nature," "nature's God," or a "supreme being" that eighteenth-century American and French constitutionalists had invoked to bless their enterprise. Agree-ment on content ought not to falter, Cassin insisted, over unsettleable differences as to what kinds of thing, metaphysically speaking, rights were, whence came their authority or what bound us to them morally. Nor, he thought, should the declaration stumble on competing pic-tures of people and society of a which-came-first kind. The draft did presume that rights were recognized rather than conferred, that they were in some sense out there, independent, and binding on us whether observed or not, and that they were accordingly less a description of actual protections than a "standard of achievement" for "all peoples and all nations." Beyond that, the declaration left open nettlesome higher questions about the precise status and general purpose of human rights.

In September 1948, Roosevelt's experts approved a draft with almost no dissent. Governments now weighed in directly on a higher UN committee that held over one hundred further meetings. The British made a halfhearted try at excluding social rights and at denying the declaration's writ within their colonies. The Yugoslavs asked Americans why they objected to South African apartheid but not to southern segregation. The Saudis resisted rights for women. The Soviets dropped all pretense and openly objected to the declaration as an interference with national sovereignty. A final draft was passed up all the same to the General Assembly, which approved it on December 10 by a vote of forty-eight to zero. The seven communist states abstained, along with Saudi Arabia and South Africa. Most of Africa and Asia was absent. Missing indeed were three-quarters of the nations that self-determination and decolonization would soon bring to the world.

The achievement was large nevertheless, and so recognized at the time. The moral climate was palpable. Since the 1930s the world had witnessed "relapses into barbarism, on all sides, which shocked humanity into a realization of what, for all its supposed civilization, it was capable of doing," as human rights lawyer James Fawcett—the author's father, who was at the UN in 1948 for the British Foreign Office and who was later president of the European Human Rights Commission—wrote in *The Law of Nations* (1968). Seen in that light, the Declaration of Human Rights was an atonement. It was equally a global charter for a new politics. December 1948 may properly be counted as a moment when liberal democracy was recognized as a global, not a narrowly Western, aspiration.

Recognition, though widespread, was not universal. Other political aspirations persisted. The declaration's private property and free elections in particular separated liberal-democratic principles from communist, exclusionary, or autocratic ones, as the final vote underlined. Many colonial nations were more interested in independence and self-determination than in rights for their future citizens. Even among liberal democrats it did not take long for excitement at having found as it seemed a recognized fixed point within the morality of politics to give way to questioning and disenchantment. Doubts set in about the declaration as they did about human rights broadly. The doubts were legal, intellectual, and political. Each kind was overdrawn. But they are worth dwelling on for they were—and remain—widely felt.

The legal doubts turned on what looked an unpalatable choice. Either human rights were to be encoded in enforceable law, when they faced the danger of overformalization as almost technical matters, far removed from the core concern to protect people from evident maltreatment and abuse of power. Or human rights were to stay as speech material for use by governments as sticks with which to beat each other: third world peoples against colonialism, communists against Western iniquities, and Westerners against communist and third world despots.

To doubters and deniers, the worst of both alternatives occurred. West Europeans took the route of enforcement. In 1950 they agreed to their own human rights convention with a court empowered to hold governments in breach. Soon citizens could appeal against human rights abuses directly. Hopes were rightly high. Many feared all the same that what European human rights law gained in traction it risked losing in focus and lucidity. A convention to prevent cruel and flagrant abuse began to turn, as critics had feared, on formal and procedural infractions that their government perpetrators might not even be aware of. In time even civil contracts between private parties became subject to human rights constraints. Before long the backlog of cases grew to more than one hundred thousand.

At the UN, the problem with human rights was not overuse but misuse. As aspiration, the UN Declaration of Human Rights provided for neither implementation nor enforcement. A tangle of UN human rights bodies nevertheless grew up, which generated further paper commitments. Westerners complained that newly independent nations exploited the UN rights machinery more to berate the West than to respect their own citizens. Third world countries riposted that the West was guilty of the same fault. Both in a sense were correct, for the deeper problem lay in expecting governments of any stripe to honor or promote human rights except under sustained pressure. In his 1975 study of the UN the British scholar Herbert Nicholas acidly remarked on "the inherent absurdity of an organization of governments dedicating itself to protect human rights when in all ages and climes it is governments which have been their principal violators." All governments could be counted on to preach human rights, the suggestion ran, but none should be expected to defend them.

Intellectual disenchantment with human rights grew with a seeming failure to find stable, publicly available defenses for them against mockers, debunkers, and deniers. In 1948 a UNESCO panel, which included the French philosopher Jacques Maritain, the British historian E. H. Carr, and the Indian leader Mahatma Gandhi, was asked to review the philosophical foundations of human rights. On reaching their conclusion that those foundations were a vexing topic on which agreement was improbable, readers did not faint from shock. The Declaration of Human Rights was drafted in something of an intellectual vacuum about the nature of the civic and political rights it recognized or called into being. Ancient and early modern thought about justice and rights was available but interpretable as a rule only by specialists. In English-speaking traditions, an articulate philosophy of rights, particularly universal human rights, barely existed. The richest legal thinking was German, but few in 1948 were looking to Germany for thoughts about human rights.

The early liberals, we saw, clamored on behalf of people against power. They demanded protections, permissions, and voice. They rarely made such claims in terms of what we now call common, universal, or human rights. Private rights were taken generally to arise from contract or custom, adjudicated in a country's courts. Political rights—to vote, assemble, and hold office, for example—were rights of citizens. Either way rights were national. Insofar as defendable claims about the proper treatment of people crossed borders, they were less rights than declaratory hopes. Insofar as legally entrenched rights were political they were national, not universal.

Civic and political rights existed in the United States, but the 1791 Bill of Rights bore on protections for citizens only from the federal government, not from the governments of states, many of which recognized the Bill of Rights selectively if at all. American constitutional law in the nineteenth century faced a primary task, pressing for business and finance, of creating national law out of a patchwork of state and federal law. When constitutional cases did involve citizens directly, American nineteenth-century courts tended, as seen, to read the Bill of Rights as more a defense for freely struck contracts than as a charter for civil liberties. Until the 1930s, the Supreme Court champions of civil liberties, Holmes and Brandeis, commonly formed a dissenting minority of two. Nor were matters greatly different in Britain, where a legal conception of civil liberties and political rights enforceable in court against the will of Parliament was largely foreign. Taken as a whole, the ringing French declarations from the 1790s had little direct impact on the practical task that faced French lawyers drafting the early nineteenth-century civil and administrative codes: shaping a discordant mass of existing Roman, feudal, and customary rules into a single body of national law.

Much as Cassin did during the drafting of the Declaration, liberal thinkers before 1945 had tended to avoid philosophical questions of where to fit rights in the furniture of the world and where to trace the source of their authority. By the time of liberalism's birth early in the nineteenth century, the idea of natural rights (the sort people anywhere had simply by being people, or at any rate European men) had fallen away with the decline of natural law (unarguable standards of justice for laws and peoples everywhere). There were several reasons for that decline as for other universalist doctrines of rights in the nineteenth century. If natural law was taken for a compendium of God's commands, it was vulnerable to the spread of secularism. If its source was taken to be our inborn sociability, then its guidance was no longer clear. For though it might be natural to belong to society, whatever actual society people "naturally" belonged to was now in permanent upheaval. Social manners and material expectations of the kind that gave claims to rights specific content were shifting in turn. "Natural," in addition, was ceasing to imply "universal," and was coming to blur in people's minds with "national." The rise of the modern nation-state put a premium on the rediscovery or invention of national features that partitioned the world into recognizably distinct societies each supposedly with its own ethical customs that underlay distinct legal traditions. Kant, it is true, handed down into liberal thought a competing universalist vision of human reason and law, according to which standards of justice lay not in commands imposed by God, nation, or society but in rules that any self-interested yet reasonable creature would accept on a *tu quoque* basis as binding on everyone. For all its theoretical power and intellectual appeal, Kantianism seemed too abstract to justify the kinds of legally backed permissions and protections people actually demanded or required. Neither tradition appeared to offer what liberals wanted from a philosophy of law: ready-to-hand justifications for a flexible source of order and sword of reform in ceaselessly changing societies. For such purpose, natural law was too silent, too universal or too fixed, and Kantianism too abstract.

Insofar as earlier liberals had or felt need of a legal philosophy, it tended to come from a workaday Utilitarianism, particularly in Britain. Utilitarianism had served well in practice as critic and razor of superannuated or contested law. Nobody knew it in the 1940s to 1950s, but as the British legal theorist Herbert Hart later put it, the philosophy of law and politics in the English-speaking world was beginning its rough crossing from "the old faith in Utilitarianism" to "the new faith in rights." A later chapter on the work and influence of John Rawls notes how, on reaching shore, legal philosophers found fresh justifications for human rights in profusion. That prompted the ungrateful complaint that, having had no theory of human rights, liberal thinkers now had too many.

Political disappointment with the 1948 Declaration of Human Rights focused on "mission creep." The discourse of rights encouraged the spread of entitlement claims into ever wider areas. Soon virtually any political issue became posable as a matter of rights. Such ran the complaints, and there was material aplenty in support. At the UN, "rights inflation," as it was called, proceeded in biblical sequence: the first generation of civic and political human rights begat a second of social and economic rights, which begat a third of group and minority rights. Each generation had a UN birth certificate in successive covenants agreed to in the General Assembly on racial discrimination (1965), economic, social, and cultural rights (1966), discrimination against women (1979), and rights of children (1989). Social and economic rights, sketched in 1948 but now spelled out in detail, came under fire as too expensive, too burdensome to poor countries, and too big a stretch for the idea of right. The problem of overstretch paralleled that of "over-legalization" with human rights in Europe. If any political demand became posable as a human rights claim, the risk was that a movement to shield people from flagrant abuses of power might shout itself out in open-ended demands and insatiable desirabilities. Such was the concern.

By an odd historical turn, those disappointments conspired in a second coming of human rights. It took shape in civic activism, in the taking of matters into people's own hands. Perhaps human rights were now entangled in law, co-opted and exploited by governments, lacking in agreed theoretical foundations and weakened by overstretch. The core demands against inhuman treatment and abuse of power had lost none of their moral or political force. Such was the profound conviction of Peter Benenson, a British lawyer who in 1961 started a campaign in London on behalf of political prisoners called Amnesty.

Benenson's aim in defending "forgotten prisoners" was humane, not geopolitical or doctrinal. Prisoners of conscience required defending not to promote their views or to attack those of their oppressors but because imprisoning people for their views was wrong. At the same time, he was strict about not standing up for every political offender. There was no point, Benenson thought, in defending the rights of prisoners who once in power would jail their opponents. Nor did he propose to defend from state violence those advocating violence of their own.

Peter Benenson (1921–2005) was born to unorthodoxy and dissent. His mother Flora Solomon was a socialist and Zionist who organized workers at Marks and Spencer's department stores. His home tutors included the poet W. H. Auden. In his teens Benenson organized relief for civil war victims in Spain. After the 1939–45 war, during which he deciphered codes at Bletchley Park, he joined the Bar. In the 1950s he campaigned against British abuses in Cyprus and against the murderous excesses of Western-backed dictatorships in Spain and Portugal. Amnesty grew in time into a worldwide campaign. Much as had Roger Baldwin at the ACLU, Benenson worked by charisma rather than method. He was the wrong person to manage a body that grew eventually into an organization with thousands of volunteers and a staff of over five hundred. Benenson resigned in 1966, complaining that Britain's secret services had infiltrated his campaign, which, whatever the truth, they were quite capable of having done.

That same year a new yet tougher phase of civic activism began, focused on prisoners of conscience in the communist world, and two in particular, Yuli Daniel and Andrei Sinyavsky, jailed in 1966. In Amnesty's footsteps, the campaign on behalf of Soviet dissidents gathered international strength from small beginnings, pressured governments in East and West and in 1975 bore fruit in the human rights provisions of the Helsinki Accords that formalized East-West détente after the First Cold

War (1947–70). Human rights activists on both sides pressed governments to comply with their commitments. They were flanked by antinuclear campaigners calling on governments to honor their promises on arms control. In Czechoslovakia, the campaign's focus was Charter 77, started by the playwright Vaclav Havel, who soon found himself in prison. Noncommunist activists took note. In New York, Aryeh Neier, a former director of the ACLU, founded Human Rights Watch to speak up for prisoners like Havel.

Prodissident movements in the West played their part in the dissolution of Soviet Communism. As Western governments took up the human rights cry, Western skeptics adopted a deflationary story of human rights. As they told it, human rights were invisible before 1945, mouthed in 1948, discarded for three decades, and then seized by Western governments as a weapon in the Second Cold War (1978–85). Not only did such human rights skeptics simplify a complex history, they neglected the force of declarative words and undertakings in politics. They belittled the entrenchment of human rights in Western European legal practice, itself a model for international criminal justice that many claimed would never, but in the 1990s did, establish itself as a new, uncontested norm in a world criminal court. The skeptics underestimated the influence of nonstate "actors" in world politics. A fault that underlay those skeptical mistakes was that the skeptics failed to understand the power of outrage.

"A humanitarian movement," Benenson once said, "should decide its actions from the heart not from the book of law." Debunkers pounced on such talk for lacking what they call "realism." What debunkers missed was that outrage mobilized people. It mobilized in particular people whose moral imaginations made special place for the figure of an exemplary or sacrificial victim. Two hundred years earlier, the Deist Christian Voltaire had understood that fact about people's moral intuitions better than debunkers did. For his *Treatise of Toleration* (1763) Voltaire is justly remembered as an intellectual godparent of the modern movement for the defense of human rights. A striking feature of the *Treatise* was that it appeared to defend a man already dead. The victim was Jean Calas, an obscure Protestant, horribly sacrificed to Catholic bigotry in a gross miscarriage of justice the previous year at Toulouse. Voltaire's campaigning book did, it is true, lead to the dead man's posthumous vindication, to acquittal of his family falsely charged with the same crime, and to handsome compensation for them from the French crown. Voltaire's *Treatise* looked forward more than it looked back. It offered all the same a lesson about the value of singling out exemplary wrongs, which two centuries later Peter Benenson fully understood.

Voltaire saw that without a *Here, look at this!* to rivet attention, people might miss the kind of outrage by power that ought to be absolutely forbidden. People might, Voltaire suggested, reflect that the death of one person was always small in the scale of things. They might settle back on the expedient thought that soldiers die by the thousand without provoking outrage. To put Voltaire's fear in modern terms, people might conclude in Utilitarian spirit that working up moral emotion over one death overweighed a single wrong in the scale of bad outcomes. They might conclude in even more modern terms that focusing on a single miscarriage of justice involved a "salience" mistake of focusing on its horror rather than its rarity. Without pursuing them, Voltaire brushed such doubts aside. He understood the significance of martyrdom. If one death was to be weighed against other deaths, martyrdom was pointless. But evidently martyrdom had a point. The martyr's message was to challenge and unmask power.

The first liberals absorbed Voltaire's lesson. They scrupulously kept a Book of Liberal Martyrs. It included the Duc d'Enghien, kidnapped and shot in 1804 to the indignation of Napoleon's former supporters after a kangaroo trial on the emperor's nod. It included the Saxon liberal executed by Austrian firing squad in the revolution of 1848, Robert Blum, who became a hero in death across the German lands. The Book of Liberal Martyrs ran on with Dreyfus, Sacco and Vanzetti, the Scottsboro Boys, Caryl Chessman, and beyond. Such cases were different on their face. Many of the victims were guilty as charged. Martyrs commonly are. Each sacrifice to power became a cause all the same—against discrimination and intolerance, against racialism, against the death penalty—to which power in time had to respond. Lincoln and Gladstone understood liberal outrage. So, Utilitarian though he was, did Mill. In his *Autobiography* Mill singled out among the many admirabilities of his wife, Harriet Taylor, "a burning indignation at everything brutal or tyrannical." You are a strange sort of liberal if you cannot give in to indignation and outrage.

The achievement of December 1948 was lasting and considerable. Disenchantment arose in large part from undue expectations of justice from the law, of final arguments from philosophers, and of moderation from the political marketplace. Whatever precise form the standards took, there grew after 1948 an acceptance across the world that the rule of law included high standards in the proper treatment of people. It was no longer to be accepted as an excuse for maltreatment, discrimination, or abuse that they were permitted under a country's laws or excused in its courts. It became widely accepted that states and their highest office holders might be held responsible for crimes, an abandonment of an idea about relations among states that had prevailed since the seventeenth century. States or societies that behaved wickedly to their own people were no longer safe from outside judgment or interference simply because their wickedness did not disturb the neighborhood. It became widely noticed that power was shameable and that, with exceptions, even habitual abusers preferred to commit their crimes out of sight, a recognizable step on the upward path from brute behavior to human conduct. Cross-border civic activism of the kind pioneered by Amnesty on behalf of human rights and international justice was accepted as a player in world politics, even by the "realists" of international political thought who had previously admitted to the game of power only states and their agents. None of that progress was complete or irreversible. Still, it was a victory for principles liberals had long stood behind and for liberal practice. For principle, since whatever human rights rested on in the end, as now expressed they reflected the core liberal tenets of resistance to power and civic respect for people, whoever they were. For practice, because experience after 1945 taught that law, government, activists, and outrage all had their part to play in the defense and application of those principles.

One country that did not participate in the victory for human rights in 1948 was Germany. In defeat, occupied, and by now divided, it had lost its status as a sovereign nation and was absent from the drafting and signing of the Declaration of Human Rights. In the western part of Germany nevertheless constitutional talks were underway. The immediate aim was to create a viable and self-governing semi-independent state. The talks led to the creation of an exemplary liberal democracy. As it took shape that new liberal order exemplified much of the declaration's spirit. It put Germany on a path toward recovery of a moral reputation in the world.

ii. German Postwar Liberals: The 1949 Basic Law as Liberal Democracy's Exemplary Charter

It would be neat, if true, to say that victorious Western allies after 1945 airlifted liberal democracy into a broken Germany. It is tempting also, given the scale of what had happened, to treat the postwar recovery of liberal principles as a historical wonder, the political equivalent of Germany's 1950s economic "miracle" only harder to explain. We have glimpsed enough of liberalism's roots in the modern German past, however, to beware of treating liberal democracy in the Federal Republic as a foreign import or a historical wonder. In rebuilding a liberal-democratic life, postwar Germans had three things to draw on. They had a morally ruinous, self-inflicted experiment with extremes of illiberalism. They had a Soviet countermodel which a fourth victorious ally was imposing on eighteen million eastern compatriots next door. And, though almost everyone had reason to doubt it at the time, Germans had strong liberal traditions of their own to draw on.

The constitution that emerged was less the dutiful execution of Western allies' wishes than a German creation that successfully brokered German conflicts. Each ally, it was true, had priorities. Security from Germany preoccupied France. Britain wanted to end the economic drain of occupation. The Americans focused on the overarching Western contest with Soviet Russia. Deteriorating conditions in Germany preoccupied everyone. Although the great capital stock Germany had built up from 1936 to 1942 was largely intact at the end of the war, Russians had begun removing industrial equipment from the East, markets were breaking down, and in places Germans had come close to starving. Conditions at first improved but worsened again in the winter of 1947. Those several postwar concerns converged in June 1948 on a call from the Western allies for a self-governing West German state. Shorn of Austria, the new state was to be liberal, democratic, and decentralized. That much the allies insisted on. Beyond that, they left matters to the

Germans. In July the allies instructed the prime ministers of the western *Länder* or states, which had been reconstituted with their own governments after 1945, to send delegates to a parliamentary council to draft a federal constitution. It was renamed a basic law to honor the letter of the allies' fast-unraveling agreements with the Russians, but also to hold open the prospect of eventual unity.

Much as in 1787 in Philadelphia or 1848 in Frankfurt, the German drafting council reflected social and political divisions. In the industrial, urban north, left and right wanted an effective central authority. The southerners wanted regional autonomy. Catholic Bavaria was suspicious of the Protestant north, and a tradition of liberal localism remained strong in the craft industries and small farms of Baden and Württemberg. The Social Democrats wanted more centralized taxation and revenue-sharing than did the Christian Democrats, the majority party on the right. With remarkable speed, such conflicts were bargained away in mutual concessions that proved more durable than the rotten compromises of Philadelphia. It was easier than expected, as liberal-democratic principles were broadly accepted from the start.

In looking for durable ways to tame power constitutionally, the drafters of Germany's Basic Law in 1949 had the historical memory of liberal resistance to authoritarianism. They had the military budget quarrels of the 1860s and the anti-Bismarck stands of Richter's liberals in the 1870s to 1880s. More directly, they had the Weimar constitution as a model, both to copy and avoid. The aim was that of 1919, to create a government that was responsive but effective, yet shorn of the Weimar constitution's flaws.

At Weimar in 1919 the drafters had aimed to temper authoritarian tradition and executive *diktat* by entrenching popular sovereignty with a variety of constitutional devices. Their results were not stable. In the presidency, they had given Germany a directly elected head of state. They had made referendums comparatively easy to call. Their parliamentary voting system encouraged minority voices and small parties. Against that, they had given the president emergency powers to override parliament. To the drafters of 1949, those several weaknesses contributed to Hitler's constitutional rise to power.

The Basic Law of 1949 built on and corrected Weimar precedent. The new Germany was to be democratic, federal, republican, and "social," meaning committed in some degree to the welfare state. The principles guiding government were popular sovereignty, rule of law, separation of powers, and human rights. Those foundations were made constitutionally unassailable by an "eternity clause." The legislative mainspring of the federal government was the Bundestag, to which chancellor and ministers were responsible. The Bundestag was popularly elected on a double-vote arrangement that combined first-past-the-post constituency voting and party-list proportional representation. An artful compromise, it avoided recognized drawbacks with pure versions of either system. It linked voters to a particular representative, which did not happen with pure proportional representation. At the same time, it gave a parliamentary voice to small parties, which pure constituency systems tended unfairly to exclude. Five percent of the party-list vote was set as a threshold for obtaining seats so as to exclude fringe parties and discourage fragmented coalitions. Though the federal government held the main powers of taxation, an attempt was made to balance central and regional authority. Federal responsibilities included foreign affairs, defense, and the economy. The states retained wide powers on schools, planning, police, and local affairs. The states were represented federally in an upper house, the Bundesrat.

The drafters agreed that Germany's new parliament would be stronger than under Weimar and its president weaker. Dissent was essential, but opposition must not become obstruction. Successive ministries needed to govern and they could not continually fall or be foiled as they had been from 1918 to 1933. Governments would now be overturned in parliament only if an opposition majority existed to form a replacement ("constructive no-confidence"). The president would be an indirectly elected national figurehead. Scope for direct appeal to voters in national referendums would be limited. On left and right alike, it was agreed that liberal democracy should this time be able to defend itself. In addition to the "eternity" clause entrenching liberal democracy—much like the American constitution's insistence on republican, that is nonmonarchical, government, there was to be no "suicidal" article 48, giving the president in the Weimar Republic emergency powers to suspend parliamentary rule and making him in effect a temporary dictator.

The drafters showed "the courage to be intolerant of those who seek to use democracy to kill it," as a Social Democrat, Carlo Schmid, put it.

The new constitution gave Germany's constitutional court authority to ban "anticonstitutional" parties and movements. For the first time it acknowledged citizens' legal right of resistance. If there was no other way, anyone could—and, the implication was, should—resist by force attempts to subvert or overthrow the liberal democratic order. German liberals had always found it difficult to distinguish in their minds between legitimate resistance to undue power and nakedly rebellious disorder. That confusion was gone. Obedience to legitimate authority could no longer be unconditional. The capacity for resistance had become a civic virtue.

The duty of law and society to show civic respect to people individually and not simply to people as members of groups, classes, or social types was present in the Weimar constitution's long and classical list of civil and personal rights. But those 1919 injunctions against intrusion, obstruction and exclusion were more declarations of hope than entrenched protections with the force of law. Such rights could be and were suppressed in times of emergency. They were overseen by conservative courts that brutally applied one law for insurgents on the left and another with culpable lenience for assassins on the right. In 1949 the duty of administrative and judicial authority to observe civil and personal rights became German law. The Weimar constitution began with politics and almost as an afterthought turned to people only after article 108. The 1949 constitution started with people and then moved to politics.

The drafters had not only German experience but liberal tradition to draw on. Running through the new German constitution were three guiding liberal thoughts about civic respect, the inevitability of conflict, and the need to resist power. The Basic Law's opening words pointed to a moral ground for the existence of the state's duty to respect personal rights. It lay in human dignity. "Human dignity shall be inviolable," article 1 read, "To respect and protect it shall be the duty of all state authority." The conflict of ideals and beliefs was accepted as a normal part of public life that could not be legislated away or stifled by state fiat. There was to be no repeat of the *Kulturkampf*. The states rather than the federal government were made supreme in matters of culture, religion, and education. Underpinning the whole, as the Christian Democrat drafter

Adolf Süsterhenn put it, was a wish to avoid what liberals from the beginning had feared, "a concentration of power in any one place."

Watching from afar in disgrace at his native home in a small town near Düsseldorf was the ex-Nazi constitutional expert Carl Schmitt (1888–1985). Ambiguous as ever, he bewailed himself as a "King Lear of public law" and wrote scholarly complaints about the new basic law. Those focused particularly on the powers of the constitutional court to countermand decisions of parliament and government. The 1949 Basic Law represented for Schmitt victory and defeat. As a theory-minded lawyer, Schmitt in the 1920s and 1930s had taken sides in a long-running dispute about the scope and nature of law that was particularly lively in Germany. The puzzle was this. If law is what the sovereign lawmaking authority commands, how lawfully may those commands be refused or overturned except by the sovereign?

The question was not academic. In a nation with a once justly admired civil service, a tradition of rule following and strong respect for law, it was an urgent matter to find ways for law to challenge law, indeed to give people orderly, lawful ways to challenge and resist the prevailing rules. For Germany's "legal positivists" law was whatever lawmaking authority said was law. Laws on the positivist account could be unjust, inequitable, wicked and still be law. Legal positivists might and commonly did complain of bad laws. Yet they left courts too little room to apply higher standards of right in interpreting them and citizens too little lawful means of dissent. So it had seemed to legal positivism's critics. On the left the critics included Hermann Heller (1891–1933), a Social Democrat lawyer who sought legal principles for containing the abuse of power that did not rely on contestable religious tenets or intricate moral constructions. At the center, the critics included Rudolph Smend (1882–1975), a theologian's son, who looked to social traditions for legal standards against which to judge prevailing laws.

On the German right, legal positivism's outstanding critic was Schmitt. Politics for Schmitt was about power, and law was the voice of power, but power thought of in a mischievously subtle way. The law, he believed, could indeed be "lawfully" circumvented or suspended in emergencies for the safety of the nation. For supreme authority lay, in Schmitt's view, not in the power to make ordinary laws but rather in the power to set laws aside, declare emergency, and rule by exception. Schmitt, in brief, was attempting to legitimize temporary dictatorship for the state's protection.

The drafters of 1949 agreed with Schmitt that the state should be able to protect itself against its enemies, but saw those enemies differently from Schmitt. To the drafters, the constitution needed protection from "anticonstitutional" forces intent on undermining its liberal-democratic principles. Schmitt looked on the state's enemies as enemies of the state as such, whether democratic, liberal, or whatever. The drafters agreed alike with Schmitt, Heller, and Smend in rejecting legal positivism: existing law for them was not law's last word. Unlike Schmitt, the drafters made personal rights, not power and national security, the standard by which ordinary law was to be gauged. They made a hierarchy of courts, with a constitutional court at the top, the arbiters of how far such standards were met. Much as in the United States and more clearly than in France or Britain, the 1949 German constitution made law a critic of the law.

A document that provided postwar Germany with an institutional reputation for deliberateness and caution was agreed to with executive speed. Approval was democratic, but not direct or popular. The constitution was not put to a referendum, which it was feared the Communists would exploit. On May 8, 1949, the council voted 53 to 12 for the Basic Law. Among the *Länder* Bavaria voted no, 101 to 63, but agreed to join if two-thirds of the other *Länder* assented, which they did. The Western allies accepted the Basic Law on the 12th and it was promulgated on the 23rd. In the first postwar West German election in August, parties of the right won around 60 percent of the vote.

The Basic Law of 1949 had little of the soaring voice and insatiable goals of late eighteenth-century constitutional oratory in France and the United States that ushered in the liberal era. The chastened tone and tightened scope lent weight. If you want a national model of twentieth-century liberal-democratic aims and ideals cast into realizable shape, it is hard to find a clearer statement than Germany's 1949 Basic Law.

Drastic economic measures helped provide the material conditions for that constitutional charter to survive and operate. Amid the near famine of 1946–47 punitive thoughts of Churchill, Henry Morgenthau, and Jean Monnet to divide or pillage western Germany, as the Russians were doing in the east, were put aside. In 1949 a currency reform that swapped old reichsmark for new deutsche marks at ten to one soaked up the involuntary savings of the war years when there was little to buy and averted a demand-pull inflation of the kind that had burdened the Weimar Republic in 1918–23. In 1957 Germany's central bank, the Bundesbank, won its legal independence from the federal government as a guardian of monetary stability. By 1961, in an indication of Germany's financial strength, the deutsche mark was revalued by 5 percent against the American dollar.

A three-party system recognizable from the Weimar Republic emerged to manage the bargaining. The political right gathered itself into a single broad party committed to liberal democracy, the Christian Democrats (CDU). In turbulent but lasting marriage with its Bavarian ally, the CDU bridged old divisions between North and South, Protestant and Catholic, middle class and working class. By embracing a tempered free-market economy it overcame Catholic suspicions of liberal capitalism that had lingered in the Center Party. The Social Democrats accepted in practice the same economic ground rules, though waited to admit it until the end of the 1950s. The Christian Democrats marginalized the nationalist right that had bedeviled Weimar either by excluding it from mainstream politics or by gathering it in, drained of its venom. Unlike Stresemann, West Germany's first postwar chancellor, Konrad Adenauer, was able to pursue conciliation with France in a West European setting, untroubled by the nihilism of the right or radical economic demands from the left. Naumann's liberal dream of a peaceful, negotiated European free-trading order turned westward and purged of its aversion to France, began to take shape.

As the spectrum of democratic politics in West Germany was liberal, there was strictly no need for a liberal party. Within liberal-democratic consensus there was still plenty to argue over and party totems to honor. The successors of the Weimar liberal parties regrouped as Free Democrats in November 1948, under an old Weimar journalist, Theodor Heuss (1884–1963), who had studied economics under Brentano and written a life of Friedrich Naumann. The founding meeting took place at Heppenheim, not far from Frankfurt, where the "Halves" or moderate liberals of 1848 had issued their manifesto. The Free Democrats became West Germany's swing party, winning between 6 percent and 15 percent of the vote. They brought down the Christian Democrats in 1966, judging them too laissez-faire and too hostile to détente with East Germany. In 1982, they brought down the Social Democrats, judging their economics too statist and their foreign policy too friendly to Soviet interests in the Second Cold War (1978–85). Neither was a shocking or sudden shift, but reflected the changing mood. Gradual adjustment was spelled out in lengthy letters of political intent and months of cross-party argument in a system where all parties gravitated to a slowly shifting center.

The steady sensibleness of West Germany baffled and provoked intellectual critics to right and left. Among right-wing liberals, two frustrated early stars were Alexander Rüstow (1885–1963), coiner of "neoliberalism," and his fellow economist, Wilhelm Röpke (1899–1966). Both were alumni of the Walter Lippmann Colloquium of 1938 and members of Hayek's Mont Pelerin Society, though neither of them subscribed to an ultra-liberal purism. As part of the free-market Freiburg school, the two had fallen afoul of Nazi centralism. Both left Germany in 1933 to teach in Istanbul. Rüstow returned in 1949 to Germany, where he founded the *Ordo* journal, taking its high-end name from the Latin for "order." The journal promoted a market economy underpinned by a responsible, effective state that policed rules, promoted competition, and provided within limits for social need. Under Ludwig Erhard, economics minister and later chancellor who supervised Germany's "economic miracle" in the 1950s, such ideas became known as the social-market model, a phrase coined by Alfred Müller-Armack, Erhard's adviser in the ministry.

Röpke never returned to Germany but lived and worked in Switzerland. In postwar Geneva he took a post at the Rockefeller-backed Institut Universitaire des Hautes Études Internationales as a colleague of Mises. In elegant, clear newspaper articles through the 1950s Röpke kept alive the anti-Keynesian flame, rued the compulsions of the welfare state, flagged the dangers of inflation, and—less prophetically—campaigned for a return to the gold standard. He was convinced that monetary stabilization and free-market economics in the late 1940s had saved West Germany from socialization or worse. Unlike Mises, with his nose for what his business backers wanted, Röpke was as much moralist as economist. Röpke expressed himself in prose more than equations and for a while used Latin titles, as if the German language needed time for disinfection. He suggested in *Civitas Humana* (1944) and *Beyond Supply and Demand* (1958) that there was more to liberal order than the free market. Much as Lippmann and Hayek had, Röpke blamed late nineteenth-century capitalism's excesses for the reactions of collectivism and social democracy. Mass consumerism shocked him. He dreaded the concentration of business. The snag was that Röpke's cures proved as elusive as they had for the nineteenth-century anticentralizing liberals Tocqueville and Schulze-Delitzsch. Liberals liked capitalism, but capitalism needed the large scale.

Röpke's individualism was in the nostalgic tradition of locality and the small scale. An imaginary Switzerland, with cantonal democracy and responsible, independent-minded citizenry, occupied an equivalent place in his ideal geography as that held by Denmark or Sweden in the heads of social-minded liberals. As suggested earlier at the end of Part One, robust capitalism required neither attachment to locality nor critical self-directedness among citizens. It required mobility, scale, and vast markets. Business liberalism and ethical liberalism did not neatly coincide. Conflict between commercial efficiency and what might be called moral community became preoccupying in the 1970s and after. Parties of the right adopted moral agendas. Troubled liberals dallied with communitarianism.

In Germany, Röpke's articles about the limits of the market echoed in a different movement. The Greens, founded in 1980 and with twenty-eight seats in the Bundestag three years later, agreed with *Ordo* liberals that there was more to life than growing the economy. Their concern was less harm to initiative or community than to the environment. Greens presumed that in the capitalist world at any rate people were growing rich enough. The "stationary state" of Smith and Mill was perhaps at last in sight. The old Marxist radicalism had taught that capitalism needed replacing, as it was faltering at history's tasks. Green radicalism taught that capitalism was in robust health but had completed its task and now needed to slow down. Otherwise, by continuing to add to wealth, it risked despoiling the human living space in which anyone might use and enjoy that wealth.

For eighteen million Germans who became citizens of the German Democratic Republic in 1949, normality had to wait. As two German societies grew apart, West German liberal democracy became for easterners an ever-present but unapproachable lure. The positions of the Western political parties on Germany's division did not follow neat lines. In the 1940s to 1950s, under the Catholic Rhinelander Adenauer, the Christian Democrats paid lip service to German unity, pursuing instead Western anchorage and Franco-German reconciliation. Kurt Schumacher, leader of the Social Democrats, was born in a part of Prussia that was now in Poland. His party had strong support in the east, especially industrial Saxony, now under Soviet control. Schumacher clung to hopes that Cold War might be averted and held out for a neutral, undivided Germany.

Adenauer's view prevailed. Two Germanies emerged, and it was soon hard for anyone to imagine how they might ever come together again. The divisions became so deep and visible, it became easy to forget what united them: language, family ties, land, and past. Among those things was the German state pension system. It survived the collapse of the Weimar Republic, the defeat of Nazism, and the division of Germany. It was familiar to a little known British official who had studied German welfare policies in person before the First World War. He was William Beveridge, and he gave his name in Britain to a further giant step in liberalism's economic compromise with democracy.

iii. Beveridge: Liberalism and Welfare

One of the few significant back-bench revolts in Britain's parliament during the Second World War came over government reluctance to back a comprehensive state-run scheme for postwar social insurance. The scheme was to cover everyone and provide material security throughout life. It would include unemployment insurance, old-age pensions, family allowances, and a free national health service. The Tory-Labour coalition government was cool. The start-up cost, which promised to double social spending at a stroke, appalled the Treasury. The British public saw matters differently. *The Report of the Inter-Departmental Committee on Social Insurance and Allied Services*, which outlined the scheme, sold out on publication in December 1942. Polls indicated the scheme's popularity. Parliament took note, 121 MPs voted against postponement and the government changed its mind. Two months later

Britain's prime minister, Winston Churchill, undertook to introduce postwar implementation of "national compulsory insurance for all classes for all purposes from the cradle to the grave."

Churchill's wartime deputy and post-1945 successor, the Labour leader Clement Attlee, made good on that undertaking. Legislation in 1946–48 implemented the essentials of the plan's four main provisions. The Welfare State, as the elements together were known, became a hallowed part of Britain's unwritten constitution. In one form or another—for there were many forms—the Welfare State became an irreplaceable part of postwar liberal capitalism across Western Europe. With the exception of national health insurance, which a majority of Americans in the late 1940s wanted according to opinion polls but did not obtain, a Welfare State of a kind emerged also in the United States. If Keynesianism represented liberalism's economic compromise with democracy, welfarism represented a large new step in its social compromise.

The British scheme's author was a lifelong Liberal, William Beveridge (1879–1963). He called it "revolutionary," which in a way it was, though he came to draft it almost by accident. Beveridge's father was a colonial civil servant who believed in Home Rule for India. His mother campaigned to educate Hindu women. For a clever boy from such a background it would have taken a natural catastrophe for him not to reach Balliol College, Oxford, then the intellectual forcing house of future liberal reformers. On winning a first-class degree in classics and mathematics, a top career as don or barrister opened to Beveridge. Instead he became a leader writer on the *Morning Post* and did social work in London's East End.

After an obligatory inspection tour of Germany to observe Bismarckian social reforms, Beveridge joined the Board of Trade and helped draft the unemployment provisions of Lloyd George's 1911 social insurance bill. Stiff and driven, he was a social engineer who thought in terms of aggregates and results with little regard for people in the way. At the Ministry of Munitions during the 1914–18 war, he demanded near-military discipline in arms plants and tight limits on collective bargaining. Yet Beveridge responded also to particular wrongs. In the 1930s he persuaded the government to relax work and immigration rules for German and Austrian university teachers fleeing fascism. Beveridge was by then out of Whitehall and head of the London School of Economics, a center of orthodoxy in counterpose to Keynesian Cambridge. In that contest Beveridge favored the gold standard and was doubtful about Keynesianism, but his focus of interest and true expertise lay in labor markets and social insurance. When war returned, Beveridge was back in government under Ernest Bevin at the Ministry of Labour. Beveridge asked to direct manpower. Nobody, after all, knew more about it than he did. Bevin was an enormous, immoveable presence uncowed by brains or status. He had run Britain's biggest trade union and remembered Beveridge's imperious ways from the first war. Bevin ignored his demand and pushed Beveridge sideways into, as Beveridge initially thought, a lesser job. He greeted Bevin's decision with tears in his eyes. The lesser job was drafting a report on the future of social insurance.

Though much of what Beveridge proposed was already in the pipeline, his report took two years to complete. His genius was to present several elements as a whole, to underline their urgency with copious social statistics and to unify them with an overall moral and political vision. His biographer, José Harris, described Beveridge as offering a "Bunyanesque vision" of society's battle against what he called the "five giants of idleness, disease, ignorance, squalor and want." As to what it provided, the plan's elements interlocked. Family benefit would lessen child poverty without removing the gap between wages and relief, which was essential in Beveridge's mind if welfare was not to discourage work. A health service would relieve social insurance from subsidizing absence from work through illness. Better health would slow the rise in costs of treating illness.

As did Cobden when promoting free trade, Beveridge argued that the plan made winners all round. Coverage was universal. Costs were shared. High-risk recipients benefited directly. Low-risk nonrecipients benefited indirectly from living in a healthier, securer nation. He exploited the plan's detail to narrow the ground for doctrinal objections. Gone were Chadwick's nineteenth-century legacy of "lesser eligibility" and the means-testing of Edwardian welfare, loathed by the left as demeaning. Treating the nonhealth elements as insurance, paid by contributions, was just credible enough to silence conservative fears over cost. Beveridge's scheme even straddled two views of the liberal-democratic state that were beginning to emerge: neutral ring keeper and upholder of legal equality (favored on the right) or active focus of concern and solidarity (favored on the left). National welfare schemes appealed across the board in less theoretical ways, and not only in Britain. They bought off left-wing parties. They tidied up and controlled, or so it was hoped, the costly patchwork of existing provision. They answered an ever-present concern of liberalism's better sort to improve "social health" by raising up the moral and material condition of the masses. That mix of motives and justifications for social welfare was at the start a selling point. In time the lack of any one agreed aim or commonly accepted rationale became a handicap, especially as costs rose.

Beveridge saw that without a strong economy creating work the welfare state could quickly become unaffordable. A friendship with Keynes at the Treasury helped stiffen Beveridge on the point. Beveridge followed up with a second report, *Full Employment in a Free Society* (1944). Both were thinking of the 1930s. Their dominant anxiety was a slack economy. Neither paused at the fact that the driver of universal welfare's rising cost would be better health, itself ensured by the National Health Service founded in 1948. Better health proved costly because healthier people lived longer, the old needed more doctoring than the young and because the costs of doctoring rose as medicine grew more complex and its range of treatments widened. The problem was common but by 2010, to continue with the British example, the disability-free life expectancy at birth was about four-fifths of life expectancy, a roundabout way to say that people would spend about a fifth of life ill and in need of care. On reaching 65, the average Briton could expect eight to nine years of worsening health.

Hallowed and popular as it was, Britain's health service became the object of continual study, criticism and re-engineering in an unbroken cycle of reforming reforms. In 1951, the Labour government imposed health-service charges for medicines, dental work and eye glasses. Aneurin Bevan, who pushed through the NHS as health minister, resigned in protest. In France and Germany, governments were less directly involved in paying doctors and running hospitals. Neither those countries nor the United States escaped the spiraling costs of keeping people healthy. As governments in this period undertook also to provide state pensions to the old, the bills grew. Almost nobody saw it at the time, but liberalism's social compromise with democracy became more and more expensive. In economic bad times especially, internal politics in liberal democracies often appeared to turn on little else.

The provision of universal health care raised a puzzle for liberals about progress and the dream of human betterment that Adam Smith had foreseen and Mill had dwelt on. Was a healthy society a fixed or moving target? That troublesome question arose with other boons of life: shelter, food, and schooling, for example. The question faced liberal-democratic societies however they provided for human welfare. If human well-being included such boons, as surely it did, might well-being not be forever improvable with better houses, richer and more varied food, longer and more demanding education? Or was material well-being by contrast a fixed target, an ample but achievable minimum about which it was possible to say, once fairly and universally distributed, "This is enough?"

12

Liberal Thinking after 1945

In the nineteenth century most of what was thought or said about liberalism could be expressed in terms that an interested reading public might understand. The characteristic form of liberal thought was the essay or public lecture. Constant addressed his thoughts on ancient and modern democracy to a political club. Mill wrote his political pieces for literary magazines. The liberal thinker was typically also a politician. Constant sat in the assembly, Guizot was prime minister, Mill was a member of parliament. They were writing for a wide public. They knew from experience what they were writing about. That breadth and intimacy began to lessen at the end of the nineteenth century, particularly as technical economics came to take up more space in liberal minds. After 1945 the separation of ideas and politics appeared to be complete as each side professionalized itself. Especially in the United States and Britain, liberal thought fell into the hands of full-time professionals. There it was toned and disciplined with a rigor of analysis and argument not found outside universities, though without that earlier familiarity with the political practice its ideas were intended to illuminate. Liberal politics fell into the hands of full-time politicians who, even if former think-tankers, had little time to think let alone themselves pen political thoughts.

Ideas all the same continued to flow from thinkers into politics. Terms such as "open society" from Karl Popper or "negative liberty" from Isaiah Berlin entered public debate. Friedrich Hayek's "spontaneous order" and John Rawls's "difference principle" never quite made it out of the academy, but the rough picture of society that each thinker had in mind did. Everyone could tell a society of the kind Hayek imagined where poverty was left to charity and luck from a society where, as Rawls pictured things, poverty was a matter of public priority and government policy. The climate of politics continued to influence what the thinkers thought. The emphasis on justice and rights in political thinking after 1945 made sense to people who had seen what wrongs might be done to people with the help of false appeals to the common good.

The modesty demanded of politics by Isaiah Berlin and Michael Oakeshott was partly a call for quiet after the totalitarian and patriotic bellowing of the previous twenty years. Rawls's *A Theory of Justice* was as much protest at the economic and racial unfairness of American society as an intricate piece of theoretical engineering. The flirtation among liberal thinkers with "community" in the 1980s reflected among other things concern for the social damage wrought by the stagflation of the previous decade. Nor did the universities wholly monopolize liberal ideas. The liberal writers George Orwell and Albert Camus as well as Jean-Paul Sartre, who despite his avowed and errant politics was a liberal by temperament, carried on an older practice of the political essay.

i. Oakeshott and Berlin: Letting Politics Alone and "Negative" Liberty

Oakeshott and Berlin took a modest view of what politics could accomplish or political ideas explain. In calling for political quiet, each of them fixed on an aspect of the constraints that liberals place on acceptable social order. Though liberal in tone and ethical attitudes, Oakeshott made the conservative complaint that liberals neglected tradition as a source of political order. Berlin stressed that conflict among our aims and ideals was ineradicable and that attempts to harmonize them led to ethical frustration and political calamity.

Michael Oakeshott (1901–90) was a refusenik of modern life. As a young philosopher in an empiricist and anti-idealist age, he adopted a form of philosophical idealism. On turning to political thought, he rejected the entire "new liberal" spirit behind Beveridge's welfare state. On succeeding a high priest of social engineering, Harold Laski, as professor of political science at the London School of Economics, Oakeshott's inaugural lecture, "Political Education" (1951), made plain that he did not believe in the subject. Politics belonged among the humanities, and trying to make the humanities into sciences was a mistake, Oakeshott argued. Understanding a healthy society was not a technical, let alone a purely economic, task. Material results mattered, but so did public virtues such as integrity, self-restraint, and civility. With good reason, his biographer, Paul Franco, bestowed on Oakeshott the Nietzschean accolade "untimely."

His personal life was cheerful, convivial, and eventful. He was married three times and had many affairs. He grew up just outside London in a middle-class household. His father, a civil servant and Fabian socialist, sent him to a progressive, coeducational school. He reached Cambridge, did well there, and won a fellowship. Two years at the theological schools of Tübingen and Marburg steeped Oakeshott in modern German thought, convinced him that religious faith could do without theology, and persuaded him that knowledge could get by without foundations.

In the Second World War, he served as a targeting officer for the artillery. The rest of his life he spent writing and teaching. On retirement, he left for a Dorset village where he enjoyed the pub and mending his own roof. He was by then an academic celebrity, and was offered Britain's second highest award for intellectual endeavor, the Companion of Honour. Oakeshott, a high Bohemian, refused. Though followers started societies in his name, he hated followings. His idea of fun was parties and the companionship of the young, drinking and arguing with them long into the night.

Oakeshott wrote two large, difficult books and in between a number of readable if allusive essays. The first book, *Experience and Its Modes* (1933), stepped off from the thought that the human mind makes a frame of ideas so as to order the flux of experience and guide it through an otherwise chaotic world in which it finds itself. Oakeshott saw not one frame but three: scientific, historical, and practical, in which last frame he included politics and morals. He called them "modes of experience." Each had its place and none was master. Between the modes there could be "neither dispute nor agreement"—and presumably no communication either. Instead of one how-mind-relates-to-world puzzle Oakeshott now had three. Much later in "The Voice of Poetry in the Conversation of Mankind" (1962) he added a fourth element, poetic imagination. To replace separate, noncommunicating "modes of experience,"

Oakeshott now wrote of distinctive "voices" conducting "conversations" with their own standards of aptness.

By then Oakeshott's manner of philosophy was out of style and he had left it for political thought, taking his root convictions with him. There was no one story of human conduct and no explanatory laws for it, only a giving and taking of the sorts of reason that fitted the "conversation" you were in. Oakeshott's lack of interest in foundations, indifference to close analysis and distrust of large syntheses aligned him with liberal American pragmatists such as John Dewey and Richard Rorty. The left-liberal Rorty gave traditionalist Oakeshott a bow at the end of *Philosophy and the Mirror of Nature* (1980) for best catching the "tone in which philosophy ought to be discussed."

For Oakeshott the cardinal sin of modern politics was overthinking. In "Rationalism in Politics" (1947) he described the sin's elements as believing that no social arrangement was immune to rational criticism, that remedial policies must be uniform, principled, and universally applicable, and that, given the proper policies, society as a whole was improvable. Those errors together underlay what he called the technical outlook. The "practical" outlook, which he favored, stood out by contrast chiefly with the faults of the "technical." Oakeshott gave a provocative list of the mischiefs the "rationalist" mind causes in politics: the Declaration of the Rights of Man, the merit civil service, votes for women, the destruction of the Austro-Hungarian Empire, the Catering Wages Act, and the revival of Gaelic in Ireland. The fogeyish wag was teasing the *bien pensants*, but with serious purpose. Oakeshott's suggestion was that rationalizers caused the problems their reforms were intended to correct. Examples were ever to hand. As a general truth, Oakeshott's claim was weak. His antirationalist critique of reform might appeal in a static society. In the dynamic societies of liberal capitalism, things were changing all the time, willy-nilly. Some change was for the good, some for the bad. The bad needed correcting. There are other views of the tireless reform of reforms that Oakeshott mocked. Perhaps as a philosophical idealist he exaggerated the powers of mind. He treated political managerialism as the avoidable product of rationalist folly. A more sympathetic view is to take it as a harried but sometimes effective reaction to an unavoidable modern predicament.

Oakeshott's second large book, *On Human Conduct* (1975), elaborated on the contrast of technique and practice. Two guides, he suggested, competed in modern society. One was "nomocracy," the other "teleocracy." One spoke for heeding tradition and making do with repair under broadly accepted procedural rules. The other appealed to plans, principles, goals, indeed to almost any general test by which the actual might be judged against a better possible order and found wanting. To nomocracy and teleocracy corresponded two kinds of human association. A "civil association" was civic and moral. People acknowledged membership in such an association by accepting the moral authority of its rules. An "enterprise association" was managerial and prudential. People joined it for a common purpose. Both sorts were voluntary. But the fairness and goodness of civil association might be tested only against prevailing tradition and law, not against some perfect model of society or against what improved the human lot. Oakeshott drew on both his intellectual heroes, Hobbes and Hegel. From Hobbes, Oakeshott took the thought that the absolute moral authority of civil association was no bar to liberty, understood as the absence of external constraint. From Hegel, he took the thought that morality was rooted in social tradition. Morals were a "sediment," without significance unless "suspended in a religious or social tradition." To endure, tradition must adapt to ever-changing circumstances.

Oakeshott's erudition and classical terms could not hide his political target, the "managerial state" of welfare capitalism. His picture of modern politics as presided over by a good and a bad angel was like Popper's open and closed society and Hayek's "made" and "spontaneous" order, a likeness Oakeshott was loath to admit. He was not often generous with his peers. He wounded the music-lover Berlin, whose insistence on the diversity of human concerns was very like his own, by calling Berlin "a Paganini of ideas," as if to say he was a brilliant but shallow virtuoso. Oakeshott faulted Hayek, who shared his distrust of reformist managerialism, for "the saddest of misunderstandings," suggesting that Hayek's "plan to resist all planning may be better than its opposite but it belongs to the same style of politics."

Oakeshott remained aloof. He left arresting images: the search for knowledge as a "conversation" and politics as a vessel without home port endlessly plowing the sea. What, though, were the conversational rules? Had the voyage charts and a compass? Oakeshott did not say. He foxed labelers. Was he liberal or conservative? Neither could fully claim him. He was a borderline case. Oakeshott stressed something Constant had seen in modern people: their lives were full of things besides politics. Oakeshott described listening to the news as a nervous complaint. He seemed to be reminding political thinkers how little people think about politics. It was unclear that they needed so reminding, and Oakeshott's claim was besides a half-truth. People think little about politics most of the time, but then, abruptly and with great impact, they think of it a lot. In denying that many political questions were addressable or solvable, Oakeshott left large ones hanging. His openness to distinct modes of thought, none of which dominated, was liberal in a loose way. Liberal concern for human betterment, on the other hand, Oakeshott treated as an over-general "rationalist" and "managerial" illusion. Despite their popularity and success, he was hostile to "new liberal" policies of redistribution and welfare. In age, he grew nationalistic and ignorantly disparaged the European Union. As for the content of "civility"—acting on the public virtues he prized and resisting the powers he detested—Oakeshott remained vague, though vague in the suggestive and appealing mode of poetry. Though "untimely" when he wrote, Oakeshott's suspicion of technocracy anticipated the rise of Green concerns for the damage technocracy was doing to the natural environment. Yet he disdained activism. Oakeshott's liberal quietism was apt for a ship in calm seas.

Isaiah Berlin (1909–97) was also hard to categorize. Like Oakeshott, he lived and breathed ideas but stood back from technical philosophy. Politically, the left distrusted him, while the right appropriated and distorted his ideas. He was a bookish intellectual who operated socially at the top. "I've no feelings about people I've never seen," he wrote self-mockingly to a friend in 1934, "unless they're very, very grand indeed." Yet he was unstintingly generous to all-comers with his ideas and his time. He spent a career at Oxford University without acquiring a trace of scholarly narrowness. History, philosophy, and literature were as one subject for him. Berlin had a dramatist's gift of personalizing ideas and for bringing them alive in paired opposites. Thinkers he disagreed with particularly attracted him. A child of the Enlightenment, Berlin was fascinated by anti-Enlightenment thought. Conflict preoccupied him, and conflict was easiest to dramatize digitally, in twos, on or off, black or white. As writer and lecturer Berlin grasped the irresistibility of the neat contrast. He divided political thinkers into hedgehogs with one idea and foxes with many. He split liberalism's biggest totem into negative liberty (good) and positive liberty (bad).

When Berlin was knighted, a friend congratulated him for services to conversation. He was a gifted talker and feline gossip who wrote as he spoke in a bubbling flow of erudition, malice, wit, and human insight. After the war Berlin explained he was going to "evaporate" as a full-time philosopher. That was a half-truth. In many variants and often through the voice of past thinkers who seemed present in the room with him but always in his own unstoppable prose, Berlin kept returning to three core ideas: that freedom from constraint by others (negative liberty) is more urgent or basic than freedom to flourish or "realize yourself" (positive liberty); that liberalism fails if it cannot validate the universal need to belong and find a home with others in a distinct human grouping that you have either chosen or were born into; and that our basic commitments—to friendship and truth, fairness and liberty, family and achievement, nation and principle—clash routinely and cannot be smoothly reconciled. Thinkers and politicians should admit the conflicts, Berlin implied, and not blanket them over with simplifying doctrine or tyrannical attempts to subordinate certain concerns to others. Conflict need not mean violence or aggression. Acceptance of disagreement and avoidance of violence went hand in hand for him. All violence, even the argumentative kind, terrified and repelled him. He never forgot as a child seeing an angry crowd beat a Russian policeman. An Oxford colleague, the moral philosopher and logician David Wiggins, recalled that if anyone showed the least verbal aggression in discussion, Berlin would leave the room.

Berlin's "pluralist" advice was plainly liberal in its acknowledgment of conflict and refusal of domination. It was also easy to misunderstand, for it was ethical first, political second. Berlin's point was less that people disagreed about purposes in life among each other than that life's aims competed within us. The supposed fact of diversity in moral belief was greatly exaggerated, Berlin thought. "More people in more countries at more times accept more common values than is often believed," he once told Steven Lukes. Pluralism for Berlin was less about splitting up political power or welcoming a variety of views. It was not that ethical diversity enriched society or that having a wide "menu" of ethical "choices" was good for people individually. Berlin's pluralism was a stronger, more demanding doctrine about the ethical facts. It suggested that there existed many basic ethical values not of our choosing. Each made its demands on us and any might clash with others without hope of reconciliation.

Such ethical pluralism, properly understood, had import for liberalism. If true, it offered an argument for forbearance and open-mindedness. If all of us are complex beings with irreconcilable goals, then putting people into warring social, religious, or cultural camps as if those camps were uniform, coherent wholes was absurd. It mislocated the source of conflict. In attacking others for their values and attachments you might be attacking something half acknowledged in yourself. That powerful, attractive argument echoed the preliberal argument from ignorance in favor of religious toleration. It drew on subsequent liberal tradition of accepting "difference" and not excluding dissenters or outsiders. It spoke for the more hopeful side of liberalism's acceptance of conflict as natural and fruitful for humans.

Berlin saw that most social groups depend for their appeal on denying or suspending attention to the very complexity that he insisted on. Submerging yourself in a group and listening to your heart's conflicting demands answered different human needs. Berlin recognized the tension in himself. Belonging was vital to him, as he believed it should be for all liberals. He was born in Riga, the capital of Latvia, then part of the Russian Empire. He considered his adopted England the best of countries, campaigned for a Jewish state in Palestine, and, while detesting the Soviet Union, never lost a profound attachment to Russia, from where his parents had brought him as a boy of eleven in 1920. He was staunch in his Zionism. On transfer from the Foreign Office at the British embassy in wartime Washington, where Berlin reported on American politics, he was asked to find who had leaked, and effectively killed, a proposal that Britain and America declare Palestine's future to be on hold until after the war. Berlin duly reported back in a letter of masterful ambiguity. The leaker was Berlin. Russia and its thinkers, above all his liberal hero Alexander Herzen, kept its hold. A letter to his parents from

Moscow in 1945, where he was briefly at work as a diplomat, read like an imaginary homecoming. Need he describe, he asked them, "the crunching snow" or the "timbre of soldiers singing in the distance" as they marched? To expect from Berlin an answer to the tension for liberals between individuality and belonging was to miss his aim. Pointing out the existence of the tension and insisting that everyone had to negotiate it as they went was for him the best anyone could do.

"Two Concepts of Liberty" (1957), Berlin's inaugural lecture as professor of political thought at Oxford, was a lesson in the slipperiness of a liberal banner term and about not trusting titles. The lecture touched many topics, but was remembered for canonizing a two-camps distinction between "negative" liberty and "positive" liberty. Negative liberty, Berlin insisted, was the only sort liberals should care about, but he did not believe liberals should care about nothing but liberty. The second part of Berlin's message tended to be lost, as was his belief as to why liberty mattered. Echoing Constant almost in his words, Berlin affirmed people's privacy: "some portion of human existence must remain independent of the sphere of social control." That was so because, whatever its metaphysical foundations, which were a matter of "infinite debate," there existed a core of human worth that was universal and untouched by cultural or national differences. Many things mattered in life, Berlin believed as a "pluralist," and there were no guarantees they could all be achieved or enjoyed together. What mattered, though, was much the same everywhere; Berlin was a pluralist, not a relativist.

On Berlin's polar contrast, positive liberty was a freedom of human development, to foster and exercise one's capacities or, to use a dark phrase Berlin made mischief with, "to realise one's true self." Negative liberty seemed simpler. It was freedom from external constraint to do as you wished. Commitment to negative liberty as a political ideal, he thought, was recent, difficult for Utilitarians such as Mill to allow for, and compatible with undemocratic forms of government. Negative liberty, Berlin was saying in effect, enjoined from state and society nonintrusion and nonobstruction. Here Berlin drew a line: negative liberty was the only sort liberals should pursue. The pursuit of positive liberty led to errors and evils, which Berlin proceeded to sketch with the bite of a caricaturist. They included T. H. Green's error of equating people's run-of-the-mill, actual desires with false, low desires and then treating the ascent, no doubt with bossy help from their betters, toward higher and truer desires as a form of liberation; Spinoza's illusion that impositions, the causes of which we understood, did not restrict our freedom; and the myth of "Sarastro's temple," that society itself might be "freed" to find a higher, rational order, a myth that turned on the worst mistake of all, imagining that in morals and politics there existed a single ideal order if only it might be found. Positive liberty, on Berlin's account, had a lot to answer for.

Intricate arguments about the character of political liberty ensued. External restraints on our wishes were not as simple as Berlin made out. He quickly acknowledged the difficulty of "adaptive preferences," a new name for the old wisdom that one way to free ourselves when prevented from what we want to do was to stop wanting to do it, in a sour-grapes way. It was pointed out also that we might have desires we did not want. We might hold beliefs in bad faith or convictions pressed on us by mystification. The "new liberal" objection was revived that without the means or capacity to use them, many freedoms were in themselves of little worth. It was suggested in addition that any given freedom was a triad involving people, restraints, and aims: a free person was always free from a certain kind of obstacle to pursue an aim or lead their life in a particular way. Until such details were patched in, complaints of political unfreedom and demands for political liberty lacked grip. Many people wondered how deep the conceptual distinction between "negative" and "positive" liberty really was. Much turned on what looked like verbalism. Any supposed negative freedom could be described as positive, and vice versa. Being free to walk in the park was, after all, not being made not to walk in the park. Much as when Popper urged politicians and officials to avoid the worst rather than aim for the best, Berlin was making more a political than a philosophical point. He was not so much illuminating the concept *liberty* as recommending political attitudes and priorities.

In time, "republican" liberty was added to liberal thought as a refinement of negative liberty in a "third way," spirit of compromise. Republican liberty was taken for reliable protection from domination by others. It was not enough, in the republican view of liberty, to be free of arbitrary interference. You had to be secure from it. For advocates of "republican" liberty, political freedom meant dependable freedom from arbitrary power. In a tyranny, for example, the mere fact that you were let alone might be due to luck. The secret police might have the wrong address. You might be too distant or obscure to bother with. Nonintrusion in such a tyranny could still not be counted on. A wise person would fear intrusion, and living in fear of intrusion was not living, in its republican sense, in freedom. Nor was every social restraint or political interference an act of domination. Social restraints were necessary and much state interference was both welcome and justified. The "third-way" label for republican liberty was merited. It planted the liberal banner of "Liberty" in the political center, flanked by negative liberty and laissez-faire on one side, positive liberty and "collectivism" on the other.

Berlin's was a hopeful, not despairing liberal lesson. If true, Berlin's pluralism offered hope of ethical engagement between people that relativism, if coherent, denied. Berlin pictured everyone as conflicted within themselves, hence perhaps able in reconciliatory spirit to recognize similar conflict in others. The ethical relativist pictured people as held within a frame of aims and ideals that need have nothing to say to those in other frames, perhaps even no effective, common means to communicate. As a political practice, liberalism is not tied to any particular theory about the nature of morals. Still there has to be something to explain why an ethical "monist" like Mill and an ethical "pluralist" like Berlin feel less opposed and together more liberal in spirit than relativists in ethics with their sectarian partitions of the world. Perhaps it was that, whether or not the set was complicated or simple, Mill and Berlin both spoke as if to a humankind governed by a common set of moral demands.

Oakeshott was a liberal quietist of conservative temper who distrusted the very idea of political ideas. He disliked the society he saw growing around him, but urged nobody to take offensive action. Berlin approved of how politics was moving away from large claims and undue demands toward centrist reform and conciliation. Mischief came to his mind from expecting any all-in-one answer, any overtidy ideology. The genuine liberal, Berlin was saying, accepted that meeting any serious goal in life or politics involved frustration and regret at not achieving something else. Their modest view of politics was different from that of Hayek, to whom we now return for his third incarnation as a political thinker. Hayek's antipolitics was an action program of a radical kind.

ii. Hayek (iii): Political Antipolitics

We left Friedrich Hayek in 1944 as a celebrity in America for *The Road to Serfdom*. His life now changed. On Hayek's divorce, his affronted mentor at the London School of Economics, Lionel Robbins, cut him off professionally and personally. Checked professionally in Britain, where his ideas were taken to be out of touch or cranky, Hayek looked to the United States. Mises's business friends whistled up money to make a post for Hayek at Chicago, a powerhouse of technical economics. To his disappointment, the job was in the politics department. His depressions worsened. In the youth of his old age, reputation and career were in decline. Hayek, however, was dogged and laughed last. In the policy think tanks of London and Washington, a shift in economic thinking was under way. Hayek became its intellectual godfather. In 1974 he won the Bank of Sweden's Nobel Prize in economics, sharing it with Gunnar Myrdal, a Swedish economist and Social Democrat advocate of welfare and civil rights.

Hayek finished the task left over from *Road to Serfdom*. That had told people what liberals were against. Hayek still had to say what liberals were for. That was the task of *The Constitution of Liberty* and *Law, Legislation and Liberty*. In those books, Hayek returned to three guiding themes: under the rule of law, strong general rules are better than discretionary authority; as there is no such thing as social justice, income cannot be expected to reflect need; and liberal democracy must be more than a temporary one-party dictatorship or naked competition among interest groups, which was not liberty but license. Hayek's thoughts had always played on the tension between order and freedom. The more he saw of "actual existing" capitalism, the more he stressed order, law, and limitations on democratic choice.

In *The Constitution of Liberty*, most of which he wrote in the 1950s, Hayek expanded on themes signposted in the *Road to Serfdom*: economic ignorance rendered planning and central regulation empty; law must prevail over interests; money and liberty were ethical twins, for "economic control" amounted to "control of all our ends"; only equality under law mattered, not equality of results. He invoked liberty ingeniously. Nonunionized labor markets were free in that anyone was free to choose a new boss. Monopolies might be as coercive as states. Echoing a hint in Berlin, Hayek stressed that liberalism neither required nor opposed democracy. Liberalism's foes were totalitarianism and central control of life. Democracy's foe was autocracy, which was compatible with liberty.

Though Hayek strove to answer Keynes's challenge to say where the line lay between government's "agenda" and "nonagenda," his reply took the form more of an exemplary list than a discriminating principle. Government, Hayek wrote, should not control prices, interfere with free labor bargaining to protect unions, limit freedom of contract, or pursue distributive justice with taxation designed to give to the poor from the rich. The second half of the book spelled out that restrictive agenda in various fields of policy. Hayek felt he still had to secure his liberal vision of masterless order. "The enemies of liberty," he wrote, "have always based their arguments on the contention that order in human affairs requires that some should give orders and others obey." Hayek needed something other than masters and commanders to provide order, but what? He was honest about what was missing and kept several answers in play.

One was elaborate, ambitious, and in the end unconvincing. Order evolved, Hayek believed. In *Law, Legislation and Liberty*, he contrasted "made order" or *taxis* with "found order" or *catallaxy*. As with Oakeshott, the use of names from a dressing-up box suggested anxiety on Hayek's part that the distinctions themselves were not wholly sound or convincing. As a story of present-day society, Hayek's account of the evolution of spontaneous order was not unlike Spencer's sociobiology that Sidgwick had hit so hard. One problem was Hayek's picture of social change. Imposed or "made" order in society was on his evolutionary story nonadaptive and socially inexpedient, that is, bad. As society evolved, it shed nonadaptive, inexpedient features. "Made" order, however, had nevertheless survived. It survived, for example, in overcontrolling social reformism. On their face, those claims were not mutually consistent. The evolutionary metaphor was weakest. In biology, evolution worked on vast time scale with a clear mechanism of change: random variation caused by genetic mutation. In social life, there was no obvious mechanism and change was too rapid for evolution of a biological kind to work. In biology, usefulness or expediency of features was inferred from their survival, not the other way around. Usefulness had no predictive value whatever. When biology was poetically winched into social life, evolutionary adepts turned that sequence on its head: they inferred survival from usefulness. "No institution will survive," he wrote in *The Constitution of Liberty*, "unless it performs some useful function." The social world, however, was full of antisocial, inexpedient norms that had survived but that ought not to have survived had the sieve of usefulness-directed social evolution done its work. Hayek did not make clear which of his inconsistent claims to abandon.

In *Law, Legislation and Liberty*, Hayek returned to the liberal economic critique of political democracy. It was awkward for right-wing liberals that belief in efficient markets did not fit well with support for majority rule. The two appeared incompatible. Hayek took the problem head on. Mass democracy, he allowed, could be deleterious to economic efficiency in two ways. It opened government to interests, to gaming of the system, and, in effect, to vote buying. Democracy also encouraged governments to meddle economically. It nudged them to overpromise high employment and high wages. Together those led to inflation, and with it an erosion of values and a disincentive to thrift. Against those risks, he proposed the general protection of limiting regulatory interference and official discretion of a kind that economic interests sought to manipulate. More specifically, he proposed to limit electoral democracy by creating a powerful upper chamber of men and women forty-five or older. It would make laws and supervise the rule of law. A lower chamber would administer the laws as, in effect, a subservient executive.

Law, Legislation and Liberty also restated Hayek's distrust of social justice. About distant, impersonal economic harms, Hayek took a stern line. Some suggested that, as such harms interfered with people's freedom, their causes might be regulated or forbidden without injuring canons of the free market. Not so, Hayek believed. Economic decisions by others might lose a person his or her job or wipe out their savings, so limiting their range of actions. Such decisions could not, though, be counted on as limitations of anyone's freedom. For limitations of freedom were personal and intentional, whereas the distant effects of market decisions were neither. Nobody singled you out and intended to ruin your firm or destroy your job. You were standing in the way of unintended consequences. That free-market answer as given by Hayek played on Rousseau's distinction between being shut in your house by a snowstorm and being wrongly locked in it against your will. Both obstructed your freedom. Only the second was blameworthy. Faced by limitations

to our freedom, the suggestion ran, we judged natural and human restraints differently. Bad economic outcomes, Hayek insisted, were like
snowstorms, and nobody blamed snowstorms. Try as he might to make
economics sound like a natural science, there were no natural facts here.
Hayek in effect was recommending that we should *treat* economic
harms as if they were snowstorms, blaming no one—a large moral claim
for which clear justifications from Hayek were lacking.

A lingering doubt about Hayek's liberalism was whether to his mind
there was any concern that trumped rising prosperity. The suspicion
never went away that his entire system rested on expediency—that
no concern, in other words, be it for justice, law, rights, or privacy—
mattered save as how it furthered economic growth. Hayek was alive to
the dangers. Back in Paris at the Lippmann Colloquium in 1938 he had
accepted that pure laissez-faire liberalism was dead as a political program. Making prosperity a moral be-all and end-all was not enough, he
acknowledged, to win people's allegiance. Yet making popular allegiance
the test of a morality was little or no advance on expediency. Hayek left
it unclear whether he had a principled answer to such challenges.

Instead, he ended his clearest summation, *The Constitution of Liberty*,
in zestful partisanship with a chapter, "Why I am Not a Conservative." It
was written with the verve and bite that had won *Serfdom* its following.
The chapter listed ten conservative faults, none of which Hayek said he
shared. He had not been a socialist since the age of eighteen. His reputation as a man of the right was well earned and not in question. Hayek's
checklist provided a clear line of separation to distinguish conservatives
from liberals. Conservatives, on Hayek's account, suffered from the following weaknesses. They feared change unduly. They were unreasonably
frightened of uncontrolled social forces. They were too fond of authority.
They had no grasp of economics. They lacked the feel for "abstraction"
needed for engaging with people of different outlooks. They were too
cozy with elites and establishments. They gave in to jingoism and chauvinism. They tended to think mystically, much as socialists tended to
overrationalize. They were, last, too suspicious of democracy. Hayek, as
mentioned, weakened on electoral democracy. For the rest, he was correct to mark himself a liberal. He distrusted power. He believed in progress. He insisted on civic respect, taken as a requirement for legal equality and protection of privacy. At the same time, he was ungiving in how

far liberals should have to promise their ideals to everyone. He was dogged and honest about where the problems lay, but he was not an unconditional democrat.

The political modesty of Hayek took openly political form. Unlike the skeptical Oakeshott, Hayek had a doctrine and an action program. Unlike the pluralist Berlin, Hayek appeared to run all values into one unstable equation of prosperity, well-being, and probity. His influence was all the same profound. He offered, it seemed, an all-purpose rationale for dismantling social legislation. His distinction between "constructive" and "spontaneous" order became a leitmotif for neoliberal radicals of the 1980s. It encouraged a comfortable habit of parsing any public problem into economic and political parts, and blaming the problem on politics. Herbert Stein, who advised the forgotten liberal Richard Nixon on economics, used to joke that, whatever the problem, he would tell political reporters that it was economic, and economic reporters that it was political. The difference may be minor, but Stein and his hearers realized that the remark was a joke. Perhaps Hayek's philosophy of economics has so appealed to otherwise practical-minded business people because it aimed to take the politics out of political economy.

iii. Orwell, Camus, and Sartre: Liberals in the Cold War

Liberal thinking after 1945 was not all about economics. Nor was it confined to universities and think tanks. The liberal climate at midcentury owed much to three writers of outstanding prose, George Orwell, Albert Camus, and Jean-Paul Sartre. They were all essayists who wrote novels with political themes set around the figure of the troublesome, unreconciled loner. Taking a stand against the odds or without knowing the odds was to them not evidence of imprudence but a sign of moral seriousness. Orwell had fought fascists in Spain. Camus had edited an underground paper for the French resistance. Sartre was a philosopher of stature, who for thirty years edited the leading left-wing journal of postwar France, *Les Temps Modernes*. His stands were more declarative, but Sartre too played David to a sequence of Goliaths: Western anticommunism, Western colonialism, Gaullism in France. None of the three thinkers were party men, and each was hard to pin down politically. All of them, even Sartre, were liberals by temperament.

George Orwell (1903–50), who dwelt on the use and abuse of words in politics, called himself a socialist, an anticommunist, and a Tory anarchist. Shy in person, though vehement on the page, he was an intellectual who scoffed at intellectuals and a left-wing old-Etonian who mocked privileged socialists. His two antitotalitarian parables, *Animal Farm* (1945) and *Nineteen Eighty-Four* (1949), made him into an early global star, though he died of tuberculosis before he could enjoy and no doubt deride his fame.

He was born Eric Blair in Bengal, where his father worked for the Indian colonial department that regulated China's opium trade. Sent to school in England, he was just young enough to escape the slaughter of the First World War. Instead of following Eton friends to Oxford or Cambridge, he joined the colonial police in Burma, an experience that swiftly made him an anticolonialist. He grew sick, he wrote, of locking people up for doing what he would do in their shoes. From his time in Burma came two renowned essays, "Shooting an Elephant," a self-reproach at giving in to the power of a frightened crowd, and "A Hanging," a quiet polemic against capital punishment.

Orwell's grasp of liberalism was intuitive but profound. He hated undue power, and understood that it came in myriad forms. "I have no particular love for the idealised worker of the bourgeois communist mind," he wrote, "but when I see an actual flesh-and-blood worker in conflict with his natural enemy the policeman, I do not have to ask myself which side I am on." He recognized society's exclusions when he saw them: "A fat man eating quails while children are begging for bread is a disgusting sight." Orwell saw that there was more to politics than ideals and policies. "His radicalism is of the vaguest kind, and yet one always knows that it is there," Orwell wrote of Charles Dickens. "He has no constructive suggestions, not even a clear grasp of the nature of the society, only an emotional perception that something is wrong. All he can finally say is, 'Behave decently,' which ... is not necessarily so shallow as it sounds." Orwell as a liberal recognized what socialists and conservatives found so hard to see, that fixity was unavailable and that politics never stopped: "Most revolutionaries are potential Tories, because they imagine that everything can be put right by altering the shape of society," Orwell wrote. "Once that change is effected," he went on, "they see no need for any other."

In "Politics and the English Language," Orwell expressed perhaps his single strongest conviction, that bad speech reflected bad thought, and that, since politics is conducted chiefly in words, bad speech could lead to political folly, violence, and oppression. His coinage "newspeak," introduced in the novel *1984* to describe browbeating obfuscation, was seized on without need of the least explanation by everyone who grasped the linkage between an authority's misuse of words and the misuse of its powers. Orwell's "newspeak" had many descendants, including notably "management speak." Stringent to the point of self-punishment, Orwell combined the conviction that our duty to resist injustice was virtually unbounded with a belief that our capacity to do anything about it was strictly limited. He was allergic to theory and speculation, and would have hated the word. But in a sense Orwell's no-win morality of high demands and low capacities made him an English existentialist.

Albert Camus (1913–60) was also preoccupied by the role of the naysayer in an unwelcoming, intractable society. Like Orwell, Camus was a chain smoker with bad lungs. Both were dead at forty-six, though Camus was killed returning to Paris as a passenger in an overpowered Facel Vega driven into a tree by his publisher. Camus was born to French parents in working-class Algiers and went to the University of Algiers, where he played in goal for the university soccer team. Camus would record that he learned about politics not in Marx but from poverty. Unlike Sartre, whose anti-anticommunism never added up to communism itself, Camus belonged to the Algerian Communist Party in 1935–37. During the German occupation, Camus edited *Combat*, a banned newspaper of the French resistance. As with Orwell, personal engagement mattered more to Camus in politics than policy or doctrine. Both listened to their responses and their loathings: of communism, colonialism, and capital punishment. Neither was saint nor martyr. Orwell gave the British Foreign Office names of left-wing friends he did not think it should employ in its propaganda work. Camus published during the occupation, acceding to demands from his German censors to remove mention of Kafka, as a Jewish writer, from a book of essays. Camus did not idolize Algeria's independence fighters, fearing that once in power they too might become oppressors.

Though best known for his fiction and his plays, Camus also wrote political essays. In *The Rebel* (1951), he laid out his wares as an anticommunist liberal. In characteristic French fashion, Camus posed questions of political principle historically. Why, Camus asked, had the emancipatory projects of the Enlightenment ended in revolutionary terror? Why had the modern search for liberty led not only to material progress and democracy but also to tyranny and industrial-scale slaughter? The questions were neither new nor unloaded. But they felt urgent when Camus set to writing what he called "an attempt to understand my times." Of all his political writing, Camus took most pride in *The Rebel*. It drew the scorn of better-drilled brains on the *marxisant* left and broke for good his friendship with Sartre.

Camus reposed the question conservatives had asked after the Revolution and Napoleon: were the crimes of modernity due to liberty or to its perversion? Burke mildly and Maistre savagely had blamed liberty. Once freed from custom and good sense, it was plain to Burke that people were capable of the worst crimes. Maistre thought the same once people were freed from God and his earthly ministers. Disobedience and dissent, to the conservative mind, led morally to confusion and bewilderment, politically to revolution, breakdown, and counterrevolution. The spirit of liberty made human life worse, not better. Revolt was not progressive, as the champions of liberty claimed, but regressive. Like the earliest liberals, Camus disagreed. As they had, he blamed the excesses of modernity on the perversion of liberty, not on liberty itself.

Camus, like Constant and Guizot, saw bad and good in revolution. As resistance to undue power, Camus took rebellion for a universal duty binding on all humans. Faced by the muteness of God, the indifference of nature, and the domination of man by man, the only decent reaction, Camus thought, was revolt. Rebelliousness in a sense defined our humanity. Revolt was unavoidably social and engaged us with others, or as Camus put it in an epigram that understandably did not catch on: "I revolt, therefore we are." With varying degrees of sympathy, Camus described the mind and deeds of many kinds of rebel: writers, dandies, antimoralists, nihilists, Jacobin managers of revolutionary terror, and lone, anti-tsarist bomb throwers. Welcome and necessary as rebellion was, why, Camus asked, had it led also to such calamities?

Camus's essay was richer in questions than answers. He concluded with hopes for a relaxed, humane politics not driven by ideas that he called "Mediterranean." His vision of a middle way between totalitarian oppression and Western excess was notably free of detail. The hard men of the intellectual left pounced. An editor at *Les Temps Modernes*, Francis Jeanson, wrote a damning review, titled "The Soul in Revolt." Camus, he suggested, was less concerned with injustice than purity of conscience. As a courageous member of the French underground helping anticolonial Algerians, Jeanson's credentials on the left were impeccable. Camus's liberal hesitations about the oppressive consequences of colonial independence gave Jeanson a target, for whom an Algerian Algeria was a moral absolute. Unwisely, Camus replied, sounding pompous and wounded. Sartre then stepped in with an open letter in *Les Temps Modernes* (August 1952) that still reads as a horrifying masterpiece of literary assassination. He and Camus barely spoke again.

The Rebel was significant less for its arguments or for provoking a politico-literary breach than for marking a corrective turn that liberalism was taking more generally. After the enormities of 1914–45, liberals were reminding themselves that concern for what state and society could do *for* people ought not to blind them to what state and society could do *to* people. Like *The God That Failed* (1950), a book of recantations by former Western communists, Camus's book also marked the lifting of an inhibition on the intellectual left against speaking out against Stalinist evils. The reasons for silence had not all been foolish or dishonorable. Loyalty was felt to a nation that at great cost had rescued West Europeans from Nazism. The West, too, visited grave harms and cruelties in defending itself and its liberal values. To Camus and Orwell those reasons for silence were no longer good enough. It was time to speak out. Like it or not, the Cold War imposed a choice, for or against, and they chose the West. As writers Orwell and Camus were opening up a space where it was again possible to be liberal, anticommunist, and left-wing.

Not everyone chose to inhabit that space. In France, the intellectual leader of those for whom liberal and left-wing were contradictions in terms was Jean-Paul Sartre (1905–80). Yet Sartre himself was more liberal than he cared to admit or than certain reviewers of the first edition of this book appeared to think. Calling Sartre a liberal by temperament was taken for an eccentricity or blunder. If so, it was a blunder shared by those who know and admire his work, the American political thinker Michael Walzer, for one. Walzer wrote of Sartre in an introduction to an English translation of his "Anti-Semite and Jew" (1946; 1995): "Indeed, he was a liberal, despite his Marxist sociologizing."

There was no need to cite authorities, however, to sense Sartre's liberal temper. He lived by opposition in a kind of permanent declarative revolt against ruling powers and prevailing conventions. His philosophical watchword was "Just say no." Dismal odds seemed to attract him. His intellectual projects were unmanageably vast. Not finishing was almost a mark of success. In his sixties he dashed off 2,300 pages of a study of Gustave Flaubert before declaring it incomplete. He boasted of never growing up. Indifferent to honors, in 1963 he turned down a Nobel Prize. Sartre was, in short, a character. In England, where characters are prized, Sartre might have been taken to people's hearts had he not hated pets, loathed country walks, and been French.

He had many mistresses, and one enduring love, Simone de Beauvoir, a novelist and thinker who shared his life, work, and duplicities as friend, lover, nurse, judge, and equal, though never wife. Near blind from youth in one eye, Sartre was otherwise robust. He needed to be. His daily intake included forty Boyard cigarettes, liters of coffee and alcohol, as well as a dozen corydrane tablets, a mixture of amphetamine and aspirin then available over the counter (the recommended daily dose was two).

Sartre's real drug was writing. His raw output was calculated at twenty published pages a day over a working life. He refused to reread or correct what he wrote. Once on the page, his thought was done with. Fond of one-liners, he said his best book was always the one he was about to write. Behind that quip lay an idea that colored his philosophy: the past had no authority over us. At any moment, we were free to make of ourselves what we wished.

For Sartre, the central fact of human life was a conflict between that conviction of freedom and the experience of constraint. We were free in our thoughts but trapped in our situation. Change was possible, if only at the margin: we were free to "deny" our situation by imagining it otherwise. That mental freedom was evident to us in our projects and hopes. We could, Sartre thought, hide our liberty from ourselves in self-deception or bad faith. Those took the form of accepting our social pigeonhole, our bodily limitations, or the restraints of morality as limits to our freedom. Acknowledgment of liberty became a gauge of self-awareness. Sartre laid out those thoughts in *Being and Nothingness* (1943). The book offered a sharpness of insight, expected from a novelist, into underanalyzed human experiences such as desire, disgust, and being looked at. It dwelt on familiar but underscrutinized mental phenomena such as self-deception and sincerity. It offered more broadly a strict view of the absolute priority of human autonomy and a correspondingly demanding account of moral responsibility. By the late 1940s, Sartre gave up teaching and lived off his writing. His most philosophical novel, *Nausea* (1938), sold more than 1.6 million copies in his lifetime, his play about political responsibility, *Dirty Hands* (1948), almost 2 million. In his unfinished *Critique of Dialectical Reason* (1960), Sartre attempted to reconcile his exigent view of human freedom with a highly personalized account of Marxism.

Sartre could be perversely and irresponsibly wrong: more pacifist than antifascist in the 1930s, pro-Soviet in the early 1950s, then pro-Castro in 1960 and pro-Mao after 1968. His rage against "bourgeois" convention permitted bourgeois convention to set his agenda. Sartre's rage drove him also to reckless admiration for the satanic antihero, the nihilist, even the terrorist. Sartre could also be shiningly right: condemning the Soviet invasion of Hungary in 1956, calling for an Algerian Algeria (right-wing terrorists twice bombed his apartment in Paris, once almost killing him), and supporting Israel against threats from Arab neighbors in 1967. One of Sartre's last campaigns was occasion for a joint appearance that, intended or not, was widely taken for a symbolic reconciliation. In 1979, Sartre and Raymond Aron, his old friend from the 1930s and liberal sparring partner from the 1950s to the 1960s, appeared together at the Elysée to ask the French government to help Vietnamese boat people fleeing their country after the fall of Saigon to the Communists in 1975.

Sartre was a lonely and fatherless child, raised by a doting mother and a professorial grandfather. One of a kind, self-involved, and living in his head, he longed for comradeship. He spoke of his months in a German prisoner-of-war camp in 1940 as the happiest in his life. Romance with imaginary crowds led him into totalitarian foolishness. Against that was his distrust of authority and of the violence it could always call on. "Commanding or obeying, it's all the same," he wrote in a marvelous self-examination masquerading as a memoir of childhood, *Words* (1963). The epigram could have come from Alain, whose philosophy pupils Sartre had rubbed shoulders with as a student at the École Normale. Sartre loathed liberal anticommunists. But he made more of limitless and demanding human freedom than most liberals did. Sartre never got the urges to belong and to be free into balance, but then who had? He scoffed at the thought that balance was achievable. The thing for Sartre was to keep both going, and see where each led. Among Sartre's bravest campaigns was defending the civil rights of radicals harried by the French state. Behind Sartre's antiliberal words could be spied a liberal-minded dissenter.

iv. Rawls: Justifying Liberalism

John Rawls (1921–2002) spent a career thinking about two questions: "What do we say to the losers?" and "How can we live together given our ethical disagreements?" Those questions ran as a double thread through *A Theory of Justice* (1971), Rawls's best known and in a sense his only work, which later writings largely amplified or corrected the better to defend. By way of answer, Rawls pictured a "well-ordered" or "just" society that excluded nobody from its advantages and that accepted profound disagreement about the shape of a worthwhile life in conditions nevertheless of civic peace. The kind of justice Rawls had in mind was caught in the title of a short paper, "Justice as Fairness," which he wrote in 1957 and then defended, reworked, and extended until it had grown into a book of eighty-seven closely argued sections of more than 580 pages. *A Theory of Justice* began to circulate in draft soon after Rawls reached Harvard from Cornell and MIT in 1962. When it finally came out, Rawls had worked in answers to the many objections he had heard or could think of.

That assiduity made the book hard going. A British reviewer, the moral philosopher Richard Hare, reported that he put it down many times in near despair. Rawls's deliberate pace and selfless scruple in argument also meant that his book met a test Hilary Putnam, a logician and fellow philosopher, once proposed for a philosophical classic: the smarter you got, the smarter it got. Among English-speaking political philosophers, Rawls's book quickly became a text of reference and starting point in argument. Two generations of Rawlsianism produced more than five thousand learned articles of interpretation, commentary, objection, and defense. The book became a university text with an educational reach not unlike that of Paul Samuelson's *Economics*, first published in 1948. By Rawls's death, *A Theory of Justice* had sold more than four hundred thousand copies and existed in many languages, including Chinese and Arabic.

At a high level of argument, Rawls offered a mid–twentieth century justification of two political ideals underpinning liberal democracy and commonly talked of in shorthand as liberty and equality. Rawls took for granted that the tutorial authority of "competent judges" that Mill had thought might show people better and worse forms of life was now gone. In such democratic conditions, Rawls wanted to know what principles might exist to underpin an acceptable liberal order that fair-minded modern citizens would recognize and rally to.

Rawls, like Mill, was a reconciliationist. He took people to be self-interested but open to the demands of fairness and justice. His answer to the old puzzle, "Does a just society make just citizens or vice versa?" was in effect "both." Rawls drew on varied sources for his ideas: the social-contract theory of political obligation, Kant's universalist ethics, current social science and rational-choice theory, and not least his own moral intuitions. He seemed to be doing what liberal thinkers had taught themselves not to do, to explain everything about politics in one coherent system. The intricacies of the Rawlsian machine stemmed in part from the hope that its diverse parts would mesh together.

Rawls nailed his topic in the opening sentence of *A Theory of Justice*: "Justice is the first virtue of social institutions, as truth is of systems of thought." Unjust laws and institutions might provide security and prosperity. If laws and institutions were not just, they "must be reformed or abolished." As the book went on, readers learned what else Rawls thought must happen in a fair society. Officials must be held to higher standards of moral account than ordinary citizens. There may be times when a dutiful citizen must disobey the law. Society must not neglect the shunned or disadvantaged.

Rawls's imperative tone was new. His opening paragraph sounded like Channing preaching or Thoreau campaigning. *A Theory of Justice* is possible to read as if written by a stateless and neutral intelligence of no fixed abode. Its silences and complexities are easier to grasp if it is kept in mind that Rawls was a deeply engaged citizen writing in the United States of the 1960s. He had strong convictions about the blights of American society. Its racialism and militarism appalled him. He strained nevertheless to observe the self-denying ordinance of his profession to rely on argument alone and not to take stands.

The rough field of social justice was familiar enough. Rawls's approach to it was new. Legal justice concerned punishment, compensation and due process. Social justice was about fair shares of benefits and burdens in society. Obvious questions of social justice were these: What shares were fair? Must fair shares be equal shares? If not, how much inequality was acceptable? The issues were old and contentious. Rather than answer directly, Rawls looked to the sources of fairness and unfairness. He started not with fair or unfair shares of benefits and burdens, but with procedures and institutions that dealt out the shares. He invoked the reasonable notion that a fair procedure was one people might agree to in advance without knowing the outcome. If the deal were fair, the cards could not be complained of. Fair procedures and institutions, it seemed to follow, ought not to be difficult to find: they were those procedures and institutions that people could agree to. The trouble was everyone would want institutions that favored his or her interests.

By basic institutions, Rawls had in mind the familiar constitutional furniture of executives and legislatures, but also markets, property laws, dispute procedures, and other ground rules of common life. Though commonly so pictured, those basic institutions were to Rawls's mind seldom neutral umpires. They tended to favor some people—the rich, the white, the strong, the clever, for example—rather than others. One way to make institutions fairer was to remove such bias. Fair institutions would then deliver more equal outcomes. That was too quick, Rawls insisted. Such an answer involved an opposite mistake. It would permit a less-privileged majority to restrict and handicap a privileged minority. As a mildly egalitarian liberal, Rawls wanted to identify fair institutions that would neither obstruct the wealthy and capable nor exclude the poor and less capable.

Readers looking for a quick takeaway jumped to Rawls's "principles of justice." Though oddly remembered as two, Rawls in fact gave three. First, everyone was to have the same set of inviolable liberties that were needed for a life of self-respect. Second, fair opportunities were to be equal to all. Third, although some inequalities were inevitable in a free, productive, and prosperous society, those inequalities had as a priority to permit and foster help to the disadvantaged. Rawls called the last "the difference principle."

His three principles themselves were familiar ideals for a social-minded liberal democracy. Nobody's privacy was to be intruded on, nobody's aims were to be obstructed, and nobody was to be excluded from such rights or practical means for exercising them. As if echoing the "new liberals" of the late nineteenth and early twentieth centuries, Rawls was running up a three-stripe flag of liberty, equal opportunity, and—to use Léon Bourgeois's word—solidarity. Rawls, however, added a telling rider. Late twentieth-century society was much richer than it had been when the new liberals were writing. Once society was prosperous enough, Rawls judged, the three principles of justice were to be applied in strict order. In a given case, should their guidance conflict, liberty was to best equal opportunity, and equal opportunity was to best solidarity.

To reach his principles, Rawls brought out of museum storage an antique device, the social contract. He imagined would-be citizens of an orderly society, veiled from knowledge of their talents, wealth, and allegiances, choosing from a menu of principles to guide their society, notably the common good, meritocratic excellence, or fairness. If choosing impartially without favoring their own aims and capacities, Rawls held that people would choose fairness or justice. Presented then with alternative principles of fairness or social justice, including Utilitarianism, Rawls held that people would prefer his three. In the book's second part, Rawls's imaginary citizens then picked a constitution, arrangements for the economy, and dispute procedures. The result was a modern liberal democracy as it might ideally be. Rawls's derivations were intricate and controversial. A common complaint from fellow philosophers was that Rawls's moral intuitions drove his imaginary people's choices. The output—liberal democracy—was ensured by the input—liberal democracy. The machinery did no justificatory work. The British thinker John Gray had something like that complaint in mind when calling *A Theory of Justice* "a transcendental deduction" of the politics of William Beveridge.

The complaint could be answered. Rawls, at root, wanted his "original position" as a running cross-check on the fairness of institutions. Anyone, Rawls was suggesting, could ask of a contested social arrangement—unequal pay for women, a minimum wage, racial discrimination, affirmative action to correct for discrimination—was this what anyone, setting one's own talents, interests, aims, and ideals to one side, might reasonably agree to? Intuitively, Rawls's cross-check seemed a telling gauge. The complaint of circularity came back, however, at a higher level. Might Rawls's imaginary people not reasonably refuse to set aside so much of themselves before deciding on acceptable social ground rules? It was difficult, in addition, to sharpen Rawls's intuitive cross-check into practical tests for use in law and politics. The difficulty was the greater in that liberals already had a test that they had grown used to in the nineteenth century and never really dropped: the common good or general well-being invoked by Utilitarianism.

Rawls broke tradition in abandoning that test. From Constant to Berlin, liberals had insisted on the inviolability of the human person. Few had offered in principle to say why. They had given no way to slacken the liberal tension between the progress of society as a whole and civic respect for people one by one. Mill had made the frankest attempt to square the overriding demands of the common good with the protection of personal liberty and promotion of individuality. Since then, liberals had slipped into a workaday Utilitarianism. They had, to Rawls's mind, gotten into the bad habit of treating society as progress's beneficiary. Like a baker weighing flour, Utilitarians lumped the winners' net gains in one pan and the losers' net losses in another. If the winners' pan proved heavier, society "as a whole" was better off. The second sentence of *A Theory of Justice* announced Rawls's rejection of Utilitarianism. "Each person," it read, "possesses an inviolability founded on justice that even the welfare of society as a whole cannot override."

Nobody, Rawls was objecting, experienced the progress of society itself. After a social "advance" everyone affected was either a net winner or a net loser. Utilitarianism had no way to justify who was which. In a ringing if gnomic phrase Rawls made famous, Utilitarianism did not "take seriously the distinction between persons." Utilitarianism had no answer to why certain people rather than others were singled out as losers. The winners might say, "Somebody has to pay," with which losers could agree yet still want to know, "Why us?" To which the winners might retort with Hayek, "Nobody singled you out. The results were not intended. They just happened."

For Rawls, appealing to bad luck was not good enough. It suggested that the results of social change were arbitrary, hence neither fair nor unfair. Justice, however, was blind, not arbitrary. Justice was impartial, not capricious. People wanted to live in a society where they could look losers in the eye and say more than "Bad luck." Rawls believed in life's contingency, and particularly in the lottery of talent. A telling sentence from the first edition of *A Theory of Justice* that went missing from the second in 1999 was, "In justice as fairness men agree to share one another's fate." Rawls recognized that brains, energy, and courage were needed to create prosperity, and he accepted that they should be well rewarded. He did not accept that those excellences had merit in themselves. Finally, expectations of what life might offer based on chance alone were too weak a consideration, Rawls feared, to bind fair-minded people's loyalty to society and discourage them from "free riding" or enjoying its benefits free.

Rawls's losers did not have to be poor. There were many raw deals that an unfair society might hand people besides lack of money. Losers could be rich members of an excluded sect. They could be groups habitually outvoted in majoritarian democracies with institutional biases and inadequate protections for minorities. It was not always obvious, but in *A Theory of Justice* Rawls was thinking of intolerance as well as indigence. Distributive justice was not all about money. A fair society needed mutual forbearance as well as mutual aid.

Rawls's hypothetical choosers appeared to share enough morality to agree to live in justice, but not enough to agree on good aims in life. Rawls, it seemed, presumed moral unanimity about justice and ethical disagreement on everything else. So it was widely objected. Rawls could reply that he was in no worse shape than other liberals. All of them wanted to keep politics out of private life. None of them wanted public life to be an amoral free-for-all. No liberal had knockdown answers as to where to draw the line. In a modern, open society, Rawls hoped that people might agree to be hyper-demanding about liberties and fairness, but ultra-relaxed about whether people chose to be Puritans or libertines, devout Christians or militant secularists, cosmopolitans or sectarians. Bouglé, we saw, had a similar hope at the time of the Dreyfus affair in France. It was an attractive vision. But was it credible?

Rawls leaned this way and that about the feasibility of making politics fair while keeping morality out of politics. At times he voiced doubts as to whether people shared enough moral ground to agree to, let alone stick with, fairness. He leaned this way and that about whether commitment to fairness itself was a matter of morality or prudence. In *A Theory of Justice*, he wrote as the confident Rawls. In its third part he raised a question not unlike the one that struck Mill dumb at the moment of his youthful breakdown. Mill had asked if the achievement of human happiness would make him happy. Rawls asked if a just society would encourage people to act justly. Ideally, Rawls concluded, it would: "Taking up the standpoint of justice promotes one's own good." Just institutions and just citizens would reinforce each other. Rawls's fair society would be reliably fair, or to use his term, "stable." Public knowledge that it was fair would discourage defection and free riding. A fair society would win allegiance. By implication, an unfair society with large inequities would not command loyalty and would consequently not be stable.

The thought is speculative, but it is hard not to think that Rawls's imperative tone had something to do with his background. The state of Maryland, where he was born in 1921, had a history of intercommunal prejudice in which first Catholics browbeat Protestants and then Protestants browbeat Catholics. A slaveholding border state, Maryland was kept reluctantly in the Union at the outbreak of Civil War in 1861 under martial law. Rawls's father was a wealthy Baltimore tax lawyer who shared the prejudices of his class and time. He presided on state boards that monitored a regressive, probusiness revenue and oversaw Maryland's segregated schools. The father's patron was the governor of Maryland, a conservative Democrat who took Herbert Hoover for an irresponsible spendthrift and who opposed women's suffrage. Rawls's mother was a progressive of German origin, who campaigned for women's rights and other radical causes.

In 1928, when young Rawls had diphtheria, a younger brother caught it from him and died. A year later Rawls caught pneumonia, which killed another brother. Rawls attributed his lifelong stammer to their deaths. In 1949, he married a teacher, Margaret Fox. She shared his love of books and on their honeymoon they found time to index a commentary on Nietzsche. Rawls lived with her and their two boys and two girls, enjoying the outdoor pleasures of walking and sailing.

Devout when young, Rawls had once thought of becoming a Protestant minister. Though unattached to a church and without theological beliefs, that religious background lingered in his attempts to reconcile morality and luck. Having been taught both "Everyone is equal in the sight of God" and "There but for the grace of God, go I," Rawls's suspicion of merit and sense of life's contingency remained strong. Colleagues remember his kindness and wry humor. He was widely admired, even loved. He was shy in public, declined most honors and regularly complained about the corrupting effects of privilege. On trips to Washington, DC, Rawls liked if he could to visit the memorial to his reconciling hero, Lincoln. Although in person he was self-deprecating and unpreachy, his political thought, like his view of life, was colored by a faith in morality that could be called in a sense religious. When Isaiah Berlin talked of Rawls as "Christ," there was point to his worldly tease. Rawls was authoritative evidence, as if more were needed, that there was no tight connection between political liberalism and secular nonbelief. Scholarly work since Rawls's death has confirmed the ethico-religious thread in his thinking.

Some thought Rawls overplayed human decency and underestimated selfishness. A conservative writer called him an innocent. Holier than some could have wished, possibly. Innocent, never. He saw what people were capable of first hand. In 1943, Rawls signed up as an infantry private and fought on the Pacific beaches. From a troop train taking him to occupation duty in Japan he saw the ruins of Nagasaki, obliterated only weeks earlier by an American nuclear bomb. It was not a political philosopher's task to tell people what to do or think, he believed. But in a rare public judgment in the magazine *Dissent* (1995) Rawls condemned the atomic bombing of Japan as immoral.

Rawls's work prompted a reply from across the profession, creating a virtual industry of Rawlsian and counter-Rawlsian theory. There were also less technical criticisms from those who stepped back from the machinery of argument itself. Right-wing critics asked why the middle classes should have to make good the troubles of the poor. *In a Different Voice* (1982), by the feminist philosopher Carol Gilligan, suggested that Rawls overdid the ethical value of impartiality at the expense of the ethics of care and concern for need. Postmodern critics took Rawls's appeal to justice as a typically hypocritical liberal excuse for domination, little better than erudite hectoring on behalf of interest and authority.

Egalitarians such as Gerry Cohen (1941–2009), Isaiah Berlin's successor as professor of political thought at Oxford, thought Rawls too tolerant of inequality. Cohen was a Canadian from Montreal who described himself as a "Marxist by birth." He used analytical philosophy against both free-market liberals and "middle-way" liberals like Rawls. Social justice was simpler than Rawls made it, Cohen said in effect. A fair society was an equal society. Any departure from equality was, by presumption, unjust and required an unusually strong defense. Cohen's thought was appealing. It seemed to fit better with everyday intuition and radical traditions of what really counted as to social *justice*, which was equality not simply of opportunities but of material means to make use of opportunities. Important as they were, neither rights, merit, nor need, however pressing, seemed to get to the heart of the matter.

Rawls, on Cohen's complaint, appeared to want matters all ways: to permit inequality, to show that inequality might be fair, and to insist that his ideal society might yet be on the side of the underprivileged. Cohen focused on Rawls's "difference principle": "social and economic inequalities are to be arranged so that they are reasonably expected to be to everyone's advantage." High pay for some was to everyone's benefit, Rawls's thought ran, because high pay was an incentive to initiative and hard work, from which everyone benefited. Why Cohen asked did the highly paid *need* such incentives? Was demanding them not out of keeping with the spirit of equality on which the "difference principle" supposedly rested? Cohen allowed that, as a matter of fact, incentives were needed to stir the efforts of the rich and talented. That practical concession from Cohen did not mean that high pay and incentives were fair or *just*. Cohen likened those who commanded high pay to kidnappers who said, "It is best if you pay the ransom." That is true, but it did not make the transaction just. Cohen argued in the spirit of Lincoln when questioned before the Civil War about slavery in the South. Slavery was wicked but "necessary," Lincoln said. What he meant was that there was no practical or peaceful way to end it. Slavery was to his mind still wicked. Inequality, Cohen believed, might be a practical necessity, but it was still wrong.

The Nobel economist Amartya Sen, though of philosophical mind, also thought that social justice was simpler than Rawls made it. Sen was less radically egalitarian than Cohen and believed in free markets. He shared Rawls's belief that social justice lay, crudely speaking, in liberty and equality together. Unlike Rawls, Sen did not think that to tell social justice from social injustice you needed to judge actual institutions against ideal institutions. Rawlsian constructions, Sen suggested in *The Idea of Justice* (2009), had distracted political philosophers from attention to recognizable and corrigible ills in the actual world. As an alternative to Rawls's "transcendental institutionalism," Sen offered "comparative realizations."

Theoretically speaking, Sen's emphasis on outcomes might seem to put him on the opposite side from Rawls of an old philosophical division in ethics between those who stress duties and those who stress consequences, between those, as Rawls put it, who thought like him that "right was prior to good" and those, in the tradition of Mill, who thought the reverse. In practice, lines blurred, for Sen rejected a narrowly material idea of well-being. Much as Mill had, Sen took the usable liberty to develop your capacities as lying at the core of human well-being, indeed of happiness. Sen's widened notion of welfare, coupled with his technical expertise, helped transform how economists measured and compared welfare in different countries. The United Nations Human Development Index, which Sen and fellow economists devised in the late 1980s, added to the commonly used measure of income per head life expectancy, which reflected health and education. In time the UNDP's annual report tabulated other measures of capacity or incapacity such as economic inequality and gender discrimination.

The extension of the economists' idea of a good life to include the political frame in which people found themselves was both an echo of Mill and a nod to Rawls. From the beginning Rawls had insisted that "the good" depended on "the right." In the technical language of recent philosophy, Rawls was recasting what nineteenth-century liberals in progressive but autocratic regimes such as Laboulaye and Richter had understood from experience: material betterment could come in illiberal ways. Without the respect due to people whoever they were, gross economic advance on its own was not enough.

v. Nozick, Dworkin, and MacIntyre: Responses to Rawls, Rights, and Community

Rawls's work and the responses it provoked marked a completion of the crossing for political philosophers in the liberal world that Herbert Hart had remarked on from an older trust in Utilitarianism to a new emphasis on rights. The philosophical questions that Cassin and Maritain had pushed to one side in 1948 of where human rights belonged in the furniture of the universe and what claims they made on politics were now answered in profusion. Rawls had championed rights, in the form of liberties, over the common good. Rights became a conceptual pass key in liberal thinking. Rights seemed to unlock any door. They were invoked against Rawls's social-minded liberalism and in its defense.

Robert Nozick argued in *Anarchy, State and Utopia* (1974) that Rawls's principles of justice were in irreconcilable conflict. Trying to redistribute wealth to reduce inequality was bound, Nozick believed, to infringe on personal rights. In the political market place right-wing commentators invoked Nozick's critique when suggesting that Rawls's surface concern for fair procedures unsuccessfully veiled an egalitarian desire for equal outcomes.

Building on Rawls's lead, in *Taking Rights Seriously* (1978) and in later work that culminated in *Sovereign Virtue* (2000), Ronald Dworkin took a stand on equal rights from a left-liberal point of view. Both Nozick and Dworkin were writing in the light of economic upheavals of the 1970s as postwar welfarist compromises came unstuck. For Nozick, equal rights expressed an ungainsayable natural liberty in people that no government could properly curtail save to protect their security and enforce freely struck contracts. For Dworkin, equal rights arose from a binding requirement on state and society to show everyone equal respect and concern. How sharp their differences were depended to some extent on how they were presented.

Nozick aimed for arguments to debar redistributive policies as such. Dworkin aimed to balance insistence from the political right wing on taking responsibility for one's own life with the left's concern for economic equity. There was no liberty as such, Dworkin argued, but certain particular liberties such as our moral rights were unabridgeable by government action or majority pressure. For abridging a person's rights, Dworkin argued, would mean treating him or her with less than equal respect. Among liberties people enjoyed by right, Nozick emphasized freedom from taxation, from economic regulation, from conscription or other forms of service, and from moral policing. Dworkin stressed free speech, sexual freedoms, and freedom from social discrimination. The language of rights, it seemed, could be put to notably different liberal purposes.

A different response to Rawlsianism was to ask whether the entire scholastic enterprise was not a blind alley. Far from reinvigorating a subject marred by positivism and Marxism, Rawlsianism had cut the subject's moorings in the actual world. So ran the criticism, which was one of form and one of content, though the difference was not sharp. In principle it is good to make a clear separation between political convictions themselves and the philosophical scrutiny of ideas and arguments those convictions depend on. In practice, convictions and scrutiny can be hard to disentangle.

As to form, the criticism of Rawlsianism was that academic political thinking had become detached, scholastic, and overengineered. It had forgotten the warning of the British constitutionalist A. V. Dicey in 1898 not to "weigh butcher's meat in diamond scales," a caution repeated a century later by the British philosopher Bernard Williams, that "basic ideas" in politics took rough handling and it was a mistake to try to make them "so metaphysically sensitive." The demanding, professionally satisfying new style gave liberals who believed in liberal democracy few critical tools for improving it in practice and few credible defenses against its attackers in the political market place.

As to content, we have seen in Sen's complaint one line of concern: that Rawlsianism detached progressive liberalism from the correction of actual social ills. Another line of concern was that Rawlsianism cloaked itself in a spurious impartiality. It claimed to make no judgment about good or worthwhile ways to live, yet continually did make such

judgments, which it was nevertheless unable, save in its own contestable terms, to defend or render persuasive. By exalting choice while
keeping silent on what was chosen, Rawlsians offered a shrunken picture of the liberal citizen. The best the tradition could find to commend
in people was that they were skilled and efficient at making choices, not
that what they chose was good or worthwhile. Rawlsians, above all, were
so caught in their time and its ethos, they could not imagine a different
social and moral order. Such criticisms came in sweeping and less
sweeping form.

In its less sweeping form, criticism of Rawlsianism and rights-based
liberalism came from "communitarian" critics. By exalting choice, the
charge ran, Rawlsianism short-changed society. The American thinker
Michael Sandel, for example, held in *Liberalism and the Limits of Justice*
(1982) that Rawls and modern liberals generally downplayed the moral
weight of family feeling, group loyalties, and community attachments.
Sandel's actual picture of a fair society was close to Rawls's. His complaint, amplified later, was less that liberal democracy was mistaken in
its ideals, than that actual liberal society failed to live up to them. In
particular, too many kinds of thing were now tradeable for money, as
market values threatened to exclude all other values. In "Philosophy and
Democracy" (1981) and *Spheres of Justice: A Defense of Pluralism and
Equality* (1983) another American, Michael Walzer, argued that justice
was not an equal distribution of anything. Money, office, and education
were different spheres of power and influence. The liberal aim should be
to disallow a few to dominate or anyone to be excluded from all of them.

A symptom of their intellectual unease was a movement of the late
1980s known as "communitarianism." Offered as the recovery of middle
ground between state and market, its political aims were vague. Its links
to fascism and Catholic corporativism largely forgotten, the term "community" drifted back into political argument from think tanks and universities in the 1980s. Electoral strategists were on the lookout for floating voters who liked lower taxes and limited government but felt ill at
ease with the egoism of the Thatcher-Reagan years. Community and
attendant watchwords of voluntarism, civic virtue, and neighborly responsibility seemed handy for "redefining" government, which commonly meant shuffling off long-standing responsibilities, "outsourcing,"
and public-private partnerships. Flanking fiscal unrest was a moral

alarm about the apparent erosion of "social capital." The ills ranged from poverty, street crime, and degraded public housing to less tangible ailments such as urban anomie and not joining bowling leagues.

The persuasiveness of "social capital" arguments was sensitive to the economic cycle. When good times returned, crime fell, incomes of poor people rose, and squalid public places were cleaned up. The movement's moral message also came into question. Separateness did not have to mean selfishness. Some people were joiners, some not. It would be grim, it was pointed out, if everyone was a joiner or everyone an outsider. The metaphors of social "unraveling" and "hollowing out," in addition, looked tendentious and nostalgic. As old forms of association died, new ones took their place. Social groups, last, could be stifling, self-seeking, and indeed vicious.

A suspicion never died that communitarians were looking for social virtue on the cheap. When the British student of politics R. M. MacIver wrote *Community* (1917) he had been thinking of the kind of civic commitment that underlay the democratic compromises of the social-minded "new" liberalism. Nor did communitarianism shake off its reputation for interfering moralism. The American liberal thinker Amy Gutmann once joked that communitarians wanted people to live in a Puritan Salem but not believe in witches.

A more sweeping rejection of Rawlsian liberalism, indeed liberalism of any kind, was due to Alasdair MacIntyre, a British-American moral philosopher. In *After Virtue* (1981), MacIntyre objected that liberalism rested on a false picture of morality. Liberals assumed that what people happened to want fixed their values and ideals, whereas in truth, values and ideals fixed what people ought to want. Values and ideals, in addition, grew out of shared practices in society, which alone gave people a purpose in life. Liberal modernity had dislocated society and shattered its practices. Without shared practices that gave people purpose, to talk even of values and ideals was a kind of nonsense, an echo of moral discourse that once, but no longer, had coherence.

Moral incoherence was to MacIntyre liberalism's original sin. The stain passed down to Marxists and liberal Utilitarians alike. Liberalism, for MacIntyre, closed off ways of life. Far from being a philosophy of freedom, liberalism was a doctrine of constraint. Liberals had inherited its fatal flaw from the eighteenth-century Enlightenment, "a machine for demolishing outlooks." By abandoning an Aristotelian picture of man as finding purpose in his social nature, the Enlightenment had broken the link between morality and society.

A "disorder of moral discourse" prevailed in liberal society, the symptoms of which were abstractness, lack of social anchorage, impersonality, and indecisiveness. Morals were supposedly authoritative, but, MacIntyre complained, liberal argument about them was interminable. The only guides left were "the aesthete" and the "the therapist" in private morality and "the manager" in public morality. Under "managerialism," society's primary task became the impartial and efficient balancing of people's wants. Emptied of purpose, moral talk continued under liberalism in three characteristic forms: claims to rights, which MacIntyre likened to the posting of "no trespassing" notices by squatters on common land; unmasking or the exposure of true interests behind their moralistic disguise; and protest, which was all that was left to dissent now that civil war was no longer an option and hope of persuasion by argument had gone.

MacIntyre rejected the label of communitarian. Communitarianism was to him a quarrel among liberals. A better reference point was perhaps postmodernism. MacIntyre's bleak account of a disordered moral predicament paralleled the postmodernist story of present-day thought in general. Both stressed theoretical incoherence and practical fragmentation. In *The Post-Modern Condition* (1978), the French thinker Jean-Paul Lyotard depicted present-day science much as MacIntyre treated liberal morality. To Lyotard, scientific knowledge in postindustrial society had become a force of production among others. It had lost both of science's old sources of legitimation. Nobody, so it was held, believed the Enlightenment "metanarrative" of humanity's liberation through the advance of knowledge. Nor did they believe the German Idealist super-tale, typified by Hegel, of truth and freedom unfolding together in a progressive historical two-step. Scientific knowledge, to Lyotard, now justified itself in use pragmatically. Knowledge, he predicted, would grow more dispersed, depersonalized, computer-readable, and commercially tradeable. MacIntyre's picture of moral disorder, in which values appeared to people as matters of choice and capitalist managerialism set the limits of practical reason, mirrored Lyotard's depiction of technical and scientific knowledge as in effect tradeable commodities.

In his personal convictions, MacIntyre moved from left liberalism to antiliberal Marxism and thence to left-wing, antiliberal Catholicism. What struck some as fashionable vagabondage struck others as an authentic search in the spirit of Mill's experiments in living. Friendly critics suspected that MacIntyre was, in effect, a closet liberal. Allowing for his concessions and provisos, MacIntyre's virtuous society was not radically different from the sort of place local-minded liberals such as the German cooperativists had hoped for, though perhaps with more mental conformity than liberals were generally happy with. MacIntyre hoped for an ethic of "moral resistance" in "small communities," for example self-managed societies or confessional universities.

To leave it there, however, would be to underplay MacIntyre's doubts. Why, he asked, was liberal society so rich in unrealized dreams of its own and so full of damage to things of value that everyone, liberal or not, ought to cherish? Why, he wanted to know, was liberal society so effective in ruining collegial institutions, eroding excellence, commodifying culture, and marginalizing the needy? Such ills, MacIntyre suggested, were not failures to meet liberal ideals. They arose as predictable consequences of liberal ideals. The liberal sin, to MacIntyre, was urging society to let go of people and encouraging people to go their own way. To liberals who objected that MacIntyre overplayed the ills of modern society and ignored its achievements, he replied that liberals were so confused by their "moral individualism" that they could no longer see the faults. Orwell, Camus, and Sartre had a picture of the morally scrupulous loner, painfully aware of their freedom, but crushed by a Moloch of social forces beyond their control. MacIntyre pictured liberal society as a kindergarten of self-interested, isolated selves no longer even able to recognize the collective goods they were destroying.

In blaming liberalism's flaws on "moral individualism," MacIntyre offered a way out he himself chose not to take. MacIntyre's entire attack tied liberalism tighter to a contentious picture of morality when equally he could have broken the link. A calmer view was taken by the British philosopher Joseph Raz in *The Morality of Freedom* (1986). Raz strongly favored the liberal practice of politics but wanted to free it from contentious ethical baggage it did not need. He leaned away from the Rawlsians in denying that liberalism could be conjured out of rights or that it required from politics strict silence about better or worse pursuits in life. He leaned toward MacIntyre in his suspicion of "moral individualism," a doctrine implying that collective goods such as learning, art, or law had strictly speaking no value in themselves but only as instruments of satisfaction for those who valued them. Acton's recognition of conflicting liberal duties to let people alone and to teach them echoed in Raz's liberalism. "It is the goal of all political action," Raz wrote, "to enable individuals to pursue valid conceptions of the good and to discourage evil or empty ones." In rejecting moral individualism, Raz thought of himself as jettisoning doctrinal cargo that liberals did not need. MacIntyre hoped that the cargo would sink the liberal ship.

A friend and academic colleague of Rawls, Thomas Nagel, once wryly commented that Rawls had "changed the subject." It is open to argument how much Rawls changed the world outside the universities. His impact was often contrasted with that of Oakeshott, say, or Hayek. Their academic influence was slight but strong in politics. With Rawls, it was said, the opposite was true. That was unfair to Rawls. He contributed to a broader understanding of human betterment among economists and political scientists, and thence to policy makers. He insisted that liberals not forget, as they can be minded to, society's losers. He left a rough gauge of fairness that anyone could use as a running cross-check on contentious social arrangements: "Is this the kind of thing that any of us might have chosen, whoever we were?"

13

The Breadth of Liberal Politics in the 1950s–1980s

i. Mendès-France, Brandt, and Johnson:
Left Liberalism in the 1950s–1960s

The "fundamental problems of the industrial revolution have been solved: the workers have achieved industrial and political citizenship." The American student of politics Seymour Martin Lipset wrote that in "The End of Ideology?", the final chapter of *Political Man* (1960). His book, which dealt chiefly with Western Europe and the United States, offered copious statistical evidence to confirm the virtuous, mutually reinforcing links Lipset saw among prosperity, urbanization, education, and "stable" democracy, generously understood as the kind of politics found in Britain, the United States, Switzerland, and Scandinavia. Much of Lipset's work was done somewhat before the book was published, and he kept French and German postwar democracy on probation, including them among "unstable democracies." Of the upheaval American politics was about to undergo, there was little sign, though Lipset prudently concluded by allowing that material success still left plenty of unfinished liberal business.

Liberal endism was in the air. Lipset took his chapter title from an article, "End of Ideology?" in *Encounter* (November 1955), an outstanding left-liberal magazine, which though readers did not know it at the time was indirectly paid for by the American intelligence services. The article reported on a conference that year in Milan on "The Future of Freedom," at which liberal intellectuals and social thinkers had gathered to mark the resolution of class struggle and the Western achievement, as one Swedish Social Democrat had it, of making politics "boring."

Things did not feel boring to three left-liberals then in the thick of politics, Pierre Mendès-France in France, Willy Brandt in West Germany, and Lyndon Johnson in the United States. In the West of the 1950s, the liberal dream of human betterment, materially speaking, was beginning to look achievable. Economies were growing strongly. Industrial conflict of the kind that had vexed liberal capitalism from 1880 to 1945 was starting to decline even in ill-managed, poorly educated Britain. The quarrel between economic collectivists and individualists had lost its fire. Parties to left and right were converging on a liberal capitalism primed and supported by an attentive state.

Material success still left plenty of work to secure the kind of order liberals hoped for. Mendès-France, Johnson, and Brandt stand out as practitioners who set to that work in the 1950s to 1970s. All three were postideological and disenchanted—the kind of left-liberal that Max Weber had hoped for. They represented something else Weber had said about responsibility in politics. It was not all log-rolling and bureaucratic routine, Weber insisted. Politics also required defending ideals and taking a stand. Mendès, Johnson, and Brandt had liberal ideals. They took stands.

They were born within six years of each other just before the 1914–18 war. All were outsiders and understood early on in person about exclusion, whether ethnic, social, or economic. Mendès-France was Jewish, Brandt was illegitimate, and Johnson was the son of a bankrupted farmer-politician from Texas Hill Country. All of them were driven by ambition and climbed over anyone in their way. Each reached the very top, Mendès-France fleetingly, Brandt by twenty years of up-and-down hard grind, and Johnson by accident. Each stamped politics with their distinctive voice and style. Each had a foil against which to stand out. Mendès had Charles de Gaulle, the dominating figure of postwar French politics—prime minister from 1944 to 1946 and again in 1958, president from 1959 to 1969. Brandt had two foils, the wily Social-Democrat Party operator Herbert Wehner and the policy-minded doer, Helmut Schmidt, Brandt's successor as West German chancellor. Lyndon Johnson had John Kennedy. Their records included large failures as well as successes. Even admirers add a qualifying "but." Each nevertheless had a distinctive liberal style. Each had an encompassing picture of what liberal-democratic politics should be like.

Pierre Mendès-France (1907–82) left his mark on three French republics and illustrated their liberal continuities. In the Third Republic

(1870–1940), Mendès led the Young Turks attempting to revivify an aging Radical Party by returning to its progressive roots. In the Fourth (1944–58), he was prime minister for the relatively long stretch of eight months from June 1954, when he both confronted and was undone by the challenge of French decolonization. In the Fifth, which began in 1958 under the dominating figure of Charles de Gaulle, Mendès opposed de Gaulle's great-man approach to power and great-nation approach to France.

A lawyer trained at the elite schools of Paris, Mendès showed early promise. Gifted and courageous, he combined the skills of an elite technocrat with personal engagement, a marriage of qualities that won him an enduring place in the hearts of France's center-left. At twenty-five Mendès entered parliament as France's youngest deputy. At thirty-one he was advising Léon Blum on economic retrenchment. In speeches, he was witty and direct. He grasped that public finances were now key. He was undogmatic, always superlatively briefed, and personally brave, volunteering in 1939 when, as a member of parliament, he was exempt from military service. On the Fall of France, Mendès joined the resistance in Morocco but was arrested by the Vichy authorities and sentenced to prison for desertion. On escape to England, he inexpertly navigated bombers for the Free French.

France's years under German occupation left France two paths to recovery from national shame: de Gaulle's appeal to nationhood and grandeur and Mendès-France's lessons in frankness and ordinary decency. Most French people were neither active resisters nor active collaborators. Speaking in Marcel Ophuls's documentary film on the occupation, *The Sorrow and the Pity* (1969), Mendès was among the first of France's nationally known politicians to puncture the counterpart myths of heroic opposition and spineless collapse.

An obstinate habit of assuming he was right and a love of opposition for its own sake were the faults of Mendès's virtues. He was clearer at seeing than at selling his solutions. Parliament refused his plan for economic rescue in 1938. At the Treasury in 1945, he drafted a well-argued counterinflationary proposal that de Gaulle rejected as overzealous and rigid. Reconciled to Franco-German cooperation, Mendès favored military and economic cooperation in Europe, but not without Britain, which rebuffed the first and was not ready for the second. Mendès was a lifelong Anglophile who like other French liberals, left or right, looked to Britain as an ally only to be disappointed. Decolonization was Mendès's high point and his undoing. In 1954, on the defeat of France's forces at Dien Bien Phu in Vietnam, Mendès recognized that France had lost the war in Indochina. His first step as prime minister was to open peace talks with the Vietnamese. The outbreak of anticolonial violence in Algeria early the following year caught Mendès, by contrast, unawares. He reacted with coercion and conciliation, uniting left and right against him, which ensured his fall.

He stood down for Edgar Faure, a more negotiable radical. Mendès called his memoir of the time *To Govern is to Choose*. Faure called his *Being Right All the Time is a Big Mistake*. When the Algerian crisis led to parliamentary deadlock in 1958, de Gaulle took power in what Mendès and the rest of the French left greeted as a coup. Nobody had seized power, was de Gaulle's dismissive riposte. He had simply "swept it up" from where a hapless parliament had scattered it across the floor. De Gaulle reflected a strand of providentialism in French politics, evident when the party of order entrusted power to a strongman, as in 1799, 1848, and 1940. Mendès spoke for a countervailing tradition of resistance to concentrated power, a tradition known locally as "republican," though thoroughly liberal in substance. A follower of Alain, Mendès was not to be taken in by the visage of "the important personage" and distrusted undue power, especially when concentrated in a charismatic leader. He objected less to the mechanics of the Fifth Republic, which favored executive initiative over parliamentary responsibility, than to de Gaulle's personalization of governmental authority. The Fifth Republic's actual working soon showed that its mechanics were not as top-down and presidential as de Gaulle made them appear.

Actor as well as technocrat, Mendès held the stage as dissenter and oppositionist, not always to his advantage. When demonstrations rocked Paris in May 1968, Mendès was drawn to the theater of protest, marching with students and addressing the crowds. He and his rival on the parliamentary left, François Mitterrand, talked publicly as if power had fallen. The right-wing liberal Raymond Aron reproved them both. In a liberal democracy, the removal of a popularly elected president, Aron argued, could not be conducted like dethroning a king. The snap election de Gaulle called in June brutally punished the parliamentary left and confirmed his authority as president.

Mendès stood up to de Gaulle, but his own party undercut him when he showed strong leadership. He believed in the force of persuasion but lost his big arguments. A hostile witness could reasonably claim that, for a liberal, Mendès opposed the personalization of state power more than state power itself, put undue trust in experts like himself and yet, somewhat contradictorily, allowed no higher authority than a popularly elected parliament. His liberal outlook was not free of purism. A believer in European integration, he opposed the Common Market in the 1950s because it was economically too liberal and politically too much a club of national governments.

More broadly, Mendès's politics was widely shared in France and proved enduring. It was a liberalism of middle-class aspiration, compromise, and pragmatic balancing of private enterprise and public need. It was antinationalist in its openness to the world in trade and culture, in European reconciliation and integration. "We are a party of the left," Mendès told a Radical Party conference in 1955. He saw no contradiction in adding, "We have always defended the interests of the middle classes." Mendès represented the gravitational center of French politics that Guizot had ruefully dreamed might form once the battles of "cap and hat, cassock and jacket" were done. Mendès represented a liberal centrism that a former finance student of his, Valèry Giscard d'Estaing, pursued as president from 1974–81. Mitterrand, Mendès's rival, followed Giscard as president in 1981–95. After a brief tactical flirtation with "socialist" economics to placate his own left wing, he pursued a similar liberal centrism.

Mendès was a systems man and a one-off, a technocrat, and a political sport. As an anti-ideological intellectual, he grasped the politics of gesture, which was perhaps part of why Camus admired him and the Marxist left, awash in theory, detested him. Mendès in his person seemed to answer the old anxiety of Tocqueville and Alain that in a complex, democratic society little one person did in politics ever mattered. Much of Mendès's liberal appeal was that he treated democratic government seriously and yet took personal stands.

As West German chancellors, Konrad Adenauer and Willy Brandt each accomplished two historic tasks. Adenauer united the German right in a single, democratic party broadly tolerant of liberal ideals and anchored West Germany in the West. Brandt secured the Social Democrats as a governing party of the center-left and regained respect for Germany in the world.

Willy Brandt (1913–92) was born out of wedlock in 1913 in working-class Lübeck, the other side of town from the fictional Buddenbrooks family of the novelist Thomas Mann. The boy's grandfather had been a tied laborer in Mecklenburg, a notably backward part of northern Prussia. Bismarck, who was from them there himself, advised, "When the world ends, go to Mecklenburg. News gets there a century late." As a scholarship boy with a left-wing mother and an absent father, young Brandt learned to look after himself early at a middle-class school among conservative schoolmates who did not like his pro-Weimar views. He plunged with extraordinary precocity into left-wing politics, found a patron among the Social Democrats but broke with the party in 1932 over its passivity in face of the threat from the extreme right. When the Nazis took power, Brandt escaped, a wanted man at twenty, to Norway. When Norway was occupied in 1940, he escaped a second time to Sweden. In the 1930s he lived for a time under cover in Berlin, worked as a reporter in Spain during the civil war, and, posing as Norwegian, carried messages for anti-Nazis abroad.

On return to Berlin in 1945, Brandt expected, perhaps naïvely, that the Western allies would welcome people from the left like him to help rebuild democracy. To his rage, Brandt took the Western allies to be treating all Germans as Nazi sympathizers. Brandt had no illusions about Communists. He had seen them fecklessly at work to split the Prussian left in the 1930s. He had seen them crush the non-Communist left in Barcelona in 1937. He now saw the Communists doing the same in Berlin. When the Social Democrats trounced the Communists in city elections of 1945, the Russians in their sector simply subordinated the winners to the losers and merged the rival parties by *force majeure*.

Brandt became a protégé of Ernst Reuter, a Westernizer and a Social Democrat modernizer. Reuter's adversary was Kurt Schumacher, a stiff veteran of 1914–18. Schumacher saw the Social Democrats as a workers' party, knew that the socialist vote was strong in the East, especially Saxony, and held out for a united Germany. Brandt, like Reuter, took this for a fantasy that ignored the evident wishes of the occupying powers, Western and Soviet. Brandt was for anchorage in the West now, unity later. He was anti-Communist in his bones but believed in talking to Communists. That characteristic "but-on-the-other-hand" approach of Brandt's caused him trouble in an atmosphere where everybody was suspected of being other than they seemed, but it also kept him allies in many camps.

Brandt's line gradually prevailed among Berlin's Social Democrats. The party did badly in two elections in the 1950s, which allowed the modernizers at Bad Godesberg to drop all but the thinnest veil of pretense that they were a socialist, let alone Marxist, party, rather than a party of left-liberal democrats. Though they took longer to admit it, the Socialists in France and the Labour Party in Britain were following a similar path. Modernizing the Social Democrats and making it a national rather than class party paid off at the polls. When in 1966 a mini-recession upended the government of Ludwig Erhard, master of West Germany's postwar economic miracle, the Christian Democrats and Social Democrats formed a coalition. The crossbred new government included an ex-Nazi, Kurt Kiesinger, as chancellor, an ex-Communist, Wehner, and a right-wing Bavarian, Franz-Josef Strauss. Brandt had preferred a coalition with the Free Democrats. But Germany's liberals were divided about open compromise with social democracy. Three years later, the Free Democrats' left had prevailed. They formed a government with the Social Democrats. Brandt was chancellor.

He had achieved his first aim, of making the Social Democrats a party of government. He turned to Germany and the world. After the crisis of 1961 and the building of the Berlin Wall, the West and the Soviet Union agreed in effect to freeze the status quo, including the division of Berlin. Brandt had a short and a long view. His short-term aims were for détente with the East while keeping West Germany clearly aligned with the West. Further ahead, he hoped, as Stresemann had hoped, for a united Germany to win back its freedom of maneuver in a "European order of peace." Brandt's opening to East Germany and the Communist bloc in 1970–72 won praise and blame in equal measure. It gave concessions to East Germany, Poland, and the Russians too cheaply. It legitimized an illegitimate system. Such were the criticisms. As in 1945–49 and again in 1989–90, it was easier to play "what-if" and second guess the handling of the German question than to make decisions. As Brandt liked to point out, his critics had an advantage in argument in that their favored alternatives were never tried. Perhaps opening to the East did prop it up longer than needed. Perhaps, on the other hand, delay brought a quieter end than otherwise. When in 1989 the end did come, and East Germany collapsed into West Germany's arms, it happened peacefully with almost no violence. It is hard to think the end could have come quietly without earlier relaxations and exchanges. Few had expected or even pictured such an outcome. In the Second Cold War of the late 1970s and early 1980s, a learned distinction that had a vogue in the West was drawn between authoritarian regimes such as General Pinochet's in Chile, which was murderous but removable, and "totalitarian" systems such as the Soviet Union, which were oppressive and irremovable. Brandt, to his credit, saw deeper, though even his confidence in change wavered toward the end.

What most of the world remembered from Brandt's Eastern policy was not strategic vision or diplomatic detail, but a simple gesture in Warsaw in December 1970. At the Monument to the Heroes of the Warsaw Ghetto Uprising, Brandt dropped to his knees and hung his head. An opinion poll of West Germans found that almost half those asked found the gesture overdone. To the wider world, Brandt had reminded people that not all Germans were bad. In 1972 Brandt's party beat the Christian Democrats for the first time since 1949. It was his high point.

The 1973 oil crisis and subsequent recession ended the liberal West's glorious postwar run. An Arab oil embargo in the Arab-Israeli war tipped overheated economies into recession. Brandt was unable to bridge Euro-American quarrels. The Social Democrats slumped in the polls. German public workers struck. When an East German spy was revealed in Brandt's private office, Brandt resigned as chancellor but remained as head of the party. He had held it at the center, and now he watched as working-class voters drifted to the Christian Democrats and young radicals joined the environmental Greens or the extra-parliamentary opposition. He turned his interests outward. He headed the Socialist International and became a fixture in international groups to promote development and democracy across the world. Brandt was already looking beyond the confines of the Cold War to how liberal democracy might spread. Nor was it all talk. The German Social Democrats under his leadership played a vital part in supporting Spanish and Portuguese democrats in the tricky 1970s as their dictatorships ended, at a time when American officials were worrying needlessly about Eurocommunism.

If Lyndon Johnson (1908–73) had a rule in politics it was that doing good mattered more than being right, though to do either you first had to get ahead. Once he had got ahead, Johnson broke a political dam that was holding American society back. The changes reshaped liberal democracy in the United States, making it fairer, more attentive to society's losers, more comfortable for the middle class, and more like Europe, which is one reason why "liberal" and "European" became virtually interchangeable terms of abuse on the lips of right-wing Republicans. Half a century later Americans were still angrily arguing over that legacy from the 1960s.

Johnson was politically smarter than intellectuals who derided him and probably smarter than John Kennedy, whose assassination in 1963 put Johnson in the White House. Kennedy worked down to democratic politics from newfound ease in a liberal elite that his Boston-Irish father had climbed into. Johnson knew the muck of democracy from childhood as the son of a liberal populist from the Texas backwoods. His roots were less obscure than he made out. He too had help from a political father, who served three terms in the Texas legislature, where opinion divided on whether Johnson Sr. fought or served the big interests. Home life was hard at first but the father regrouped and bought a farm, a hotel, and a newspaper press. Johnson's college-educated mother encouraged wide reading, and on second try Lyndon entered a teacher's college. His father's connections landed him an office job with a Texan congressman in Washington. He climbed the pole sucking up to rich Texans first to get his own seat in Congress, then to Sam Rayburn, the House Speaker and workaholic bachelor who treated Johnson like a son, and finally to Richard Russell, the dean of the southern Dixiecrats in the Senate, whose power Johnson courted, conciliated, and in 1964–65, with his historic civil rights legislation, overcame.

Johnson used more than flattery. He knew how to sell, a talent that won him New Dealers' attention. Federal works were not popular with

Texan businessmen. Johnson used a simple argument to nudge them round: money spent in Texas on federal projects came from taxes raised from easterners, whereas, Johnson reminded them, "we don't pay taxes in Texas." To critics to his left who complained that he was siphoning projects to the big interests, he answered that big interests were big hirers. Johnson won his seat in the U.S. Senate in 1948 by stealing more votes than the opposition, and if once there, as defenders claimed, he was a liberal reformer waiting his moment, he took his time to show it. He toed the southern line and was slow to act against the red-baiting senator from Wisconsin, Joe McCarthy. His procedural finesse was unsurpassed. He could calculate almost to the hour when a northern liberal would bend on principle or a southern conservative standing in the way of some pressing reform would for a price lift his veto.

Commanding skill in the Senate, though, did not yield large results, either legislatively or for Johnson. In 1956 he fumbled an attempt to win the Democratic nomination for president, badly underestimating the toughness of the actual candidate, Adlai Stevenson, a liberal Democrat whom Johnson mistook, as he put it, for "a nice man with too much lace on his drawers." In 1960 Kennedy, a Catholic northerner, picked Johnson as his vice presidential running mate, partly to balance the ticket in the Protestant South but also to break Johnson's hold in the Senate. The upper house had been contrived originally as a "cooling off" chamber to temper the democratic urges of the lower house. Since the Civil War southerners had, when necessary, turned the Senate with consummate skill into a deep freeze against change that threatened regional interests. Kennedy was not sure which was the true Johnson, if there was one, the liberal reformer or the loyal southerner.

Johnson's personality awed and repelled. He had to be the center of attention and dominate every encounter, whether that took charm, bullying, profanity, crudity, cornering, lapel grabbing, elbow pawing, or shin kicking. Ben Bradlee, the editor of the *Washington Post*, likened "the Johnson treatment" to being licked all over by a Saint Bernard. Johnson employed the spoken word the way he used his giant, domineering frame. He sensed in an instant what people wanted to go home with, not just in their pockets but in their heads. When he told people what he thought they wanted to hear, it was for him a form of telling the truth. As vice president, Johnson made a thankless job worse for himself by crawling to Kennedy's men, few of whom trusted or respected him. But for an unhinged gunman's bullet, Johnson would probably have been remembered, if at all, as an original, a throwback, a failed enormity. Once in the White House, Johnson seized his chance. He arrived there by accident, but he understood the office. He grasped a puzzling truth about the world's strongest liberal democracy: when party forces were aligned, opinion was mobilized and the moment was right, the power of an American president had no clear bounds.

In his State of the Union Address on January 8, 1964, Johnson intoned, "The administration today, here and now, declares unconditional war on poverty." It was the start of a burst of legislative reform known as the Great Society, a ringing phrase passed down through the American liberal Lippmann from his Harvard teacher, the British Fabian, Graham Wallas. A shift in liberal-democratic government that had taken place in Europe twenty years earlier and in certain northern states now occurred nationally. Many of the legislative changes had pended for years. Johnson neither thought of them nor drafted them, but he got them into law.

The reforms included state-provided medical insurance for the old (Medicare) and poor (Medicaid), public housing money, consumer-protection laws, new limits on pollution, school-support programs (Head Start), cultural promotion (National Endowments for the Humanities and for the Arts), a Corporation for Public Broadcasting, the Freedom of Information Act, and the opening of the Office of Equal Opportunity. Johnson also faced down the southerners in the Senate and won passage of a Voting Rights Act and a Civil Rights Act. "There is no Negro problem. There is no southern problem. There is no northern problem. There is only an American problem," Johnson told a joint session of Congress in March 1965 to ask for the VRA: "[R]eally it is all of us, who must overcome the crippling legacy of bigotry and injustice. And we shall overcome." Taken together the two acts stripped segregation of its legal shields in the southern states and for the first time put all American citizens, black and white, within the protections of the federal Bill of Rights.

In parallel, a liberal Supreme Court enjoined legal desegregation in the South and de facto segregation in the North. It extended protections for people under arrest and for defendants in criminal trials. It strengthened freedoms of press and speech, and forbade legal restrictions on the sale of contraceptives. Seen by its supporters, the liberal Court got the state out of people's lives and extended the range of privacy, in the tradition of Holmes and Brandeis. Seen from another angle, the Court brought the federal law with its Bill of Rights into the states. It is exaggerating only slightly to say that until the 1960s the United States, in its exclusions and restrictions of civic respect, was the least completely *democratic* society of the four liberal countries under discussion here. It takes imagination for anyone who did not know the United States before that postwar shift of political culture to sense their scale or appreciate the strength of the conservative countermovement they created.

Several factors combined to deny Johnson credit for his achievements. The largest was the Vietnam War, which the American left blamed Johnson for continuing, the right for losing, and Wall Street for fighting without raising taxes. By 1968, antiwar street protest punctuated by city riots in black neighborhoods had made middle American voters eager for calm and open to calls for order. Johnson declined to run for a second full term and retired to Texas. His reputation was shattered and he was ignored as a party elder. He grew his hair, neglected to care for an overweight, overtaxed body, and died of a heart attack, the last of several, at sixty-four. No twentieth-century American president had done more to change American politics with as many new laws in so short a time. A reaction was to be expected, and its impact was great.

The most obvious impact was on Johnson's own party. In national politics, civil rights and the Great Society would lose the Democrats the South for a generation, Johnson predicted. He underestimated by half a century or more. In a "white backlash," the Democratic Party lost the South and much of the working-class North, especially after courts ordered cross-town busing to neighborhood schools that were all-black or all-white because of housing patterns. The Democrats' progressive liberal core, held previously in place by Roosevelt and the New Deal, split into a "rainbow" coalition of special causes with the rise of "identity politics," black, feminist, and later gay. Those several campaigns were liberal in their aim. They were part of a traditional liberal cause: to blind public power to the many social markers of "difference" and to make civic respect more thoroughly inclusive. In its more immediate effects, identity politics weakened political liberalism in the United States. Not only did identity politics divide liberals, especially Democrats, from each other. It strengthened a moralizing conservative backlash.

Social changes were driving politics, which played back into society. The South was becoming richer and ceasing to be a backwater. Across the nation, a baby-boom generation was entering adulthood with more schooling and more spending money than their parents had had. Old sources of authority were drying up or going unheard. Business was quick to exploit and promote a more permissive, less deferential ethical climate. American life was in many ways getting better for more and more people. But politics does not work neatly by aggregates. Enough people felt shaken and affronted by change to cry "stop," especially when change was happening so fast.

The impact on the Republicans was delayed. As president from 1969 to 1974, the Republican Richard Nixon deepened and extended the liberal reforms of the 1960s, throwing sops to the Republican Right while conducting himself as the Hidden Liberal, in line of descent from Hoover, the Forgotten Liberal. Nixon tended to rate dissembling as more effective in politics than openness. Characteristically he told his staff, in private, that he was a "do-more-than-we-can-promise liberal."

The Johnson years in the United States were a historic achievement in the search for an acceptable liberal order. Decades later its essentials were still in place. Much the same was true of the 1950s to 1970s in France, Britain, and Germany. People's lives, by measures of health, diet, and schooling, were improving fast. Inequalities were lessening, opportunities growing. People were less bossed about than their parents had been and ethically freer to behave as they chose. In Britain, criminal penalties for homosexual conduct were abolished. In France censorship of broadcasting and the state monopoly of television were ended. Divorce by consent and, later, abortion became legal. One outstanding debt to the liberal cause remained to be acquitted. It was as good a single test as any of a thoroughly liberal attitude to the limits of state power. Condorcet had proposed the measure in his rejected draft for France's 1793 constitution. Germany, to recall, had entrenched it in the 1949 Basic Law. France and Britain now joined the West Germans and abolished capital punishment.

Postwar material progress lessened economic conflicts and gave content to civic respect in new ways. It did not quiet politics. New conflicts arose over the powers of the state and the liberties of citizens, the just measure of civic respect, and the accommodation of profound ethical disagreements. Once the postwar run of economic good times ended in 1973, material conflict itself returned over what those at the peak and in the middle of the social diamond owed to those at the bottom. The changes of the 1950s to 1970s were for many a welcome upheaval. Still, they were an upheaval. They raised expectations. They disturbed familiar patterns. They stored up a powerful counterreaction mixing wrathful opposition and disappointed hopes.

ii. Buchanan and Friedman: Liberal Economists against the State

In a vote heard round the liberal world, Californians in November 1978 chose by a margin of two to one to cut their property taxes. Some years before the California Supreme Court had directed prosperous localities to share revenues with poor localities. The matter was nettlesome as property taxes paid for schools, which were good in prosperous neighborhoods and bad in poor ones. The court's decision barely touched the richest Californians. It enraged middle-class Californians, especially as inflation in the 1970s continued to push up the value of their houses and with it their property taxes. Voters in the middle could not see why they should have to short-change their children's schools to pay for the schools of the poor. The fact of considerable overlap between the categories of "white" and "middle class" on the one hand and on the other between "black or Latino" and "poor" did not help. Anger grew, and Proposition 13, as the proposal to write a property tax cap into the state constitution was known, passed everywhere save in one thinly populated rural county, in the Democrat-dominated state capitol Sacramento, and in left-liberal San Francisco.

The ballot initiative used in California and other states in the Upper Midwest and West gave voters a measure of direct democracy. It was a legacy of the Progressive movement before the First World War, when good-government liberals and popular democrats sought state and local ways to circumvent the corruptions of electoral politics. Proposition 13 now announced a swelling countermovement against seventy years of progressive change. California's Proposition 13 represented in microcosm a conflict that came to dominate liberal-democratic politics both in the United States and, with local variations, in Britain and later, though less divisively, in France and Germany.

The tax revolt of November 1978 had fiscal and intellectual roots that ran deep and wide. Both stretched far beyond California. A first factor was material progress itself. As society's shape grew less like a pyramid and more like a diamond, the bite of taxation widened. When first introduced in Europe and the United States in the 1880s to 1910s, progressive income tax had broad appeal because few people earned enough to have to pay. Governments liked income tax, as it was a handy revenue raiser. Middle-class voters liked it because it soaked the idle rich. After 1945 income tax began to soak the hard-working middle classes. In addition, the moralizing contrast between hard-earned and unearned money that Mill had invoked, and that progressive reformers had drawn on to win support for their proposals, now sounded quaint. Virtually everyone worked. Unearned income paid not just for the furs and polo ponies of coupon clippers. It paid the pensions of middle-class people, many of whom saved for retirement through investment funds. Liberal democracy had broken the tax resistance of the rich earlier in the century. The tax resistance of the middle classes was a new order of difficulty, for the middle classes were now, in representative terms, a democratic majority.

A third factor was the rigidity of fiscal structures. The difficulty took its own form in each country. The broad problem was common. No tax is wholly neutral in its effects. Tax may bite incomes or sales. It may favor the rich or the poor. It may hit households or firms. Every fiscal system has its own mix of taxes. To take examples, the United States relies heavily for federal revenues on income taxes, France pays for central government more from sales tax and social-security contributions, almost 70 percent of which employers pay. A quite general problem is that once a pattern of taxation is set, it is politically hard to change. It is a wisdom as old as Machiavelli that people will put up with exactions they have grown used to but will fight those they do not expect. Shifting the bite of taxation from one group of people to another is provocative enough when the overall level of tax is steady. In the 1970s, inflation was everywhere pushing up not only taxes people paid on their property but also taxes they paid on their incomes, as higher earnings pushed them into higher tax brackets. By the end of the decade, those three factors— the breadth of taxation, the replacement of the idle rich with the taxman as a focus of public anger, and structural rigidity—had combined to create a fiscal explosion.

Inflation was no longer primarily a national phenomenon. Internationally speaking, the postwar economic balance in which Western Europe and the United States had grown rich had broken down. Inflation in the 1950s was broadly under control. By the end of the 1960s, it was recognized as a growing danger, especially in Britain and the United States. After the Second World War, dollars flooded the world. People to begin with wanted dollars. They traded and invested in dollars. Accordingly they wanted to believe in dollars. The more dollars there were, however, the harder it became to sustain their belief. By the end of the 1960s, when the United States was borrowing heavily to pay for a war on poverty and a war in Vietnam, the dollar came under sustained pressure. A weakness of the Bretton Woods currency system was that the pressure on debtor currencies to devalue was greater than that on creditor countries to revalue. By the late 1960s Germany and Japan had become large creditors, reluctant to import higher prices by cheapening the deutsche mark and the yen. In 1971–72, the United States, banker to the world, suspended gold payments, and the Bretton Woods system broke apart. In time, the globalized system would prove an engine of new prosperity. In the 1970s, it meant that shocks traveled from country to country without hindrance.

The intellectual roots of the middle-class revolt against government lay in free-market economics. In the 1930s, it fell out of favor. Economically, it offered no answer to the slump. Politically, right-wing ideas became tainted, fairly or not, with the odor of failure and extremism. In the 1960s, the intellectual climate began to change. Right-wing ideas recovered from disregard and disgrace. The weight of "radical" and "conservative" shifted. The social-minded advisers to the Democrat Johnson and the Republican Nixon now represented a vulnerable status quo. They had a thirty-year record for their radical rivals on the right to attack. Among economists, two radicals who hit hardest were James Buchanan, a founder of public-choice theory, and Milton Friedman, the anti-Keynesian monetarist.

James Buchanan (1919–2013) urged people to think once more of the state as wolf. Buchanan viewed "politics without romance," as he put it, in a "hard-nosed way." In more technical language, Buchanan recast the skeptical thoughts of previous economic critics of democracy such as Michels and Schumpeter. His own background was hard. He grew up on his father's farm in Murfreesboro, Tennessee, which as he might remind listeners, was the site of the Civil War's single deadliest battle. After a naval staff job in the Second World War, Buchanan studied at Chicago, the American center of free-market economics. Buchanan came away determined to apply economics to politics. Peacetime governments were spending one-third to two-fifths of the national income, he noticed, but economists were not looking hard at how or why. A year's study in Italy exposed Buchanan to economics teachers who shared an ancient Italian suspicion of government power and who treated politicians and officials not as advocates of the common good but as self-interested foxes and wolves.

Buchanan returned to a post at the University of Virginia, where he met Gordon Tullock. His new colleague was looking into Duncan Black's studies of agenda control on committees and Kenneth Arrow's work on voting paradoxes. Black's results suggested how electoral outcomes might be manipulated by the manner or order in which choices were presented. Refining Condorcet's paradox of self-defeating, circular majorities, Arrow in 1950 had suggested that on plausible assumptions about fair voting methods there were no clear ways to derive a consistent "collective" choice from individual preferences. Majority voting, it seemed, was manipulable and not decisive. To Buchanan that was welcome news. For in the steps of Schumpeter, he treated majoritarian democracy as a problem. It held out a prospect that had occupied Madison and haunted Calhoun: the semipermanent domination of outvoted minorities. Buchanan and Tullock combined those several thoughts in *The Calculus of Consent: The Logical Foundations of Constitutional Democracy* (1962).

If their suspicions of government were correct, the authors suggested, it was likely that public goods such as roads, hospitals, and state schools would be oversupplied. The prevailing wisdom was that there need be no link between what a taxpayer paid and the benefits he or she received. In such conditions, politicians and officials controlling the supply of public goods would "sell" them for votes or tenure. If on the other hand everyone who got a service from the state had to agree to pay for it, public goods would be undersupplied. The requirement would work as a unanimity rule, giving everyone a veto. Free riders, who wanted only public services they did not have to pay for, and libertarians, who opposed public spending on principle, would block any spending proposal.

Responsible taxpayers on the one hand deserved protection from majoritarian pork barrel that oversupplied public goods. Society's needs on the other ought not to be frustrated by libertarian zealots or freeloaders. If given a veto, they would create an undersupply of public goods. Somewhere between those extremes, Buchanan and Tullock looked for "workable unanimity." To find it, Buchanan took his search to a higher level. The rules of the game, he concluded, ought to be unanimously agreed to. Once such rules were at work, majority voting could prevail. Buchanan's construction was remarkably like Rawls's. At opposite points on the liberal spectrum, they even drew similar conclusions from their thought experiments. Rawls thought that, obliged to choose as if for everyone, people would pick rules that protected the worst off. Buchanan thought that, if unanimity were required, nobody would agree to rules that threatened to make them into permanent losers.

Buchanan and Rawls were close in another way. As Americans began to quarrel more openly about manners and morals, Buchanan grew glum, as did Rawls, about the chances of agreement on matters of principle. Unlike Hayek, Buchanan did not think that ethical and social cohesion could simply be counted on in the way, for example, that Adam Smith and David Hume had counted on it in the apparent historical stillness before capitalism upturned social and ethical stability for good. Unlike Rawls, Buchanan's impact outside the universities was large. Directly or indirectly, Buchanan's ideas for constitutional limits on taxing and spending spread from California to Washington. There Republicans began to explore self-limiting ordinances to limit or reduce the size of government spending. Buchanan's work lent academic weight to a growing antipolitical mood among the American public at large, especially when explained in clear and simple public lectures in his wry, Border drawl.

No economist did more than Milton Friedman (1912–2006) to shift the focus of public debate from keeping employment high to holding inflation low. A historian of money as well as a first-rate economic theorist, Friedman believed like Irving Fisher that bad monetary management had turned a business recession in the late 1920s into a decade-long depression. Getting monetary policy right was the government's primary economic task, on Friedman's view. Often he sounded as if it were government's only economic task. For the other tasks people had come to expect of government were to Friedman's mind either positively damaging when done by government or better done in other ways. Born in Brooklyn to first-generation immigrants from the Austro-Russian borderlands, Friedman shot through school and on to Chicago, where he was quickly recognized for his outstanding twin gifts in mathematics and disputation.

Friedman knew how to market ideas. Unlike Hayek, who after *Road to Serfdom* worked wholesale through think tanks and lobbying groups, Friedman sold retail. As a salesman of ideas, Friedman was gleeful and electric. His free-market tract, *Capitalism and Freedom* (1962), was a world best seller. Friedman and his wife, Rose, had a successful television show—on public television—called *Free to Choose*. For eighteen years, Friedman wrote a column in *Newsweek*. His attack on Keynesianism was sharper and less oblique than Hayek's. Keynesians taught that governments should spend and borrow when needed to keep demand in the economy buoyant and unemployment at bay. No, Friedman answered. Government should provide monetary stability and leave it there. Lack of work was the ill to be cured in the 1930s, as Friedman recognized. He himself worked in Roosevelt's Washington, helping to bring in withholding taxes during the war. Times and economic thinking had now changed. Inflation was the danger. Friedman offered to explain how it arose and how it was to be stopped.

"There is always a temporary trade-off between inflation and unemployment. There is no permanent trade-off." Those words of Friedman's in a speech to fellow American economists, published as "The Role of Monetary Policy" (1968), marked a turning point in postwar thinking about the economy. Rising inflation created jobs, Friedman was saying. High inflation killed them. Keynesian wisdom taught that with looser money or more spending, governments could buy a touch less unemployment for a slight rise in inflation. Friedman disagreed. As radicals must, Friedman set up Keynesians as a discredited opposition and exaggerated how far he and they differed. Keynes had done no less with his "classical" foe. The mathematical economist in Friedman combined with the star debater to great effect.

Heeding Marshall's advice, Friedman insisted that the time scale of adjustment mattered. Keynesians, he complained, ignored the medium term. Firms and consumers took it seriously. They saw government borrowing or tax reductions now as promise of inflation to come. Having more spending money might at first prompt people to buy more. Pushing demand harder than supply was bound soon to raise prices. The gain, it would be clear, was empty. Buying would slacken. Unemployment would again rise. As everyone could see that coming, Friedman argued that the Keynesian's favored tool, fiscal policy, was either inflationary or ineffective. Friedman was echoing Fisher's quantity theory of money. The only lasting effect of creating more money was to push up prices. The effect on output and jobs was minor. Friedman had argued that himself in "The Quantity Theory of Money" (1956).

Friedman's disbelief in fiscal policy, his conviction that "inflation is always and everywhere a monetary phenomenon," and his explanation for the Great Depression combined in a positive recommendation. Money was too important to be left to the discretion of central bankers. Instead, governments should fix a "monetary rule" for growth in the money supply. The idea of "rules not authorities" was in the air. Hayek thought rules might control interfering officials and reformers. Buchanan thought they might curb democratic majorities. To tame inflation in Britain, Margaret Thatcher's government tried but soon abandoned Friedman's monetary targets during the 1980s. No measure of the amount of money in the economy seemed to work. Hayek was not surprised. He no more believed in Friedman's monetary targets than in any macroeconomic aggregates. Friedman grumbled that the British Treasury had misunderstood his ideas.

Friedman's cure in Britain perhaps fell victim to Goodhart's law, named after a British economist, Charles Goodhart: "Any observed statistical regularity will tend to collapse once pressure is placed upon it for control purposes," or as a fellow economist put it, "When a measure becomes a target, it ceases to be a good measure." A parallel thought underpinned a new school of economics known as "rational expectations." That school too cast doubt on government's capacity to guide the economy. Its suggestion was that people's guesses about future prices and wages were more right than wrong. If that were true, government steps now to affect future prices and wages would be ineffective. For people's broadly correct guesses about the future had already taken government action into account. The expected effect of present action to shift futures prices was already reflected, in other words, in present prices. Monetarists, to schematize, taught that Keynesian demand management was self-defeating. Rational expectations taught that all government interventions in markets were self-defeating.

In 1973, the welcome postwar boom that the Germans called the *Wirtschaftswunder* and the French the *Trentes Glorieuses* ended. Trouble had brewed in Britain and the United States. A quadrupling of oil prices and an oil embargo after a third Arab-Israeli war in 1973 stopped the Western economies dead. It did not stop inflation. The new malady was called "stagflation." Keynesians had not said it could not occur. Only that it was improbable and avoidable. Friedman had said stagflation was both probable and hard to avoid if government pushed up spending power artificially. The course of the 1970s appeared to prove Friedman right.

Friedman's popular manifesto was *Capitalism and Freedom* (1962). As had Hayek, he argued that political freedom required economic freedom. Markets were blind to people's nonmonetary differences. Markets encouraged mutual forbearance and acceptance. The more markets spread within society, the less room there was for intolerance, oppression, and harmful political factionalism. After 1973, the corrupt and murderous Pinochet regime in Chile offered a test bed for that claim. The regime adopted Friedmanite ideas with mixed economic results, though Friedman personally was not involved. Were it true that political liberty required economic freedoms, the reverse was not necessarily the case. Pinochet's regime lasted seventeen years. To link economic and political freedom more convincingly, more needed to be said about the timescale of adjustment. How long might a free-market tyranny be held to continue before it became a counterinstance to the commonly heard claim that markets themselves fostered political liberty?

Governments, Friedman thought, should limit themselves to enforcing contracts, promoting competition, protecting "the irresponsible, whether madman or child," and ensuring stable money. Those strictures on the state paralleled Hayek's, save the last, which Hayek took for illusory. Friedman in *Capitalism and Freedom* listed fourteen things government should *not* do, including subsidize farms, control rents, run national parks, compel state pension contributions from people, permit licensing of doctors—one of Spencer's bugbears—conscript young men, and regulate banks. Many went unheard. On the other hand, in a proud moment for Friedman, the American military draft was ended in 1973. Banks were later deregulated. Both reforms had unintended consequences. The book was prescient internationally. In chapter 4, *Capitalism and Freedom* recommended floating exchange rates. The proposal seemed academic. Ten years later the Bretton Woods currency system that Keynes had helped to found broke down. A globalized economy Friedman hoped for in which labor, goods, and capital flowed freely across national borders came in view. Schuman and Hallstein had set France and Germany on the path to creating an open Europe. Friedman, thinking globally like an American, wanted an open world.

In the 1970s, the center of gravity shifted in liberal attitudes to the state. Nearly one hundred years of acceptance and embrace now made way for distrust and withdrawal. Liberals, who had focused on how much governments could do, now thought more about what they should not do. Before, several assumptions were widely shared in and out of government. Budget constraints were "soft": as reliable borrowers, states could reach deep into lenders' pockets. Markets had a bias to unemployment and tended to operate unfairly to the disadvantage of the poor. Economic conflict was lessening, as management and labor saw mutual advantages in cooperating. Modern success in business depended less on besting rivals than on organization and command of scale. Competition was not at odds with regulation. Nor was all social life a competition. Markets were part of society, not all of society.

From the work of Buchanan, Friedman, and others, a stripped-down job description for government emerged. Its only big-ticket macroeconomic job was to keep prices down. Otherwise, governments should stop sharing richer people's money with the poor. They should lower taxes to encourage work and cut spending to avoid borrowing. They should ensure the rule of law and property rights but limit other tasks. Markets were better at providing many services people and businesses had come to expect from government. A new economic vocabulary entered politics. Citizens became clients, hospital patients became customers. The subversive idea spread that because any transaction between people could be described in economic terms, it was thereby subject to the laws of the market.

Winning and timely as they were, the ideas of such thinkers did not prevail on their own. Universities and, above all, think tanks transmitted their ideas into politics. Market liberals in the nineteenth century had popularizers and the business press. Reform liberals had universities, where the scholar's gown had not long since replaced the cleric's frock. Now neoliberals ideas fermented in institutes, commonly paid for by business money and energized by gifted intellectual entrepreneurs. They included William Baroody at the American Enterprise Institute in Washington (founded 1943), Anthony Fisher of the Institute of Economic Affairs (1955), and Alfred Sherman of the Centre for Policy Studies (1974), both in London.

The liberal climate changed later and more gradually in Germany and France, but new ideas also filtered into political life from institutes and think tanks. German postwar parties all had active research arms. The oldest was the Social Democrats' Friedrich Ebert Foundation (1925). The Christian Democrats set up the Konrad Adenauer Foundation (1955), the Free Democrats the Friedrich Naumann Foundation (1958). German banks and companies also promoted the traffic in ideas through foundations and research departments. Notable was the Bertelsmann Foundation, set up by the publisher Reinhard Mohn in 1977 to promote free-market centrism. The research departments of the Bundesbank and of Deutsche Bank, before its transformation into a global giant, played an active part in German economic debate.

Despite French allergy to the word "liberal" and undue attention to *marxisant* intellectualism, liberal ideas played a central role in postwar French politics. A roster of the bankers, business people, officials, politicians, and journalists in Le Siècle, a nonpartisan political club founded in 1944 with an office on the Avenue de l'Opéra, offered a better idea of the liberal center of gravity in French public life than the writings of left-bank critics. By the 1980s, the economic case for more competition and less regulation was winning adepts on center-right and center-left alike. Journals sprang up also with a politically liberal outlook. They included *Commentaire*, founded by Raymond Aron in 1978 and edited by Jean-Paul Casanova, an adviser to the center-right prime minister Raymond Barre, and *Débat*, founded in 1980 by the historian Pierre Nora and edited by the Benjamin Constant scholar Marcel Gauchet.

Ideas need expert messengers. But expert messengers are not enough. Something more is required. A shift in political attitudes also takes outstanding politicians. Not that they create a new climate. Nobody does that, although the will to believe in the powerful figure who "stamps their time" seems unbreakable. A political shift, rather, needs politicians to show people that they are in a new climate. In the 1970s, neoliberalism had two such leaders.

iii. Thatcher, Reagan, Mitterrand, and Kohl:
Right Liberalism in the 1970s–1980s

The Centre for Policy Studies in London was the creation of Sherman, an ex-communist writer and journalist who had fought for the Republicans in the Spanish Civil War, and Keith Joseph, a lawyer, Oxford don, and Conservative MP. Both men believed that post-1945 consensus was crippling Britain. Soon after the center's launch in 1974, Joseph asked a fellow MP, the little-known Margaret Thatcher, to be vice-chairman of their campaign against compromise and muddle-through. A year later, to broad surprise, she became leader of the Conservatives, then in opposition. In 1979, at the end of wearing years of inflation and unemployment, the Conservatives won power. Their victory and Thatcher's premiership, which lasted until 1990, coincided with a radical shift in how state and government were thought about. Although Thatcher did not cause people to think of government more as foe than as friend, her courage, feel for politics, and determination gave that new attitude voice. With oratorical skill, she daunted critics and questioners in her own party as well as in the Labour and Liberal opposition. Although she did not need think tankers to know what to think, colleagues like Joseph gave her convictions policy detail and economic rationale. The convictions were hers.

As to her larger picture of politics and society, Thatcher is said to have shown colleagues a copy of Hayek's *Constitution of Liberty*, tapped hard on its cover and announced, "This is what we believe in." Whatever the lines of influence, her thoughts paralleled his. "Who is society?" she asked an interviewer rhetorically in 1987. "There is no such thing! There are individual men and women; and there are families and no government can do anything except through people, and people look to themselves first. It is our duty to look after ourselves and then also to help look after our neighbour."

Thatcher's command of her brief and her words were vital to her rise in the Tory Party, her success with British voters and her reputation in the world. As if ignoring the odds, she stood up to opposition. As if indifferent to opinion, she stood up for what she believed. Vexing as it was for left-minded liberals in the West, the Western politician whom Easterners in the communist world probably most admired in the 1980s as that world broke up was Margaret Thatcher.

In encouraging people to look favorably on markets and unfavorably on the state, Thatcher spread the thought that politics was the problem, economics the answer. To effect such a change, however, took not only influence and charisma, both of which Thatcher had in abundance. It took power. And there lies a first puzzle about the character of Thatcher's liberalism. Her governments broke the power of industrial trade unions, broke the closed shop of British banking, broke the power of local councils, and broke the esprit de corps of ministerial departments. Though commonly spoken of as a victory for "freedom," those changes concentrated economic power in the hands of large business enterprises, particularly banks, government power in the central administration at Whitehall, and Whitehall power in the prime minister's office. Few prime ministers since the "new" liberal Lloyd George had done as much to concentrate power as Thatcher had. It was a strange legacy for a prime minister surrounded by neoliberal intellectuals committed to dispersing power and promoting spontaneous order.

Another notable element that colored Thatcher's liberalism was her national feeling. On her death in 2013, David Cameron, an ex–public relations man and later Conservative premier, called Thatcher "the patriot prime minister." The phrase was apt. More than anything, she appealed to British, or strictly English, pride. Thatcher loved England with a divisive passion. She and her followers told a beguiling story of rescuing Britain from national decline brought on by its adversaries, inside as well as out. Their radical narrative of impotence and decay echoed the anti-parliamentary rightism of the 1920s and 1930s. It was supported neither by the events of the 1970s, when Britain was suffering from a general crisis of Western economies, nor by Britain's subsequent failure, despite the luck of North Sea Oil, to match its northern continental partners, especially Germany, in price stability, job creation, or labor productivity.

The economic facts did not detract from the patriotic epic in which Thatcher sincerely believed. She played effectively to English—not British—pride, and to suspicion of foreigners, especially suspicion of the French and Germans. She played to an obstinate national taste for gambling against odds and for punching above the country's weight in the confidence, not always well placed, that the United States would pick up the pieces. In all that, Thatcher was the least Cobdenite of liberals. In other ways, she was Cobdenite through and through: unimpressed by class or status and keen to let men and women with initiative get on in their various enterprises without envy or vested interests standing in their way. A natural in politics, she was ever more flexible in practice than she sounded in speeches. "Never negotiate with terrorists," she intoned in public. Secretly and successfully, her officials talked on her behalf to "terrorists" in Ireland and Southern Africa.

When, in 1990, Thatcher's growing weakness threatened her party, it moved to the kill with customary efficiency. On resigning from her government, a close colleague, Geoffrey Howe, spoke in the Commons as a Roman senator might have spoken of a would-be tyrant in the days of the Republic. Thatcher's hostility to Europe and her deafness to dissent were endangering not only her party but her country. At the end of her rule, such criticisms from a quiet spoken ex-minister were fatal. They pointed at the same time to sources of Thatcher's former strength: conviction and willpower.

In the United States, think tanks played their due part in the Republican realignment of 1980. In Washington, two Catholic conservatives, Edwin Feulner and Paul Weyrich, started the Heritage Foundation (1973), and the following year Murray Rothbard, a libertarian thinker, founded with friends the Cato Institute. Both institutions struck political Washington to begin with as a rest home for aging cranks. Political Washington had soon to think again. Under Ronald Reagan, libertarian economics and conservative moralism entered the pamphlets and speeches of Republicans. Soon libertarians, antigovernment campaigners, and moralizers became the party's mainstream, pushing moderate Republicans to its fringe or out of the party altogether.

Thatcher attacked the state while using its power to free that of the market. Reagan similarly ran against government so as to run government with like purpose. Whereas Thatcher made government sound selfish or naughty, Reagan made it sound comical. "The nine most ter-rifying words in the English language," he used to say, "are, 'I'm from the government and I'm here to help.' " The differences ran deeper. In Britain the arguments of the 1970s and 1980s were among liberals. It was a rerun of the old inner-liberal argument, met many times in this liberal story, between more government and less government. Thatcher was right-wing and for all her talk of freedom was overfond of power, but she was still liberal. Despite her party label, Thatcher passed Hayek's check-list for not being conservative with relative ease. In the United States, matters were more complicated, for the American right had liberal and nonliberal streams.

Politically speaking, in the 1950s Democrats and Republicans con-verged at the liberal center. The liberal historian Hartz and the liberal student of politics Lipset were not alone in treating the United States as if it in fact was as John Rawls thought it ought to be: a country of man-ageable disagreements framed by overarching liberal concord. Ameri-can politicians had always wrapped themselves in the flag of liberty. Equally they had claimed to stand for America above party. At midcen-tury, to left and right, it was possible to believe in an opportune pairing of liberalism and Americanism, that mix of civic pride, national loyalty, and provident superiority that had served as an image of unity in a pe-riod of rapid immigration before 1914 and in two world wars.

By the 1970s, the pairing of liberalism and Americanism was more contested than believed. Each element was under challenge. To the left, identity politics helped split the old Roosevelt-Truman Democratic co-alition. The party began to caucus less by state and city than by color, ethnic group, and gender. To the right, moral politics began to harden and narrow the Republican Party, making a once minority wing into a dominant, illiberal core. Crudely, you no longer needed to be all-American to be a good Democrat. To be a good Republican, you no lon-ger needed to be all-American. You simply needed to be good, which meant upright, God-fearing, and, in a partisan shift of meaning, liberal-loathing. Whether as the description of a historic achievement, the de-lineation of a social ideal or as a partisan political label, the word "lib-eral" in American politics became a flag of war.

As the postwar American right recovered its intellectual self-regard, four groups stood out. One, mentioned earlier, was represented by market economists and old critics of the New Deal. A second group included anticommunists, smoking out collectivists in an anticollectivist society. A third group were traditional conservatives, disturbed by cultural democracy, permissiveness, and a loss of "civility." William Buckley, a quick-witted Catholic controversialist, united and modernized the anticommunists and the traditionalists. Buckley started the *National Review* (1955), which played a similar part in the right's revival as the *New Republic* had played in the liberal tide forty years earlier. Buckley had a talk show, *Firing Line*—again, on public television—in which *bien pensants* leftist guests were sometimes surprised to meet a well-informed, dialectically formidable adversary. Buckley's achievement was to weed out the crackpots and make the ideas of the intellectual right count again. A fourth group were the New York neoconservatives. Many were ex-Marxists, and all were liberals, though liberals who had been "mugged by reality," in the words of one of their luminaries, Irving Kristol. The neoconservatives cohabited with Nixon and Reagan, but mostly abandoned the Republicans when the Republicans abandoned the center.

Among Republican activists, the "antigovernment" movement had cross-cutting streams. One was a *libertarian*, almost anarchist right, with roots in the American past, in antifederalism and localism. Another was a diverse crowd of *resentful conservatives*, who had not accepted modern American society, either for its multiracialism or its permissive secularism. Suspicion of elites, dislike of the "coasts" and a discourse of states' rights or local community linked the two first groups. A larger stream than either was accounted for by *disappointed liberals*. Such voters had expected government to protect them from the ups and downs of capitalism. They had expected the United States not only to win its wars but to be loved by the world for doing so. Unlike libertarians, the disappointed did not want a political scrap. They did not telephone talk radio to bellow about big government and elite conspiracies. Politics, if anything, bored the disappointed. Many were independents, without durable party loyalty. Sometimes they had voted Republican, sometimes Democrat. They were the center of gravity in American elections, its broad, pragmatically conservative middle ground that was needed to win national elections. Unlike libertarians and resenters, the disappointed were at home with modern government in modern society. Their parents or grandparents had voted for Roosevelt-Truman Democrats. The disappointed, in the large sense, not the partisan sense, were liberals. In 1972, disappointed liberals voted for Nixon and twelve years later for Reagan. Though the term jars given present-day American usage, inclusion of the disappointed as liberals better describes the actual political ground. A fourth element in the antigovernment mood of the 1970s must not be forgotten. It came from Democratic liberals who exposed the warfare state's misuse of spies and the political abuse of power, mostly visibly in the Watergate scandal that led to Nixon's resignation in 1974. Those liberals had not meant it, but their campaigns of investigation and exposure, then as now, also encouraged disenchantment with government.

Reagan understood those many antigovernment streams. As an old Roosevelt Democrat and former head of Hollywood's actors' union, he was himself one of the disappointed. Though a divorced, nonchurchgoer, he could tell a fundamentalist Christian audience in sincerity that there was "sin and evil" and that everyone was "enjoined by scripture and the Lord Jesus to oppose it" with all their might. He knew, as Lincoln had known, how to sneak behind the proprieties and appeal to white prejudice. He rocked audiences with jibes at big government's expense so skillfully that they forgot in their glee that big government was what Reagan was asking them to let him run.

Reagan was courteous, relaxed, fun at dinner for his guests, impatient with detail, and ruthless with colleagues. It was said he made Americans feel better about themselves but was indifferent to how many of them lived. He seized rather than made his opportunities. He inherited a defense buildup started by his predecessor. He inherited a burst of high-tech creativity that buildup had nourished. He inherited a chairman of the federal reserve, Paul Volcker, who had pushed interest rates to 11.5 percent a year before Reagan took office, a brutal step which by early in the new presidency had cut double-digit inflation to 3.5 percent, so smoothing a path to the long economic boom that lasted into the new century. Reagan inherited a superpower rivalry that the United States was on course to win as its Soviet rival, mired in its own failures and shadowed by a rising China, began to implode. With practiced grace and skill, Reagan made the most of those opportunities. He knew when to push at an open door, calling dramatically in Berlin in June 1987, "Mr. Gorbachev, tear down this wall."

Reagan told his barber, Milton Pitts, that he had come to office with five aims: restoring morale, lowering tax rates, increasing spending on defense, facing down the Soviet Union, and scaling back government. He had done all but the last, he said. If so skilled a politician as Reagan, who was dealt such a good hand and who had such a popular following, was unable with all the powers of office to complete his fifth task, perhaps the answer was that America's disappointed majority did not really want it to be completed. Perhaps they did not want less government but better government, and government they could again place their confidence in.

Reagan was remarkable in combining in one body several political beings. He appealed to two wings of American liberalism, New Deal Democrats and tight-money big business Republicans. He knew how to appeal, too, to illiberal Bible Belt Christians and to beyond-the-liberal-fringe libertarians. After Reagan, Republicanism fell ever more into the hands of the religious right and antigovernment fundamentalists as a once right-wing liberal party began a transformation into something at or beyond the edge of liberalism.

In France and Germany, the shift of mood against the state at the political center was subtler to recognize, less doctrinal, and to start with less angry. In the 1970s and 1980s, top-down authority in France's Fifth Republic relaxed. In the 1970s, after the politico-cultural shocks of 1968 and de Gaulle's retirement the following year, the institutions of French politics became less rigid and top heavy. Change quickened after 1974 when the liberal right won power under Valéry Giscard d'Estaing. His party, the Republican Independents, was centrist, pro-European, and, in the words of its manifesto, liberal "in the political sense of the term," by which was meant public dialogue, freeing of the media from government influence, more say for parliament, and greater local powers for the regions. The presidential grip in France's Fifth Republic loosened further after the socialist President Mitterrand won the presidency in 1981. Five years later his party lost a parliamentary election, obliging him to "cohabit" with a right-wing government.

Whichever party was in charge, the 1970s and 1980s brought France many liberal changes. The state television monopoly and broadcasting censorship ended. Divorce by consent and abortion became legal. Powers devolved to elected regional assemblies. As Gaullism's France-first appeal faded, France committed itself to the European Union and to a single European currency. The powers of the constitutional court increased. The French state accepted that citizens could appeal directly against its misdeeds to the European Commission on Human Rights.

The liberal center exercised its pull on the French left. Mitterrand had won the presidency with Communist support and there followed a brief experiment with state-led attempts to stimulate a flagging economy. The experiment ended, as economic liberals had predicted it would, as a weakening franc and rising inflation prompted a U-turn and fiscal retrenchment. In modern conditions, of currency exposure and European integration, go-it-alone "Albanian" policies, it was concluded, were no longer possible. In 1985, a quarter of a century after the German Social Democrats at Bad Godesberg, the French Socialist Party at Toulouse formally dropped the last remnants of socialism. The doctrinal shift reflected a change in society. In 1930, the French workforce was still divided almost equally in three among farming, industry, and services. It was now overwhelmingly in services. Almost nobody worked on the land, and only 20 percent of French people lived in the countryside. The industrial workforce had shrunk. Despite the reputation of France's "street," France by the end of the twentieth century had one of the lowest rates of union membership in Europe.

A counterliberal left lived on in a ferment of radical Greens, antineoliberals and latter-day Trotskyists. None had a coherent or credible alternative of their own to liberal centrism. Each represented a sharp, effective nail to puncture liberal complacency. The far right lingered on, marginal to begin with, more threatening in time. It combined populist resentment against big government and big business, familiar on the Republican right in the United States, with French chauvinism and antique but villainous prejudices.

By 1989, the historic legend of the unfinished revolution on France's socialist left was dying, as was the myth of heroic resistance and national pride on the Gaullist right. To mark the bicentenary of the French Revolution, a spectacular parade was mounted on July 14 on the Champs-Elysées in Paris. It celebrated every aspect of French life and history imaginable. Cool and up-to-date, the mise-en-scène was due to an advertising man, Jean-Paul Goude, known for promoting the mineral water Perrier. The centenary of the French Revolution in 1889 had been an affirmation of political principle, a chance to defend France's liberal republic against its conservative enemies and to claim the mantle of Revolution from its socialist rivals. If the playful, chaotic spectacle on the Champs-Elysées had a political point, it was not to down oppressors or refight class war but to welcome openness, diversity, and "difference." The French Revolution had always been more than a complex of historical events. It was also a picture gallery of the political imagination in which red fought white, left fought right, and right fought wrong. On seizing power in 1799, Napoleon and his fellow consuls had announced, prematurely, that the revolution was over. Pictures of unbroken polar conflict colored French politics for more than a century and a half. By 1989, conflict had by no means disappeared from France. Its colors had changed. In liberal fashion, the colors of conflict were many and mixed. Conflict, as liberals had always accepted, was endless. If Goude's parade was any sign, conflict in France was no longer thought of as polar but as parti-colored and kaleidoscopic.

Nobody knew it that summer of 1989, but to the East in Germany a different revolution was brewing. In 1953, 1956, and 1968 the Soviet Union had defended Communist control in Eastern Europe by force. Economically ruined and sapped by a losing war in Afghanistan, by the mid-1980s Soviet Communists had lost the will to survive by force. By 1989, they had lost the will to survive. As dissent swept East Germany, its Communist leaders were told by the reform Soviet leader Mikhail Gorbachev that they were on their own.

In November, travel restrictions from East Germany were lifted. East Germans flooded West. In November the Berlin Wall opened. Within a year, the two Germanies were one, inside the West's defense alliance and with its Eastern border with Poland settled for good. A knot of conflicts that had set two nuclear-armed superpowers against each other for forty years was resolved by talk in an astonishingly short space of time. That a historical upheaval of such scale occurred without violence depended on a sufficient confidence and lack of fear on both sides. Many elements contributed to sustaining that climate of detente, never secure but always at risk. They included the West's unmatched military power as well as the appeal and stability of an expanding European Union. To the extent that personal credit was due for easing strategic tensions, it belonged to the German chancellor Willy Brandt. He was not pushing at an open door in Moscow in 1960 when as mayor of West Berlin he spoke on Soviet television of a German people divided by barbed wire. The First Cold War was at its height, and Brandt was bravely taking a personal first step on the long road to East-West détente.

That the November Revolution of 1989 led to German unification with such speed and decisiveness was due to another German chancellor, Helmut Kohl (1930–2017). Flawed and underrated, Kohl seized the moment. He had come to power in 1982 when the German liberals abandoned the Social Democrats to pursue a more "market" economic policy. Kohl now counted on that solidity for his masterstroke. As people East and West wondered in the winter of 1989–90 what was to happen next, Kohl decided. Germany was to become one, not in stages, but at once. It was to be one, not as a neutral, which was the only united Germany anyone could think of during the era of Two Blocs. United Germany would belong squarely in Europe and in the West. It would be one not after negotiation between two states, agreeing to unite under perhaps a new constitution. Germany would be one under the Basic Law of 1949. It would take decades for broken East Germany to be economically one with West Germany. But West Germany was prosperous enough to pay for the arduous transition. East Germans might, relatively speaking, be paupers. They were not to start out as citizens of a united Germany destitute. Their savings were worthless. The West German mark was worth perhaps ten times the East German mark. Kohl insisted, against the advice of bankers and treasury experts, that the currencies would exchange one to one. Almost nobody thought it might be done, but Kohl did it, surprising perhaps even himself.

Until 1989 Kohl had never shaken a reputation as a party manager, a fixer, and a politician without vision. Even afterward, in 1990, his party ran a successful but unworthy election campaign in Eastern Germany, blackening Social Democrats as Communists. After his retirement, old suspicions were confirmed that Kohl had long dispensed under-the-table political money. None of that cancelled Kohl's achievement in 1989–90. His decisiveness required a rare act of political imagination. He cut through the alternatives and brushed aside the difficulties, casting his mind forward to an outcome that people told him was almost impossible and, when it came, they looked back on as virtually inevitable. Kohl's decisiveness was also an act of liberal confidence, an expression of belief in liberal democracy, particularly German liberal democracy.

The achievements of the liberal leaders of 1945–89, left as well as right, were remarkable. They learned from liberal failures and mistakes. They accepted that liberal values were universal, not Western. They embedded a democratic liberalism in fairer institutions. In the welfare state they accepted that rights without the means to exercise them were shallow rights. They learned from their own reforms, as when economic actions proved perverse and when social costs grew too large. They made parties and voters see that political mentalities had changed. After years of stagflation, inflation fell and economies boomed. They brought peace and unity to a fratricidal continent. "They" did none of that, it is easy to riposte. Larger historical forces were at work. Perhaps so. But it all happened on their watch, and the common rule in politics is to credit the captains, for good or for ill and however briefly the credit lasts.

The liberals of 1945–89 learned, atoned, and delivered. They left strong results. By removing barriers, they created a globalized world. They also left, in a sense, a story about that world but a story that often sounded like no story at all. The liberal thinkers of 1945–89 left lessons in what not to do and what not to think. Besides Rawls's eminent construction and the arguments it generated, liberal thinking after 1945 tended to be negative. It urged people not to expect big, durable patterns in history or politics. It urged them to expect fluidity, endless choices and inevitable regrets. It spoke less of unbridled free choice than of particular constrained choices, of dilemmas and trilemmas. Economists taught that a nation might have any two but not three of fixed exchange rates, free flow of capital, and national control of interest rates. In a global world, a nation might hope for any two but not three of economic openness, national sovereignty, and social equity. In like spirit, liberal thought stressed that the three elements of the liberal dream were in tension with each other: human progress, civic respect for all whoever they were, and the prevention of domination by any single interest or power. Yet the lesson of experience itself was not negative. From 1945 to 1989 the liberal dream came closer to realization than before. After the 1914–18 war, Keynes had regretted the loss of liberal confidence that he had admired in their nineteenth-century predecessors. In 1989 liberals could for a time feel that confidence had returned.

"What have you learned?" a reporter asked Vaclav Havel during a press conference in Prague on December 7, 1989. Czechoslovakia's Communists were in full retreat. Their party had gone through three leaders within a month. Civic Forum, the opposition movement, was legal and at the door of power. Havel, a Czech playwright and ex–prisoner of conscience, was about to become his country's president. His answer to the journalist's question was characteristically serious and wry: "When a person tries to act in accordance with his conscience, when he tries to speak the truth, when he tries to behave like a citizen even in conditions where citizenship is degraded, it won't necessarily lead anywhere but it might." One thing was sure to get in the way of success, he added. That was agonizing about whether dissent would work. There was a lesson in Havel's words for liberal democracy.

After the collective highs of 1989, many liberals soon began to worry, with good reason. They worried whether liberal democracy was sustainable, whether the tensions among its various promises, once a strength, had not turned to weaknesses and whether across the world liberal democracy was gaining rivals faster than it was gaining allies. Faced by the rise of an illiberal right in liberal democracies themselves, liberals wondered in alarm if they were not entering a post-liberal world. Their alarm was justified. But it mattered to focus the alarm in the proper places. It mattered to distinguish corrective from destructive alarm. And it mattered, this was Havel's lesson, not to let alarm swamp itself in despair.

PART FOUR

Liberal Dreams and Nightmares in the Twenty-First Century

14

Two Decades That Shook Liberal Democracy

i. The Rise of the Hard Right

In a climate of unknowing, on June 23, 2016, 52 percent of those voting in a nationwide referendum called for Britain to leave the European Union, despite the near-unanimous collective finding of mainstream politicians on the left and right, business leaders, economists, historians, scientists, military specialists, and foreign-policy experts that withdrawal would in time prove an economic and strategic blunder. On November 8, the real estate developer and television personality Donald Trump, running a right-wing "America First" campaign as a maverick Republican, won the US presidency with a minority of the popular vote but a large majority in the electoral college, despite the caustic suspicions of his adopted party and pollsters' predictions that he would badly lose. On April 23, 2017, Marine Le Pen at the head of the National Front advanced to the second round of France's presidential election, beating conventional parties of center-left and center-right. Although she lost the runoff, Le Pen won 34 percent of the vote, a popular breakthrough for a far-right party previously contained at the extremes. On September 24, 2017, in Germany's national elections, the Alternative für Deutschland also broke out from the fringes and won 94 seats, a seventh of the total, in the Bundestag, the federal parliament. Not since the 1950s had Germany's far-right won national representation and never in such strength.

Coming together in fifteen months, those results in four nations of the Western liberal core sharpened anxieties about the health of liberal democracy itself.

Elections upsets do not normally cause such alarm. Those voting shocks, however, followed a decade and a half of bewildering events and punishing episodes: terror attacks that killed close to 3,000 people in

Washington and New York (2001), the opening assault of an unremitting campaign by militant Islamists to shake liberal societies and provoke wars of faith; a spuriously justified US-British occupation of Iraq (2003), the post-invasion failures of which deepened voters' distrust in expertise and elected leadership; a world financial crash (2008) that brought on a deep economic recession followed by a slow, tepid recovery. Throughout, right-liberal and left-liberal governments struggled alike. Economically, neither market-minded nor social-minded policies appeared to be working or to be working fast enough. Disturbing trends were detected behind the shock of events. Headline numbers that people's parents and grandparents had since 1945 become accustomed to see going up—more equal incomes, less poverty, better health, longer lives—began in many parts of Europe and the United States to go down. Discontent grew with mainstream parties and with their common presumption of a shared, if contested, political middle ground. Across the world, the tide of liberal and democratic change promised in the 1990s appeared to ebb. In liberal democracy's heartland, Europe and the United States, elected politicians looked baffled, voters grew angrier, and political observers, whatever their viewpoint, found themselves at a loss.

Not all the anxiety was well-pitched or well-placed. Election losers were more distressed than were election winners. Soaring financial markets welcomed or discounted political shocks. The immediate damage to liberal democracy was debatable. In Britain and the United States, the hard right won, but narrowly. On breaking into the mainstream, the French hard right was there roundly defeated. In Germany, support for the hard right was strong in Saxony and other eastern Länder but weak nationally. Worries about liberal democracy's health were nowhere new. Performance failures, structural flaws and disagreement about aims had been recognized by liberals and argued over for much of the previous half century or more. Sanguine accounts of liberal democracy's prospects, given necessary repairs, were available but lacked salience and plausibility amid the hammering of bad news. The political shocks of 2016–17 gave unease a new authority. Liberals listened with fresh attention as worriers laid bare liberal democracy's troubles layer by layer: the rise of a hard right, dismaying economic trends, geopolitical loneliness, conflicts of identity and nation feeling, and intellectual disaffection. In these concluding chapters, each layer will be considered in turn.

There could be little quarrel about the disruptive character of a hard, national-minded right in the United States and Britain, the unpredictable fluidity of skeptical electorates in both countries, and the disorientation of the liberal center. Clouding vision in the United States, however, was the outsized figure of a hard-to-categorize president loved and loathed on either side of politics, who—in the words of the center-right columnist David Brooks of the *New York Times*—seemed to be at once a budding authoritarian, cynical Nixonian, rabble-rouser, and big-business Republican. Clouding vision in Britain was an imaginary Europe, a historical tangle of envy and disregard, love and admiration, hated in ignorance by Brexiteers and venerated, despite the European Union's acknowledged flaws, by Remainers. The intensity of feeling in the United States and Britain caused surprise, particularly to observers who had earlier worried about popular disengagement from politics. In the contest of emotions, it was nevertheless clear that a hard right, illiberal in its attitude to power and populist in its vision of democracy, had entered the political mainstream in both countries.

In the United States, all three branches of the federal government, 32 of 50 state legislatures and more than half the state governments were after 2016 in control of a hard-right Republican party whose few moderates were isolated or cowed. In Britain, a divided Conservative government set off on a perplexing course of improvisation and error, harried by its Little England right-wing. Days after the June 2016 referendum, a new prime minister, Theresa May, committed the nation to a strategic course of unknown destination she herself had campaigned against. Some two-thirds of Conservative members of Parliament were also for staying in the European Union but, anxious for their seats and the survival of their party, loyally followed the leader. Rather than claim the radical, disruptive decision as hers, May shifted responsibility by appealing to the contestable authority of the popular will. The referendum had been advisory, the close 52 to 48 percent result showed at best not one will but two, and two devolved nations of the United Kingdom— Scotland and Northern Ireland—registered large majorities for Remain. To the charge of hazardous improvisation with liberal-democratic norms, defenders of the government's decision, which was seconded by Labour, responded that, politically, the instruction to leave was imperative and that, invoking a weasel phrase, the result left no choice. Wrong, constitutionally, on the imperative force of the referendum, the government was baffled by its content. Stay or Leave was deceptively presented as an on-off choice. As was soon plain, there was not one exit from the European Union but many, and nobody knew which led where.

As exemplified by American Republicans under Trump and by British Conservatives captured by their nativists, the new hard-right elite of politics had several common features: readiness to neglect familiar norms of representative government; impatience with the division of powers; quickness, when challenged, to answer that they were doing what the people wanted; and willingness to reverse or ignore long-standing elements of internationally agreed commitments, claiming to put their own nation first.

To supporters, the leaders of the hard right were giving divided societies direction in troubled times and using the powers of office to their full in the manner of revered, high-handed leaders of the past—Roosevelt, Churchill, or de Gaulle for example—all of whom bent or broke constitutional norms. They were speaking up for hard-working, hard-pressed families against the empty promises of entrenched, cosmopolitan elites who had for too long dominated politics. To critics, Trump Republicanism and Brexit Conservatism marked a dangerous turn for liberal democracy, now sliding with limiters and self-correctives broken towards illiberal or undemocratic forms of power. Where some critics saw governmental incompetence, improvisation, and muddle, others saw a soft authoritarianism in germ, while yet others noted that the two had often gone together. When enough rules are bent and disorder becomes the norm, electorates have often turned to strong leaders to restore order with illiberal solutions. What caused the critics alarm and justified the label "hard right" was that Trump Republicans and Brexit Conservatives were at the edge of liberal democracy, right or left, as it had become familiar since the mid–twentieth century. As awkward coalitions, each united extreme economic liberals, happy to sacrifice economic democracy, with anti-foreign nativists, happy to sacrifice liberal norms of civic respect.

Stark historical parallels and novel political categories were cast about for. Serious commentary raised questions that would earlier have sounded overwrought. A former US ambassador, Daniel Fried, interviewed on MSNBC (March 9, 2017), wondered if the atmosphere in his country was not "like the 1930s, when the very idea of liberal democracy [was] being questioned." In *Foreign Affairs* (May–June 2017), the sober, open-eyed journal of the century-old Council on Foreign Relations, it was asked if the US was still "safe for democracy." In an earlier issue devoted to populism (November–December 2016), the spectre of fascism was considered but wisely set aside as an improbable parallel to the present hard right in Europe and the US. Fascism was historically specific. It sprang up in the 1920–30s after a ruinous world war without European winners. It relied on a cult of the leader at the head of a mass party, a totalizing vision of society, a unifying Bolshevik enemy, an indifference to legality and an encouragement of violence against political opponents. The echoes were clear and disturbing, but differences of scale and context were too large to make the parallel convincing.

Liberal democracy, however, could be corroded in many ways. As a present-day corrosive, populism was widely offered as a better account of what was underway. Populism, properly understood, is not an institutional arrangement or a form of democracy but a style of political self-justification. To use its own contentious language, populism is an elite phenomenon. Although often wrongly presented as a contest between people and elites, populism is a contest among elites in which one side, the populists, claims to speak for the people. Right-wing populists claim to defend a virtuous nation, often ethnically imagined, against corrupt establishments and menacing foreigners. Left-wing populists claim to defend the working people against corrupt establishments and the rich. Right or left, populists are commonly political outs exploiting electoral odium against the ins. As insurgents they may upset familiar party patterns, lending force to the sly definition of "populist" as what losers call winners after an unexpected electoral defeat or the collapse of a well-established party. As disturbers of the political peace, populists may form a new party or capture an existing party, as the Brexit minority did in Britain to the Conservatives and Corbyn's hard-left backers did to Labour. Whichever they do and however loudly they speak for that mythical being, the people, they are activists, often from the same background—and in the case of Conservatives, the same two universities—as the opponents they aim to displace.

Populism is easy to confuse with direct or participatory democracy, in contrast to the representative kind. That is a mistake, however, as

Jan-Werner Müller made clear in *What is Populism?* (2016). Populists were for representative government, he noted, so long as they were the representatives. Once elected to power by representative means, they resorted to plebiscites or referendums to confirm courses of action already decided on. Populists were ill at ease with multi-party competition or coalition government and happiest when elected opposition was demoralized and ineffective. Populists acted as caretakers of the people's will, claiming to know it better than their competitors. Jealous of their authority, populists were indifferent or hostile to countervailing powers within state and society. In office, they tended to bully critics, favor cronies, and attack judges whose rulings they disliked.

As a description of how politics and government work in large, complex, constitutionally intricate societies, populism is inept. To the liberal mind, there was strictly no such thing as the will of the people, hence nothing for elected power to know or speak for. Popular sovereignty, as Guizot for example, understood, was a negative idea: the denial of sovereignty to any single interest or class. In speaking for the people, sovereignty spoke for the citizenry and answered to the citizenry. In speaking for all, sovereignty spoke for no one in particular. Sovereign decision resulted not from intuition or divination but from often frustrating constitutional procedure. To the populist mind by contrast, the will of the people was single, undivided, and authoritatively intuited by power. The people was not the citizenry but a blend of cultural nation, which distinguished it from foreigners, and common folk, which distinguished it from elites. If populism was understood as involving a distinctive rhetorical appeal, the right-wing government confirmed in the British election (June 2017) was populist. Social complexity and constitutional mechanism did not vanish. Institutionally, Britain remained liberal and democratic. Politically, it was for now in the hands of a party whose unspoken slogan was "We know what you want."

Matters were subtler in the United States. Historically, the American Populists were prairie radicals of the 1890s, the working-class half of a movement whose other half was middle-class Progressivism. As the term "populist" was spoken for, to call the Republican tide of 2016 "populist" was misleading without more to say. In a farsighted article written before Trump entered national politics, Walter Russell Mead had made a case for the apter label "Jacksonian." A Jacksonian, on his account, was a distinct type of voter who by class or education alone might once have been taken for a natural Democrat but who since the 1960s had tended to vote Republican. As characterized in "The Jacksonian Tradition" (2000), these lower-middle-class white Americans were hostile to federal government, to do-gooding at home or abroad, and to taxes so long as programs favoring them such as Medicare, mortgage deductions and Social Security were not jeopardized. They believed in honor, military virtues, and equality with those above them, an ethical code, Mead suggested, that many black Americans shared.

White Jacksonians were recognizable at Trump's rallies, in Trump slogans and in Trump speeches, but they were not his only voters. Powerful as Mead's ideal-type portrait was, the Trump voter could not be neatly typified, save tautologically and unhelpfully as a typical Republican. The same was true of the Brexit voter in Britain, a typical Conservative, and the voters for far-right parties in Europe, typical far-rightists. Across Europe, they were in fact a motley type, not a single type: anti-immigrant nativists, moral traditionalists, anti-EU libertarians and defenders of Western-Christian values against the feared encroachment of Islam.

As an instant explanation of the American and British votes, the Forgotten White Democrat and the Disgruntled Labour Voter won undue attention. They were distressed, it was claimed, at recent globalization, troubled by new immigrants in their neighborhoods and, when prompted by attitude-collecting enquirers, overcome by a sense of having lost control to distant forces, an echo of the reactionary Romantic cry against liberal modernity heard among all social classes since the early nineteenth century, noted by German and American political scientists studying authoritarian attitudes in the middle of the past century and now dutifully recorded on opinion surveys as if a novel discovery. That the liberal left did not own the working-class vote should have surprised nobody. A segment of the white working class previously loyal to the Democrats had been voting Republican since the late 1960s. Labour's share of the working-class vote had already in the 1970s fallen from two-thirds to a half. Unconvincing electoral sociology about neglected and marginalized voters served shaken democratic liberals as displacement, especially those liberals who had forgotten the damage done to people's solidarity and self-esteem by the erosion of industrial trade unions. The typical Trump or Brexit voter was not working class at all but comfortable, conservative, and suburban. The harsh truth was that in Britain and the United States at any rate, a voting majority of their fellow citizens had chosen the hard right. The choice was foolish but freely taken and not forced on voters by social facts.

There were more exact, less self-flagellating ways to take the 2016 votes than as consequences of cosmopolitan disdain or liberal inattention. Marginal defections from expected Democratic or Labour supporters had, it is true, led to the narrow losses. Trump carried three large states that contributed to his electoral college victory—Michigan, Pennsylvania, and Wisconsin—by less than 80,000 votes in total. These were commonly and misleadingly described as Democratic states, whereas all three had gone Republican in the Nixon (1972) and Reagan landslides (1984), and in the 1940s and 1950s Wisconsin voters had twice sent to the US Senate a red-baiting Republican bigot, Joseph McCarthy. If a one-answer explanation was insisted on for the presidential result, an equally plausible candidate was the sharp drop in the Democrats' black turnout. In Britain, similarly, age offered a better one-answer explanation than class. Young voters were heavily pro-Remain and turnout among them was, at 65 percent, only just below the national turnout of 72 percent. However, among voters over 65 years of age, who were heavily pro-Brexit, turnout was around 90 percent.

Liberal democrats could take some comfort from two open questions. The hard right was in power in the United States and Britain, but it was unclear how long they would remain or how coherently they might govern. A case could be made that both narrow victories were lucky one-offs and that the hard right's electoral coalition would be hard to pull together another time. A case also could be made that the hard right in office could not honor all its promises and was bound to disappoint one large part of an incoherent following. Like the rabble-rousing Huey Long and Father Coughlin in the 1930s, Trump undertook to help the little guy without hurting the rich. The Tories in Britain similarly undertook to help the poor and disadvantaged while continuing to squeeze public spending and favor their rich donors. The hard right was indeed an unnatural pairing. It yoked free-market, small-government conservatives who favored free trade and were open-minded about immigration to nativist, our-nation-first conservatives claiming to speak for the people against what they called the elites. Their undeliverable common program promised government handouts and low taxes, help for working people, and a free hand for business.

Thoughts of this kind were soothing for democratic liberals only to a point. The hard right might have come to power by electoral luck. It might be programmatically divided. Its core voters were old and would soon be gone. No matter, the hard right was in power. It had somehow to be voted out of power, which was where comfort stopped, for organised and effective electoral alternatives were weak or absent. In theory, the liberal right and the liberal left ought to have been able to find common cause in resisting the hard right and seizing back the middle ground. Both, however, faced severe handicaps.

In the United States, moderate conservatives, troubled equally by Trump's excesses and by the Republican politics of "No," were at a loss. They were unsure whether to drop moderation and follow Trump or drop conservatism and abandon the right. The neoconservative scion William Kristol and liberal professor of politics William Galston bravely planted a small joint flag on the political middle-ground by calling on voters to rally to a New Center.

Opinion-polling evidence had accumulated for some years suggesting that Americans were politically less divided than their politicians, that independence from party was growing and that a large middle-ground was there to be played for. Contrary evidence was also to hand, however, that Americans were not only just as divided over politics as their politicians but were angry with each other politically and unwilling to mix or marry with those of the wrong party. A new party uniting liberal-left and liberal-right at the center was good to hope for but dangerous to count on in an electoral system that was cruel to third parties. A bad choice remained for liberals, right or left, between unacceptable Republicans or unsuccessful Democrats.

Sanguine Democrats looked forward to future Democratic majorities. Republicans were old, they reasoned, whereas the young voted Democrat, a hope that seemed to miss the point that the young also age and do not reliably carry their first opinions into dotage. In Britain, a divided Labour party showed the hard right scant resistance where it counted. Labour first caved into Brexit, although most Labour members of Parliament, like most Conservative MPs, had been for staying in Europe. Then it campaigned on an attractive but uncosted help-the-people platform that in June 2017 won two-fifths of the electorate but did not put Labour in position to govern. Its leader, the underestimated Jeremy Corbyn, proved a successful campaigner, but Labour's surprising success was due more to Conservative ineptitude and discredit. Had Britain a more democratic and proportional electoral system, left-wing Labour could have won itself a permanent minority position as a needed anchor against rightward drift. Labour, however, had long fought proportional representation, clinging to its hope of again becoming a party of government. A revived Labour party might have offered Britain's national-minded hard right clear opposition. But it was itself now in the hands of a national-minded left that had colluded in the strategic recklessness of Brexit.

The center-left parties of France and Germany, pillars of post-1945 prosperity and stability, were divided and in electoral decline. Everywhere structures of working-class life on which traditional left-wing parties had depended were being hollowed out. Union membership in Britain fell from 13 million (1979) to 6 million in the mid-2010s. Similar erosions occurred in the United States. There, as Democrat working-class structures broke up, Republicans made skillful use of the right's favored structures: churches, think-tanks, and business lobbies. Oratory, conviction, and passionate calls to change the status quo still served the left, it is true. Rousing stump speeches by Bernie Sanders in the United States, Jeremy Corbyn in Britain, and Jean-Luc Mélenchon in France rallied crowds, especially young crowds, and revived radical hopes, but it was easier to see the three, whose average age was 69, as favorite uncles at the head of protest movements than future leaders of durable left-wing government. Only on a spectrum of opinion that had shifted as a whole to the right over 50 years were they in the least radical. The policies they proposed would have seemed timid to the governing parties of the 1950s and 1960s, including conservative parties.

To a bleak picture of liberal democracy's health in Britain and the United States, France and Germany offered an encouraging contrast as well as reasons for concern. Democratic liberals prevailed in France in May 2017 but as much because the left and right extremes were unacceptable as for the appeal or coherence of the liberal center itself. A centrist former Socialist and exbanker, Emmanuel Macron, won the presidency comfortably and his new political grouping swept the parliamentary elections that followed, though on a very low turnout. In Germany, the liberal center also prevailed, though its main parties, the Christian Democrats and the Social Democrats, were both weakened.

Against that political background, liberal democrats faced economic and geopolitical concerns, to be taken now in turn. The main economic question was whether the post-1945 growth-plus-welfare model of capitalism on which liberal democracy had relied economically was itself sustainable on political terms liberal democrats could accept. Geopolitically, the stature and appeal of liberal democracy was less sure than it had recently looked, not least because of its own divisions. In 2016-2017, a liberal center held in France and Germany but failed to hold in Britain and the United States. It could no longer be assumed that a once coherent West was still united by a common liberal-democratic outlook.

The first liberals in the nineteenth century had hoped for a masterless order without absolute authorities or undivided powers. Democratic liberalism in the twentieth century had extended that vision of a liberal order to include everyone, whoever they were. The economic aspect of that extended vision was a promise to protect everyone from the absolute mastery of the market or the undivided power of wealth. To the unreconciled left, such a promise was empty, and to the unbending right, an act of thievery. Yet enough of the promise was delivered in the post-1945 decades to make the liberal democracies the material envy of the world. As delivery of the promise was made possible only by strong enough economic growth, securing a future for liberal democracy meant recovering an economic pace that for two decades had eluded both Europe and the United States.

ii. Economic Discontents

In the slow, tepid recovery from deep recession that began after the financial crash of 2008, it became common to claim that, regardless of policy, liberal capitalism had entered an era of slow economic growth. If true, that was bad for liberal democracy. Since the Great Depression of the 1930s, the common assumption on center-right and center-left alike had been that the inevitable conflicts of society were manageable only if given strong economic growth.

If, whatever policies were pursued, adequate growth could not be achieved, problems of poverty, inequality, and political distrust seen across the liberal-democratic world would become harder to manage and could be reasonably expected to worsen. The post-1945 fiscal and monetary work of government at smoothing capitalism's cycles and remedying its distributional flaws would, with lower growth, be less effective and less affordable. The prestige and authority of government would go on falling and the discredit of politics would continue to rise.

If, on the other hand, with the proper policies, faster growth could be achieved, a political difficulty had to be faced. Economists might agree or disagree technically about which in practice the proper policies were, although the range of their disagreement was commonly exaggerated by noneconomists. The trouble was that opposing political camps within the liberal tent each claimed that the economic policies favored by their rivals retarded growth or worsened the social problems that faster growth was relied on to solve.

Liberals to left and right had pursued that growth argument for nearly a century. The debate began during liberal capitalism's first twentieth-century crisis (the 1930s), as described in Part Two. It carried on into liberal capitalism's second twentieth-century crisis (the 1970s), as described in Part Three. Each liberal camp, the economic right or economic left, blamed the other for pursuing the wrong kind of growth-promotion or for pursuing the correct kind for too long so that it became counterproductive.

To confuse matters, the competing political parties of the liberal middle ground, whether nominally left-wing or right-wing, had tended to cohere around a prevailing economic orthodoxy. The economic left, as was seen, had won the argument after the 1930s and guided governments of whatever color in the 1950 and 1960s. Under the post-1930s orthodoxy, governments took responsibility for supporting the economy and for correcting social ills. They combined pursuit of growth with social purpose, understood as state-supported provision of public goods, including universal health-care and help for anyone in need that markets did not naturally supply.

In the 1970s, when low or no growth combined with soaring prices, the economic right won the argument against the economic left, in large part by blaming the ruinous inflation of the 1970s on the post-1930s orthodoxy. First in Britain and the United States, then across Europe, the economic right's alternative—noninflationary growth, low taxes and balanced budgets—became, despite its internal tensions, a new orthodoxy. Aided by open trade and take-off in China and India, the new orthodoxy appeared to succeed in the low-inflation, strong-growth 1990s. It was embraced by parties of the center-left, which became hard in economic terms to distinguish from parties of the center-right.

Critics of the post-1970s orthodoxy questioned its coherence. To budget hawks it promised unmanageable deficits, to welfare advocates unacceptable spending cuts. Economists of all persuasions noted that it did little to alter worrisome underlying trends. Labor productivity continued to drop, and real wages grew slowly if at all. Not till the financial crash of 2008 and its aftermath, however, was the free-market, small-government orthodoxy finally exposed and, openly or in effect, abandoned. Pushed too far and pursued for too long, the free-market orthodoxy had failed to deliver steady growth. In addition, cuts in social spending, pursued over three decades, made the social costs worse when the crash came.

Yet nothing new replaced it. There was no one answer, be it Keynesian, Hayekian, or Friedmanite. Governments improvised. Taxes were lowered to encourage people to spend and governments increased their own spending. As taxes were already low, however, fiscal tools were of limited use. In addition, outside the dollar-issuing United States, whose credit was good to the world and who therefore needed to worry less about budget deficits, governments soon again cut spending.

Although doctrine was now confused and orthodoxies at a discount, as in the 1930s, the challenges were clear. The short-term challenge was to prevent the Great Recession from becoming a second Great Depression. The long-term challenge was to restore the economic growth in rich economies, without which liberal democracy's open-ended social promises risked becoming undeliverable.

The short-term rescue relied on central banks, nominally independent but acting in practice as part of government. To steady shaken banks, the US Federal Reserve sold them, in effect, good money for bad.

By October 2014, when its direct aid ended, the Fed had bought up $4.5 trillion in assets from weakened banks and other lenders. In 2015, a previously tight European Central Bank followed suit on smaller scale. Recovery was fitful but economic growth and, eventually, wages did rise. By spring 2017, stock markets were racing and green shoots along with other seasonal metaphors returned to economic commentary. Prematurely or not, the immediate crisis was felt to have passed.

Judgments of how liberal policy-makers performed after 2008 were colored by expectations. Those expecting a brisk return to the fast-growth 1990s were disappointed. Policy-makers in the Euro zone, who chose monetary stability over job promotion, were criticized for doing too little, too slowly. Liberal centrists were mocked from either extreme of politics for attempting to rescue the unrescuable. Hard left and hard right took welfare capitalism for doomed—the hard left because it was capitalist, the hard right because it was welfarist. There were, it was true, worse calamities avoided. In the Great Depression, output per head in the United States fell by 30 percent from 1929 to 1933 and did not fully recover for a decade. That drop was much steeper than the drop in an equivalent measure after 2008. However, the recovery since 2008 has been slower than in the 1930s. It was estimated that, twelve years after the crisis began, gross domestic product per working American adult would have grown only 11 percent.

Social corrosions linked to economic underperformance were uncontested. Poverty, low-wage growth, job insecurity, long-term joblessness and income inequality rose. The human damage was unacceptable, particularly in rich economies, but it was not evenly distributed or all the same kind. Some long-term trends noted in the 1980s—slow real wage growth, for example—worsened in the new century, but after 2015 appeared to slow if not reverse. Large cities, university towns, high-tech zones and, in the US, oil, gas, and agri-chemical regions were less affected. In Germany, strong midsized exporting firms found throughout the country, a trusted and familiar 120-year-old social safety net as well as labor-market reforms of 2005 helped ensure that the country suffered less than elsewhere. Across much of rural France, by contrast, as powerfully recorded by the antiglobalist social geographer Christophe Guilluy, once thriving towns became shells as jobs left and shops closed. In the American Rust Belt and England's industrial north, large cities were hollowed out. In the hardest hit areas of the United States, health and life expectancy declined.

The harshest corrosion was poverty, which, according to the Organisation for Economic Co-operation and Development (OECD), on absolute measures in the 2010s trapped one American in five and one Briton in eight. But poverty rarely protests with the lungs of the disappointed middle-classes, which drew more attention. The halt to half a century's material progress for the broad middle of society was a shock when it came in the 2000s and played out politically long after. The sharpest complaints varied from country to country. They came as soaring health costs in the United States, unaffordable housing in southeast England, and lasting youth unemployment of around 20 percent or more in France. In common across much of the rich West, material life for many people stopped getting easier in ways they had grown accustomed to. Both partners with children now worked, as a rule. Two incomes held up household earnings but much of the extra went to child care. For those who had them, jobs were less secure and jobs for life became treasured antiques. From society's middle 60 percent came ever louder complaints of unfairly paying taxes to help the poor, and the sense of unfairness mounted as incomes of the top 10 percent sharply rose and those of the top 1 percent ballooned to grotesque proportions.

A forgotten term, inequality, re-entered public argument, although it obscured as much as it illuminated. Inequality irked the rich as the hyper-rich raced out of sight in competition for "positional" goods, the kind that lose value as a greater number of people enjoy them. Such positional goods were goods of economic privilege. Some came with sought-after social cachet, for example, the best schools and best hospitals. Others were goods that insulated their buyers from the crowded public spaces and stretched amenities of common life, for example, access to private airports or quiet, exclusive neighborhoods. Inequality irked the middle classes, who took themselves to bear society's burdens unfairly, although a closer look by economists suggested that in the United States middle-class tax breaks—mortgage interest deductions, or business write-offs for employer health plans, for example—much lightened the burden and, when taken into account, indicated that middle-class real incomes had slowed or fallen behind less from 2000 to 2015 than headline figures suggested. Inequality, finally, irked welfare advocates for the neglected, often voiceless poor who saw ample resources available in a rich society that were not tapped or, when tapped, foolishly deployed.

It was plain that a liberal capitalism aiming to combine growth with social progress—commitment, that is, to the welfare state—was underperforming at both tasks. As to what to do, there were destructive and constructive responses. Destructive answers attracted camps opposed in theory to each other, the libertarian hard right and the anti-liberal hard left.

For the libertarian hard right, healthy capitalism was sustainable only if social progress, understood as protection against life's risks and relief of hardship at share expense, was abandoned as a political goal. As embodied in the modern welfare state, that goal was unachievable in practice and mistaken in principle. Social-minded liberals had striven to lessen poverty for more than a century. Despite their efforts, poverty was growing again. Liberals had persisted in failure, misguided by an unjust, ill-founded pursuit of equality. Neither complaint was true. Both, however, won wide currency. The complaints were illiberal in rejecting the goal of social progress for all, and in distorting the liberal call to resist power. The libertarian right wanted to limit state power in order to release market power. It answered the question of how to reconcile capitalism and welfare destructively, by denying that welfare was needed.

For the hard left, capitalism was historically doomed, either because its moral inequities would lead to political overthrow or because its incoherent mechanics would lead to economic breakdown. Tempering capitalism by welfare paid for by social insurance and progressive taxation was dismissed either as pudic cover for injustice or palliative care for a dying patient. The hard left claimed to believe, like liberals, in social progress. Yet its conviction was more theatrical than actual. By play-acting at the defense of progress, the hard left denied progress. In its eyes nothing counted as progress short of arrival at a just society, yet it did not spell out what a just society would be like. That said, it could see when social justice was missing. With good cause, it insisted that liberal society was so arranged as to create social injustice, for liberal society depended on a capitalist economy, and capitalism depended on unacceptable inequality. Progressive liberals had two replies. The weaker reply was that without more said about the destination, leaving behind unjust liberalism might well not lead to greater justice, and experience suggested it could easily lead to less. The stronger reply was that although as a harmful side-effect of beneficial wealth creation, liberal society did indeed create injustice, it created also forms of politics that could be used to correct injustice. The hard left was loath to listen. Intellectually, it obstructed liberal progress either by abandoning politics and economics for cultural criticism or by offering visionary alternatives that were not describable or, if describable, not attainable. Practically, it obstructed liberal progress by branding all liberals as economic libertarians under the false but widely used label "neoliberal." Jealous of its niche, the hard left was foolhardy to refuse cooperation with the liberal center, a natural partner in achievable reduction of capitalism's avowed social harms.

Constructive responses to liberal capitalism's underperformance aimed to save it by finding a new balance between growth and social purpose. As to ensuring growth, honest economists offered no certitudes, only open-minded experiment and distrust of magical answers. The US economy, measured as output per head, had grown historically at 2 percent a year over the past century and a half, at 2.5 percent in the glory years 1950–73 and again during the booming 1990s, only to steady again after the 2008–09 crash to a historic trend of 2 percent forecast for 2017. Against that record, the 3 percent growth target suggested early in the Trump administration looked to some wishful. Yet 2 percent growth on average over a century was compatible with sudden spurts of strong growth, which the administration's supporters trusted the United States was about to enjoy.

Why the economy recovered so slowly met a variety of answers. The former head of the Federal Reserve, Ben Bernanke, blamed slowness on the painful working down of a savings glut created by growth in India, China, and other rapidly advancing economies. Larry Summers, a leading voice of the secular stagnation school, took the rich economies to be suffering from chronic oversaving and underinvestment. Governments, he thought, should step in with "expansionary fiscal policy": bigger deficits, more spending, especially on repair and overdue public works, and lower business taxes, to bring faster growth and higher wages for the nonrich, who saved less and spent more, relatively speaking, than the rich did.

Economic historians foresaw a dismal future judged against a golden past. The French economist Thomas Piketty in *Capital in the 21st Century* (2014) took liberal democracy's good years in the second half of the last century for exceptional and unrepeatable. In a capitalist economy, he argued, capital's share in income tended to grow, depressing economies in the long run as savings outran growth. Piketty's projections stretched 80 years into the future, which even sympathetic economists took for little more than guessing. His book was nevertheless a world best seller. Parallel discouragement to thinking that the post-1945 years could be repeated came from American economist Robert Gordon in a study of technical change and productivity, *The Rise and Fall of American Growth* (2016). Compared with the productive innovations that had helped multiply the size of the American economy by seven or eight in the "special century" (1870–1970)—electricity, automobiles, vaccines, chemicals and their like—the vaunted internet technology revolution of the 1980s, Gordon argued, had given the American economy far less measurable push.

Techno-optimists answered Gordon by conjuring up future putative breakthroughs in medicine, which if realized would presumably prolong life and worsen the economic burden of the nonproductive on the productive, or breakthroughs in artificial intelligence, which would presumably make it harder to find idled people purposeful work. The truth was that both sides were guessing. Gordon's more careful critics pointed out that technical innovation had always driven capitalist advance and that, as Popper had argued against economic determinism in the 1940s, future innovation together with its economic effects were not knowable. That argument from uncertainty was telling but not decisive. Perhaps Gordon's predictions would turn out wrong. Perhaps they would turn out right. If he was wrong and strong growth returned, welfare capitalism could continue to afford itself. If he was right and strong growth did not return, either welfare or capitalism would suffer. The trouble for liberal democrats was that they had, in ignorance, to be ready for either eventuality.

Besides the threat of unaffordability, welfare capitalism faced charges, just noted, of ineffectiveness and perversity, to which social-minded liberals had answers. The charge of ineffectiveness was true of some social programs in some places in some countries. It was not true of all programs in all places in all countries. The gross claim that welfare states did not work was historically false. More than a century of experience suggested that making everyone insure themselves through government against life's risks (social security) or paying a needy minority directly out of taxation (welfare) did pull people out of poverty or stopped them from falling in. The undeniable social costs noted by economic liberals were seldom adequately netted against the undeniable social benefits. Nor had economic liberals credible stories of how post-1945 Western societies might have developed without the cushion of the welfare state.

Social security and welfare, that is, could work but much depended on what kind they were. Rich nations could spend money to social purpose well or foolishly. Some societies had socially more efficient economies than others. They used national wealth, that is, to better human effect. Denmark, for example, ranks lower in income per head than the United States, but on the 2016 UN Human Development Scale, it ranked higher on human development. Northern Europe generally had coherent, transparent, and effective welfare systems. The United States spent much tax money for social purposes, but spent it incoherently and ineffectively. That criticism was a commonplace and had been since the 1960s, but in the clash of interests, lobbies, and partisanship, no reform had ever been broad enough and no narrow reform succeeded in its aim for long. Setting cohesive small societies like Denmark against divided large societies like the United States made, it is true, for false comparisons. On the other hand, a federal system had advantages in that several states could experiment with different programs.

No iron law existed to set social aims against pursuit of growth. A 2014 International Monetary Fund study using multidecade data on income inequality from 173 nations collated by the political scientist Frederick Solt suggested that in developed, democratic nations, large income inequalities probably slowed growth and that a degree of government redistribution could correct some inequality, but that persistent, large-scale distribution made sustained strong growth harder than otherwise to achieve. Such findings were helpful to a point, but took politicians and voters little distance beyond the banality: don't go too far.

Shaken by hard economic years, by the political shocks of 2016-2017, and by the structural weaknesses of welfare capitalism, liberals were tempted to tell a grim story of what lay ahead. That story told of vanishing job growth amid spreading automation, rapid fiscal deterioration as society aged and social dependency grew, a further weakening of economic sovereignty as globalization accelerated, intensification of social conflict, more flight from the political center, and louder calls for coercive order. There was also hopeful story to tell. It looked forward to a return of job growth, a stabilization of budgets, an easing of trade imbalances, and restoration of liberal-democratic stability.

Nobody knew which was closer to what in fact lay ahead. A blithe liberal politics would tell the hopeful story. It would say, for example, that future new gadgets and free markets, if allowed to work, would bring growth with which to provide for social need. A cautious liberal politics would stress the grim possibility and aim to cover for it.

The dilemma was not unlike that with climate change. The climatic future was uncertain. Inaction at little or no cost might lead to calamity later. Prevention at heavy cost might turn out to have been pointless. So with welfare capitalism. Liberal democrats could do nothing, save trusting future blessings and facing up to social conflict when blessings failed to arrive. Or, to ensure a socially peaceable future, they could take socially costly steps to promote economic growth that the blessings of gadgets and markets were about to deliver anyway. Economists might agree on what technical steps would promote growth. There was little political agreement on how the social costs of those steps were to be borne. If magical answers were set aside, a renegotiation of the historic compromise between liberalism and democracy would be needed. It would involve market and government, economics and society.

Besides imagination, daring, and patience, such a renegotiation would take several things, in ascending order of difficulty. It would need to rethink, not simply adjust, the welfare state. Liberal democracies since the 1900s had, either by state-supported insurance or directly, promised care or support for a lengthening list of the old, the sick, the disabled, the poor, the unemployed, the unhoused, the university student, the young couple with children. To ensure that the promise was deliverable, radical change would be needed. Ideas were in ample supply. A universal basic income, for example, could replace a tangle of separate programs barnacled with lobbies and interests. If a universal basic income were not to be a promise to the world, however, it would be limited to citizens. Alternatively, means-testing could be accepted and middle-class benefits limited. Or the ancient liberal prejudice against handouts to the needy without making them work, seen in

Chadwick's "lesser eligibility" in the 1830s and revived in post-1980s welfare reforms, could be abandoned in favor of welfare that did not stigmatize poverty.

Jobs were a next order of difficulty. People want to escape need but even more they want rewarding work. A new economic compromise would have to recognize that many people who had lost their jobs and who would not get those jobs back, either because of globalization or automation, wanted not just an income but rewarding work. If instead of steady, decently paid and well-regarded work, more and more people were to look forward only to insecure, poorly paid and ill-regarded work, then two remedies only were open. Either there must be a revalorization of labor that imparted satisfaction and esteem to low-paid, menial work, or ways had to be found to resupply the kind of rewarding, productive jobs that had been lost. Short of improbable changes in social attitudes and ambitions, a revalorization of poorly regarded labor looked like another magical answer. Resupplying productive, rewarding jobs, on the other hand, raised the challenge on which all else rested: restoring stronger economic growth and higher output per hour than the rich economies had enjoyed since the end of the 1960s.

Talk of balancing growth with social purpose would be empty if growth in one of the scales was not enough to balance the open-ended social promises in the other scale. Talk of rewarding work would be empty if, bar an upheaval in capitalist values that radically upgraded noneconomic rewards, the work was not economically productive. A final level of difficulty was balancing faster growth, if achievable, for the peoples of the present, with preventive action, if needed, against catastrophic climate change that may blight future generations. Cast in simple terms, here was a conflict of goals—faster growth or protecting the environment—which neither liberals nor anyone else had as yet stable, convincing ways to think about or resolve. The tasks looked daunting and voices abounded claiming that liberal democracy was no longer equal to them. As those same voices could not say what alternative practice of politics was equal to the task of balancing economics and environment, the claim was less a serious critique of liberal democracy than a cry of bewilderment.

Daunting tasks had not proved beyond the imagination of liberal intellectuals or the improvisations of liberal governments before. Liberalism had survived by a combination of strategic vision, local experiment, and learning from often ruinous mistakes. The economic challenge now was less technical than political.

The first liberals dreamed of an economic order free of crown or state domination, monopoly privileges, and local obstacles to national markets. By the end of the nineteenth century, that dream had been largely realized. Amid social conflicts that market capitalism caused, early twentieth-century liberals negotiated a historic compromise from which came electoral democracy and welfare capitalism. After the compromise failed catastrophically in the 1930s across much of Europe and came close to failing in Britain and the United States, post-1945 chastened liberals successfully renegotiated that historic compromise. For post-1989 liberals, the social and economic challenges were of similar order, but it remained open whether they had the political will to address them. It remained open whether democratic liberals could hold the center ground against political extremes. It remained open whether welfare capitalism could be defended against a hard right that wanted it to fail because it disbelieved in welfare and a hard left that wanted it to fail because it disbelieved in capitalism.

At the end of the 2010s, nobody knew what patterns of economic growth lay ahead. Nobody knew if the post-war international liberal order that had benefited the West would now survive to benefit the world or break up to leave hostile, mercantilist blocs. Nobody knew if the democratic liberalism of 1945–89 that had prevailed in the West would prove a passing phase, to be followed by devil-take-the-hindmost societies of growing inequality. In a climate of uncertainty, nobody knew if the angry, nativist-tinged politics of Britain and United States or the more convergent, pragmatic politics of France and Germany would prevail. Nothing, however, was fated. There were no necessities here. A sure way for liberals to lose the argument was by leaving it.

iii. Geopolitical Loneliness

The first liberals dreamed of an international order in which trade prevailed over war and treaty prevailed over force. Constant and Cobden hoped that among equal, independent, postimperial nations a peaceful world order might become self-reinforcing as mutual gains from trade and openness outgrew the spoils of war. That hopeful liberal dream survived late nineteenth-century imperial competition among Europe's trading powers and the 1914–18 mutual slaughter to which it led. As war ended, the historically minded economist Schumpeter surveyed liberal capitalism and judged it, despite appearances, to be pacific. Wars, he wrote in "The Sociology of Imperialisms" (1919), were caused by backward powers struggling to preserve their "atavisms" in the only way they knew how, that is by expansion and conquest. In capitalist society, by contrast, everything including national advantage was bargainable. Democratic culture made it hard to rally people to the flag. As nations became capitalist and democratic, war would grow less probable and more absurd.

Liberal hopes for a pacific commercial order survived the 1939–45 war. That war had come about, so self-flattering liberals might tell themselves, from the mutual quarrels and predations of Bolshevik Russia, Nazi Germany, and Imperialist Japan, which had dragged in reluctant liberal democracies out of self-defense. The liberal dream then survived the ceaseless warfare of the 1945–89 era: Greece, Israel-Palestine, Korea, Kenya, Malaya, Indochina, Algeria, Congo, Indonesia, India-Pakistan, Nigeria, Central Africa, Central America, and Afghanistan. Those wars, so post-1945 liberals reasoned, were wars of decolonization, wars between predemocratic nations or civil wars within them. They were, for all their horrors, not world wars among the powers but local, containable wars. Nor was liberal hope disturbed by the hypergrowth of the liberal warfare state, notably in the United States, for its destructive power and global reach defended liberalism and democracy from an equally hyperarmed Soviet warfare state.

When the Soviet empire, though not its warfare state, collapsed and a capitalist China opened itself to the world, many liberals looked forward to a global spread of liberalism and democracy. In that promising moment, liberals took comfort from a third visitation of Constant's and Cobden's dream. Schumpeter had in effect been right after all, the American foreign-policy theorist Michael Doyle suggested in books and articles that won a wide following in the 1980s and 1990s: liberal democracies did not make war against each other. Doyle's careful warning that liberals nevertheless went to war against nonliberals to defend or extend liberalism was paid less heed. After 1989 in a world rich with possibility, a liberal complacency set in that, like the three Graces, liberalism, democracy, and peace would now bless a stable but vigorous modernity. Although doubters scoffed, the dream was not entirely wishful. Liberals had learned much in the past 100 years about their dream of peace and international order.

Historical experience suggested that rising trade and wealth across the world could not themselves be counted on to keep the peace. Without an acknowledged rule-setter and policeman, war had broken out in 1914 among the powers in a global economy marked, as now, by high cross-border trade, foreign investment, and migration. When global growth slowed and crashed in the 1920–30s, uncontainable political conflict led to a second global war. The plea of free-market purists that the global economy would in time recover if left to itself was, if true, unhelpful. Neither politically nor humanly was there enough time.

Those historical lessons were uppermost in the minds of the post-1945 liberals who, under American leadership as rule-setter and policeman, established a new liberal economic order. On trade, money and defense, it negotiated with its allies to set up multilateral arrangements that sacrificed a degree of national sovereignty for mutual advantage: the tariff-lowering General Agreement on Tariffs and Trade (GATT), which later became the World Trade Organization, the post-1945 fixed-rate and floating monetary systems each with their dollar anchor, stated or presumed; and NATO, the military alliance that engaged members to defend each other if attacked. Guiding the architects of those econo-strategic arrangements was a conviction that openness fostered prosperity and that nations accordingly should bind themselves not to disrupt openness.

That Western, American-led economic order was globalized in the 1980 and 1990s to include Asia, Latin America, and much of Africa; the label "Western" was dropped and it became known as the Liberal International Order (LIO). In 1949, 13 countries had taken part in the first postwar tariff talks. By 2001, 159 were negotiating open trade among themselves. The LIO promised to the world the benefits economic openness had brought the West. However, differences between liberal Westernism and liberal globalism were quickly apparent. From a frozen Cold War order emerged not peaceable fluidity but geopolitical disorder, full of promise but also full of fractures and danger. An open-trading, global-ized economy had between the 1980s and 2010s made poor countries richer and lifted more than a billion people out of poverty. That open-ness was nevertheless now at risk from slower-growing economies, creeping trade protection and financial strains between debtor and creditor nations. Nor was economic order alone in danger. Much as slower growth made all conflicts harder to contain within nations, so global contraction or disruption promised to inflame geopolitical fric-tions among nations.

Liberals worried that for all its attractions, liberal globalism was frag-ile and untested. They wondered how it could be policed, no longer by a single, unchallenged power but by five or six competing powers. Global victory for capitalism, they realized, had ended ideological conflict, not geopolitical conflict. They worried that political support which many believed vital for a liberal economic order—the global spread of liberal democracy—had slowed or reversed. They feared that anti-globalism was growing and with it a hybrid hard right, committed in theory to international business but, to pacify local discontent, pursuing in prac-tice a disruptive unilateralism. By the late 2010s, disorder, not order, looked self-reinforcing.

Two revisionary powers and three status-quo powers faced each other without recognized boundaries of conduct or clear understand-ing of each other's intentions. Of the revisionary powers, Russia was constructively weak but destructively capable and in unpredictable hands. China was strong and, if the grip lasted, in steady, determined hands. Of the status-quo powers, the United States was unmatched strategically in across-the-board hard power but uncertain of its world role and unpredictably led. Europe was strong in soft power, but politi-cally not yet coherent enough to throw its economic weight and social appeal into the geopolitical contest. Japan was economically strong but like Europe aging and unsure of its strategic partnerships. India hov-ered as a potential sixth power, neither obviously revisionary nor obvi-ously status-quo.

The end of ideological conflict did not mean the global contestants no longer had ideologies—political outlooks under another name. It meant that they no longer strove openly to impose their ideologies on others. If international order was to emerge after the end of the Cold

War, it promised to be more like that after the Treaty of Westphalia (1648), when the European powers ended a century and a half of religious warfare by agreeing that nations should choose their own Christian faiths and tolerate non-conforming Christians, or more like the post–Napoleonic Concert of Europe after 1815, when it was agreed that national powers should not interfere with each other's political arrangements unless they disturbed international peace, an avowedly large loophole. Once faith and politics were removed as justifications for conflict, the powers of the seventeenth through nineteenth centuries still had plenty to quarrel about, and so it was in the twenty-first century.

Capitalist, one-party China vied with the capitalist, democratic United States for which one of them was to set and police the monetary-commercial norms of global capitalism. The two argued over trade and deficits, which worked in principle to mutual advantage but which, given their scale, were fraught with potential for conflict. In 2016 the United States bought $350 billion more goods from China than it sold, and at year end China held $1.1 trillion in American official debt with perhaps as much again in other dollar instruments. Capitalist, illiberal Russia and capitalist, liberal Europe engaged in age-old competition across a European heartland rich in territorial flashpoints and vengeful memories. China and Japan pressed at each other's strategic interests in their neighboring seas. Across the Middle East, civil wars within Islam ran on without prospect of settlement at a growing cost in lives, displacement, and poverty, with the risk of extraregional contagion, as the combatants had patrons among the powers.

Far from diminishing after the 1990s, liberal loneliness grew. Instead of liberal democracy to the horizon, people talked of "democratic rollback" and the "retreat of liberalism." International indexes of liberal and democratic progress showed stagnation or reversal. The Economist Intelligence Unit's Democracy Index (2016) recorded that whereas half the world's people lived in full or flawed democracies, only 4.5 percent lived in full democracies, a smaller share than a decade earlier, partly because the United States had been demoted to "flawed," as its score on public trust in politics had collapsed. The decoupling of political and economic progress ought to have been no surprise. Historical experience suggested that a flourishing liberal economy required open trade, property rights, independent courts to defend those rights, uncorrupt government, and popularly accepted taxation. Such an economy could take various political forms, liberal or illiberal, democratic or non-democratic.

Whereas the Cold War had consolidated each of the competing blocs politically, post–Cold War disorder now revealed fault lines within the former blocs, notably in the West. Cold War frictions among the three Western powers had been pervasive but manageable. The same was no longer true as Europeans and Japanese watched the emergence of a go-it-alone United States and a self-isolating Britain. The rise to dominance of a hard right in both countries contrasted starkly with liberal-democratic continuity in Europe and Japan. Not only was a once-coherent West breaking up. A new segmentation appeared within the nations of the former West. It divided globalists from localists, multilateralists from unilateralists, the immediate winners from immediate losers. Those internal divisions raised the irksome topics of nationhood and patriotism that twentieth-century liberals had commonly been silent or confused about. The division was starkest in the United States.

Thanks to unmatched economic, monetary and strategic power, the prc-1989 US had been first among equals, always acknowledged although often contested. As understood by successive American administrations, leadership of Western liberal multilateralism involved a happy coincidence of national self-interest and liberal mission. Open markets, cheap borrowing and global stationing of its armed forces served American interests. Liberal economic values were extended and sustained across the West by freer trade and easier financial flows. Liberal political values were served in turn as American defenses protected the West against antiliberal Communism. In a remarkably durable American foreign policy consensus, accepted in essentials by Democrats and Republicans alike, Americanism blended smoothly with Westernism and liberalism. Political consolidation within the United States was never total. On the left, liberal mission was taken as cloak for imperial self-interest, on the right, particularly once the Cold War ended, for fruitless and thankless idealism. Yet for 70 years, broad agreement held that liberal order was good for the United States and good for the world.

Whether the end of the Cold War broke the geopolitical frame that made foreign-policy consensus in the United States possible, whether after the Vietnam war consensus was now on borrowed time, or whether, to the contrary, consensus renewed itself in the 1980–90s only to be broken by the Iraq War, are questions for future historians. By 2016, American consensus had gone. A president was elected who promised to put America first and who quickly acted to show the world that the promise was more than an electoral slogan. Not only did the new president divide the United States from its European allies and withdraw from multilateral agreements, he did so in manner calculated to cast doubt on the worth of alliances and multilateralism themselves. His White House, it is true, was divided between America Firsters competing for the ear of a cannily unpredictable president and defenders of an older foreign policy consensus, yet that only added to the outside world's uncertainties.

America Firstism was not as new or strange as it was widely made to seem. It had roots in an original conviction of American self-sufficiency and suspicion of foreign entanglement as well as in early twentieth-century American unilateralism. After the First World War, the Republican Cabot Lodge, as noted in Part Two, had led the rejection of American participation in the League of Nations. After the Second World War, his successor at the head of conservative Republicanism, Robert Taft, had led the party's opposition to NATO. Such attitudes were less nationalist or isolationist than unilateralist. Trump's presidency marked a reassertion of the unilateralist tradition in American policy towards the rest of the world. In terms made familiar by Walter Russell Mead, Trump reintroduced American Jacksonianism. He put nation first, revered military strength, and preferred command to persuasion. For the law-and-peace internationalism of Wilson he had no time and was happy to question Hamiltonian open commerce. In the eyes of the Trump administration and the Republican Right, the Liberal International Order could no longer be assumed to serve the interests of the United States. Liberalism and Americanism had for the moment come apart.

As tested understudy and prospective replacement for the United States in its role as liberal democracy's champion, Europe had strengths and weaknesses. If hard power was the standard, Europe could not compete. It was a weakling beside the United States, whose $611 billion on defense (2016) was more than the world's next six most heavily armed nations combined. However, in geopolitical soft power—the power of attraction, co-option and persuasion—Europe was equal to the United

States, if not superior. European nations collectively topped every international index of human well-being, social openness, and political accountability. Its citizens were not as well-paid on average as Americans. But if leisure time, health and longevity were costed in the calculation, French and British citizens, who earned about a fifth less than Americans in money terms, almost reached American levels of material well-being. As a model of society, Europe was admired not only by democratic liberals. People across the world, liberal or not, wanted to live there. Nor were they drawn only by money or driven by warfare. On almost any comparative test, Europe was an open, fair, and decent place to live. By atoning for moral enormities and curing historic ills, Europeans since 1945 had created a continental normality that was easy to take for granted. The accomplishments included democratization of dictatorial Spain, Portugal, and Greece, the peaceful enlargement the European Union on a once-divided continent, and the unifying of Germany, a credit to patient, far-sighted government and responsible democratic politics.

Europe's weaknesses tripped off hostile Anglo-American tongues, dripped from headlines of the anti-European press, and rallied national-minded Europeans on left and right. Many were caricatures, a mixture of jingoism, envy and monophone ignorance, but many were genuine complaints. The economic complaints included low growth, sluggish productivity, high youth unemployment and the monetary travails of a single currency. Political complaints included the institutional opacity of the European Union, its lack of democratic legitimacy and the uneven commitment of member nations to liberal values. Many of Europe's problems were common to the rich world and not all were equally felt across the continent. Taken nevertheless as a whole, Europe showed three clear lines of strain: between a wealthy, creditor north and a less wealthy, debtor south; between a liberal west and a less liberal or frankly illiberal east; between pro- and anti-Europeans, a political more than geographic line running less between Europe's core and its periphery than within national electorates.

Strains of like kind had been present in the European project from the beginning. They had shaped its novel architecture and affected its history. Enlargement—from an original six nations (1950s) to nine (1970s), 12 (1980s), and 28 (1990s–2000s)—had added to the strains. Whether strains would be worsened or relieved by Britain's departure, Europeans were unsure. The Franco-German core remained, strengthened out of mutual need by America's turning of its face, by Britain's decision, and by steady eastern pressure from Russia. Despite patent difficulties, it was not foolish to think that the shocks of 2016-2017 would prove salutary for Europe. In partnership, France and Germany had an opening, in hoped-for calmer political water after 2017, to face Europe's deeper challenges. Franco-German disagreements about monetary burden-sharing and Germany's tight purse looked more tractable, the often-predicted death of the euro less sure, and a many-speed Europe, with closer and less close union, no longer taboo.

A Europe of 27 nations, if shorn of Britain, equal in voice but unequal in fact, was not stable in its current form. A single market of 450 million people, a eurozone of 340 million, and a hybrid supranational association of small and big states could not happily cohere without either stronger, more accountable central institutions or looser, more flexible terms of membership. If Europe took the first course towards closer union, it could become an active champion of liberal democracy, not the passive champion it had become, a geopolitical player, not a sociopolitical model. That first course towards closer union was the less probable course, but not an impossible course. Europe's capacity for strategic vision and bold action was matched by habits of compromise and a proneness for the historic blunder. Recent blunders had included Germany's giving in to early membership in the euro of debt-prone Spain, Portugal, Italy, and Greece. Europe, on the other hand, was capable also of diplomatic success, notably its patient shepherding of the nuclear deal with Iran. Much was going to depend on the strength of the Franco-German partnership. France and Germany had created the European Union and brought it success, but each also played Europe for its own advantage. Germany's $280 billion trade surplus (2016), equivalent to 8 percent of gross domestic product, remained a source of contention over which less thrift-bound European partners shared a grievance with the United States. It looked, nevertheless, as if sudden isolation might yet shock Europe into finding some of the daring that drove its founders, provided energy and attention needed for reform were not drained by negotiating Britain's exit, should that folly be carried through.

The Franco-German duo should have been a trio of France, Germany, and Britain. Such a trio would have strengthened the EU's voice and capacities in the world. Neither of Britain's two leading parties, Conservative and Labour, were fully committed, however. After 1989, the British played a destructive long-game, a new variation on the old British strategy of resisting the emergence of a dominant continental power. In the seventeenth and eighteenth centuries, that power was France; in the nineteenth century it was Germany, and in the late twentieth century, Europe itself. To weaken Europe's Franco-German core, the British pressed for immediate expansion to include excommunist Easterners. True to a narrowly economic vision of Europe, they pressed simultaneously for a rapid creation of a single market, with free movement of goods, services, capital, and people. All the while, they obstructed steps towards closer political integration without which such economic arrangements were not sustainable, guided by a delusory faith in markets' self-correcting capacities. When markets failed to correct in 2008, Europe's lack of coordination made the cost of recovery deeper than needed. The anti-EU wing of Britain's Conservatives, then preparing their takeover of a shakily pro-European party, seized on the continent's travails to boast of Britain's supposed superiority and gather financial support in the City of London from hedge funds that make money from uncertainty. The anti-Brexiteers rallied popular support by calling to stop immigration from Europe, a direct consequence of the single European market for which the Conservative Party had fought.

The mendacity of the Brexiteers and the complacency of the Remainers spoke ill of both campaigns. The national security, institutional integrity, and future well-being of the British people were at stake. The underlying choice was clear. It could be put in terms of a trilemma made current by Lawrence Summers. Nations, he suggested, could have two, not three, of economic openness, national control, and public purpose, by which he meant government provision of needs markets did not supply. The aim of the European Union was to cede national control for the sake of economic openness and public purpose, sustained at European level. The European ideal was to balance free trade and economic competition with social welfare. In rejecting that ideal, Brexiteers were wishing on Britain one of two outcomes: government social provision in a penurious closed economy or an open economy without public purpose where the devil took the hindmost. That second outcome had been the strategic aim of the economic hard right since the 1970s. It was as if, judging Britain unable to compete with stronger, fairer Germany, the economic hard right wished Britain to compete for low wages and social insecurity with India and China. Whether they grasped that underlying strategy or not, Brexit voters were turning their backs on the world's most hopeful experiment in post-national liberal democracy.

The Brexit referendum and the election of President Trump prompted a cascade of bogus sociology about political disaffection among neglected, left-behind voters. The social speculation appeared to miss that working-class voters had been voting on the right since the 1960s. Although Trump was not a classic Republican, his win was in ways a classic Republican victory. The rich in 2016 voted right, most of the less rich voted left. Most whites voted right, most nonwhites who did vote voted left. Only among whites with higher degrees, in fact, did the Democrat candidate for president win majority support. In Britain, the Brexit vote was similarly a classic Tory win, carried off with a skill that surprised even the victors among the old in the suburbs and the countryside.

Republican and Brexit support came also, it is true, from a small share of hard-up voters in hollowed-out towns and distressed areas who played an outsize part in explanations of the results. Such voters told pollsters that free trade and export of jobs were to blame for their plight, although automation and technical change were as likely culprits. As a Pew survey of global attitudes to trade and investment (September 2014) confirmed, hostility to free trade had been growing in rich nations since the early 2000s. In the United States and France, for example, the survey reported that around half the people polled believed that trade killed jobs and lowered wages. In poor nations, where globalization was raising people out of poverty, the survey found unsurprisingly that close to 90 percent of those polled favored free trade, and only small percentages thought that trade hurt jobs and wages. Discontented voters in rich nations, however, judged their situation not by the standards of poor nations but against a customary expectation, now frustrated, of steady material progress. After allowance for those familiar truths, what the instant sociology failed to explain was why economic discontent took nationalistic form. History, by contrast, offered precedents. Liberal societies had suffered storms of nativist anger before. They had swept over Europe and the United States in the 1890s and again in the 1920s and 1930s. Liberals were puzzled, but that again was nothing new. Liberals had often found themselves at a loss to grasp the appeal of exclusionary nationhood.

iv. Nationhood, Citizenship, and Identity

Faced by an angry reversion to xenophobia and intolerance during the 1890s, the French social thinker Célestin Bouglé asked in "The Crisis of Liberalism" (1902) how liberals should respond when people, left as they should be to decide for themselves, chose to be bigoted, illiberal, and exclusionary. Bouglé, as was said in Part Two, urged complacent liberals not to count on earlier progress in establishing openness and acceptance of others. Liberal modernity, then as now, was turning familiar economic and social patterns upside down. Newcomers from the countryside and migrants from other lands were upsetting familiar patterns of life in crowded neighborhoods. Not only in France but across Europe and the United States, the political right nursed and encouraged nativist reactions against immigrants and social outsiders as an illiberal, exclusionary nationalism took hold.

Bouglé detested patriotism of the foreigner-hating kind but acknowledged the conservative complaint that liberals underplayed love of nation and the desire to belong. For conservatives, the nation gave citizenship focus and society coherence. Without a strong sense of nationhood, too little bound people together for a durable political order to exist. Liberals, the complaint ran on, overstressed what society owed people and what people owed each other. Their ideals of standing up to power and standing up for people were too negative or too thin to create the required social bonds on their own. Liberals stood aloof from patriotism, that is, but presumed on the nation. Without a nation, a citizenry had no more cohesion than a busy market or crowded train station. The challenge for liberals was to find a patriotism that answered those conservative complaints but was not bigoted and exclusionary.

In "Teaching Patriotism" (1904), Bouglé argued for a patriotism that would blend shared political ideals with historical memory and common sentiment of a kind that society would share. That liberal patriotism was in the line of descent from Guizot's hope to combine liberal principle with imaginative reverence for the French past. It ran parallel to Mill's conviction, expressed in *On Representative Government* (1861), that at the core of the "fellow-feeling" required for a liberal and democratic political order lay "possession of a national history" and a "community of recollections."

The first half of the early twentieth century was unkind to liberal patriotism. In 1914, war silenced politics and society was called on to unify. Clemenceau proclaimed in Paris, "When our soldiers march towards the enemy, radicals must march with reactionaries." In Berlin, the kaiser announced: "I no longer recognize any parties or any confessions; today we are all German brothers and only German brothers." When, at the end of a second war, Western nations abandoned mutual slaughter, foreigner-obsessed chauvinism gave way to liberal patriotism. The nation after 1945 was at a discount and international neighborliness at a premium. Many liberals found themselves ready to agree with the cynical old adage cited by the Prague-born American scholar Karl Deutsch, in *Nationalism and its Alternatives* (1956), that a nation was a group of people united by a common mistake about their ancestry and a shared dislike of their neighbors.

The exclusionary, foreign-hating kind of patriotism survived, it is true, but underground or in disguise, for example as McCarthyite anticommunism in the United States or as right wing procolonialism during vain French and British wars to keep a hold on their broken empires. By the 1990s, even those lingering passions appeared to have died. Foreign objects of hatred were no longer needed to rally citizens and stir national feeling. Among universal-minded liberals, hopes revived of a liberal patriotism in a postnational world. Such a patriotism would combine cultural reverence for local or national gods with political commitment to universal ideals of economic openness, human rights, and planetary care. Blending conflicting goals and attachments into an aspirational object of global affection might look a noble but foolish dream. Yet there were reasons for postnational liberals to think a start could be made.

Liberal economic and humanitarian ideals were spreading. Attachments of place and memory were growing less national and becoming again more local, as they had been before the nineteenth century. With cheap transcontinental travel, global commerce, and instant communication, national ways of life and attitudes to life had blurred, first across the rich world and then among the middle classes of the less rich world. Government itself was changing as national responsibilities spread downward in centralized systems like Britain and France to component nations or regions, or in federal systems like the United States and Germany to the states. National sovereignty was at the same time being shared upwards with supranational bodies, in Europe notably with the European Union. By the early twenty-first century, the large Western nations had renounced their single greatest hold over citizens, the command of young lives. Compulsory military service ended in hard-up Britain, which found training young reservists too expensive (1960), in the United States after its politico-military failures in Vietnam (1973), then in France (1996), and finally in a united Germany (2011). National rivalry survived in displaced, pacific forms such as World Cup soccer, but by the end of the century the greater rivalries were among postnational club teams, whose players came from across a globalized soccer-playing world.

The liberal mood of postnational confidence after 1989 was clouded by a noxious combination of terror, war, and hard times that followed in the new century. As the atmosphere turned defensive, a desire grew for shelter, partiality, and reassurance, which liberalism's ideals seemed poor at supplying. Complaints against liberalism's failure to recognize people's attachment to nation and community had resurfaced in a detached way among thinkers and writers in the 1980s but had found little immediate grip and soon died away. Now doubts about the drawing power of liberal ideals returned. The liberal outlook, it was charged, was either too weak to replace love of country as a common anchorage among citizens or, if strong enough within a country, drained to emptiness when stretched beyond a country's borders. The critics hoped in such way to face liberals with a dilemma. If thinned and universalized to the world at large, in country-blind commitment to human rights and ending global poverty, for example, the liberal demands to resist undue power and respect everyone became too vaporous to serve as focus of a durable patriotism. If, on the other hand, those two liberal ideals were to be given enough practical body to win a people's lasting attachment, they could not be stretched without limit beyond a nation's borders.

As democratic liberalism's prestige fell further after the financial crash of 2008, its difficulties with nationhood worsened. First liberals had overstressed cultural diversity. Now they had oversold economic openness. In both ways, liberals had forgotten what nations were and why they mattered, so it was widely complained. Without a strong sense of the nation, liberals were foxed by three topics in particular that festered in political imagination and clouded public debate: immigration, Muslim assimilation, and the divisive claims of identity politics. Each posed questions for liberals about nationhood. Immigration posed the question of who belonged in a nation, assimilation posed questions of what those who belonged in it owed to the nation, and identity politics posed questions of what the national group owed to smaller groups within it, whether recognized or self-avowed.

Although liberals had answers to the charge of not understanding the nation, in a climate of rancor and impatience they found the charge hard to beat off. They were nagged also by fears of their own that their critics might after all be right. They worried that the originating liberal dream of a masterless social order sustained by economic progress and personal contentment was indeed empty without a hostile foreign Other to give a society needed cohesion. Without a real or imagined enemy, liberals worried that their dream of self-sustaining order was empty even in its successful post-1945 democratic version. That success had relied heavily on shared commitment to social inclusion and common welfare. But both were now under challenge. Perhaps the early twenty-first century, like the early twentieth century, was not going to be kind to liberal patriotism.

Modern nations, to schematize, have cultural and political aspects. They might be thought of as ethico-cultural entities of some kind or as the body politic. A nation, that is, might be taken for an *ethos*, a people who share ethical ideals and cultural attachments. Or it might be taken for a *demos*, a body of citizens. Conservatives have stressed the ethico-cultural aspect of the nation, liberals the political aspect, although any actual nation, certainly any modern nation, involved both. Each side tended to build its political ideals into its preferred idea of the nation. The nation for conservatives was unifying, for liberals the nation was useful.

Conservatives have taken nationality to be a given rather than chosen, and nations to be immemorially ancient, ethnic in composition, and valuable not for other purposes but in themselves, hence objects of admiration and piety. Liberals by contrast have taken nationality to be chosen rather than given, and nations as modern, civic, and political. The nation as such merited neither admiration nor piety. For the nation in liberal eyes was a fruitful resource. The nation was a bounded territory, a usable field cleared and readied for the pursuit of people's chosen ends, whether capitalist enterprise, private interest, or liberal progress.

Liberals were quite able to see the non-political ties of imagination and affection that bound people to their countries. Liberals denied only that those ties could be captured in a formula or that there was an authoritative answer as to which ties, if any, mattered more than others. Most people had an imaginative picture of their country, often several, but not everyone had or needed to have the same picture. To stress in conservative manner, continuity, roots, and shared history as a vital element in national consciousness, faced the difficulty, acknowledged by Mill, that every national past was also one of rupture, uprooting and disputed history.

The United States was imagined biblically by Winthrop as a "city on a hill," prophetically by Tocqueville as a democratic laboratory, poetically by Whitman as a "teeming nation of nations" and reprovingly by Douglass as the impossible pairing of freedom and slavery. It is idle to ask which alone was right. Three songs have claim to be national songs: Katharine Lee Bates's hymn to the land, "America the Beautiful" (1893), Woody Guthrie's call to brotherhood, "This Land is Your Land" (1944) or Bob Dylan's elegy to American restlessness, "Like a Rolling Stone" (1965).

As for Englishness, to the Conservative prime minister, Stanley Baldwin, who had owned a Midlands ironworks employing 4,000 people, England evoked "the tinkle of the hammer on the anvil," "the sound of the scythe against the whetstone" and "the wild anemones in the woods in April, the load at night of hay." A love of those sights and sounds he wrote in "On England" (1926) were "innate and inherent in our people." When by contrast the British film maker Danny Boyle choreographed an evocation of Britishness for the opening ceremony of the London Summer Olympics, *Isles of Wonder* (2012), the nation's green and pleasant land morphed into industrial grime before nurses, patients, and doctors jitterbugged on giant hospital beds in celebration of the National Health Service, a widely acknowledged object of patriotic admiration.

In France and Germany, national attachment à la carte of the kind here suggested was exemplified in two massive literary productions. The historico-literary evocation of France and Frenchness *Les Lieux de Mémoire* (1984–92), edited by Pierre Nora, ran to seven volumes with 130 essays. A German sequel, *Errinerungsorte* (2001–08), edited by Etienne François and Hagen Schulze, had 122 essays allocated to one or other of 18 disparate categories into which national sentiments and reflections might reasonably be taken to fall: the realm and the territory, writers and thinkers, peoples, enemies, divisions, guilt, revolution, freedom, discipline, efficiency, law, modernity, education, feeling, faith and denominations, homeland, romanticism, and identities.

A patriotic conservative might retort that such productions show not love of nation but the scholar's detachment or the tourist's taste for heritage kitsch. The jibe would miss the mark. Liberals do not ignore or deny the nation. They have a different understanding of the nation from that of conservatives, which they take for truer to history and to people's actual attachments. Where conservatives in accounting for the nation appeal to piety and mystique, liberals as they see it appeal to history and principle. For liberals, the ethico-cultural nation grew up together with the nation-state and national market in the nineteenth century, each fostering the others.

Those contrasting conservative and liberal views of the nation were framed by the political ideals each held themselves to stand for. Conservatives took nations, like societies, as uncreated or natural unities of a kind. They accepted the authoritative, unargued hold of nations on their members. Liberals took nations as artificial creations of state and society, themselves fields of conflict. A nation's character, to liberals, was inevitably disputed and its claims on members in need of justification. Liberalism offered people protection from the nation's demands, including liberty to leave the nation and adopt a new nationality. Conservatism took nationality for given or imposed and changeable only in superficial, legally formal ways. For conservatives, the nation understood as a cultural unity was a source of political order, for liberals its consequence. The British philosopher Roger Scruton stressed the point in *How to be a Conservative* (2014). Political order, he wrote, required "cultural unity, something that politics itself can never provide."

Tidy as those contrasts looked, a reconciliation was possible. If by cultural unity was meant a narrow, exclusive set of cultural attachments, liberals could not agree. They would not accept one version of French-ness, Britishness, German-ness or American-ness, particularly not a version silently loaded with an exclusionary Other or with nonliberal political ideals. If, on the other hand, cultural unity meant a broad, open-ended set of cultural attachments together with shared commitment to liberal-democratic ideals, then many liberals might agree. Cultural unity and liberal patriotism, as understood by social-minded conservatives and democratic liberals, would not then be far apart. Each could make room for what they feared the other left out. Liberals could accept, as conservatives insisted, that citizens belonged like it or not to a larger national whole with claims on their moral sentiments, notably solidarity and pride, and on their acceptance, like it or not, for liberal-democratic norms. Conservatives could acknowledge, as liberals insisted, that national solidarity and national pride were not unconditional. They could agree, that is, that a nation's political ideals mattered and that when a nation had the wrong ideals or the right ideals it failed to live up to, national pride should turn to shame and solidarity to dissent. In the space of ideas there was room at the center for a love of the nation that conservatives and liberals could agree on.

That was all very well, but however tightly or loosely nations were imagined and thought about, practical questions had to be answered about who belonged in the nation, as well as questions about what rights and duties came with nationality. However far the patriotic liberal went to meet the patriotic conservative in argument, the awkward fact remained that there never had been a tidy national "Us" and tidy foreign "Them." There were rarely stable answers to who could settle in a country (immigration) or what status people had once there (nationality). The history of nationality and immigration revealed not gemlike facts about distinctive national characters but a tangle of changing laws and definitions. Part of why both topics remained politically divisive and seemingly immune to fair-minded negotiation was a lasting mismatch between the passion each provoked and the technicality involved in sure-handed knowledge of either.

Countries that needed more people, new hands or fresh soldiers have tended to welcome foreigners. After the Revolution, when social ranks were abolished and a citizenry created, Frenchness was legally defined as born to a French father. Worry about underpopulation and lack of young men for soldiering led in 1889 to an extension of French nationality to those born in France of non-French fathers. In 1927, war-bled France relaxed restrictions on immigration, only to be villainously attacked on the right for letting in the wrong kind of foreigner, notably Jews, an exclusion codified in Vichy's nationality laws. Decolonization, particularly Algeria, presented France with vexing puzzles of who from the ex-empire could come to France.

War and decolonization shaped Britishness also. Britain did without legislative definitions of nationality until 1915, when to distinguish loyal subjects from enemy aliens Parliament first defined who was and who was not British. Granting colonies independence after 1945 then left post-imperial Britain with a tangle of national categories and resident statuses, which it continued to refine and confuse in more than half a dozen major revisions of its nationality laws over the following decades. Membership in the EU brought a degree of coherence and stability, but the British government's decision to leave the EU threw into question which Europeans could continue to live and work there, once again upsetting rooted expectations and jeopardizing counterpart rights in Europe to which British citizens had grown accustomed. Britain's European commitments, on the other hand, had narrowed opportunities for ex-imperial, commonwealth citizens to settle in Britain. Freedom from European restrictions would allow for that exclusion to be corrected, an argument pressed by Brexiteers for openness to a non-European world linked to Britain by family and memory. Either way, Britishness was again proving a contingency open to legal re-adjustment and shifting political winds.

Europe in turn was open in ways, closed in others. In the stagflationary 1970s, its nations shut their borders to foreign migrants. When the EU expanded in the 1990s and 2000s, it kept its outer borders closed but opened its inner borders to free movement by any EU citizen from country to country. Pressure of economic migrants from North Africa and refugees from the Syrian war would, it was predicted, break the EU apart. But, as with predictions that conflicts over the euro would break the EU apart, the horizon of Europe's calamity kept receding.

In the United States, where capital was historically plentiful and labor scarce, its borders were open to the world until the 1920s, then closed, only to be reopened somewhat in the 1960s, after which immigration became again an unresolved political contest, although a contest in which the partisan sides had switched. In the 1970s–80s, industries and growers from Texas to California wanted cheap hands. "Open borders!" was the Republican cry. Northern unions, still a force among Democrats, resisted to protect American wages. Michael Walzer, who argued for immigration controls in *Spheres of Justice* (1983), was not a lone voice on the liberal left. Positions then reversed. Republicans began to call for a tightening of America's borders, Democrats to keep them open, or at any rate not close them in discriminatory ways. Soon middle ground was lost. To a Republican, anyone against controls was anti-American, to a Democrat, anyone who failed to resist controls was antiliberal.

That political fluidity was reflected intellectually. Among liberal thinkers there was no one philosophy of citizenship and nationhood. Universalist liberals proposed a global, not national, understanding of the civic respect required for people from state and society. Respect was owed, they held, for people no matter where they found themselves or what nation they belonged to. There was, they would claim, no good argument against open borders. The Canadian philosopher Joseph Carens, for example, defended open borders on the Nozickian ground that they were a universal right, on the Rawlsian ground that they were a requirement of fairness and on the Utilitarian ground they were of greater general benefit than were closed borders. The strict universalist insisted that the needs of the poor Bangladeshi peasant must be weighed equally with those of the laid-off worker in Sunderland or Lille. Among liberal economists, the net benefits of open borders were insisted on, which though diffuse and gradual, could be relied on in time. The challenge for the liberal politician was to make either philosophical or economic claim while looking a laid-off local worker in the eye.

National-minded liberal thinkers were more ready to accept the claims of partiality and the needs of the locale. The British political thinker David Miller, for example, argued in *On Nationality* (2005) that a liberal-democratic nation was united by, among other things, a shared commitment to political ideals and social achievements they had an interest in keeping and protecting. Universalist liberals were no doubt correct that all human lives were of equal value and that everyone shared equally in human rights. Nevertheless, refugees excepted, Miller held that states did not coerce would-be immigrants by closing its borders to them. Refusing a request was not imposing an undue demand. Immigration controls in themselves were accordingly not unjust. All states had humanitarian duties to human welfare, Miller accepted, but their exercise might justifiably be limited by appeal to capacities and local obligations. That said, national-minded liberals tended to agree with universal liberals that it was wrong to control immigration in nakedly illiberal ways that discriminated against people on religious or ethnic grounds.

Passionate disagreement about who and how many to let in stretched to how people who settled in a new country might be called on to behave. Angry, question-begging argument about immigration was matched by angry, question-begging argument about assimilation, particularly Muslim assimilation. Just as the intricacies of immigration were simplified in public argument by national and foreign stereotypes, so the complexities of assimilation were simplified by Muslim and Western stereotypes. The West was under threat from Islam, it was insisted, and anyone who did not get it, particularly the well-meaning liberal, was blind. That was the message shouted on the right in Europe and the United States for 20 years or more. Under such a barrage, it was not surprising that 43 percent of people interviewed for a French poll (2012) thought that the country's Muslims constituted a "menace to the identity of France"; 51 percent of respondents to a German poll (2013) thought Islam threatened the German way of life, and 27 percent of 18- to 24-year-olds in a British radio poll (2013) professed not to trust Muslims, whereas only 13 percent distrusted Buddhists and 12 percent distrusted Christians.

The right-wing narrative of an Islamic threat drew strength from its simplicity. It was much like the racial narrative in the post–Civil War United States. That racial narrative divided poor whites from poor blacks by playing up and to an extent inventing a binary racial opposition that encouraged and encoded prejudice. The Islamic-threat narrative depended on two falsehoods, each of which contained just enough truth to keep the larger untruth alive.

The first falsehood was that immigration and the social difficulties it caused were new, in character or scale. Tensions over immigration had flared in the United States in the (1890–1900s), France (1920s), Britain (1950s) and Germany (1960s) among the poorly paid people competing for scarce housing in crowded cities and underserviced neighborhoods. History of large movements of people and the deleterious changes they were held to have brought was invoked, but it was usually history of a safely distant and largely picturebook kind—fourth-century German tribes on the Roman borders, for example, or sixteenth-century Ottomans pressing against Vienna.

The second falsehood was that there existed a homogenous Western society under threat from a homogeneous people, the Muslims. The falsehood's purveyors were unsure how to characterize the social homogeneity under threat. Was it liberalism, secularism, Christianity, Judeo-Christianity, Westernism or some mixture of them all given the presumptuous and slippery label of "Christian-heritage society"? As to the cohesive threat, the falsehood's purveyors were unsure whether it was a people (Muslims in all their diversity) or a faith (Islam in its many streams).

It was estimated that in 2010 around 5 million citizens of North African origin lived in France. A majority, surveys suggested, were secular, and of the 40 percent who considered themselves observant, only a quarter attended Friday prayers. Their grandparents in the 1960s–70s had been known not as Muslims, but as *Arabes* or *beurs*. They were from all classes and had widely varying views. To say, in other words, that there were 5 million to 6 million Muslims in France was as underinformative about present-day French society and politics as saying that there were 44 million Christians. Nor was anyone sure of the number. Some surveys suggested 6 million Muslims, some 3.5 million. There was no official count. Unlike Britain and the United States, since 1978 France had, with exceptions, forbidden by law the collection and distribution of ethnic or religious statistics. Mindful of France's shameful treatment of Jews under the Vichy régime (1940–44), the French state did not wish to credit contentious, potentially prejudicial categories. Although such self-denial made it harder to refute the French right's claim that the number of Muslims in France was underestimated, the policy of "equality through invisibility" was upheld. France's belief in gradual assimilation was stiffened by *laïcité*, a hard-fought, long-standing principle that not only required the legal separation of church and state, as in the

United States, but also expressed a determination to keep religion out of public argument.

Rather than follow France in pursuing religion-blind assimilation, Britain adopted a limited multiculturalism, the policy of extending certain cultural protections and local privileges to immigrant groups or their nominated leaders. Its institutional context for absorbing Islam was different from France's. Though British society was as thoroughly secularized as that of France, Britain did not separate church and state; its monarch was head of the Church of England, and religious office-holders had a recognized, if marginal, voice in public life. Liberal respect made it wrong to treat a Muslim imam differently from an Anglican vicar. Unlike France's Muslims, Britain's came mostly from Pakistan and Bangladesh, with their own backgrounds and traditions. A need for action was acknowledged after urban riots between Muslim Asians and blacks in the 1970s and 1980s shook hopes that competing minority neighborhoods would blend by themselves in civic peace. A degree of social separation was acknowledged. Community leaders took representative part in civic affairs. In large cities, Pakistani and Bangladeshi enclaves grew where a small minority of local leaders encouraged frank separatism and a still smaller minority spoke up for militant violence. Germany's approach lay between multiculturalism and assimilation. It had a large, socially settled Turkish population, the children and grandchildren of guestworkers brought over in the 1960s, now with citizenship rights.

Given the tensions and social problems, predictions of civic corrosion and breakdown had been heard in all three countries for four or five decades. British riots in the 1980s and French riots in 2005 got more attention than positive trends. Although slow, imperfect integration was hard to make topical, the public face of Islam in Europe was more varied, more familiar and less disturbing than the Islam-threat story suggested. Awkwardly and incompletely, Europe was absorbing newcomers on terms that balanced acceptance with defense of liberal values. David Miller had expressed such terms in his 2005 work on nationality. A national-minded liberalism, he had written, should demand from newcomers a "willingness to accept current political structures and engage with the host community so that a new identity can be forged." By the 2010s, there were signs that something like that hope was indeed being realized. Islamic community and religious leaders had begun to play a larger part in local and government decision-making in return for readier public acknowledgement of liberal-democratic norms. London voters in 2016 elected as mayor a London-born, moderate Labour ex-MP, Sadiq Khan, son of Sunni Muslim immigrants in the 1960s from Pakistan. An observant Muslim, Khan by profession was an anti-discrimination lawyer. His election was a reminder of culture's openness and adaptability. It was often said that global communication, which let immigrants keep in touch with an old culture in their mother tongue, discouraged learning the language and ways of their new country. That was perhaps true but overlooked the point that global communication was also changing the old culture with which they kept in touch.

There were reasonable grounds, that is, for thinking that the Islamic-threat story was wrong. European society was not being overwhelmed, demographically, culturally or politically. The Islamic-threat story took old birth rates and straight-lined them 50 years or more into the future. It ignored the social complexity and cultural seduction of liberal modernity. It called on far-fetched historical parallels of migration and conquest from pre-modern times. It confused the issue of what threatened the West by aligning Muslims with anti-liberal Islamists and anti-liberal Islamists with militant Islamists. If liberal-democratic principles were under strain in Europe and the United States, it was because liberal democracy was failing at its own promises, not because of Islam.

Europe, like the United States, was nevertheless exposed to a violent backwash from the civil wars engulfing Islamic societies in the Middle East. The backwash took the form of unremitting terror attacks, which both alarmed and mobilized. Though commonly perpetrated by Western born or Western educated recruits, terror attacks were inspired by antiliberal movements within the Middle East. Terror was a tactic in a strategic campaign to impose a rigid, imprisoning interpretation of faith on Islamic societies and block them from more open forms of modernity. Terror's double purpose was to shake Europeans and Americans into treating their Muslim citizens as a hostile, alien bloc and to shake those same Muslim citizens into treating acknowledged social grievances as cause for war with Western society. Terror's destabilizing effects were never to be underestimated, but a small, encouraging sign was that imams and Muslim community leaders in Europe showed a growing willingness to join the mourning and displays of solidarity after terror attacks committed in the name of militant Islamism.

The extent and character of militant Islamism's appeal within Europe and the United States was disputed. Some observers stressed the disorganized, copycat character of the attacks and the social isolation of the assailants. Others stressed the ideological purposes behind terror. The contrast of views was vivid in France, where two noted students of Islam, Olivier Roy and Gilles Kepel, took opposite corners. For Roy, the terror afflicting Europe was more criminal than political. He wrote of it as an Islamization of marginality and petty crime. Kepel took militant Islamism for an antiliberal movement, led by politicians and intellectuals who had read the West's fascist writers of the 1920–30s and who grasped the power of terrorist violence. Study of British jihadists in recent years by the International Centre for the Study of Radicalisation at King's College, London, suggests that many are educated and from comparatively comfortable backgrounds, but adrift, nihilistic in outlook, and in search of a cause. Though religious in name, they were not unlike the unanchored young Europeans who in the 1970s joined the Red Army Faction and the Red Brigades, or in the 1920s formed fascist flying brigades.

Liberals as ever could tell themselves a hopeful story. Terror might die out, when exposed and harried by police-intelligence work and when confronted by failure to ignite social warfare among peoples who, despite friction and lack of understanding, would rather live together in grudging tranquility. Liberals could also tell themselves a grim story. Terror could leave people unable to gauge the scale of the threat. It could leave them at a loss to say if the known and heavy cost to civil liberties of counterterrorism was outweighed by its invisible and disputable gains. Terror could succeed in dividing liberal democracies further into hostile camps.

Questions of unity and difference arose for democratic liberalism in less alarming but more pervasive ways by identity politics. Out of the momentous campaigns of civil rights and nondiscrimination, once the principles behind those campaigns had taken root in law, new movements arose that were categorized together as identity politics. The politics of identity stressed not social class but gender, race, faith, ethnicity, and nationality. Nonclass elements had figured in politics immemorially. Yet the label "identity politics," borrowed from social psychology and the liberalism of recognition, was new. The first relevant citation for "identity politics" in the *Oxford English Dictionary* was for 1989.

In its modern versions, the politics of identity dates from the 1960s. In recent years, it was linked exclusively with the left and hung on the left by its critics as an albatross. In truth, identity politics was played from the beginning by both sides in politics, often more skillfully by the right. When, in the United States, Democrats pushed civil rights and antidiscrimination, Republicans won "ethnic" votes from the 1970s onwards in a white working-class backlash. Using "ethnic" as code for "white," Republicans created the Nixon Democrat, who in the 1980s became the Reagan Democrat only to be rediscovered as if never heard of as the Trump Democrat in 2016. Something similar occurred in Britain and the rest of Europe in the 1970s as the left began to lose working-class support over immigration to nativist parties of the right. The voters in question might reasonably have bridled at being taken for bigots, but rightwing campaign managers, early adept at identity politics, nevertheless sought out such voters as bigots and appealed to them in bigoted ways.

On the left, particularly in the United States and Britain, identity politics was divisive in other ways. As a slogan and category, identity took wing only in the last of three distinct phases in historic campaigns to make civic respect for everyone more than a limited hope. The first phase was against discrimination and for equal rights, particularly for black Americans, a campaign with which most liberals agreed. The second phase was for selective help towards equalizing opportunities in jobs and education, known as affirmative action or positive discrimination. With that most left-wing liberals agreed. In the third phase, however, a quite new demand was heard. Not just for protection from prejudice. Not just for help in repairing damage from past prejudice. The demand now was to recognize, respect, and celebrate previously stigmatized groups as such, and with that few liberals of any stripe agreed. On the thinking left, a battle line was drawn: for identity politics or against.

Defenders of identity politics put a negative case against liberal universalism and a positive case for a new kind of group loyalty. Negatively, it was charged that liberal ideals of difference-blindness and equal respect were incoherent or oppressive. Difference-blindness was discriminatory in practice. Equal respect was either so encompassing as to be empty or, when given content, suffocating in its uniformity. A classic attack on liberal principle of the kind was Iris Marion Young's "Polity and Group Difference: A Critique of the Ideal of Universal Citizenship" (1989). Positively, the claims of identity politics were well summarized later by Sonia Kruks, an expert on the thought and writing of Simone de Beauvoir. Kruks took identity politics, in her words, "as a demand for recognition on the basis of the very grounds on which recognition has previously been denied." It was as women, as blacks, as lesbians, Kruks wrote, that groups demanded recognition. None were asking for respect, as she put it, "despite their difference." The new demand, Kruks said, was "respect for oneself as different."

Interpreting that dark phrase would take a return to the clinical idea of a desirably integrated self, which was popularized in the 1950s by two Freudian psychiatrists, one from the liberal center, Erik Erikson, the other from the radical left, Frantz Fanon. It would take going back to the Heideggerian and existentialist ideas of an authentic self and back to the recently revived Hegelian idea of nonrecognition as a common unit of account for every form of social or political oppression. In those mists, however, a nagging thought would never vanish: wasn't demanding respect for one's *self* a sign, not of solidarity, but of conceit? Wasn't demanding respect for oneself as *different*, a kind of radical individualism behind a collectivist mask? If wrongful inequalities of power were at issue, which they were, then talk of selves and identity was a lamentably indirect and confusing way to pursue the argument.

The politics of identity, properly understood, is one way to practice the politics of categorization, and liberals are allergic, or should be, to putting people into social categories and keeping them there. Liberals are not daft. They recognize categories of need and status. Over a life cycle, people are young, old, single, married, well, ill, better off, worse off, able, less able. Those are social categories liberals pay attention to, or ought to. Liberals are blind, or should be, to socially loaded identities that drench a person at birth and cloak them throughout life.

If identity politics involved the claim that nobody should be demeaned or discriminated against because of their social clothes, and if it celebrated the replacement of cultural monopoly by cultural diversity, well and good. If identity politics meant acknowledgment that cultural groups and their traditions had nourishing worth of their own, well and good. If identity politics called on liberal politics to reaffirm its promises of civic respect for everyone with solid protections and empowerments, then well and good. If on the other hand, identity politics was understood divisively and individualistically in ways that diluted or denied common citizenship and shared political morality, then identity politics threatened democratic liberalism at its roots.

After such a catalogue of challenges, it might seem that little was left to hope for from the liberal patriotism with which this chapter began. Hard-eyed doubters and mockers abounded who took liberals for sleepwalkers. Faced by a return of nationalistic passion, liberals had for all that no need to despair. What counted was to be clear about liberal-democratic ideals, to stick to them without flinching or apology, and above all to avoid distracting simplicities.

One such distracting simplicity was the suggestion in "The Clash of Civilisations" (1993) by the American student of politics Samuel Huntington that ethico-cultural conflict had replaced class competition. Civilizations were difficult to define, let alone map convincingly into geopolitics. The idea that culture had replaced class and economics as sources of conflict in politics was premature, as the years after 2008 have made clear, when class and inequality returned to politics in strength. There need be no civilizational war unless such a war is sought and promoted.

A second simplicity was to suppose that liberalism came with a Western passport. That was as much a caricature as claiming that liberalism came in nineteenth-century clothes. The jeering suggestion "universalism to the West, imperialism to the rest" distracted from who "the rest" were. The "rest" who claimed that liberal values were Western or imperialist were commonly self-selected leaders, usually male, claiming to speak for others with less power and little or no voice of their own, who had been typed with a contentious identity-label they did not necessarily accept. The claim that liberalism can flourish only in the West is as empty as the claim that it must somehow sweep the globe.

The final simplicity to avoid was the caricature of the liberal without passionate attachments. Among the falsehoods of the Brexit campaign was a falsehood about national feeling. The French loved France. Germans loved Germany. The English loved England. They did not love

Europe. Nor could they love Europe, for Europe was the wrong kind of object for patriotic affection. Europe was not a nation, but a distant, bureaucratic tangle of ill-defined committees without common history or culture.

So it was charged, but the charge was false, as the big European votes of 2016–17 showed. After the Brexit defeat in Britain, the outburst of political emotion was widely remarked on. The feelings were many but one of the feelings was a sense of wounded patriotism for Europe. Love of Europe showed itself in France in sound defeat for the anti-European far right. In the 1950s and 1960s, De Gaulle had silenced and absorbed France's far right into Gaullist conservatism by appealing to love of France. In 2017, Macron soundly defeated France's far right by appealing to love of Europe. European patriotism was striking among the European young. They loved Europe with the kind of liberal patriotism mixing memory and ideals that Bouglé had looked forward to. They loved Europe because of and despite its past, much as any patriot whose pride in country implied a capacity for shame. They loved Europe because it embodied liberal-democratic ideals that they feared were threatened in their own country and because it represented, for all its flaws, attachment to an open society underpinned by social concern. They loved Europe because they loved their own countries and thought their own countries would be better and safer in a Europe of like-minded neighbors.

The claims that people have only one social identity and cannot feel supranational patriotism are false. Neither nation nor subnational group has a final, decisive claim on anyone's loyalty or sense of themselves. If all that is true, liberals can insist, against their critics, that they do understand the nation and are indeed patriotic, albeit in a liberal way. When their critics complain that by insisting on choice and responsibility in matters of national attachment, liberals are endorsing detachment in disguise, liberals can respond that the critics are confusing the strength or origin of a bond with what the bond ties you to. There is a risk that the range of ways to hold or voice national attachments can widen to a point where treating them as shared attachments is emptied of sense. There is a bigger risk that fluid national attachments will freeze into two hostile halves matching the partisan camps, one half claimed by liberals, the other by an implacable, flag-waving right.

v. Intellectual Doubts and Disaffection

Despite liberalism's reputation for complacency, self-criticism is its second name. Liberalism hides its flaws neither from itself nor its opponents. If you take any decade since the 1930s, you will find liberals anxiously checking liberalism's vital signs or nonliberals calmly pronouncing the patient dead. In between George Dangerfield's *The Strange Death of Liberal England* (1935) and H. W. Brands's *The Strange Death of American Liberalism* (2001), John Hallowell judged in "The Decline of Liberalism" (1942) that mass society had rendered obsolete the "individualistic *Weltanschauung*" on which liberalism had rested; Arthur Ekirch worried in *The Decline of American Liberalism* (1955) that from Lincoln to Eisenhower the American warfare state had undermined liberal resistance to overbearing power; Theodore Lowi worried in *The End of Liberalism* (1969) that civic-minded liberalism was being sapped by bureaucratic clientelism, government favors to business, and the growing burdens of the welfare state as interest-group politics stifled liberalism's larger ideals; Daniel Bell worried in *The Cultural Contradictions of Capitalism* (1976) that the virtues of hard work, thrift, and social responsibility on which liberal capitalism had relied for its historic successes were giving way to ethical permissiveness, self-preoccupation, and a childlike short-term spirit of play; Samuel Huntington, writing with fellow French and Japanese scholars on behalf of the Trilateral Commission, worried in *The Crisis of Democracy: On the Governability of Democracies* (1975) that liberal-democratic governments were setting themselves up for failure by undertaking too many tasks and by the resulting burden of unmeetable expectations; echoing a concern voiced by the German liberal historian Friedrich Meinecke in the late 1920s, Ronald Terchek worried in a chapter from *Liberals on Liberalism* (1986) called "The Fruits of Success and the Crisis of Liberalism" that liberal achievements were too easily taken for granted and that liberalism's survival was being complacently presumed on; Roger Kimball and Hilton Kramer complained in their collection of essays, *The Betrayal of Liberalism* (1999), that the divisive, exclusionary claims of identity politics and the spread of unearned entitlements had debauched the worth of liberal respect for people and their chosen projects; in "Liberalism and its Discontents" (2002) and *Philosophy and*

Real Politics (2008), Raymond Geuss, a political diagnostician from the intellectual left, drew up an ominous list of ailments from which contemporary liberalism was widely taken to be suffering: it was passionless and uninspiring; it could not replace the old social bonds it dissolved; it embodied commercialism at its worst; it promised the planet only damage, not protection; it cloaked Western privilege in spurious universalism, and had no answers to poverty or inequality. In *Why Liberalism Failed* (2018), the American Catholic scholar Patrick Deneen charged liberalism with promulgating equal rights but creating material inequality, with resting its legitimacy on consent but discouraging civic commitment and with claiming to stand for personal autonomy while sustaining a state with the deepest reach yet known.

Not all those writers were having the same argument. Some were friendly to liberalism, some hostile. Some wanted to own liberalism and deny its label to other liberals. Some wanted to foist on liberalism a caricature or a contentious defense of liberalism in order to discredit liberalism itself. Some wanted to defeat or replace liberalism altogether. Laid out, nevertheless, from nearly 100 years of self-analysis and criticism was a generous selection of complaints on which twenty-first century worriers and critics could draw, and draw on them they did—with gusto. That almost all twenty-first century doubts and criticisms had been heard before did not mean they were ill-founded. That liberal doubts and critical voices of disaffection came from many quarters and in a variety of registers did not mean that they cancelled each other out. Just about everybody could agree that something was wrong with the present state of liberal democracy even if there were many ways to show how.

Sympathetic political scientists worried about how liberal democracy was to be shored up politically. Sympathetic philosophers questioned how best to defend it philosophically. Although without settled or palatable alternatives of their own, hostile intellectuals to the right and left picked away at liberal democracy's evident flaws.

To confuse a muddled scene further, non-political accounts of current political conflicts became popular, which encouraged people to give in to what could be called the lure of mechanism, the belief that politics was governed by deep forces beyond anyone's control, be it the history of the implausibly *longue durée*, evolutionary biology, long-term demographic change, or a global cultural geography that treated political disputes as hard-to-broker differences of ethics and culture.

The attraction of such accounts was to resolve argument by changing the subject from politics to something else. It was suggested by the history of human inequality since the Stone Age, for example, that political action to reduce inequality worked briefly if at all. Again, it was proposed that differences of opinion between liberals and conservatives could be understood less in terms of fact, argument, and conflicting interests than in terms of contrasting ingrained moral responses passed down genetically from early humans. Or again, it was suggested that political variety across the world could be best seen culturally and mapped according to a people's survey-measured degree of commitment to "traditional" or "secular-rational" values on the one hand and to "survival" or "self-expression" values on the other. Despite their imposing factual range and explanatory appeal, those were kinds of reductive tales in which no liberal could wholly believe. They were too general to provide a grip on practical disputes. At best they offered confirmation in new guise of what had always been believed about flawed humanity, at worst excuses for treating political conflict as beyond control. Such tales left little or no room for argument or negotiation, and to the liberal mind without either there was no politics.

Heard on all sides was the common thought that the twentieth century's historic compromise between liberalism and democracy was under serious strain. However it was expressed and whether ruefully or gleefully held, a belief was spreading that the democratic promise of liberalism for all rather than the nondemocratic promise of liberalism for a few might be undeliverable on its old, familiar terms.

Among liberals themselves, the work of Francis Fukuyama offered a core sample of the liberal shift from guarded hope in the 1990s to anxious concern in the 2010s. As the Cold War ended, Fukuyama, then a researcher at the Rand Corporation in Santa Monica, California, wrote a bold essay, "The End of History?" (1989), the punning title of which was easy to misunderstand and that lost its question mark when a lengthened version appeared in book form as *The End of History and the Last Man* (1992). The collapse of Soviet communism, Fukuyama argued, had left the liberal-democratic outlook as the only political outlook with broad, lasting appeal. Other outlooks existed, he accepted: authoritarianism, state capitalism, gangster capitalism, theocracy, strong-man populism. None, in his view, was durable. Each had decisive failings: destructive inner conflicts, incurable economic inefficiencies and an inability to satisfy people's everyday demand for what liberals have called "liberty" or "freedom," and what Fukuyama, writing in neo-Hegelian mode, called a yearning for recognition. By recognition, he meant respect from the powers of society for each of us as self-possessed people with lives and commitments of our own.

Although Fukuyama was writing of liberal democracy's aims and ideals, not the West's achievements, he was widely mistaken for a Western triumphalist. Ignoring the caricature, Fukuyama began a twenty-year study of civic attitudes, social patterns, and governmental institutions that he believed necessary for strong liberal democracies. He widened his view to the world and went far back in time to produce two massive studies on how political order grew and how it could break down. The second of those books, *Political Order and Political Decay* (2014), focused on capitalist modernity since the industrial revolution. It suggested that popular accountability, a healthy economy, and social progress depended on an uncorrupt state serving the public interest according to recognized laws. The liberal democratic United States had gone a distance towards creating such a model republic in the later twentieth century but was now, he judged, in "political decay."

Fukuyama generalized that lesson. Liberal democracy, he said, in effect, could weaken or break down if not kept in repair and protected from capture by corrupt interests. Sensing the coming economic backlash against established parties, he wrote "Can Liberal Democracy Survive the Decline of the Middle Class?" (2012). In answer to his title question, Fukuyama doubted whether liberal democracy could survive unless "the middle classes of the developed world" abandoned the prevailing narrative of the past 30 years that their interests were best served by "by ever-freer markets and smaller states." Despite sharing its social concerns, he had by now abandoned earlier sympathies for neoconservatism because its hopes of spreading democracy by force were, whatever else, delusory, and because its economic hostility to government ignored an essential element of political order.

Two years later there followed Fukuyama's grim account of political gridlock and governmental failure in the United States, "America in

Decay" (2014). Soon after, however, writing of the Trump and Sanders insurgencies in 2016, he saw signs that American democracy might be "in some ways in better working order than expected." He did not believe in either candidate, particularly not Trump, "a singularly inappropriate instrument" for reform. Nevertheless, he saw opportunity in popular anger. Voters, Fukuyama took it, were trying to "wrest control" of the political narrative from a "vetocracy" representing "organised interest groups and oligarchs." Popular mobilization was welcome, he concluded, but not enough on its own to restore liberal-democratic health, and not without danger. Widespread anger and good government, as in the Progressive Era and New Deal, brought "great things." Widespread anger and bad government, however, were capable also of "terrible things," as in Europe in the 1930s.

A loss of confidence after 1989 was noticeable also among philosophers of liberalism but a loss perhaps of limited bearing on politics. To an unwary eye the philosophical shift of mood could be mistaken for a shaking of political faith. But the doubts had more to do with how to defend liberalism than with liberalism itself. The object of questioning was less liberal democracy than the Rawlsian liberalism of justification that had dominated English-speaking political philosophy in the 1970s and 1980s. Among outstanding doubters were Judith Shklar, Richard Rorty, John Gray, John Skorupski, and Bernard Williams. They did not make a philosophical school, although the multitasking label "realist" was commonly attached to them. Nor did they make a political group, although all of them, save the hard-to-place Gray, were left-wing liberals of a kind. What grouped them as thinkers when it came to defending political ideas was a preference for philosophical modesty as opposed to Rawlsian ambition.

A familiar objection to the Rawlsian defense of liberal principles was that the justification appeared to move in a circle—liberal democracy in, liberal democracy out. The circle was harmless if Rawlsianism was taken to offer democratic, social-minded liberals philosophically more articulate reasons for believing in democratic, social-minded liberalism. If Rawlsianism, on the other hand, was taken as an argument to all comers, it presumed too much of what it was hoping to convince them of. The liberalism of justification demanded of a legitimate political order that it be "justifiable to all citizens" (Rawls), justifiable to "everyone who is required to live under it" (Thomas Nagel) or "rooted in the consent of all those who have to live under it" (Jeremy Waldron). In a society of "deep diversity," as critics called it, where people disagreed about what mattered to them most, particularly faith and morals, it was unreasonable to expect that they would accept common political ground rules. They might put up with them, but that did not mean they took them for justifiable or legitimate. The Rawlsian school was alive to the difficulty and fertile with solutions, none of which, however, laid the suspicion that high-level argumentative pleas for liberalism were not going to budge nonliberals, even the reasonable kind who were open to argument.

In *Contingency, Irony and Solidarity* (1989), Richard Rorty argued instead for an "ironical" stance of wholehearted commitment to social-minded, liberal-democratic beliefs coupled with acceptance that philosophy offered no ladder by which people could climb out of their times to justify those beliefs in Kantian fashion to rational-minded all-comers. In "The Liberalism of Fear" (1989), another American thinker, Judith Shklar, called in like spirit for a lowering of philosophical sights and for sharper practical focus. The liberal tasks, she suggested, were to avoid the worst harms (rather than promote the greatest good, presuming the two could be prized apart), to stick to politics (rather than pursue ethical uplift by attempting to improve a coarsened democratic culture), and above all to resist the abuse of power. "The governments of this world," Shklar wrote, "with their overwhelming power to kill, maim, indoctrinate and make war are not to be trusted unconditionally." The "what-to-avoid" tone of Shklar's liberalism had been heard in Popper and Berlin. Her suspicion of power took liberalism's royal road opened by Constant and Guizot.

Parallel thoughts were voiced in Britain. In *Liberalisms* (1989) and *The Two Faces of Liberalism* (2000), John Gray opened a direct attack on Rawlsian liberalism, which he judged "hubristic and defective." It suffered, Gray claimed, from spurious universality, took liberal theory to guide liberal practice rather than the other way around, failed to provide clear tests of what was acceptable and unacceptable in politics, and pretended to ethical neutrality while seeking to impose on people liberalism's own ethic of life. Gray's quarrel was more one of method and tone than liberal aim. His "modus vivendi" liberalism of peaceful coexistence among people who disagreed about which gods to worship and which ways of life to pursue was little different from Rawls's hope for an "overlapping consensus" on political ground rules amid irreconcilable moral and religious disagreement. Gray held fast to the tradition of toleration on which liberalism had drawn and on the "historic inheritance of liberal civil society," but in time appeared to drift further from liberalism altogether. Not only did he think its ideas could not be justified philosophically, he rejected a liberal faith in progress as "delusion."

In less caustic vein, John Skorupski argued in "Liberalism's Hollow Triumph" (1999) that like a stone arch, liberalism could stand up without metaphysical falsework if its elements held together in mutual support. Springing, to continue Skorupski's metaphor, from the twin abutments of equality under law and the feeling of common humanity, liberalism's ideals of civic decency, personal responsibility and impartial concern could, he believed, hold each other up without the whole collapsing.

Lack of ambitious philosophical support was not itself troubling. So-called realist defenses of liberalism were, after all, philosophical in their own way. There had never been, in any event, one philosophy of liberalism. Utilitarianism served early nineteenth-century liberals, neo-Hegelian idealism served late nineteenth-century liberals, science-minded, anti-metaphysical philosophy served mid–twentieth century liberals, and rights-based neo-contractarianism served late twentieth-century liberals. The more political worry was for the public credit of liberalism itself. However democratic liberalism was defended philosophically, the question remained of how well it could stand up politically without persuasive champions amid such widespread intellectual disaffection to its right and left.

Despite a complacent liberal picture of conservatives as the thoughtless party, antiliberal thinking on the right was abubble with new magazines, new books, and new foundations as well as new thoughts or revived thoughts. Conservative thinking tended to divide into cultural criticism of liberal society and criticism of liberal-democratic politics, although the distinction was not tight.

Cultural conservatism had never come to terms with liberal modernity. Evergreen conservative complaints, planted in the late eighteenth and early nineteenth centuries, were heard again against commercialism, me-firstism, and secular impiety. More nationalistic complaints were heard as well about liberal corrosion of the cultural nation.

American conservatives had two stories about what ailed present-day culture, one hopeful, one bleak. The hopeful story told of liberal capture. In the 1950s and 1960s, the story ran, an unrepresentative secular-liberal elite seized the churches, universities, media, and courts from a fundamentally god-fearing and virtuous people. The task for conservatives was to win them back. That aim inspired the Christian right in its fight for the soul of the Republican Party. At its peak in the Reagan-Bush years of the 1980s, the Christian right came close to believing that it had realigned America's political majority with an underlying moral majority. The bleak view was that secular decadence was too seductive not to prevail. Even when conservatives controlled all three branches of government after 2016, holders of the bleak view did not expect the sweeping changes in laws to do with private morality of the past 40 years to be rolled back.

According to the bleak view, bluntly stated, the United States had an immoral majority and righteous people could do little about it. The proper response was not political resistance but spiritual and intellectual renewal. Intellectually, a flagship publication was *First Things*, an ecumenical but strongly Catholic magazine, which was founded by the late Father John Neuhaus, a neoconservative critic of liberal society. *First Things* was notable for publishing work by neo-Thomist thinkers centered at Notre Dame University hoping to recreate a new morality of politics freed from, as they took it, liberal error. Less philosophically, Rod Dreher took the bleak view of political action in *The Benedict Option* (2017), which called on devout American families to withdraw from a corrupted society and lead a monastic routine of prayer, home-schooling and shopping, where possible, only in stores run by other spiritual refugees. Both the philosophical and the self-improvement versions of religious resistance took inspiration from MacIntyre's call in the 1980s, noted in chapter 12 of Part Three, for an archipelago of nonliberal institutions, especially colleges or universities, to serve as shelters from hostile, secular society where countertraditions could be kept alive, perhaps later to prevail again.

A British critic of liberal society, the philosopher Roger Scruton, offered four essays in *On Human Nature* (2017) that drew together complaints he had been making since his classic *The Meaning of Conservatism* (1980). Every political outlook presupposed a philosophical picture of the human person, Scruton wrote. A picture widely accepted in liberal societies rested on three mistakes. They could be labelled, though Scruton himself did not use the terms, scientism, philosophical libertarianism, and transactionalism. Scientism mistakenly took biology and evolutionary psychology to promise the whole truth about who we were. Science explained our animal selves. It could not explain the irreducibly personal perspective by which we recognized who we were and held each other accountable for how we acted. Libertarianism was correct that we were each morally free and personally accountable, but wrong in neglecting unchosen social ties that imposed duties and fleshed out who we were. Transactionalism treated anything of value as having acquired value by choice or consent, a mistake that threatened to equate value with price and render everything that mattered open to trade. Scruton countered that many things mattered by themselves, regardless of who favored them, for example, beauty, learning, the natural environment, and a person's nation. Such "lasting things" needed to be cherished and protected. The proper attitude to them was not to ask "What is this for?" but to show what, in a nonreligious sense, Scruton called piety, that is, unquestioning recognition and respect. A sickened liberal culture, he believed, need not be abandoned. It could be cured if more people returned to piety.

Many liberals could agree with Scruton's ethico-cultural criticism, his concern for the environment, and his belief in intrinsic values. They did not need to agree with his suggestion that the liberal outlook depended on scientism, libertarianism, or an out-and-out economic liberalism according to which anything that mattered in human life was tradeable at a market price for something else that mattered. As suggested often in these pages, liberalism depended in principle on none of those three errors, although honest liberals would want to ask themselves why the errors were so widely credited, perhaps fostered, in latter-day liberal society and so easy for critics to hang around liberals' necks.

In Germany and France, the right's cultural critique of liberal democracy blended with politics and took a nativist tone. Two best sellers in the 2010s revived a popular tradition of national-decline books stigmatizing despised outsiders or corrupt insiders that had flourished in both countries during the 1920s–30s and had never fully died. In twenty-first century Germany, the culprits were immigrants and welfare recipients. In *Deutschland schafft sich ab: Wie wir unser Land aufs Spiel setzen* (2010) (*Germany is Destroying Itself: How We're Gambling with our Country*), the German ex–central banker Thilo Sarrazin wrote that failure to assimilate immigrants from Muslim and African nations was undermining German society and that the welfare state was becoming unsustainable. In *Le suicide français* (2014), Eric Zemmour blamed the 1960s generation for the "derision, dismantlement and destruction" that he believed had sapped France's "virility." The irresponsible, antiauthoritarian foolishness of well-educated *soixante-huitards* had in Zemmour's view become the guiding outlook of the nation's elites. The list of ills in his tirade included women's liberation, abortion, gay rights, immigrants, and American business practices. Sarrazin's and Zemmour's books were models of illiberal, exclusionary patriotism, the kind that Bouglé had lamented. Both in their time were runaway best sellers.

In the United States, the electoral shock of Trump's victory left thinkers and writers of the center-right at a loss. The conservative columnists George Will of the *Washington Post* and David Brooks of the *New York Times* might have been expected to favor a Republican. Yet they disavowed Trump in brutal terms. Citing Trump's "dangerous inability," Will called on the American public in May 2017 to "quarantine this presidency." The headlines alone of Brooks's columns in the spring months of 2017 indicated his wounded sense of moderate conservatism betrayed: "The Trump elite: like the Old Elite but Worse!", "The Crisis of Western Civilisation," and "When a Child is Leading the World." Their difficulty was that for the moment open-minded, ready-to-bargain conservatism was homeless. Most Republicans had rallied to Trump and party loyalty was rapidly normalizing his presidency. The New Center of William Galston (liberal) and William Kristol (conservative)—a centrist movement launched in November 2016 with a brief statement of purpose that spoke of the "institutions and principles of liberal democracy" as "under assault"—was as yet little more than a shelter for the politically displaced. Something similar was observable in Britain, where moderate conservative opinion appeared to have collapsed in the face of the Brexit hard right on the one side and on the other the popular leftism of Corbyn-led Labour.

Not all conservatives in the United States suffered the anti-Trump agonies of the center right. At the Harvard Club in New York early in 2017, a young right-winger, Julius Krein, who had welcomed Trump's victory and earlier helped run an online magazine, *The Journal of American Greatness*, launched a new magazine, *American Affairs*. Although he later cooled to Trump himself, the magazine, Krein indicated, would offer a platform for the thinking right to provide a Trump Doctrine to replace the post-1989 American foreign policy consensus.

Nor was Trump's victory alone responsible for concern on the intellectual right about the wisdom of electoral democracy. The libertarian right had been concerned for a long time. In *Against Democracy* (2016), Jason Brennan of Georgetown University in Washington, DC, drew on recent work in political studies to revive old doubts raised by Schumpeter and Hayek about the compatibility of liberal capitalism and electoral democracy. Combining argumentative skill with appeal to survey research, Brennan argued for "epistocracy," that is, competent government by those who knew what they were doing as opposed to ignorant government confirmed by ignorant voters. Citizens had a right, Brennan argued, to be protected from incompetent government. Correct political theory showed what kind of governments were competent: the small, low-tax free-market-minded and socially liberal kind. Political surveys showed that most voters could not identify the correct theory and in their ignorance were unable to tell competent from incompetent governments. Brennan was open-minded about how voting was to be filtered so that citizens' right to protection from incompetence might be upheld. His suggestions included stripping ignorant voters from the rolls, giving informed voters extra votes or giving panels of experts a veto over the decisions of elected bodies, particularly on money and finance. Brennan's book, like Krein's new magazine, were good examples of a revived intellectual confidence on the American right and an unapologetic readiness to direct academic firepower, often to their opponents' surprise, at deeply held liberal-democratic assumptions.

Antiliberal thinking on the left tended to greet the travails of democratic liberalism in "we-told-you-so" spirit. If democratic liberalism was washed up, neo-Marxists and post-Marxists professed few regrets. Expressions of left-wing antiliberalism ranged from the mischief-making of the ex-Maoist philosopher Alain Badiou, who urged French voters in

June 2017 to abstain rather than vote for a centrist liberal against the far-right National Front, through the anti-EU, anticapitalist German political economist Wolfgang Streeck, to a stoical neo-Marxist believer in a yet-to-glimpse post-liberal future, the historian Perry Anderson, who from the 1960s edited or guided *New Left Review*, the English-speaking flagship journal of the unreconciled left.

In "How will Capitalism End?" (2014), Streeck suggested that capitalism was no longer compatible with democracy. Schumpeter had worried 75 years earlier about democracy's drag on capitalism but had concluded that the two could probably in the end get along. Streeck's account of capitalism's drag on democracy was much starker. The historic compromise between liberal capitalism and democracy that had underpinned post-1945 Western success was broken, he believed. Capitalism had run out of ways to temper the social harms it caused. First it had tried to limit the damage by inflating wages (1970s) and then by borrowing to pay for health and welfare (1980s–90s). Unsustainable debt caused by slowing economic growth and rising social costs led governments to abandon their efforts and accept unremitting austerity (2000s–2010s). Streeck's story ignored variations among rich economies. It made debt-obsessed governments prisoners of economic necessity, whereas they were likelier prisoners of Hayekian economists. Most striking, however, was Streeck's economic nationalism, which was representative of a novel left-wing trend. Antiliberalism on the left was by tradition internationalist. Marxism had fought capitalism for ownership of the world, not the nation. Now that capitalism had won the world, Streeck looked for rescue to the nation. The postnational European Union offered none. The euro was in Streeck's eyes undemocratic, and he opposed German membership in the EU. Only the democratic nation, he believed, could win back power from globalized capital, and even there he was unsure. He sensed breakdown was imminent, although he left unclear whether democracy or capitalism would crack first. Streeck hesitated between saying that capitalism would destroy itself, opening the way to a truly democratic future, and saying that capitalism would crush democracy. He suggested the second outcome was likelier, as democratic resistance, however needed, was probably vain.

Not everyone on the anti-liberal left was daunted by the capitalist behemoth or resigned to be crushed by its power. Like Corbyn in Britain and Sanders in the United States, Jean-Luc Mélenchon in France combined rousing stump speeches that stirred especially young crowds with policies that would have seemed timid to parties of the liberal left in the 1950s–60s. In *L'ère du peuple* (2014), Mélenchon wrote in simple, popular tones of free trade as a "fatal poison" and of a "financial oligarchy" that vetoed people's decisions. Fear of populism, he wrote, amounted to fear of the people, the new political actor of the times. France, he urged, should have a "Sixth Republic" established by a constituent assembly that would draft a new constitution with proportional representation, a welcome idea to bring minority voices into Parliament. Like Corbyn in Britain, Mélenchon offered the sketchiest ideas of how to govern or pay for proposals but promised a spirited presence on the political street.

Surges of popular discontent with liberal capitalism had always enthused the editors of *New Left Review*, but rarely for long. Anderson particularly kept a commanding eye on the intellectual heights where, as a latter-day Gramscian, he believed the true battle was to be fought, not in the street. There was no worse fault in a general, he grasped, than underestimating the enemy's forces. When the *New Left Review* relaunched itself at the millennium with a symbolic renumbering of Issue 239 as Issue One, Anderson wrote a fresh editorial prospectus, "Renewals" (2000), in which he acknowledged liberalism's dominance: "It is unlikely the balance of intellectual advantage will alter greatly before there is a change in the political correlation of forces. . . . Little short of a slump of inter-war proportions looks capable of shaking the parameters of the current consensus." The intellectual left, by contrast, had suffered, he judged, the "uprooting of all the continuities of a socialist tradition" and, despite "impressive theoretical energy and productivity" had produced no "social sum," by which meant a credible vision of an achievable alternative to liberal democratic society. Anderson, nevertheless, voiced a stalwart faith that something would turn up.

Soon after, Anderson wrote a rueful survey of the political scene in France, "Dégringolade" (2004). In elegiac vein he lamented the absence of ambitious post-1945 French thinkers belonging to a "rejectionist" left, which his magazine had done much to introduce to English-speaking readers. Grand, explain-everything narratives had fallen out of fashion in France by the 1970s–80s. Thinkers had rediscovered French liberalism, and old battle lines separating a Marxist-dominated left and a rigidly establishment right dissolved. Anderson's picture of what had followed in the next decades presented a thinned out, consensual, and uncritical landscape, for which the discussion of political ideas on television appeared to share undue blame. Others less regretful for the past saw a ferment of voices stretching from the unreconciled far left to the thoughtful center-right, a picture of vitality in France well drawn by Emile Chabal's "Intellectuals and the Crisis of Democracy" (2017).

Without winning the street, liberalism in France long ago won the heights in terms of ideas. The word "liberal" remained for many a term of abuse, synonymous with unchecked capitalism at its most corrosive. Liberalism itself, the practice of politics that France bar Vichy had pursued since the late nineteenth century, was now openly embraced and avowed. Liberal magazines such as *Commentaire, Débat*, and *Pouvoirs* displaced Marxist publications of one variant or another as the authoritative and informed voice of progress, although there remained antiliberal redoubts, for example, the weekly *Le Monde diplomatique*. Pierre Rosanvallon, a center-left historian of liberalism and democracy and animator of the discussion group *La République des idées*, exemplified the change of climate. His *Society of Equals* (2011, 2013) traced the rise and fall of democratic equality from the late eighteenth-century revolutions to industrial capitalism's recreation of inequality, democratic liberalism's twentieth-century rediscovery of equality, and equality's later retreat, with which liberal democracy in the 2010s was struggling. After the election of Macron, to whom Rosanvallon gave guarded welcome, he told *Le Monde* that France's choice was no longer liberalism or antiliberalism, but which kind of liberalism to pursue. The choice, Rosanvallon in effect suggested, was between social-minded liberalism and market-minded liberalism.

From that rapid overview of a mist-filled landscape, a lesson to end with is that intellectual liberals had reasons for hope and reasons for despair, but that neither should detain them long. What mattered was not the liberal mood but how liberals understood and defended liberal democracy. Liberals, after all, had always cycled between hope and de-

spair. Such thoughts underlay the political historian David Runciman's
*The Confidence Trap: A History of Democracy in Crisis from World War I to
the Present* (2013). It offered a historical parallel to the list of intellectual
complaints about liberalism at the beginning of this chapter. Using "democracy" as a shorthand for liberal democracy and limiting his study to
Britain and the United States, Runciman looked back at seven critical
episodes when confidence in liberal democracy was badly shaken: unforeseen war (1914), unexpected slump (1933), threats to postwar Europe (1947), possible annihilation in the Cuba missile crisis (1962), economic stagflation (1974), short-lived triumphalism (1989) and financial
meltdown (2008). Liberal democracy had come through, although Runciman accepted, that it was too early to say how far it had come through
the last crisis.

The lesson of history for liberals, Runciman suggested, was not to rely
on history. Old problems recurred, but seldom in the same form. Unlike
people in autocracies, which were "fatalistic" and inflexible, those in democracies expected the future to be different. Adapting to ceaseless
change had given liberal democracies a resourcefulness at muddling
through. Runciman acknowledged that inequality, fiscal overstretch,
climate change, and China's power were testing liberal democracies
hard. He did not think liberal democracy was bound to muddle through
or bound not to muddle through. As a historian, he did not believe in
iron laws of history. He did not give in to the lure of mechanism to explain political change. If liberal democracy did come through, however,
it would be in ways that took people by surprise. Runciman's point was
a strong point, but it could be put in a way that stressed more what liberals did than what surprised or happened to them. If liberal democracy
came through, it would be because of what democratic liberals did or
failed to do in its defense. In pursuing their ideals and getting out of the
holes they had dug for themselves, liberals when being true to themselves had always accepted the primacy of politics.

15

The Primacy of Politics

Amid social and economic upheavals on a scale not previously imagined, the first liberal thinkers and politicians in 1830–80 laid the groundwork of a new political order guided by distinctive aims and ideals, which together formed a flexible and appealing quadrilateral. Its four elements, referred to in shorthand throughout this book, were recognition of conflict, resistance to power, belief in progress, and civic respect for everyone.

As described in Part One, the first liberals grasped that moral and material conflict was now inevitable in society. Rather than trying to contain conflict with unchecked power, they sought on the contrary durable ways to resist power's monopolizing grasp, be it the power of the state, money or majority opinion. As believers in progress, the first liberals looked instead to human betterment for a surer source of social peace. Conflict, they hoped, could be tamed as competition and put to fruitful use in argument, experiment, and exchange. They trusted, lastly, that the liberating endorsement of individuality, innovation, and cultural variety could be combined with a common civility as well as with enforceable standards of how people should be treated and, above all, not mistreated.

In 1880–1945, as described in Part Two, liberals faced the challenge of extending those aims and ideals democratically to everyone, whoever they were, beyond the interested circles of educated, propertied men from which liberalism had sprung. In 1945–89, as described in Part Three, chastened liberals built and defended a new liberal democratic order, mindful of twentieth-century calamities of war, political breakdown and worse that liberalism had either brought on the world or failed in its irresolution to prevent. Liberal thinkers offered intellectual vindication of post-war achievements in which liberals could take justified pride. As the previous chapters of Part Four have shown, liberal hopes soon darkened, however, and in the first decades of the twenty-first century liberal confidence drained away. Liberals began to worry whether, far from marking a new liberal age, the year 1989 had not marked the dawn of an unwelcome postliberalism. They worried that liberal democratic success in 1945–89 had been an improbable, unrepeatable interlude between historically more typical periods of disruption, inequality, and war.

The lure of prophecy should be resisted. It would be nice to be able to tell ourselves what lies ahead. It would be nice to be able to delve, for example, into human prehistory, into the evolutionary roots of our moral responses, into the global geography of shifting demographics or discordant political cultures and find there laws or trends that would show us what was in store for liberal democracy. It would be nice if the hydraulic principles of self-stabilizing markets or the iron laws of capitalist decline could tell us if liberal democracy was or was not going to be able to pay its bills. It would be nice, that is, to give in to the lure of mechanism and take politics for a matter of necessities rather than a tiresomely endless argument and negotiation governed by contingency and choice in often unforeseen circumstances.

It would be nice, but not liberal. For just as liberals insist on pursuing their aims together even as those aims conflict, so liberals insist on taking politics for what it is and not turning it into something else. Liberals believe in the primacy of politics. To them, politics is a workaday human practice where argument, bargaining, and compromise ought to prevail. When insisting on the primacy of politics, liberals recognize the force of contingency and choice in the public sphere. Appealing to mechanisms and to prophecies that call on mechanism is a way to deny the primacy of politics. What happens next with liberal democracy will depend on many things, some unforeseen, some in nobody's control, but whatever the circumstances, it will depend also on how well liberals understand and defend liberal democracy.

In asking themselves what they stand for and what is going wrong, liberals have behind them arguments, traditions, and experience. Over the past two centuries liberals have learned, or ought to have learned, several lessons. As the history of liberalism in these pages has suggested, universal education and cultural progress do not ensure human reasonableness. Liberal zeal to enlighten and improve can harden into an urge to control and dominate. Modern economies do not reliably stabilize by themselves. International trade and financial exchange do not guarantee peace. Runaway capitalism and imperial domineering do not, as hostile critics claim, constitute liberalism, but they are habitual vices of its virtues, to be acknowledged and fought against. Early twentieth-century liberals learned to their shock that liberalism's peaceful order could slide back into war and barbarism on a scale that the very successes of liberal capitalism had done much to make possible. Early twenty-first century liberals learned that liberal democracy was neither self-sustaining nor spreading happily across the globe. If those lessons were to be put into one lesson, it was that liberal democracy did not look after itself but had to be defended and kept in repair.

One obvious thing is for shaken liberals to steady their intellectual nerve. The first chapters of this fourth part dwelt in detail on a daunting list of anxieties and alarms: political discredit, economic unsustainability, geopolitical loneliness, and the inspirational disadvantage of liberal ideals when set against the stronger pull of nationhood or group identity. The chapter on intellectual disaffection listed a small lexicon of antiliberal complaints and liberal self-criticisms. They ranged from sweeping and dismissable complaints, through the pointed but answerable to the pointed and not yet answerable kind.

The sweeping but dismissable criticisms were the nuclear sort aiming at obliteration in a first strike. They are worth briefly recalling not because they are effective but because they are widely made. Their common tactic is to bundle every difficulty with liberalism into one and declare the liberal project not just flawed but hopeless. Two such sweeping criticisms have stood out. One was programmatic incoherence, the other a false picture of people and society.

Liberalism was incoherent, it was charged, in that its aims and ideals were not jointly meetable. Liberalism offered social progress, restraints on power, and civic respect for people. But resources, including time, were limited. You could have more social progress in the form say of super-rapid economic growth. You could have more restraint on power in the form of local rights and popular consent. You could not have both at the same time. Commitment to unachievable goals made liberals into sincere Utopians or manipulative hypocrites.

Liberals could answer that the complaint of conflicting goals was not serious or not unique to liberalism. Everyone had conflicting goals, even when choosing to pursue one at the expense of others. Politics, like life, made conflicting demands. Politics asked attention to a variety of tasks. Liberalism was characteristic in accepting all the tasks. It did not sacrifice one to others at the outset or rank them in advance as more or less urgent in order to make unavoidable hard choices look simpler. Liberals could drop one task to make others easier to reach: say, more restraint on power and more civic respect for people at the cost of slower progress or quelling conflict and ensuring order by giving free rein to state power. Dropping a conflicting aim in that way, however, would be dropping liberalism. Aiming to meet several conflicting demands in politics made liberalism not only distinctive. It made liberalism attractive.

A second sweeping complaint was that liberalism's picture of people and society was inept. It had no credible philosophical anthropology or political sociology. Liberals, in simple terms, were clueless about their fellow humans. The charge took several forms. Philosophically, it was complained, liberalism was individualist in its picture of people, and individualism was false. However, as the chapter on civic respect, toleration, and "the individual" argued, individualism on inspection was a congeries of discordant beliefs, either inessential for political liberalism or if essential—moral concern for people one by one, for example—not peculiar to liberalism.

As for the liberal picture of society, it was complained that liberals relied on an idealized citizen that had never existed. The same may be said of every political outlook, but it was also unclear which type of over-idealized citizen liberalism was wrong to rely on. Was it the power-leery, civic republican that preliberal sixteenth- and seventeenth-century thinkers had celebrated, Kant's dutiful universalist, Mill's experimenter in living or Schumpeter's self-interested, rational calculator? Tying liberalism to any one of those stereotypes would deny liberalism its breadth. Tying liberalism to them all could be seen as a strength, namely having in hand a diversified portfolio of many ideal-citizen types.

Historically, it was complained that liberalism was anachronistic. Liberalism had worked in the nineteenth century, it was claimed, because its social virtues of responsibility and independence suited a self-directed, strong-minded citizenry. It could not work in the fluid, biddable citizenry of mass society. As Part One of this book amply showed, there was no socially typical nineteenth-century liberal. Liberals came as factory owner-managers and factory workers; as landowners and freed slaves; as bankers, brokers, newspaper editors, professors, and clerics; and as campaigners against slavery and colonialism, for free trade, women's rights, suffrage extension, or world peace. Some liberals were several of those things at the same time. Humboldt's belief in the growth of human capacities and Mill's insistence on the protection of individuality were not prisoners of a class or time. Contrary to caricature, liberalism was an enduring practice of politics in which people of various social types with a normal range of diverse personal attitudes and temperaments engaged. It was not a neatly encapsulable set of off-the-rack opinions, a final extra that could be added to a putative social type like a top hat.

On the other side of the contrast, the post–nineteenth century citizen supposedly ill-adapted to liberalism's stiff social demands was hard to get into view. He or she was pictured alternately as robbed by mass society of independent will and purpose or as locked away in their own lives, socially irresponsible and disengaged. The typical modern citizen was so weak as to be crushed by society or so detached as to disband society. The more artful theories of liberalism's social ineptness insisted that what appeared to be two types of flawed modern citizen were in fact one. Self-absorption, on such view, was really a loss of self, for a true sense of self could be found only by engagement in society.

Such criticisms failed to allow for what people in the variety of their inclinations and temperament were really like. It was, besides, rarely clear what implied standard of civic self-possession and social engagement the modern citizen failed. The complaint of retreat into privacy and withdrawal from community had been made against liberal modernity since the early nineteenth century, yet liberalism had survived. The flash mob, online fund-raising and presidential tweeting were reminders that new forms of political engagement emerge as others die out. Most people pay politics little attention most of the time, although they are capable of suddenly paying it a lot.

The greatest weakness with sociological critiques of liberalism was to confuse political consent with political engagement. These critiques left unclear how many active, engaged citizens a healthy liberal democracy needed for durable success. To have lasting legitimacy, liberalism required consent. It did not require that there be a mass, let alone a majority, of active, engaged liberals. At any moment, the practitioners of politics, that is its politicians, government officials, donors, activists, and volunteers are always a small minority. For its institutions to be kept in repair and its flaws fought against, liberal democracy needed a vigorous minority of active liberals and reliable majorities of passive support. It did not need more, although asking for either was already asking a lot.

Less sweeping and more pointed but still answerable were charges from the antiliberal left and antiliberal right. The antiliberal left took liberalism for hypocritical. Liberalism professed to offer equal respect and the inclusion of all, but in fact licensed and encouraged the creation of inequality because it depended on capitalism, and capitalism depended on creating inequality and exclusion. Honest liberals could agree that as unwanted by-products of fruitful prosperity, capitalism did create inequality and exclusion. But they could add, against the antiliberal left, that liberalism devised political means to temper capitalism, redress inequality, and reduce exclusion.

For the anti-liberal right, liberalism's promise of progress was empty. In terms of material progress, liberalism had failed to lessen poverty and material inequity despite a century of trying. Poverty in rich societies remained and was in places getting worse. Liberal welfare, besides, undermined the family, weakened responsibility, and generally made life for poor people worse. Libertarians liked such claims, for they did not believe anyone should be made to assist the poor as liberal taxation required. Traditional conservatives liked such claims either because they thought the poor should buck up and not fall back on handouts or because they disbelieved in progress generally and accepted that the poor were always with us. Both those two families of the modern right liked such claims because they promised less social spending and a continuation of low taxes. Liberals had answers to them both, rehearsed at several points in this book. Most so-called welfare was not a handout but obligatory insurance that had improved lives. Good policies had historically reduced poverty. Where poverty was rising again, it was due more to low wages and job insecurity than to growth-diminishing taxes and morally corrosive welfare.

As for cultural progress, antiliberal conservatives complained that liberal permissiveness and contempt for standards were in fact sapping cultural and intellectual life. Honest liberals could here again agree that an open, liberal society throws up severe cultural problems. Free speech is often vulgar, hateful, or irresponsible. Encouraging the school and university young to grow up and take responsibility for themselves makes them hard to teach when they think themselves grown-up and responsible before they are. In a diverse culture of wide choice, common pursuits are often lost to view, the canon forgotten, and great institutions that have grown over time left to neglect, traduced by managerialism, and financially strangled.

The conservative mistake was to run all cultural problems into one lump of civilizational trouble. Keeping in repair and out of the hands of special interests the working elements of a shared culture—schools, universities, the media, the arts, intellectual life, pure research, a nation's "places of memory"—was not one task, but many tasks. None was ever over and each needed paying for. All involved conflict and politics for which there were few if any simple, partisan answers. The conservative cultural critique of liberalism was as old as Chateaubriand and Coleridge. For all its elegiac charm, the critique was never politically candid. Conservatives tended to write of culture as a mysteriously free bestowal or inheritance that liberals thoughtlessly squandered. A culture, however, is not an heirloom but a work in progress. Like liberal democracy, it must be sustained and kept in repair. The conservative cultural critique of political liberalism underplays the cost, work and steady resistance to interests and their managing agents that the upkeep of a varied culture and rich intellectual life demands.

Pointed and not yet answerable complaints were felt by liberals themselves. Running through the preceding five chapters was concern for liberal democracy's sustainability. Liberals worried with reason about how the liberal and the democratic elements might hold together. Liberalism for a few, the undemocratic or predemocratic kind, was comparatively easy to sustain. Liberalism for all, the democratic kind, was always going to be difficult.

When going well, liberal democracy relies on politics and government to keep its two elements, liberalism and democracy, together. When liberal democracy is going badly, politics and government become captured by the interests of a few. If liberal democracy is to be repaired, a first task is not less government but better government. Polling surveys show a collapse in public trust in government, which is unsurprising after half a century in which governments have been cut, people have been told that government is not the solution but the problem, and clever young people have chosen almost any career but government service.

Liberal democracy will not be shored up unless authority and prestige is restored to liberal government, a large task with many elements. Liberals, for one, need to be clearer and tougher about the respective duties of citizens and government. Just as they should spurn the libertarian fantasy of no government, so they should fight the populist perversion of government as the voice of the people. In representative democracies, citizens choose governments and governments rule citizens.

In practical terms, a requirement of fiscal equity ought to be acknowledged. People get the government and public goods they pay for. Liberals fall too easily into the trap of having to justify taxation as if it can be treated as a presumptive exaction in isolation from the public provision of schools, hospitals, roads, courts, and social order. If, on the other hand, entitlements grow without taxes keeping pace, people expect too much from government for too little. Candid liberals should admit that a fairer society with strong public provision requires higher taxes. Candid conservatives should admit that if taxes are to remain low, society must be less fair and public provision more beggarly.

No slogan has done more damage to society than "Government is the problem." When people now take liberalism for a small-government doctrine, liberals themselves share the blame. By focusing too long on undue state power (1970s–2010s), a dogmatic, free-market liberalism contributed to the political challenges liberal democracy now faces in the overconcentration of wealth and unanchored popular distrust of government.

It is now widely agreed among liberals of the center-right and center-left that economic inequality is in danger of pulling liberal democracies apart. As a shorthand, that is correct, but open to misunderstanding. The main economic difficulty is not inequality as such and the trouble with inequality is not purely economic. As an earlier chapter in Part Four stressed, the underlying economic difficulty is that growth is too slow, wages too low, and the precariousness of work higher than official unemployment figures suggest. The underlying social and political difficulty is an entrenchment of privilege and indifference to its exclusions, two ills of which inequalities in income and wealth are symptoms.

In the liberal vision, the powers of a nation—state, wealth and society—ought to be balanced against each other to people's advantage. It was not enough that no single interest should be permitted to capture any one of the three powers and exercise them in their own interest. The three powers should in addition not be allowed to ally together for the benefit of a few. They should not, that is, be permitted to create privileged castes with the triple protection of untroubled wealth, social sanction, and political indulgence. The starkest failing of liberal democracy in the past 30–40 years is to have allowed a running together of economic, social, and political power in the service of a few, not the many.

The first liberals dreamed of an unobstructed social order providing ladders to social heights that anybody might climb. In time, that ideal became known as equality of opportunity or meritocracy. It was in ways an admirable ideal, but not an ideal that could be reached and then set aside as a job done. It may be human when scrambling up the ladder of opportunity to kick it away to stop others below from following you up. The job of politics and government is to put ladders back.

Since the 1970s, ladders have been kicked away and not replaced. A concentration of wealth, a rise of private and commercial values at the expense of public or social values, and an erosion of governmental capacity have encouraged a clustering of unchallenged privilege among a favored few who enjoy undue command of the resources that make lives go well: not just money but education, ease, connections, and prestige. If the slogan figure of one percent is apt, the privileged of the rich world number around 10 million. They are too many to be a clique and too varied in location and attitude to be an establishment or even an elite, let alone a liberal elite or a cosmopolitan elite. Even when offered as social description rather than partisan invective, such labelling misses the point. Talk of elites overpersonalizes and mislocates the problem. The creation of unacceptable privilege comes not from greed or egoistical indifference but from political failure. Liberals ought to stand for a separation of state, economic, and social power. Instead, they have permitted a growing alliance among the three powers to protect not the many, but a lucky few.

The story of liberalism told in these pages is open to two obvious objections. One objection is that it is not a story of liberalism. For liberalism is all about liberty or equality, which have barely appeared in this book's pages. It may be answered that liberty and equality in their manifold variety have appeared throughout, but not under those names.

Faced by the interferences and exactions of rulers, landowners, and priests, reliable protection from power, even authorized power, was what people, immemorially, have spoken of as liberty. Such protection for everyone was what, immemorially, they have spoken of as equality. The first liberals, it was said at the outset, were hoping for ethical order without appeal to divine authority, established tradition, or parochial custom. Drawing on the experience of toleration, they were hoping, that is, for acceptance of moral liberty. They hoped for social order without legally fixed hierarchies or privileged classes. They were hoping, that is, for legal equality. They were hoping for an economic order free of crown or state interference, monopoly privileges, local obstacles to national markets, or international tariffs blocking trade among nations. They were hoping, that is, for economic liberty. They were hoping for a political order without absolute authorities or undivided powers that citizens might understand, accept, and to a degree control. They were hoping, that is, for political liberty. When pressed democratically, liberalism extended those hopes so that nobody was to be excluded from what liberal hopes promised. Democratic liberals, that is, were aiming for an equality of moral, economic, and political liberty. As all those terms were contested and none were transparent in meaning, it seemed simpler to tell the story in unfamiliar but more straightforward terms.

The other obvious objection is that the story told here is not a story of liberalism but of liberalisms. It is a story of distinct traditions each given the label "liberal" but only loosely and confusingly related to each other if at all. When faced with the word "liberal," there are no decisive semantic facts that will settle whether there is one liberalism or many. There are no agreed conceptual facts as to whether "liberalism" names one practice or tradition or many practices or traditions. There is, however, a persuasive historical answer to the one-liberalism-or-many-liberalisms question.

Over the past century, four distinct Western countries serving here as an exemplary but non-exclusive core—France, Britain, Germany, and the United States—converged on a shared practice of politics that is uncontroversially recognized in its continuity and distinctiveness. That is true especially now that the health and survival of the practice is the object of such widespread concern, among both liberalism's friends and enemies. Calling the practice in question "democratic liberalism" is more descriptive, but "liberal democracy" closer follows ordinary usage. Either way, what matters is the thing named, not the name. If it is insisted that what liberalism is remains obscure, it can be answered that the wrong kind of clarity is being asked for or that clarity is sought in the wrong place—semantic or conceptual space rather than in history, where it can be found. Liberalism is what led to liberal democracy, a political practice that by historical standards is, or was, successful, even admirable, but is now at risk from misappreciation and neglect.

To defend and repair liberal democracy, liberals should keep in mind what it has achieved. Looking back in old age, the philosopher Karl Popper praised liberal democracy's successes in "The History of Our Time: An Optimist's View" (1986), a lecture in memory of the British social reformer and campaigner for child benefit in Britain, Eleanor Rathbone. His celebration merits citing for self-critical liberals to remember. Without ifs or buts and using "men" in the old-fashioned manner to mean men and women, Popper told his listeners: "At no other time, and nowhere else have men been more respected, as men, than in our society. Never before have their human rights, and their human dignity, been so respected, and never before have so many been ready to bring great sacrifices for others, especially for those less fortunate than themselves. I believe that these are facts."

There are other, less flattering facts about liberal democracy, including the warfare state, an imperial urge to teach and domineer, persistent inequalities, and crisis proneness, for example, which were highlighted throughout this book. In writing a life of liberalism that stressed its weaknesses and failings as well as its strengths, the aim was to be objective, not neutral. This book has presumed, not argued, that among known practices of politics that have actually been tried liberal democracy was the least flawed. The aim was not to write *Liberal Democracy: For or Against?* The aim was to see better what liberalism was, so as to be clearer about what was going wrong. In his *Notebooks*, the writer-doctor Anton Chekhov said of his fellow humans that they would get better only if made to see what they were like. *Liberalism: The Life of an Idea* was written with that advice in mind. If twenty-first century liberals can avoid aping their critics in piling all their difficulties into one insurmountable heap, if like earlier liberals they can rethink their aims of resistance, progress, and respect to suit new challenges, if they can find the political will to begin fixing even some of the many flaws in liberal democratic societies, then it may yet be too early to bury liberalism under a statue of hope.

WORKS CONSULTED

For this essay in political history and ideas I have relied on writings of liberal thinkers and politicians themselves as well as on interpretations and commentaries by many scholars and commentators. I am in their debt and thank them all. Except where quoted directly, I have not cited them in the text itself. Below is a list of works that I consulted for each chapter or section, including, at the start of this bibliography, some general works and reference sources. Book titles and publication names are in italics; article, speech, and pamphlet titles are in quotation marks. For changeable online sources, month and year of download are given. In the main text, for ease of reading, all titles are in English. Here non-English titles are in the original, with translation where relevant or available. To mark notable debts of interpretation, assessment, and argument I have singled out certain works at the head of sections, immediately after the writings or speeches of my principal liberals. There then follow other works that readers besides me may find helpful, arranged by date of first publication.

General works: Guido de Ruggiero, *Storia del liberalismo europeo* (1924); trans. Collingwood, *The History of European Liberalism* (1927); Harold Laski, *The Rise of European Liberalism* (1936); C. B. Macpherson, *The Political Theory of Possessive Individualism* (1962); Kenneth Minogue, *The Liberal Mind* (1963); Larry Siedentop, "Two Liberal Traditions," in *The Idea of Freedom* (1979), ed. Ryan; Rudolf Vierhaus, "Liberalismus," in *Geschichtliche Grundbegriffe, Vol. III* (1982), eds. Brunner, Conze, and Koselleck; Gerald Gaus, *The Modern Liberal Theory of Man* (1983); Steven Seidman, *Liberalism and the Origins of European Social Theory* (1983); Ronald J. Terchek, "The Fruits of Success and the Crisis of Liberalism," in *Liberals on Liberalism* (1986), ed. D'Amico; Jeremy Waldron, "Theoretical Foundations of Liberalism," *Philosophical Quarterly* (April 1987); Stephen Macedo, *Liberal Virtues* (1990); J. Q. Merquior, *Liberalism Old and New* (1991); Richard Bellamy, *Liberalism and Modern Society: An Historical Argument* (1992); Richard Bellamy and Martin Hollis, "Liberal Justice: Political and Metaphysical," *Philosophical Quarterly* (January 1995); Immanuel Wallerstein, *After Liberalism* (1995); Michael Freeden, *Ideologies and Political Theory* (1996); Ralf Dahrendorf, "Squaring the Circle: Prosperity, Civility and Liberty," in *Liberalism and Its Practice* (1999), eds. Avnon and Shalit; Jörn Leonhard, *Liberalismus* (2001); Jörn Leonhard, "Semantische Deplazierung und Entwertung: Deutsche Deutungen von 'liberal' und 'Liberalismus' nach 1850 in europäischen Vergleich," *Geschichte und Gesellschaft* (January–March 2003); Gaus, *Contemporary Theories of Liberalism* (2003); Freeden, "Twentieth-Century Liberal Thought: Development or Transformation?" in *Liberal Languages* (2005); *Histoire du libéralisme en Europe* (2006), eds. Nemo and Petitot; Susan James, "The Politics of Emotion: Liberalism and Cognitivism," in *Political Philosophy* (2006), ed. O'Hear; Cathérine Audard, *Qu'est-ce que le libéralisme?* (2009); Alan Ryan, *The Making of Modern Liberalism* (2012).

Anthologies and dictionaries: *The Liberal Tradition* (1956), eds. Bullock and Shock; *Western Liberalism: A History in Documents from Locke to Croce* (1978), eds. Bramsted and Melhuish; *Blackwell Encyclopedia of Political Thought* (1987), eds. Miller et al.; Simon Blackburn, *The Oxford Dictionary of Philosophy* (1994); *A Companion to Contemporary Political Philosophy* (1995), eds. Goodin and Pettit; *The Routledge Encyclopedia of Philosophy* (1998), ed. Craig, disc version *REP 1.0* (2001); *Liberalism, Critical Concepts in Political Theory: Vol. I, Ideas of Freedom, Vol. II, Rights, Property and Markets, Vol. III, Justice and Reason, Vol. IV, The Limits of Liberalism* (2002) (English-speaking journal articles 1950s–1990s), ed. Smith; Roger Scruton, *Dictionary of Political Thought* (3rd 2007); Ian Adams and R. W. Dyson, *Fifty Major Political Thinkers* (2007); *Freedom: A Philosophical Anthology* (2007), eds. Carter, Kramer, and Steiner; *Les Penseurs libéraux* (2012), eds. Laurent and Valentin; *Dictionnaire du libéralisme* (2012), ed. Laine.

Online sources: *Stanford Encyclopedia of Philosophy Online*; The Online Library of Liberty, a Project of the Liberty Fund; *German Historical Documents & Images* (*GHDI*), website of the German Historical Institute (Washington, D.C.); INSEE online database (France); *Social Trends* (2008–13), Office for National Statistics (Britain); *Destatis*, online database of Statistiches Bundesamt (Germany); *Statistical Abstract 2012*, Census Bureau (United States); OECD Data Lab (OECD statistics online); *American National Biography Online* (*ANB Online*); *Oxford Dictionary of National Biography Online* (*ODNB Online*).

Liberalism in France: Michel Chevalier, "Power and Liberty," in *Society, Manners and Politics in the United States* (1835, trans. 1839); Charles Renouvier, *Manuel républicain des droits de l'homme et du citoyen* (1848); Edouard Laboulaye, *Le parti libéral: son progrès et son avenir* (1863); Emile Ollivier, *L'empire libérale* (1895–1907); Emile Faguet, *Le libéralisme* (1903); André Siegfried, *Tableau des partis en France* (1930); René Rémond, *Les droites en France*

(1954; 3rd 1982); Raymond Aron, *Dix-huits leçons sur la société industrielle* (1962); *Démocratie et Totalitarianisme* (1965); *Trois essais sur l'âge industrielle* (1966); *Politics and Society in Contemporary France 1789–1971: A Documentary History* (1972), ed. Eric Cahm; Bertrand de Jouvenel, *Du pouvoir* (1972); Theodore Zeldin, *France 1848–1945: Vols. I & II, Ambition and Love (1973); Vol. III, Politics and Anger* (1973); *Vol. IV Intellect and Pride* (1977); Joseph Amato, *Mounier and Maritain: A French Catholic Understanding of the Modern World* (1975); "Etat libéral et libéralisation économique," Adeline Daumard in *Histoire économique et sociale de la France III/2* (1976), eds. Braudel and Labrousse; William Logue, *From Philosophy to Sociology: The Evolution of French Liberalism, 1870–1914* (1983); Louis Girard, *Les libéraux français: 1814–75* (1985); John Godfrey, *Capitalism at War: Industrial Policy and Bureaucracy in France, 1914–18* (1987); Vincent Wright, *The Government and Politics of France* (3rd 1989); Stephen Davies, "French Liberalism," in *A Dictionary of Conservative and Libertarian Thought* (1991), eds. Ashford and Davies; Rémond, *Notre Siècle, 1918–88* (1988) and "Liberal Models in France 1900–1930," in *Liberty/ Liberté: The American and French Experiences* (1991), eds. Klaits and Haltzel; Jean Rivero, "The Jacobin and Liberal Traditions," and George Armstrong Kelly, "The Jacobin and Liberal Contributions," in *Liberty/Liberté*; Sudhir Hazareesingh, *Political Traditions of Modern France* (1994); Nicolas Roussellier, "Libéralisme," in *Dictionnaire historique de la vie politique française au XXème siècle* (1995), ed. Sirinelli; Jean-Claude Casanova, online interview, nonfiction.fr (June 2010); Iain Stewart, "Raymond Aron and the Roots of the French Liberal Renaissance," doctoral submission to Manchester University (2011); Jeremy Jennings, *Revolution and the Republic: A History of Political Thought in France since the Eighteenth Century* (2011); Aurelian Craiutu, "Raymond Aron and the Tradition of Political Moderation in France"; Raf Geenens and Helena Rosenblatt, "French Liberalism, an Overlooked Tradition?"; William Logue, "The 'Sociological Turn' in French Liberal Thought"; Cheryl B. Welch, " 'Anti-Benthamism': Utilitarianism and the French Liberal Tradition"; all in *French Liberalism from Montesquieu to the Present Day* (2012), eds. Geenens and Rosenblatt.

Liberalism in Britain: A. V. Dicey, *Lectures on the Relation between Law and Public Opinion in England in the Nineteenth Century* (1898); Elie Halévy, *La Formation du radicalisme philosophique* (1901–4); trans. Morris, *The Growth of Philosophic Radicalism* (1928); George Dangerfield, *The Strange Death of Liberal England* (1935); John Plamenatz, *The English Utilitarians* (1949); Crane Brinton, *English Political Thought in the 19th Century* (1949); Stephen Koss, *Asquith* (1976); John Dinwiddy, "The Classical Economists and the Utilitarians," in *Western Liberalism*, eds. Bramsted and Melhuish (1978); Koss, *The Rise* and Fall of the Political Press in Britain: Vol II, The Twentieth Century (1984); Peter Stansky, "The Strange Death of Liberal England: Fifty Years," Albion: A Quarterly Journal Concerned with British Studies (Winter 1985); Jonathan Clarke, English Society 1688–1832 (1985); David Cannadine, "The Passing of the Whigs," in The Decline and Fall of the British Aristocracy (1990); Stefan Collini, Public Moralists: Political Thought and Intellectual Life in Britain, 1850–1930 (1991); Jonathan Parry, The Rise and Fall of Liberal Government in Victorian Britain (1993); Martin Daunton, Progress and Poverty: An Economic and Social History of Britain 1700–1850 (1995); Conrad Russell, An Intelligent Person's Guide to Liberalism (1999); G. R. Searle, The Liberal Party: Triumph and Disintegration 1886–1929 (2001); G. R. Searle, A New England? Peace and War 1886–1918 (2004); Boyd Hilton, A Mad, Bad, Dangerous People? England 1783–1846 (2006); Parry, The Politics of Patriotism: English Liberalism, National Identity and Europe, 1830–86 (2006); Collini, Absent Minds: Intellectuals in Britain (2006); Steve Pincus, 1688: The First Modern Revolution (2009); Brian Harrison, Seeking a Role: The United Kingdom 1951–70 (2009) and Finding a Role? The United Kingdom 1970–90 (2011).

Liberalism in Germany: Paul von Pfizer, "Liberal, Liberalismus," in Staatslexikon (1840); John Hallowell, "The Decline of Liberalism," in Ethics (April 1942); Irene Collins, "Liberalism in 19th-Century Europe" and Franz Schnabel, "The Bismarck Problem," in European Political History 1815–70: Aspects of Liberalism (1966), ed. Black; Geoffrey Barraclough, "Mandarins and Nazis," New York Review of Books (NYRB) (October 19, 1972); Wilfried Fest, Dictionary of German History 1806–1945 (1978); James Sheehan, German Liberalism in the Nineteenth Century (1978); Gordon A. Craig, Germany 1866–1945 (1978); Thomas Nipperdey, Deutsche Geschichte, 1800–1866: Bürgerwelt und starker Staat (1983); trans. Nolan, Germany from Napoleon to Bismarck, 1800–1866 (1996); H. W. Koch, A Constitutional History of Germany (1984); E. L. Jones, German Liberalism and the Dissolution of the Weimar Party System, 1918–33 (1988); Jarausch and Jones, "German Liberalism Reconsidered"; Marion W. Gray, "From the Household Economy to 'Rational Agriculture': The Establishment of Liberal Ideals in German Agricultural Thought"; Geoffrey Eley, "Notable Politics, the Crisis of German Liberalism, and the Electoral Transition of the 1890s"; Jarausch, "The Decline of Liberal Professionalism"; Thomas Childers, "Languages of Liberalism"; all in In Search of a Liberal Germany (1990), eds. Jarausch and Jones; Lothar Gall et al., Bismarck: Preussen, Deutschland und Europa (1990), show catalog, German Historical Museum, Berlin; Mary Fulbrook, A Concise History of Germany (1990); Winkler, "Nationalismus, Nationalstaat und nationale Frage in Deutschland seit 1945," in Politik und Zeitgeschichte (September 1991); Stephen Davies, "German Liberalism," in A

Dictionary of Conservative and Libertarian Thought (1991), eds. Ashford and Davies; Peter Pulzer, "Political Ideology," in *Developments in German Politics* (1992), ed. Smith; Otto Dann, *Nation und Nationalismus in Deutschland 1770–1990* (1993); Richard Bessell, *Germany after the First World War* (1993); Horst Möller, "Bürgertum und bürgerlich-liberale Bewegung nach 1918," in *Historische Zeitschrift*, Sonderheft 17 (1997), and Introduction by Gall; David Blackbourn, *Germany 1780–1918: The Long Nineteenth Century* (1997); August Winkler, *Der lange Weg nach Westen* (2000); trans. Sager, *Germany: The Long Road West* (2006); *Liberalism, Anti-Semitism and Democracy: Essays in Honor of Peter Pulzer* (2001), eds. Tewes and Wright; John Zmirak, *Wilhelm Röpke* (2001); Jonathan Wright, *Gustav Stresemann: Weimar's Greatest Statesman* (2002); William Hagen, *Ordinary Prussians* (2002); Niall Ferguson, "Max Warburg and German Politics," in *Wilhelminism and Its Legacies* (2003), eds. Eley and Retallack; Gerd Habermann, "La 'mesure humaine' ou 'l'ordre naturel,' " in *Histoire du libéralisme en Europe* (2006), eds. Nemo and Petitot; Jonathan Steinberg, *Bismarck* (2011).

Liberalism in the United States: John Dewey, *Liberalism and Social Action* (1935); Richard Hofstadter, *The American Political Tradition* (1948); Arthur Schlesinger Jr., *The Vital Center* (1949); David Riesman, Nathan Glazer, and Reuel Denney, *The Lonely Crowd* (1950); Louis Hartz, *The Liberal Tradition in America* (1955); Arthur Ekirch, *The Decline of American Liberalism* (1955); C. Wright Mills, *The Power Elite* (1956); Bernard Crick, *The American Science of Politics* (1959); Seymour Martin Lipset, *Political Man* (1960); Daniel Bell, *The End of Ideology* (1960); Christopher Lasch, *The New Radicalism in America 1889–1963* (1965); Hofstadter, *The Progressive Historians* (1968); Robert Paul Wolff, *The Poverty of Liberalism* (1968); Barton J. Bernstein, "The Conservative Achievements of Liberal Reform," in *Towards a New Past: Dissenting Essays in American History* (1968), ed. Bernstein; Theodore Lowi, *The End of Liberalism* (1969); Gordon S. Wood, *The Creation of the American Republic* (1969); John Dunn, "The Politics of Locke in England and America in the Eighteenth Century," in *John Locke: Problems and Perspectives* (1969), ed. Yolton; Charles Reich, *The Greening of America* (1970); J.G.A. Pocock, "The Americanization of Virtue," chap. 15 of *The Machiavellian Moment* (1975); Bell, *The Cultural Contradictions of Capitalism* (1976); Ann Douglas, *The Feminization of American Culture* (1977); Lasch, *The Culture of Narcissism* (1979); Daniel Walker Howe, *The Political Culture of the American Whigs* (1979); William Galston, "Defending Liberalism," *American Political Science Review* (September 1982); Steven Dworetz, *The Unvarnished Doctrine: Locke, Liberalism and the American Revolution* (1990); J. Isaac Kramnick, *Republicanism and Bourgeois Radicalism* (1990); Lasch, "The Fragility of Liberalism," *Salmagundi* (Fall 1991); *Debates on* *the Constitution I & II* (1993), ed. Bailyn; David Greenstone, *The Lincoln Persua-sion: Remaking American Liberalism* (1993); *A Companion to American Thought*, eds. Fox and Kloppenberg (1995); Howe, *The Making of the American Self* (1997); Robert Remini, "The Age of Jackson and Its Impact," in *The Liberal Persuasion* (1997), ed. Diggins; David Kennedy, *Freedom from Fear: The Ameri-can People in Depression and War, 1929–45* (1999); John Silber, "Procedure or Dogma: The Core of Liberalism," in *The Betrayal of Liberalism* (1999), eds. Kramer and Kimball; H. W. Brands, *The Strange Death of American Liberalism* (2001); James Hurtgen, *The Divided Mind of American Liberalism* (2002); Charles Noble, *The Collapse of Liberalism* (2004); *American Speeches I & II* (2006), ed. Wilmer; Thomas Bender, *A Nation Among Nations: America's Place in World History* (2006); Paul Starr, *Freedom's Power: The True Force of Liberal-ism* (2007); Arthur Schlesinger Jr., *Journals 1952–2000* (2007); Alan Wolfe, *The Future of Liberalism* (2009); Norman Podhoretz, *Why Are Jews Liberals?* (2009).

Humboldt: Wilhelm von Humboldt, *Ideen zu einem Versuch, die Grenzen der Wirksamkeit des Staats zu bestimmen* (written 1791–92; pub. 1852); trans. Coulthard, *The Limits of State Action* (1969), rev. and ed. Burrow; Peter Berglar, *Wilhelm von Humboldt* (1970); Paul Sweet, *Wilhelm von Humboldt: A Biography I* (1978) and *II* (1980). Other works: Friedrich Meinecke, *Weltbürgertum und Nationalstaat* (1908); trans. Kimber, *Cosmopolitanism and the National State* (1970); Eduard Spranger, *Wilhelm von Humboldt und die Reform des Bildung-swesens* (1910); F. Schaffstein, *Wilhelm von Humboldt: Ein Lebensbild* (1952); E. V. Gulick, "The Final Coalition and the Congress of Vienna, 1813–15," in *New Cambridge Modern History IX* (1965); Nicola Abbagnano, "Humboldt," in *Ency-clopedia of Philosophy*, ed. Edwards (1967); Manfred Geier, "Die Brüder Hum-boldt," in *Deutsche Erinnerungsorte III* (2001), eds. François and Schulze; Det-mar Doering, "Wilhelm von Humboldt et les origines du libéralisme allemand," in *Histoire du libéralisme en Europe*, ed. Nemo and Petitot (2006); Charles Esdaile, *Napoleon's Wars: An International History 1803–15* (2007); Frederick Beiser, "Humboldt," in *REP 1.0*; Kurt Mueller-Vollmer, "Humboldt," in *SEP Online* (December 2010); Franz-Michael Konrad, *Wilhelm von Hum-boldt* (2010).

Constant: Benjamin Constant, "De la force du gouvernement actuel de la France et de la nécessité de s'y rallier" (1796); "Des réactions politiques" (1797); "Des effets de la terreur" (1797), all in *Des réactions politiques*, ed. Raynaud (1988); "De la perfectibilité de l'espèce humaine" (1805); "De L'esprit de conquête et de l'usurpation" (1814); "Principes de politique" (1815); "De la liberté des anciens comparée à celle des modernes" (1819); "Du développe-ment progressif des idées religieuses" (1826); all in *Ecrits Politiques* (1997), ed. Marcel Gauchet; *Adolphe* (1816); *Journaux Intimes*, eds. Roulin and Roth

(1952); Stephen Holmes, *Benjamin Constant and the Making of Modern Liberalism* (1984); Pierre Manent, "Benjamin Constant and the Liberalism of Opposition," in *Histoire intellectuelle du libéralisme* (1987); trans. Balinski, *An Intellectual History of Liberalism* (1994); *The Cambridge Companion to Constant* (2009), ed. Rosenblatt. Other works: Harold Nicolson, *Benjamin Constant* (1949); Gall, *Benjamin Constant: Seine Politische Ideenwelt und der deutsche Vormärz* (1963); Georges Poulet, *Benjamin Constant par lui-même* (1965); *Benjamin Constant (1767–1830), Une Vie au Service de la Liberté* (1980), show catalog, Lausanne; Kurt Kloocke, *Benjamin Constant: Une Biographie Intellectuelle* (1984); Etienne Hoffman, "Constant," in *Dictionnaire Napoléon* (1988), ed. Tulard; Tzvetan Todorov, "Freedom and Repression during the Restoration," in *A New History of French Literature* (1989), ed. Denis Hollier; Biancamaria Fontana, *Benjamin Constant and the Post-revolutionary Mind* (1991); Dennis Wood, *Benjamin Constant, A Biography* (1993); Maurice Cranston, review of Wood, *Times Literary Supplement* (*TLS*) (September 3, 1993).

Guizot: François Guizot, *Histoire des origines du gouvernement représentatif en Europe* (1821–22); trans. Scoble, *Origin of Representative Government in Europe (1861); Histoire de la civilisation en Europe* (1828); trans. Hazlitt, *The History of Civilization in Europe*, with Introduction by Siedentop (1997); Douglas Johnson, *Guizot: Aspects of French History 1787–1874* (1963); *Guizot: Historical Essays and Lectures* (1972), ed. Mellon; Laurent Theis, *François Guizot* (2008). Other works: Manent, "Guizot," in *Histoire intellectuelle du libéralisme* (1987); Pierre Rosanvallon, "Guizot," in *Dictionnaire Critique de la Révolution Française* (1989), eds. Furet and Ozouf.

Madison and Calhoun: James Madison, in *Federalist Papers* (1787–88); Letter to Jefferson (October 24, 1787), in *Debates on the Constitution, Vol. I* (1993), ed. Bailyn; John Calhoun, *Disquisition on Government* (posth.), ed. Lence, Library of Liberty Online; Senate speeches: "On Anti-slavery Petitions" (1837); "On Compromise Resolutions" (1850), in *American Speeches* (2006), ed. Ted Wilmer.

Chadwick and Cobden: Edwin Chadwick, *The Poor Law Commissioners' Report* (1834); Pamphlets (later as books): on enthusiasm for America and Commerce as "Grand Panacea," in *England, Ireland and America* (1835); Against Regulation of Trade in "Russia" (1836); Against Annexation of Burma and Britain's Culpability for "Imperial Crimes" in "How Wars Are Got Up in India" (1853); Against British Part in Ottoman-Russian Conflict and "Don Quixotes of the World" (1854); Campaigning Speeches: Free Trade as Fair to Laborers (February 8, 1844); Free Trade versus Landed Interest (July 3, 1844); Free Trade as Moral Principle and "I Have a Dream" (January 15, 1846); House of Commons Speeches: Against Armaments (June 12, 1849); On Liberal

Economic Doctrines, Nonintervention, Reform (August 1862); In Support of North in American Civil War and Against British Empire in India (November 24, 1863); Richard Cobden, *Letter to His Brother from Prussia* (September 11, 1838) in *Richard Cobden's German Diaries* (2007), ed. R. J. Davis; John Morley, *Life of Cobden* (1879). Antony Brundage, *England's "Prussian Minister": Edwin Chadwick and the Politics of Government Growth, 1832–54* (1988); Peter Mandler, "Chadwick, Sir Edwin," *ODNB Online* (December 2010); Myles Taylor, "Cobden, Richard," *ODNB Online*. Other works: Frank Trentmann, *Free Trade Nation: Commerce, Consumption and Civil Society in Modern Britain* (2008); Jonathan Parry, review of *Letters of Richard Cobden*, *TLS* (December 10, 2010).

Tocqueville and Schulze-Delitzsch: Tocqueville, *De la Démocratie en Amérique* (1835 and 1840); *Souvenirs* (1850), ed. Monnier (1942); *L'Ancien Régime et la Révolution* (1858); Hugh Brogan, *Alexis de Tocqueville: Prophet of Democracy in an Age of Revolution* (2006). Other works: Alexander Herzen, *My Past and Thoughts* (1854–66); trans. Garnett, rev. Higgins (1968); André Jardin, *Aléxis de Tocqueville: 1805–1859* (1984); Alan S. Kahan, *Aristocratic Liberalism: The Social and Political Thought of Jacob Burckhardt, John Stuart Mill and Alexis de Tocqueville* (1992).

"Schulze-Delitzsch," in *Dictionary of German Biography* (2001), eds. Killy and Vierhaus; Ulrike Laufer, "Schulze-Delitzsch," in *Gründerzeit 1848–71: Industrie und Lebensträume zwischen Vormärz und Kaiserreich* (2008), show catalog, German Historical Museum, Berlin. Other works: Léon Walras, *Les associations populaires de consommation, de production et de crédit* (1865); James Sheehan, *German Liberalism in the 19th Century* (1978) and *German History 1770–1866* (1989); R. J. Bazillion, "Liberalism, Modernization, and the Social Question in the Kingdom of Saxony, 1830–90," in *In Search of a Liberal Germany* (1990), eds. Jarausch and Jones; Timothy W. Guinnane, "A 'Friend and Advisor': External Auditing and Confidence in Germany's Credit Cooperatives, 1889–1914," *Business History Review* 77 (2003).

Smiles and Channing: Samuel Smiles, *Self-Help* (1859); *Thrift* (1875); H.G.C. Mathew, "Smiles, Samuel," *ODNB Online* (February 2013). William Ellery Channing, "Self-Culture" (1838); Daniel Walker Howe, "Channing, William Ellery," *ANB Online* (February 2013). Other works: Herbert Wallace Schneider, "Intellectual Background of William Ellery Channing," *Church History* (March 1938); Sydney E. Ahlstrom, *A Religious History of the American People* (1975); Howe, *The Making of the American Self* (1997).

Spencer: *The Proper Sphere of Government* (1843), in *Spencer: Political Writings* (1994), ed. Offer; *Social Statics* (1851); *The Man Against the State* (1884) in Offer; *"Justice," Part IV of Principles of Ethics* (1891); *An Autobiography* (1904); David Miller, *Social Justice* (1976); José Harris, "Spencer, Herbert,"

ODNB Online (May 2012). Other works: Henry Sidgwick, "The Theory of Evolution in Its Application to Practice," *Mind* (January 1876); "Mr Spencer's Ethical System," *Mind* (April 1880); F. W. Maitland, "Mr Herbert Spencer's Theory of Society, I & II," *Mind* (July and October 1883); D. G. Ritchie, "The State v. Mr Herbert Spencer," LSE Pamphlet (1886); Hillel Steiner, "Land, Liberty and the Early Herbert Spencer," *History of Political Thought* 3 (1982); Tim Gray, "Herbert Spencer's Liberalism," in *Victorian Liberalism* (1990), ed. Bellamy; James Meadowcroft, *Conceptualising the State: Innovation and Dispute in British Political Thought 1880–1914* (1995); Tim Gray, "Herbert Spencer," in *REP 1.0*; Mark Francis, *Herbert Spencer and the Invention of Modern Life* (2007); Steven Shapin, "Man with a Plan: Herbert Spencer's Theory of Everything," *New Yorker* (August 13, 2007); Jonathan Rée, "How to Be Happy," *TLS* (November 30, 2007), both reviews of Francis.

J. S. Mill: *Principles of Political Economy* (1848; and later editions); *On Liberty* (1859); *Utilitarianism* (1861); *Representative Government* (1861); *The Subjection of Women* (1869); *Autobiography* (1873); all in the Toronto Edition of *Collected Works of John Stuart Mill* (1963–91) in Library of Liberty Online; *Letters of John Stuart Mill* (1910), ed. Eliot; Michael St. John Packe, *Life of J. S. Mill* (1954); John Gray, Introduction to *John Stuart Mill: On Liberty and Other Essays* (1991); Richard Wollheim, "J.S. Mill and Isaiah Berlin," in *J. S. Mill "On Liberty" in Focus* (1991), eds. Gray and Smith; Roger Crisp, *Mill on Utilitarianism* (1997). Other works: James Fitzjames Stephen, *Liberty, Equality, Fraternity* (1873); John Skorupski, "J.S. Mill," in *REP 1.0*; William Stafford, *J.S. Mill* (1998); Alan Ryan, Introduction to *J.S. Mill's Encounter with India* (1999), eds. Moir, Peers, and Zastoupil; Ten Chin Liew, *Was Mill a Liberal?* (2004); David Weinstein, "Interpreting Mill," in *J.S. Mill and the Art of Life* (2011), eds. Eggleston, Miller, and Weinstein; Agnar Sandmo, "Consolidation and Innovation: John Stuart Mill," in *Economics Evolving* (2011); José Harris, "Mill, John Stuart," *ODNB Online* (March 2012).

Lincoln: Richard Hofstadter, "Lincoln," in *The American Political Tradition* (1948); James McPherson, *Battle Cry of Freedom: The Civil War Era* (1988); Eric Foner, *Reconstruction* (1988); *Speeches and Writings, 1832–58 & 1859–65* (1989), ed. Fehrenbacher; David Donald, *Lincoln* (1995); *Our Lincoln: New Perspectives on Lincoln and His World* (2008), ed. Foner.

Laboulaye and Richter: Edouard Laboulaye, *Le parti libéral: son progrès et son avenir* (1863); Rosenblatt, "On the Need for a Protestant Reformation: Constant, Sismondi, Guizot and Laboulaye," in *French Liberalism from Montesquieu to the Present Day* (2012), eds. Geenens and Rosenblatt. Eugen Richter, *Sozialdemokratischen Zukunftsbilder, frei nach Bebel* (1891); trans. Wright, *Pictures of a Socialistic Future* (1907), in Library of Liberty Online; Ina Susanne

Lorenz, *Der entschiedene Liberalismus in wilhelminischer Zeit 1871 bis 1906* (1981), *Historische Studien, Heft 433*; Theodore Hamerow, review of Lorenz, *Journal of Modern History* (September 1983).

Gladstone: David Bebbington, "The Nature of Gladstonian Liberalism," in *The Mind of Gladstone* (2004); H. G. C. Mathew, "Gladstone, William Ewart," in *ODNB Online* (December 2010). Other works: Bullock and Shock, Introduction to *The Liberal Tradition* (1956); *Gladstone Diaries V, 1855–60 (1978)*, ed. Mathew; Gerhard Joseph, "The Homeric Competitions of Tennyson and Gladstone," *Browning Institute Studies* 10 (1982); Andrew Adonis, "Byzantium and Liverpool: Marx's Critique of Gladstone—and Gladstone's Refutation by Example," *TLS* (February 9, 1996); Hoppen, *The Mid-Victorian Generation, 1848–1886* (1998).

Civic respect, individuals, and individualism: Steven Lukes, *Individualism* (1973); Colin Bird, *The Myth of Liberal Individualism* (1999). Other works: William Blackstone, "On the Nature of Laws in General," *Commentaries on the Laws of England* (1753); Bentham, "Attacks upon Security," in *Principles of the Civil Code* (post. 1843), ed. Bowring; Henry Sidgwick, *Elements of Politics* (1891); Zeldin, "Individualism and the Emotions," in *France 1848–1945: Intellect and Pride* (1977); Jon Elster, "Marxisme et individualisme méthodologique," in *Sur l'individualisme* (1986), eds. Léca and Birnbaum; Philip Pettit, *The Common Mind* (1993); Roy Porter, *Rewriting the Self* (1997); Lars Udehn, "The Changing Face of Methodological Individualism," *Annual Review of Sociology* 28 (2002); Carol Rovane, "Why Do Individuals Matter?," *Daedalus*, "On Identity" (Fall 2006); "Law of Persons: Family and Other Relationships," pt. 4 of *The Oxford History of the Laws of England XIII 1820–1914: Fields of Development*, eds. Cornish et al. (2010); Marion Smiley, "Collective Responsibility," in *SEP Online* (February 2010); Joseph Heath "Methodological Individualism," in *SEP Online* (December 2011); Jeremy Waldron, "Liberalism," in *REP 1.0*.

Toleration: John Milton, *Areopagitica: A Speech for Liberty of Unlicensed Printing* (1644); John Goodwin, "Independency of God's Verity or the Necessity of Toleration" (1647); Benedict Spinoza, *Tractatus Theologico-Politicus* (published anon., 1670); Pierre Bayle, *Commentaire philosophique sur "Contrains-les d'entrer"*; trans. *Philosophical Commentary on "Compel Them to Come in That My House May Be Full"* (1686); John Locke, *Letter Concerning Toleration* (trans. from Latin, 1689); Daniel Defoe, "The True-Born Englishman" (1701); Ashley Cooper, Earl of Shaftesbury, "On Enthusiasm," *Characteristics* (1711); Thomas Gordon, *Cato's Letters* (1720); Montesquieu, *Notes sur l'Angleterre* (1730); Voltaire, *Traité sur la tolérance* (1763); Mill, *On Liberty* (1861); *On the Subjection of Women* (1869); Gerhard Besier and Klaus Schreiner, "Toleranz," in *Geschichtliche Grundbegriffe VI*, eds. Brunner, Conze, and Koselleck (1990);

Bernard Williams, "Toleration: An Impossible Virtue?" in *Toleration: An Elusive Virtue* (1996), ed. Heyd; John Horton, "Toleration," *REP 1.0*; Cécile Laborde, "Toleration and laïcité," in *The Culture of Toleration in Diverse Societies: Reasonable Tolerance* (2003), eds. McKinnon and Castiglione; Rainer Forst, "Toleration," *SEP Online* (July 2012); John Christian Laursen, "Toleration," Encyclopedia.com (August 2012). Other works: Charles Mullett, "Some Essays on Toleration in Late 18th-century England," *Church History* 7 (1938); Herbert Marcuse, "Repressive Tolerance," in Marcuse, Barrington Moore, and Robert Paul Wolff, *A Critique of Pure Tolerance* (1965); Robert N. Bellah, "Civil Religion in America," *Daedalus*, "On Religion in America" (Winter 1967); Henry Kamen, *The Rise of Toleration* (1967); Hilary Putnam, "Reason and History," chap. 7 of *Reason, Truth and History* (1981); Joseph Raz, "Freedom and Autonomy," chap. 15 of *The Morality of Freedom* (1986); *On Toleration* (1987), ed. Mendus; *Justifying Toleration* (1988), ed. Mendus; Thomas Nagel, *Equality and Partiality* (1991); Jonathan Rauch, *Kindly Inquisitors* (1993); Alain Bergounioux, "La laïcité, valeur de la République"; Gérard Defois, "La laïcité vue d'en face"; Rémond, "La laïcité et ses contraires"; Jacques Zylberberg, "Laïcité, connais pas," all in *Pouvoirs 75*, "La laïcité" (1995); *Toleration* (1996), ed. Heyd; Michael Walser, *On Toleration* (1997); Thomas Nagel, "Concealment and Exposure," *Philosophy and Public Affairs* (1998); Jeremy Waldron, "Political Neutrality," *REP 1.0*; *Toleration in Enlightenment Europe* (2000), eds. Grell and Porter; Christopher Hill, "Toleration in 17th-Century England: Theory and Practice," in *The Politics of Toleration in Modern Life* (2000), ed. Mendus; *Toleration, Neutrality and Democracy* (2003), ed. McKinnon; *Daedalus*, "On Secularism and Religion" (Summer 2003); Ronald Dworkin, *Is Democracy Possible Here?* (2006); Catriona McKinnon, *Toleration* (2006); Paul Starr, "Religious Liberty and the Separation of Church and State," in *Freedom's Power: The True Force of Liberalism* (2006).

Political democracy: Sièyes, "Qu'est-ce-que c'est le tiers état?" (1789); Condorcet, "Sur l'admission des femmes aux droits de Cité" (1790); Moisei Ostrogorski, *Democracy* (1902); Acton's letter of April 24, 1881, to Mary Gladstone in *Letters of Lord Acton* (1904), ed. Paul; Georges Sorel, *Réflexions sur la violence* (1908); trans. Jennings, *On Violence* (1999); *Les Illusions du progrès* (1908); Joseph Schumpeter, *Capitalism, Socialism and Democracy* (1942); Richard Wollheim, "A Paradox in the Theory of Democracy," in *Philosophy, Politics and Society* (1962), eds. Laslett and Runciman; Max Weber, *Political Writings*, eds. Lassman and Speirs (1994); Richard Bellamy, "The Advent of the Masses and the Making of the Modern Theory of Democracy," in *The Cambridge History of Twentieth-Century Political Thought* (2003), eds. Ball and Bellamy; John Dunn, *Setting the People Free: The Story of Democracy* (2005); Andreas Fahrmeir, *Citizenship: The Rise and Fall of a Modern Concept* (2007). Other works: Denis Brogan, *Citizenship Today* (1960); Robert A. Dahl, "Democracy," in *Blackwell Encyclopedia of Political Institutions* (1987), ed. Bogdanor; Benjamin Barber, "Democracy," in *Blackwell Encyclopedia of Political Thought* (1987), eds. Miller et al.; Russell L. Hanson, "Democracy," in *Political Innovation and Conceptual Change* (1989), eds. Ball, Farr, and Hanson; Amy Gutman, "Democracy," in Goodin and Pettit (1995); Joseph Femia, "Complexity and Deliberative Democracy," *Inquiry* 39 (1996); Charles Tilly, *Democracy* (2007); Adam Przeworski, *Democracy and the Limits of Self-Government* (2010); David Runciman, *The Confidence Trap: A History of Democracy in Crisis from World War I to the Present* (2013); Stein Ringen, *Nation of Devils: Democracy and the Problem of Obedience* (2013).

Economic democracy: Hermann Levy, *Economic Liberalism* (1913); H. A. Shannon, "The Limited Companies of 1866–1883," *Economic History Review* (October 1933); Pierre Caron, *Histoire économique de la France, XIXème–XXème siècle (1973)*; trans. Bray, *Economic History of Modern France* (1979); Wolfram Fischer and Peter Lundgren, "The Recruitment of Administrative Personnel," in *The Formation of Nation States in Western Europe* (1975), ed. Tilly; *United States Historical Statistics: Bicentennial Edition, Bureau of Census* (1976); W. H. Greenleaf, *The British Political Tradition (I): The Rise of Collectivism* (1983); Eberhard Kolb, review of Abelshauser, *Die Weimarer Republik als Wohlfahrtsstaat* (1987), *Historische Zeitschrift* (June 1989); Angus Maddison, *The World Economy in the 20th Century* (1989); H. J. Braun, *The German Economy in the Twentieth Century* (1990); Gosta Esping-Andersen, *The Three Worlds of Capitalism* (1990); Niall Ferguson, "Public Finance and National Security: The Domestic Origins of the First World War Revisited," *Past and Present* (February 1994); H. Berghoff and R. Moller, "Tired Pioneers and Dynamic Newcomers? English and German Entrepreneurial History, 1870–1914," *Economic History Review* (May 1994); *The Boundaries of the State in Modern Britain* (1996), eds. Green and Whiting; Clive Trebilcock, "The Industrialization of Modern Europe" and Harold James, "Fall and Rise of the Economy," in *Oxford Illustrated History of Modern Europe* (1996), ed. Blanning; *Creating Modern Capitalism* (1997), eds. Thomas McCraw; Vito Tanzi and Ludger Schuknecht, *Public Spending in the 20th Century: A Global Perspective* (2000); Niall Ferguson, *The Cash Nexus* (2001); Daunton, *Just Taxes: The Politics of Taxation in Britain, 1914–1979* (2002); John Micklethwait and Adrian Wooldridge, *The Company* (2003); Werner Abelshauser, *Deutsche Wirtschaftsgeschichte seit 1945* (2004); *Cambridge Economic History of Modern Britain 1939–2000* (2004), eds. Floud and Johnson; Toni Pierenkemper and Richard Tilly, *The German Economy during the 19th Century* (2004); Christopher Kopper, "Continuities and Discontinuities," *Contemporary European History* (special issue, November 2005); Maddison, *The World Economy* (2006); Daunton, *Wealth and Welfare: An Economic and Social History of Britain, 1850–1951* (2007); *State and Market in Victorian Britain: War, Welfare and Capitalism* (2008); *The European Economy in an American Mirror* (2008), eds. Eichengreen, Landesmann, and Stiefel; Carmen Reinhart and Kenneth Rogoff, *This Time is Different: Eight Centuries of Financial Folly* (2009); Philip Coggan, *Paper Promises: Money, Debt and the New World Order* (2011).

Ethical democracy: Célestin Bouglé: "Crise du libéralisme" (September 1902); *Solidarisme et libéralisme* (1904), with Introduction by Alain Policar (2009); "Le solidarisme" (1907); "Marxisme et sociologie" (November 1908); "Remarques sur le polytélisme" (September 1914); Georges Davy, "Célestin Bouglé, 1870–1940," *Revue française de sociologie* 8 (January–March 1967); William Logue, "Sociologie et politique: le libéralisme de Célestin Bouglé" and W. Paul Vogt, "Un durkheimien ambivalent: Célestin Bouglé (1870–1940)," both in *Revue française de sociologie*, "Les Durkheimiens" (January–March 1979); Lavinia Anderson, *Windthorst: A Political Biography* (1981); David Blackbourn, "Catholics and Politics," pt. III of *Populists and Patricians: Essays in Modern German History* (1987); Ronald Ross, *The Failure of Bismarck's Kulturkampf* (1998).

Walras and Marshall: Léon Walras, *Eléments d'économie politique pure* (1874); "L'Etat et le chemin de fer," *Revue du Droit public et de la Science politique* (1875); "Théorie de la propriété," *Revue Socialiste* (June 1896), cited in *The Origins of Left-Libertarianism* (2000), eds. Vallentyne and Steiner; B. Bürgenmeier, "The Misperception of Walras," *American Economic Review* (March 1994); Donald A. Walker, "Walras, Léon," in *The New Palgrave: A Dictionary of Economics* (2nd 2008), eds. Durlauf and Blume; Sandmo, "The Marginalists: Léon Walras," in *Economics Evolving* (2011). Alfred Marshall, *The Principles of Economics* (1890); J. M. Keynes, "Alfred Marshall," *The Economic Journal* (September 1924); Sandmo, "The Marginalists: Alfred Marshall," in *Economics Evolving* (2011); Rita McWilliams Tullberg, "Marshall, Alfred," *ODNB Online* (June 2012); on freedom of contract: P. S. Atiyah, *The Rise and Fall of Freedom of Contract* (1979).

Bastiat, Martineau, Bagehot, and Leroy-Beaulieu: Harriet Martineau, *Illustrations of Political Economy, Vol. 1: Life in the Wilds, Hill and the Valley, Brooke and Brooke Farm* (1832); Frédéric Bastiat, *Sophismes Economiques* (1845); Margaret G. O'Donnell, "Harriet Martineau: A Popular Early Economics Educator," *Journal of Economic Education* (Autumn 1983); Eric Hobsbawm, Introduction to *The Communist Manifesto: A Modern Edition* (1998).

Walter Bagehot, "Letters on the French coup d'état of 1851 in France," *The Inquirer* (1852); *The English Constitution* (1867); "Mr Robert Lowe as Chancellor of the Exchequer" (1871); *Physics and Politics* (1872); *Lombard Street*

(1873); "The Metaphysical Basis of Toleration" (1874); *Postulates of English Political Economy* (1876); "Adam Smith as a Person" (1876); "Adam Smith and Our Modern Economy," in *Economic Studies* (posth. 1915); Joseph Hamburger, "Bagehot, Walter," *ODNB Online* (November 2012).

Paul Leroy-Beaulieu, *De la colonisation chez les peuples modernes* (1874); *L'Etat moderne* (1890); *Les Etats Unis au XXième siècle* (1891); Zeldin, *France 1848–1945: Politics and Anger* (1973). Other works: Dan Warshaw, *Paul Leroy-Beaulieu and Established Liberalism in France* (1991); Sharif Gemie, "Politics, Morality and the Bourgeoisie: The Work of Paul Leroy-Beaulieu (1843–1916)," *Journal of Contemporary History* (April 1992); Pierre Lévêque, review of Warshaw, *Annales* (January–February 1996).

Hobhouse and Britain's "new liberals": T. H. Green, *Lectures on the Principles of Political Obligation* (1879–80); "Liberal Legislation and Freedom of Contract" (1881); Herbert Samuel, *Liberalism: Its Principles and Proposals* (1902); Leonard Hobhouse, *Morals in Evolution* (1906); *Liberalism* (1911); *The Metaphysical Theory of the State* (1918); J. A. Hobson and Morris Ginsberg, *L. T. Hobhouse* (1931); Collini, *Liberalism and Sociology: L. T. Hobhouse and Political Argument in England, 1880–1914* (1979); Michael Freeden, "Hobhouse, Leonard Trelawney," *ODNB Online* (December 2011). Other works: Gareth Stedman-Jones, *Outcast London* (1971); Collini, "Hobhouse, Bosanquet and the State: Philosophical Idealism and Political Argument in England 1880–1918," *Past and Present* (August 1976); Freeden, "The New Liberalism and its Aftermath," in *Victorian Liberalism* (1990), ed. Bellamy.

Naumann and German social liberals: Friedrich Naumann, *Demokratie und Kaisertum* (1900); *Mitteleuropa* (1915); Tomas Masaryk, *The New Europe: The Slav Standpoint* (1917, trans. 1918); Theodor Heuss, *Friedrich Naumann: Der Mann, das Werk, die Zeit* (1937); Peter Theiner, *Sozialer Liberalismus und deutsche Weltpolitik: Friedrich Naumann in Wilhelminischen Deutschland, 1860–1919* (1983). Other works: Richard Nürnberger, "Imperialismus, Sozialismus und Christentum bei Friedrich Naumann," *Historische Zeitschrift* 170 (1950); William O. Shanahan, "Friedrich Naumann: A Mirror of Wilhelmine Germany," *Review of Politics* (1951); Heuss, *Vorspiele des Lebens* (1953); trans. Bullock, *Preludes to a Life* (1955) and "Naumann, Friedrich," *Neue Deutsche Biographie* (1955, rev. 1997); Shanahan, "Liberalism and Foreign Affairs: Naumann and the Pre-War German View," *Review of Politics* (January 1959); Beverly Heckart, *From Bassermann to Bebel: The Grand Bloc's Quest for Reform in the Kaiserreich 1900–14* (1974); Moshe Zimmermann, "A Road Not Taken: Friedrich Naumann's Attempt at a Modern German Nationalism," *Journal of Contemporary History* (October 1982); Hans Fenske, review of Theiner, *Historische Zeitschrift* 240 (1985); A. J. Nicholls, review of Theiner, *English Historical*

Review 101 (1986); Michael Freeden, review of Schnoor, *Liberalismus zwischen 19. und 20. Jahrhundert, am Beispiel von Friedrich Naumann und Leonard Hobhouse* in *English Historical Review* (September 1994); George Steinmetz, "The Myth of the Autonomous State: Industrialists, Junkers, and Social Policy in Imperial Germany," in *Society, Culture and State in Germany 1870–1930* (1996), ed. Eley; Frederic Schwartz, *The Werkbund: Design Theory and Mass Culture before the First World War* (1996); Chris Thornhill, *Political Theory in Modern Germany* (2000); Margaret Lavinia Anderson, *Practising Democracy: Elections and Political Culture in Imperial Germany* (2000); Joachim Radkau, *Max Weber* (2005), trans. Camiller (2009); Andrea Orzoff, *Battle for the Castle: The Myth of Czechoslovakia in Europe* (2009).

Bourgeois and French Solidarism: Léon Bourgeois, *Solidarité* (1896); Zeldin, "Solidarism," chap. 8 of *France 1848–1945: Politics and Anger* (1974); James Kloppenberg, *Uncertain Victory: Social Democracy and Progressivism in European and American Thought, 1870–1920* (1986). Other works: Charles Renouvier, *Manuel républicain des droits de l'homme et du citoyen* (1848); Emile Durkheim, *De la division du travail social* (1893); Charles Gide and Charles Rist, "Les Solidaristes," V, iii, in *Histoire des doctrines économiques* (1909); trans. Richards, *A History of Economic Doctrines* (1915); Léon Duguit, *Souveraineté et liberté* (1922); Maurice Hamburger, *Léon Bourgeois* (1930); J.E.S. Hayward, "Solidarity: The Social History of an Idea in 19th Century France," *International Review of Social History* (August 1959); David Wiggins, "A First-Order Ethic of Solidarity and Reciprocity," lecture nine in *Ethics: Twelve Lectures on the Philosophy of Morality* (2006); Wiggins, "Solidarity and the Root of the Ethical," *Tijdschrift voor Philosophie* (June 2010); Nicolas Delalande, "Le solidarisme de Léon Bourgeois: un socialisme libérale?" on website la vie des idées. fr (April 2012).

Croly, Weyl, and American Progressives: Croly, *The Promise of American Life* (1909); Walter Weyl, *The New Democracy* (1912); Charles Forcey, *The Crossroads of Liberalism: Croly, Weyl, Lippmann and the Progressive Era 1900–1925* (1961); "Herbert Croly," in *A Companion to American Thought* (1995), eds. Fox and Kloppenberg; Steven L. Piott, *American Reformers 1870–1920: Progressives in Word and Deed* (2006); David W. Levy, "Croly, Herbert David," *ANB Online* (August 2010); David W. Levy, "Weyl, Walter Edward," *ANB Online* (August 2010).

Chamberlain, Bassermann, and liberal imperialism: P. M. Kennedy, *The Rise of the Anglo-German Rivalry 1860–1914* (1980); Gall, *Bürgertum in Deutschland* (1989); Peter T. Marsh, "Chamberlain, Joseph," *ODNB Online* (December 2009). Other works: Friedrich Fabri, *Bedarf Deustchland der Kolonien?* (1879); Gustav Schmoller, *Studien über die wirtschaftliche Politik Friedrich des*

Großen (1884); introduction trans. Ashley, *The Mercantile System and Its Historical Significance* (1896); J. A. Hobson, *Imperialism* (1902; 2nd 1905); V. I. Lenin, *Imperialism: The Highest Stage of Capitalism* (1917); Winston Churchill, "Joseph Chamberlain," in *Great Contemporaries* (1937); William E. Leuchtenburg, "Progressivism and Imperialism," *Mississippi Valley Historical Review* (December 1952); George Lichtheim, *Imperialism* (1971); Sidney Morgenbesser, "Imperialism: Some Preliminary Distinctions," *Philosophy and Public Affairs* (Autumn 1973); Ian L. D. Forbes, "Social Imperialism and Wilhelmine Germany," *Historical Journal* (June 1979); Mathew Burrows, " 'Mission Civilisatrice': French Cultural Policy in the Middle East, 1860–1914," *Historical Journal* (March 1986); Anthony Pagden, *Lords of All the World: Ideologies of Empire in Spain, Britain and France c. 1500–1800* (1995); Douglas Porch, *Wars of Empire* (2000); Alan Ryan, "Liberal Imperialism," in *The Future of Liberal Democracy* (2004), eds. Fatton and Ramazani; Henk Wesseling, "Imperialism and the Roots of the Great War"; Robin Blackburn, "Emancipation and Empire from Cromwell to Karl Rove"; Anthony Pagden, "Imperialism, Liberalism and the Quest for Perpetual Peace"; Kenneth Pomeranz, "Empire and 'Civilizing Missions,' Past and Present"; all in *Daedalus*, "On Imperialism" (Spring 2005).

Clemenceau, Lloyd George, and Wilson: Woodrow Wilson, *Congressional Government* (1885); *The State* (1889); *The New Freedom* (1913); Henry Cabot Lodge, "Speech to Senate Against League of Nations" (August 1919), in *American Speeches* (2006), ed. Wilmer; *Lloyd George* (1968), speeches, writings, and assessments ed. Martin Gilbert; H. W. Brands, *Woodrow Wilson* (2003); Michel Winock, *Clemenceau* (2007); Kenneth O. Morgan, "George, David Lloyd," *ODNB Online* (January 2011). Other works: Keynes on Clemenceau in *Economic Consequences of the Peace* (1919); Churchill, "Clemenceau," in *Great Contemporaries* (1937); E. M. Hugh-Jones, *Woodrow Wilson and American Liberalism* (1947); Georges Wormser, *Clemenceau vu de près* (1979); *Clemenceau (1841–1929): Exposition du cinquantenaire* (1979), show catalog, Palais des Beaux-Arts, Paris; Niall Ferguson, "Germany and the Origins of the First World War: New Perspectives," *Historical Journal* (September 1992); Stephen Constantine, *Lloyd George* (1992); Ian Packer, *Lloyd George* (1998); Margaret Macmillan, *The Peacemakers* (2001); Ronald Steele, "The Missionary," on Wilson, *NYRB* (November 20, 2003); D. R. Watson, *Georges Clemenceau* (2008); Christopher Clark, *The Sleepwalkers: How Europe Went to War in 1914* (2012).

Alain, Baldwin, and Brandeis: Alain, *Propos* (1906–36) (Pléiade ed. 1956); *Souvenirs de guerre* (1937); Ramon Fernandez, "Propos sur Alain," *NRF* (July 1941); *Politique* (1951); *Les Passions et la Sagesse* (Pléiade ed. 1960); Paul Foulquié, *Alain* (1952); Raymond Aron, "Alain et la politique," in *NRF "Hommage à Alain"* (September 1952); Ronald F. Howell, "The Philosopher Alain and

French Classical Radicalism," in *Western Political Quarterly* (September 1965); Simone de Beauvoir, on Alain's pupils, *La cérémonie des adieux* (1981); John Weightman, "Alain: For and Against," *American Scholar* (June 1982); Thierry Leterre in "Alain Colloque, 2009," *ENS Paris website* (October 2010). Peggy Lamson, *Roger Baldwin: Founder of the American Civil Liberties Union: A Portrait* (1976); Norman Dorsen, "Baldwin, Roger Nash," *ANB Online* (January 2012). Louis Brandeis, *Brandeis and America* (1989), ed. Dawson; *Brandeis on Democracy* (1995), ed. Strum; Philippa Strum, "Brandeis, Louis Dembitz," *ANB Online* (January 2012). Other works: Arthur Schlesinger Jr., *War and the American Presidency* (2004); Geoffrey R. Stone, *War and Liberty: An American Dilemma, 1790 to the Present* (2007).

Keynes, Fisher, and Hayek: J. M. Keynes, *The Economic Consequences of the Peace* (1919); "Am I a Liberal?" (1925); "The End of Laissez-Faire" (1926); *The General Theory of Employment, Interest, and Money* (1936); Robert Skidelsky, *John Maynard Keynes: Vol. I: Hopes Betrayed, 1883–1920* (1983); *Vol. II: The Economist as Saviour, 1920–37* (1992); *Vol. III: Fighting for Britain* (2000). Other works: Skidelsky, *Keynes* (1996); Samuel Brittan, "Keynes's Political Philosophy," in *Cambridge Companion to Keynes* (2006), eds. Backhouse and Bateman; Sandmo, "John Maynard Keynes and the Keynesian Revolution," in *Economics Evolving* (2011).

Irving Fisher, *Booms and Depressions* (1932); "The Debt-Deflation Theory of Great Depressions," *Econometrica* (October 1933); "Destructive Taxation: A Rejoinder," *Columbia Law Review* (March 1943); James Tobin, "Fisher, Irving," in *The New Palgrave: A Dictionary of Economics* (2nd 2008), eds. Durlauf and Blume. Other works: William J. Barber, "Irving Fisher of Yale," and Robert W. Dimand, "Fisher, Keynes and the Corridor of Stability," *American Journal of Economics and Sociology* (January 2005); "Out of Keynes's Shadow," on Fisher, *The Economist* (February 14, 2009); Theodore M. Porter, "Fisher, Irving," *ANB Online* (August 2012).

Friedrich Hayek, "Economics and Knowledge," *Economica* (1937); *The Road to Serfdom* (1945); "The Uses of Knowledge in Society" (1945); "Individualism, True and False" (1948); *The Constitution of Liberty* (1960); "Principles of a Liberal Social Order" (1966); *Law, Liberty and Legislation: Vol. I: Rules and Order* (1973); *Vol. II: The Mirage of Social Justice* (1976); *Vol. III: The Political Order of a Free People* (1979); Andrew Gamble, *Hayek: The Iron Cage of Liberty* (1996); Samuel Brittan, "Hayek, Friedrich August," *ODNB Online* (June 2011). Other works: Jacob Viner, "Hayek on Freedom and Coercion," *Southern Economic Journal* (January 1961); Lionel Robbins, "Hayek on Liberty," *Economica* (February 1961); Fritz Machlup, "Friedrich Hayek's Contribution to Economics," *Swedish Journal of Economics* (December 1974); John Gray, "Hayek on Liberty,

Rights and Justice," *Ethics* (October 1981); Jeremy Shearmur, "Hayek," in *Blackwell Encyclopedia of Political Thought* (1987), eds. Miller et al.; Richard Cockett, *Thinking the Unthinkable: Think-Tanks and the Economic Counter-Revolution, 1931–1983* (1994); Edna Ullman-Margalit, "The Invisible Hand and the Cunning of Reason," *Social Research* (Summer 1997); Mario Sznajder, "Hayek in Chile," in *Liberalism and Its Practice*, in Avnon and de-Shalit (1999); Alan Ebenstein, *Friedrich Hayek: A Biography* (2001); Bruce Caldwell, *Hayek's Challenge: An Intellectual Biography* (2003); Roger W. Garrison, "Over-Consumption and Forced Savings in the Mises-Hayek Theory of the Business Cycle," *History of Political Economy* (2004); Kim Phillips-Fein, *Invisible Hands: The Businessman's Crusade Against the New Deal* (2009).

Hoover and Roosevelt: Herbert Hoover, speeches: "Business Ethics" (1924); "Rugged Individualism" (1928), "The Meaning of America" (1948); William Leuchtenburg, *Herbert Hoover* (2009); Joan Hoff, "Hoover, Herbert Clark," *ANB Online* (June 2012).

Franklin D. Roosevelt, *The Roosevelt Reader* (1957), selected speeches, messages, press conferences, and letters, ed. Rauch; Alan Brinkley, "Roosevelt, Franklin Delano," *ANB Online* (June 2012). Other works: Ray T. Tucker, "Is Hoover Human?" *North American Review* (November 1928); Richard Hofstadter, "The Ordeal of Herbert Hoover," in *The American Political Tradition* (1948); Charles Kindleberger, *The World in Depression: 1929–39* (1973); David U. Romasco, "Herbert Hoover: The Restoration of a Reputation," *Reviews in American History* (March 1984); Barry Eichengreen and Peter Temin, "The Gold Standard and the Great Depression," NBER Working Paper 6060 (June 1997); David Kennedy, *Freedom from Fear: The American People in Depression and War, 1929–1945* (1999); Amity Shlaes, *The Forgotten Man* (2007); Andrew B. Wilson, "Five Myths about the Great Depression: Herbert Hoover Was No Proponent of Laissez-Faire," *Wall Street Journal* (November 4, 2008); H. W. Brands, *Traitor to His Class: The Privileged Life and Radical Presidency of Franklin Delano Roosevelt* (2008).

Lippmann: Walter Lippmann, *Drift and Mastery* (1914); *Public Opinion* (1922); *The Good Society* (1937); G. J. Morton Blum, *Public Philosopher: Selected Letters of Walter Lippmann* (1985); Ronald Steel, "Lippmann, Walter," *ANB Online* (August 2010). Other works: Christopher Lasch, "Walter Lippmann Today," *NYRB* (December 9, 1965); and Steel, *Walter Lippmann and the American Century* (1980); François Denord, "Aux Origines du néo-libéralisme en France: Louis Rougier et le Colloque Walter Lippmann de 1938," *Le Mouvement Social* 195 (2001); Daniel Stedman-Jones, *Masters of the Universe: Hayek, Friedman and the Birth of Neo-liberal Politics* (2012).

Popper: *Die Logik der Forschung* (1934); trans. author, *The Logic of Scientific Discovery* (1959); "The Poverty of Historicism Vol. I" (myth of prophecy) and Vol. II (piecemeal social engineering), *Economica* (May and August 1944); "The Poverty of Historicism Vol. III" (laws and trends), *Economica* (May 1945); *The Open Society and Its Enemies* (1945); "Intellectual Autobiography," in *The Philosophy of Karl Popper* (1974), ed. Schillp; Anthony Quinton, "Popper: Politics without Essences," in *Contemporary Political Philosophers* (1975), eds. Crespigny and Minogue; Anthony O'Hear, *Karl Popper* (1980). Other works: Hilary Putnam, "The 'Corroboration' of Theories"; William C. Kneale, "The Demarcation of Science," and W. V. Quine, "On Popper's Negative Methodology," in Schillp; Manfred Geier, *Karl Popper* (1994); Stephen Thornton, "Karl Popper," *SEP Online* (Winter 2011).

Human rights: William Paley, "The Division of Rights," in *Principles of Moral and Political Philosophy* (1775); Jeremy Bentham, *Anarchical Fallacies: An Examination of the Declarations of Rights Issued during the French Revolution* (1796); Max Weber, "Zur Lage der bürgerlichen Demokratie in Rußland" (1906); trans. Speirs, "On the Situation of Constitutional Democracy in Russia" (1994); Hannah Arendt, "The Perplexities of the Rights of Man," chap. 9, ii of *Origins of Totalitarianism* (1951); Herbert Hart, "Are There Any Natural Rights?" *Philosophical Review* (April 1955); J. E. S. Fawcett, *The Law of Nations* (1968); *Historical Change and Human Rights* (1995), ed. Hufton; Mary Ann Glendon, *A World Made New: Eleanor Roosevelt and the Universal Declaration of Human Rights* (2001); Tom Bingham, *The Rule of Law* (2010); Samuel Moyn, *The Last Utopia: Human Rights in History* (2010); Andrew Vincent, *The Politics of Human Rights* (2010).

German Basic Law of 1949: J. F. Golay, *The Founding of the Federal Republic of Germany* (1958); Carlo Schmid, *Politik und Geist* (1961); Peter Merkl, *The Origin of the West German Republic* (1963); H. W. Koch, *A Constitutional History of Germany* (1984).

Beveridge: William Beveridge, *Social Insurance and Allied Services* (1942); José Harris, *William Beveridge* (1997); Michael Freeden, "The Coming of the Welfare State," in *Cambridge History of 20th-Century Political Thought* (2003), eds. Ball and Bellamy; Harris, "Beveridge, William Henry," *ODNB Online* (September 2012).

Oakeshott and Berlin: Michael Oakeshott, *Experience and Its Modes* (1933); *The Social and Political Doctrines of Contemporary Europe* (1939); *Rationalism in Politics and Other Essays* (1962), containing "Rationalism in Politics" (1947); "Political Education" (1951); "The Voice of Poetry in the Conversation of Mankind" (1959); "Political Discourse" (1962); *On Human Con-*

duct (1975); Paul Franco, *Michael Oakeshott* (2004). Other works: *The Intellectual Legacy of Michael Oakeshott* (2005), eds. Abel and Fuller; Andrew Gamble, "Oakeshott's Ideological Politics: Conservative or Liberal?" in *The Cambridge Companion to Oakeshott* (2012), ed. Podoksik.

Isaiah Berlin, "Two Concepts of Liberty" (1957); *Personal Impressions* (1981), ed. Hardy; *Flourishing: Letters, 1928–46* (2004); *Enlightening: Letters 1946–60* (2009), eds. Hardy and Holmes; *Building: Letters 1960–75* (2013), eds. Hardy and Pottle; Michael Ignatieff, *Isaiah Berlin* (1998). Other works: Gerald C. McCallum, "Negative and Positive Freedom," *Philosophical Review* (July 1967); J. P. Day, "On Liberty and the Real Will," *Philosophy* (July 1970); John Gray, "On Liberty, Liberalism and Essential Contestability," *British Journal of Political Science* (October 1978); Charles Taylor, "What's Wrong with Negative Liberty," in *The Idea of Freedom* (1979), ed. Ryan; Amartya Sen, "Individual Freedom as a Social Commitment," *NYRB* (June 14, 1990); Chandran Kukathas, "Liberty," in *A Companion to Contemporary Political Philosophy* (1995), eds. Goodin and Pettit; *The Legacy of Isaiah Berlin* (2001), eds. Dworkin, Lilla, and Silvers; Ian Carter, "Positive and Negative Liberty," in *SEP Online* (December 2012).

Orwell, Camus, and Sartre: *Homage to Catalonia* (1938); *The Collected Essays, Journalism and Letters Vols. I–IV* (1968–2000), eds. Sonia Orwell and Angus; Bernard Crick, *Orwell: A Life* (1980); Jeffrey Meyers, *Orwell: Wintry Conscience of a Generation* (2000); George Orwell, *Orwell and the Dispossessed: "Down and Out in London and Paris" and Other Essays* (2001), ed. Peter Davison.

Albert Camus, *Le mythe de Sisyphe* (1942); *L'Homme révolté* (1951); trans. Bower, *The Rebel* (1954); Francis Jeanson, "Albert Camus ou l'âme révoltée," *Temps Modernes* (May 1952); Camus, "M. le directeur," *Temps Modernes* (June 1952); Sartre, "Mon cher Camus," *Temps Modernes* (August 1952); Ronald Aronson, *Camus and Sartre: The Story of a Friendship and the Quarrel That Ended It* (2004).

Jean Paul Sartre: *L'Imaginaire* (1940); *L'être et le néant* (1943); trans. Barnes, *Being and Nothingness* (1957); *Les Mots* (1963); *Carnets de la drôle de guerre* (1983); Ronald Hayman, *Writing Against: A Biography of Sartre* (1986). Other works: *The Philosophy of Jean-Paul Sartre*, ed. Cumming (1968); Raymond Aron, *Mémoires* (1983); Annie Cohen-Solal, *Sartre 1905–1980* (1985); Nicolas Baverez, *Raymond Aron: un moraliste au temps des idéologies* (1993); Jean Sirinelli, *Deux Intellectuels dans le siècle: Sartre et Aron* (1995).

Rawls and Rawlsianism: John Rawls, *A Theory of Justice* (1971); *Political Liberalism* (2nd 1996); *Collected Papers* (1999), ed. Freeman; Chandran Kukathas and Philip Pettit, *A Theory of Justice and Its Critics* (1990); G. A. Cohen,

Rescuing Justice and Equality (2008). Other works: *Reading Rawls: Critical Studies on Rawls's "A Theory of Justice"* (1975), ed. Daniels; *The Philosophy of Rawls, a Collection of Essays: Vol. I, Development and Main Outlines of Rawls's Theory of Justice*; *Vol. II, The Two Principles and their Justification*; *Vol. III, Opponents and Implications of a Theory of Justice* (1999), ed. Richardson; *Vol. IV, Moral Psychology and Community*; *Vol. V, Reasonable Pluralism* (1999), ed. Weithman; David Wiggins, "A Fresh Argument for Utilitarianism" and "Neo-Aristotelian Reflections," in Wiggins, *Ethics* (2006); Paul Graham, *Rawls* (2006); Thomas Pogge, *John Rawls* (2007), trans. Kosch; Joshua Cohen and Thomas Nagel, "Faith in the Community: A Forgotten 'Senior Thesis' that Signals John Rawls's Future Spiritual Force", TLS (March 20, 2009).

Nozick, Dworkin, and MacIntyre: Robert Nozick, *Anarchy, State and Utopia* (1973); Ronald Dworkin, *Taking Rights Seriously* (1978); *Sovereign Justice* (2000); *Justice for Hedgehogs* (2011); Alasdair Macintyre, *A Short History of Ethics* (1967); *After Virtue* (1981); *Whose Justice, Which Rationality?* (1988); *Three Rival Versions of Moral Enquiry* (1990); *After MacIntyre* (1994), eds. Horton and Mendus; *The MacIntyre Reader* (1998), ed. Knight; Leif Wenar, "Rights," *SEP Online* (December 2010).

Mendès-France, Brandt, and Johnson: "Mendès-France, Pierre 1907–1982," in *Historical Dictionary of the French IIId Republic 1870–1940* (1980), ed. Hutton; and in *Dictionnaire de la résistance* (2006), eds. Marcot, Leroux, and Levisse-Touze; Jean Lacouture, *Mendès-France* (1981); *Pierre Mendès-France: La morale en politique* (1990), eds. Chêne et al.; Eric Roussel, *Pierre Mendès-France* (2005); Richard Vinen, "Writer's Choice," review of Roussel, *TLS* (May 18, 2007).

Willy Brandt, *Erinnerungen* (1989); trans. Camiller, *My Life in Politics* (1992); *Die Spiegel-Gespräche, 1959–1992* (1992); Barbara Marshall, *Willy Brandt: A Political Biography* (1997).

Merle Miller, *Lyndon: An Oral Biography* (1980); Robert Caro, *The Years of Lyndon Johnson: Means of Ascent* (1990); *Master of the Senate* (2002); *The Passage of Power* (2012); Lloyd Gardner, "Johnson, Lyndon Baines," *ANB Online* (December 2012). Other works: Rowland Evans and Robert Novak, *Lyndon Johnson: The Exercise of Power* (1966); Robert Dallek, *Lone Star Rising: Lyndon Johnson and His Times, 1908–60* (1991); James T. Patterson, *Grand Expectations: The United States 1945–74* (1996); Dallek, *Flawed Giant: Lyndon Johnson and His Times, 1961–73* (1998).

Buchanan and Friedman: James Buchanan and Gordon Tullock, *The Calculus of Consent* (1962); Buchanan, "The Justice of Natural Liberty," *Journal of Legal Studies* (January 1976); Lecture at Francisco Marroquin University, FMU website (March 2011); Steven Pressman, "What is Wrong with Public Choice,"

Journal of Post Keynesian Economics (Autumn 2004). Friedman, *Capitalism and Freedom* (1962); with Anna J. Schwartz, *A Monetary History of the United States 1867–1960* (1963); "The Role of Monetary Policy," *American Economic Review* (March 1968).

Thatcher, Reagan, Mitterrand, and Kohl: *Sincerely, Ronald Reagan* (1976), sayings, thoughts, and letters, ed. Helene von Damm; Richard Reeves, *President Reagan: The Triumph of Imagination* (2005). "D'où venons nous? Que sommes nous? Où allons nous?: A Survey of France," *The Economist* (March 12, 1988); Franz-Olivier Giesbert, *Le Président* (1990), on Mitterrand. Horst Teltschik, *329 Tage* (1991), on Kohl and German unification; "Not as Grimm as it Looks: A Survey of Germany," *The Economist* (May 23, 1992).

Vaclav Havel: *Letters to Olga* (1983; trans. Wilson 1988); *Living in Truth* (1986, trans. various); *Disturbing the Peace* (1990; trans. Wilson); *Open Letters* (1991; trans. Wilson); *To the Castle and Back* (2005; trans. Wilson 2007); Mark Frankland, *The Patriots' Revolution* (1990); Tony Judt, "Living in Truth," *TLS* (October 11, 1991); Michael Simmons, *The Reluctant President* (1991); John Keane, *Vaclav Havel: A Political Tragedy in Six Acts* (1999).

The Rise of the Hard Right: Michael Mann, "The Social Cohesion of Liberal Democracy," *American Sociological Review* (June 1970); Charles Peters, "A Neo-Liberal's Manifesto, *Washington Monthly* (September 5, 1982); Fareed Zakaria, "The Rise of Illiberal Democracy," *Foreign Affairs* (November-December 1997); Marc Plattner, "Liberalism and Democracy: Can't Have One Without the Other," *Foreign Affairs* (March-April 1998); Morris Fiorina, *Culture War? The Myth of Polarized America* (2004); Tony Judt, "What is Living and What is Dead in Social Democracy?" *NYRB* (December 17, 2009); Lane Kenworthy, "America's Social Democratic Future," *Foreign Affairs* (January-February 2014); "What's Gone Wrong with Democracy," *The Economist* (March, 4 2014); Thomas Meaney and Jascha Mounk, "What was Democracy?" *The Nation* (May 13, 2014); "Beyond Distrust: How Americans View their Government," Pew Research Center (November 2015); Michael Ashcroft, "How the United Kingdom Voted on Thursday . . . and Why," lordashcroftpolls.com (June 24, 2016); Ronald F. Inglehart, "The Danger of Deconsolidation: How Much Should We Worry?" *Journal of Democracy* (July 2016); Max Ehrenfreund and Jeff Guo, "A Massive New Study Debunks a Widespread Theory for Donald Trump's Success," *Washington Post* (August 12, 2016); Victor Davis Hanson, "Why Trump Won," *Hoover Daily Report* (November 11, 2016); William A. Galston and William Kristol, "A New Center," *The Weekly Standard* (November 29, 2016); Kelefa Sanneh, "A New Trumpist Magazine Debuts at the Harvard Club," *New Yorker* (February 25, 2017); Jennifer Schuessler, "Talking Trumpism: A New Political Journal Enters the Fray," *NYT* (March 8, 2017); Ross Mc-

Kibbin, "Labour in Crisis: The Red Sag," *Prospect* (March 10, 2017); Christopher Caldwell, "The French: Coming Apart," *City Journal* (Spring 2017); David Brooks, columns on Trump, *NYT* (March 24, April 21, May 16, 2017); Suzanne Mettler, "Democracy on the Brink: Protecting the Republic in Trump's America," *Foreign Affairs* (April 2017); Robert Mickey, Steven Levitsky, and Lucan Ahmad Way, "Is America Still Safe for Democracy? Why the United States is in Danger of Backsliding," *Foreign Affairs* (May-June 2017); Michael Lind, "The New Class War," *American Affairs* (May 20, 2017); "Macron's Victory in Charts," *Financial Times Online* (June 2017); Fiorina, "The 2016 Presidential Election: Identities, Class and Culture," Hoover Institution Essays 11 (June 22, 2017); "La France périphérique: comment on a sacrifié les classes populaires," on Christophe Guilluy, fr.wikpedia (June 2017).

Populism, neo-authoritarianism and fascism: Seymour Martin Lipset, "Democracy and Working-Class Authoritarianism," *American Sociological Review* (August 1959); Robert Paxton, "Les fascismes: essai d'histoire comparée," lecture at École des Hautes Études en Sciences Sociales (June 13, 1994); *The Anatomy of Fascism* (2004); Jan-Werner Mueller, *What is Populism?* (2016); Other works: *Fascists and Conservatives* (1990), ed. Blinkhorn; Pierre Milza, "Le Front National," in *Histoires des droites: Vol. I, Politique* (1992), ed. Sirinelli; Edwy Plenel and Alain Rollat, *La République ménacée: dix ans d'effet Le Pen* (1992), ed.; *Histoire de l'extrême droite en France* (1993), ed. Winock; Tim Mason, *Nazism, Fascism and the Working Class* (1995); Jonathan Marcus, *The National Front and French Politics: The Resistible Rise of Jean-Marie Le Pen* (1995); Axel Schildt, *Konservatismus in Deutschland* (1998); Walter Russell Mead, "The Jacksonian Tradition," *National Interest* (Winter 1999–2000); Slavoj Zizek, "Why We All Love to Hate Haider," *New Left Review* (March-April 2000); Peter Davies, *The Extreme Right in France, 1789 to the Present* (2002); Catherine Fieschi, *Fascism, Populism and the French Vth Republic* (2004); "Le Front National," *Pouvoirs* 157 (2016); Sheri Berman, "Populism is Not Fascism: But it Could be a Harbinger," *Foreign Affairs* (November-December 2016); Hajo Funke, *Von Wutbürgern und Brandstiftern: AfD, Pegida, Gewaltnetze* (2016); Joshua Green, *Devil's Bargain* (2017); Martin Wolf, "The Economic Origins of the Populist Surge," *Financial Times* (June 27, 2017).

Economic discontents: Fred Hirsch, *The Social Limits to Growth* (1976); Richard Posner, *The Economics of Justice* (1981); Robert Skidelsky, "Thinking about the State and the Economy" (1996), in *The Boundaries of the State in Modern Britain* (1996), eds. Green and Whiting; John Williamson, interview on Washington Consensus and Neo-liberalism, *Washington Post* (April 12, 2009); John Cassidy, "After the Blowup: Laissez-faire Economists Do Some Soul-Searching, and Finger-Pointing," *New Yorker* (January 10, 2010); Skidelsky, "Where Do We Go from Here?" *Prospect* (January 17, 2010); Posner, *A Failure of Capitalism: The Crisis of '08 and the Descent into Depression* (2010); Zanny Minton Beddoes, "For Richer, for Poorer: Special Report on the World Economy," *The Economist* (October 13, 2012); Kimberley J. Morgan, "America's Misguided Approach to Social Welfare: How the Country Could Get More for Less," *Foreign Affairs* (January-February 2013); Martin Wolf, *The Shifts and the Shocks: What We've Learned—and Have Still to Learn—from the Financial Crisis* (2014); "Inequality v Growth," *The Economist* (March 3, 2014); Eugene Steuerle and Sisi Zhang, "Impact of the Great Recession and Beyond: Disparities in Wealth Building by Generation and Race," Urban Institute Working Paper (April 2014); Thomas Piketty, *Capital in the 21st Century* (2014); Charles J. Jones, "The Facts of Economic Growth," *Stanford GSB and NBER* (April 6, 2015); Daron Acemoglu and James A. Robinson, "The Rise and Decline of General Laws of Capitalism," *Journal of Economic Perspectives* (Winter 2015); Robert Gordon, *The Rise and Fall of American Growth* (2016); Tyler Cowan, "Is Innovation Over?" review of Gordon, *Foreign Affairs* (March-April 2016); Ben Bernanke and Lawrence Summers, Exchange on Secular Stagnation, Ben Bernanke's Blog/brookings.edu (June 2016); Lawrence Summers, "The Age of Secular Stagnation," *Foreign Affairs* (March-April 2016); J. Tomilson Hill and Ian Morris, "Can Central Banks Goose Growth?" *Foreign Affairs* (March-April 2016); Laurence Chancy and Brina Seidel, "Is Globalization's Second Wave about to Break?" *Brookings Global Views* (October 2016); "Income Inequality Update: Table 1. Key Indicators on the Distribution of Household Disposable Income and Poverty," *OECD* (November 2016); "Inequality or Middle Incomes: Which Matters More?" *The Economist* (January 7, 2017); "From Deprivation to Daffodils: The World Economy is Picking Up," *The Economist* (March 18, 2017); "Union Membership has Plunged to an All-Time Low, says DBEIS," *Guardian* (June 1, 2017); Jason Furman, "Looking Backward and Forward at the US Fiscal Trajectory," lecture at Peterson Institute for International Economics (June 29, 2017); *Human Development for Everyone: UNDP Human Development Report 2016* (2017).

Geopolitical loneliness: Joseph Schumpeter, "The Sociology of Imperialisms" (1919); Michael Doyle, "Liberalism and World Politics," *APSR* (December 1986); Stewart Patrick, "The Unruled World: The Case for Good Enough Global Governance," *Foreign Affairs* (January-February 2014); "Faith and Scepticism about Trade, Foreign Investment," Pew Research Center (September 2014); "Why is World Trade Growth Slowing?" *The Economist* (October 12, 2016); Robert Niblett, "Liberalism in Retreat: The Demise of a Dream," *Foreign Affairs* (January-February 2017); "Donald Trump, Trade and the New World Order," *The Economist* (March 25, 2017); John Peet, "Creaking at 60: The Future of the

European Union," *The Economist* (March 25, 2017); *Democracy Index 2016,* Economist Intelligence Unit (April 2017); Anatole Kaletsky, "Theresa May's Pyrrhic Victory," projectsyndicate.org (April 29, 2017); "What Donald Trump Means by Fair Trade"; "The Trump Trilemma: The Contradiction at the Heart of Trumponomics," *The Economist* (May 13, 2017); "Why Trade is Good for You," *The Economist* (May 27, 2017); "What the German Economic Model can Teach Emmanuel Macron" (May 27, 2017); "An Interview with Wolfgang Ischinger," *The Economist Online* (May 30, 2017); Richard Haass, *A World in Disarray: American Foreign Policy and the Crisis of the Old Order* (2017).

Nationhood, citizenship, and identity: W. H. Walsh, "Pride, Shame and Responsibility," *Philosophical Quarterly* (January 1970); Ernest Gellner, *On Nations and Nationalism* (1983); Eric Hobsbawm, *Nations and Nationalism since 1780* (1990); Fritz Gschnitzer, Reinhart Koselleck, Bernd Schönemann, and Karl Ferdinand Werner, "Volk, Nation, Nationalismus, Masse" in *Geschichtliche Grundbegriffe* 7 (1992), ed. Koselleck; David Miller, *On Nationality* (1995), *The Nationalism Reader* (1995), eds. Dahbour and Ishay; Miller, *Citizenship and National Identity* (2000); Patrick Weil, *Qu'est-ce qu'un Français?: Histoire de la nationalité française depuis la Révolution* (2002; 2005); trans. *How to be French: Nationality in the Making since 1789* (2008); Miller, "Democracy's Domain," *Philosophy and Public Affairs* 37, 3 (2009); Nenad Miscevic, "Nationalism," *SEP Online* (December 2015); Dominique Leydet, "Citizenship," *SEP Online* (December 2015); Sabine Corneloup, "Les modes actuels d'acquisition de la nationalité française"; Dominique Schnapper, "Nationalité et citoyenneté"; Serge Slama, "Jus soli, jus sanguinis, principes complémentaires et consubstantiels de la tradition républicaine"; Hugues Fulchiron, "Les enjeux contemporains du droit français de la nationalité à la lumière de son histoire"; all in "La Nationalité," *Pouvoirs* 1 (2017).

Free Movement: Ethical Issues in the Transnational Migration of People and Money (1992), eds. Barry and Goodin; Michael Walzer, *Spheres of Justice* (1983); Joseph Carens, "Aliens and Citizens," *Review of Politics* 49 (1987); *International Handbook on the Economics of Migration* (2013), eds. Constant and Zimmermann; Samuel Scheffler, "Immigration and the Significance of Culture," *Philosophy and Public Affairs* (Spring 2007); Stephen Macedo, "Should Liberal Democracies Restrict Immigration?" in *Citizenship, Borders, and Human Needs* (2011), ed. Smith; Chandran Kukathas, "Expatriatism: The Theory and Practice of Open Borders," in ibid.; Christopher Caldwell, "The Hidden Costs of Immigration," *Claremont Review of Books* (November 8, 2016).

Multiculturalism Reconsidered (2002), ed. Paul Kelly; Will Kymlicka, *Liberalism, Community and Culture* (1989); *The Rights of Minority Cultures* (1995) and *Politics in the Vernacular: Nationalism, Multiculturalism and Citizenship*

(2001); Kenan Malik, "The Failures of Multiculturalism," *Foreign Affairs* (March-April 2015); and "Britain's Dangerous Tribalism," *INYT* (July 11, 2015); Michael Ignatieff, *The Lesser Evil: Political Ethics in an Age of Terror* (2005); Malise Ruthven, "How to Understand Islam," *NYRB* (November 8, 2007); Panka Mishra, "Islamism," *New Yorker* (June 7, 2010); "Uneasy Companions: Islam and Democracy," *The Economist* (August 6, 2011); Timothy Garton-Ash, "Freedom and Diversity: A Liberal Pentagram for Living Together," *NYRB* (November 22, 2012); Malise Ruthven, review of Claire Adida, David Laitin, and Marie-Anne Valfort, "Why Muslim Integration Fails in Christian-Heritage Societies," *Financial Times* (January 29, 2016); Adam Nossiter, "That Ignoramus: Two French Scholars of Radical Islam Turn Bitter Rivals," *NYT* (July 12, 2016); Cécile Laborde, Liberalism's Religion (2017).

Eric Hobsbawm, "Identity Politics and the Left," *New Left Review* (May-June 1996); Brian Barry, *Culture and Equality* (2001); Amy Gutmann, *Identity and Democracy* (2003); Anthony Appiah, *The Ethics of Identity* (2005); Natalia Stoljar, "Feminist Perspectives on Autonomy," *SEP Online* (January 2016); Mark Lilla, "The End of Identity Liberalism," *NYT* (November 18, 2016); Cressida Heyes, "Identity Politics," *SEP Online* (December 2015); Somogy Varga and Charles Guignon, "Authenticity," *SEP Online* (December 2015);

Intellectual doubts and disaffection: George Dangerfield's *The Strange Death of Liberal England* (1935); John Hallowell, "The Decline of Liberalism," *Ethics* (April 1942); Arthur Ekirch, *The Decline of American Liberalism* (1955); Theodore Lowi, *The End of Liberalism* (1969); Daniel Bell, *The Cultural Contradictions of Capitalism* (1976); Samuel Huntington, Michel Crozier, and Joji Watanuki, *The Crisis of Democracy: On the Governability of Democracies* (1975); Ronald Terchek, "The Fruits of Success and the Crisis of Liberalism," in *Liberals on Liberalism* (1986); Meinecke citation, Rudolf Vierhaus, "Liberalismus," in *Geschichtliche Grundbegriffe 3* (1982), ed. Koselleck; Roger Kimball and Hilton Kramer, *The Betrayal of Liberalism* (1999); H. W. Brands, *The Strange Death of American Liberalism* (2001); Raymond Geuss, "Liberalism and its Discontents," *Political Theory* (2002) and *Philosophy and Real Politics* (2008); Patrick Deneen, *Why Liberalism Failed* (2018); Jonathan Haidt, *The Righteous Mind: Why Good People are Divided by Politics and Religion* (2012); Thomas Nagel, "The Taste for Being Moral," review of *The Righteous Mind*, *NYR* (December 6, 2012); Ronald Inglehart and Scott C. Flanagan, "Value Change in Industrial Societies," *APSR* (December 1987); Ronald Inglehart and Chris Welzel, "The WVS Cultural Map of the World," World Values Survey website (July 2017); Walter Scheidel, *The Great Leveller: Violence and the History of Inequality from the Stone Age to the 21st Century* (2017); Francis Fukuyama, "The End of History?" *National Interest* (Summer 1989); *Political Order and Political Decay*

(2014); "Can Liberal Democracy Survive the Decline of the Middle Class?" *Foreign Affairs* (January-February 2012); "America in Decay," *Foreign Affairs* (September-October 2014); "American Political Decay or Renewal? The Meaning of the 2016 Election," *Foreign Affairs* (July-August 2016); Samuel Huntington, "The Clash of Civilizations?" *Foreign Affairs* (Summer 1993); *"The Clash of Civilizations": The Debate, 20th Anniversary Edition, Foreign Affairs* (August 2013); Azar Gat, "The Return of Authoritarian Great Powers," *Foreign Affairs* (July–August 2007); Daniel Deudney and G. John Ikenberry, "The Myth of the Autocratic Revival: Why Liberal Democracy Will Prevail," *Foreign Affairs* (January–February 2009); Azar Gat, "Which Way is History Marching? Democracy's Victory is Not Preordained," *Foreign Affairs* (July–August 2009); Ikenberry, "The Future of the Liberal World Order," *Foreign Affairs* (May–June 2011); "The Plot Against American Foreign Policy: Can the Liberal Order Survive?" *Foreign Affairs* (May-June 2017); Andrew Levine, "A Conceptual Problem for Liberal Democracy," *Journal of Philosophy* (June 1978); Richard Rorty, *Contingency, Irony and Solidarity* (1989); Judith Shklar, "The Liberalism of Fear," in *Liberalism and the Moral Life* (1989), ed. Rosenblum; John Gray, *Liberalisms* (1989); Richard Bellamy and John Zvesper, "The Liberal Predicament: Historical or Logical?" *Politics* (February 1995); John Skorupski, "Liberty's Hollow Triumph," *Royal Institute of Philosophy Supplements* 45 (March 2000); Gray, *The Two Faces of Liberalism* (2000); Raymond Geuss, "Liberalism and Its Discontents," *Political Theory* (June 2002) and *Philosophy and Real Politics* (2008); Jeremy Waldron, *Torture, Terror and Trade-Offs: A Philosophy for the White House* (2010); Marc Stears, "Liberalism and the Politics of Compulsion," *British Journal of Political Science* (July 2007); Matt Sleat, "Liberal Realism: A Liberal Response to the Realist Critique," *Review of Politics* (Summer 2011); Edward Hall, "Contingency, Confidence and Liberalism in the Political Thought of Bernard Williams," *Social Theory and Practice* (October 2014); Steven Pinker and Andrew Mack, "The World is Not Falling Apart," *Slate* (December 22, 2014); Charles Kenny, "2015: The Best Year in History for the Average Human Being," *The Atlantic* (December 18, 2015); Peter Vallentyne and Bas van der Vossen, "Libertarianism," *SEP Online* (May 2017); "Le suicide français," fr .wikipedia.org (September 30, 2016); Alexander Stille, "The French Obsession with National Suicide," *New Yorker* (December 11, 2014); Regina Krieger, "Wie Sarrazin Millionär wurde," *Handelsblatt* (May 21, 2012); "Deutschland schafft sich ab," de.wikipedia.org (September 30, 2016); Jason Brennan, *Against Democracy* (2016); Roger Scruton, *On Human Nature* (2017); Rod Dreher, *The Benedict Option* (2017); Albert O. Hirschman, "Rival Interpretations of Market Society: Civilizing, Destructive or Feeble?" *Journal of Economic Literature* (December 1982); Wolfgang Streeck, "How Will Capitalism End?" *New Left Review*

(May-June 2014); "Le retour des évincés," in *L'âge de la régression* (2017), ed. Geiselberger; on Streeck, Adam Tooze, "A General Logic of Crisis," review of Streeck's work, *London Review of Books* (January 5, 2017); Jean-Luc Mélenchon, *L'ère du peuple* (2014); Perry Anderson, "Renewals," *New Left Review* (January-February 2000); "Dégringolade," *London Review of Books* (September 2, 2004); Emile Chabal, "Les intellectuels et la crise de la démocratie," *Pouvoirs* 2 (2017).

NAME INDEX

Acton, John Dalberg-Acton, Lord: *History of Freedom,* 15; on universal suffrage, 152–53
Adenauer, Konrad, 305, 308, 357
Ahmad, Muhammad, 204
Alain (Emile Chartier, 1868–1951), 29, 226–27; anti-war liberalism of, 226–27; Aron's criticism of, 228–29; background and career of, 226–27, 227–28; Baldwin and, 227; character and outlook of, 227–28; influence on Weil, 228; liberal dissent of, 229; Mendès-France and, 344, 356; *Propos,* 226; Rousseauan idealism of, 228
Amendola, Giovanni, 272
Anderson, Perry, 451–52; *New Left Review* editor, 450
Arnoldt, Hans, 67
Aron, Raymond, 167; founding *Commentaire,* 374; liberal dissent of, 228–29, 231–32; Mendès-France and, 355–56; Sartre and, 334
Arrow, Kenneth, 368
Asquith, Herbert, 186, 215
Asquith, Margot, 217
Attlee, Clement, 309
Auden, W.H., 295

Bagehot, Walter (1826–1877), 109, 182–84; background and character of, 182–83; *The English Constitution,* 183; fear of the masses, 183; Gladstone on, 184; reconciling liberalism and tradition, 184; on *Weltpolitik,* 202–3. *See also* Leroy-Beaulieu, Paul
Baldwin, Roger Nash (1884–1981), 29, 295; ACLU and, 229–30, 230; anti-war liberalism of, 227; liberal dissent of, 229
Baldwin, Stanley, 425
Balzac, Honoré de, 37
Barker, Ernest, 127

Baroody, William, 374
Barre, Raymond, 374
Bassermann, Ernst (1854–1917), 29, 192, 239; background and character of, 208, 211–12; on German nationalism, 212–13. *See also* Chamberlain, Joseph
Bastiat, Frédéric, 66, 180–81
Bates, Katharine Lee ("America the Beautiful"), 425
Beaverbrook, Max, 217
Bebel, August, 67; *Women under Socialism,* 113
Bell, Daniel, *The Cultural Contradictions of Capitalism,* 439
Bell, John, 103
Benenson, Peter, 295, 296–97
Bentham, Jeremy, 70, 71; J.S. Mill and, 90–91; Utilitarianism of, 91–92
Benz, Karl, 142
Bergson, Henri, *Two Sources of Morality and Religion,* 276–77
Berle, Adolf A., *The Modern Corporation and Private Property,* 270
Berlin, Isaiah (1909–1997), 124; background and character of, 318–19, 320–21; on "negative" and "positive" liberty, 321–22; Oakeshott on, 317; pluralism of, 319–20, 321; "republican" liberty concept of, 322–23; "Two Concepts of Liberty," 321; Zionism of, 320–21
Bernanke, Ben, 260, 405
Bernhard, Georg, 239
Bernstein, Eduard, 140
Bevan, Aneurin, 157
Beveridge, William (1879–1963), 25; abandoning "lesser eligibility" welfare test, 310–11; background and character of, 309–10; creating British Welfare State, 308, 309–11; *Full Employment in a Free*

Beveridge, William (*cont.*)
Society, 311; welfare reforms of, 74. *See also* Chadwick, Edwin
Bismarck, Otto von, 111–13; anti-socialist laws of, 113; *Memoirs,* 112; progressive reforms of, 163; Reichstag and, 111–12; Richter and, 110–11; on scramble for Africa, 202; on universal suffrage, 148; wars of, 113; Wilhelmine liberals and, 164
Black, Duncan, 368
Blackstone, William, 122
Blum, Léon, 161
Blum, Robert, 297
Bodin, Jean, 8, 49–50
Bonaparte, Napoleon, 51, 383; Constant and, 44–45; as elected despot, 54; press freedom and, 110
Bouglé, Célestin (1870–1940), 29, 167–68, 438; background and character of, 170–71; defense of "principles of 1789," 170–71; "Egalitarian Ideas," 168; liberal patriotism of, 421–22; "Polytelism" essay, 171; on religion and anticlericalism, 171; study in Germany, 169; "Teaching Patriotism," 421–22; "The Crisis of Liberalism," 168, 421. *See also* Rawls, John
Bourgeois, Léon (1851–1925), 10; background and character of, 194–95; *Solidarité,* 194; taxing for imperial expansion, 202
Bowring, John, 214, 225
Boyle, Danny, London Summer Olympics opening ceremony of, 425–26
Bradlee, Ben, 361
Brandeis, Louis (1856–1941), 29; background and character of, 233; liberal dissent of, 233–34; Wilson and, 234
Brands, H. W., *The Strange Death of American Liberalism,* 439
Brandt, Willy (1913–1992), background and character of, 353, 357–59; in East-West détente, 384; left-liberalism of, 352–53; promoting international democracy, 359–60
Breckinridge, John, 103
Brennan, Jason, *Against Democracy,* 449
Brentano, Lujo, 165, 305
Briand, Aristide, 220
Bright, John, 75
Brogan, Hugh, 62; *History of the United States,* 221
Brooks, David, 448
Brown, Florence, 139
Bryan, William Jennings, 163, 222, 259

Buchanan, James (1919–2013), 156; anti-government views of, 367–69; background and character of, 367–68; *The Calculus of Consent,* 368; limited government of, 373
Bucher, Lothar, 112
Buckley, William, Jr., 263, 379
Burgess, John, *Comparative Constitutional Law,* 166
Burke, Edmund, 92, 331

Caillaux, Joseph, 161, 220
Calas, Jean, 296
Calhoun, John, 135, 368
Cameron, David, 376
Camus, Albert (1913–1960), 26, 314, 328; anticommunist liberalism of, 331; background and character of, 330–31; on good and bad revolutions, 331–32; *The Rebel,* 331–32
Carens, Joseph, 429
Carlyle, Thomas: on J.S. Mill, 89; *Past and Present,* 73
Carr, E. H., 292
Casanova, Jean-Paul, 374
Cassin, René, 288
Castlereagh, Robert Stewart, Viscount, 16–17
Chadwick, Edwin (1800–1890), 10, 28, 71–74, 74, 98; background and character of, 71; Bentham and, 71; centralizing attitudes of, 72–73; creation of single market, 73; on deserving and undeserving poor, 189; "lesser eligibility" concept of, 310, 408–9; liberal reforms of, 72; moralization of poverty of, 73–74; Nassau and, 72; Poor Laws report of, 73–74; reputation of, 71–72; on society and government, 71–72; on state vs. market, 135. *See also* Cobden, Richard
Chamberlain, Joseph (1836–1914), 29, 154; background and character of, 208–9; on British Empire, 210–11; Gladstone and, 210; radicalism of, 209–10
Chang, Pen-Chun, 288
Channing, William Ellery (1780–1842), 10, 28, 81–82; background of, 81; liberal Protestantism of, 81; moral self-improvement, 78; on moral self-improvement, 82; on personal progress, 135; on political engagement, 82; on self-cultivation, 81–82
Charrière, Isabelle de, 44
Chartier, Emile. *See* Alain
Chase, Salmon, 108

Chekhov, Anton, 465
Chessman, Caryl, 297
Churchill, Winston: *Great Contemporaries,* 158; implementing national compulsory insurance, 309; on Lord Rosebery, 158; in modernized British politics, 211; on Sudan massacre, 204
Clemenceau, Georges (1841–1929), 26, 161; admiration for "Anglo-Saxon" world, 219; anticlerical sentiment of, 171; background and character of, 217–21; belief in capitalism, 218; call for unity, 422; Dreyfus affair and, 219; French Revolution and, 218; as liberal hawk, 213, 217–21; on *Weltpolitik,* 203
Clémentel, Etienne, 161
Cobden, Richard (1804–1865), 10, 28, 37–38, 71, 74–77, 135; admiration of for Prussian government, 164; in America, 74; on American civil War, 77; background of, 74; class war of, 75–76; "everyone wins" position of, 76; on free enterprise, 76–77; on free trade, 75, 76; on incorporation of boroughs, 75; on land reform, 75; on landed aristocracy, 75; liberal causes of, 74–75; liberal dream of, 410–11; on local self-government, 74–75; on Ricardo's labor theory, 76; on theory of value, 76. *See also* Chadwick, Edwin
Cohen, Gerry, 343–44
Comte, Auguste, 89, 278
Condorcet, Nicholas de, Marquis, 147, 364, 368
Constant, Benjamin (1767–1830), 8, 10–11, 27, 40–43, 65, 126, 134, 153, 313, 318, 321; *Adolphe,* 45; background and career of, 40, 43; belief in new society, 45; character and outlook of, 40; on civic respect for people, 135; de Staël and, 44; direct democracy and, 47; human personhood and, 45–46; and the individual, 44–45; liberal dream of, 410–11; liberalism and, 48; *Liberty Ancient and Modern,* 47; Louis Philippe and, 43; Mill and, 48; Mme de Charrière and, 44; Napoleon and, 44–45; on power, 47; *Principles of Politics,* 40, 152; on progress, 46; resistance to power, 46–47; Rousseau and, 47; on sovereignty of the people, 152; on undesirability of direct democracy, 150–51; on vigorous civil society, 65
Corbyn, Jeremy, 398
Courbet, Gustave, 218

Cournot, Antoine, 174
Croly, Herbert (1869–1930), 10; background and career of, 190; "Crolier than thou" tone of, 191; *The Promise of American Life,* 190–91

Dangerfield, George, *Strange Death of Liberal England,* 439
Daniel, Yuli, 295
Darwin, Charles, 37
Daumier, Honoré, 51, 54
Davies, David, 224–25
de Beauvoir, Simone, 333, 435
de Gaulle, Charles, 353, 354; far right and, 438; Mendès-France and, 355–56
Debs, Eugene, 103
Defoe, Daniel: on religious sectarianism, 133; *Robinson Crusoe,* 133
Delacroix, Eugène, *Liberty Leading the People,* 53
Delaroche, Paul, Guizot portrait by, 51
Deneen, Patrick, *Why Liberalism Failed,* 440
Deutsch, Karl, *Nationalism and its Alternatives,* 422
Dewey, John, 150, 316
Dicey, A. V., 346; *Lectures on Law and Public Opinion in England in the Nineteenth Century,* 120
Dickens, Charles, 329
Disraeli, Benjamin, 97–98
Dohm, Hedwig, 141
Dow, Charles: creating Dow-Jones stock index, 143; *Wall Street Journal,* 181
Doyle, Michael, 411–12
Dreher, Rod, *The Benedict Option,* 446
Dreyfus, Alfred, 168, 219, 297, 341
Duguit, Léon, 195
Dunn, John, *Setting the People Free,* 157–58
Durkheim, Emil, 167, 187, 195
Dworkin, Ronald: response of to Rawls, 345–47; on rights, 345–46; *Sovereign Virtue,* 345; *Taking Rights Seriously,* 345

Ebert, Friedrich, 241
Ekrich, Arthur, *The Decline of American Liberalism,* 439
Eliot, George (Mary Ann Evans), 83
Eliot, T. S., 25–26
Elton, Godfrey, 214–15, 215n.1
Emerson, Ralph Waldo, 37
Engels, Friedrich: *The Communist Manifesto,* 13, 181; on *doctrinaires,* 54

Enghien, Louis-Antoine, Duc d', 297
Erhard, Ludwig, 306
Erikson, Erik, 435
Erzberger, Matthias, 239

Fabri, Friedrich, *Does Germany Need Colonies?*, 203–4
Faguet, Emile, 17
Fanon, Frantz, 435
Faure, Edgar, 355
Fawcett, Henry, 67–68, 164
Fawcett, James, 290
Ferry, Jules, 203
Feulner, Edwin, Heritage Foundation of, 377
Fisher, Anthony, 374
Fisher, David Hackett, *Liberty and Freedom*, 102
Fisher, Irving (1867–1947), 29, 140, 244; in America's Great Depression, 256–58; background and character of, 257–60; *Booms and Depressions*, 244; on depression's cause and cure, 244; financial ruin of, 259–60; *How to Live*, 258; influence of on policy, 245–46; *The Nature of Capital and Income*, 259; quantity theory of money of, 371; Schumpeter and, 258; solution to slump, 247–48; world of, 246–47
Fourier, Charles, 66
Fox, Margaret, 342
Franco, Paul, 315
François, Etienne, *Errinerungsorte*, 426
Freud, Sigmund, 141
Fried, Daniel, 392–93
Friedman, Milton (1912–2006), 156, 260; background and character of, 370; *Capitalism and Freedom*, 370, 372–73; Goodhart's law and, 371–72; on inflation, 369, 370, 371; on Keynesianism, 370–71; on limited government, 372–73; Margaret Thatcher and, 371; Marshall and, 370–71; on monetary policy, 369–70; stagflation and, 372; "The Quantity Theory of Money," 371
Fukuyama, Francis: "America in Decay," 441–42; "Can Liberal Democracy Survive the Decline of the Middle Class?", 441; *The End of History and the Last Man*, 440–41; *Political Order and Political Decay*, 441
Fuller, Margaret, 80

Galston, William, 397, 448
Gandhi, Mahatma, 203, 292

Garrison, William, *The Liberator*, 37–38
Gauchet, Marcel, 374
Gentz, Friedrich von, 16
Geuss, Raymond: "Liberalism and its Discontents," 439–40; *Philosophy and Real Politics*, 439–40
Gide, Charles, 195; *History of Economic Doctrines*, 68
Gilligan, Carol, *In a Different Voice*, 343
Giscard d'Estaing, Valéry, 356, 381
Gladstone, William Ewart (1809–1898), 3, 25, 26, 28, 101, 115–19; on Bagehot, 184; on British imperialism, 203; Chamberlain and, 210; character of, 116–19; on education reform, 116–17; on free market and free trade, 115–16; on Home rule for Ireland, 116; as Liberal Party leader, 115; liberal reforms of, 98; liberal rhetoric of, 136; moral vision of, 117–19; as progressive "inequalitarian," 117–18; reforms of, 116
Goldman, Emma, 230
Gompers, Samuel, 140
Goodhart, Charles, 371–72
Gorbachev, Mikhail, 383
Gordon, Robert, *The Rise and Fall of American Growth*, 406
Gossen, Hermann, 174
Goude, Jean-Paul, 382–83
Gramsci, Antonio, 272
Grant, Sir Hamilton, 203
Gray, John: *Liberalisms*, 444–45; on Rawlsian liberalism, 443, 444–45; *The Two Faces of Liberalism*, 444–45
Greeley, Horace, 18
Green, T. H., 186–88, 321–22
Grey, Edward, 186
Guizot, François (1787–1874), 3, 9, 10, 25, 26, 47, 49–51, 52, 136, 313, 356; on absolute power, 50, 56–57; background and career of, 52; belief of in representative government, 52–53; Bouglé and, 170; and Bourbon Ultras, 53; on bourgeois man, 159; on conflict and disorder, 49–50, 59–61; conservatives and, 57, 59; on containing power, 55–56; and *doctrinaires*, 52–53; in exile, 54–55; on French Revolution, 52, 53; on the French Revolution, 50, 51; on good government vs. tyranny, 50; images of, 51; in July Monarchy, 49, 53–54; *Lectures on Representative Government*, 55; liberal patriotism pf, 422; love of

France, 55; Marx and Engels on, 54; on masterless order, 135; Mill on, 49; Napoleon and, 54; on need for governing classes, 153–54; place of in liberal thought, 55; on popular sovereignty, 57–58; as reactionary, 59; retirement of, 55; on Robespierre, 51; sacking and flight of, 51–52; on sharing of power, 56–57; socialists and, 57, 59–60; on sovereignty of people, 56; on sovereignty of the people, 152; Tocqueville and, 49; on tyranny, 50–51; on unbridled power, 49–50, 51
Gutmann, Amy, 348

Halévy, Elie, 17
Hallowell, John, 439
Hallstein, Walter, 284, 373
Hamilton, Alexander, 270
Hankey, Maurice, 217
Hare, Richard, 335–36
Harris, José, 310
Hart, Herbert, 294
Hartz, Louis, 378; *The Liberal Tradition in America,* 104
Havel, Vaclav, 296, 386
Hayek, Friedrich (1899–1992), 29, 156, 244; antitotalitarianism of, 274–76; background and character of, 260–61, 264, 324; on business cycles, 262; on collectivism, 260; on conservatism, 327–28; *The Constitution of Liberty,* 260, 275–76, 324–25, 326, 327–28; on depression's cause and cure, 244, 262–63; on economic ignorance, 263; *Economica,* 277; on evolution of order, 325–26; expediency of, 327; Friedman and, 370, 371; on government's agenda and nonagenda, 325; influence of on policy, 246; *versus* Keynes and Fisher, 262; Keynes on, 276; *Law, Legislation and Liberty,* 260, 324, 325, 326–27; liberal capitalism of, 280; on limited government, 372; at Lippmann Colloquium, 272, 327; Ludwig Mises and, 261–62; Oakeshott on, 317; political antipolitics of, 324–28; on right-wing liberalism, 260; *The Road to Serfdom,* 260, 274–75, 324; on social justice, 326–27; solution to slump, 247–48; world of, 246–47; writing style of, 263–64
Hegel, Georg Wilhelm Friedrich, 4, 12, 14, 27, 264, 130134; Oakeshott and, 317; *The Philosophy of Right,* 159
Heidegger, Martin, 287

Heller, Hermann, 303, 304
Heraclitus, 277
Herzen, Alexander, 63, 320
Heuss, Theodor, 305
Hicks, John, 254
Hitler, Adolf, rise to power of, 112, 217, 250–51, 272, 300
Hobbes, Thomas, 121–22, 317
Hobhouse, Emily, 205
Hobhouse, Leonard (1864–1929), 10, 74, 164, 188–91; background and character of, 188; *Liberalism,* 188; on resistance to authoritarian order, 188–89; on state regulation and social intervention, 189–90; on Utilitarianism and laissez-faire, 189
Hobson, J.A.: background and character of, 206–7; *Imperialism,* 207; on imperialism, 207–8
Holmes, Oliver Wendell Jr., 235
Hoover, Herbert (1874–1964), 25; *American Individualism,* 268; on business ethics, 269–70; character of, 267, 268–70, 341; as the Forgotten Liberal, 265–66, 364; New Deal and policies of, 266; "ordered liberty" of, 103; on role of government, 266; Roosevelt and, 256, 265–66; Smoot-Hawley tariff-raising bill and, 258; stock market crash and, 266–67
House, Edward, 222
Howe, Geoffrey, 377
Howe, Louis, 268
Hugenberg, Alfred, 241
Humboldt, Wilhelm von (1767–1835), 10, 27, 134, 139, 140; background and career of, 33–35; belief in limitations of law and government, 34–35; character and outlook of, 34–35; on civic respect for people, 135; conditions during lifetime of, 34–35; detachment of, 42; French Revolution and, 35; on growth of human capacities, 458; liberalism and, 48; *The Limits of the Effectiveness of the State,* 39; Mill's admiration of, 41–42, 94; in peace talks of 1813–15, 42; on progress as growth of human capacities, 35, 39–43; self-standing civility ideal of, 145; on the state, 34–35; views of on liberal education, 41
Hume, David, 1, 134–35, 263–64
Humphrey, John, 288
Huntington, Samuel: *The Crisis of Democracy,* 439; on ethico-cultural conflict, 437
Huxley, Thomas, 87

Jackson, Andrew, 80, 103
Jaurès, Jean, 161, 219–20
Jeanson, Francis, 332
Jefferson, Thomas, 102, 270
Jevons, Stanley, 174
Johnson, Hiram, 226
Johnson, Lyndon (1908–1973), 25; background and character of, 353, 360–62; Great Society of, 362–64; Kennedy and, 360, 361; left-liberalism of, 353
Joseph, Keith, 375
Justi, Ludwig, 181

Kant, Immanuel, 1, 457; on British state, 152; *Groundwork to the Metaphysic of Morals*, 130; on noninstrumentality of persons, 130
Kellogg, J.H., 258
Kennedy, John, 353; Johnson and, 360, 361
Kepel, Gilles, 434
Ketteler, Wilhelm von, *The Labour Question and Christianity*, 122
Keynes, John Maynard (1883–1946), 29, 221, 244, 284, 385; background and career of, 139–40, 248–51; Bretton Woods currency system and, 372; on capitalism, 243; on classical economics, 251–53; on Conservatives, 249; on depression's cause and cure, 244; *The Economic Consequences of the Peace*, 250–51; *Essays in Persuasion*, 249; on future interest rates, 254; G. E. Moore and, 264; *General Theory of Employment, Interest and Money*, 251–52, 253–54; on government's agenda and nonagenda, 325; on government's role in economy, 250; on Hayek, 276; Hicks on, 254; idolization and scapegoating of, 248; on imperialism, 207; influence of on policy, 245–46; on Marshall, 179; in modern liberal politics, 254–56; on money wages, 253–54; politics of, 249–50; solution to slump, 247–48; on supply-side theory, 252–53; *A Tract on Monetary Reform*, 251; *A Treatise on Money*, 253; on virtues of economic liberalism, 252–53; world of, 246–47
Keynes, Neville, 139
Khan, Sadiq, 433
Kiesinger, Kurt, 358
Kimball, Roger, *The Betrayal of Liberalism*, 439
King, Martin Luther, Jr., 103
Kipling, Rudyard, 204

Kohl, Helmut, 384–85
Kohn, Hans, 272
Kramer, Hilton, *The Betrayal of Liberalism*, 439
Krein, Julius, 449
Kristol, Irving, 379
Kristol, William, 397, 448
Kropotkin, Peter, 230
Kruks, Sonia, 435

Laborde, Cécile, 17
Laboulaye, Edouard (1811–1883), 25, 48, 109–10, 114–15, 136; admiration for American democracy of, 109–10; on democratic liberalism, 110, 152, 153; *The Liberal Party*, 110
Lamarck, Jean-Baptiste, 84–85
Laroque, Pierre, 162
Lassalle, Ferdinand, 67
Le Pen, Marine, 389
Learned Hand, 235
Lecky, W.E.H., *Democracy and Liberty*, 153
Lenin, Vladimir, *Imperialism: The Highest Stage of Capitalism*, 207
Leo XIII (Pope), 13
Leroy-Beaulieu, Paul (1843–1916), 182, 184–86, 247; background and career of, 184–85; jingoism of, 203–4; *The Modern State*, 185–86. *See also* Bagehot, Walter
Liebermann, Max, 192
Lieven, Dorothée, 51
Lincoln, Abraham (1809–1865), 25, 26, 101–8; background and career of, 106–7; character of, 105, 106–7; Civil War and, 107–8; creation of warfare state, 101; democratic liberalism of, 105–6; Gettysburg Address of, 102, 105; keeping the South in the Union, 108; liberal rhetoric of, 136; meaning of liberty and freedom to, 101–4; progressive values of, 106–7; on slavery, 343–44
Lincoln, Mary Todd, 106
Lippmann, Walter (1889–1974), 190; antitotalitarianism of, 273–74; *The Good Society*, 273; liberal capitalism of, 280
Lipset, Seymour Martin, 378; *Political Man*, 352
Lloyd George, David (1863–1945), 26; Asquith and, 215–16; background and career of, 215–17; Hitler and, 217; as liberal hawk, 213, 215–17, 221; in modernized British politics, 211; People's Budget of,

162; progressive reforms of, 163; on *Welt-politik*, 203

Locke, John, 104, 148

Lodge, Henry Cabot, 223

Lohmann, Theodor, 163

Loucheur, Louis, 161–62

Louis Napoleon, 49, 63, 110; Bagehot's weakness for, 182; coup of, 182; as reforming autocrat, 109

Louis Philippe, king of the French, 43, 53, 54

Louis XVI, execution of, 53

Louis XVIII, king of France, 52, 55

Lowe, Robert, 97, 149

Lowi, Theodore, *The End of Liberalism*, 439

Lukes, Steven, 124–25, 320

Lyotard, Jean-Paul, *The Post-Modern Condition*, 349

Macaulay, Thomas: on British rule in India, 204; *History of England*, 15

MacIntyre, Alasdair: *After Virtue*, 348; background and character of, 349–50; call for nonliberal institutions, 446; on community and moral incoherence, 348–49; on moral individualism, 350–51

MacIver, R. M., *Community*, 348

Macron, Emmanuel, 18, 398–99; election of, 452; far right and, 438

Madison, James, 57, 135; *Federalist X*, 150; on representative democracy, 150; on sovereignty of the people, 152

Maine, Henry Sumner, *Popular Government*, 153

Maistre, Joseph de, 26, 331

Malesherbes, Guillaume de, 62

Malik, Charles, 287–88

Mallett, Bernard, 153

Malthus, Thomas Robert, 77

Mann, Golo, 235

Maritain, Jacques, 292, 345

Marlio, Louis, 273–74

Marshall, Alfred (1842–1924), 10, 173–74, 176–79; background and career of, 173–74, 177; on competitive markets, 246; on ethics and economics, 179–80; free-market triangle and, 179–81; Friedman and, 370–71; on individualism, 123; marginalist ideas of, 174–75, 177–78; on poverty, 179; *The Principles of Economics*, 140, 177–78, 179; on supply and demand, 177–78

Martineau, Harriet, 180–81

Marx, Karl, 25, 26, 37, 66, 183; Bagehot on, 183; on classlessness, 58; *The Communist Manifesto*, 13, 181; on *doctrinaires*, 54; in First Working Men's International, 231; on solidarity, 194

Masaryk, Tomas, *New Europe*, 194

Maurras, Charles, 26

May, Theresa, 391

McCarthy, Joseph, 361

McCraw, Thomas K., 142

Mead, Walter Russell, 394–95

Mehta, Hansa, 288

Meinecke, Friedrich, 239, 439

Mélenchon, Jean-Luc, 398; *L'ère du peuple*, 451

Mendès-France, Pierre (1907–1982): background and character of, 353–56; *To Govern is to Choose*, 355; left-liberalism of, 352–53

Menger, Carl, 174

Mercier, Ernest, 273–74

Metternich, Prince, 16

Michelet, Jules, 54; *History of the French Revolution*, 53

Michels, Robert, *Political Parties*, 154

Mill, James, 89, 90, 92

Mill, John Stuart (1806–1873), 8, 10–11, 25, 28, 88–100, 134–35, 174, 313, 339, 457; admiration of for Humboldt, 41–42; on the American Civil War, 97; *Autobiography*, 78, 89, 297; background and career of, 89–91; Bentham and, 91; on Benthamite Utilitarianism, 93–94; Berlin and, 323; on British liberals, 164; Coleridge and, 91; Constant and, 48; defense of British control in India, 203; at East India Company, 92, 201; with East India Company, 92–93; German co-operativism and, 67–68; on Guizot, 49; on hard-earned vs. unearned money, 365; "harm" test of, 95–96; on Humboldt, 94; on individuality, 94–96; on laissez-faire and noninterventionism, 99; on liberal outrage, 297; liberalism of, 88–89; *On Liberty*, 41, 94–95; *Liberty, Equality, Fraternity*, 96; marriage of, 92; on Martineau, 181; mental world of, 91; on national past, 425; on nonintrusion, 126; in Parliament, 97–98; *Political Economy*, 98–99, 126, 181; *Principles of Political Economy*, 65; on progress and prosperity, 99–100; on proportional representation, 96–97; on protection of individuality, 458; rejection of

Mill, John Stuart (*cont.*)
one template for human flourishing, 95–96; *On Representative Government,* 96–97, 422; on social conflict, 98; on social progress and individuality, 135–36; on stationary state, 100; *On the Subjection of Women,* 98; *System of Logic,* 95; on Tocqueville, 61; on Tocqueville's America, 145–46; on universal suffrage, 152, 153; *Utilitarianism,* 93; Utilitarianism of, 93–95, 189; on women and marriage, 98
Miller, David, 429–30, 432–33; *On Nationality,* 429–30
Millerand, Alexandre, 161
Milner, Alfred, 186
Milton, John, *Paradise Lost,* 130
Mises, Ludwig, 260–61
Mitterrand, François, 355, 356, 381
Mohn, Reinhard, 374
Moltke, Helmut von, 24
Monnet, Jean, 304–5
Montesquieu, Charles-Louis, Baron de, 133
Moore, G. E., 264
Morel, Edmund, 205
Morgenthau, Henry, Jr., 304–5
Müller, Jan-Werner, *What is Populism?,* 393–94
Müller-Armack, Alfred, 306
Mussolini, Benito, 13, 272
Myrdal, Gunnar, 324

Nagel, Thomas, 351, 443–44
Napoleon III. *See* Louis Napoleon
Nassau, William Sr., 72
Naumann, Friedrich (1860–1919), 10, 112, 186, 187; background and career of, 192–93; character of, 192–93; *Democracy and Empire,* 193; *Die Hilfe,* 192; dream of free-trading order, 305; on German patriotism, 193–94; hope for grand coalition of business liberals and moderate socialists, 239; liberal dissent of, 231–32; *Mitteleuropa,* 193–94; Weber and, 193
Neier, Aryeh, 296
Neuhaus, Father John, 446
Nicholas, Herbert, 291
Nicholas of Cusa, 132
Nietzsche, Friedrich, 26; *Thus Spake Zarathustra,* 141
Nora, Pierre: founding *Débat,* 374; *Les Lieux de Mémoire,* 426
Nozick, Robert: *Anarchy, State and Utopia,*

345; response of to Rawls, 345–47; on rights, 345–46

Oakeshott, Michael (1901–1990), 25; background and character of, 314–15, 317–18; on Berlin, 317; *Experience and Its Modes,* 315–16; on Hayek, 317; on Hobbes and Hegel, 317; *On Human Conduct,* 317; liberal quietism of, 317–18, 323; on modern politics and rationalism, 314–16; pragmatism of, 316–17
Ollivier, Emile, 110
Ophuls, Marcel, 354
Oppenheim, Louis, 167
Orwell, George (1903–1950), 26, 198, 314, 328; anticommunism of, 332; background and character of, 329; on Dickens, 329; intuitive liberalism of, 329–30; "newspeak" of, 330; "Politics and the English Language," 330
Ostrogorski, Moise, 154

Packe, Michael St. John, 99
Parker, Theodore, 102
Pasquier, Etienne, 62
Paul, Alice, 163
Peel, Robert, 75
Phillips, Wendell, 65, 82, 99
Piketty, Thomas, *Capital in the 21st Century,* 406
Pinochet, Augusto, 359, 372
Pitts, Milton, 381
Place, Francis, 89
Plummer, Mary, 218
Popper, Karl (1902–1994), 142, 274; antidefinitionalism of, 277–78; Hayek and, 277–78; on historicism, 277; on liberal democracies' achievements, 464; on limits of science, 278–80; open liberalism of, 276–80; on open society, 276–77, 313; *The Open Society and Its Enemies,* 276–77
Preuss, Hugo, 239
Putnam, Hillary, 336

Rathbone, Eleanor, 464
Rathenau, Emil, 142
Rathenau, Walter, 239
Rauschenbusch, Walter, 163
Rawls, John (1921–2002), 25, 335–45, 385; background and career of, 335–36, 341–42; Buchanan and, 369; criticism of, 342–43; "difference principle" of, 313–14, 338,

343; Gerry Cohen on, 343–44; impact of, 351; justifying liberalism, 335–45; on liberal principles, 443–44; on need for reconciliation, 336; principles of justice of, 338–39; responses to, 345–51; on social justice, 336–38; *A Theory of Justice,* 260, 314, 335–37, 339; on Utilitarianism, 339–40. *See also* Bouglé, Célestin

Rayburn, Samuel, 360

Raz, Joseph, *The Morality of Freedom,* 350–51

Reagan, Ronald (1911–2004): antigovernment views of, 377–78, 380; background and career of, 377–78, 380–81; libertarian economics and conservative moralism of, 377

Reuter, Ernst, 357–58

Ricardo, David, 76, 77, 189, 206

Richter, Eugen (1838–1906), 25, 110–15, 136; background and career of, 112; Bismarck and, 110, 163; failure of, 114; opposition to *Kulturkampf,* 170; oppositionism of, 231; *Pictures of the Socialistic Future,* 113; on social insurance, 114; socialists and, 113; on trade and tariffs, 114; on *Weltpolitik,* 203; Wilhelmine liberals and, 110–11, 112–13

Robbins, Lionel, 262, 324

Robespierre, Maximillian, 53

Rockefeller, John D., 142

Roosevelt, Eleanor, 268, 288

Roosevelt, Franklin (1882–1945), 25; character and outlook of, 267–68, 270–71; economic policy of, 256; Four Freedoms of, 103; Great Depression and, 256–57, 267; Hoover and, 265–66; New Deal of, 265–66; on role of government, 266. *See also* Fisher, Irving

Roosevelt, Theodore, 163, 176, 190

Röpke, Wilhelm (1899–1966), 306–7, 307. *See also* Rüstow, Alexander

Rorty, Richard: *Contingency, Irony and Solidarity,* 444; on Oakeshott, 316; *Philosophy and the Mirror of Nature,* 316; on Rawlsian liberalism, 443, 444

Rosanvallon, Pierre, *Society of Equals,* 452

Rosebery, Archibald Primrose, Earl of Rosebery, 158

Rothbard, Murray, 377

Rousseau, Jean-Jacques, 43, 47, 130; Constant and, 43, 47, 228; on ideal society, 43, 56, 130; snowstorm image of economic harms, 326–27

Roy, Olivier, 434

Ruggiero, Guido de, *History of European Liberalism,* 14

Rumbold, Richard, 130

Runciman, David, *The Confidence Trap,* 453

Russell, Lord John, 149

Russell, Richard, 360

Rüstow, Alexander, 273, 306

Sacco, Nicola, 229–30, 297

Samuelson, Paul, *Economics,* 336

Sandel, Michael, *Liberalism and the Limits of Justice,* 347

Sanders, Bernie, 398

Sarrazin, Thilo, *Deutschland schafft sich ab,* 448

Sartre, Jean-Paul (1905–1980): background and career of, 332–33, 334–35; *Being and Nothingness,* 334; on Camus, 332; *Critique of Dialectical Reason,* 334; on freedom and constraint, 333–34; as semi-liberal or temperamental liberal, 25, 26, 314, 333; *Words,* 335

Schacht, Hjalmar, 272

Schatz, Albert, *L'individualisme économique et sociale,* 123

Schinkel, Karl-Friedrich, 33

Schmidt, Helmut, 353

Schmitt, Carl, 26, 303–4

Schmoller, Gustav, 140, 163–64, 165–66; on free trade, 206; *The Mercantile System and Its Historical Significance,* 206

Schulze, Hagen, *Errinerungsorte,* 426

Schulze-Delitzsch, Hermann (1808–1883), 28, 65–69, 99; background of, 65; on balanced, localized liberal society, 67–68; Bismarckian state welfare and, 67; on capitalism, 66–68; on collectivism, 66–67; on cooperativism, 68; on failed German revolution, 66; German cooperativism and, 67–68; Gide on, 68; on "golden middle ranks," 65–66; ideal society of, 65–66; on industry and trade, 66, 67; on middle-way progress and voluntarism, 68; on mutualism, 67; on socialists, 66–67

Schumacher, Kurt, 308, 357–58

Schuman, Robert, 372

Schumpeter, Joseph, 140, 367, 457; *Capitalism, Socialism and Democracy,* 155–56; on capitalism and popular sovereignty, 155; criticism of democracy, 145, 367, 368, 450; on entrepreneurial risk, 255; Fisher and,

Schumpeter, Joseph (*cont.*)
258; on liberal capitalism, 145, 411, 449–50; "The Sociology of Imperialism," 225
Schurz, Carl, 108
Scopes, John, 229
Scruton, Roger: ethico-cultural criticism of liberalism, 446–47; *On Human Nature*, 446–47; *The Meaning of Conservatism*, 447
Sen, Amartya: *The Idea of Justice*, 344; on Rawlsianism, 346
Shaftesbury, Earl of, *Characteristics*, 133
Sherman, Alfred, 374, 375
Shklar, Judith, 443, 444
Sidgwick, Henry, 85, 86–87; *The Elements of Politics*, 122–23, 190; on individualism, 122–23; on Spencer, 88
Sièyes, Abbé, *What Is the Third Estate?*, 147
Simon, Jules, 48
Sinyavsky, Andrei, 295
Siodmak, Robert, 236
Skidelsky, Robert, *John Maynard Keynes: Hopes Betrayed*, 255
Skorupski, John, 443, 445
Smend, Rudolph, 303, 304
Smiles, Samuel (1812–1904), 10, 78–81; on character, 78–79, 80–81; on hard work and self-help, 78–80; on individualism, 78; material self-improvement, 78; on progress, 79–80; on social vices, 127; *Thrift*, 80; on virtues of drudgery, 79
Smith, Adam, 1–2, 70, 176, 285; Bagehot on, 183; on business and government, 143–44; on ethical stability in society, 100, 369; on mercantile doctrine, 206; political economy theory of, 70, 77; on wages, 176–77
Solomon, Flora, 295
Sonnemann, Leo, 181; *Frankfurter Zeitung*, 181
Sorel, Georges, 183; *The Illusions of Progress*, 155; on liberal democracy as sham, 155; radical anarchism of, 230; *Reflections on Violence*, 155
Spencer, Herbert (1920–1903), 82–88; *Autobiography*, 83, 88; background and career of, 82–83; on bad government, 84; character of, 83–84; *Data of Ethics*, 85; defensive conservatism of, 87–88; on equal freedom principle, 84; on evolution of human character, 85–87; on evolution of natural forms, 85; on evolutionary progress, 135; Huxley on, 87; on need for relaxation, 88; *Principles of Ethics*, 85; progressive ethics

of, 85–87; *The Proper Sphere of Government*, 82; radical ideas of, 82–83; Sidgwick on, 85, 86–87, 88; on social Darwinism, 84–85; *Social Statics*, 82, 84, 87; "The Development Hypothesis," 84
Spender, Stephen, 26
Spinoza, Baruch, 132, 322
Spooner, Lysander, 230–31; *No Treason*, 230–31
Staël, Germaine de, 44
Standing Bear, 141
Stanton, Elizabeth Cady, 80
Stein, Herbert, 328
Stendhal, *The Charterhouse of Parma*, 17
Stephen, James Fitzjames, 96
Stephens, Alexander, 13
Stevenson, Adlai, 361
Stevenson, Frances, 216
Stöcker, Adolf, 192
Straight, Willard, 190
Strauss, Franz-Josef, 358
Streeck, Wolfgang, 450
Stresemann, Gustav (1878–1929), 236, 237–43; annual reports to his party, 241; background and career of, 237, 240; Bassermann and, 211; death of, 237–38, 242; defending democratic republic, 239–40; hope for united Germany, 358; political growth of, 241; on reconciliation with France, 241
Strong, Benjamin, 256
Summers, Lawrence, 405, 419
Sumner, William Graham, 258
Süsterhenn, Adolf, 302–3

Taft, Robert, 416
Taft, William Howard, 233–35, 234
Tardieu, André, 161
Tawney, R. H., 180
Taylor, Harriet, 92, 93, 297
Taylor, Helen, 93
Terchek, Ronald, *Liberals on Liberalism*, 439
Thatcher, Margaret (1925–2013): background and character of, 375–76; Milton Friedman and, 371; nationalism of, 376–77; pro-market anti-state views of, 376–78; right liberalism of, 376–78
Thiers, Adolphe, 48–49; in July Monarchy, 54; in literal press, 53
Thoreau, Henry David, 337; on civil disobedience, 229, 232
Thünen, Johann, 174

Tobin, James, 260
Tocqueville, Aléxis de (1805–1859), 8, 10–11, 25, 27–28, 47, 61–65, 126, 134, 136; on Algerian revolt, 201; on America as democratic laboratory, 425; background and career of, 62–63; in Bourbon restoration, 62–63; *Democracy in America,* 37–38, 64; on excellence and democratic mediocrity, 63; on French Revolution, 64; Guizot and, 49; on individualism, 61; J.S. Mill on, 145–46; in July Monarchy, 61; on mass democracy, 135; on middle-class society, 64–65; *Recollections,* 63; in Second Empire, 63; in second republic, 63; on spread of democracy, 61–62; on threats of state and mass society, 68; on voting, 65
Tolstoy, Leo, *Anna Karenina,* 25
Trotha, General Lothar von, 205
Trotsky, Leon, *The Revolution Betrayed,* 272
Truman, Harry S., 108, 378
Trump, Donald: America Firstism of, 389, 416; "dangerous inability" of, 448; election of, 396; intellectual right and, 448–49; Jacksonians and, 395; populism of, 396–97; Republicanism of, 392; typical supporters of, 395–96
Tugwell, Rexford, 266
Tullock, Gordon, 368–69; *The Calculus of Consent,* 368
Twain, Mark, 163

Ulmer, Edgar, 236
Urabi, Ahmed, 203

Vanzetti, Bartolomeo, 229–30, 297
Veblen, Thorstein, *The Theory of the Leisure Class,* 191
Veuillot, Louis, 171
Virchow, Rudolf, 170
Viviani, René, 220
Volcker, Paul, 380
Voltaire (François-Marie Arouet), *Treatise of Toleration,* 296–97

Waldeck-Rousseau, Pierre, 161
Waldron, Jeremy, 444
Wallas, Graham, 362
Walras, Léon (1834–1910), 10, 67–68, 140, 173–76, 178–79; on association, justice, and fraternity, 178–79; background and career of, 173–74, 175–76; on competi-

tive markets, 246; on efficiency and equity, 178; *Elements of Pure Economics,* 175, 176; on ethics and economics, 179–80; free-market triangle and, 179–81; on free trade and competition, 175, 176; on individualism, 123; on limits of economics, 179–80; marginalist ideas of, 174–75, 178; on rights and duties of social life, 178–79; "The Theory of Property," 178–79
Walzer, Michael: on immigration control, 429; on Sartre as liberal, 333; *Spheres of Justice,* 347, 429
Ward, Mrs. Humphry, 117
Watt, James, 33–34
Weber, Max, 25, 123, 183; in German Democratic Party, 239; left-liberalism of, 353; on liberal democracy, 154–55; Naumann and, 193
Wehner, Herbert, 353
Weil, Simone, 228
Welcker, Carl, 152
Wells, H. G., 157–58
Wells, Ida B., 163
Weyl, Walter, 190, 191; *The New Democracy,* 191–92
Weyrich, Paul, 377
White, Harry Dexter, 284
Whitney, William, 190
Wiggins, David, 319
Wilde, Oscar, *De profundis,* 96
Wiley, H. W., 163
Will, George, 448
Williams, Bernard, 346, 443
Wilson, James, 83, 183
Wilson, Woodrow (1856–1924): on American Founders, 222; background and character of, 221–22; Brandeis and, 234; Henry Cabot Lodge and, 223; Hoover and, 267; League of Nations and, 223–24; as liberal hawk, 221–24; *The New Freedom,* 222; presidency of, 163; Progressive policies of, 163; Red scares and, 229; Selective Services Act and, 227; Utopianism of, 221
Wolff, Theodor, 239
Wright, Jonathan, 238
Wycliffe, William, 132

Young, Iris Marion, 435–36

Zemmour, Eric, *Le suicide français,* 448

SUBJECT INDEX

Americanism, 378–79, 389, 416
anarchism, 23–24; and dissent, 230–31; liberalism and, 23, 230–32
authoritarianism: progressive, 24; resistance to, 188–89; soft, 300, 392; *as against* totalitarian systems, 359
authority: anarchism and, 230–31; conservatism and, 19, 57, 327–28; diffuse character in modernity, 159; dissent and, 83, 217–18, 226–32; ethical, decline or withdrawal of, 28, 61, 96, 131, 136, 145, 171; national, emergence of, 144; power and, 9, 23, 57, 288, 303–304

Britain, liberals and liberalism in, 115–19, 364; in 1914–18, 215–17; after French July uprising, 54–55; European Union and, 389–92, 418–20; business press and, 182–84; centralizing attitude of, 72–73; in Cold War, 328–30; disaffection of, 446–47; on free trade, 75–77, 208–11; liberal imperialism of, 200–201, 210–11; Liberal Party's decline in, 157–58; Liberal Party's rise and heyday in, 115; on mass democracy, 152–53; on nationality and assimilation, 428, 430, 433; as "new" liberals, 186–90; northern trade and Christian nonconformism of, 115; on public interest and common good, 70–72; reform legislation of, 162; on slavery and serfdom, 34; social reforms of, 195–96; on social responsibility, 186–88; state authority and, 144; on suffrage extension and mass democracy, 157, 158; Thatcherism and, 375–78; on voting rights, 149; war preparations of, 166; in welfare state, 308–12; Whig aristocracy and, 115
business press: significance for free-market liberalism, 173, 180–84

capitalism, liberal, 8, 30, 280; democracy and, 61, 64, 68–69, 145–46; industrial, 118–19
categorization, social: politics of, 436. *See also* identity
civic respect. *See* respect, civic
civil society, 61, 64–66; localized, 67–69, 72
class conflict, 28–29, 58–59, 75, 104, 153
communism: end of, 21, 261, 296, 383–84, 441–42; *as against* liberalism, 20–21
community and communitarianism, 347–51
companies and corporations: legal recognitions and protections of, 143, 180, 269
compromise with democracy. *See* democracy, liberalism's compromise with
confidence, business, 253–4; liberal. *See also* self-confidence
conflict, class, 28–29; contrasting conservative attitudes toward, 59–60; false belief in diminishment of, 286; inevitability of as liberal guiding idea, 2, 5–6, 7–8, 21, 59, 60–61, 411–12; over state power and civil liberties, 364–65; search for political order in, 4–5; contrasting socialist attitudes toward, 19, 21–22, 59–60; hopes for taming without arbitrary power, xii, 7–8, 58–60, 454
conservatism, *as against* liberalism, 19, 459–60; on civic respect, 128; on conflict, 7, 59; on human capabilities, 19; on liberal society, 445–48; on nations and nationhood, 425–28; on power, 57; as practice of politics, 27; on progress, 21, 69–70, 249; Romantic, 91–92; in 1970s–80s Britain, 375–78; in 20th-century U.S., 377–81; weakness of, 327–28; on worth of personhood, 128–29
contract, freedom of, 180; as element of free-market or business liberalism, 173; indif-

contract (*cont.*)
ferent to contractual parties or contractual content, 180; limits to, 234; as means, not end, 187; unions feared as threat to, 153
cooperativism, 28, 61, 67–69, 240

democracy, *as against* liberalism, 3; bureaucratization of, 153–54; capitalism and, 449–51; direct, 150–51; economic, 160–67, 250, 285–86; economic critique of, 97, 326; electoral, 96–97; ethical, 167–72; four limits on (representation, articulation, bureaucratization, insulation), 152–54; liberal concession to, 150; liberal ethics and, 167–72; liberal parties' decline in, 148, 156–57, 242; liberalism's compromise with, 28, 140, 144–46, 147–60, 441; local, 118, 228, 240, 268; mass, 61, 64, 68–69; participatory vs. populism, 393–94; political, 147–60; representation in, 150–52; spread of, 61–62; suffrage restriction and extension of, 19, 71, 78, 105, 109–11, 136, 147–60; as "who?" not "how?" question, 149–50. See also liberal democracy
democratic liberalism. See liberal democracy
dissent: anarchism and, 230–31; anti-Soviet, 296; attitudes toward authority and, 132, 231–32; in Germany's Federal Republic, 301–2; in liberal democracies, 232–35; libertarianism and, 230–31; as political duty, 231–34; warfare state and, 226–35
diversity, 8, 29, 58–59, 128, 131, 383; cultural, 424, 436; moral: exaggerated degree of, 320
doctrinaires. See under France, liberals and liberalism in

economists, liberal, 177–78; in inflation of 1970s, 400–401; marginalist of 1880s–90s, 123; in 1930s slump, 243–64; since 2008, 399–410; against the state, 365–75
equality, 48, 168, 288; civil rights and, 362–63; economic, 461–62; fairness and, 337–39, 343–44; of human worth, 128–30; under law, 324; of moral, economic and political liberty, 463; of opportunity, 462–63. *See also* nonexclusion
ethics: of care and concern as against impartiality, 343; disagreements over, 441; of duties or of consequences, 344; Kantian, 130, 336; liberal hopes for order of without authorities, 5–6, 28; Millian, 93–96; Nietzschean, 141; pluralism or monism in distinguished from relativism, 323; speculative evolution of, 84–86, 441, 455
European Union, 194, 261, 417, 419, 423, 450; Britain and, 389–392, 418–20; France and, 382, 418; Germany and, 384, 418,

fascism, 20–21; liberal opposition to, 272–73
France, liberals and liberalism in, 17–18, 43, 184–85; in 1914–18, 217–21; admiration of for Anglo-Saxon world, 219; as anti-Jacobin Girondins or proto-liberals, 51; anticlericalism and, 170–71; attitudes of toward French Revolution, 49, 50, 52, 53, 382–83; as broad center of modern politics, 356, 374, 381–83; on citizenship and immigration, 431–32; dissenting, 226–28; as *doctrinaires,* 52–54; ever-present except in name, 59; in Fifth Republic (1958 on), 353–56; in Fourth Republic (1944–58), 330–35, 355; on free trade, 206–7; in July Monarchy (1830–48), 49–61, 184; liberal economists and, 374; liberal imperialism of, 201–2; in Napoleonic republic, 36; as Radicals or Republicans, 53–54, 161; restored reputation of, 452–53; right wing and in 20th century, 381–83; rise of hard right and, 398–99; in 1950s–1960s, 353–56; in Second Empire (1852–70), 109–10; on solidarity, 194–95; state authority and, 144; suffrage extension in, 148; in Third Republic (1870–1940), 44–45, 160–62, 194–95, 354–55; Tribunate and, 44
free markets/free trade, 75–77; seen as engine of prosperity and progress, 99–100; expansion of, 28; imperialism and, 207–8
freedom and liberty, 12–15. *See also* liberty

Germany, liberals and liberalism in, 17, 36–37, 41–42, 140–41, 206; 1848 revolution and, 24, 66; admiration of for British constitution, 152; after Napoleonic Wars, 41–42; anti-religious sentiment and, 169–70; Bismarck and, 110, 111–13; business press and, 181; calling for representative government, 54; critics of, 205–6; disaffection of, 447–48; in Federal Republic (1949 on), 299–308, 385; Free Democrats and, 17, 305–6, 358, 374; as *Freisinnigen* or Independents, 17; German Democratic Party and, 17, 239; in German Empire (1871–

1918), 110–15, 191–94; German People's Party and, 17, 157, 239; influence of on 1949 constitution, 302–3; liberal economists and, 374; liberal imperialism of, 202, 205; as National Liberals, 111, 211–13; November Revolution of 1989 and, 384; Progressive, 110–11, 164–67; right wing and in 20th century, 383–85; rise of hard right and, 398–99; in 1950s–1960s, 357–60; as Social Democrats, 140; on suffrage expansion, 156–57; tangled party structure in, 17, 239, 305–6; in Third Republic, 144; unmerited poor reputation of, 165–66; on voting rights, 148; wedge issues for, 113–14; in Weimar Republic (1918–33), 235–43; Wilhelmine, 112–13, 165–67

government: bad accounted for in diverse traditions, 64, 84; modern, centralized, 64, 72–73, 110, 115, 118, 121, 135, 144, 154, 196, 217, 250, 268–69, 278, 299–300, 307, 423; good *as against* tyrannical, 50–51; need to restore authority and prestige of, 460–61

guiding ideas of liberalism, 7–12, 21–23, 39–100; *as against* conservatism and socialism, 24–25, 26–28; diverse grounds for, 5–6; *as against* fascism and communism, 20–21; as liberal answers to basic political questions, 21–22; social sentiments and moral emotions strengthening, 26; *as against* 21st-century rivals, 21, 24; tensions and cross-supports of, 9–12, 21–23. *See also* conflict; power; progress; respect

hard right: in Britain and U.S., 390–92; common features of, 393–97; fascism and, 393; in France and Germany, 398–99; intellectual right and, 448–49; and Jacksonianism, 80–81, 394–95; populism and, 393–97; rise of, 30, 389–99

historical periods of liberalism: 1835 as time slice, 36–38; 1883 as time slice, 140–43; achievements of in 1945–89, 2, 385–86, 410–11, 455; fears and challenges to after 1989, 423–24; new start after 1945, 283–351; new world of ceaseless change (1930–80), 29, 33–38, 454; world liberals were making (1880–1945), 139–46

human character, 445–47; liberal hopes for progress of, 77–78; progress of as material self-improvement, 78–82; progress of as moral growth, 43, 81–82; releasing capac-

ity of, 39–49; varied nature of, 85, 93, 95–96

human rights, 287–99; 1948 Universal Declaration, 287–90; campaigns for, 294–96; legal, intellectual and political doubts about, 291–94. *See also* rights

identity: divisive politics of, 435–37; as muddled category, 434–38; national ideas of, 421–38; origins of in non-discrimination, 435; as politics of categorization, 436; recognition and, 130–33, 434–36, 442, 447

imperialism, liberal, 29, 198–213, 239; British, 200–201; civilizing mission of, 203–5; critics of, 202–3; economic roots of, 207; French, 201–2, 206–7; free trade and, 207–8; German, 202, 206; U.S., 200, 202, 205; as threat to peace, 207–8

individualism: assorted doctrines and obscurities of, 121–25, 268–69, 274–75; civic respect and, 120–31; conservative understandings of, 128–29; economic, 123–24; freedom of contract and, 173, 180; introduction of term, 61; liberal concerns for people mislabeled as, 125–30; as method of study, 123–25; moral, 350–51; charactering modern people, 27

individuality, 23, 27, 39, 41, 60, 83, 94–96, 120, 128, 136, 339, 458; and group belonging, 320; threatened by social conformity, 94

individuals: anachronistic use of term, 121–22; ordinariness of concept of, 122; loaded usage of, 122

intolerance, persistence of, 28–29, 168–72, 421

Jacksonianism, 148; liberty and, 102–3. *See also* hard right, Jacksonianism and

Kulturkampf, 168–70, 237

laissez-faire, 206; arguments for, 99–100; failures of, 209, 251; fluctuating belief in, 243, 365–85, 399–410; in liberal democracy, 161; of Manchester-school liberalism, 189; as misleading label for liberal outlook, 82–83; Law, rule of, 303–4; democratic understanding of, 111, 289, 298, 324; *as against* discretionary authority, 324; equality and, 108–9, 127–28, 188, 212–13, 275, 288–89, 324, 327–28; liberal understanding of, 275; post-1945 understanding

laissez-faire (*cont.*)
of, 288–89, 298, 324; as protection of property rights, 53, 64, 198, 373; social justice and, 336–45

liberal (as word): contested use and abuse of, 17–18; emergence of word in politics, 16–19; (as political kind): who is and who isn't, 24–25

liberal democracy, 18–19; achievements of, 464; capitalist modernity and, 30; conflicts with national and social identity in, 389–99; criticisms and disaffection with, 392–93, 439–53; dissent in, 232; economic concerns in, 155–56, 399–410; emergence of, 2; geopolitical loneliness of, 410–21; guarded acceptance of, 154–55; guiding liberal ideas in, 3, 7–12; historic compromise creating, 24, 28–29, 140; as openness and experiment, 276–80; post-1989 challenges to, 412–39; as post-1945 common form of politics, 283–351; rejection of, 155; suffrage extension in, 147–60; sustainability of, 460–61; threats to in 1918–33, 235–43

liberal internationalism, 29, 223–24, 284; Americanism and, 415–16; divisions in, 415–16; of idealists, realists, and cosmopolitans, 225–26; post-1945 humanitarian movement and, 296–99; retreat from after 2016, 413–14; unilateralist, 223; WWI shock as spur to, 224–25

liberal outlook. *See* guiding ideas of liberalism; liberalism, four guiding ideas of; social sentiments

liberalism, 1; as anachronistic, 457–58; broken up into "liberalisms," 286; centrist, 356; characteristics of, 19–21; in Cold War era, 328–35, 352–65; compromise of with democracy, 28, 140, 144–46, 147–60, 158–59; on conflict, 7–8; conflicting goals of, 456–57; conflicting ideals of, 199–200; *as against* conservatism and socialism, 21–22; deviations and alliances of, 23–24; doubts and disaffection with, 379–81, 439–53; emergence of, 34–35; equality and, 25–26; extension of, 454–55; failures of, 28–29; four guiding ideas of, 2–4, 7–12, 21–23, 39–100 (*see also* conflict; power; progress; respect); four periods of, 2; free-market, 173–86; idealized citizen of, 457; intellectual and moral sources of, 1–2, 4; justifying, 335–45; left-wing, 98–99; moral

foundation of, 348–51; non-Western, non-bourgeois character of, 30; as openness and experiment, 276–80; or "liberalisms," 463–64; passions of, 25–26; as practice of politics, 26–28; restabilization and success of, 29; rights and, 345–48; in the round, 30; *as against* small-government doctrine, 461; sociological critique of, 354–59; sources of, 2–4; in 21st century, 30; successes and failures of, 28; temperamental, 25–26; unity and shape of, 21–23

libertarianism, 23–24; dissent and, 230–31; philosophical, 447; present-day political influences of, 24, 368–69; in 1970s–80s U.S., 377

liberty, 36, 288–89; acknowledgment of, 333–34; ancient and modern, 47; as banner term, 4, 30, 36, 103, 183–84, 321–23; character and, 78; as check against power, 13; democratic, 15; disputed shape of, 319–23; diverse concepts of in politics, 187–88; economic, 15; freedom and, 12–15, 187–89; liberal belief in, 13; "negative," 319–23; perversion of, 331; political, 4, 14, 15, 320–23; "positive," 321–22; as protection from power, 463; pursuit of, 4–5; "republican," 322–23; uses of exemplified in U.S., 101–5; as wrong idea to start liberal story, 12–15

marginalism, economic, 123, 173–86; ethical neutrality of, 178–80; dropping preoccupation with supply, 175–78; specifying economic choice, 174–75

markets: dampening localist hopes, 68–69; local and cooperative, 28, 65–67; mass, 28, 61, 64, 68–69; nation-state and, 207, 426; national, 5, 73, 142, 410, 426, 463; power of, 28; resisting on behalf of society, 186–97; social progress through, 70–77; taming state, 173–86, 376

martyrs, liberal, 297

masses, fear of, 149–54

masterless order, liberal dream of and hopes for, 6–7, 64–65, 135–36, 149, 152, 325, 399; articulated in five domains, 9–12; doubts about, 149–54

mutualism, 66–67

nationalism, 29; imperialism and, 211–13; internationalism and, 415–17, 422; multilateral, 415–16; *as against* nativism, 392–93,

395–97, 421–22, 435, 447–48; in 1970s–80s Britain, 376–77; unilateral, 416; in Weimar Republic, 239–42

nations and nationality: assimilation and multiculturalism in, 430–34; citizenship and identity in, 421–38; exclusive and inclusive ideas of, 391–92; immigration and, 428–31; liberal and conservative ideas of, 246, 425–28

nativism. *See* nationalism; nations and nationhood

nonexclusion, as element of civic respect, 3, 11; equality and, 362–63; moral, 126, 128–31; political, 127–28; to socialists, 128; in welfare state, 310–11. *See also* democracy

nonintrusion, as element of civic respect, 3, 11, 125–26, 289; arguments for, 99–100; in human progress, 46; individuality and, 40–49; as legal concept, 131–33; liberty and, 126, 321–23; *as against* need to improve people, 23; privacy and, 3, 126, 128; respect for principle of, 39–49; right to, 233–34

nonobstruction, as element of civic respect, 3, 11, 125–27, 289; economic liberty and, 127; as liberal novelty in politics, 131; liberty and, 321; socialist and conservative hostility toward, 128

patriotism: citizenship and identity in, 421–38; in France, 171–72 (*see also under* Bouglé, Guizot, and Mendès-France *in name index*); in Germany, 193–94 (*see also under* Bassermann and Naumann *in name index*); liberal and nonliberal, 417–18, 421–22, 426; in 1900s, 193–94; in 1970s–80s Britain, 376–77; shared political ideals and, 421–22

peace: after WWI, 221, 223, 224; liberal belief in normality of, 214–15; imperialism as threat to, 207–8; postwar errors of, 250–51. *See also* war

personhood, untouchable worth of human: 3, 40, 121, 124, 127–31, 287–88, 321; and human dignity, 129–30, 288, 302, 464

political obligation, 232, 336–37

popular sovereignty: as nonsovereignty of any one entity, class, or interest, 55–58; "republican" understanding of, 151–52. *See also* democracy

populism, 163, 393–95, 443; elite character of, 393; fascism and, 393; hard right and,

391; Jacksonian, 394–95; *as against* participatory democracy, 393–94

poverty: as blight on nation, 209; British Poor Law reforms and, 73–74; industrial capitalism and, 118–19; inequality and, 403–4; "lesser eligibility" rule and, 409–10; liberal concern with, 179; moralization of, 73–74. *See also* social welfare

power, of some humans over others, political, economic or social, 8–9; decentralized, 302–3; diverse forms of, 329; divided, 3; exclusive and obstructive, 11; fluid, ever-present character of, 49–51; liberal defenses against, 9–12; liberal distrust of, 2–3, 5, 226–35; limits to, 10–11; as majoritarian bullying, 9, 98, 340, 368–69; as market exaction, 9, 61; need to be shared, 55–57; positive aspects of, 23; public forms of, 9; resistance to aiming at nondomination by one class, interest, or section, 9; resistance to as liberal principle, 51, 55–57; resistance to as refusal of submission, 9, 83–84; restraint of, 46–47; in restraint of conflict, 49–61; socialists on, 19–20; as state coercion, 9–10, 82–83; tension between people and, 21–22; tyrannous, 47

practice, liberalism as practice of politics, 26–27, 463–65

primacy, of politics for liberals, 30, 454–65

privacy. *See* nonintrusion

progress, as liberal guiding idea, 3, 8–10; conflicting with civic respect, 23, 24; conservative and socialist views on, 20, 21, 69–70; cost and sustainability of, 5–6, 10; free markets as engine of, 99–100; by government action, 28; of human character through material self-improvement, 28, 37, 78, 248; of human character through moral self-improvement, 10, 28, 78–82, 248, 446; individual happiness and, 90–91; in liberal democracy, 3; liberal hopes for, 3, 69–71; nonintrusion and, 46; in nonliberal regimes, 108–15; privacy and, 40–49; respect for individual and, 94–95; social, through governments, 69–77, 92–93; social, through markets, 69–77; social sentiments and moral emotions and, 26; winners and losers in, 339–40

progressives. *See under* Germany, liberals and liberalism in; United States, liberals and liberalism in prosperity: free markets as engine of, 99; social welfare and, 248–49; war and military spending as enemies of, 74–75

radicals, 104, 161; as left-wing liberals, 24, 68, 98–99, 111, 136–37, 168, 194, 239, 256, 311, 328–33, 350, 393, 398, 435, 443, 449–50. *See also under* Clemenceau *in name index*: Britain, liberals and liberalism in; France, liberals and liberalism in
rational expectations, in economics, 371–72
recognition, liberalism of: 12, 435, 442. *See also* identity
religion: Christianity and liberal empire, 200; coercive laws backing, 131–32; intolerance of, 168–72; *Kulturkampf,* 168–70, 237; liberal Protestantism and, 81–82; politics and, 117–18; toleration (*see* toleration, religious); on worth of human person, 129–30
republicanism, 17, 59, 161, 381, 392, 416
republicans. *See under* France, liberals and liberalism in; United States, liberals and liberalism in
resistance to power, as liberal guiding idea, 9–10; 55–56, 333, 454; civic respect and, 22–23; necessity of, 331–32; as neverending work, 51; as refusal of submission, 83–84; social sentiments and moral emotions and, 26; as voluntary outlawry, 84, 87–88; in warfare state, 226–35
respect, civic, as liberal guiding idea, 3, 22–23; for all people, 29, 48; conflicting with progress, 23; conservatives on, 19; exclusions and restrictions of, 362–63; indifference of to personal characteristics and social status, 133–34, 168; for individual, 40–49, 120–35, 265; liberty and, 12–15; moral nonexclusion and, 128–31; natural rights and, 11–12; for private citizen, 45–46; progressive authoritarianism and, 24; as public, not private, requirement, 125–26, 129–33; in religious toleration, 130–35; resistance and, 22–23; as restraint on power, 10–11; *as against* social progress, 94–95; *as against* social reform, 92–93; social sentiments and moral emotions and, 26; to socialists and conservatives, 128; triple structure of, 12–15, 125–26. *See also* Nonexclusion; Nonintrusion; Nonobstruction

revolution, 35; "bad," 51, 148, 151, 331–32; "good," 53, 148, 331–32
rights: civil, in Prussia, 34; civil, in U.S., 18, 29, 108, 141, 362–63; equal, 127–28, 132–33, 345; human, common or universal, 11–12, 29, 122, 287–99; natural, 293; philosophical views on nature of, 11–12, 45–46, 293, 345–46; liberalism of, 12, 123–24, 294; political rights and suffrage extension, 146–60; trade union, 98; women's, 80–82

self-confidence, liberal: gains and losses in, 136, 146, 385, 423, 453, 455
social contract, 338–39
social sentiments, liberal, 26. *See also* conflict; progress; resistance; respect
social welfare: Bismarckian, 39, 209–10, 309–10; of "deserving" poor, 189–90; government responsibility for, 255–60; means-testing for, 409–10; negative and positive, 39–40; in post-1945 welfare state, 301, 308–12; post-1970s disputes over costs of, 399, 401–4, 407–9; progressive reforms and, 69–70; prosperity and, 248–49; taxation for, 208–10; through late 19th century–early 20th century reforms, 28–29, 67, 91–93; through nonliberal reforms, 106–7
socialism, *as against* liberalism, 142, 219–20; class war and, 113; on conflict, 19, 21–22, 59–60; contesting civic respect, 128; of Fabians and Webbs, 189; in French Third Republic, 161; on human progress, 20, 70; municipal, 208–9; as practice of politics, 27; as reaction to liberalism, 19–20, 213; on resistance to power, 19–20; in Weimar Republic, 237
state: 19th-century attitudes toward, 67–68, 185–86; distrust of, 372–75; levels and overlapping authorities of, 72–73, 159–60, 166, 445; limitations of, 325, 372–73; local vs. centralized, 268–69; markets used to tame, 99–100, 268–70, 376; middle-class revolt against, 365–75; new liberalism and, 160–67; resisting on behalf of markets, 173–86; as twin growth with national market, 143–44; used to tame markets, 100, 270–71

taxation, 115, 300–301; liberal trilemma concerning, 39–40; necessity of, 461; rigidities of, 365–67; for social welfare, 208–10, 407, 459

toleration, religious, 121, 130–35, 168–72; arguments for from ignorance and perversity, 132; conceptual shape of, 133–34; history of, 3–5, 15, 121, 131–35; hoped to be irreversible and self-abolishing, 133–34; and liberal Protestantism, 81–82; persistence of intolerance and, 168–72, 421; as precedent for civic respect and nonexclusion, 126, 131–35

totalitarianism: *as against* authoritarianism, 359; liberal theories of, 274–76; as negative liberalism, 272–76

United States, liberals and liberalism in, 18, 37–38; in 1914–18, 221–24; ACLU and, 228–30; antigovernment movements and, 378–81; during Civil War, 103; conservative right in, 18; democratic, 105–8; disaffection of, 445–46; on dissent, 231–35; on free trade, 75; in Gilded Age, 162–64; in Great Depression and WWII, 264–71; hard right and, 448–49; on immigration, 429, 430; *as against* Jacksonian democrats, 80–81, 102–3; liberty's meaning to, 101–5; middle-class, 64–65; New Deal and, 256–60; Pro-

gressive, 163–64, 190–92, 394; Protestant, 81–82; reform legislation of, 162–64; religious right and, 381, 445–46; as Republicans in Civil War, 106–7; rise of right and in 20th century, 377–81; in 1950s–1960s, 360–65; on suffrage extension, 147–48, 156; on unbridled individualism, 190–91; as Whigs or early liberals, 80, 106–7

utilitarianism, 4, 70–71, 90–91, 93–95; rights and, 123–24, 294, 339–40

voluntarism, 178–79, 347; appeal of, 65; limitations of, 67–69, 270

war: ceaseless, 411–12; as enemy of prosperity, 74–75; explanations for 1914–18, 214–26; imperialism and, 207–8; liberal prowess at, 55, 112–16, 217; and liberal self-image as pacific, 214–15; reparations for, 224

warfare state, liberal, 214–26, 464; abuses of, 380; liberal dissent and, 226–35

welfare state: capitalism and, 10; to contain socialism, 211; difficulties of reforming, 407–408; in Germany's Federal Republic, 301; in postwar Britain, 308–12. *See also* social welfare

Liberalism

THE LIFE OF AN IDEA

Liberalism

THE LIFE OF AN IDEA
SECOND EDITION

Edmund Fawcett

Princeton University Press
Princeton & Oxford

Requests for permission to reproduce material from this work
should be sent to Permissions, Princeton University Press

Published by Princeton University Press,
41 William Street, Princeton, New Jersey 08540

In the United Kingdom: Princeton University Press,
6 Oxford Street, Woodstock, Oxfordshire OX20 1TR

press.princeton.edu

COVER IMAGES: *Row 1*: Wilhelm von Humboldt; Sir Isaiah Berlin (Library of Congress, Prints & Photographs Division, reproduction number LC-USZ62-112715); Walter Lippmann (Walter Lippmann Papers, Manuscripts and Archives, Yale University Library). *Row 2*: John Maynard Keynes, 1883–1946 (print collection, Miriam and Ira D. Wallach Division of Art, Prints and Photographs, The New York Public Library, Astor, Lenox and Tilden Foundations); Alexis Charles Henry de Tocqueville (lithograph, 1848, by Théodore Chassériau. Rosenwald Collection, 1952.8.215. Courtesy of the National Gallery of Art, Washington); Franklin Delano Roosevelt, photograph by Harris & Ewing (Library of Congress, Prints & Photographs Division, reproduction number LC-DIG-hec-47325). *Row 3*: Friedrich von Hayek (Courtesy of the Ludwig von Mises Institute); John Stuart Mill.

Original edition published 2014
Fifth printing, and first paperback printing, 2015
Second edition published 2018

Library of Congress Control Number 2017954566
ISBN 978-0-691-18038-0

British Library Cataloging-in-Publication Data is available

This book has been composed in Kepler Std

Printed on acid-free paper. ∞

Printed in the United States of America

10 9 8 7 6 5 4 3 2 1

TO MARLOWE,

AND IN MEMORY OF ELIAS

CONTENTS

Preface to the Second Edition   xi

Acknowledgments   xv

INTRODUCTION   The Practice of Liberalism   1

PART ONE   THE CONFIDENCE OF YOUTH (1830–1880)

1 Historical Setting in the 1830s: Thrown into a World of
   Ceaseless Change   33

2 Guiding Thoughts from Founding Thinkers: Conflict,
   Resistance, Progress, and Respect   39
   i. Humboldt and Constant: Releasing People's Capacities and
      Respecting Their Privacy   39
   ii. Guizot: Taming Conflict without Arbitrary Power   49
   iii. Tocqueville and Schulze-Delitzsch: The Modern Powers
      of Mass Democracy and Mass Markets   61
   iv. Chadwick and Cobden: Governments and Markets as
      Engines of Social Progress   69
   v. Smiles and Channing: Personal Progress as Self-Reliance or
      Moral Uplift   77
   vi. Spencer: Liberalism Mistaken for Biology   82
   vii. J. S. Mill: Holding Liberalism's Ideas Together   88

3 Liberalism in Practice: Four Exemplary Politicians   101
   i. Lincoln: The Many Uses of "Liberty" in the Land of Liberty   101
   ii. Laboulaye and Richter: Tests for Liberals in Semiliberal
      Regimes   108
   iii. Gladstone: Liberalism's Capaciousness and the Politics
      of Balance   115

4   The Nineteenth-Century Legacy: Liberalism without
     Caricature   120
     i. Respect, "the Individual," and the Lessons of Toleration   120
     ii. The Achievements That Gave Liberals Confidence   135

PART TWO   LIBERALISM IN MATURITY AND
THE STRUGGLE WITH DEMOCRACY (1880–1945)

5   Historical Setting in the 1880s: The World Liberals
     Were Making   139

6   The Compromises That Gave Us Liberal Democracy   147
     i. Political Democracy: Liberal Resistance to Suffrage Extension 147
     ii. Economic Democracy: The "New Liberalism" and Novel Tasks
         for the State   160
     iii. Ethical Democracy: Letting Go Ethically and the Persistence
          of Intolerance   167

7   The Economic Powers of the Modern State and
     Modern Market   173
     i. Walras, Marshall, and the Business Press: Resisting the State
        on Behalf of Markets   173
     ii. Hobhouse, Naumann, Croly, and Bourgeois: Resisting
         Markets on Behalf of Society   186

8   Damaged Ideals and Broken Dreams   198
     i. Chamberlain and Bassermann: Liberal Imperialism   198
     ii. Lloyd George, Clemenceau, and Wilson: Liberal Hawks
         of 1914–1918   214
     iii. Alain, Baldwin, and Brandeis: Liberal Dissent and the
          Warfare State   226
     iv. Stresemann: Liberal Democracy in Peril   235
     v. Keynes, Fisher, and Hayek (i): Liberal Economists in the Slump 243
     vi. Hoover and Roosevelt: Forgotten Liberal and Foremost Liberal 264

9   Thinking about Liberalism in the 1930s–1940s   272
     i. Lippmann and Hayek (ii): Liberals as Antitotalitarians   272
     ii. Popper: Liberalism as Openness and Experiment   276

PART THREE   SECOND CHANCE AND SUCCESS (1945–1989)

10 Historical Setting after 1945: Liberal Democracy's New Start   283

11   New Foundations: Rights, a Democratic Rule of Law,
       and Welfare   287
     i. Drafters of the 1948 Declaration of Human Rights: Liberal
        Democracy Goes Global   287
     ii. German Postwar Liberals: The 1949 Basic Law as Liberal
         Democracy's Exemplary Charter   299
     iii. Beveridge: Liberalism and Welfare   308

12   Liberal Thinking after 1945   313
     i. Oakeshott and Berlin: Letting Politics Alone
        and "Negative" Liberty   314
     ii. Hayek (iii): Political Antipolitics   324
     iii. Orwell, Camus, and Sartre: Liberals in the Cold War   328
     iv. Rawls: Justifying Liberalism   335
     v. Nozick, Dworkin, and MacIntyre: Responses to Rawls,
        Rights, and Community   345

13   The Breadth of Liberal Politics in the 1950s–1980s   352
     i. Mendès-France, Brandt, and Johnson: Left Liberalism in the
        1950s–1960s   352
     ii. Buchanan and Friedman: Liberal Economists against the State 365
     iii. Thatcher, Reagan, Mitterrand, and Kohl: Right Liberalism in
          the 1970s–1980s   375

PART FOUR   LIBERAL DREAMS AND NIGHTMARES
IN THE TWENTY-FIRST CENTURY

14   Two Decades That Shook Liberal Democracy   389
     i. The Rise of the Hard Right   389
     ii. Economic Discontents   399
     iii. Geopolitical Loneliness   410
     iv. Nationhood, Citizenship, and Identity   421
     v. Intellectual Doubts and Disaffection   439

15   The Primacy of Politics   454

Works Consulted   467

Name Index   495

Subject Index   507

PREFACE TO THE SECOND EDITION

To shore up a weakened building, you need to understand its foundations. You need to grasp what it rests on, why it arose, and what it is for. So it is with democratic liberalism, or to use the more familiar name, liberal democracy. Nobody who witnessed recent political shocks and watched antiliberal successes in Europe and the United States can doubt that liberal democracy is under challenge from inside and out. As discrepancies of wealth and power widened in recent decades, disaffected citizens questioned liberalism's aims and ideals. A great structure of historic wealth and shelter that lately appeared to be the envy of the world showed weaknesses and flaws. As the pride of its occupants gave way to self-doubt, people on all sides asked, were those flaws reparable or fatal? Across the world, liberalism's geopolitical prestige was dimmed by rising powers that offered attractive-looking nonliberal paths to material progress and stability. The liberal democratic world itself appeared to be splitting as the United States and Britain took illiberal paths politically and unilateralist paths internationally, leaving a shaken France and Germany as European standard-bearers for the liberal order.

The original edition of *Liberalism: The Life of an Idea* in a final chapter mentioned, without dwelling on, the present weaknesses of liberal democracy. The book's aim was to show what liberalism is, the better to see what we should be worrying about. This updated new edition contains an expanded final part, written after the upsets of 2016–17, on liberalism's present ills and doubts about its prospects. A new Introduction makes clearer the book's underlying assumption that liberalism, although complex and diverse, is easy to recognize and distinguish from its rivals, especially in times as now when liberalism looks as if it is in jeopardy and needs defending.

Liberalism is an enduring practice of politics guided by distinctive aims and ideals. It began in the early nineteenth century, not before as often claimed, in a previously unimagined predicament. Amid the ceaseless change of capitalist modernity, the first liberals sought durable new ways to secure ethical and political stability. That liberal search, then as now, was guided by four broad ideas: acceptance that moral and material conflict in society cannot be expunged, only contained and perhaps in fruitful ways tamed; hostility to unchecked power, be it political, economic or social; faith that social ills can be cured and that human life can be made better; and law-backed respect by state and society for people's lives and projects, whatever they believe and whoever they are.

More follows in the Introduction about each of those ideas—in shorthand, *conflict, power, progress* and *respect*. They distinguish liberalism point-for-point from its chief rivals in the nineteenth century, conservatism and socialism; from fascism and communism in the twentieth century and from their diverse twenty-first-century competitors: authoritarians, populists of right and left, theocrats and one-party state-capitalists. Much of the unending conflict among liberals that runs through this book is about how to think about their ideals and realize their aims. Because liberalism's guiding ideas set such high hopes, they also cause swings of mood from triumphalism to despair—and back.

Despite its wide variety of parties, camps, interests, philosophies and dominant characters, liberalism has for two centuries shown a high degree of unity and continuity. In secure times, liberalism's variety has struck people as too bewildering to count as variation in a single political practice. Surely, it is said, the term "liberalism" names different practices. Surely, there are many liberalisms. Surely, there is no one settled concept *liberalism* or *liberal*. Although arresting when first heard, such claims are much exaggerated and hard to press without raising the suspicion that the claimant recognizes liberalism well enough but is foxed by the wealth of diverse ways to think and talk about liberalism. Fear of loss, however, sharpens the mind. In insecure times, as now, definitional puzzles are less worrisome than the blunt matter of liberalism's survival.

In aiming for a rounded picture, the story here does not start with liberty, as books on liberalism often do. It does not labor back upstream to track liberal ideas to a remote preliberal past. It does not sequester liberal thought within economics or moral philosophy. It distinguishes liberalism from democracy and describes the arduous, ever negotiable compromise that produced liberal democracy. It does not treat liberalism provincially as a British and American monopoly but gives due weight to liberal traditions in France and Germany, treating all four countries together as a representative but nonexclusive core. Polemical energy is wasted on showing that liberalism's aims and ideals are narrowly Western, secular-Enlightened, bourgeois-individualist, procapitalist or—to use a fashionable term of abuse—rootlessly cosmopolitan. None of these slurs or labels stick. No sect or party owns liberalism's aims and ideals. They serve every nation, gender and class. If that brands liberals as universalists, so be it. They may wear their scarlet "U" with pride.

This is a book for the concerned common reader. There are no regular footnotes and no endnotes. The speed and generosity of the web has lightened the task of checking facts or following up quotations. Save for recent books not translated, titles of works are given in English with the date of original publication. A list of works consulted and drawn upon can be found at the end.

Liberals have been searching for acceptable points of stability amid bewildering change for 200 years. No point of stability has lasted. New ones, as now, were in time always needed. Conflict was never resolved, only mitigated. The search goes on, and liberals can blame themselves if they stop looking. They are not searching blindly. For behind them they have arguments, traditions, and experience. They have a history. That history is vital for understanding what liberalism is, why it matters and what, amid the shocks of the present, we risk losing. To recall that history is why I wrote this book.

Edmund Fawcett
January 2018

ACKNOWLEDGMENTS

For this chronicle of liberalism, I have plundered widely from the works of many writers and scholars. I am in their debt and thank them all. In person, I thank wholeheartedly Oliver Black, Donald Franklin, Charles Hope, Howard Naish, Chaim Tannenbaum, Tony Thomas, and David Wiggins, who read all or part of drafts, caught errors, and made valuable suggestions; Catherine Clarke, my agent, who encouraged me to "tell a story"; Al Bertrand at Princeton University Press, who saw the point and who urged me to update the story with liberalism's present travails in this new edition; my editor, Sarah Caro, and her ever helpful Princeton University Press colleagues; Marlowe Fawcett, who shared his film skills; and Natalia Jiménez, my wife, who gave unflagging support and never shied, on reading drafts, from "I don't get it" and "Where is this going?"

Liberalism

THE LIFE OF AN IDEA

Liberalism

THE LIFE OF AN IDEA
SECOND EDITION

Edmund Fawcett

Princeton University Press
Princeton & Oxford

Requests for permission to reproduce material from this work
should be sent to Permissions, Princeton University Press

Published by Princeton University Press,
41 William Street, Princeton, New Jersey 08540

In the United Kingdom: Princeton University Press,
6 Oxford Street, Woodstock, Oxfordshire OX20 1TR

press.princeton.edu

COVER IMAGES: *Row 1*: Wilhelm von Humboldt; Sir Isaiah Berlin (Library of Congress, Prints & Photographs Division, reproduction number LC-USZ62-112715); Walter Lippmann (Walter Lippmann Papers, Manuscripts and Archives, Yale University Library). *Row 2*: John Maynard Keynes, 1883–1946 (print collection, Miriam and Ira D. Wallach Division of Art, Prints and Photographs, The New York Public Library, Astor, Lenox and Tilden Foundations); Alexis Charles Henry de Tocqueville (lithograph, 1848, by Théodore Chassériau. Rosenwald Collection, 1952.8.215. Courtesy of the National Gallery of Art, Washington); Franklin Delano Roosevelt, photograph by Harris & Ewing (Library of Congress, Prints & Photographs Division, reproduction number LC-DIG-hec-47325). *Row 3*: Friedrich von Hayek (Courtesy of the Ludwig von Mises Institute); John Stuart Mill.

Original edition published 2014
Fifth printing, and first paperback printing, 2015
Second edition published 2018

Library of Congress Control Number 2017954566
ISBN 978-0-691-18038-0

British Library Cataloging-in-Publication Data is available

This book has been composed in Kepler Std

Printed on acid-free paper. ∞

Printed in the United States of America

10 9 8 7 6 5 4 3 2 1

TO MARLOWE,

AND IN MEMORY OF ELIAS

CONTENTS

Preface to the Second Edition   xi

Acknowledgments   xv

INTRODUCTION   The Practice of Liberalism   1

PART ONE   THE CONFIDENCE OF YOUTH (1830–1880)

1   Historical Setting in the 1830s: Thrown into a World of
    Ceaseless Change   33

2   Guiding Thoughts from Founding Thinkers: Conflict,
    Resistance, Progress, and Respect   39
    i. Humboldt and Constant: Releasing People's Capacities and
       Respecting Their Privacy   39
    ii. Guizot: Taming Conflict without Arbitrary Power   49
    iii. Tocqueville and Schulze-Delitzsch: The Modern Powers
       of Mass Democracy and Mass Markets   61
    iv. Chadwick and Cobden: Governments and Markets as
       Engines of Social Progress   69
    v. Smiles and Channing: Personal Progress as Self-Reliance or
       Moral Uplift   77
    vi. Spencer: Liberalism Mistaken for Biology   82
    vii. J. S. Mill: Holding Liberalism's Ideas Together   88

3   Liberalism in Practice: Four Exemplary Politicians   101
    i. Lincoln: The Many Uses of "Liberty" in the Land of Liberty   101
    ii. Laboulaye and Richter: Tests for Liberals in Semiliberal
       Regimes   108
    iii. Gladstone: Liberalism's Capaciousness and the Politics
       of Balance   115

4   The Nineteenth-Century Legacy: Liberalism without
    Caricature   120
    i. Respect, "the Individual," and the Lessons of Toleration   120
    ii. The Achievements That Gave Liberals Confidence   135

PART TWO   LIBERALISM IN MATURITY AND
THE STRUGGLE WITH DEMOCRACY (1880–1945)

5   Historical Setting in the 1880s: The World Liberals
    Were Making   139

6   The Compromises That Gave Us Liberal Democracy   147
    i. Political Democracy: Liberal Resistance to Suffrage Extension   147
    ii. Economic Democracy: The "New Liberalism" and Novel Tasks
    for the State   160
    iii. Ethical Democracy: Letting Go Ethically and the Persistence
    of Intolerance   167

7   The Economic Powers of the Modern State and
    Modern Market   173
    i. Walras, Marshall, and the Business Press: Resisting the State
    on Behalf of Markets   173
    ii. Hobhouse, Naumann, Croly, and Bourgeois: Resisting
    Markets on Behalf of Society   186

8   Damaged Ideals and Broken Dreams   198
    i. Chamberlain and Bassermann: Liberal Imperialism   198
    ii. Lloyd George, Clemenceau, and Wilson: Liberal Hawks
    of 1914–1918   214
    iii. Alain, Baldwin, and Brandeis: Liberal Dissent and the
    Warfare State   226
    iv. Stresemann: Liberal Democracy in Peril   235
    v. Keynes, Fisher, and Hayek (i): Liberal Economists in the Slump   243
    vi. Hoover and Roosevelt: Forgotten Liberal and Foremost Liberal   264

9   Thinking about Liberalism in the 1930s–1940s   272
    i. Lippmann and Hayek (ii): Liberals as Antitotalitarians   272
    ii. Popper: Liberalism as Openness and Experiment   276

PART THREE   SECOND CHANCE AND SUCCESS (1945–1989)

10   Historical Setting after 1945: Liberal Democracy's New Start   283

11 New Foundations: Rights, a Democratic Rule of Law,
    and Welfare   287
    i. Drafters of the 1948 Declaration of Human Rights: Liberal
       Democracy Goes Global   287
    ii. German Postwar Liberals: The 1949 Basic Law as Liberal
       Democracy's Exemplary Charter   299
    iii. Beveridge: Liberalism and Welfare   308

12 Liberal Thinking after 1945   313
    i. Oakeshott and Berlin: Letting Politics Alone
       and "Negative" Liberty   314
    ii. Hayek (iii): Political Antipolitics   324
    iii. Orwell, Camus, and Sartre: Liberals in the Cold War   328
    iv. Rawls: Justifying Liberalism   335
    v. Nozick, Dworkin, and MacIntyre: Responses to Rawls,
       Rights, and Community   345

13 The Breadth of Liberal Politics in the 1950s–1980s   352
    i. Mendès-France, Brandt, and Johnson: Left Liberalism in the
       1950s–1960s   352
    ii. Buchanan and Friedman: Liberal Economists against the State 365
    iii. Thatcher, Reagan, Mitterrand, and Kohl: Right Liberalism in
       the 1970s–1980s   375

PART FOUR   LIBERAL DREAMS AND NIGHTMARES
IN THE TWENTY-FIRST CENTURY

14 Two Decades That Shook Liberal Democracy   389
    i. The Rise of the Hard Right   389
    ii. Economic Discontents   399
    iii. Geopolitical Loneliness   410
    iv. Nationhood, Citizenship, and Identity   421
    v. Intellectual Doubts and Disaffection   439

15 The Primacy of Politics   454

Works Consulted   467

Name Index   495

Subject Index   507

PREFACE TO THE SECOND EDITION

To shore up a weakened building, you need to understand its foundations. You need to grasp what it rests on, why it arose, and what it is for. So it is with democratic liberalism, or to use the more familiar name, liberal democracy. Nobody who witnessed recent political shocks and watched antiliberal successes in Europe and the United States can doubt that liberal democracy is under challenge from inside and out. As discrepancies of wealth and power widened in recent decades, disaffected citizens questioned liberalism's aims and ideals. A great structure of historic wealth and shelter that lately appeared to be the envy of the world showed weaknesses and flaws. As the pride of its occupants gave way to self-doubt, people on all sides asked, were those flaws reparable or fatal? Across the world, liberalism's geopolitical prestige was dimmed by rising powers that offered attractive-looking nonliberal paths to material progress and stability. The liberal democratic world itself appeared to be splitting as the United States and Britain took illiberal paths politically and unilateralist paths internationally, leaving a shaken France and Germany as European standard-bearers for the liberal order.

The original edition of *Liberalism: The Life of an Idea* in a final chapter mentioned, without dwelling on, the present weaknesses of liberal democracy. The book's aim was to show what liberalism is, the better to see what we should be worrying about. This updated new edition contains an expanded final part, written after the upsets of 2016–17, on liberalism's present ills and doubts about its prospects. A new Introduction makes clearer the book's underlying assumption that liberalism, although complex and diverse, is easy to recognize and distinguish from its rivals, especially in times as now when liberalism looks as if it is in jeopardy and needs defending.

Liberalism is an enduring practice of politics guided by distinctive aims and ideals. It began in the early nineteenth century, not before as often claimed, in a previously unimagined predicament. Amid the ceaseless change of capitalist modernity, the first liberals sought durable new ways to secure ethical and political stability. That liberal search, then as now, was guided by four broad ideas: acceptance that moral and material conflict in society cannot be expunged, only contained and perhaps in fruitful ways tamed; hostility to unchecked power, be it political, economic or social; faith that social ills can be cured and that human life can be made better; and law-backed respect by state and society for people's lives and projects, whatever they believe and whoever they are.

More follows in the Introduction about each of those ideas—in shorthand, *conflict*, *power*, *progress* and *respect*. They distinguish liberalism point-for-point from its chief rivals in the nineteenth century, conservatism and socialism; from fascism and communism in the twentieth century and from their diverse twenty-first-century competitors: authoritarians, populists of right and left, theocrats and one-party state-capitalists. Much of the unending conflict among liberals that runs through this book is about how to think about their ideals and realize their aims. Because liberalism's guiding ideas set such high hopes, they also cause swings of mood from triumphalism to despair—and back.

Despite its wide variety of parties, camps, interests, philosophies and dominant characters, liberalism has for two centuries shown a high degree of unity and continuity. In secure times, liberalism's variety has struck people as too bewildering to count as variation in a single political practice. Surely, it is said, the term "liberalism" names different practices. Surely, there are many liberalisms. Surely, there is no one settled concept *liberalism* or *liberal*. Although arresting when first heard, such claims are much exaggerated and hard to press without raising the suspicion that the claimant recognizes liberalism well enough but is foxed by the wealth of diverse ways to think and talk about liberalism. Fear of loss, however, sharpens the mind. In insecure times, as now, definitional puzzles are less worrisome than the blunt matter of liberalism's survival.

In aiming for a rounded picture, the story here does not start with liberty, as books on liberalism often do. It does not labor back upstream to track liberal ideas to a remote preliberal past. It does not sequester liberal thought within economics or moral philosophy. It distinguishes liberalism from democracy and describes the arduous, ever negotiable compromise that produced liberal democracy. It does not treat liberalism provincially as a British and American monopoly but gives due weight to liberal traditions in France and Germany, treating all four countries together as a representative but nonexclusive core. Polemical energy is wasted on showing that liberalism's aims and ideals are narrowly Western, secular-Enlightened, bourgeois-individualist, procapitalist or—to use a fashionable term of abuse—rootlessly cosmopolitan. None of these slurs or labels stick. No sect or party owns liberalism's aims and ideals. They serve every nation, gender and class. If that brands liberals as universalists, so be it. They may wear their scarlet "U" with pride.

This is a book for the concerned common reader. There are no regular footnotes and no endnotes. The speed and generosity of the web has lightened the task of checking facts or following up quotations. Save for recent books not translated, titles of works are given in English with the date of original publication. A list of works consulted and drawn upon can be found at the end.

Liberals have been searching for acceptable points of stability amid bewildering change for 200 years. No point of stability has lasted. New ones, as now, were in time always needed. Conflict was never resolved, only mitigated. The search goes on, and liberals can blame themselves if they stop looking. They are not searching blindly. For behind them they have arguments, traditions, and experience. They have a history. That history is vital for understanding what liberalism is, why it matters and what, amid the shocks of the present, we risk losing. To recall that history is why I wrote this book.

Edmund Fawcett
January 2018

ACKNOWLEDGMENTS

For this chronicle of liberalism, I have plundered widely from the works of many writers and scholars. I am in their debt and thank them all. In person, I thank wholeheartedly Oliver Black, Donald Franklin, Charles Hope, Howard Naish, Chaim Tannenbaum, Tony Thomas, and David Wiggins, who read all or part of drafts, caught errors, and made valuable suggestions; Catherine Clarke, my agent, who encouraged me to "tell a story"; Al Bertrand at Princeton University Press, who saw the point and who urged me to update the story with liberalism's present travails in this new edition; my editor, Sarah Caro, and her ever helpful Princeton University Press colleagues; Marlowe Fawcett, who shared his film skills; and Natalia Jiménez, my wife, who gave unflagging support and never shied, on reading drafts, from "I don't get it" and "Where is this going?"

J.S. Mill P.98

Channing, P. 81